Drug Design

Drug Design

Balkishen Razdan

Former Dean
Postgraduate Studies and Research
Birla Institute of Technology
Mesra, Ranchi, Jharkhand

and

Former Director
S Bhagwan Singh Postgraduate Institute
of Biomedical Sciences and Research
Balawala, Dehradun, Uttarakhand

CBSPD

CBS Publishers & Distributors Pvt Ltd

New Delhi • Bengaluru • Chennai • Kochi • Kolkata • Lucknow • Mumbai
Hyderabad • Jharkhand • Nagpur • Patna • Pune • Uttarakhand

Disclaimer

Science and technology are constantly changing fields. New research and experience broaden the scope of information and knowledge. The author has tried his best in giving information available to him while preparing the material for this book. Although, all efforts have been made to ensure optimum accuracy of the material, yet it is quite possible some errors might have been left uncorrected. The publisher, the printer and the author will not be held responsible for any inadvertent errors, omissions or inaccuracies.

Drug Design

ISBN: 978-81-239-2217-1

First Edition: 2012
Reprint: 2018, 2020, 2023, 2025

Published by Satish Kumar Jain and produced by Varun Jain for

CBS Publishers & Distributors Pvt Ltd
4819/XI Prahlad Street, 24 Ansari Road, Daryaganj, New Delhi 110 002, India
Ph: 011-23289259, 23266838 Website: www.cbspd.com
e-mail: delhi@cbspd.com

Corporate Office: 204 FIE, Industrial Area, Patparganj, Delhi 110 092
Ph: 011-4934 4934 Fax: 011-4934 4935 e-mail: publishing@cbspd.com; publicity@cbspd.com

Branches

- **Bengaluru:** Seema House 2975, 17th Cross, K.R. Road, Banasankari 2nd Stage, Bengaluru 560 070, Karnataka, India
  Ph: +91-80-26771678/79 Fax: +91-80-26771680 e-mail: bangalore@cbspd.com
- **Chennai:** 18/8B, Subbarayan Street, Shenoy Nagar, Chennai 600 030, Tamil Nadu, India
  Ph: +91-44-42032115, 26681266 e-mail: chennai@cbspd.com
- **Kochi:** 42/1325, 1326, Power House Road, Opp KSEB, Power House, Ernakulam 682 018, Kerala, India
  Ph: +91-484-4059061-65 Fax: +91-484-4059065 e-mail: kochi@cbspd.com
- **Kolkata:** 147, Hind Ceramics Compound, 1st Floor, Nilgunj Road, Belghoria, Kolkata-700056, West Bengal, India
  Ph: 033-25633055, 033-25633056 e-mail: kolkata@cbspd.com
- **Lucknow:** Basement, Khushnuma Complex, 7-Meerabai Marg (Behind Jawahar Bhawan), Lucknow 226001, India
  Ph: 0522-4000032 e-mail: tiwari.lucknow@cbspd.com
- **Mumbai:** PWD Shed. Gala no. 25/26, Ramchandra Bhatt Marg, Next to JJ Hospital Gate no. 2, Opp. Union Bank of India Noorbaug Mumbai-400009, Maharashtra, India
  Ph: 022-66661880/89 e-mail: mumbai@cbspd.com

Representatives

- **Hyderabad** 0-9885175004 • **Jharkhand** 0-9811541605 • **Nagpur** 0-8692091830
- **Patna** 0-9334159340 • **Pune** 0-9664372571 • **Uttarakhand** 0-9716462459

Printed at Glorious Printers, Delhi, India

Preface

This book is an extension of my earlier book *Medicinal Chemistry*. In the present book an attempt has been made to incorporate the various concepts used in drug design. Further, at the end of each chapter references to literature have been provided for further study.

This book is addressed mainly to undergraduate and postgraduate students of pharmacy and to the students of other streams who offer drug design as one of their elective.

Sufficient care has been taken so that there are no mistakes in structures or text. However, if any reader detects any mistake, the author would appreciate if it is brought to his notice.

I am thankful to Dr Swastika Ganguly for contributing two chapters on 'QSAR' and 'Molecular Modelling'. I take this opportunity of expressing my gratitude to my elder brother, my wife, and my children for their support and encouragement during the writing of this book.

In the end, I would like to thank Mr YN Arjuna, Senior Director—Publishing, Editorial and Publicity, and his team at CBS Publishers & Distributors, for bringing out the book in the present form.

Balkishen Razdan

Contents

1

Drug–Receptor Interactions and Theories of Drug Action

The drugs which are non-specific in their action and show their pharmacological effect due to physico-chemical properties require large doses to show their effect. On the other hand, drugs which are structurally specific show their pharmacological action in small doses. Thus, structurally specific drugs cannot act on all the molecules of the body but on specific structures known as receptors. Their interactions with specific receptors results in the pharmacological response.

QUANTITATIVE ASPECTS OF DRUG–RECEPTOR INTERACTIONS

In order to show its effect, the drug first complexes reversibly with the receptor and this complexation is governed by the Law of Mass Action. Suppose the total number of receptors in a tissue to which the drug is applied is R_T and when this tissue is exposed to D concentration of the drug, the number of receptors occupied by the drug will be R_D and the number of unoccupied or vacant receptors would be $R_T - R_D$. Since the number of drug molecules applied to tissue greatly exceeds the total number of receptors (R_T), the binding does not appreciably reduce the drug concentration.

The drug-receptor complexation can accordingly be represented by (Eq. 1):

$$D + \underset{\substack{\text{vacant receptors} \\ (R_T - R_D)}}{R} \rightleftharpoons DR \qquad \text{... (Eq. 1)}$$

thus,

1. Rate of forward reaction $= k_{+1}\ [D][R_T - R_D]$ ... (Eq. 2)
2. Rate of backward reaction $= k_{-1}\ [DR]$ ... (Eq. 3)

at equilibrium,

$$k_{+1}[D][R_T - R_D) = k_{-1}[DR] \qquad \text{... (Eq. 4)}$$

The proportion of receptors occupied or occupancy $p_D = R_D/R_T$ is independent of R_T and is given by the (Eq. 5):

$$p_D = \frac{[D]}{[D] + k_{-1}/k_{+1}} \qquad \text{... (Eq. 5)}$$

Since the equilibrium constant $K_D = k_{-1}/k_{+1}$, (Eq. 5) can be written as (Eq. 6).

$$p_D = \frac{[D]/K_D}{[D]/K_D + 1} \quad \text{... (Eq. 6)}$$

This is known as Hill-Langmuir equation.

The equilibrium constant, K_D is characteristic of a drug and receptor and is defined as the concentration of drug which occupies 50% of the receptor i.e. when $D = K_D$, $p_D = 0.5$.

The higher the affinity of the drug for the receptors, the lower will be the K_D. Equation 6 thus, describes the relationship between the occupancy and the drug concentration. A plot of occupancy against drug concentration in a linear scale results in a hyperbolic curve (Fig. 1.1) while in semilogarithmic scale a sigmoid curve (Fig. 1.2), is obtained.

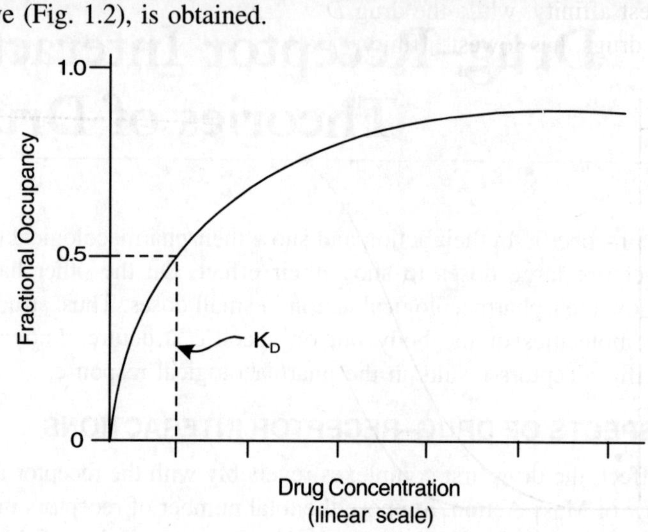

Fig. 1.1 Relationship between receptor occupancy and drug concentration (linear scale)

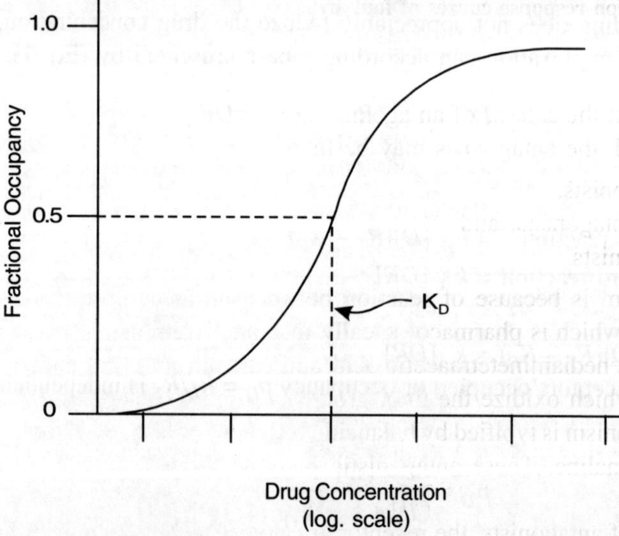

Fig. 1.2 Relationship between receptor occupancy and drug concentration (log. scale)

In order that a structurally specific drug shows effect, it is necessary that it should bind to a receptor first and then be able to elicit a response. The characteristic which enable the structurally specific drug to bind to a receptor is known as its "affinity" and the ability to elicit a pharmacological response is its "intrinsic activity". A drug which possesses both affinity and intrinsic activity is an agonist. An agonist, thus, can be defined as "a drug that binds to the receptor and mimics the regulatory effects of endogenous signalling compound and possesses both affinity and intrinsic activity." However, in a pharmacological related series of agonists acting on the same receptor, all the members of the series may not possess same affinity. This is illustrated by the log concentration-response curves of drugs *A*, *B*, *C* and *D* (Fig. 1.3). All the drugs produce the same maximal effect indicating that all of them possess same intrinsic activity. However, they differ in their affinities. Thus, the drug *A* which produces maximal response at lowest dose has highest affinity, while the drug *D* which produces maximal response at highest dose level among the four drugs, has lowest affinity.

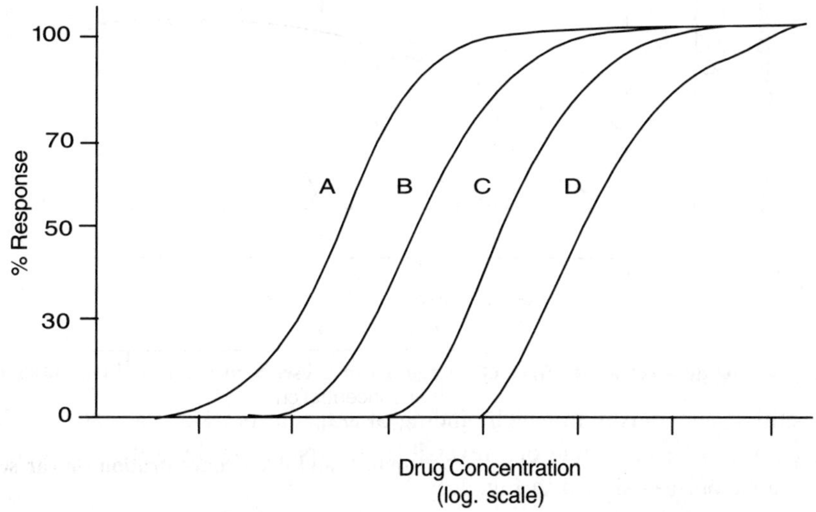

Fig. 1.3 Log concentration-response curves of four hypothetical drugs A, B, C, and D with different affinities

Antagonists

Molecules which inhibit the actions of an agonists are known as antagonists. Depending upon how the antagonism is achieved, the antagonists may be further classified as:

(a) chemical antagonists,
(b) physiological antagonists, and
(c) receptor antagonists.

Chemical antagonism is because of reaction between an antagonist and agonist. Such a reaction results in a compound which is pharmacologically inactive. Examples of chemical antagonism include reaction between ethylenediaminetetraacetic acid and calcium ions and antibacterial action of certain oxidizing substances which oxidize the thiol groups of certain bacterial enzymes.

Physiological antagonism is typified by balancing influence of hormones such as insulin and glucagon, acetylcholine and adrenaline. These antagonistic pairs oppose the action of each other by acting at different receptors.

The third category of antagonists, the receptor antagonists act by binding either to the site where the agonist bind (the active site) or another site (allosteric site). Binding at the active site prevents the binding of the agonists. On the other hand, binding at allosteric site prevents the conformational changes required for receptor activation and subsequent binding of the agonist to it.

Binding at the active site can be reversible or irreversible. When it is reversible, it is competitive antagonism and it can be overcome by increased addition of an agonist. The effect on the log dose-response curve of an agonist in presence of a competitive antagonist results in shifting of the curve towards right (Fig. 1.4). Thus, a competitive antagonist reduces the potency of an agonist without affecting the efficacy. Irreversible binding to the active site cannot be overcome by increased addition of an agonist.

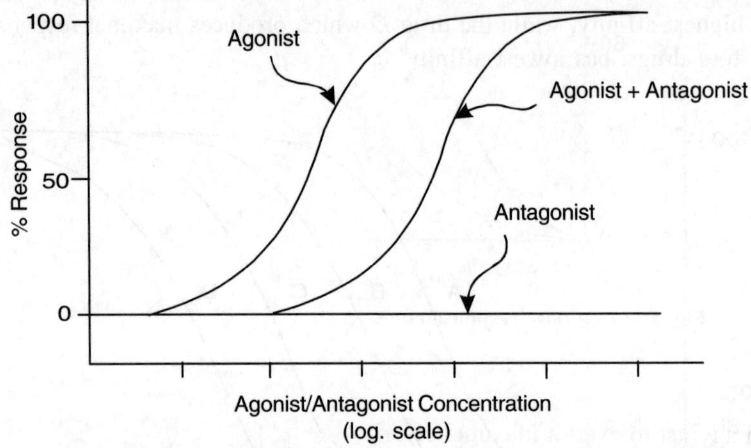

Fig. 1.4 Log dose-response curve of an agonist in presence of a competitive antagonist

A non-competitive antagonism, in which binding of antagonists takes place at site other than active site (allosteric site), can be reversible or irreversible. A typical log dose-response curve in case of a non-competitive antagonist is shown in Fig. 1.5.

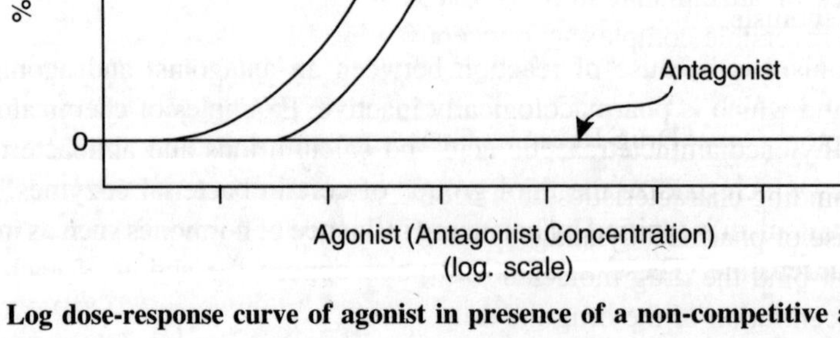

Fig. 1.5 Log dose-response curve of agonist in presence of a non-competitive antagonist

Partial Agonists

A partial agonist produces only a partial response even when all the receptors are occupied (Fig. 1.6). Partial agonists act as competitive antagonist of an agonist. Thus, in presence of partial agonist, the maximum response of an agonist is reduced.

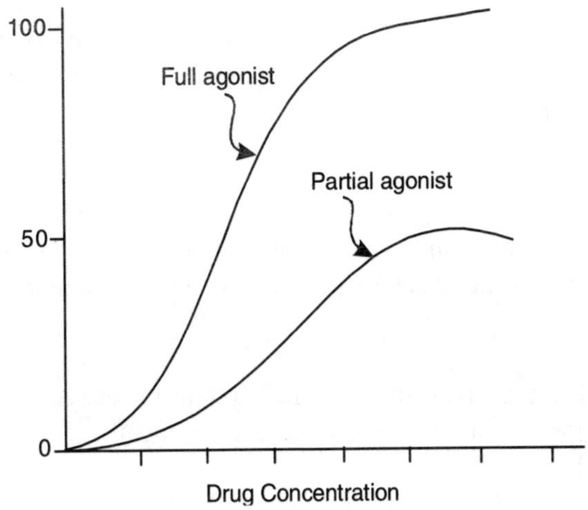

Fig. 1.6 Log dose-response curve of an agonist and partial agonist

Spare Receptors

Normally, for an agonist to exert a maximal effect, 100% receptor occupancy is required. However, a maximal response can also be achieved with less than 100% occupancy. This is due to presence of spare receptors. In presence of spare receptors, less than half the receptors are occupied to elicit a maximum response. Thus, maximal response in presence of spare receptors is obtained with lower concentration of an agonist. The phenomenon of spare receptors is thought to be due to two mechanisms. One of them probably is that the receptor remains activated even after the agonist leaves the receptor, allowing one molecule of agonist to activate several receptors simultaneously. The other mechanism could be due to amplification of relatively small signal and activation of only few receptors to produce a maximal response.

Drug-Receptor Interactions

Most of the drugs show their effect by forming a complex with a macromolecule commonly known as receptor. In order to reach the receptor in the cell, the drug molecule has to pass through many barriers including other sites of attachment, storage, and also avoid metabolic changes. After it reaches the receptor, it forms a reversible complex with receptor which then triggers the pharmacological response (Eq. 7).

$$\text{Drug + Receptor} \rightleftharpoons \text{Drug-Receptor Complex} \longrightarrow \text{Pharmacological Response} \quad \text{...(Eq. 7)}$$

For favourable binding characteristics, it is necessary that equilibrium of the complex formation lies towards right. In case of pharmacodynamic agents it is desired that the effect does not last long. In such cases the forces that bind the drug molecule to the receptor are weak and not permanent so that with the decrease in concentration of the drug the drug molecule is cleaved from the drug-receptor complex and is metabolized and excreted. In case of chemotherapeutic agents, where it is desired that the drug is toxic to the parasite, the forces that bind the drug molecule to the receptor in the parasite are irreversible.

The different types of bonds which are involved in drug-receptor complexation include:

1. covalent bond,
2. ionic bond,
3. dipole-dipole interactions,
4. hydrogen bond,
5. hydrophobic bonding, and
6. van der Waal's forces

Covalent bonds are the strongest bonds with a bond strength of 40-110 kcal/mole, van der Waal's interactions on the other hand are the weakest interactions with a bond strength of 0.5-1 kcal/mole.

Covalent Bond

Covalent bonds are formed and cleaved in the living system by enzymes. Covalent bond formation between the drug and receptor is desired in case of chemotherapeutic agents and insecticides where the death of the parasite is goal.

Examples

Cholinesterase (Ach-Ser-OH) is an enzyme responsible for the hydrolysis of acetylcholine (1) (Fig. 1.7). Inhibition of cholinesterase results in increased levels of acetylcholine which results in death of the cell. Organo-phosphorus compounds are irreversible inhibitors of cholinesterase. The enzyme cholinesterase contains serine, the hydroxyl group of which acts as a nucleophile and hydrolyzes the acetylcholine. Organo-phosphorus compounds phosphorylate the hydroxyl group of serine thereby blocking the hydrolysis of acetylcholine. Since phosphorylation of hydroxyl group of serine involves covalent bond formation, it is irreversible which results in death of the parasite.

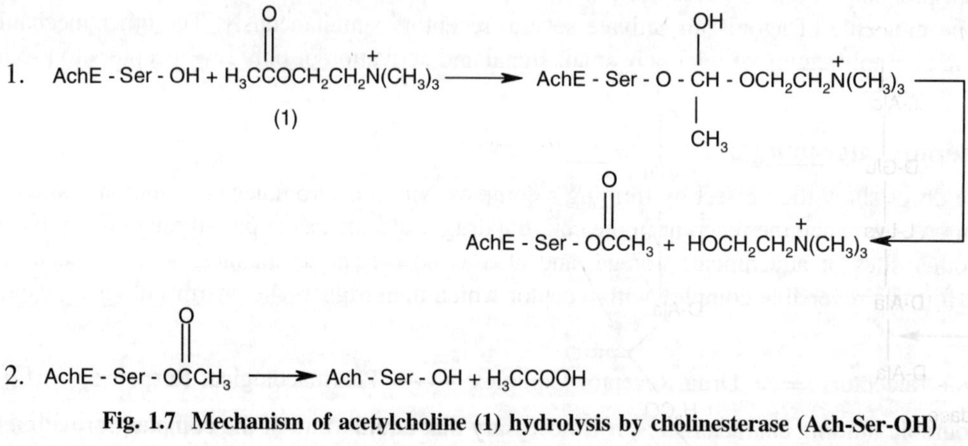

Fig. 1.7 Mechanism of acetylcholine (1) hydrolysis by cholinesterase (Ach-Ser-OH)

The anticancer activity of nitrogen mustards (2) is due to alkylation of proteins and nucleic acids (Fig. 1.8).

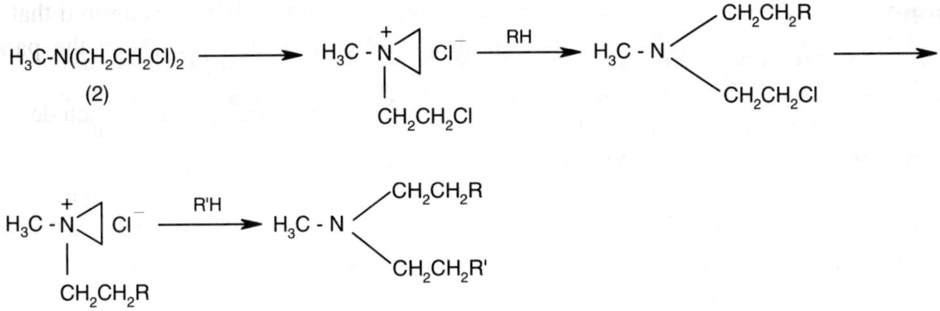

Fig. 1.8 Mechanism of alkylation by nitrogen mustards

The antibacterial activity of penicillin and other β-lactam antibiotics is due to acylation of serine hydroxyl of transamidase by penicillins (Fig. 1.9). This acylation is irreversible. As a result the terminal D-Ala unit of the pentapeptide strand of muramic acid is not cleaved and cross-linking of the cell wall does not take place. This results in lysis.

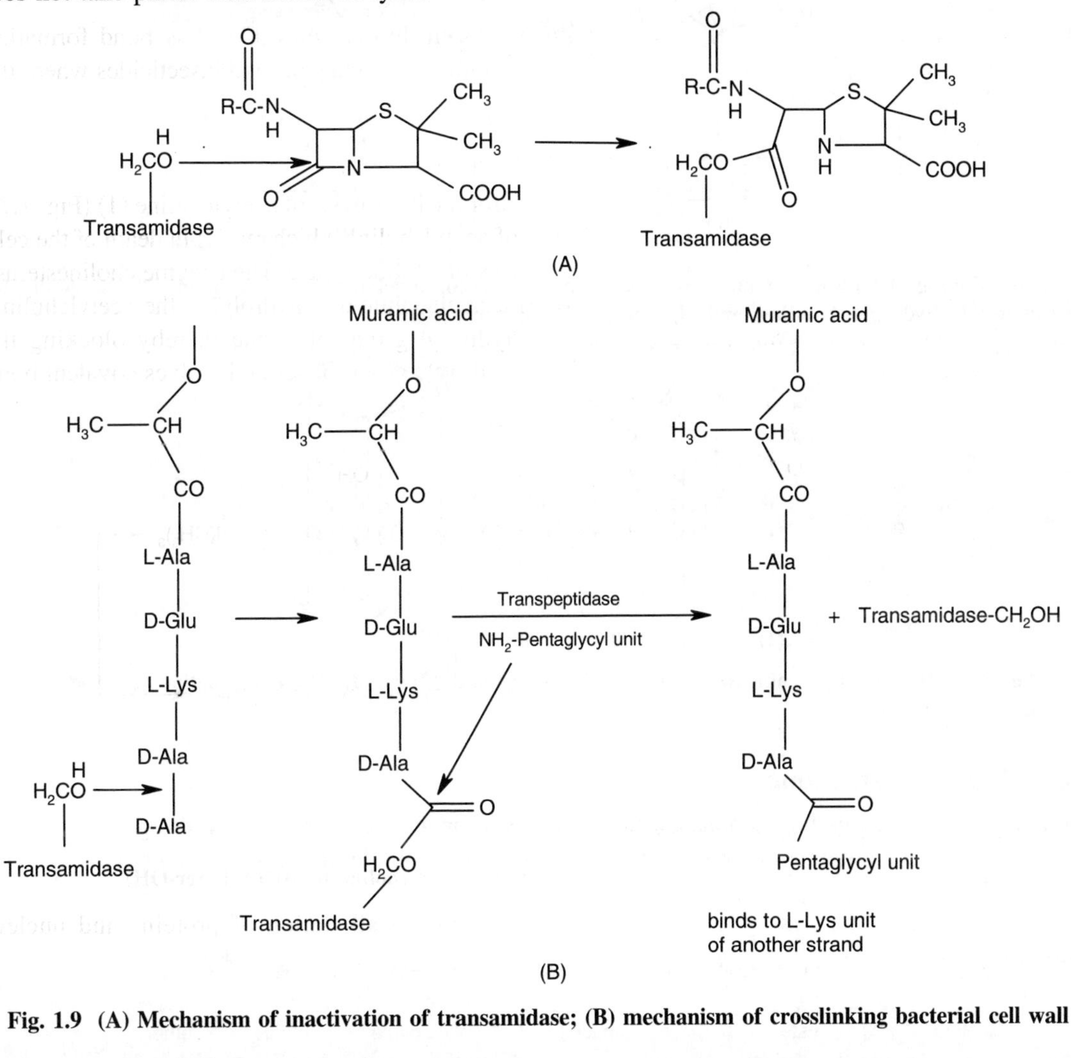

Fig. 1.9 (A) Mechanism of inactivation of transamidase; (B) mechanism of crosslinking bacterial cell wall

Ionic Bond

Most of the drugs are either weak acids or weak bases. At physiological pH the weak acids such as carboxylic acid remain ionized as carboxylate ion. Similarly, an amino group remains as a positively charged species. The receptors, which are made up of proteins, contain free amino and free carboxylic groups, which also remain ionized at physiological pH as ammonium and carboxylate ions, respectively. Thus, the drug molecules can interact with the receptors through these cationic and anionic interactions. However, these interactions last only a fraction of a second (10^{-5} sec). But when these interactions are reinforced with other interactions, simultaneously, they last longer.

Example

Binding of (-)-*S*-hyoscyamine with muscarinic receptor (Fig 1.10) and local anaesthetic procaine with its receptor (Fig. 1.11).

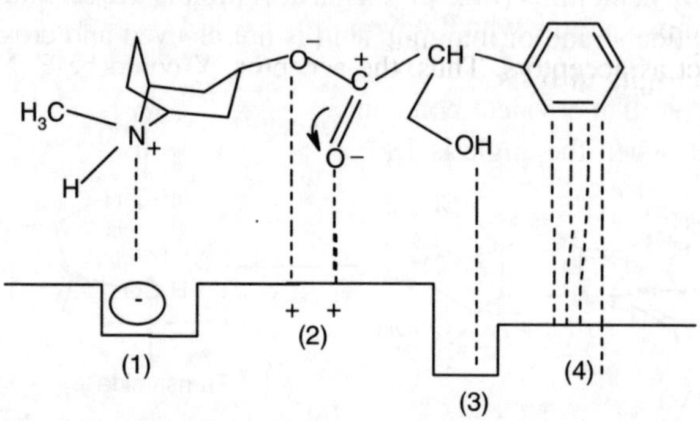

Fig. 1.10 Binding of (-)-S-hyoscyamine with muscarinic receptor involving (1), ionic bond, (2), dipole-dipole-interaction, (3), hydrogen bonding, and (4), van der Waal interaction

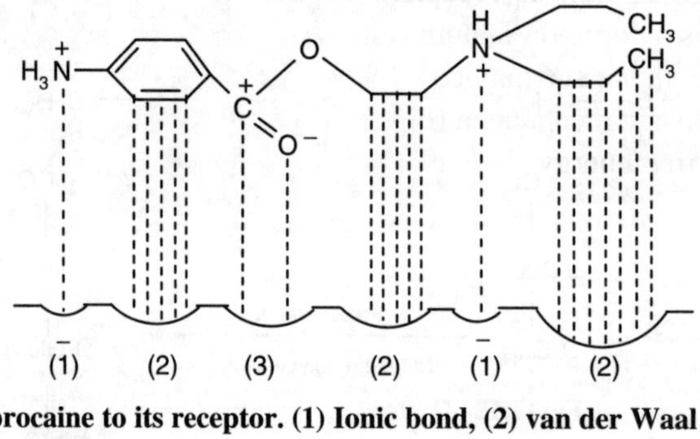

Fig. 1.11 Binding of procaine to its receptor. (1) Ionic bond, (2) van der Waal interaction, (3) dipole-dipole interaction

Dipole-Dipole Interactions

A dipole results when carbon is attached to a more electronegative atom such as nitrogen or oxygen. Examples of such dipole are carbonyl group of ketone, ester, amide, a nitrile or even ether.

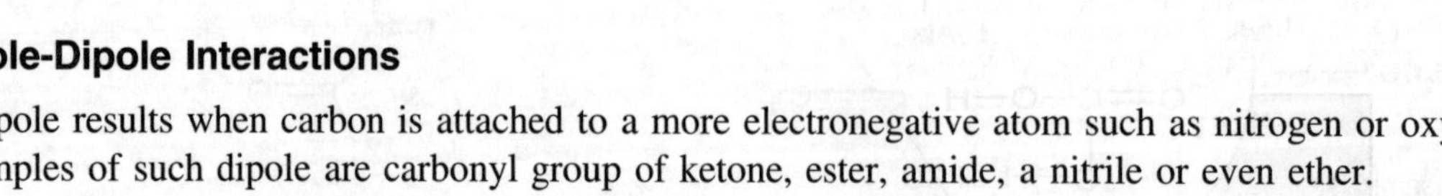

Since proteins, which constitute receptors, also contain carbonyl functions, a dipole is created in them also. Thus, drugs with dipole can align themselves with the dipole of the protein, resulting in dipole-dipole interactions. Similarly, ions can also interact with the dipole in a protein resulting in ion-dipole interaction. Such interactions are frequently encountered in drug-receptor interactions.

Hydrogen Bond

A hydrogen bond is formed between two electronegative atoms, one of them donating a proton and another accepting this proton. The donor molecule, X-H could be F – H, O – H, or N – H. The

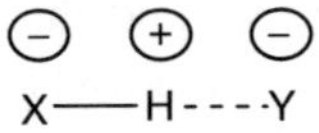

molecules which can also act as donors are Cl – H, S – H, and P – H, but they form very weak hydrogen bonds. Carbon in its sp-hybridization is highly electronegative and therefore can act as a donor.

Among acceptors, all those atoms, which have an extra pair of electron and are ready to share this pair with a proton, can act as acceptors. Thus, the acceptor, Y could be F, N, and O.

Hydrogen bond is weaker than covalent bond but is stronger than van der Waal's forces. A hydrogen bond is highly directional, when the angle is 180^0 it is strongest and when less than 180^0, it is weak.

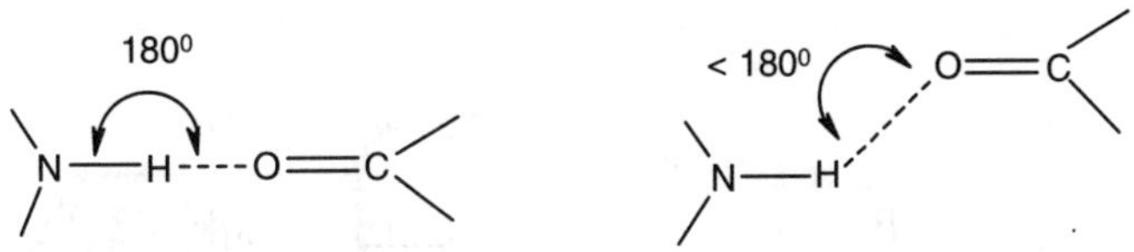

In biological system, one encounters groups like NH, OH, C=O, as a result hydrogen bonds are common feature. Hydrogen bonding stabilizes the helical structure of protein and double helical structure of DNA. Since both drugs as well as receptors contain the groups like NH, OH, C=O, hydrogen bonding between the two is a common feature of binding of a drug to a receptor. Before a drug (D-H) binds to the receptor (R) both are surrounded by water molecules in the body. The interaction between the two takes place by exchange mechanism (Fig. 1.12). This exchange is favourable and occurs readily with very little change in free energy.

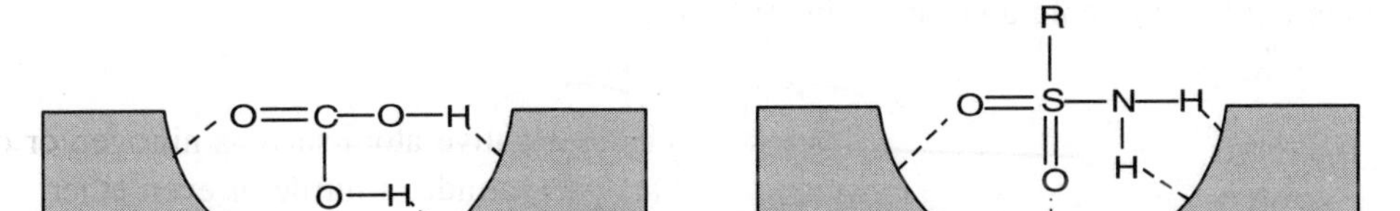

Fig. 1.12 Hydrogen bond formation

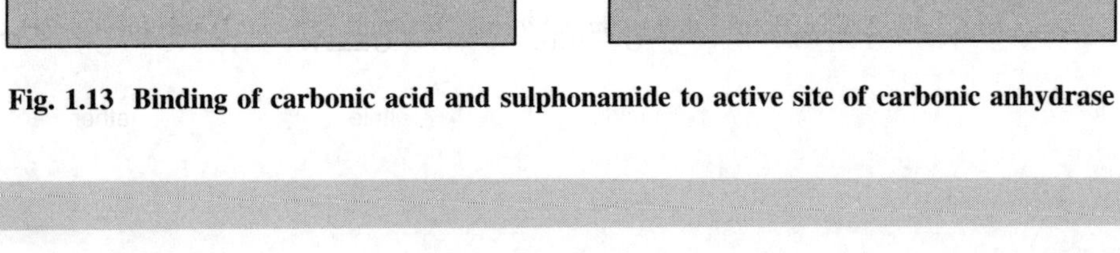

Fig. 1.13 Binding of carbonic acid and sulphonamide to active site of carbonic anhydrase

An example of the involvement of hydrogen bond in drug action is the diuretic activity of sulphonamides. The sulphonamide competes with the carbonic acid for the active site on carbonic anhydrase and binds to the receptor through hydrogen bonding (Fig. 1.13).

Hydrophobic Bonding

Both macromolecules as well as drug molecules have hydrophobic regions. These regions can be aryl or alkyl residues and they interact with each other and the interaction can be of appreciable magnitude. Such interaction between the non-polar regions is known as hydrophobic bonding. Before such an interaction takes place, the macromolecule (M) and the drug molecule (D) are surrounded by water molecules (o) in an orderly fashion. The interaction between the two takes place by displacement of water molecules (Fig. 1.14). The water molecules displaced are disordered as a result there is increase in entropy which results in stabilization of the system

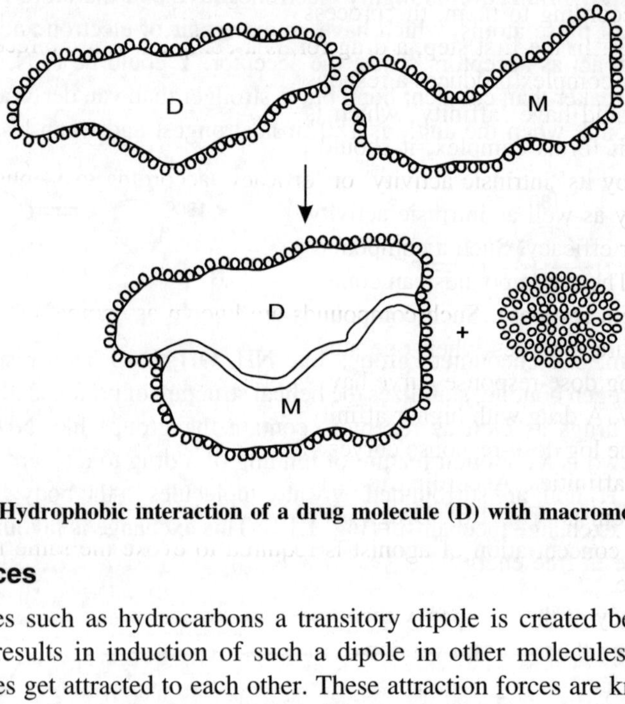

Fig. 1.14 Hydrophobic interaction of a drug molecule (D) with macromolecule (M)

van der Waals Forces

In non-polar molecules such as hydrocarbons a transitory dipole is created because of distortion of electron cloud. This results in induction of such a dipole in other molecules also. Because of this induction the molecules get attracted to each other. These attraction forces are known as van der Waals forces or London forces (Fig. 1.15). van der Waals forces are effective when the interacting atoms are at a distance of 4-6 Å. Further, they are of short duration and last for about 10^{-6} seconds. van der Waals forces operate in alkyl chains and aromatic rings and contribute significantly in the drug-receptor interactions reinforcing ionic and dipole interactions.

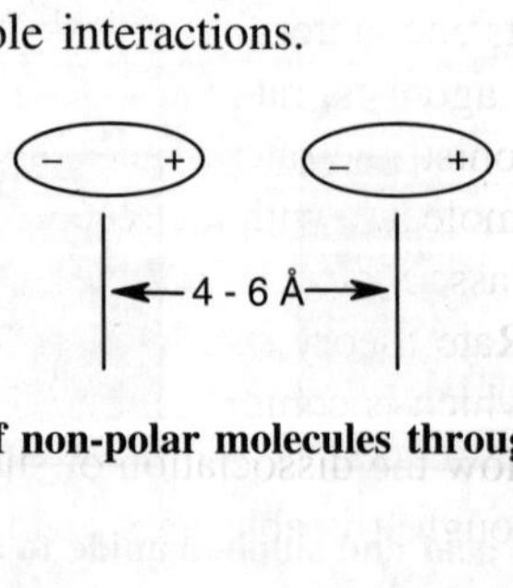

Fig. 1.15 Interaction of non-polar molecules through van der Waals forces

THEORIES OF DRUG ACTION

Most of the drugs act by interacting with specific sites, commonly known as receptors which results in a pharmacological response. Many theories have been proposed to explain as to how the drugs show their effect after interacting with the receptors. Some of these theories will be discussed here.

Occupancy Theory

According to occupancy theory, which was proposed by Clark and Gaddum, the intensity of the pharmacological response was directly proportional to the number of receptors occupied by the drug. Thus, the drug effect will be more intense as the number of occupied receptors increases and the maximum action will correspond to the occupation of all receptors. However, it has been observed that maximum response in some cases is never obtained even when the dose is increased indefinitely. To overcome this and other inconsistencies, Ariens and Stephenson proposed a modification of original occupancy theory. According to them, the process of production of a response by a drug essentially consisted of two stages. In the first step, a drug forms a complex with the receptor and in the second step, the drug-receptor complex produces a response. In order that it is able to form a complex with the receptor, the drug should have 'affinity' which is manifested in it through complimentary structure characteristics. After it forms complex, it should be able to generate a response which according to Ariens is manifested by its 'intrinsic activity' or 'efficacy' according to Stephenson. Thus, an agonist possesses both affinity as well as intrinsic activity or efficacy. A compound may possess affinity but no intrinsic activity or efficacy. Such a compound can form a complex with the receptor but is unable to produce response. These compounds can compete with the agonist for binding with the receptor but are unable to produce a response. Such compounds are known as competitive antagonists.

A more clear picture emerges when one studies the log dose-response curve. Thus, compounds which show similar log dose-response curve have similar intrinsic activity or efficacy (Fig. 1.3). Such drugs differ in affinity. A drug with higher affinity and higher efficacy will evoke a higher response at a lower dose. When the log dose-response curves differ in their shape, the drugs have differing intrinsic activities but similar affinities. According to Ariens, such compounds are dualistic and according to Stephenson partial agonists (Fig. 1.6). Drugs which do not show any response are antagonists and in their presence higher concentration of agonist is required to evoke the same intensity of response as without their presence.

One of the deficiency of the occupancy theory is its failure to explain the mechanism of drug action at molecular level. Even the modified version of the occupancy theory is not able to explain this aspect of drug action.

Rate Theory

This theory was proposed by Patton and coworkers. According to this theory, the pharmacological response of a drug is the function of its encounters per unit time with the receptor and not the formation of a stable complex. Thus, in case of agonists, rates of association and dissociation are fast as a result there is stimulation. In case of antagonist, the rate of dissociation is very slow as a result the number of encounters per unit time of a drug molecule with the receptor is much less as compared to an agonist. In case of partial agonist the rate of association is intermediate.

Like occupancy theory, Patton's Rate theory suffers from inconsistencies. One of these is the fact that a drug molecule has a structure which is complimentary to the receptor. As a result, it should form a stable complex with the receptor. How the dissociation of such a complex can take place, this theory is not able to explain. Secondly, although it is able to explain the differences between agonist, partial agonist, and antagonist, this theory is not able to explain the mechanism of drug action at molecular level.

Induced Fit Theory

This theory which was proposed by Koshland *et al* assumes that the active site of an enzyme or receptor need not be complimentary to the substrate/drug. The active site instead is flexible and elastic. When a substrate comes near this active site, it induces conformational changes in the enzyme or receptor molecule and this results in alignment/non alignment of the substrate molecule to the active site (Fig. 1.16). This hypothesis has been extended to explain the action of drugs. According to this theory, after the drug molecule binds to the receptor it causes reversible perturbation or changes in the tertiary structure of the protein which results in pharmacological response.

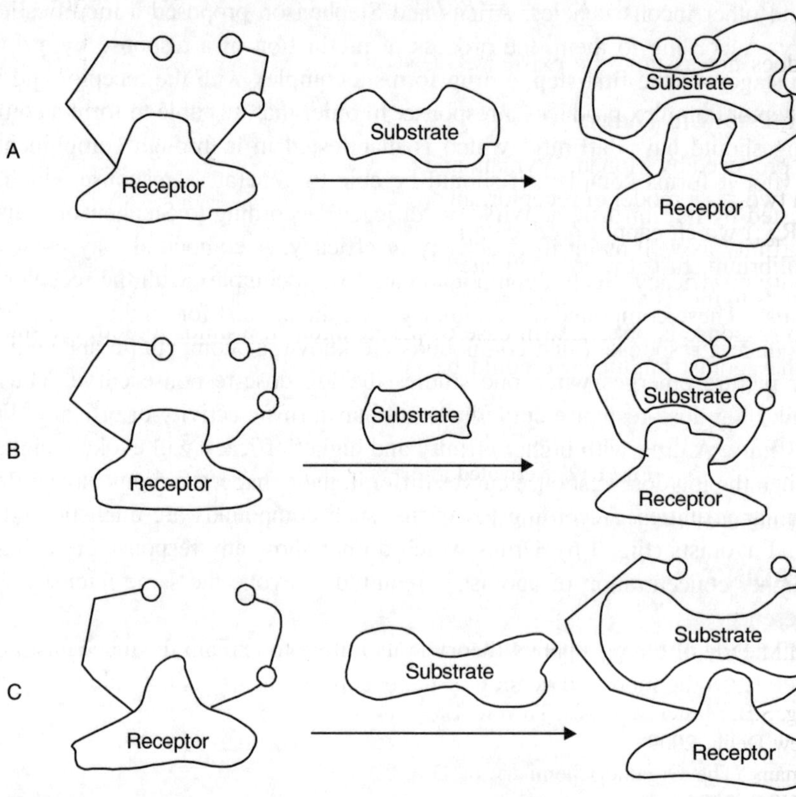

Fig. 1.16 Model of plastic active site. (A) denotes proper fitting of the substrate on the active site, while (B) and (C) shows improper fitting

Macromolecular Perturbation Theory

Macromolecular Perturbation Theory was proposed by Balleau in 1964. According to this theory when a drug molecule (D) interacts with the receptor (R) two types of conformational perturbations can occur and these include specific conformational perturbation and non-specific conformational perturbation. In case of specific conformational perturbation, the R*D (Eq. 8) complex can adsorb certain molecules (M) related to substrate and convert this substance to product (P) (Eq. 9) which is responsible for the pharmacological response. This happens in case of an agonist. Another type of conformational

$$R + D \longrightarrow R^{*}D \qquad \text{...(Eq. 8)}$$

$$R*D + M \rightleftharpoons R*DM \rightleftharpoons R*D + P \qquad \text{...(Eq. 9)}$$

perturbation, which is non-specific, may result because of complexation of an inhibitor (I) with receptor (R) (Eq. 10). This complex is not able to convert a molecule (M) to the product (P) (Eq. 11) and a pharmacological response is not generated. This happens in case of antagonist. If the drug has both the characteristics, i.e. it is able to generate both specific and non-specific perturbations then it can act as a partial agonist to antagonist.

$$R + I \longrightarrow R^{\#}I \qquad \text{...(Eq. 10)}$$

$$R^{\#}I \rightleftharpoons R^{\#}IM \not\rightleftharpoons R^{\#}IM + P \qquad \text{...(Eq. 11)}$$

This theory does not assume the existence of affinity and intrinsic activity in a drug molecule.

Activated–Aggregation Theory

This theory was proposed by Monad, Wyman, and Changeux in 1965 and Karlin in 1967. These authors have proposed a two-state model of receptor, an activated state (R_{act}) which can produce a response and a resting state (R_{rest}) which cannot produce a response (Fig. 1.17). As soon as an agonist binds to the receptor the equilibrium shifts towards activated state (R_{act}) and a response is obtained. Similarly, when the antagonist binds to the receptor in resting state, the equilibrium shifts towards the resting state (R_{rest}) as a resulting no response is obtained. In case of partial agonist, it binds to both the states. According to this theory, the agonist binding site could be different from the site where an antagonist binds.

$$R_{rest} \rightleftharpoons R_{act}$$

Fig. 1.17 Activated and resting state of receptor

As is evident none of the theories are able to explain the drug action at molecular level.

FURTHER READING

1. A. Korolkovas, "Essentials of Molecular Pharmacology," Wiley Interscience, New York, 1970.
2. H.P. Rang, M.M. Dale, J.M. Ritter, and P.K. Moore, "Pharmacology," 5th ed. Churchill Livingstone, Edinburgh, 2003.
3. B.G. Katzung, S.B. Masters, and A.J. Trevor, "Basic and Clinical Pharmacology," 11th ed., Tata McGraw-Hill Pvt. Ltd., New Delhi, 2009.
4. R.B. Silverman, "The Organic Chemistry of Drug Design and Drug Action," 2nd ed., Academic Press, Burlington, USA, 2004.

2

Sites of Drug Action

The various sites for drug action include:

(a) Receptors,
(b) Ion-channels, and
(c) Enzymes.

RECEPTORS

The various types of receptors include

(a) G-protein coupled receptors,
(b) Kinase linked receptors, and
(c) Nuclear receptors.

G-Protein Coupled Receptors (GPCR, 7-TM Receptors)

They are also called metabotropic receptors and are membrane bound. At present more than 100 receptors are known to be coupled with G-proteins and some of these include adrenergic receptors, serotonin (5-HT) receptors, muscarinic acetylcholine receptors, dopamine receptors, neurokinin peptide receptors, light receptors (rhodopsin) and their subtypes.

G-proteins serve as a link between the membrane bound receptor and the effector responsible for signal transduction. At present at least 13 G-proteins are known and these are of four types namely G_s, G_i, G_q, and G_{12} (Table 2.1).

Table 2.1 G-Proteins and their effectors

G-protein	*Receptor*	*Effector*
G_s	β-adrenergic, histamine serotonin	adenylyl cyclase and Ca^{2+} channel stimulation
G_i	α_2-adrenergic, muscarinic, opioid	adenylyl cyclase inhibition and activation of K^+ channels
G_q	muscarinic, serotonin (5-HT_{1C})	phospholipase C stimulation
G_{12}	aldosterone	modulates Na^+/H^+ exchanger

The G-protein coupled receptors consist of a single polypeptide chain. Since this chain traverses the plasma membrane seven times, they are also known as Seven Trans Membrane Receptors (7-TM Receptors) (Fig. 2.1). The N-terminal end of the polypeptide chain is extracellularly located and the C-terminal end intracellularly. There are two sites for binding of agonist/ligand. The smaller ligand binds in the extracellular region and the larger ligand on the region within the plasma membrane. The G-protein coupling domain is located intracellularly (Fig. 2.1). After the binding of a ligand these receptors either activate/inhibit G-proteins which in turn activate/inhibit the various effectors or the activity of an ion channel.

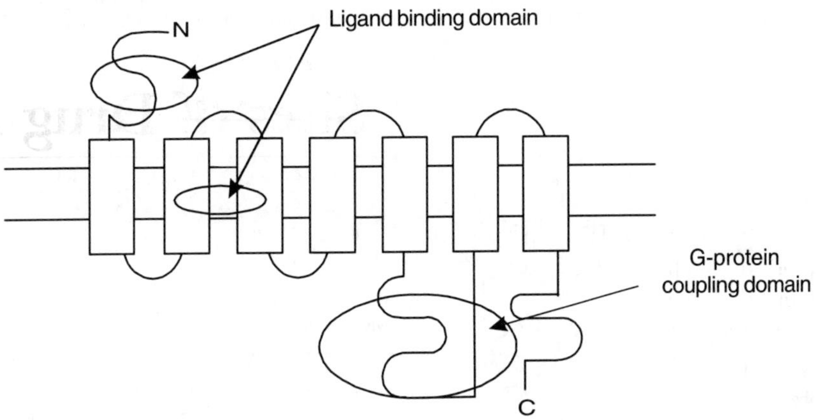

Fig. 2.1 G-protein coupled receptor

The G-proteins consist of three subunits namely, α, β and γ. After an agonist has bound to the receptor the α-subunit binds to it. Next, the bound GDP of α-subunit is exchanged with the cellular GTP. The G-α-GTP complex then dissociates and couples with the target protein where it activates the effector. The interaction with the target activates the GTPase which hydrolyzes the GTP. The G-α-GDP then joins the G-βγ-subunit (Fig. 2.2).

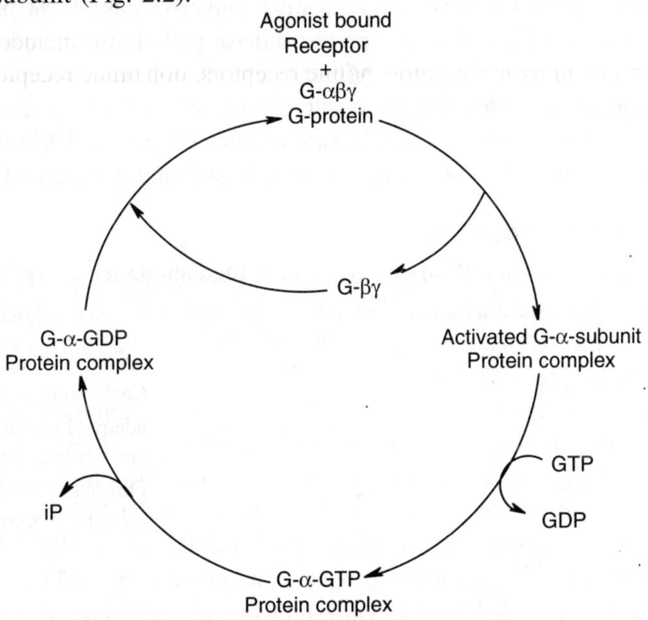

Fig. 2.2 The receptor G-protein cycle

The G-protein coupled receptors control different aspects of cell function through:
(a) adenylate cyclase/ cyc. AMP system, and
(b) phospholipase C_β Inositol system.

Adenylyl Cyclase/ cyc. AMP System

The association of Gsα-GTP protein complex with adenylyl cyclase stimulates the enzyme which converts adenosine triphosphate (ATP, 1) into cyclic adenosine monophosphate (cyc.AMP, 2). The cyc.AMP in turn activates the inactive protein kinase (PKA). The active protein kinase regulates various enzymes involved in various metabolisms by phosphorylation of these enzymes. Thus, phosphorylation

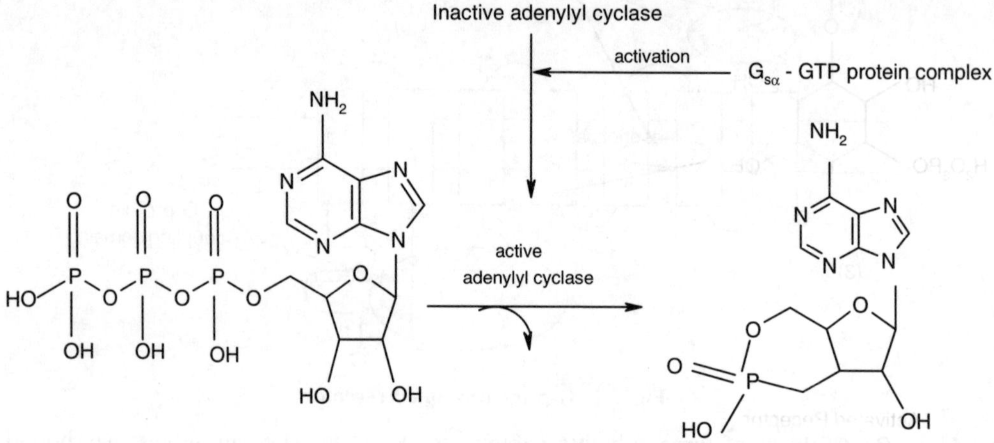

(1) (2)

of lipase activates it and this results in increased lipolysis. Phosphorylation of active glycogen synthase results in inactive glycogen synthase which results in reduction of glycogen synthesis. Phosphorylation of phosphorylase kinase activates it, this inturn activates phosphorylase b, the enzyme responsible for glycogen breakdown. Other effects of active protein kinase include phosphorylation of myosin light chain kinase, which results in its inactivation. Myosin light chain kinase is required for the contraction of smooth muscle. Inactivation of this enzyme results in relaxation of smooth muscle. Receptors linked to G_i –protein inhibit adenylyl cyclase which results in reduced cyc. AMP levels. Examples of these include α_2-adrenergic receptors, M_2-muscarinic receptors, and opiate receptors.

Phospholipase C_β/ Inositol System

Another enzyme which is activated through G-protein is phospholipase C_β (PLC_β). PLC_β hydrolyses phosphatidylinositol 4,5-diphosphate (PIP_2, 3) to diacylglycerol (DAG, 4) and inositol 1,4,5-triphosphate (IP_3, 5). Both of these act as second messengers. Phospholipase D hydrolyses PIP_2 (3) to phosphatidic acid (6) and inositol diphosphate (7).

The activation of phospholipase C_β takes place in the same fashion as adenylyl cyclase. After the agonist binds to the receptor, the receptor-agonist complex catalyzes GTP-GDP exchange on an associated protein, G_q. The activated G_q then activates the membrane bound phospholipase C_β which catalyzes the production of DAG (4) and IP_3 (5) by hydrolyzing PIP_2 (4). The IP_3 (5), which is water soluble, diffuses from plasma membrane to endoplasmic reticulum where it binds to specific IP_3 receptors and causes Ca^{++} channels within endoplasmic reticulum to open, resulting in increased Ca^{++} levels in cytosol. The elevated Ca^{++} levels activate protein kinase C. Diacylglycerol also activates the protein kinase C. Protein kinase C catalyzes the transfer of phosphoryl groups of specific residues in one or more target proteins, thereby altering their activity and the cell metabolism (Fig. 2.3).

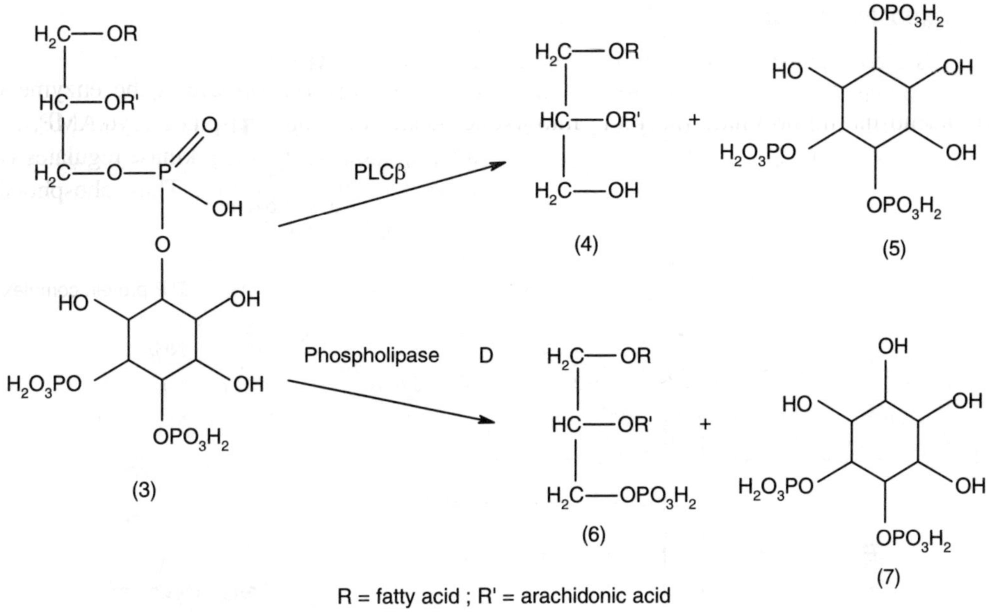

(3) (4) (5) (6) (7)

R = fatty acid ; R' = arachidonic acid

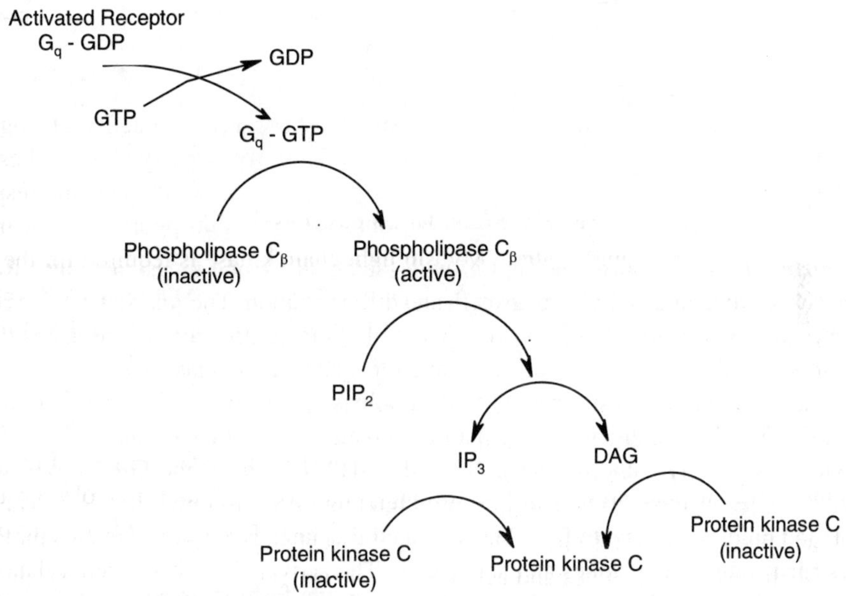

Fig. 2.3 Phospholipase C_β PIP_2 system

There can be multiple G-protein coupled receptor types for a single agonist/ligand. In such a situation same agonist/ligand can activate variety of effector pathways and thus produce different cellular responses. For example, norepinephrine binding to β_1-adrenergic receptor results in stimulation of adenylyl cyclase system which is responsible for increase in heart rate. Binding of norepinephrine to α_2-adrenergic receptor on the other hand results in activation of IP_3 system which results in contraction of smooth muscle. Thus, a single agonist/ligand can give rise to wide variety of responses by binding to different receptor subtypes.

Kinase-linked Receptors

They constitute receptors for various hormones (insulin), various cytokines, and growth factors. They comprise of extracellular ligand binding domain (N-terminal) linked to intracellular catalytic domain (carboxy terminal) linked by a single transmembrane helix (Fig. 2.4). The intracellular domain is enzymic in nature with protein kinase or guanylate cyclase activity. Tyrosine kinase constitutes the

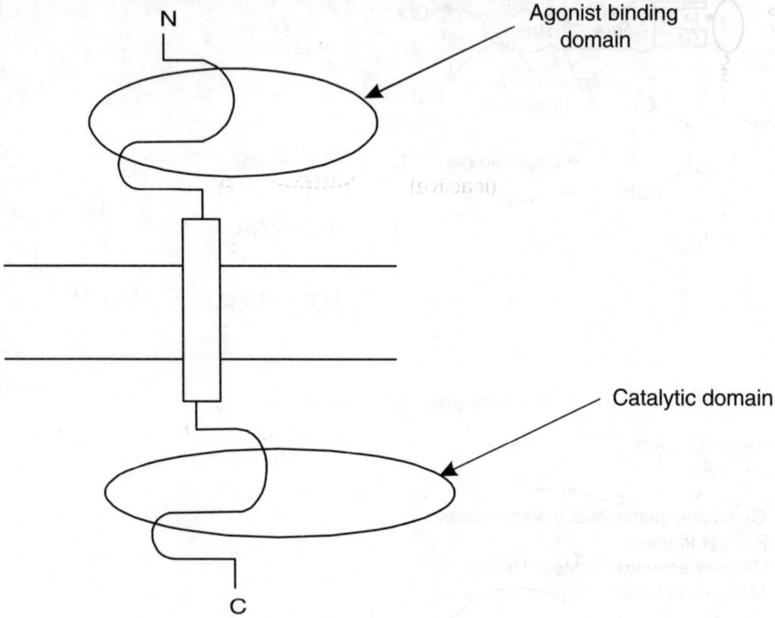

Fig. 2.4 Kinase-linked receptors

intracellular domain of various hormones and growth factors. Tyrosine kinase activates Ras/Raf/Map pathway which is important in cell division, growth and differentiation. The Jak/Stat pathway is activated by cytokines and this controls the synthesis and release of some inflammatory substances. Some of the hormone receptors (atrial natriuretic factor) are linked to gaunylate cyclase..

The signal transduction mechanism in Ras/Raf/Map kinase pathway involves binding of a ligand to its receptor (Fig. 2.5). Next, there is conformational change and dimerization. This is followed by autophosphorylation of the tyrosine residues. Next, the SH2 domain of the Grb2 protein bind to the phosphorylated tyrosine residues. This is followed by binding of Sas to Grb2 then Ras. This causes the release of GDP and binding of GTP to Ras. The activated Ras next, binds and activates the Raf and Raf phosphorylates MEK on serine residues and activates it. The activated MEK phosphorylates MAPK on the threonine and tyrosine residues, thereby activating it. The activated MAPK enters nucleus where it phosphorylates proteins such as Elk-1. This along with SRF stimulates transcription and translation of genes nedded for cell division.

The Jak/Stat pathway involves binding of cytokines to the receptor and subsequent dimerization. Next, it attracts Janus kinase (Jak) and phosphorylates the receptor dimmer. The Jak then phosphorylates the SH2 domain of Stat. After phosphorylation and dimerization they move to nucleus where they bind to specific DNA sequence and stimulate the expression of specific target genes (Fig. 2.6).

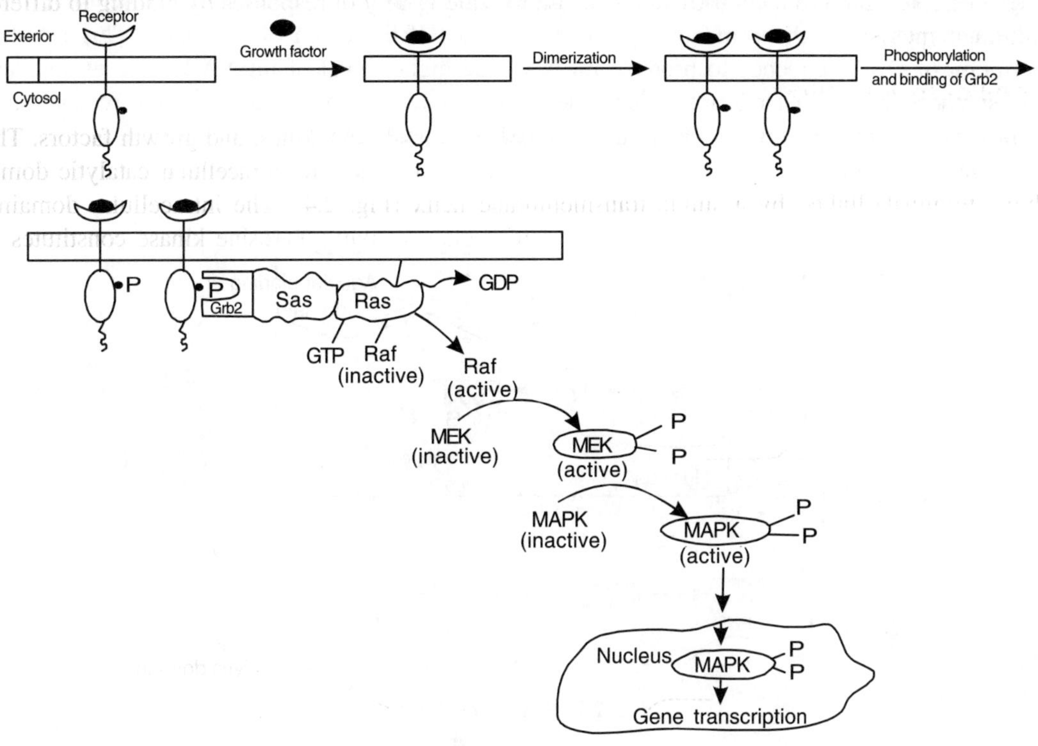

Ras - Guanisine nucleotide binding protein
Raf1 - Protein kinases
MAPK - Mitogen activated protein kinase
MEK - Mitogen activated extracelluar regulated kinase

Fig. 2.5 Ras/Raf/MAP kinase pathway

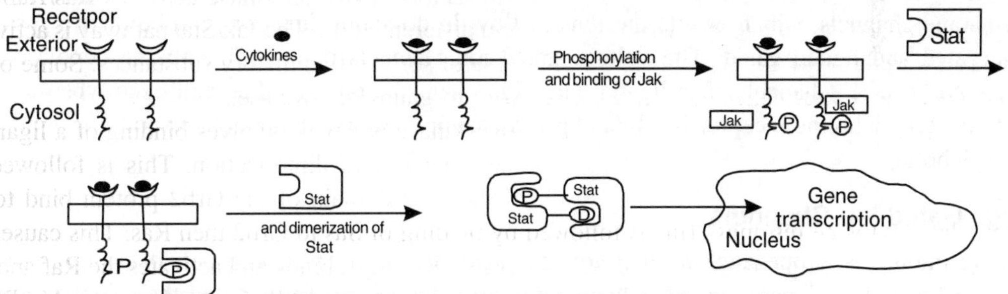

STAT - Signal transduction and activators of transcription

Fig. 2.6 The Jak/Stat pathway

Nuclear Receptors

Steroid and thyroid hormones exert their effects in nucleus and alter the gene expression. After their release these hormones are carried by specific carrier proteins to their target tissues. In target cells, they pass the plasma membrane and bind to specific receptor proteins in nucleus (Fig. 2.7). This binding of steroid to receptor initiates a conformational change resulting in formation of steroid-receptor dimmer. The dimmer interacts with hormone-responsive element (HRE) region of the DNA. This results in transcription of DNA sequence to produce mRNA. The higher level of mRNA lead to an increased protein synthesis in endoplasmic reticulum. The proteins synthesized include enzymes, receptors, and other factors that subsequently result in the steroidal hormonal response regulating the cell function, growth, and differentiation.

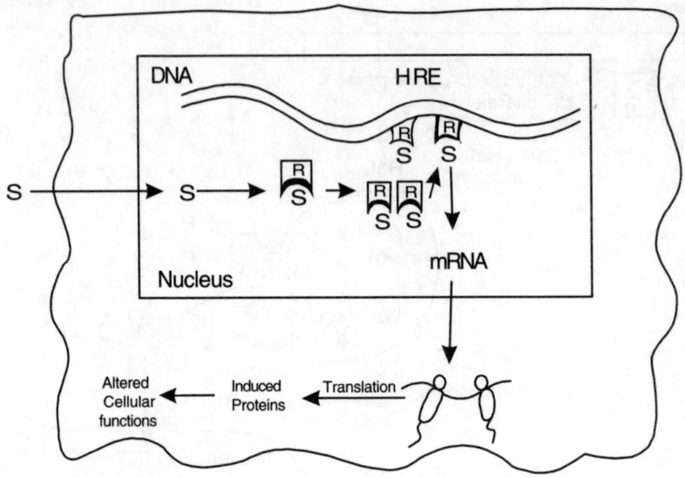

Fig. 2.7 Steroid receptor

ION CHANNELS

The lipid bilayer of biological membrane is impermeable to ions or polar molecules. They are transported across the membrane by pumps and channels. Pumps use the energy such as ATP or light to drive the thermodynamically uphill transport of ions or molecules. Examples of pumps are Ca^{++}-ATPase and Na^{+}-K^{+}-ATPase. This is active transport. Channels on the other hand enable ions to flow rapidly through membrane in downhill direction. This is an example of passive transport or facilitated diffusion.

Membrane channels, which enable the ions to flow in downhill direction, can be of two types the voltage gated and ligand gated. The voltage gated ion channels open by membrane depolarization. Example Na^{+} and K^{+} channels. The ligand gated ion channels, on the otherhand open when a ligand binds to it. Acetylcholine receptor is a ligand gated channel because it opens in response to binding of the acetylcholine.

Voltage Gated Ion Channels

The nerve impulse is propagated through voltage gated channels. These channels open in response to an electrical impulse. Three types of voltage gated ion channels are known and these include voltage gated Na^{+} channel, K^{+} channel and Ca^{++} channel.

Signalling in nervous system is achieved through neuron. The axon of neuron are separated by a gap called synaptic cleft. The communication across the cleft is through small molecules called neuro-transmitters such as acetylcholine. The end of presynaptic axon is filled with synaptic vesicles filled with acetylcholine molecules.

In the resting state the presynaptic neuron is polarized (inside negative –60 to –70 mv). This state is achieved by pumping 3 Na^{+} out for every 2 K^{+} pumped into neuron by Na^{+}-K^{+}-ATPase. A nerve

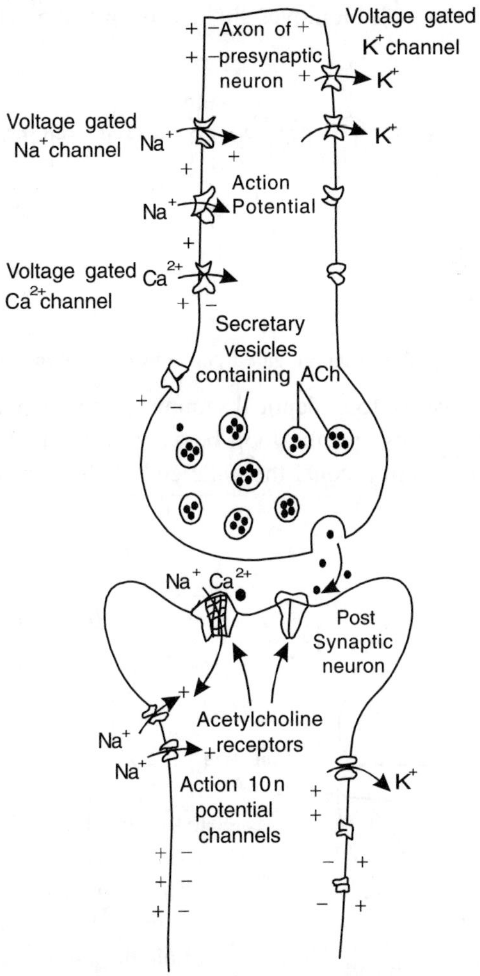

Fig. 2.8 Voltage gated ion channels

impulse or action potential is generated when the membrane potential goes beyond threshold value of –60 to –40 mv. The generated action potential travels along the axon (Fig. 2.8). This results in opening of the Na^+ channels leading to depolarization. The membrane potential becomes positive within a millisecond and attains a value of +30 mv. When the wave of depolarization reaches axon tip, voltage gated Ca^{++} channels open allowing the entry of Ca^{++}. The increased concentration of Ca^{++} at the tip of presynaptic axon results in the release of acetylcholine from vesicles by a process of exocytosis. The binding of acetylcholine to the axon of presynaptic neuron results in opening of Na^+ and Ca^{++} channels resulting in depolarization of the presynaptic cell. The electrical impulse is thus propagated from one neuron to other.

Molecular Architecture of Na^+, K^+, and Ca^{++} Channels

The voltage gated Na^+ and Ca^{++} channel comprise of a single polypeptide chain (1,840 amino acids) with four repeating units. Each repeating unit is composed of six transmembrane helices. The loops between helices 5 and 6 form the pore (Fig. 2.9). One of the helix contains more of basic amino acids.

This region acts as a voltage sensor and it moves slightly towards the outer surface resulting in opening of the channel.

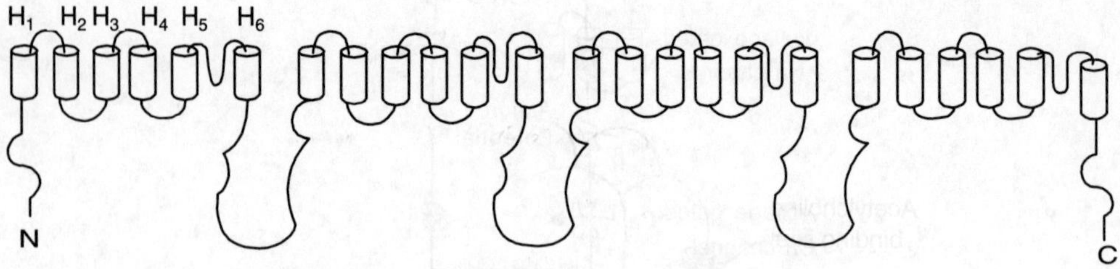

Fig. 2.9 Voltage gated Na^+ and Ca^{2+} channels

The potassium channel consists of four identical subunits rather than a single long chain (Fig. 2.10a). Each subunit consists of six helices and the loop between 5th and 6th helices form part of the gate (Fig. 2.10b). The four subunits form a cone, the wide end of the cone facing the extracellular region (Fig. 2.10a)

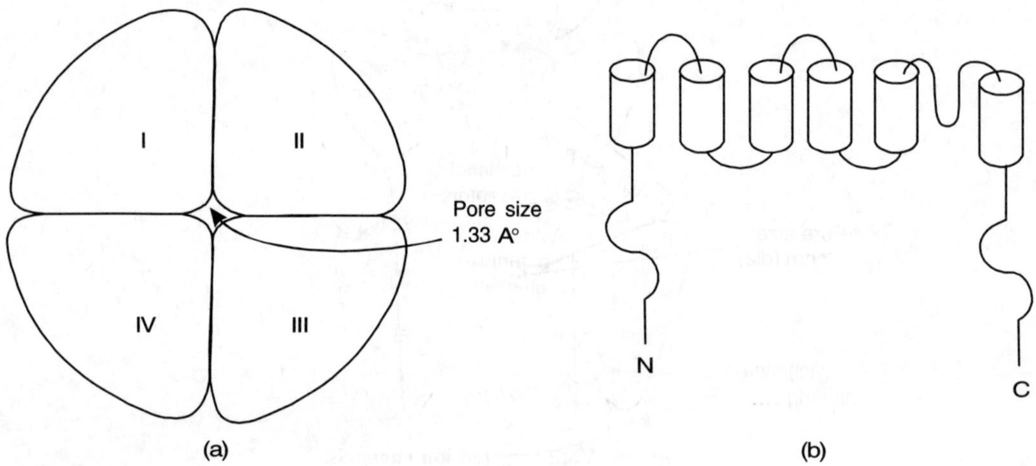

Fig. 2.10 Voltage gated potassium channel

Ligand Gated Ion Channel

They are also known as ionotropic receptors. They are membrane proteins having structure similar to voltage gated ion channel and have a ligand binding site (receptor) in extracellular domain. The channel opens when the ligand binds to the receptor. The ligands which bind on the receptors are fast acting neurotransmitters. Some of the receptors include nicotinic acetylcholine receptors, $GABA_A$ receptors, 5-hydroxytryptamine ($5\text{-}HT_3$) receptors, and inositol triphosphate receptors (IP_3R).

One of the very well studied ligand gated ion channel is the nicotinic acetylcholine receptor. It is a pentamer of four kinds, α_2, β, γ, δ arranged to form a ring. The five subunits each posssss four membrane spanning helical domain and one of these (M_2) from each subunit defines the central pore (Fig. 2.11). There are two acetylcholine (Ach) binding sites in the extracellular portion of the receptor and at the interface between the α- and adjoining subunit. The five M_2 helices form the pore. In the closed state, bulky leucine side chains block the channel. After the acetylcholine binds to its receptor, a conformational

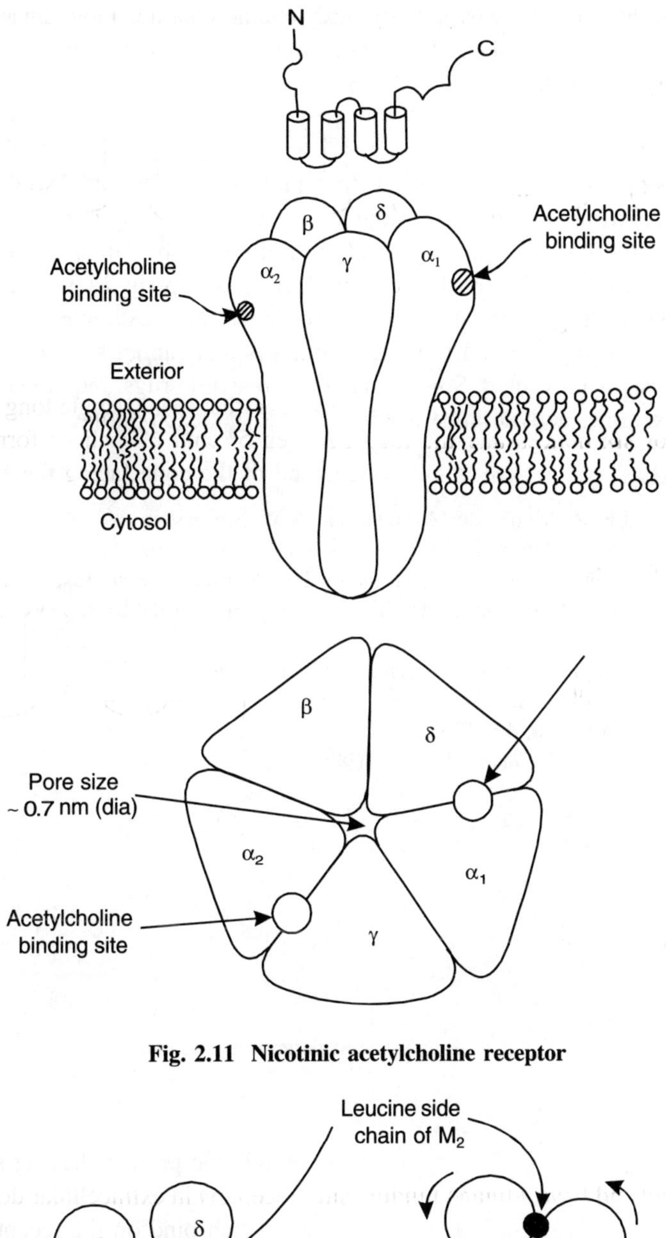

Fig. 2.11 Nicotinic acetylcholine receptor

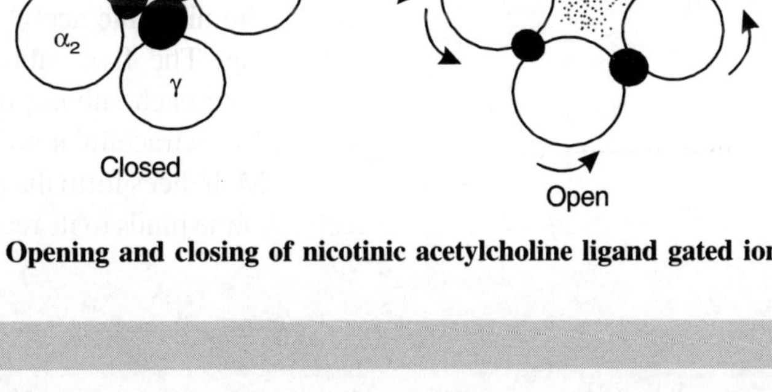

Fig. 2.12 Opening and closing of nicotinic acetylcholine ligand gated ion channel

change occurs. The five M_2 helices twist slightly, and leucine residues move away from the channel and smaller polar residues take their place. This results in opening of the channel, allowing the passage of Na^+, K^+, and Ca^{++} (Fig. 2.12).

ENZYMES

Enzymes are also the sites of action of drugs. A drug molecule when bound to an enzyme catalyzes the production of a second messenger, thus stimulating enzyme activity. The drug can also act as a competitive inhibitor of the enzyme either reversibly or irreversibly. Some of the examples include neostigmine as irreversible inhibitor of acetylcholine and aspirin as irreversible inhibitor of cyclooxygenase. Similarly drugs may also act as antimetabolites, examples include 5-fluorouracil which acts as an antimetabolite of uracil in purine synthesis and cannot be converted to thymidylate. As a result DNA synthesis is prevented. Some drugs known as prodrugs, require activation by enzyme before they can act, example, activation of azathioprine to mercaptopurine.

FURTHER READING

1. E.J. Ariens, A.J. Beld, J.F. Rodrigues de Miranda, and A.M. Simons, in the "Receptors, A Comprehensive Treatise," R.D. O'Brien, Ed., Plenum Press, New York, 1979, pp. 33-91.
2. E.M. Ross and T.P. Kenakin in "Goodman & Gilman's The Pharmacological Basis of Therapeutics," 10th ed. (Intern.), J.G. Hardman and L.E. Limbird, Eds., McGraw-Hill Medical Publishing Division, New York, 2001, pp. 31-43.
3. M.E. Linder and A.G. Gilman, *Scientific American*, July 1992, p. 56.
4. T. Kenakin, *Nature Rev. Drug Discovery*, **1**, 103 (2002).
5. D.R. Waud, *Pharmacol. Rev.*, **20**, 49 (1968).
6. A.M. Speigel, *Ann. Repts. Med. Chem.*, **23**, 235 (1988).

3

Adrenergic Receptors

Autonomic nervous system controls the involuntary functions of the body. It consists of two major divisions, the sympathetic and parasympathetic. Adrenergic drugs exert their effect on sympathetic portion of the autonomic nervous system. The principal neurotransmitter of the sympathetic division is norepinephrine (1) epinephrine (2), a hormone of the adrenal medulla is closely related to norepinephrine (1) and shows similar pharmacological actions. Both norepinephrine (1) and epinephrine (2)

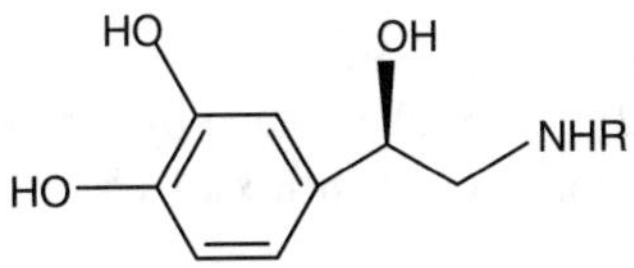

(1), R = H

(2), R = CH_3

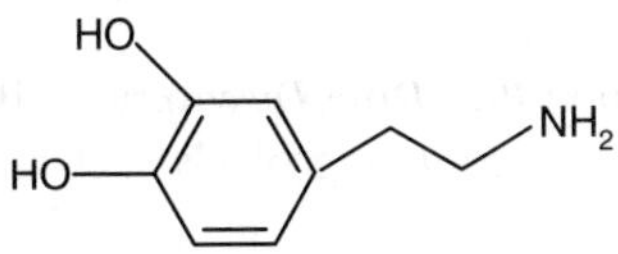

(3)

along with dopamine (3), the predominant neurotransmitter of mammalian extrapyramidal system and mesolimbic neuronal pathway, constitute what are known as catecholamines.

Stimulation of sympathetic nervous system causes increased rate and force of heart contraction, rise in blood pressure, shift of blood flow to skeletal muscles, dilation of bronchioles and pupil, and an increase in blood glucose levels through gluconeogenesis and glycogenolysis. All these physiological and metabolic effects are mediated through the neurotransmitter norepinephrine (1). As a part of response to stress, adrenal medulla is also stimulated, this results in increased levels of epinephrine (2) in blood. The actions of norepineprine (1) and epinephrine (2) are similar at some sites but differ at others. Thus, both stimulate myocardium, however, norepinephrine (1) causes constriction of blood vessels in skin, mucosa and kidney while as epinephrine (2) dilates the blood vessels.

The biosynthesis of norepinephrine (1) takes place in adrenergic neuron (Fig. 3.1). The precursor is L-tyrosine (4) which is taken up by the adrenergic neurons by an active transport system. In the adrenergic neurons, it is converted to dihydroxy phenylalanine (DOPA, 5). This is the rate determining step. In the next step DOPA (5) is converted to dopamine (3) by the action of aromatic aminoacid decarboxylase. The dopamine (3) formed is taken up in storage vesicles where it is converted to norepinephrine (NE, 1) by dopamine β-hydroxylase by introducing a hydroxyl group at β-position in *R*-configuration. The norepinephrine (1) is stored in storage vesicles along with ATP in the ratio of 4:1

complex (Fig. 3.1). The norepinephrine (1) is converted to epinephrine (2) by the action of phenylethanolamine N-methyltransferase which transfers the methyl group of S-adenosylmethionine to norepinephrine (1).

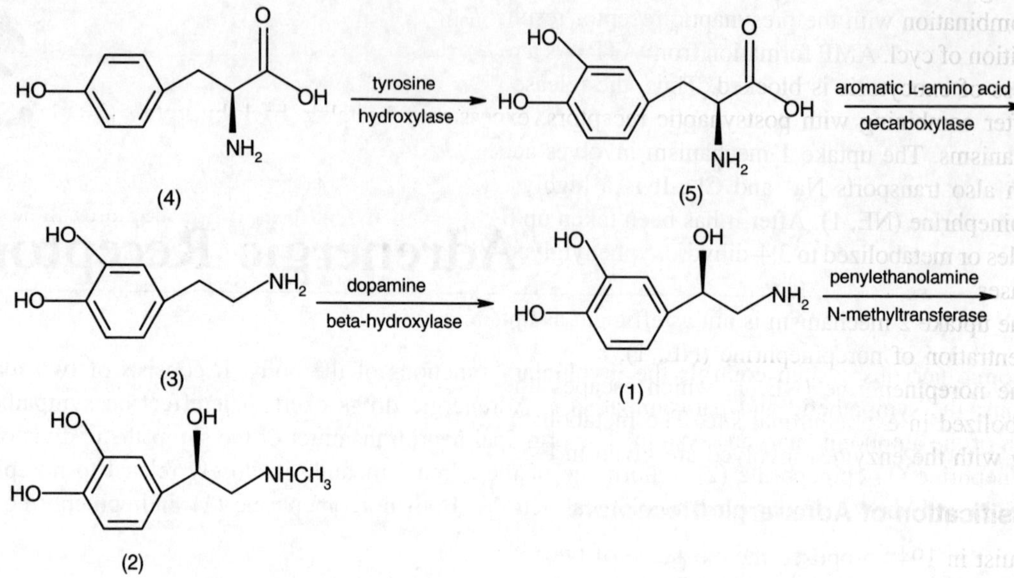

The release of norepinephrine (1, Fig. 3.1 NE) into synapse takes place by a process of exocytosis. Depolarization results in opening of Ca^{++} channel and consequent influx of Ca^{++}. The Ca^{++} promotes

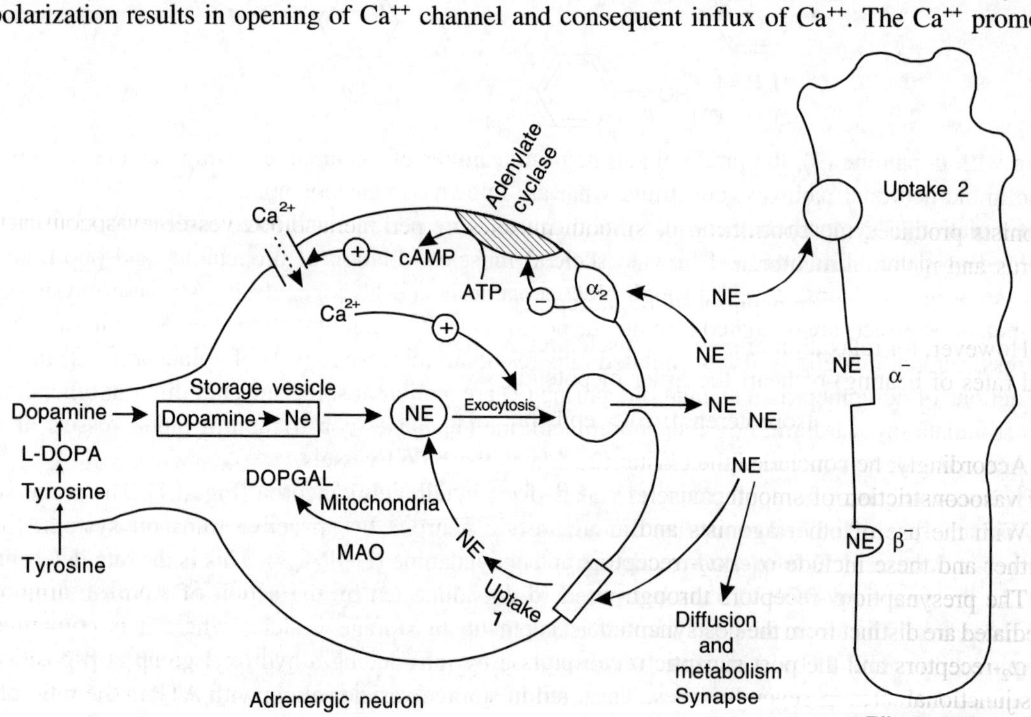

Fig. 3.1 Biosynthesis, storage and release of norepinephrine (NE, 1)

the fusion of storage vesicles to neuronal cell membrane and by process of exocytosis the neurotransmitter norepinephrine (NE,1) along with ATP is spilled in synapse.

The released norepinephrine (NE,1) can combine either with the presynaptic receptor located in the adrenergic neurons or receptors located in the effector cell.

Combination with the presynaptic receptor results in inhibition of adenylyl cyclase and consequent inhibition of cycl. AMP formation from ATP. As a result the opening of Ca^{++} channel is blocked and the process of exocytosis is blocked. Thus, the release of norepinephrine (NE, 1) is autoregulated.

After combining with postsynaptic receptors, excess may be taken back by uptake 1 or uptake 2 mechanisms. The uptake 1 mechanism involves active transport by neurotransmitter transport protein which also transports Na^+ and Cl^-. It is a highly efficient transport mechanism and is selective for norepinephrine (NE, 1). After it has been taken up by uptake 1 mechanism, it may be stored in storage vesicles or metabolized to 3,4-dihydroxyphenylglycoaldehyde (DOPGAL) by mitochondrial monoamine oxidases.

The uptake 2 mechanism is not as efficient as uptake 1 mechanism and operates in presence of high concentration of norepinephrine (NE, 1).

The norepinephrine (NE, 1) which escapes uptake processes may diffuse from synapse and get metabolized in extraneuronal site. The metabolism of norepinephrine (NE, 1) and epinephrine (E, 2) along with the enzymes involved are given in Fig. 3.2.

Classification of Adrenergic Receptors

Ahlquist in 1948 proposed the existence of two adrenergic receptors. He determined the responses of norepinephrine (1), epinephrine (2), and isoproterenol (6) on isolated organs. He found that these

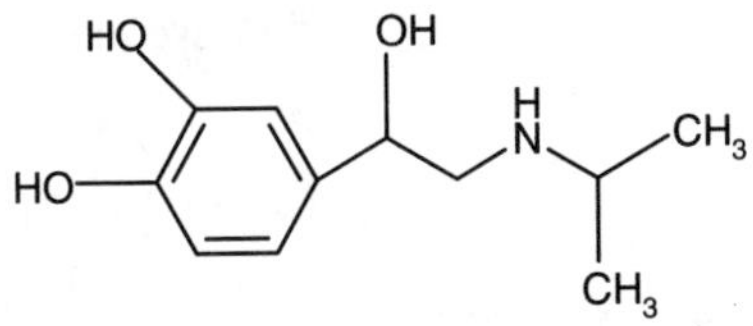

(6)

agonists produced the contraction of smooth muscles of peripheral blood vessels (vasoconstriction), uterus and nictating membrane with an order of potency:

epinephrine (2) > norepinephrine (1) >>isoproterenol (6)

However, for relaxation of smooth muscle preparation and excitation (increase in force of contraction and rates of beating) of heart the order of potency was:

Isoproterenol (6) > epinephrine (2) > norepinephrine (1)

Accordingly, he concluded the existence of two types of adrenergic receptors and named them as α- for vasoconstriction of smooth muscles and β- for vasodilation of smooth muscles.

With the use of other agonists and antagonists, it has been possible to classify the two receptors further and these include α_1-, α_2- receptors and β_1-, β_2-, and β_3- receptors.

The presynaptic α-receptors through which the feedback inhibitory effect of norepinephrine (1) is mediated are distinct from the postsynaptic α-receptors, The presynaptic α-receptors have been designated as α_2-receptors and the post synaptic α-receptors as α_1-receptors. The α_2-receptors are also present at postjunctional sites in several tissues. Thus, stimulation of postjunctional sites in brain are associated with reduced norepinephrine (1) release. Infact this is the mode of action of clonidine (7)

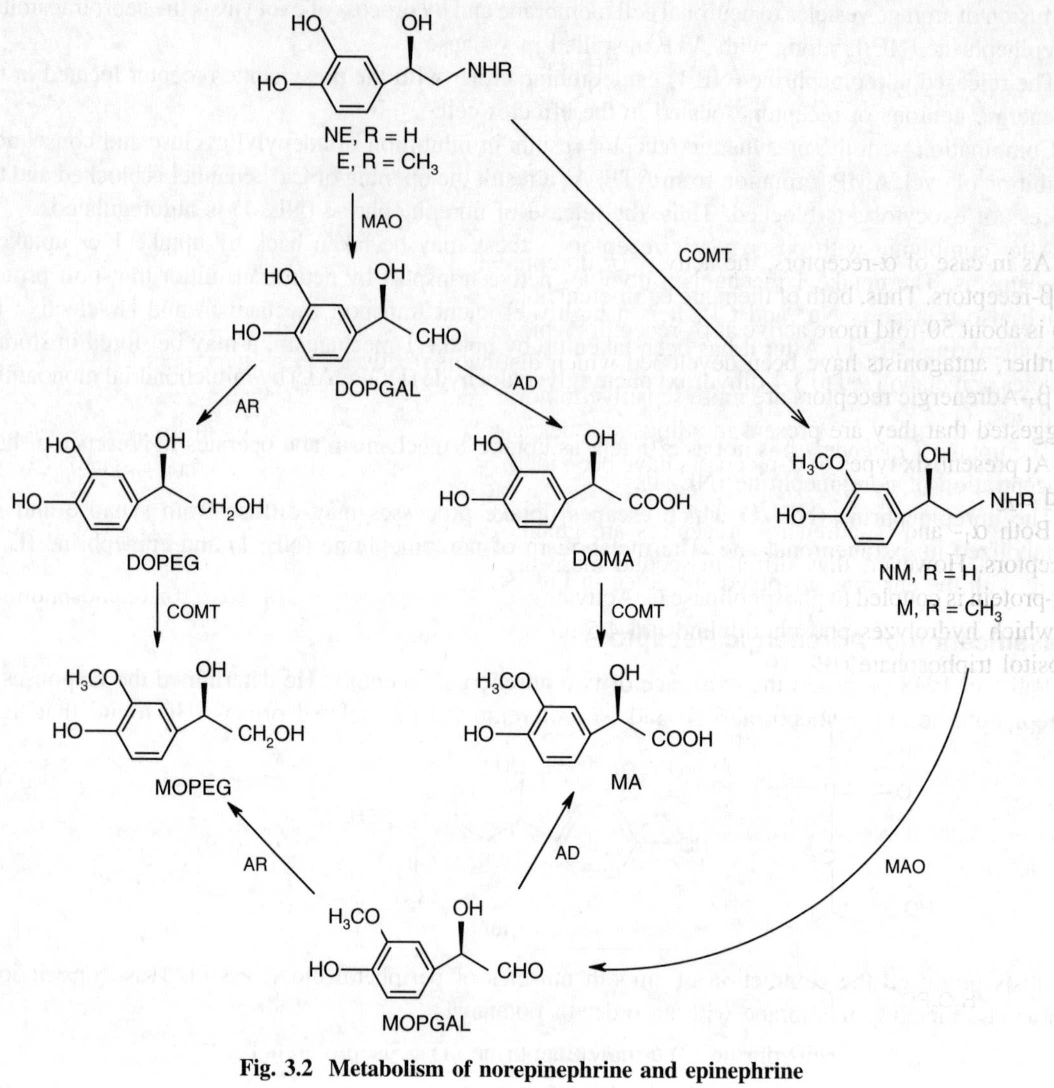

Fig. 3.2 Metabolism of norepinephrine and epinephrine

(**AD** - aldehyde dehydrogenase; **AR** - aldehyde reductase;
COMT - catechol-O-methyltransferase;
DOMA - 3,4-dihydroxymandelic acid; **DOPEG** - 3,4-dihydroxyphenylethyleneglycol;
DOPGAL - 3,4-dihydroxyphenylglycoaldehyde;
E - epinephrine
M - metanephrine; **MA** - 3-methoxy-4-hydroxymandelic acid; **MAO** - monoamine oxidase;
MOPEG - 3-methoxy-4-hydroxyphenylethyleneglycol; **MOPGAL** - 3-methoxy-4-hydroxyphenylglycoaldehyde
NE - norepinephrine; **NM** - normetanephrine)

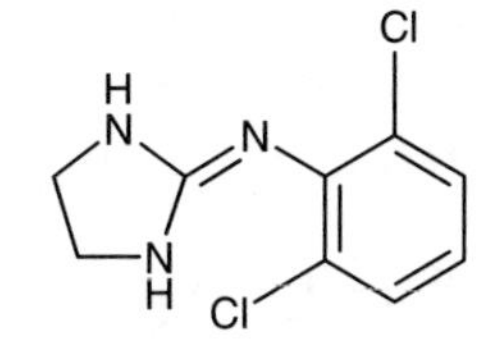

(7)

As in case of α-receptors, the activity of norepineprine (1) and epinephrine (2) also differs in case of β-receptors. Thus, both of them are equipotent at β_1-receptors (in myocardium), however, epinephrine (2) is about 50-fold more active at β_2-receptors which are found in smooth muscles and most other sites. Further, antagonists have been developed which distinguish between these two types of receptors.

β_3-Adrenergic receptors are more sensitive to norepinephrine (1) than to epinephrine (2). It has been suggested that they are present in adipose tissues and their stimulation results in lipolysis.

At present six types of α-receptors have been identified and these include α_{1A}, α_{1B}, α_{1D} and α_{2A}, α_{2B}, and α_{2C}.

Both α_1- and α_2-adrenergic receptors are guanine-nuceotide-regulatory protein (G-protein) linked receptors. However, they differ in second messenger system. In case of α_1-adrenergic receptor, the G_q-protein is coupled to phospholipase C. Activation of α_1-receptor results in activation of phospholipase C which hydrolyzes phosphotidylinositol-4,5-diphosphate (PIP_2, 8) into diacyglycerol (DAG, 9) and inositol triphosphate (IP_3, 10).

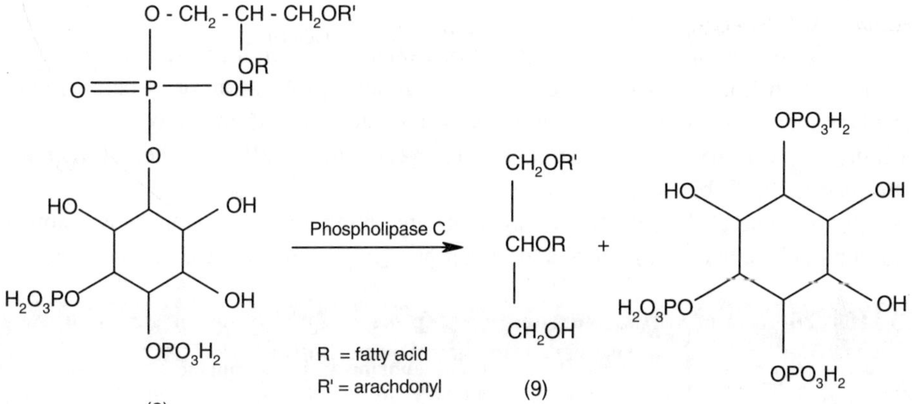

(8) (9) (10)

Both of these function as second messengers. Production of DAG (9) results in activation of membrane bound kinase which causes phosphorylation of proteins. IP_3 (10), on the other hand causes release of Ca^{++} from intracellular stores, the endoplasmic reticulum. The endoplasmic reticulum is coupled to calcium channel, which open after IP_3 binds to receptor in endoplasmic reticulum. Increased free intracellular Ca^{++} results in smooth muscle contraction, increased force of contraction of cardiac muscles and transmitter release.

The α_2-adrenergic receptors are G_i-linked. Activation of these receptors results in inhibition of adenylyl cyclase which is responsible for converting ATP (11) to cyc.AMP (12). This results in lowering of cyc. AMP levels which results in inhibition of norepinephrine (1) release.

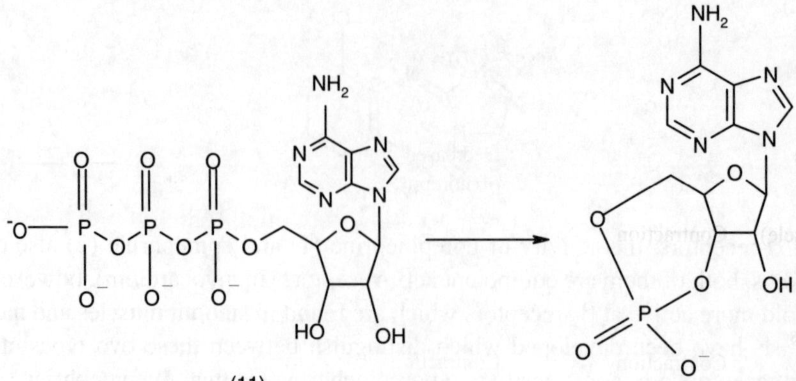

(11) (12)

In summary, the stimulation of α_1-adrenergic receptors results in vasoconstriction, relaxation of gastrointestinal smooth muscles, salivary secretion and hepatic glucogenolysis. While as stimulation of α_2-adrenergic receptors results in inhibition of norepineprine (1) release, platelet aggregation, contraction of vascular smooth muscles and inhibition of insulin release.

All the three types of β-receptors are linked to guanine nucleotide Gs and the second messenger in all the three subtypes is adenylyl cyclase which catalyzes the formation of cyc. AMP (12) from ATP (11). The increased levels of cyc. AMP (12) results in activation of protein kinase which phosphorylates myosin-light-chain-kinase, thereby inhibiting the contraction. Activation of β-receptors also reduces the intracellular Ca^{++} through efflux.

The effect of stimulation of β_1-adrenergic receptors, thus, results in increased cardiac rate and force, β_2-receptor stimulation leads to bronchial dilation, vasodilation, relaxation of visceral smooth muscles and hepatic glycogenolysis and the stimulation of β_3-receptors results in lipolysis.

The distribution of various classes of adrenergic receptors and the effect of their stimulation on some organs is summarized in Table 3.1.

The structures of some of the selective α_1-agonists and antagonists, α_2-agonists and antagonists, β_1-agonists and antagonists, and β_2-agonists and antagonists are listed in Figs. 3.3 to 3.10.

Table 3.1 Distribution of various adrenergic receptors in some tissues/organs and the effects observed on their stimulation

Tissue/organ	*Receptor type and the effect observed on its stimulation*			
	α_1	α_2	β_1	β_2
Heart	–	–	Increased force and rate of contraction	–
Liver	Glycogenolysis and glyconeogenesis	–	–	Glycogenolysis and glyconeogenesis
Pancreas (β-cells)	–	Decreased secretion of insulin	–	–
Platelets	–	Aggregation	–	–

(Contd.)

(Table 3.1 contd.)

Tissue/organ	*Receptor type and the effect observed on its stimulation*			
	α_1	α_2	β_1	β_2
Nerve terminals	–	Decreased release of norepinephrine	–	Increased release of norepinephrine
Eye (radial muscle)	Contraction	–	–	–
Skeletal muscles	–	–	–	Glycogenolysis
Smooth muscles				
(a) vascular	Contraction	Contraction	–	Relaxation
(b) gentiourinary	Contraction	–	–	Relaxation
(c) bronchial	Constrict	–	–	Relaxation
(d) gastrointestinal	Hyperpolarization and relaxation	–	–	– Relaxation

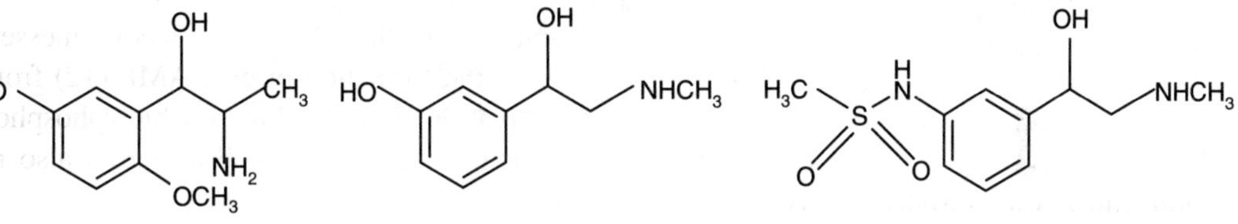

Methoxamine Phenylephrine Amidephrine

Fig. 3.3 Some of the selective α_1-adrenoreceptor agonists

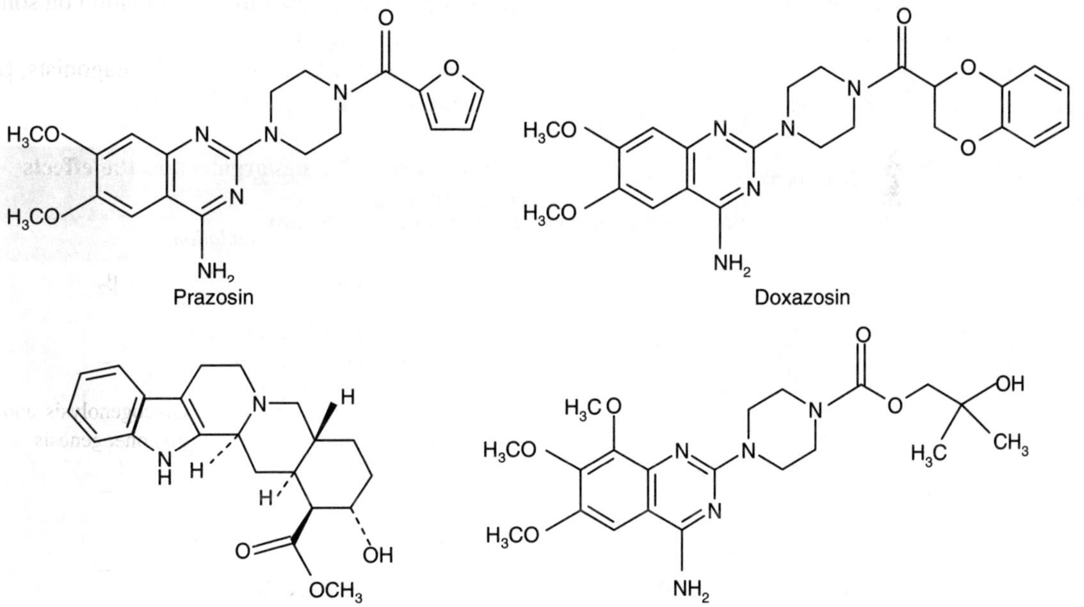

Prazosin Doxazosin

Corynanthine Trimazosin

Fig. 3.4 Some of the selective α_1-adrenoreceptor antagonists (*contd.*)

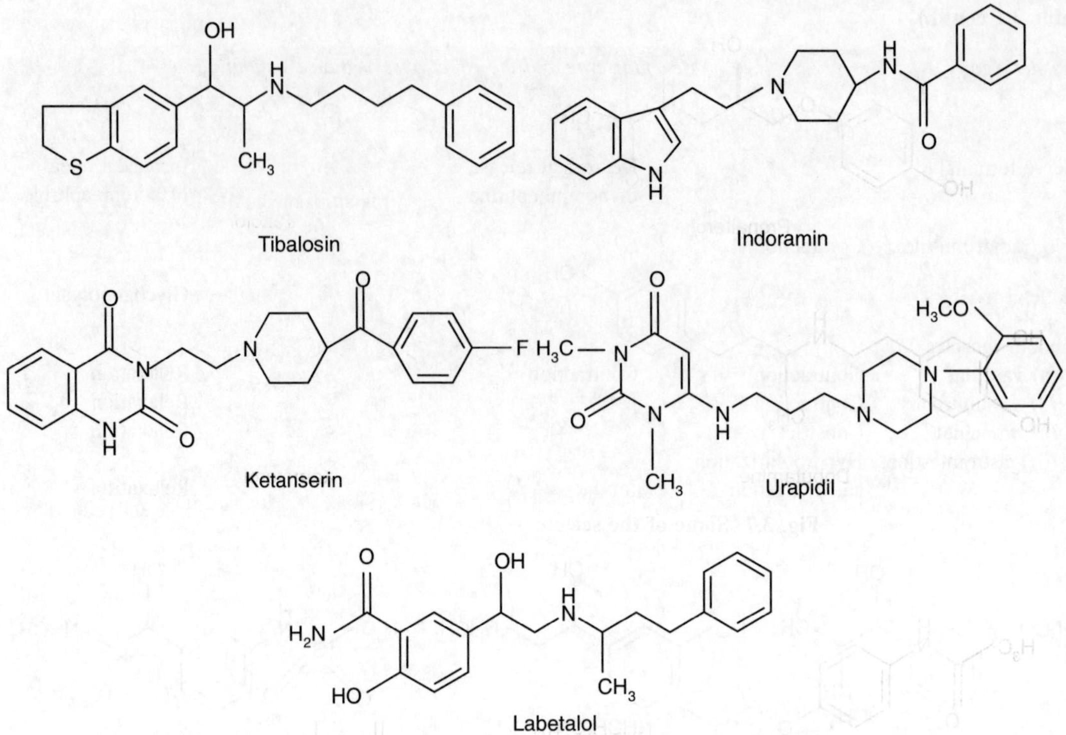

Fig. 3.4 Some of the selective α_1-adrenoreceptor antagonists

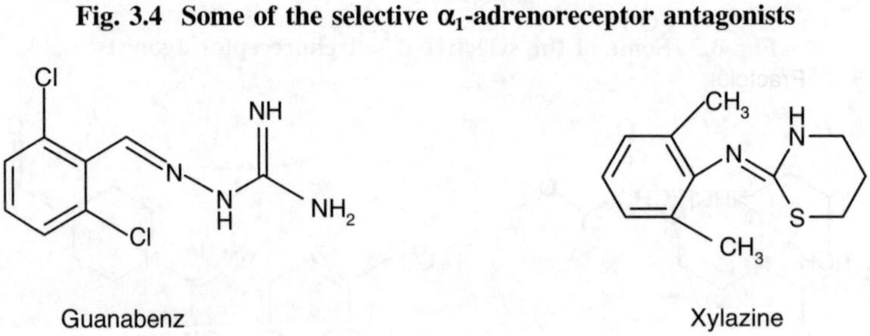

Fig. 3.5 Some of the selective α_2-adrenoreceptor agonists

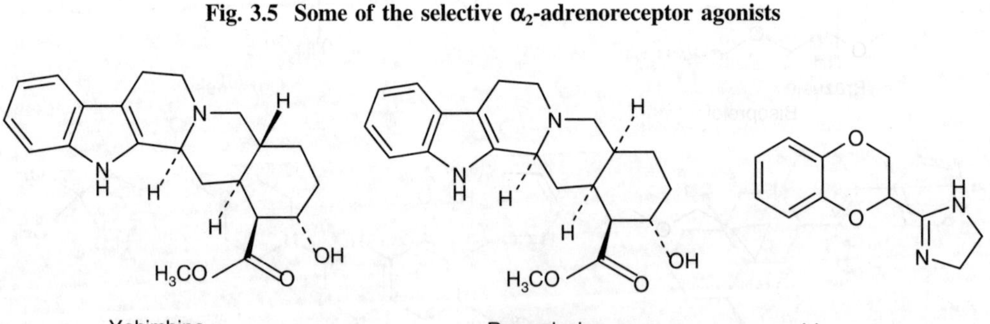

Fig. 3.6 Some of the selective α_2-adrenoreceptor antagonists

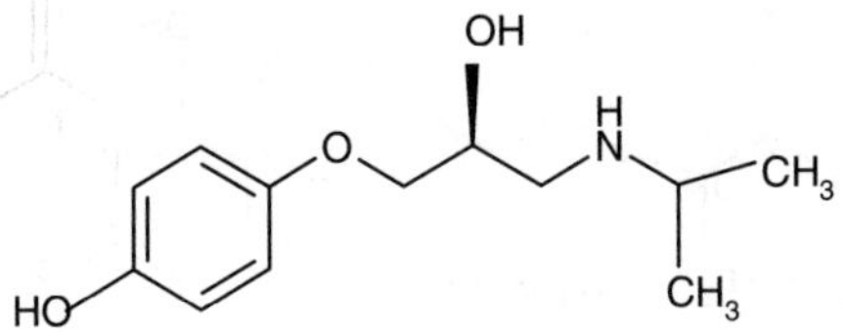

Prenalterol

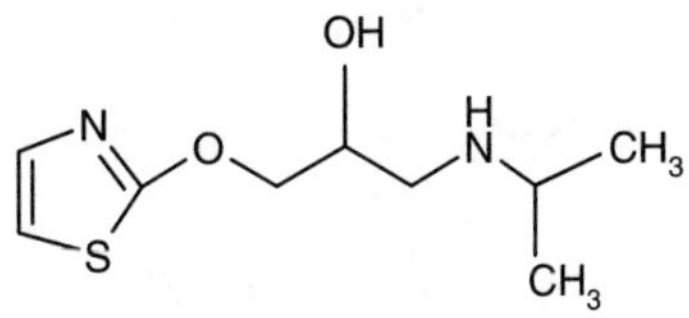

Tazolol

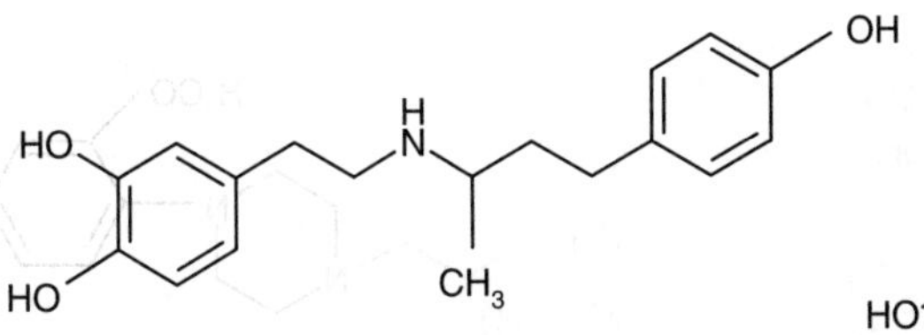

Dobutamine

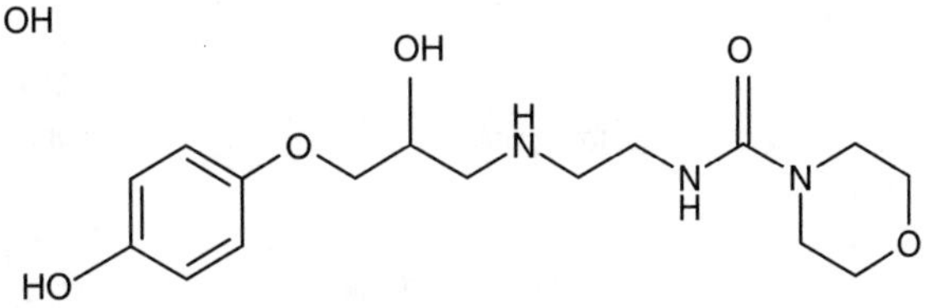

Xamoterol

Fig. 3.7 Some of the selective β_1-adrenoreceptor agonists

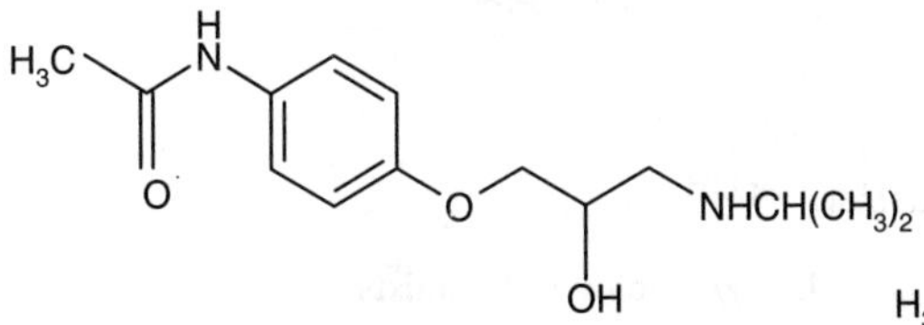

Practolol

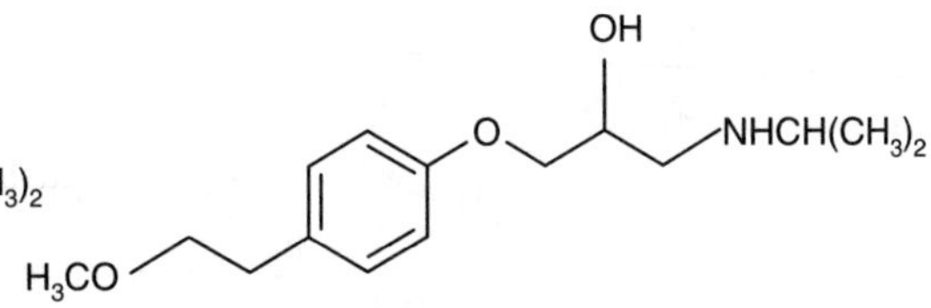

Metoprolol

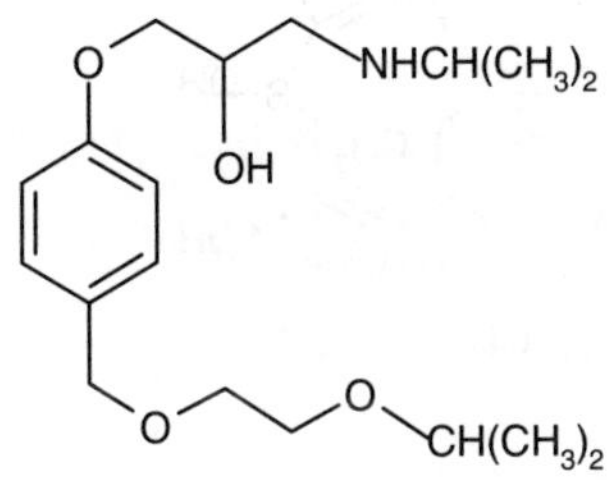

Bisoprolol

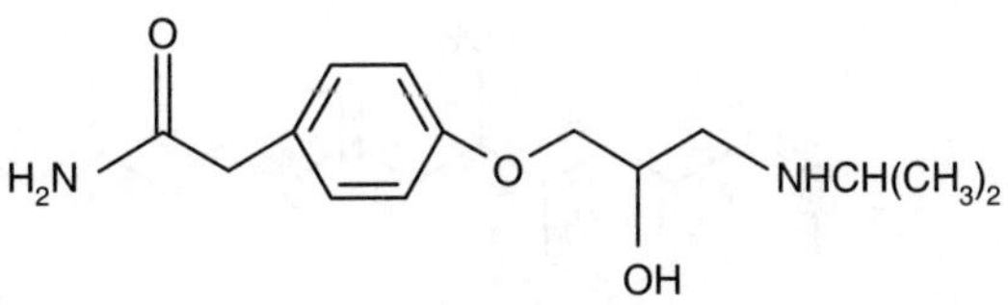

Atenolol

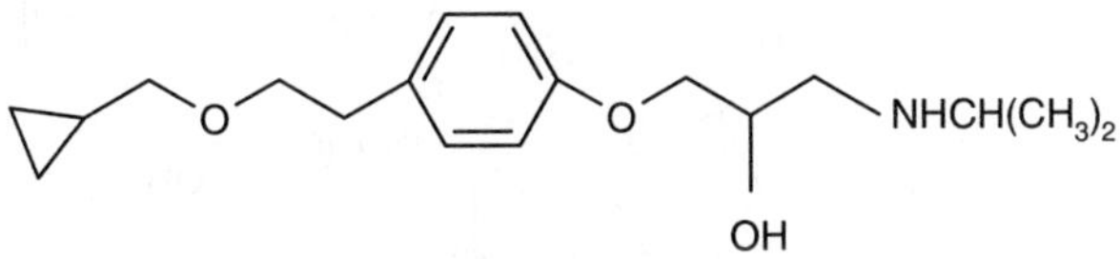

Betaxolol

Fig. 3.8 Some of the selective β_1-adrenoreceptor antagonists

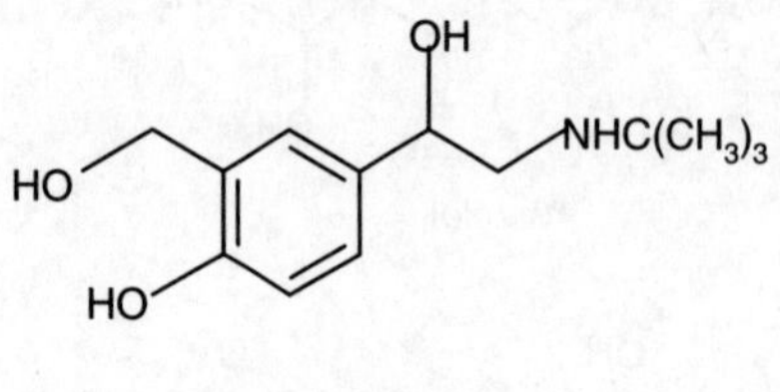

Salbutamol

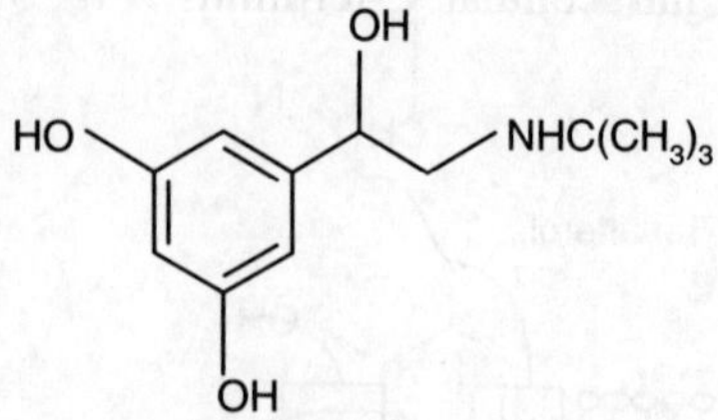

Terbutaline

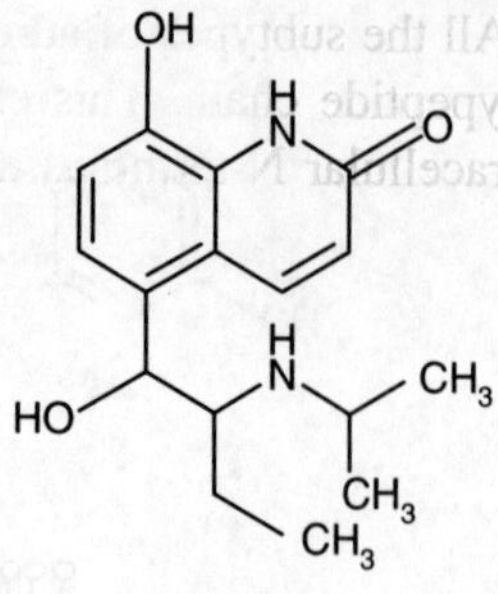

Procaterol

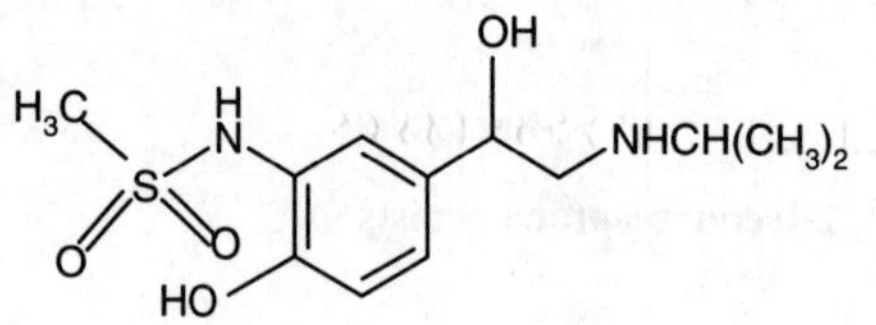

Soterenol

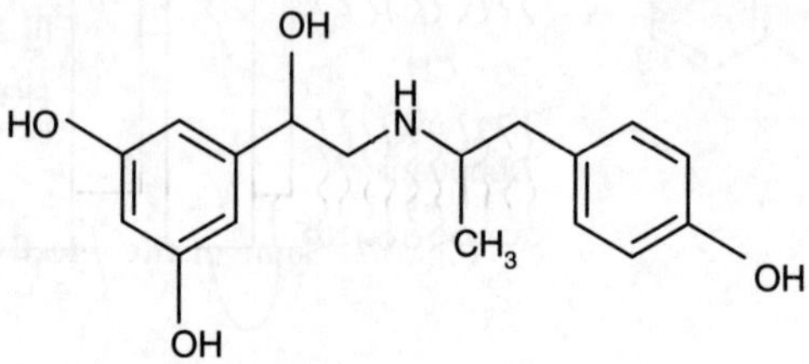

Fenoterol

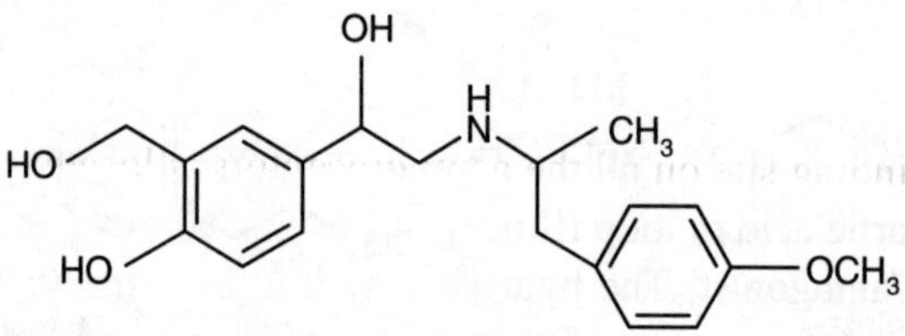

Salmefamol

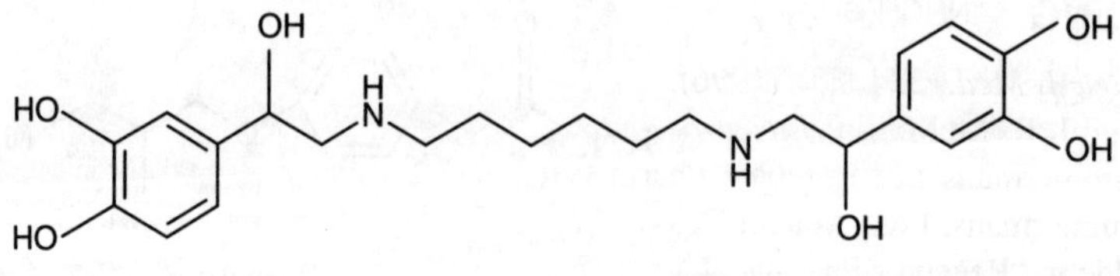

Hexoprenaline

Fig. 3.9 Some of the selective β_2-adrenoreceptor agonists

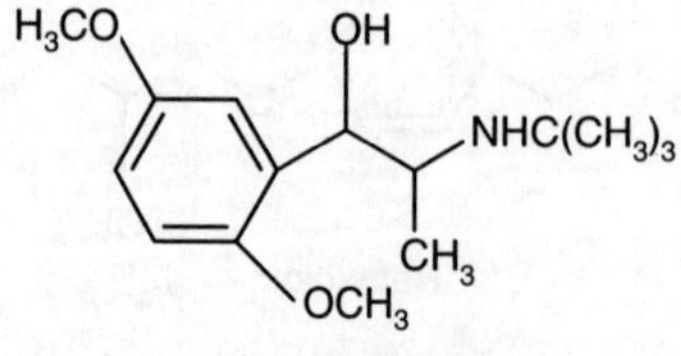

Butoxamine

Fig. 3.10 Some of the selective β_2-adrenoreceptor antagonist

All the subtypes of adrenergic receptors i.e. α_{1A}, α_{1B},α_{1D}, α_{2A}, α_{2B}, α_{2C}, β_1, β_2, and β_3 have a single polypeptide chain. This chain is looped back and forth through cell membrane seven times with an extracellular N-terminus and intracellular C-terminus (Fig. 3.11).

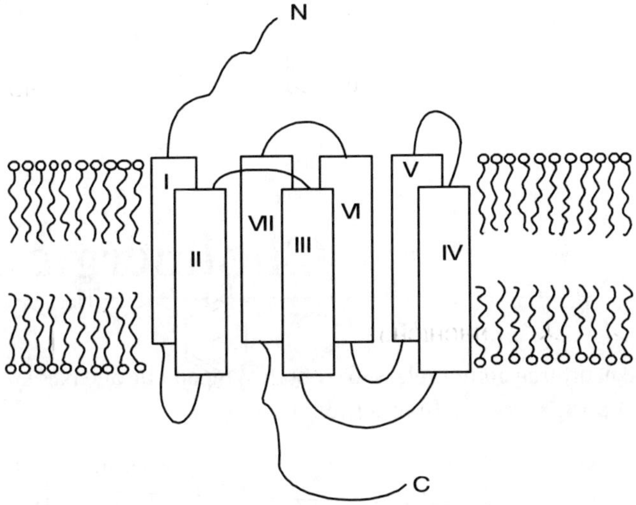

Fig. 3.11 Adrenergic receptor

The agonist/antagonist binding site on all the adrenoreceptors is located within the membrane bound portion of the receptor. Aspartic acid in loop III has been implicated in binding of the positively charged amino group of the agonist/antagonist. The hydroxyls of the two serine residues in loop V have been implicated in hydrogen bond formation of the catechol hydroxyl groups of the agonist. Further phenylalanine in the transmembrane domain VI is involved in binding of the catechol ring.

FURTHER READING

1. P.A. Insel, *N.Engl. J. Med.*, **334**, 580 (1996).
2. R.J. Summers and L.R. McMartin, *J. Neurochem.*, **60**, 10 (1993).
3. P.B.M.W.M. Timmermans in "Receptor Pharmacology and Function," M. Williams, R.A. Glennon, and P.B.M.W.M. Timmermans, Eds., Marcel Dekker Inc., New York, 1989, p. 173.
4. Otto-Erich Brodde in "Receptor Pharmacology and Function," M. Williams, R.A. Glennon, and P.B.M.W.M. Timmermans, Eds., Marcel Dekker Inc., New York, 1989, p. 207.
5. M.E. Linder and A.G. Gilman, *Scientific American*, July 1992, p. 56.
6. T. Kenakin, *Nature Rev. Drug Discovery*, **1**, 103 (2002).

4

Cholinergic Receptors

Acetylcholine (1) is the neurotransmitter released by both sympathetic and parasympathetic preganglionic fibres as well as by all postganglionic fibre terminals.

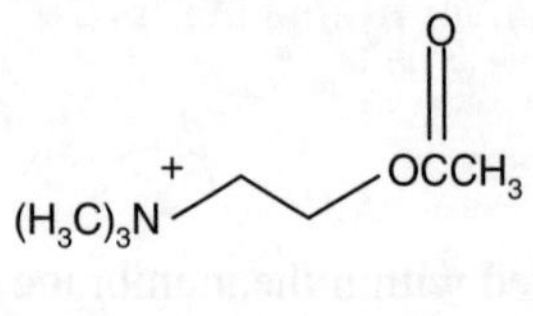

(1)

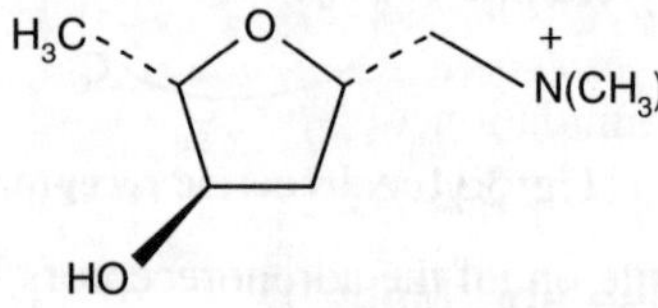

(2)

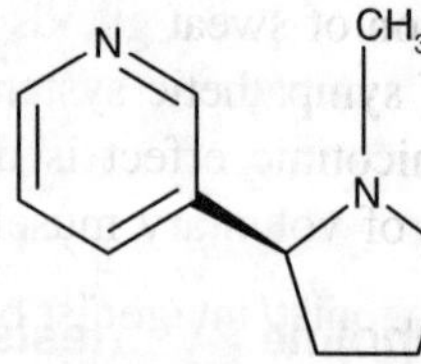

(3)

While studying the pharmacological actions of acetylcholine (1), Dale observed two types of actions, the muscarinic and nicotinic. The muscarinic effects were similar to the effects produced by (2*S*, 3*R*, 5*S*) (+)-muscarine (2), an alkaloid obtained from mushroom, *Amanita muscaria*. The nicotinic effects were similar to that produced by the alkaloid (S)(-)-nicotine (3) obtained from dried leaves of *Nicotiana tobacum*. Thus, in small doses, acetylcholine (1) produced muscarinic effects which included, vasodilation and slowing of heart. These effects were abolished or blocked by atropine (4). When acetylcholine is given in large doses it produces nicotinic effects which resulted in initial rise in blood pressure due to stimulation of sympathetic ganglia and consequent vasoconstriction and secondary rise resulting from secretion of epinephrine (5). This is blocked by d-tubocurarine chloride (6).

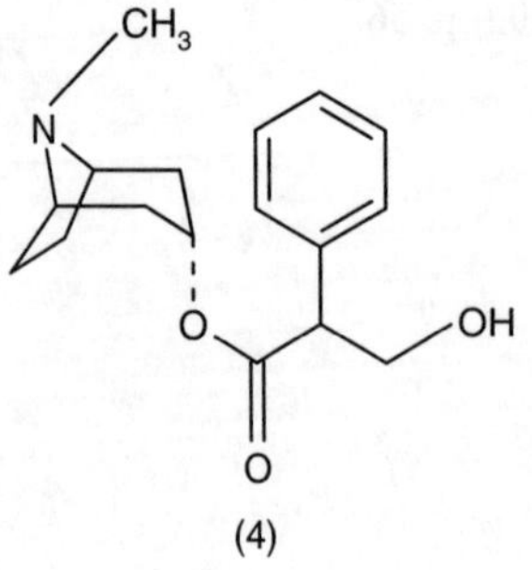

(4)

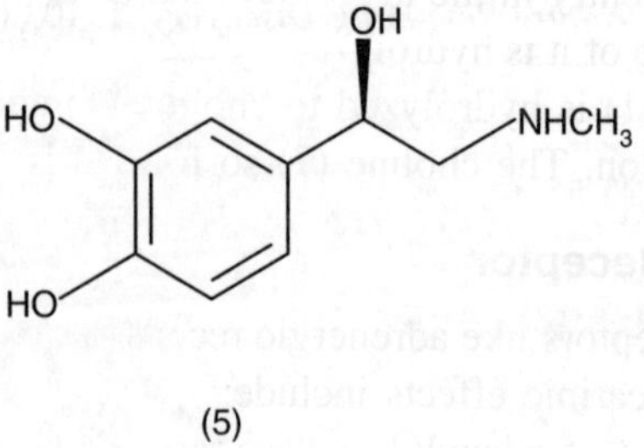

(5)

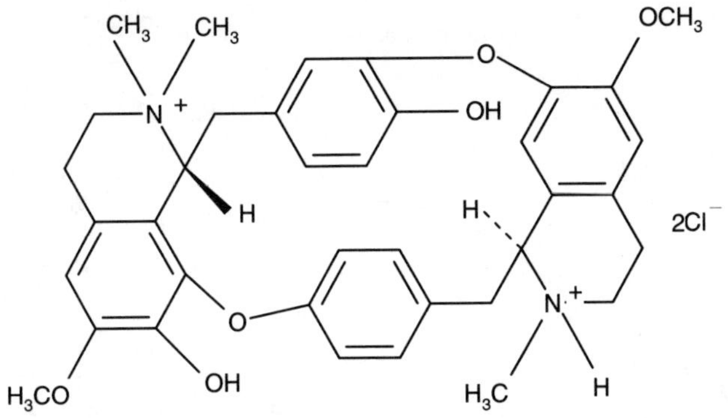

(6)

The muscarinic actions are similar to the actions produced by acetylcholine (1) on postganglionic parasympathetic nerve endings with the exception of action on blood vessels and sweat glands. Although the blood vessels do not have parasympathetic innervations, yet acetylcholine (1) causes vasodilation which is because it causes release of smooth muscle relaxant, nitric oxide, from endothelial cells. The stimulation of sweat glands by acetylcholine (1) is because these glands are innervated by cholinergic fibres of sympathetic system.

The nicotinic effect is due to stimulation of sympathetic and parasympathetic ganglia, motor – endplate of voluntary muscles, and secretory cells of medulla.

Acetylcholine Synthesis Release and Metabolism

Acetylcholine (1) is synthesized in nerve terminal from choline (7). The choline (7) is transported into the nerve terminals by active transport system. It is, next, acylated by choline acetyltransferase which

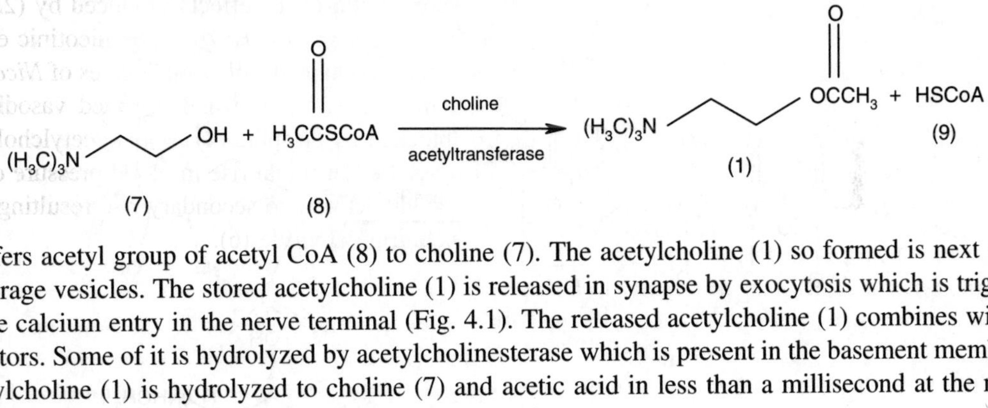

transfers acetyl group of acetyl CoA (8) to choline (7). The acetylcholine (1) so formed is next stored in storage vesicles. The stored acetylcholine (1) is released in synapse by exocytosis which is triggered by the calcium entry in the nerve terminal (Fig. 4.1). The released acetylcholine (1) combines with the receptors. Some of it is hydrolyzed by acetylcholinesterase which is present in the basement membrane. Acetylcholine (1) is hydrolyzed to choline (7) and acetic acid in less than a millisecond at the neuromuscular junction. The choline (7) so formed is inactive.

Muscarinic Receptor

Muscarinic receptors like adrenergic receptors are G-protein coupled receptors. The biochemical events leading to muscarinic effects include:

(a) inhibition of adenylyl cyclase, and
(b) increased turnover of diacylglycerol (DAG) and inositol triphosphate (IP_3) from phosphatidyl inositol-4,5-diphosphate (PIP_2).

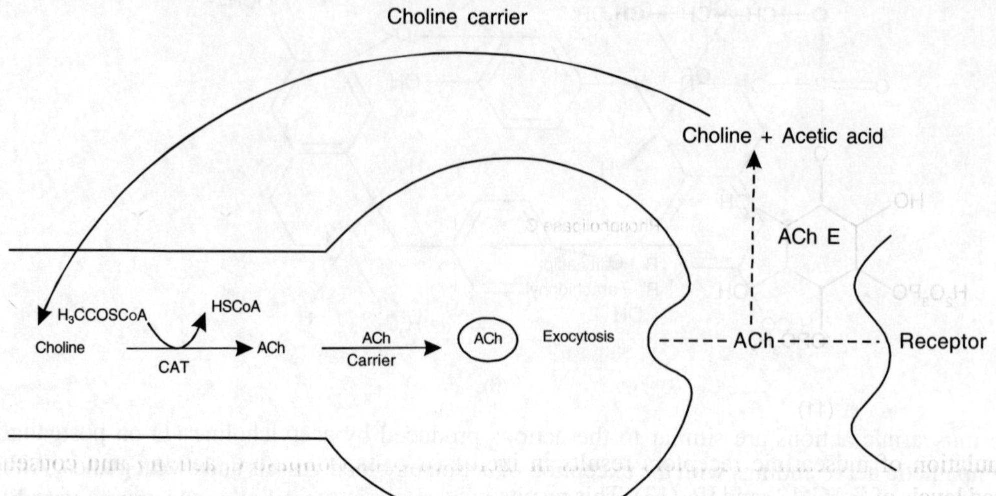

$H_3CCOSCoA$ - AcetylCoA; HSCoA - enzyme CoA; ACh - Acetylcholine
CAT - Cholineacetyl transferase; AChE - Acetylcholinesterase

Fig. 4.1 Biosynthesis, release, and metabolism of acetylcholine

Adenylyl cyclase is responsible for conversion of ATP (9) to cyc. AMP (10). Inhibition of adenylyl cyclase results in decreased cyc. AMP (10) levels, decreased Ca^{++} conductance and increased K^+ conductance resulting in cardiac inhibition.

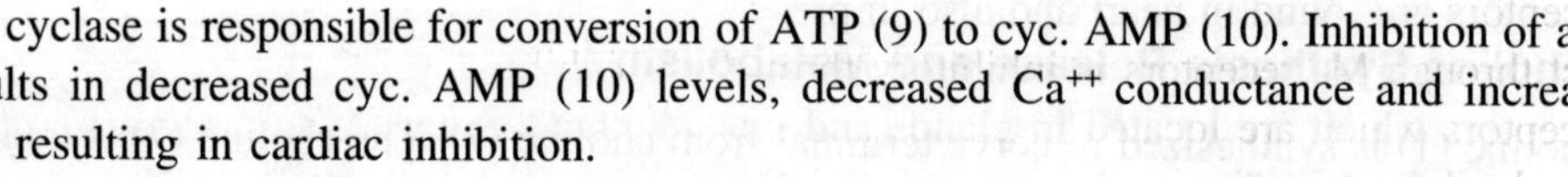

(9) (10)

Phospholipase C is an enzyme responsible for hydrolysis of phosphatidylinositol-4,5-diphosphate (PIP_2, 11) to diacylglycerol (DAG, 12) and inositol triphosphate (IP_3, 13).

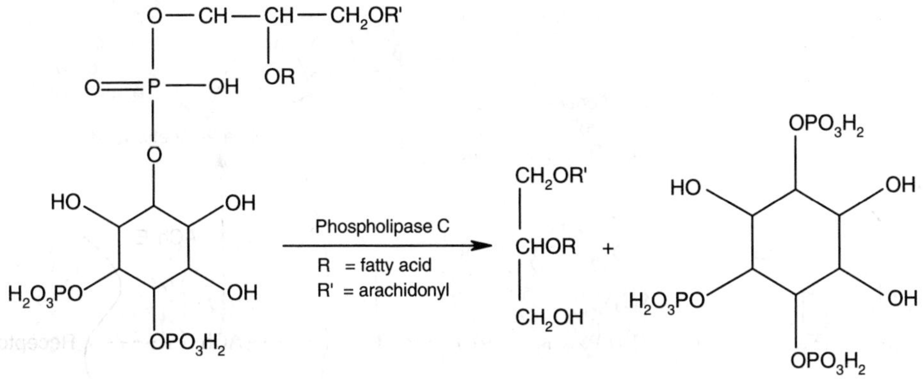

(11) (12) (13)

Stimulation of muscarinic receptors results in increased phospholipase C activity and consequent increased levels of DAG(12) and IP_3 (13). This results in increased mobilization of Ca^{++} from intracellular stores which results in contraction of smooth muscles, depolarization, and gastric secretion.

Gene cloning has revealed five distinct types of muscarinic receptors and include M_1, M_2, M_3, M_4, and M_5 receptors.

M_1 receptors are mainly located in CNS and peripheral neurons. They mediate mainly the excitatory effects.

M_2 receptors are found in heart and also in presynaptic terminals of peripheral and central neurons. The effect through M_2 receptors is inhibitory through the inhibition of Ca^{++} channels.

M_3 receptors which are located in glands and smooth muscles have stimulatory effect resulting in increased glandular secretion and increased peristalsis.

M_4- and M_5-receptors are located in CNS, however, their role is not well understood.

The second messenger in case of odd numbered receptors i.e. M_1-, M_3-, and M_5-receptors is DAG (9) and IP_3 (10) while in case of even numbered receptors that is M_2- and M_4-receptors act through inhibition of adenylyl cyclase.

The N-terminal of all the five types of muscarinic receptors is extracellular and the C-terminus intracellular. There are 7-transmemberane domains. The binding of acetylcholine involves aspartate, threonine, and tyrosine of 3rd, 5th, and 6th transmembrane domain, respectively (Fig. 4.2).

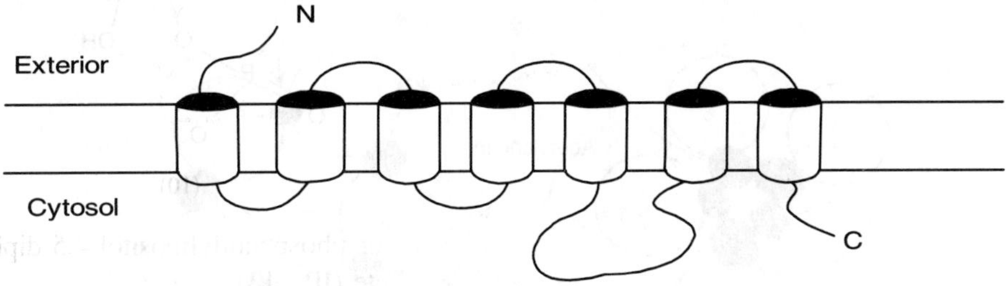

Fig. 4.2 Muscarinic receptor

Nicotinic Receptors

Nicotinic receptors are ligand-gated ion channels. They are located in muscles, ganglion, and CNS. The receptor which is a glycoprotein, consists of four different subunits namely α, β, γ, and δ. In a

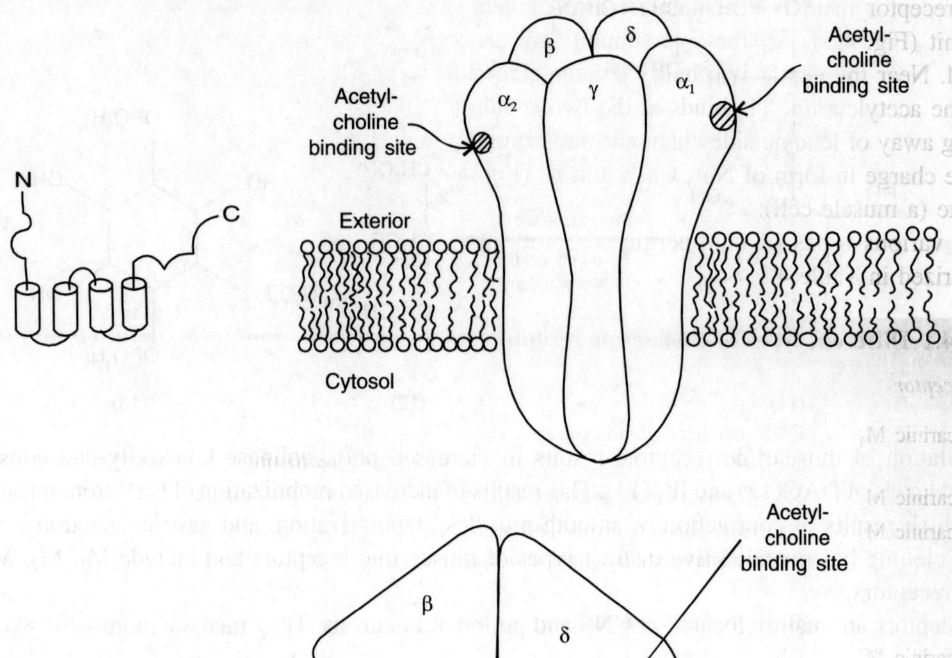

Fig. 4.3 Nicotinic receptor

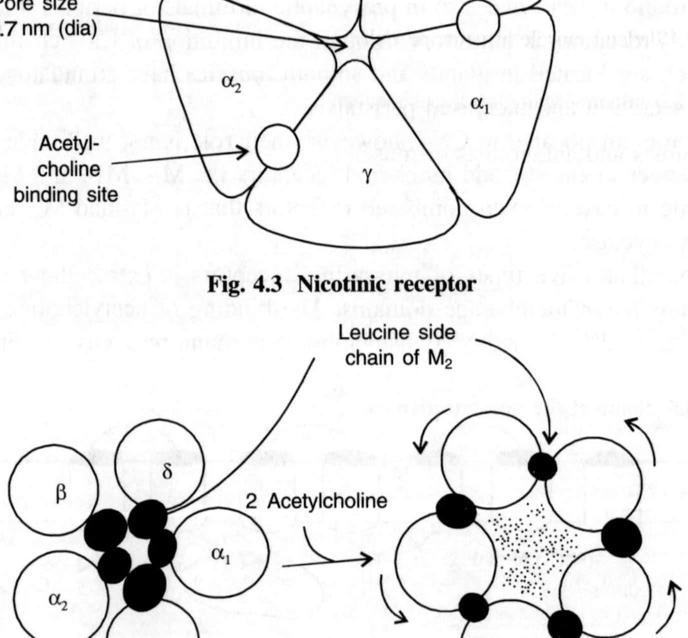

Fig. 4.4 Opening and closing of nicotine acetylcholine ligand gated ion channel

single receptor there is a pentameric arrangement of two α- subunits with one each of β-, γ-, and δ-subunit (Fig. 4.3). All the five subunits are arranged around a central pore that serves as an ion channel. Near the center is a bulky leucine side chain which acts as an opening and closing device. After the acetylcholine (1) binds at the two α-subunits, there is a conformational change resulting in drawing away of leucine side chain and subsequent opening of the ion channel and allowing of inward positive charge in form of Na^+, Ca^{++}, and K^+ (Fig. 4.4). This depolarizes the plasma membrane of the myocyte (a muscle cell).

The various types of cholinergic receptors and the effects observed after their stimulation are summarized in Table 4.1.

Table 4.1 Different types of cholinergic receptors, their location and effects observed after excitation

Receptor	*Location*	*Response after excitation*
Muscarinic M_1	CNS, exocrine glands (gastric, salivary)	CNS excitation, gastric and salivary secretion
Muscarinic M_2	Heart, atria, smooth muscles, G.I. tract, CNS	Cardiac inhibition, tremors, hypothermia
Muscarinic M_3	Exocrine glands (salivary and gastric)	Increased salivary and gastric secretion
	Smooth muscles (G.I. tract and eye)	Contraction of smooth muscles, ocular accommodation
	Blood vessels (endothelium)	Vasodilation
Muscarinic M_4	CNS	As M_2
Muscarinic M_5	CNS	As M_3
Nicotinic N_1	Skeletal muscle at neuromuscular junction	End-plate depolarization, skeletal muscle contraction
Nicotinic N_2	Autonomic ganglia/adrenal medulla	Depolarization secretion of catecholamines

Some of the agonists and antagonists of muscarinic and nicotinic receptors are listed in Figs. 4.5 to 4.9.

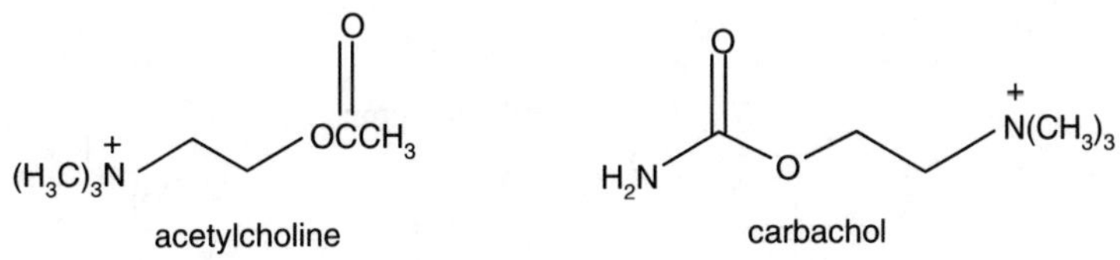

Fig. 4.5 Some of the non-selective cholinergic agonists (muscarinic and nicotinic)

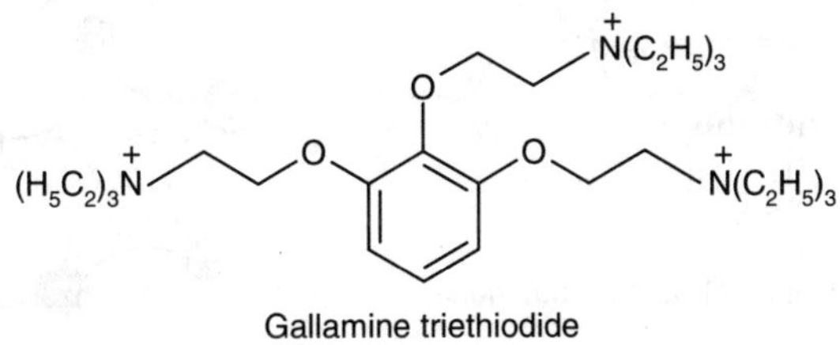

Fig. 4.6 Some of the non-selective cholinergic antagonists (muscarinic and nicotinic)

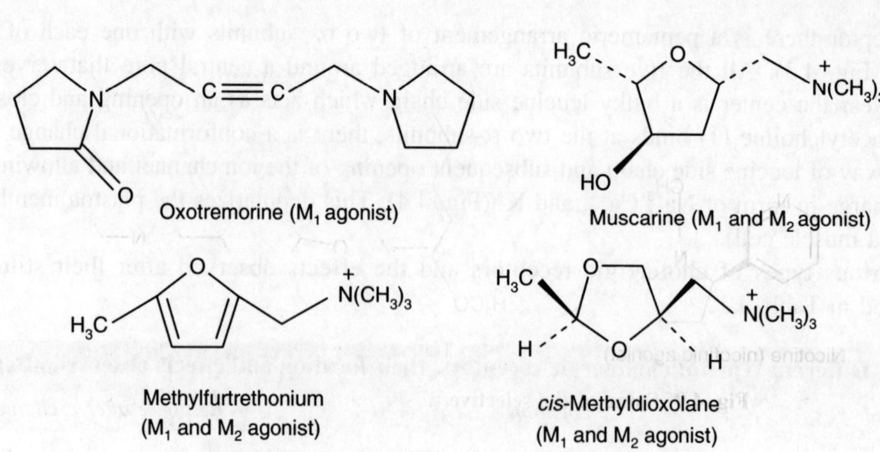

Fig. 4.7 Some of the selective muscarinic agonists

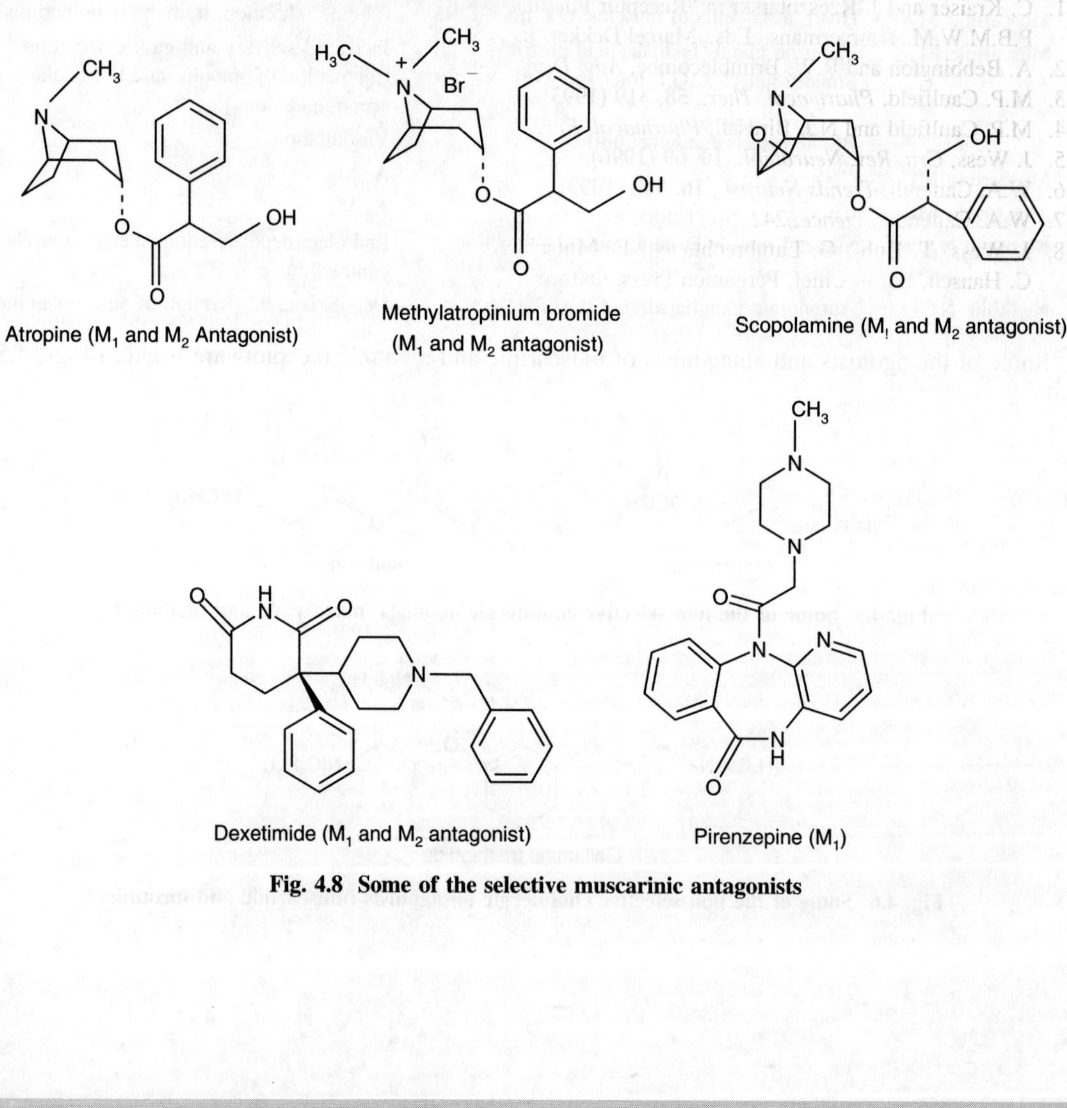

Fig. 4.8 Some of the selective muscarinic antagonists

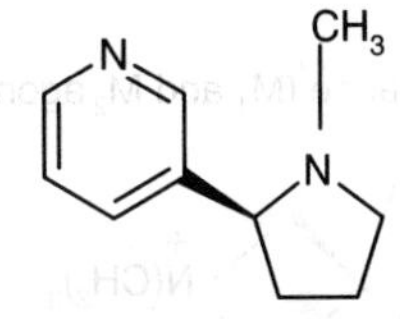

Nicotine (nicotinic agonist)

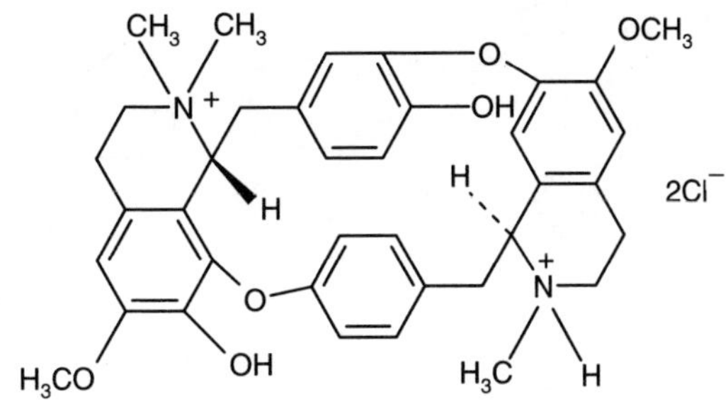

Tubocurarine chloride (nicotinic antagonist)

Fig. 4.9 Some of the selective nicotinic agonists and antagonists

FURTHER READING

1. C. Kraiser and J. Rzeszotarski in "Receptor Pharmacology and Function," M. Williams, R.A. Glennon, and P.B.M.W.M. Timmermans., Eds., Marcel Dekker, Inc., New York, 1989, p. 503.
2. A. Bebbington and R.W. Brimblecombe, *Adv. Drug Res.*, **2**, 143 (1965).
3. M.P. Caulfield, *Pharmacol. Ther.*, **58**, 319 (1993).
4. M.P. Caulfield and N.J. Birdsall, *Pharmacol. Rev.*, **50**, 279 (1998).
5. J. Wess, *Crit. Rev. Neurobiol.*, **10**, 69 (1996).
6. W.A. Catterall, *Trends Neurosi.*, **16**, 500 (1993).
7. W.A. Catterall, *Science*, 242, 50 (1988).
8. J. Wess, T. Buhl, G. Lambrecht, and E. Mutschler in "Comprehensive Medicinal Chemistry," Vol. 3, C. Hansch, Ed. in Chief, Pergamon Press, Oxford, 2005, p. 423.

5

The Opioid Receptors

The term opioid is a general term and includes substances, whether endogenous or synthetic, that produce morphine-like effects that are blocked by antagonists like naloxone. Opiate is an older term and is restricted to morphine like drugs with non-peptide like structures.

Opium is dried milky exudates obtained from unripe fruits of poppy, *Papaver somniferum*, family *Papaveraceae*. About 23 alkaloids have been isolated from opium and these constitute about 20% of the weight of opium. The alkaloids of opium are of two types, one those which contain partially hydrogenated phenanthrene nucleus and the other containing 1-benzylisoquinoline system. Alkaloids with partially hydrogenated phenanthrene nucleus include morphine (1), codeine (2), and thebaine (3). The benzyliso-quinoline type of alkaloids include papaverine (4) and narcotine (5).

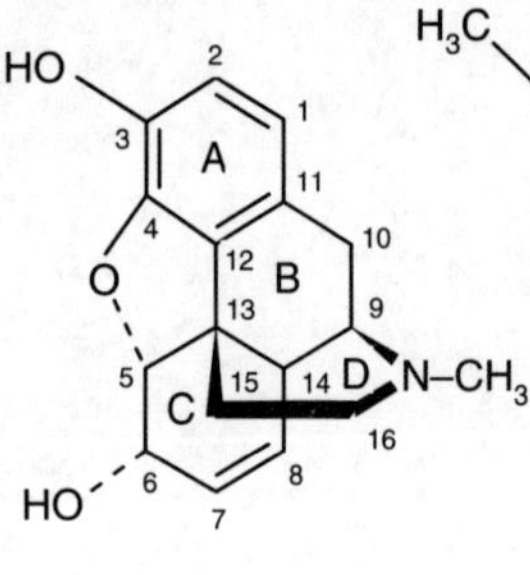

(1)

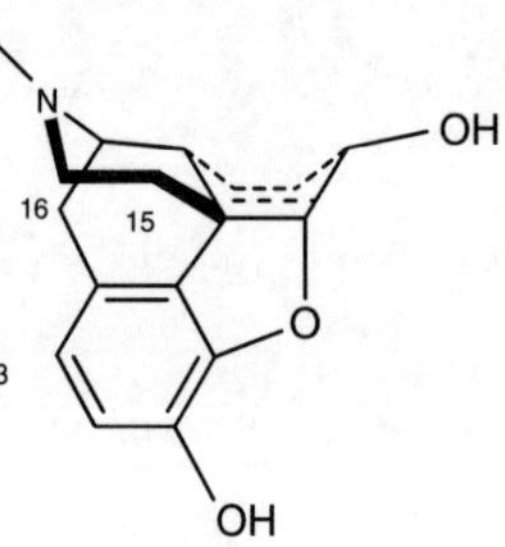

(1a)

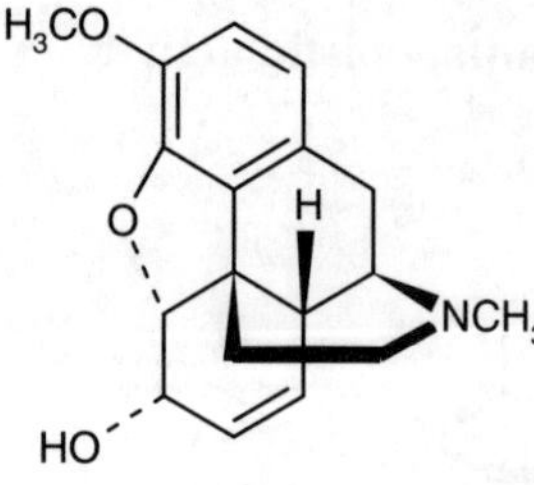

(2)

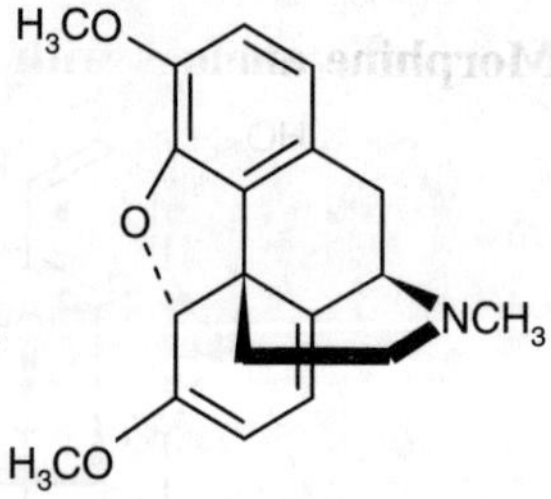

(3)

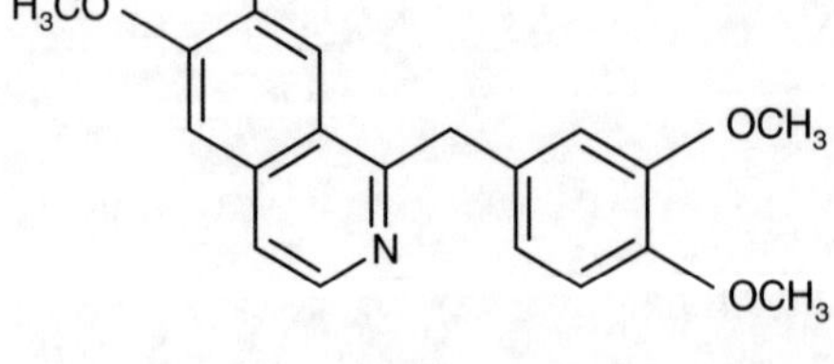

(4)

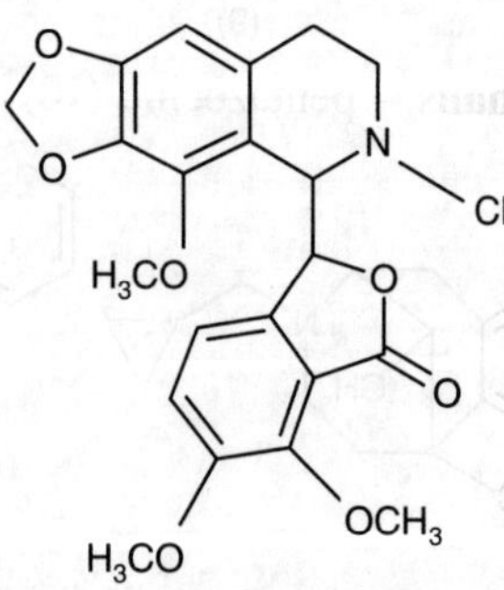

(5)

The action of opium is mainly due to morphine (1). In addition to its excellent analgesic properties, it also possesses undesirable side effects such as euphoria, which is responsible for its addiction liability, gastrointestinal disturbances, respiratory, and circulatory depression. Codeine (2) which has excellent cough suppressant properties has weak analgesic activity. It is usually used as an antidiarrheal and cough suppressant. Thebaine (3) does not possess any analgesic activity but is convulsant. Pappaverine (4) possesses smooth muscle relaxant properties and narcotine (5) is used as antitussive.

Morphine (1) has five asymmetric centres and include 5,6,9,13, and 14. The absolute configuration of these cenres is 5*R*, 6*S*, 9*R*, 13*S*, and 14*R*. The conformation of cycloalkene ring, which constitutes ring C is boat while as the piperidine ring which constitutes ring D, is in chair form (1a).

Structure-activity relationship studies have resulted in number of synthetic analogs which also show good analgesic activity. Some of these include:

Morphine analogs - codeine (2) and diamorphine (6).

Morphine analogs with partial agonistic activity - nalorphine (7) and levallorphan (8).

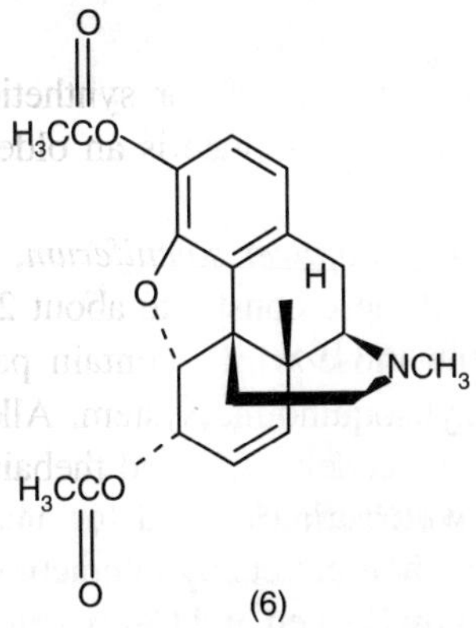

(6)

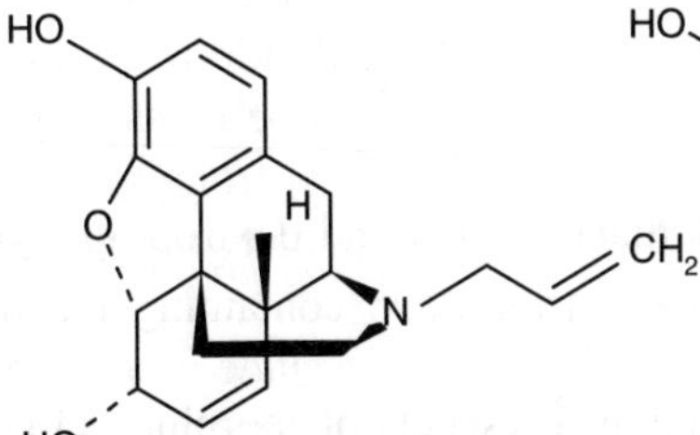

(7)

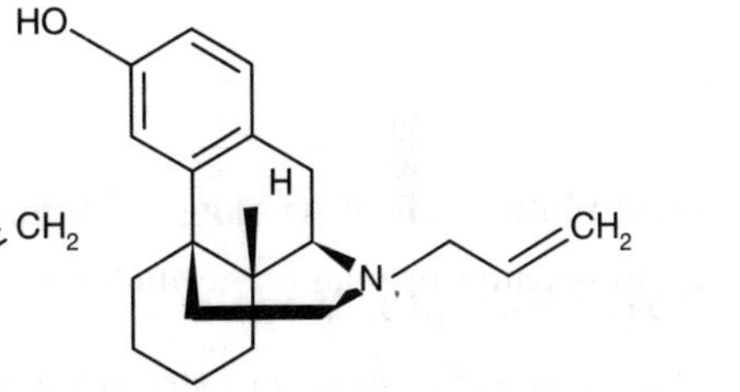

(8)

Morphine analogs with antagonistic activity - naloxone (9).

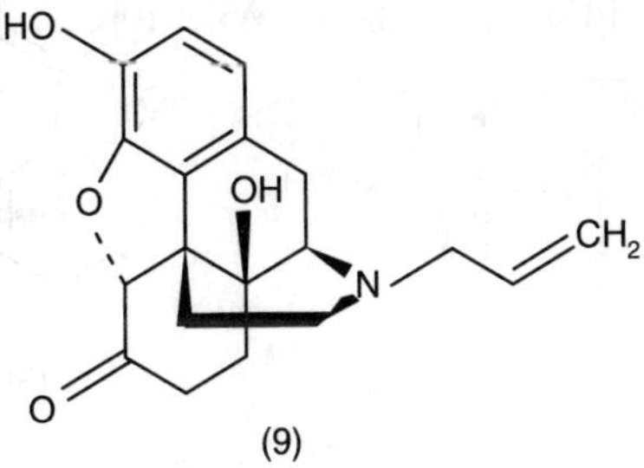

(9)

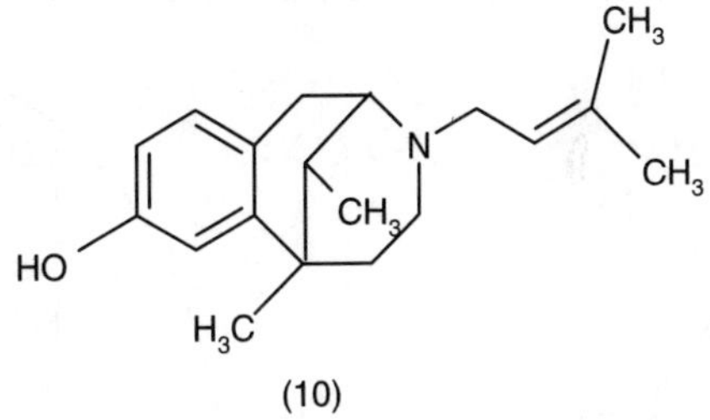

(10)

Benzomorphans – pentazocine (10) and cyclazocine (11).

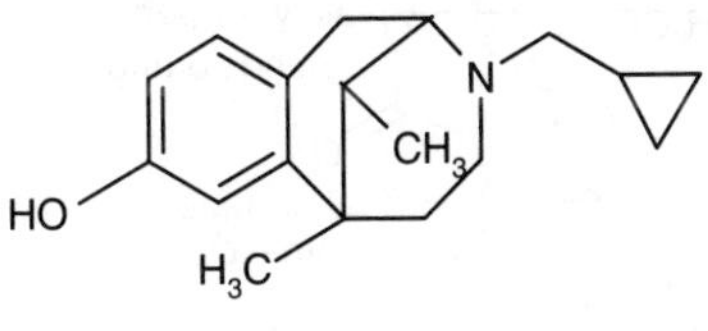

(11)

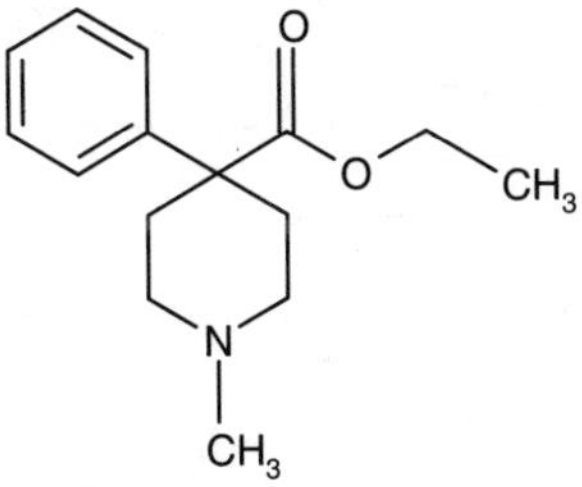

(12)

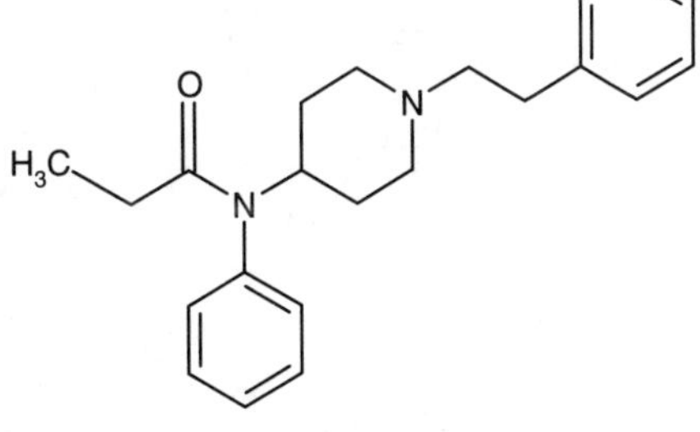

(13)

Phenylpiperidines – pethidine (12), Fentanyl (13), and sufentanil (14).

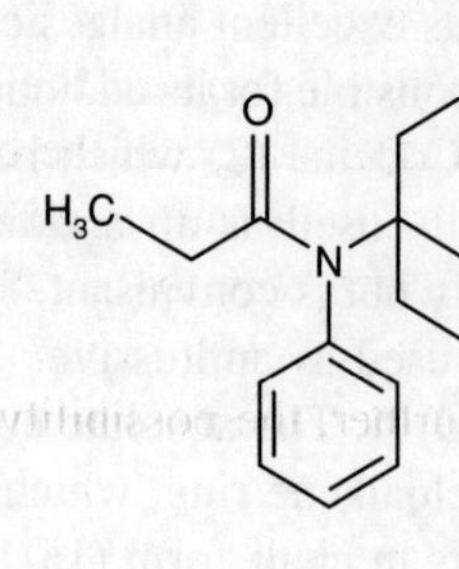

(14)

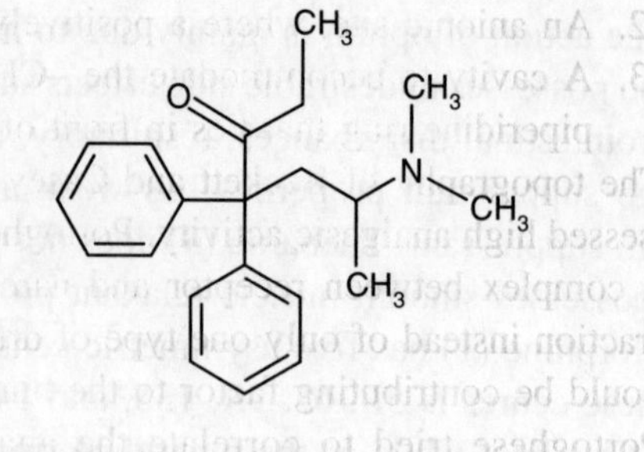

(15)

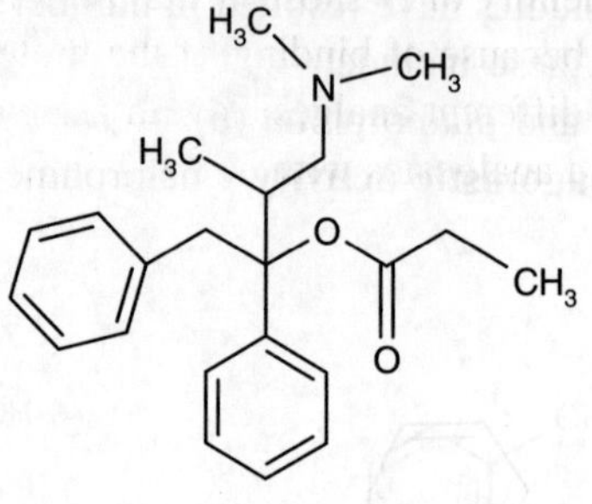

(16)

Methadone and its Analogs – Methadone (15) and dextropropoxyphene (16).

Opioid Receptor Models

The structural rigidity and stereochemical aspects of morphine (1a) which are essential for analgesic activity of morphine (1) and related opioids suggests that they produce their effects by interacting with a specific receptor. The earliest model of such a receptor was proposed by Beckett and Casey (Fig. 5.1). According to them, there are essentially three sites at the receptor (Fig. 5.1):

1. A flat structure, where the aromatic ring is bound through van der Waal forces.

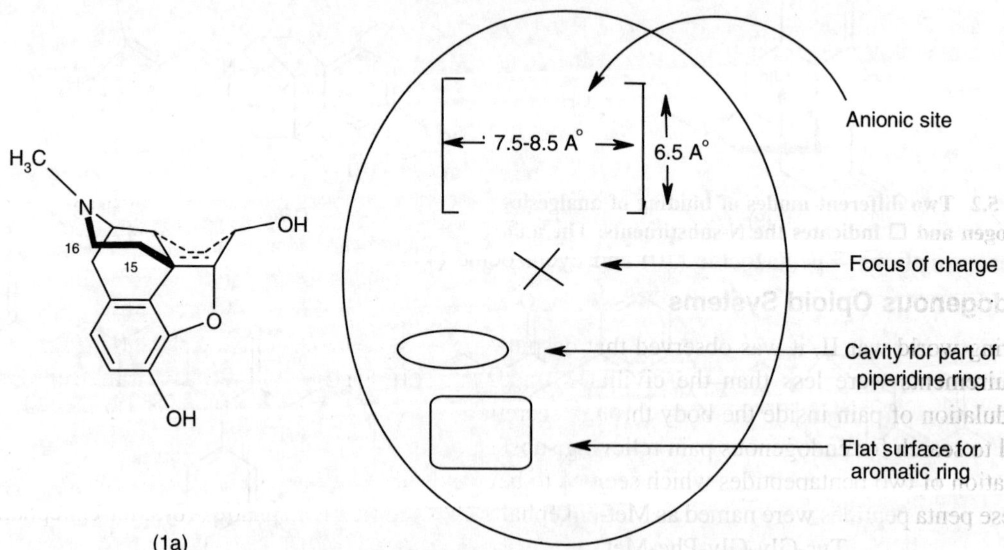

(1a)

Fig. 5.1 Beckett and Casey's model of opioid receptor

2. An anionic site, where a positively charged nitrogen is able to bind.
3. A cavity to accommodate the $-CH_2-CH_2-$ portion relative to carbon15 and 16 projecting from piperidine ring that lies in front of the plane containing the aromatic ring and the basic centre.

The topography of Beckett and Casey model was not complimentary to certain compounds which possessed high analgesic activity. Portoghese proposed another model. According to this, the formation of a complex between receptor and narcotic analgesics, in many cases, invoved different modes of interaction instead of only one type of drug-receptor complexation. Further, the possibility of induced fit could be contributing factor to the binding of analgesic to the receptor.

Portoghese tried to correlate the analgesic activity of various structures such as methadones, mepridines, prodines, etc to the identity of N-substituents. According to him, the analgesic response of two different molecules could be because of binding of the molecules to the receptor stereoselectively in two different modes. Thus two different analgesics with identical N-substituents bind to the receptor in a similar way. On the other hand analgesics with entirely different N-substituents bind to the receptor in different way (Fig. 5.2).

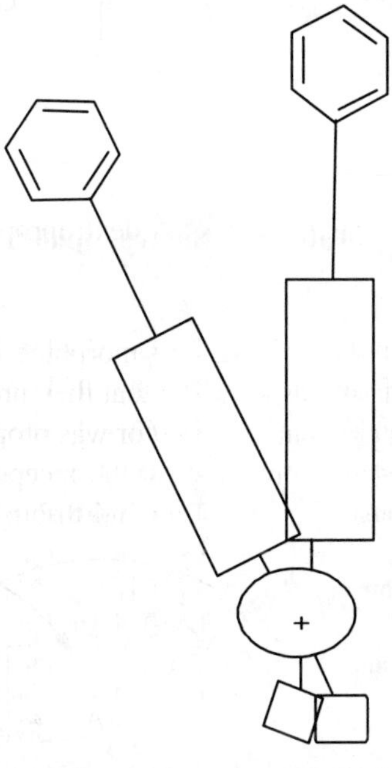

Fig. 5.2 Two different modes of binding of analgesics with different N-substituents, ⊕ indicates the protonated nitrogen and □ indicates the N-substituents. The anionic site lies beneath the protonated nitrogen

Endogenous Opioid Systems

During world war II, it was observed that despite greater severity of soldier's wounds, their analgesic requirements were less than the civilian's undergoing surgery. This indicated that there must be modulation of pain inside the body through secretion of pain relieving substances. These observations lead to search for endogenous pain relieving substances. In 1975, Huges and his associates reported the isolation of two pentapeptides which seemed to be responsible for most of the observed opioid activity. These penta peptides were named as Met-enkephalin (17) and Leu-enkephalin (18). Met-enkephalin (17)

Tyr-Gly-Gly-Phe-Met (17)

Tyr-Gly-Gly-Phe-Leu (18)

sequence has been reported to be present as amino acid residues in pituitary hormone β-lipoprotein. The opioid activity of pituitary has also been reported.

The discovery of another polypeptide endorphin (Table 5.1) has been reported by various workers. Several other opioid peptides have been reported and the most important among them is the dynorphine. Some of the natural opioids together with their precursors and amino acid composition are given in Table 5.1. All of these naturally occurring opioid peptides contain either Met-enkephalin or Leu-enkephalin in their N-terminal and include:

Met-enkepalin containing peptides

1. heptapeptide
2. octapeptide
3. α-endophin
4. γ-endorphin
5. β-endorphin

Leu-enkephalin containing peptides

1. α-neoendorphin
2. dynorphin
3. dynorphin A
4. dynorphin B

Table 5.1 Natural opioids

Precursor	*Peptide*	*Structure*
Proenkephalin	Met-enkephalin	Tyr-Gly-Gly-Phe-Met_5
	Leu-enkephalin	Tyr-Gly-Gly-Phe-Leu_5
	Heptapeptide	Tyr-Gly-Gly-Phe-Met-Arg-Phe_7
	Octapeptide	Tyr-Gly-Gly-Phe-Met-Arg-Gly-Leu_8
Pro-Opio-Melanocortin	α-Endorphin	Tyr-Gly-Gly-Phe-Met-Tyr-Ser-Glu-Lys-Ser-Glu-Thr-Pro-Leu-Val-Thr_{16}
	γ-Endorphin	Tyr-Gly-Gly-Phe-Met-Thr-Ser-Glu-Lys-Ser-Glu-Thr-Pro-Leu-Val-Thr-Leu_{17}
	β-Endorphin	Tyr-Gly-Gly-Phe-Met-Thr-Ser-Glu-Lys-Ser-Gln-Thr-Pro-Leu-Val-Thr-Leu-Phe-Lys-Asn-Ala-Ile-Ile-Lys-Asn-Ala-Tyr-Lys-Lys-Gly-Glu OH_{31}
Prodynorphin	α-Neoendorphin	Tyr-Gly-Gly-Phe-Leu-Arg-Lys-Tyr-Pro-Lys_{10}
	Dynorphin	Tyr-Gly-Gly-Phe-Leu-Arg-Arg-Ile_8
	Dynorphin A	Tyr-Gly-Gly-Phe-Leu-Arg-Arg-Ile-Arg-Pro-Lys-Leu-Lys-Trp-Asp-Asn-Gln_{17}
	Dynorphin B	Tyr-Gly-Gly-Phe-Leu-Arg-Arg-Gln-Phe-Lys-Val-Val-Thr_{13}

Opioid Receptors

The existence of more than one opioid receptor was demonstrated from the dual action of synthetic opioid nalorphine (7). Nalorphine (7), not only antagonizes the analgesic actions of morphine (1) but also shows analgesic action. According to Martin the analgesic action of nalorphine (7) was mediated through kappa (κ)-opioid receptor.

At present there are known at least three types of opioid receptors and these include mu (μ)-, kappa (κ)-, and delta (δ)-receptors. There is evidence that each of these receptors have subtypes.According to recent nomenclature of opioid receptors, δ-receptors are OP_1- receptors, κ-receptors are OP_2-receptors, and μ-receptors are OP_3-receptors. Some of the selective agonists and antagonists of these three types of receptors are listed in Figs. 5.2 to 5.4, respectively.

All the three types of opioid receptors belong to the family of G-protein coupled receptors. Stimulation of all the three opioid receptors result in inhibition of adenylyl cyclase and consequent decrease in cyc. AMP. The mechanism of inhibition of adenylyl cyclase appears to be due to activation of guanine nucleotide regulatory protein, Gi. However, in locus coeruleus, the opioid effects may be mediated through via a pertusis toxin sensitive cyc. AMP independent mechanism, possibly through a Go rather than a Gi-protein.

Stimulation of three receptors also results in an effect on ion-channels through a G-protein coupling to the channel. This results in opening of K^+ channel and inhibition of opening of voltage gated Ca^{2+} channels. These effects at membrane level reduce both neuronal excitability due to increased outward K^+ conductance and transmitter release due to inhibition of Ca^{2+} entry. The overall effect is inhibitory at the cellular level. The opening of K^+ channels is triggered through μ- and δ-receptors and inhibition of Ca^{2+} channel through κ-receptors.

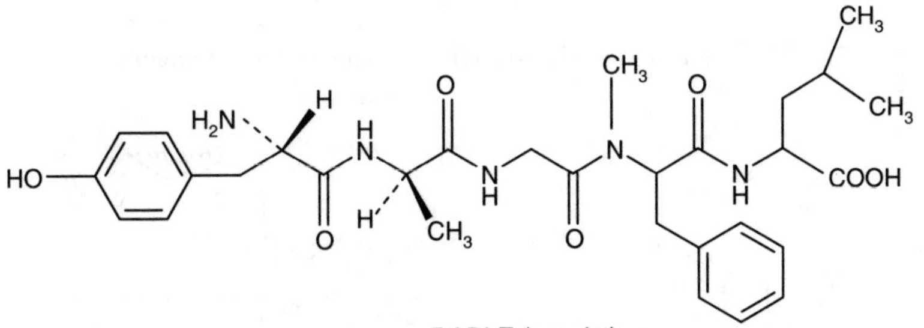

DADLE (agonist)

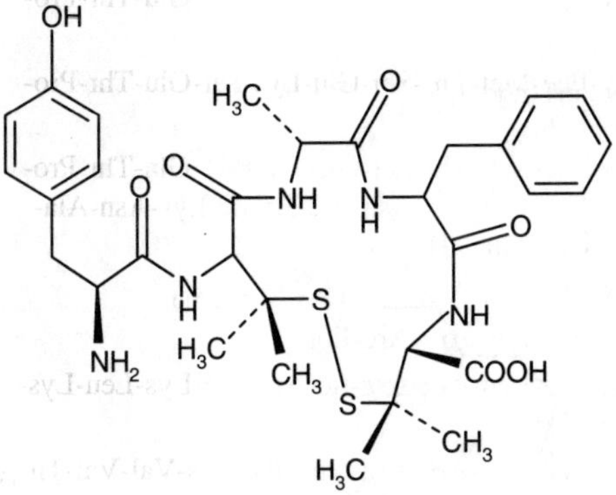

DPDPE (agonist)

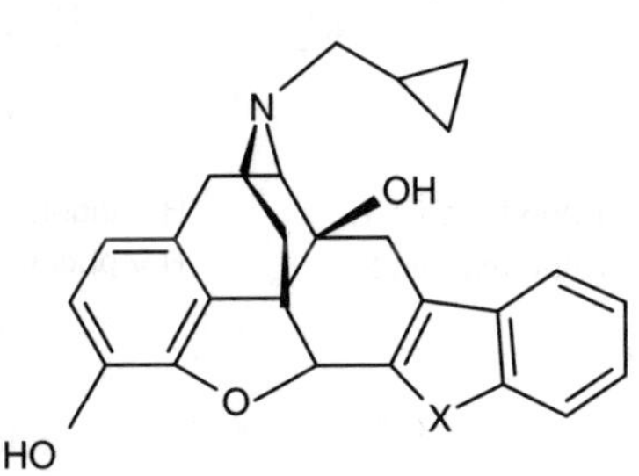

Naltrindol, X = NH antagonists
Naltiben, X = O antagonists

Fig. 5.2 Some of the selective OP_1 (δ) agonists and antagonists

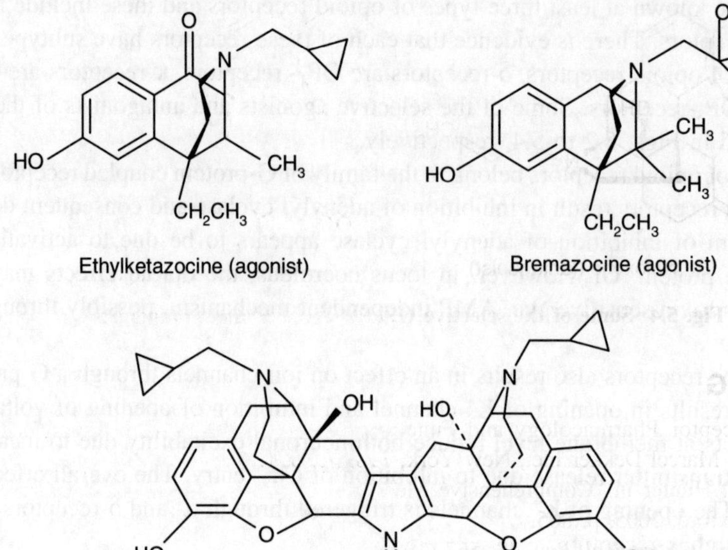

Fig. 5.3 Some of the selective OP_2 (κ) agonists and antagonists

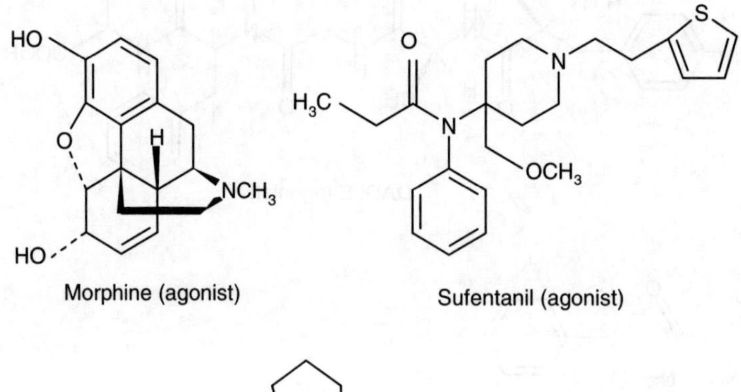

Endomorphin 1, R = indolyl (agonist)
Endomorphin 2, R = phenyl (agonist)

(Contd.)

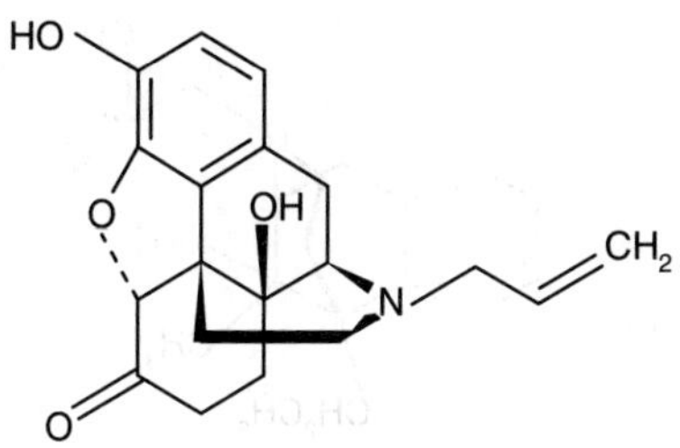

Naloxone ((antagonist)

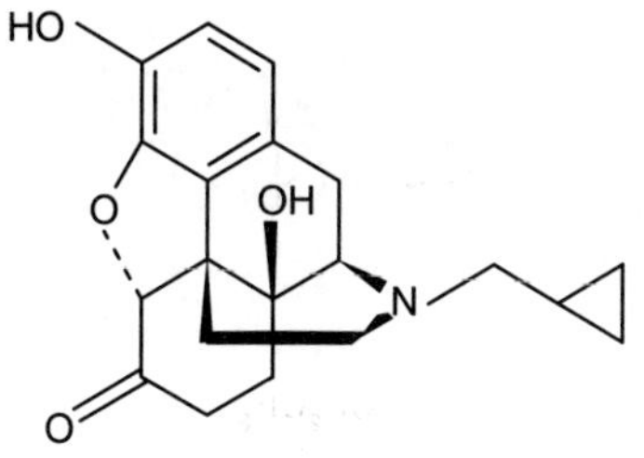

Naltrexone ((antagonist)

Fig. 5.4 Some of the selective OP_3 (μ) agonists and antagonists

FURTHER READING

1. S.W. Tam in "Receptor Pharmacology and Function," M. Williams, R.A. Glennon, and P.B.M.W.M. Timmermans, Eds., Marcel Dekker Inc., New York, 1989, p. 571.
2. D.C. Rees and J.C. Hunter in "Comprehensive Medicinal Chemistry," Vol. 3, C. Hansch, Ed. in Chief, Pergamon Press, Oxford, 2005, p. 805.
3. B.N. Dhawan, et. al., *Pharmacol. Rev*, **48**, 567 (1996).
4. G. Henderson and A.T. McKnight, *Trends Pharmacol. Sci.*, **18**, 293 (1997).
5. H.B. Gutstein and H. Akil in "Goodman and Gilman's The Pharmacol-ogical Basis of Therapeutics," 10th ed. (Intern.), J.G. Harman and L.E. Limbird, Eds., McGraw Hill, New York, 2001, p. 569.

6

Serotonin Receptors

Serotonin or 5-hydroxytryptamine (1) is widely distributed in plants and animals. It exists in gastrointestinal tract and in CNS, where it functions both as neurotransmitter and as a local hormone

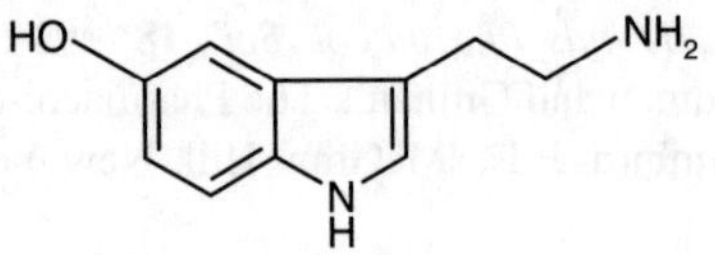

(1)

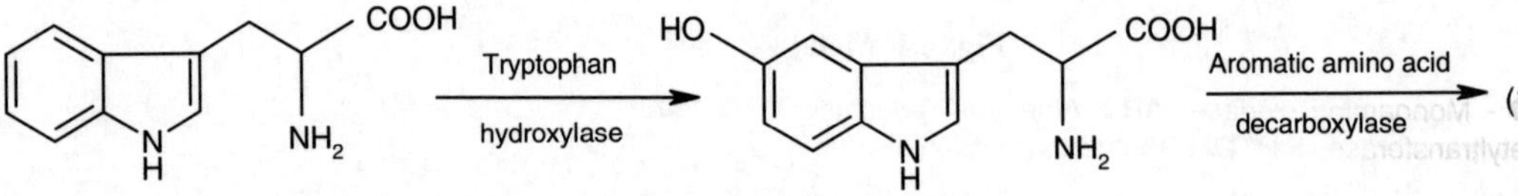

(2) (3)

in the peripheral vascular system. It is biosynthesized from the amino acid tryptophan (2), which is converted to 5-hydroxytryptophan (3) by the action of tryptophan hydroxylase in serotogenic neurons. Decarboxylation of 5-hydroxy-tryptophan by aromatic amino acid decarboxylase results in the formation of serotonin (1). Serotonin (1) appears to regulate its own synthesis through autoreceptors. After its synthesis it is stored in storage vesicles from which it is released in synapse by exocytosis under appropriate conditions. The released serotonin (1) binds to postsynaptic receptors. The excess of serotonin (1) diffuses away from the synapse and gets metabolized. The major metabolic pathway is through oxidative deamination by monoamine oxidase (MAO) which results in the formation of 5-hydroxyindole-3-acetaldehyde (4), its reduction product, 5-hydroxyindole-3-ethanol (5) and its oxidation product 5-hydroxyindole-3-acetic acid (6). The other metabolic products include N-acetyl-5-hydroxytryptamine (7) and its methyl ether analog, melatonin (8). The various pharmacological actions of serotonin are summarized in Table 6.1.

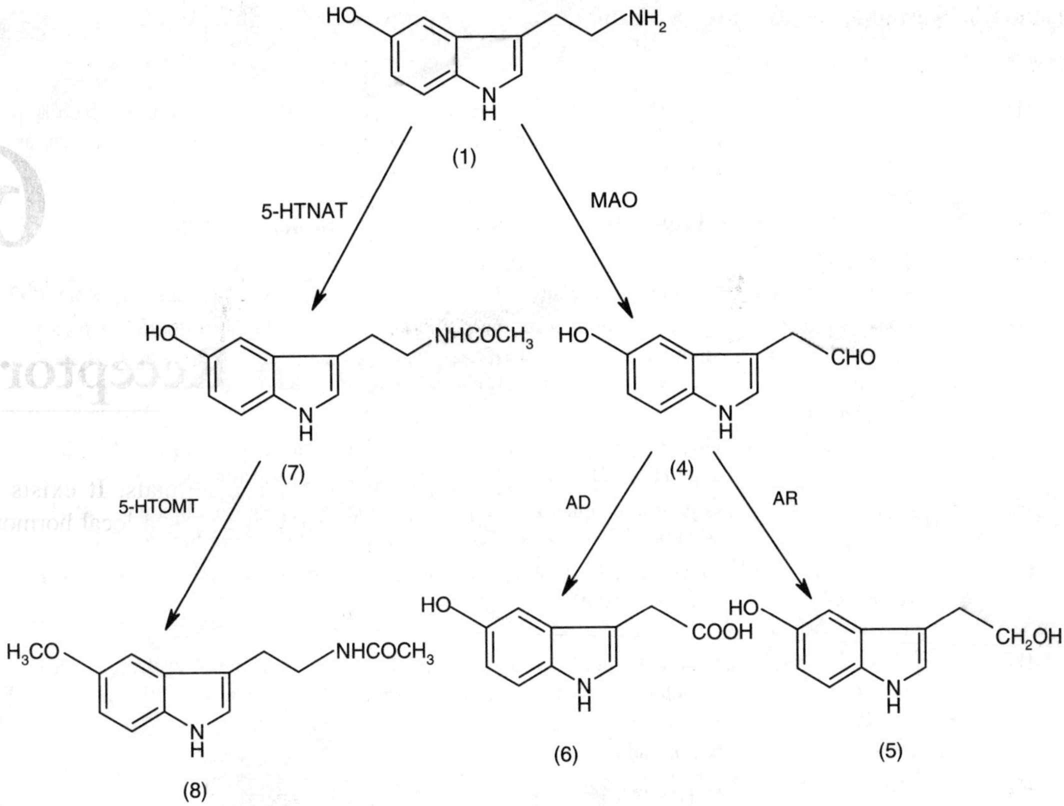

Fig. 6.1 Metabolism of serotonin

(**MAO** - Monoamine oxidase; **AR** - Aldehyde reductase; **AD** - Aldehyde dehydrogenase; **5-HTNAT**-5-hydrotryptamine N-acetyltransferase; **5-HTOMT**-5-hydroxytryptamine O-methyltransferase)

Table 6.1 Pharmacological actions of serotonin (1) on various organs

Organ	*Pharmacological Actions*
GI Tract	Increased motility due to direct effect on smooth muscles of GI tract. Release of serotonin (1) from chromaffin cells and by vagal stimulation which results in vagal reflex.
Uterus, brochial tree	Minor stimulation in case of humans
Blood Vessels	Constriction mediated through 5-HT_{2A}, vasodilation mediated through 5-HT_{1A} receptors.
Blood Platelets	Serotonin (1) causes platelet aggregation. This effect is mediated through 5-HT_{2A} receptors.
CNS	Serotonin (1) excites some neurons and inhibits others. Different receptors have been implicated in these effects.

Serotonin Receptors

At present seven families of serotonin receptors have been identified. They have been identified as 5-HT_1 – 5-HT_7. These seven families are further subdivided in various subclasses. All of these except 5-HT_3 are G-protein coupled receptors. The $5HT_3$-receptor is a ligand gated cation channel. The various receptors along with the second messengers are listed in Table 6.2.

Table 6.2 Serotonin receptors their location and second messenger and pharmacological actions

Receptor type	*Location*	*Second Messenger and Pharmacological Actions*
5-HT_{1A}	CNS	G-protein coupled receptor.Second messenger-adenylyl cyclase which is inhibited. The main effect is neuronal inhibition, on thermal regulation, and anxiety.
5-HT_{1B}	CNS	G-protein coupled receptor. Second messenger-adenylyl cyclase which is inhibited. The main effect – presynaptic inhibition and on behavior.
5-HT_{1D}	CNS and blood vessels	G-protein coupled receptor. Second messenger-adenylyl cyclase which is inhibited. The main effects – cereberal vasoconstriction and on locomotion.
5-HT_{2A}	CNS, peripheral nervous system, smooth muscles, and platelets	G-protein coupled receptor. Second messenger-Phospholipase C which is stimulated. The main effects- neuronal excitation, platelet aggregation, smooth muscle contraction and vasoconstriction and vasodilation.
5-HT_{2B}	Gastric fundus	G-protein coupled receptor. Second messenger-Phospholipase C, which is stimulated. The main effect-contraction of gastric fundus.
5-HT_{2C}	CNS	G-protein coupled receptor. Second messenger-Phospholipase C, which is stimulated. The main effect-increased secretion of cerebrospinal fluid.
5-HT_3	CNS and peripheral nervous system	Ligand gated cation channel. Stimulation results in anxiety, emesis, and neuronal excitation.
5-HT_4	CNS, peripheral nervous system, and G.I.T.	G-protein coupled receptor. Second messenger-adenylyl cyclase which is stimulated. The main effect-increased gastrointestinal motility and neuronal excitation.
5-HT_5	CNS	Not known.
5-HT_6	CNS	Not known.
5-HT_7	CNS, G.I.T, and blood vessels	G-protein coupled receptor.Second messenger-adenylyl cyclase which is stimulated.

The G-protein coupled receptors consist of 7-transmembrane (TM) helical portions (TM). The amino end of the chain is extracellular and the carboxy end intracellular (Fig. 6.2). The large intracellular loop between transmembrane 5 and 6 is the binding site to the second messenger.

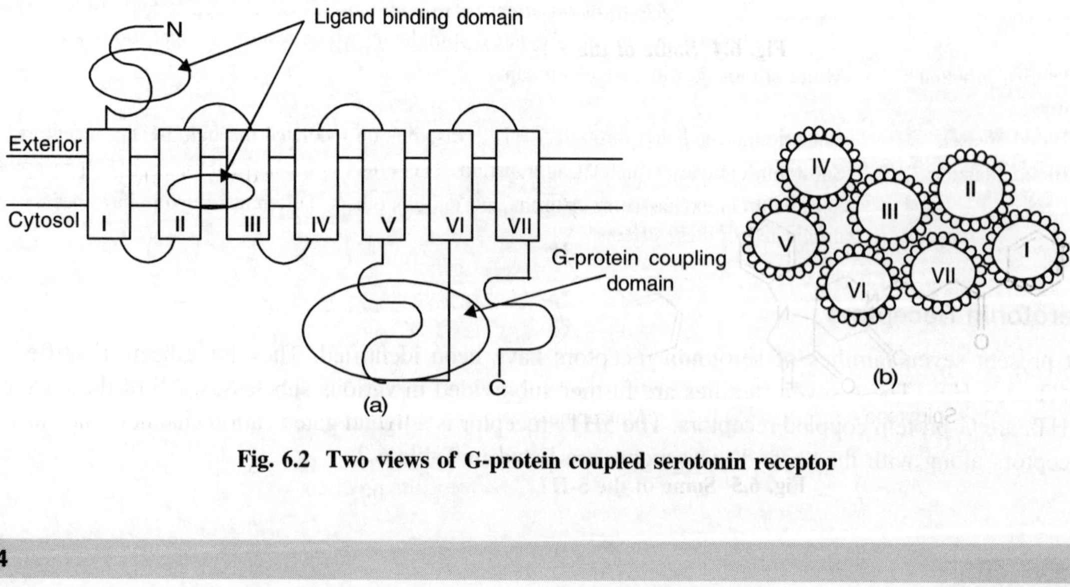

Fig. 6.2 Two views of G-protein coupled serotonin receptor

The 5-HT_3 is a ligand gated cation channel. The channel is a pentameric and each subunit consists of transmembrane-spanning amino acid chains (Fig. 6.3), the amino and carboxy end of which are extracellular.

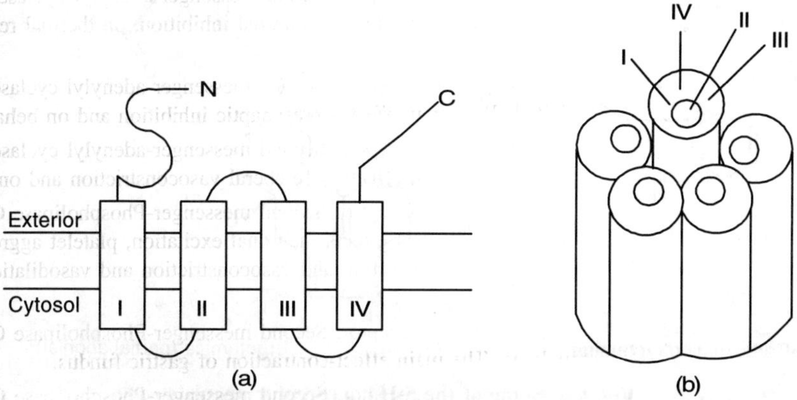

Fig. 6.3 Two views of the ligand gated 5-HT_3 cation channel

The various agonists and antagonists of serotonin receptors are listed in Figs. 6.5 to 6.14.

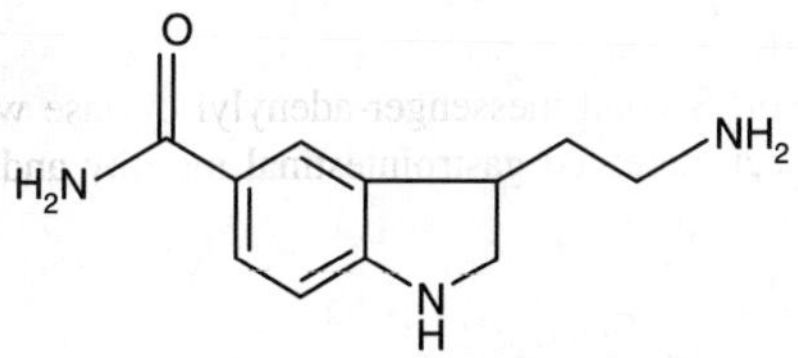

5-Carboxamidotryptamine

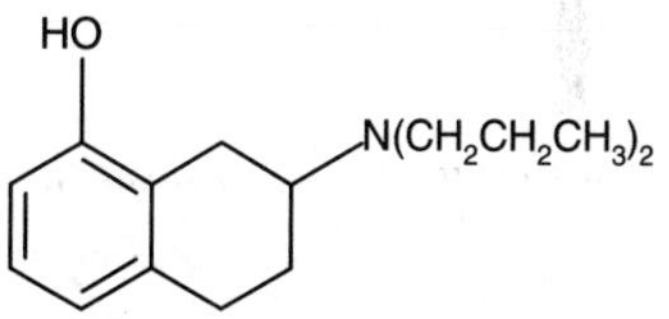

8-Hydroxy-N,N-di-n-propyl-2-aminotetralin

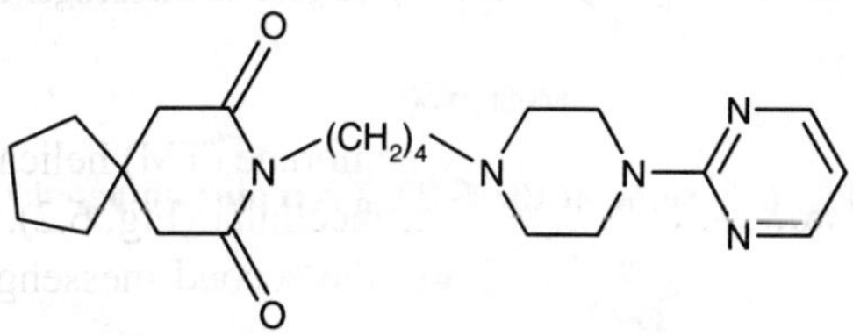

Buspirone (partial agonist)

Fig. 6.4 Some of the 5-HT_{1A} receptor agonists

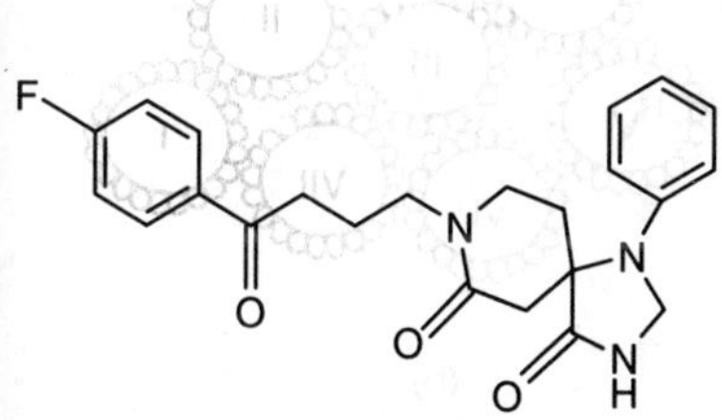

Spiperone

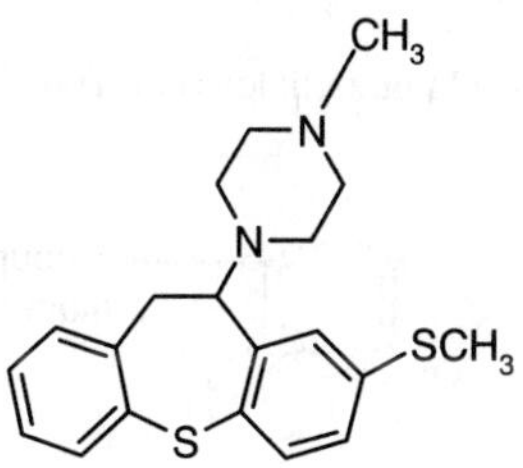

Metitepine

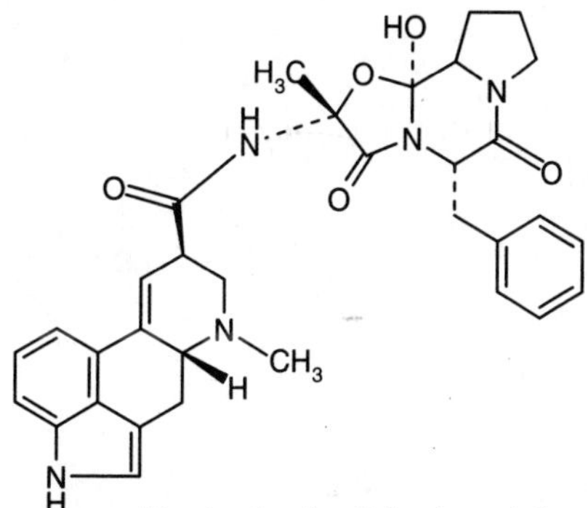

Ergotamine (partial antagonist)

Fig. 6.5 Some of the 5-HT_{1A} receptor antagonists

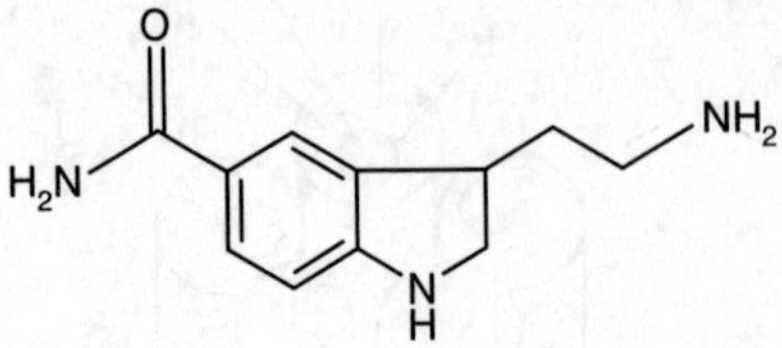

5-Carboxamidotryptamine

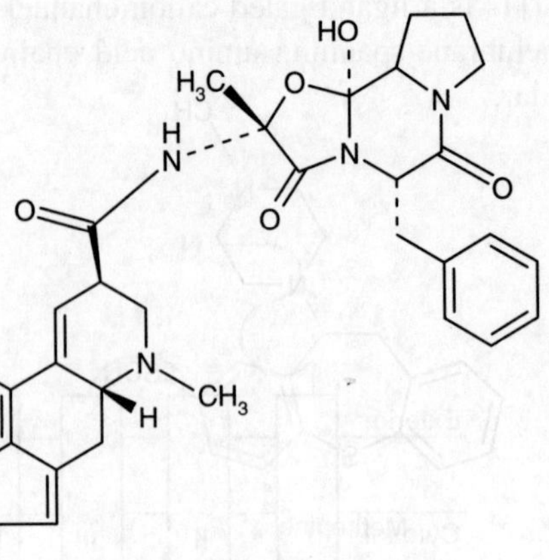

Ergotamine (partial agonist)

Fig. 6.6 Some of the 5-HT$_{1B}$ receptor agonists

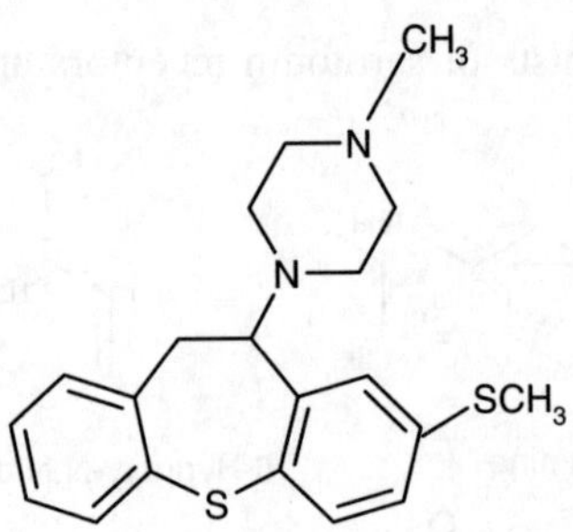

Metitepine

Fig. 6.7 Some of the 5-HT$_{1B}$ receptor antagonist

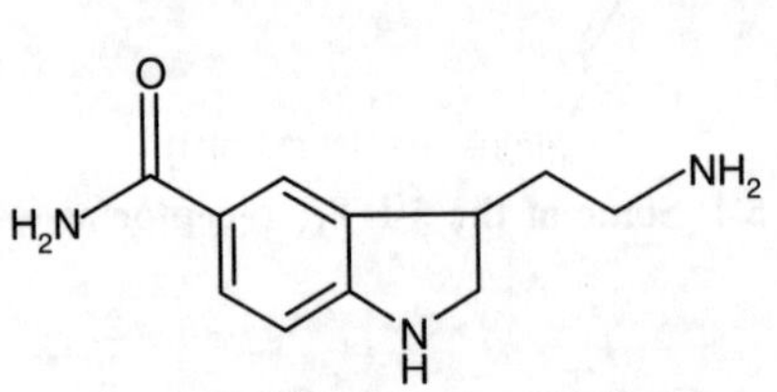

5-Carboxamidotryptamine

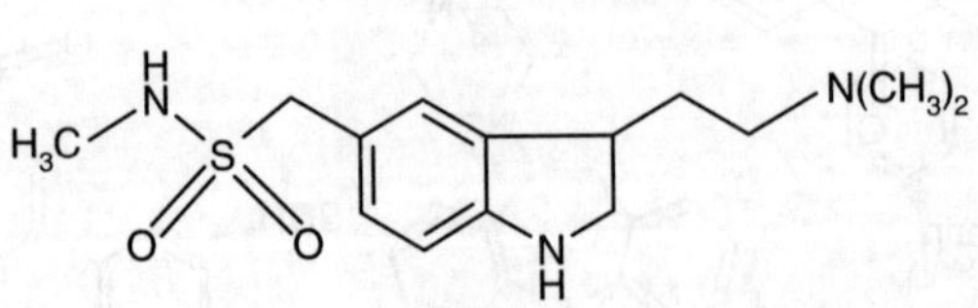

Sumatriptan

Fig. 6.8 Some of the 5-HT$_{1D}$ receptor agonists

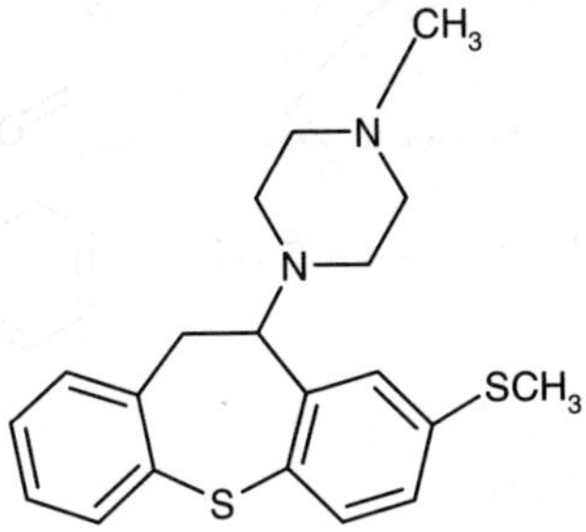

Metitepine

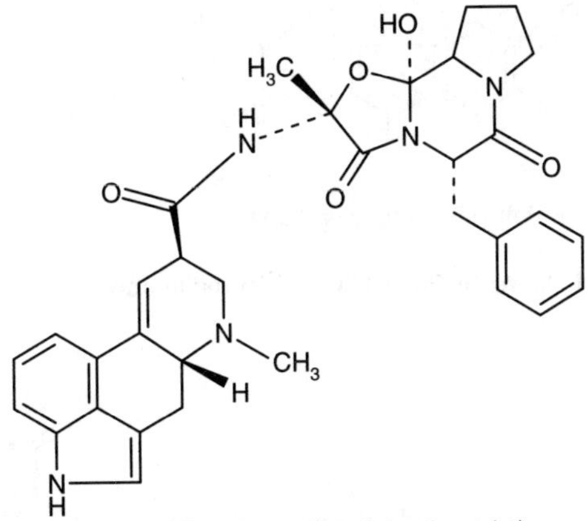

Ergotamne (partial antagonist)

Fig. 6.9 Some of the 5-HT$_{1D}$ receptor antagonists

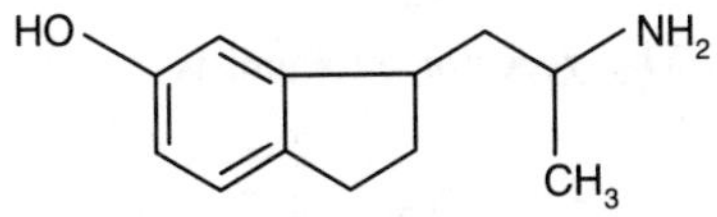

α-Methyl-5-hydroxytryptamine

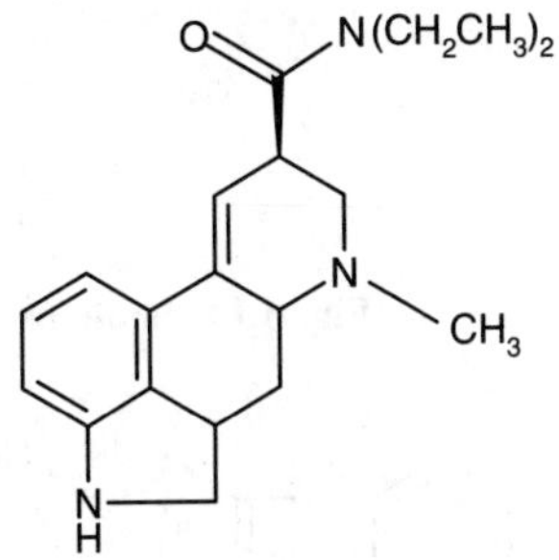

D-Lysergic acid diethylamide

Fig. 6.10 Some of the 5-HT$_{2A}$ receptor agonists

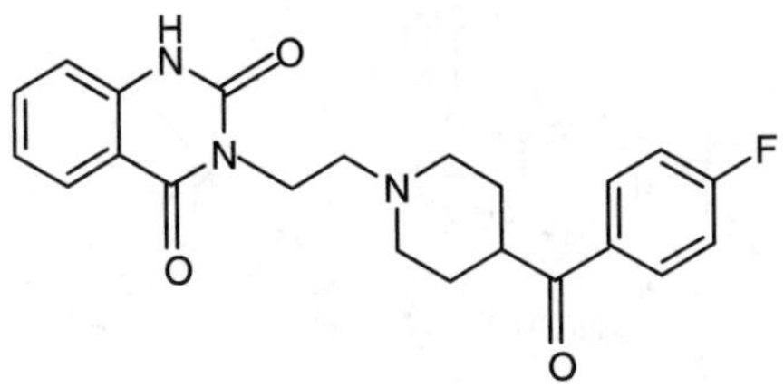

Ketanserin

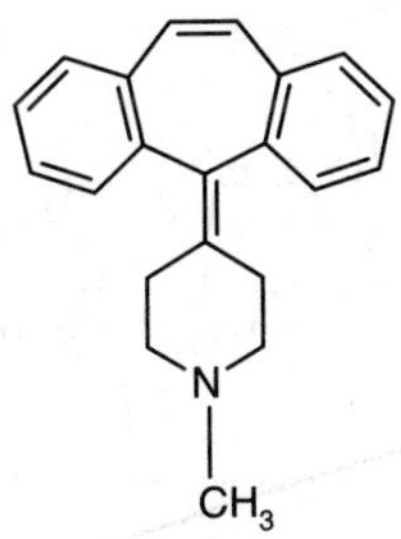

Cyproheptadine

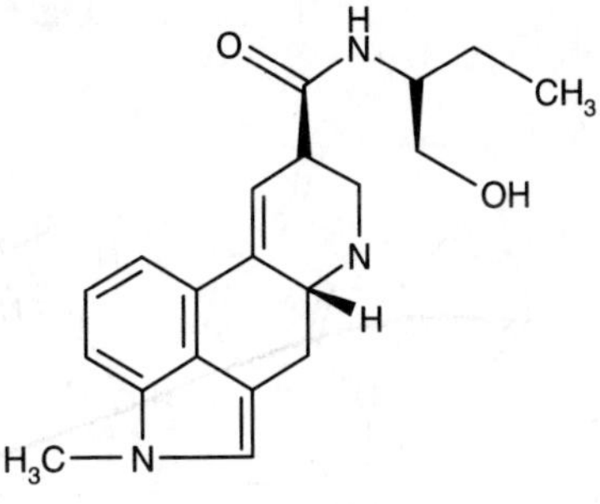

Methysergide

Fig. 6.11 Some of the 5-HT$_{2A}$ receptor antagonists

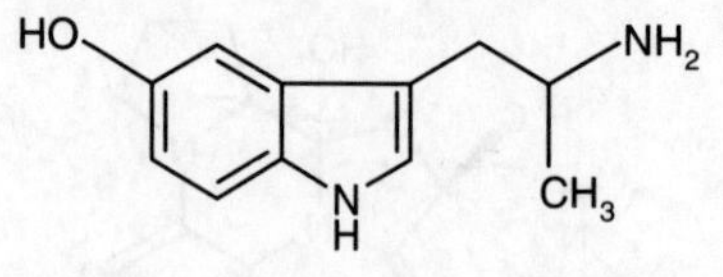

α-Methyl-5-hydroxytryptamine

Fig. 6.12 Some of the 5-HT_{2B} receptor agonists

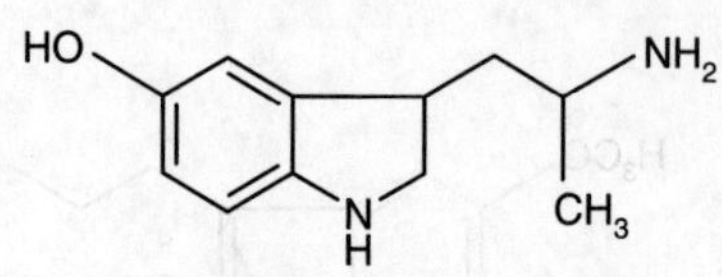

α-Methyl-5-hydroxytryptamine

Fig. 6.13 Some of the 5-HT_{2C} receptor agonists

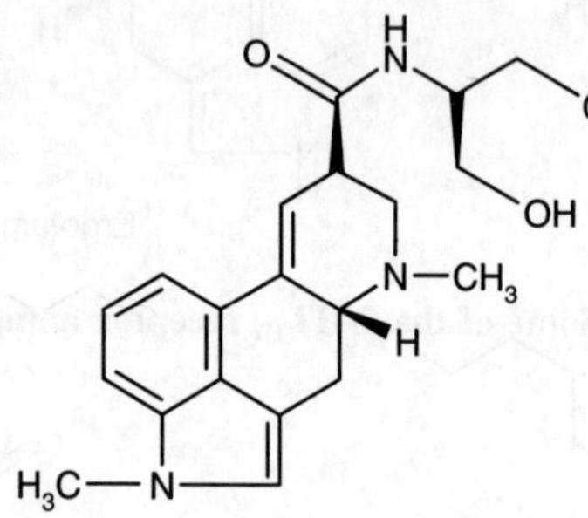

Methysergide

Fig. 6.14 Some of the 5-HT_{2C} receptor antagonists

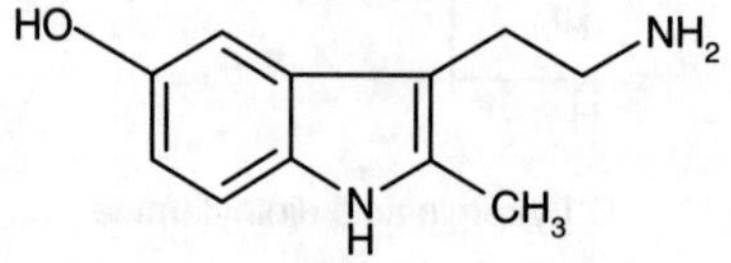

2-Methyl-5-hydroxytryptamine

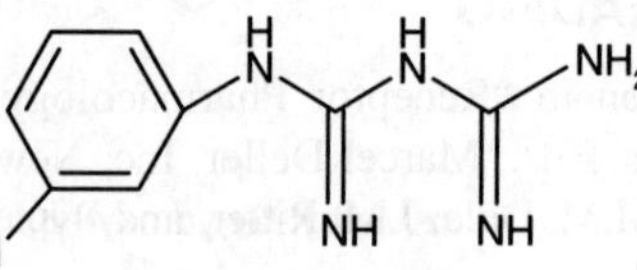

m-chlorophenylbiguanide

Fig. 6.15 Some of the 5-HT_3 receptor agonists

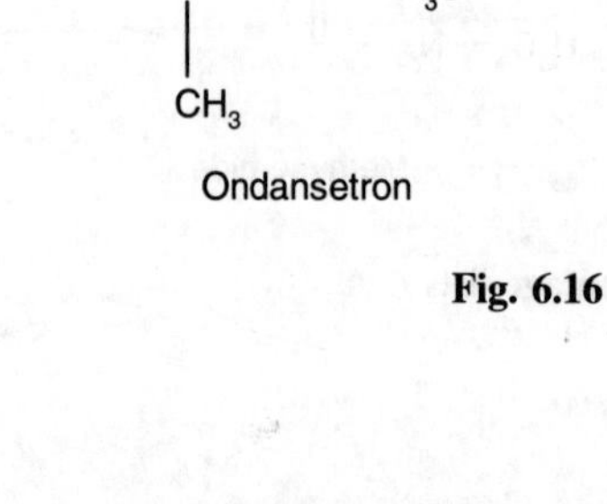

Ondansetron

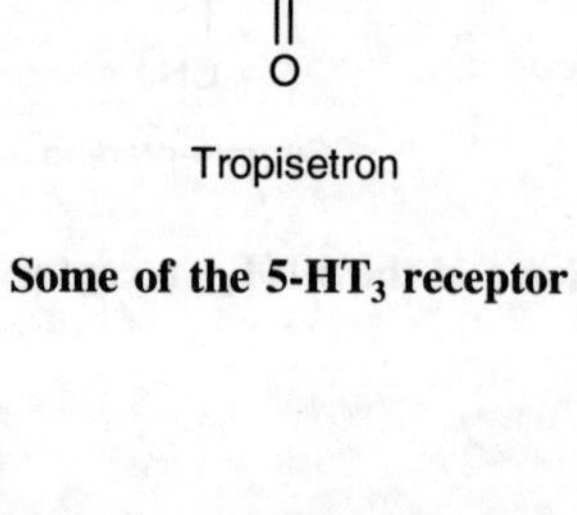

Tropisetron

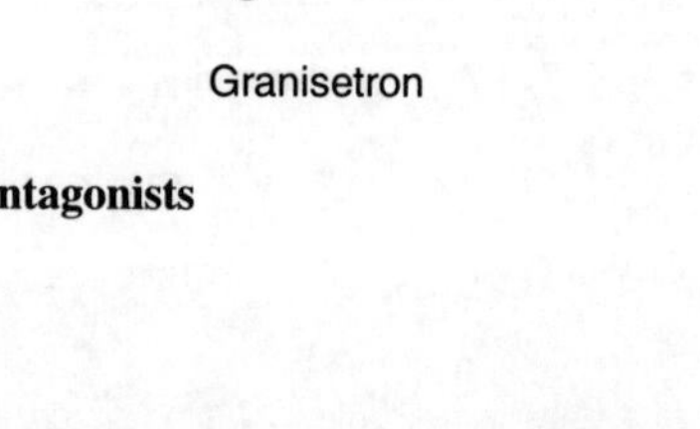

Granisetron

Fig. 6.16 Some of the 5-HT_3 receptor antagonists

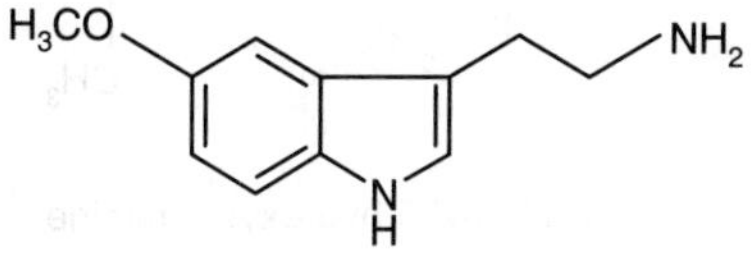

5-Methoxytryptamine

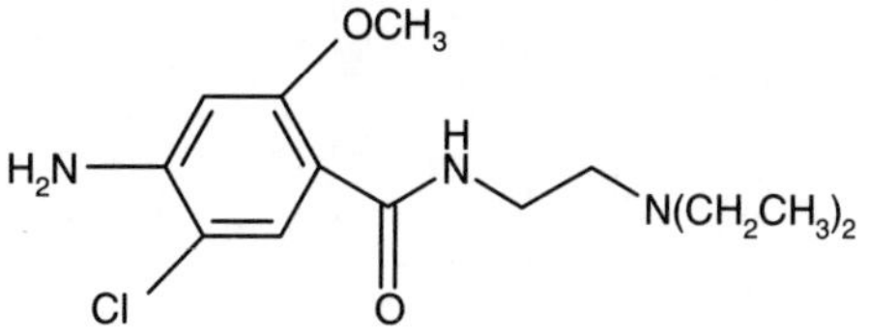

Metoclopramide

Fig. 6.17 Some of the 5-HT$_4$ receptor agonists

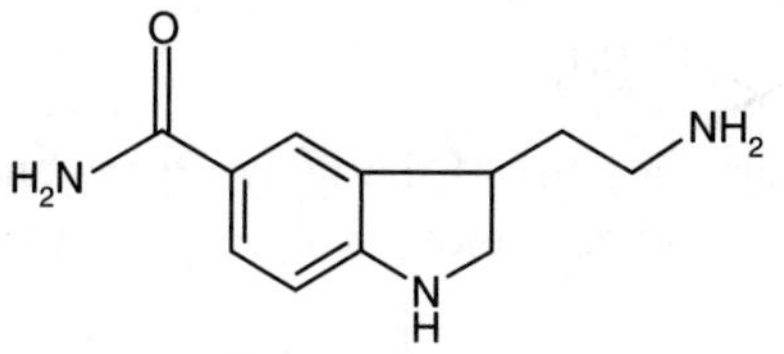

5-Carboxamidotryptamine

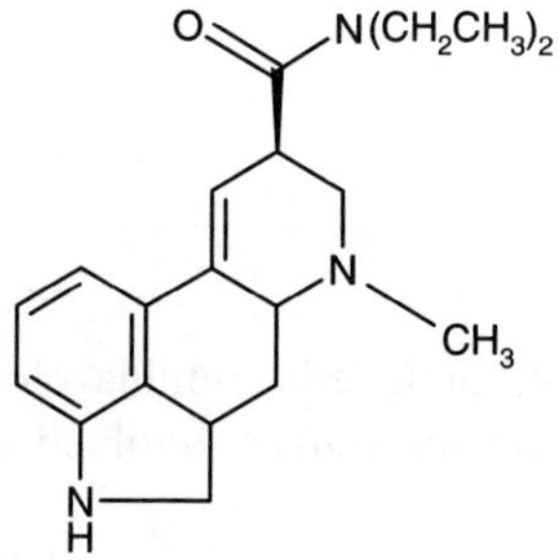

D-Lysergic acid diethylamide

Fig. 6.18 Some of the 5-HT$_7$ receptor agonists

FURTHER READING

1. R.A. Glennon in "Receptor Pharmacology and Function," M. Williams, R.A. Glennon, and P.B.M.W. Timmermans, Eds., Marcel Deller, Inc, New York, 1989, p. 257.
2. H.P. Rang, M.M. Dale, J.M. Ritter, and P.K. Moore, "Pharmacology," 5th ed., Churchill Livingstone, London, 2003, p. 184.
3. N.M. Barnes and T.Sharp, *Neuropharmacology*, **38**, 1083 (1999).
4. J.R. Cooper, F.E. Bloom, and R.H. Roth, "The Biochemical Basis of Neuropharmacology," Oxford University Press, New York, (1996).
5. M.F. Hibert, A.K. Mir, and J.R. Fozard in "Comprehensive Medicinal Chemistry," Vol. 3, C. Hansch, Ed. in Chief, Pergamon Press, Oxford, 2005, p. 567.

7

Histamine Receptors

Histamine, 4(5)-(2-aminoethyl)-imidazole (1), occurs in most of the body organs and body fluids. It acts as a chemical messenger involved in various complex biological actions. The two methylene

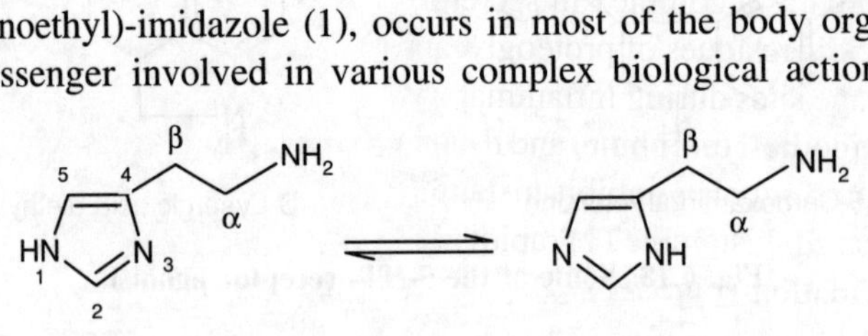

(a) (b)

(1)

carbons through which the amino group is attached are designated as α- and β-. It exists in two tautomeric forms (1a) and (1b). In aqueous solution the equilibrium is towards left, favouring (1a) by 4:1. Histamine (1) has two pKa of 9.40 (due to aliphatic primary amino group) and 5.80 (due to NH).

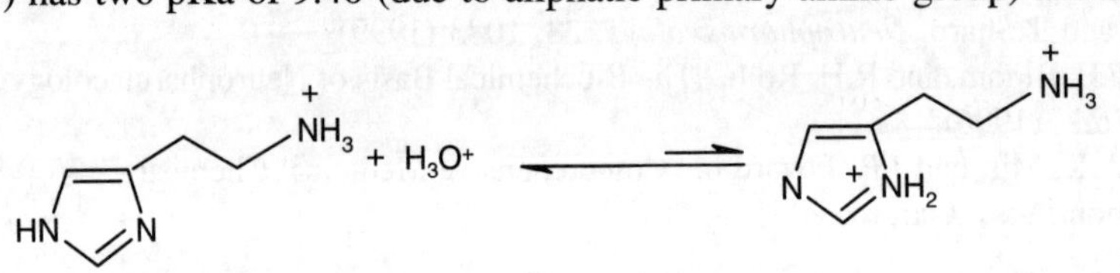

(2) (3)

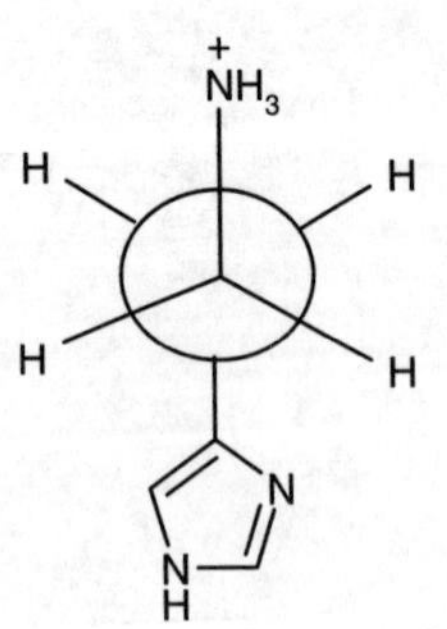

(4)

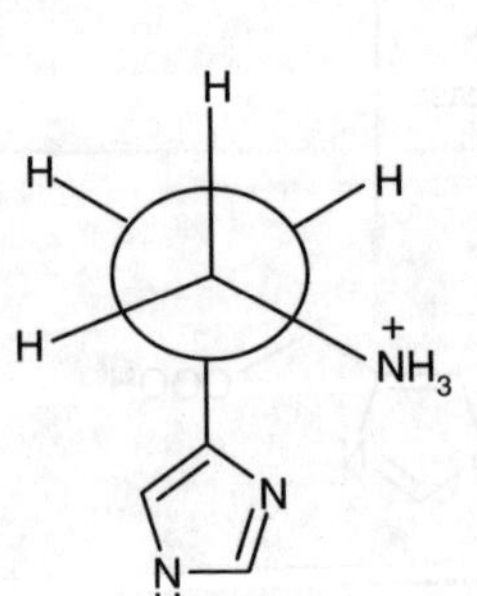

(5)

At physiological pH it exists as equilibrium mixture of monocation (2)(96%) and a dication (3)(30%). Conformational studies have shown that it exists in trans (4) and gauche (5) conformations.

Biosynthesis Storage and metabolism of Histamine (1)

Histamine (1) is synthesized from the amino acid L-histidine (6) in the Golgi apparatus of mast cells and basophils. The reaction involves decarboxylation of L-histidine by L-histidine decarboxylase with pyridoxal phosphate serving as the co-factor.

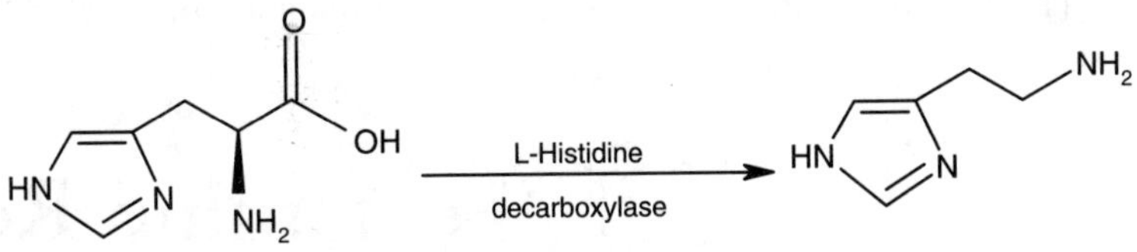

(6) (1)

Histamine (1) is stored as a complex in secretory granules of mast cells and basophils. In mast cells it is complexed with acidic residues of proteoglycan, heparin, and in basophils with chondroitin sulphate. It is released from storage sites during inflammatory or allergic reactions. The stimuli include interaction of antigen with IgE antibodies, morphine, and d-tubocurarine. Agents which inhibit cyc. AMP formation, such as β-adrenoreceptor agonists inhibit histamine (1) release.

As soon as it is released, histamine (1) rapidly undergoes metabolism to inactive metabolites through N-methylation and oxidation (Fig. 7.1).

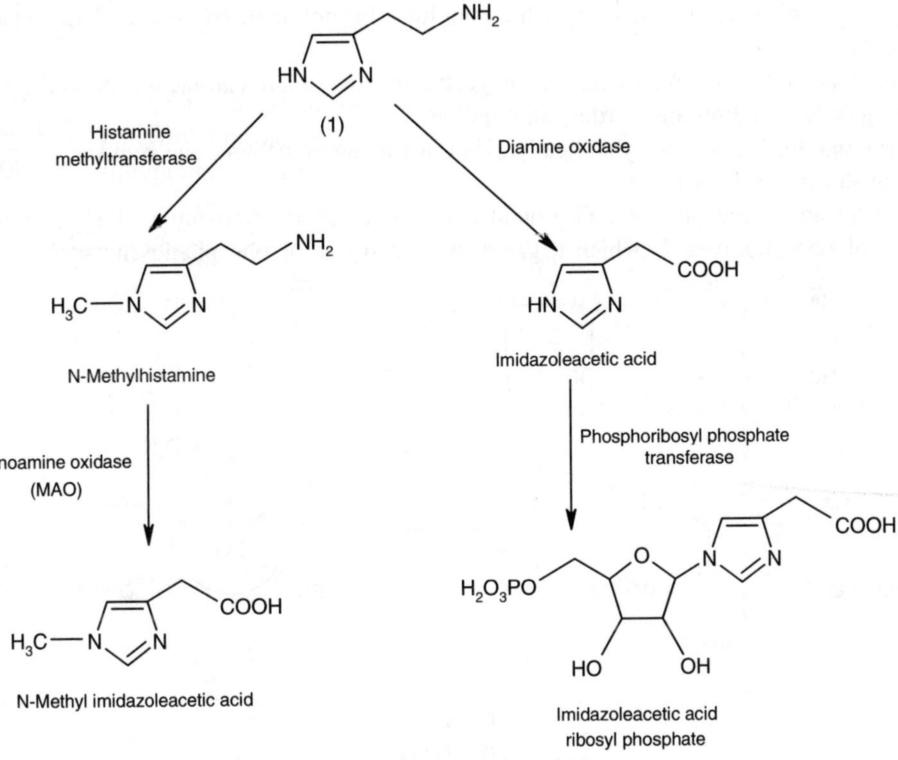

Fig. 7.1 Metabolism of histamine (1)

Histamine Receptors

After its release, histamine (1) exerts its effects on smooth muscles and glands. It causes contraction of smooth muscles of ileum, bronchii and brochioles, and uterus.

Histmine (1) stimulates the secretion of gastric acid which may result in ulcers. The cardiovascular effects of histamine (1) include dilation of blood vessels, increase of vascular permeability, and increased rate and output of heart.

Many of the earlier antihistaminics such as mepyramine (7) were not able to antagonize some of the effects of histamine (1) such as stimulation of gastric juice, stimulation of isolated atria, inhibition of

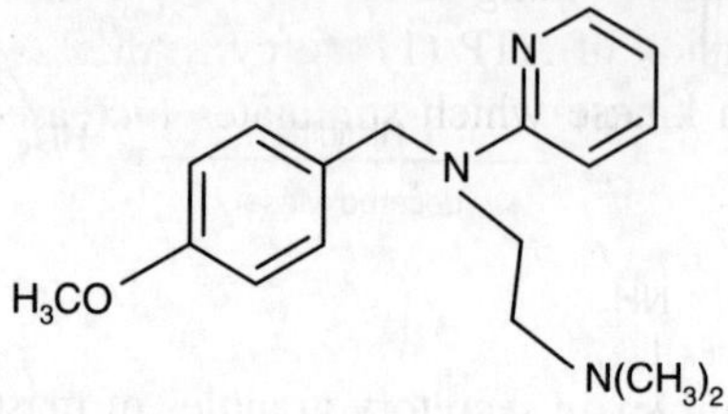

(7)

uterus and vasodilatory effects of large doses of histamine (1). These observations led to suggestions for the existence of more than one histamine (1) receptors. At present there are known three types of receptors, namely H_1-, H_2-, and H_3-receptors.

H_1-receptors are found mainly in smooth muscles, vascular endothelial cells, and in presynaptic histaminergic neurons in hypothalamus where they function as autoreceptors. H_1-receptors mediate inflammatory and allergic reactions which include bronchoconstriction and increased vascular permeability.

H_2-receptors are located in parietal cells in gastric mucosa and in cardiac muscle cells. They mediate increased gastric secretion and cardiac stimulation.

H_3-receptors are located presynaptically. They act as autoreceptors and regulate histamine release through feedback mechanism.

All the histamine receptors are G-protein coupled receptors. Activation of H_1-receptors leads to activation of phospholipase C which triggers the hydrolysis of phosphatidylinositol (8) resulting in

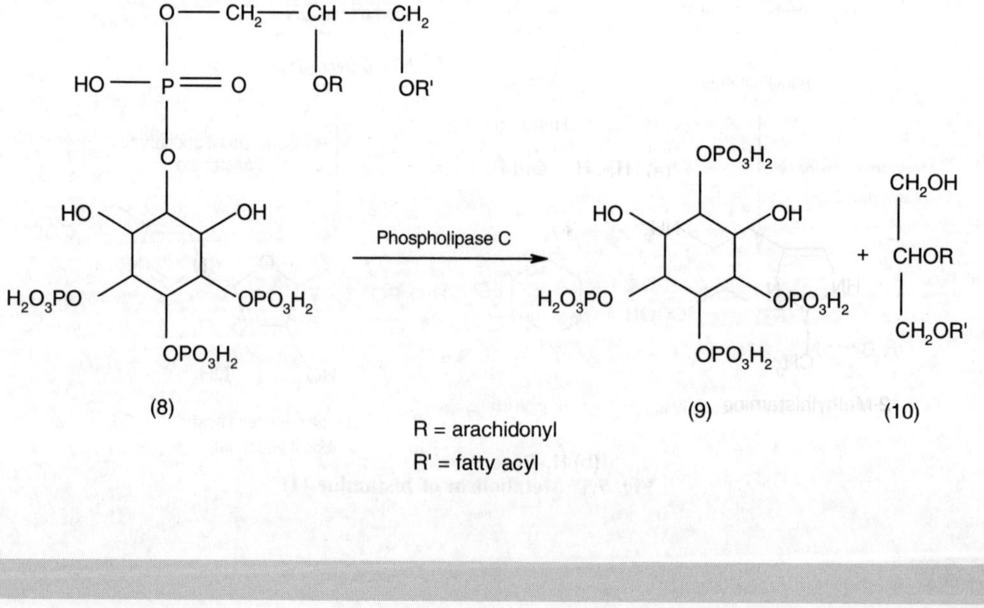

(8) (9) (10)

R = arachidonyl

R' = fatty acyl

increased levels of inositoltriphosphate (IP_3, 9) and diacylglycerol (DAG, 10). Increased levels of IP_3 (9) result in release of Ca^{2+} from intracellular stores leading to increased cytosolic Ca^{2+} levels. This results in smooth muscle contraction by Ca^{2+}/calmodulin –mediated phosphorylation of myosin-light-chain. However in other tissues, such as postcapillary vanules, increased cytosolic Ca^{2+} results in the synthesis of nitric oxide which relaxes the smooth muscles.

Increased Ca^{2+} levels also result in increased cyc. GMP, glycogenolysis, and neuronal excitation.

DAG (10) activates protein kinase C leading to phosphorylation and consequent activation of contractile proteins.

Activation of H_2-receptors through binding of H_2-agonists results in activation of adenylyl cyclase, an enzyme responsible for conversion of ATP (11) to cyc. AMP (12). Increased levels of cyc. AMP (12) result in actvation of protein kinase which stimulates increased gastric secretion, lipolysis, and formation of contractile proteins.

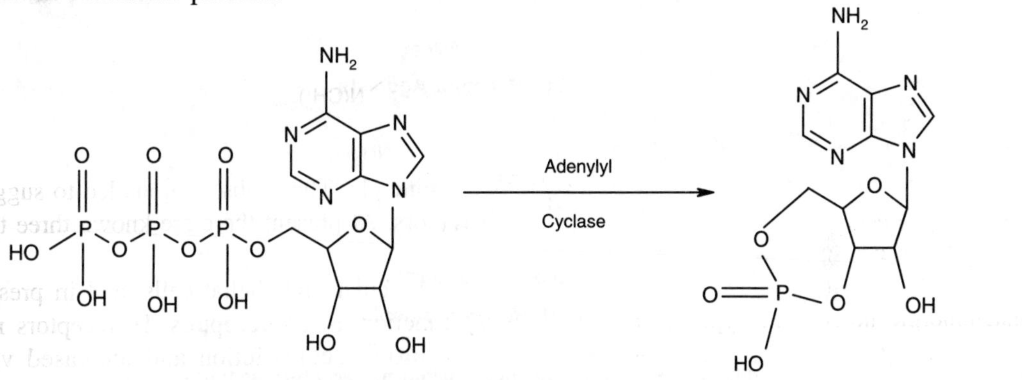

(11) (12)

Activation of H_3-receptors results in decreased cyc. AMP formation. This results in decreased neuronal firing and histamine release.

Some of the agonists and antagonists of histamine receptors are listed in Figs. 7.2 and 7.3 respectively.

Of the two conformations, trans- (4) and gauche- (5), trans-conformation is complimentary to H_1-receptor and gauche-conformation complimentary to H_2-receptor.

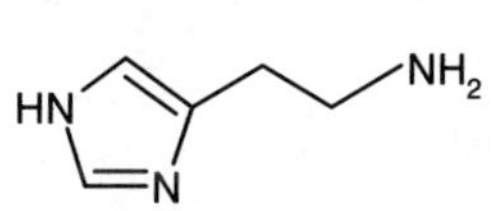

Histamine (1)

(a) H_1-, H_2-, and H_3-Receptor Agonists

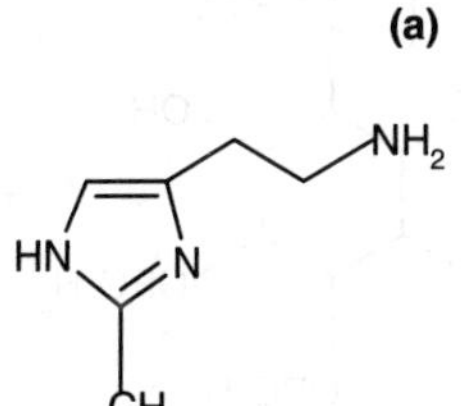

2-Methylhistamine

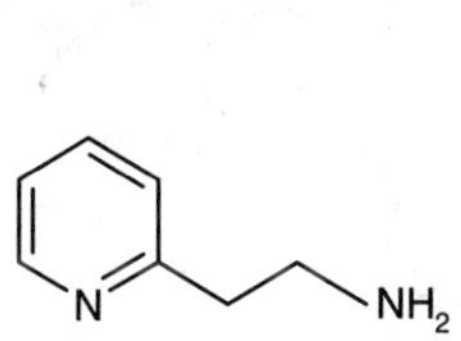

2-Pyridylethylamine

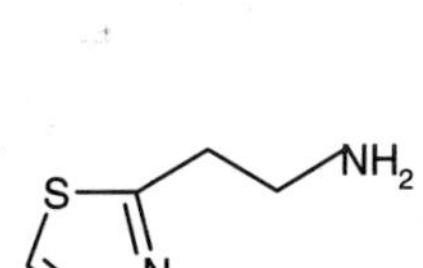

2-Thiazolylethylamine

(b) H_1-Receptor Agonists

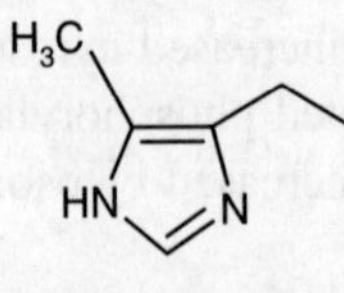

4(5)-Methylhistamine

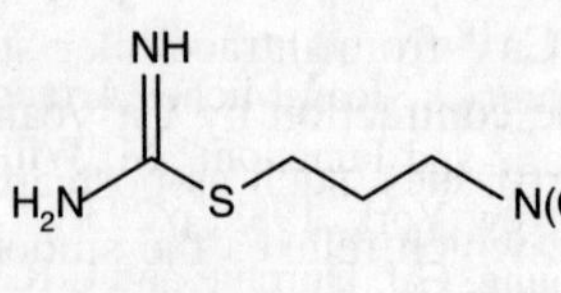

Dimaprit

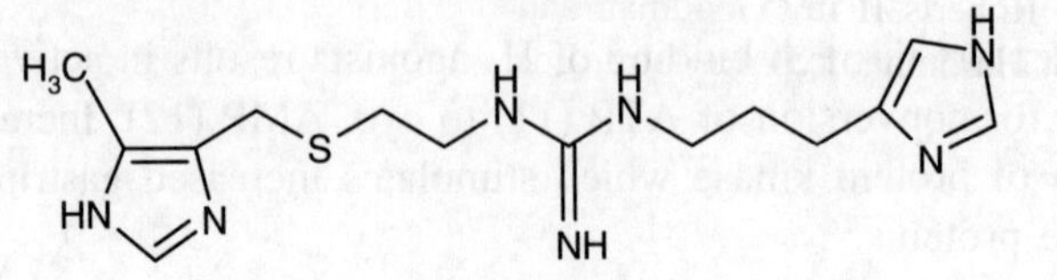

Impromidine

(c) H_2-Receptor Agonists

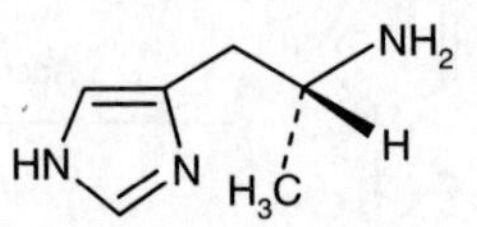

(R)-α-Methylhistamine

(d) H_3-Receptor Agonist

Fig. 7.2 Structures of some histamine receptors agonists

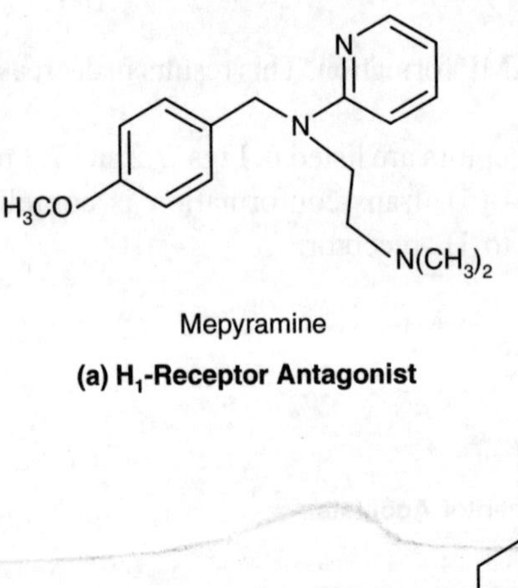

Mepyramine

(a) H_1-Receptor Antagonist

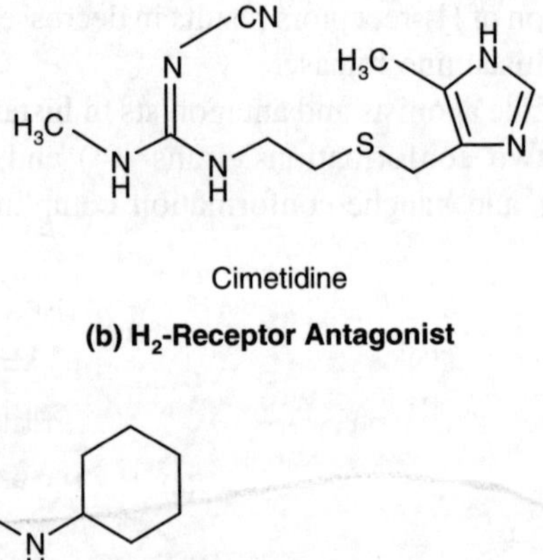

Cimetidine

(b) H_2-Receptor Antagonist

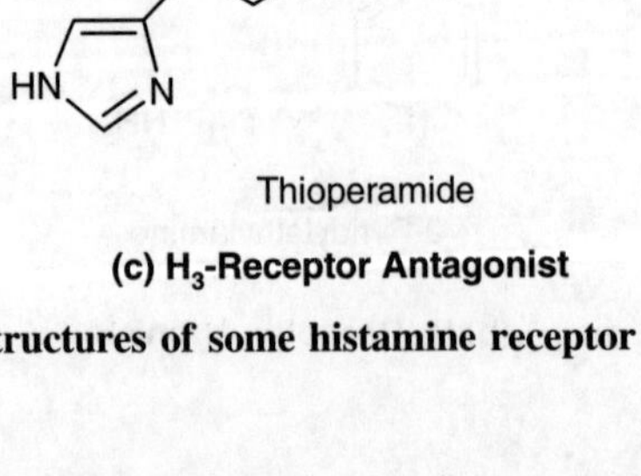

Thioperamide

(c) H_3-Receptor Antagonist

Fig. 7.3 Structures of some histamine receptor antagonists

FURTHER READING

1. A. Buschauer, W. Schunack, Jean-Michel Arrang, M.Garbarg, Jean-Charles Schwartz, and J.M. Young in "Receptor Pharmacology and Function," M. Williams, R.A. Glennon, and P.B.M.W.M. Timmerman, Eds., Marcel Dekker, Inc., New York, 1989, p.293.
2. D.G. Cooper, R.C. Young, G.J. Durrant, and C.R. Ganellin in "Comprehensive Medicinal Chemistry," Vol.3, C. Hansch, Ed. in Chief, Pergamon Press, Oxford, 2005, p. 323.
3. C.R. Ganellin M.A. Parsons, Eds., "Pharmacology of Histamine Receptors," PSG, Bristol, 1982.
4. N.J. Brown and L.J. Roberts II in "Goodman and Gilman's The Pharmacological Basis of Therapeutics," 10th ed. (Intern.), J.G. Hardman, L.E. Limbird, Eds. McGraw Hill, New York, 2001, p. 645.

8

Dopamine and Steroid Hormone Receptors

DOPAMINE RECEPTORS

Dopamine (1) is involved in several disorders of brain function, particularly in Parkinson's disease, schizophrenia, as well as in drug dependent and in certain endocrine disorders. The biosynthesis of

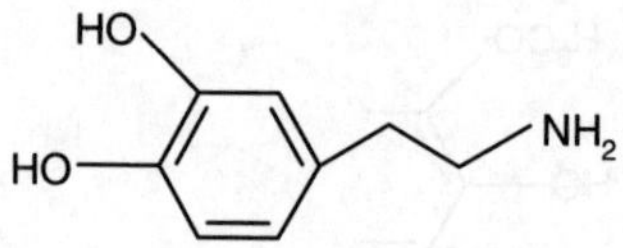

(1)

dopamine (1) starts with the amino acid tyrosine (2), which after getting hydroxylated with tyrosine hydroxylase is converted to L-Dopa (3). The L-Dopa on decarboxylation in presence of aromatic amino acid decarboxylase yields dopamine (1).

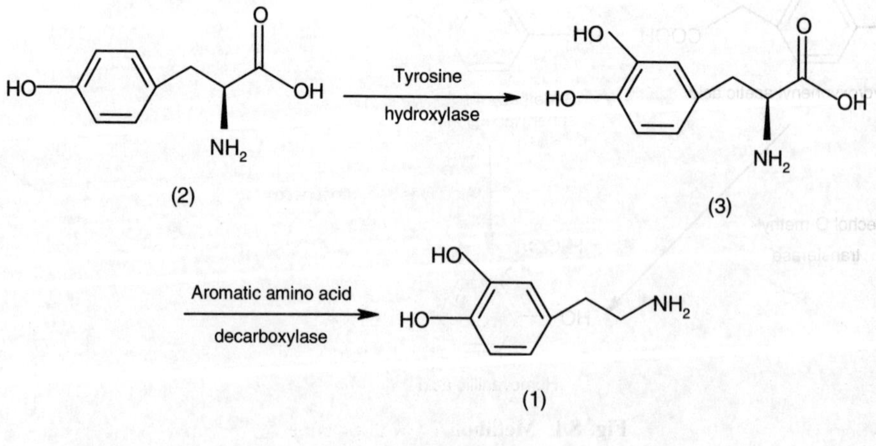

The synthesized dopamine (1) is stored in vesicles which are located in nerve endings. It is stored as a complex with chromogranins, divalent ions like calcium and magnesium and ATP. Evidences of free storage pools of dopamine in cytoplasm are there. The free storage pools of dopamine seem to control the synthesis of dopamine (1) by controlling the activity of tyrosine hydroxylase.

Dopamine (1) is released from nerve endings by exocytosis. This release of dopamine (1) is calcium dependent.

The metabolism of dopamine (1) involves oxidation with monoamine oxidase and aldehyde dehydrogenase and methylation of phenolic hydroxyl group by catechol-O-methyltransferase (Fig. 8.1). Another route of metabolism involves conversion to norepinephrine and epinephrine (Fig. 8.1).

Dopamine (1) has been associated with Parkinson's disease and schizophrenia. In Parkinson's disease, there is depletion of dopamine (1) in the corpus luteum. On the basis of indirect evidences, release of

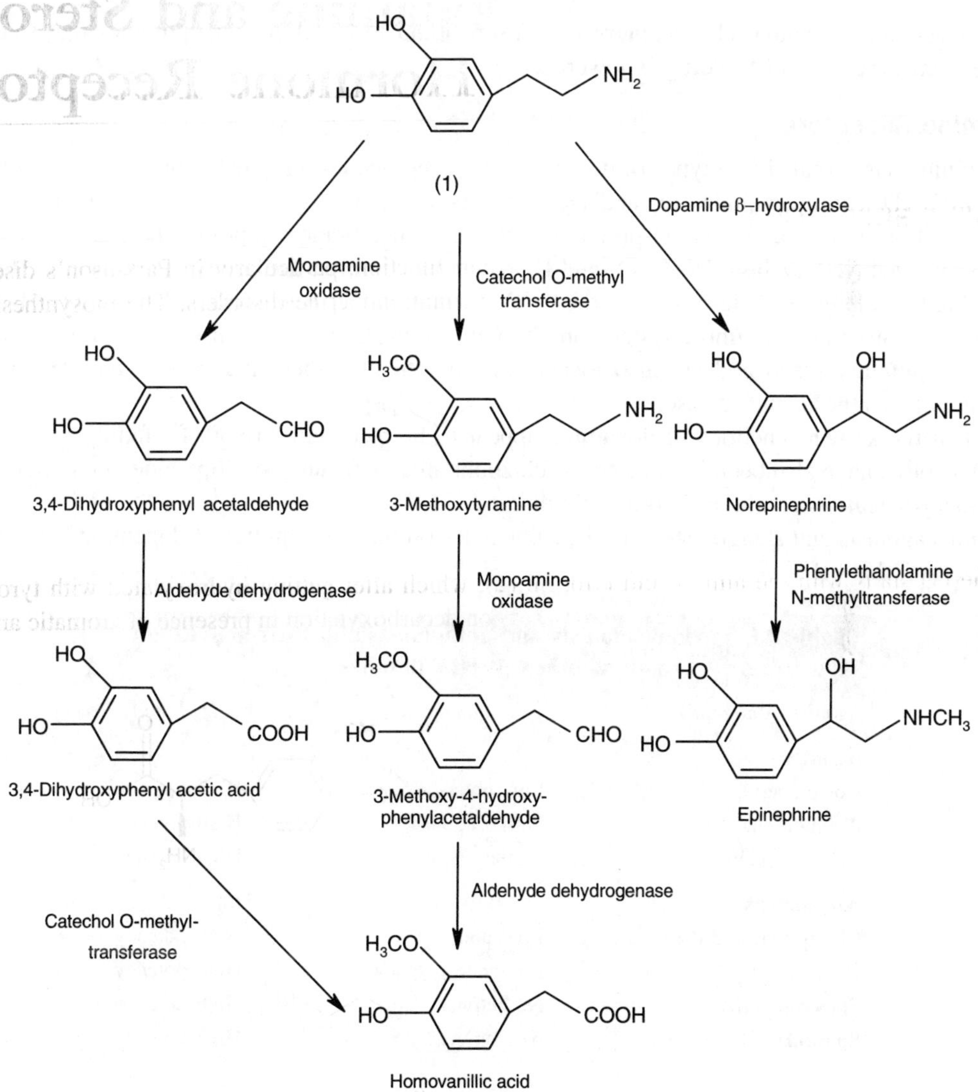

Fig. 8.1 Metabolism of dopamine

dopamine (1) or activation of dopamine receptors has been proposed as the cause of schizophrenia. Thus, drugs such as amphetamine (4), cocaine (5), and apomorphine (6) which incease dopamine (1)

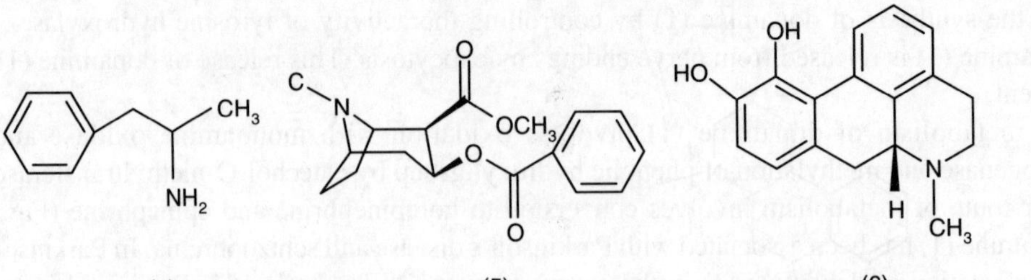

(4) (5) (6)

levels or activate dopamine (1) receptors have been found to develop schizophrenic- like state that subsides when the dose of the drug is lowered.

Dopamine Receptors

Gene cloning has revealed five types of dopamine (1) receptors, D_1 – D_5, belonging to two families D_1 and D_2. The D_1 family includes D_1 and D_5 receptors while as D_2 family includes D_2, D_3, and D_4 recptors. All of these receptors are G-protein coupled transmembrane receptors. The signal mechanism is linked via adenylyl cyclase. While D_1 and D_5 receptors stimulate the adenylyl cyclase, D_2, D_3, and D_4 inhibit the adenylyl cyclase and increase IP_3 formation. D_1 Receptors are most abundant and widespread in striatum, the limbic system, and hypothalamus. D_2 receptors also occur in these areas as well as in pituitary gland and are also located presynaptically where they act as autoregulators of dopamine (1) synthesis and release.

Most of the known functions of dopamine appear to be mediated through D_2-family of receptors. These receptors have also been implicated in schizophrenia. Deficiency of dopamine (1) in nigrostratal dopaminergic neurons results in Parkinson's disease.

Various agonists and antagonists with their potencies on the two families of dopamine (1) receptors are listed in Table 8.1.

Table 8.1 Various agonists and antagonists and their activity on dopamine receptor families

Agonist/ Antagonist	*D_1 Family*	*D_2 Family*
Agonist		
Dopamine (1)	Low potency	High potency
Apomorphine (6)	Partial agonist	High potency
Bromocriptine(7)	Partial agonist	High potency
Antagonists		
Chlorpromazine (8)	Low potency	High potency
Haloperidol (9)	Moderate potency	High potency
Spiperone (10)	No activity	High potency
Sulpiride (11)	No activity	High potency

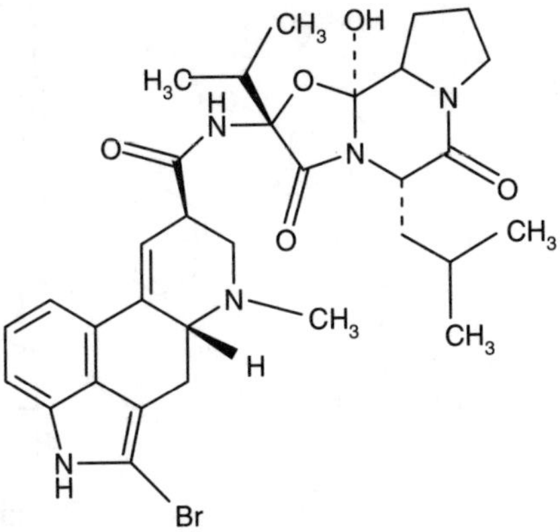

(7)

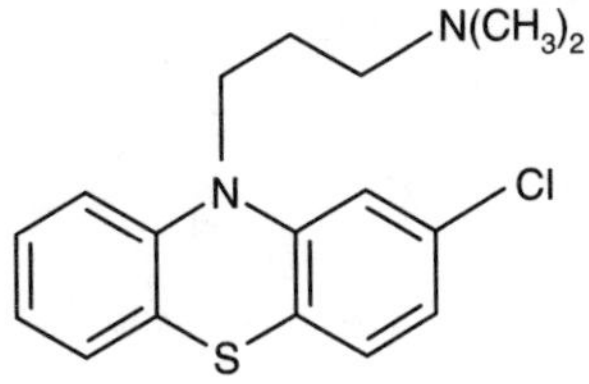

(8)

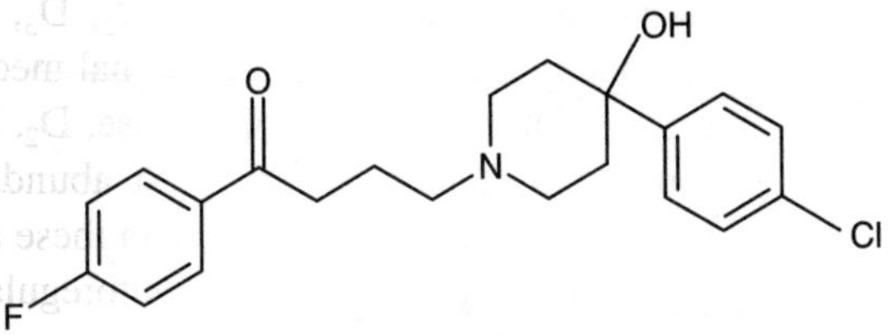

(9)

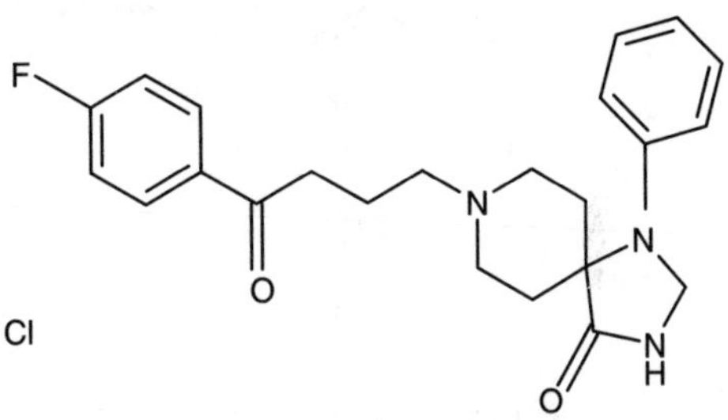

(10)

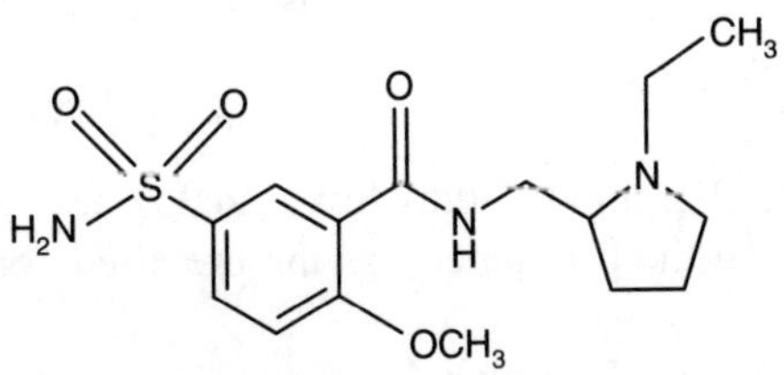

(11)

Dopamine (1) can assume either *gauche*-(12a and 12b) or a *trans*- conformations (13a and 13b). The *trans*- conformation (13a), in which the catechol moiety is perpendicular to $-CH_2NH_2$ is *trans*-α and in another *trans* -conformation (13b) where the catechol moiety is coplanar to $-CH_2NH_2$ is *trans*-β. The energy difference between the *gauche*- and the *trans*-conformations is only 4-8 k Jol mol^{-1}. The pharmacological studies on rigid and semirigid analogs of dopamine (1), suggests that the *trans*-conformation is the preferred conformation for binding to the receptor. The crystal structure and the molecular orbital calculations of NMR coupling constants further indicate that the catechol moiety is perpendicular to $-CH_2NH_2$, indicating a *trans*-α (13a) conformation. However, since apomorphine (6) is a planar molecule, one can conclude that receptor-prefered conformation must be *trans*-β (13b).

The preferred conformation of catechol in *trans*-β isomer could either be (14, α-rotamer) or (15, β-rotamer). This was resolved by studying the pharmacological activities of semirigid analogs, 2-amino-5,6-dihydroxytetralin (14a) and 2-amino-6,7-dihydroxytetralin (15a) corresponding to α-rotamer

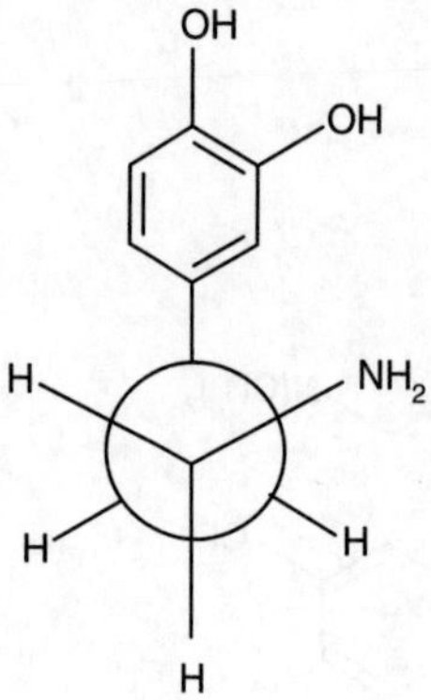

(12a)

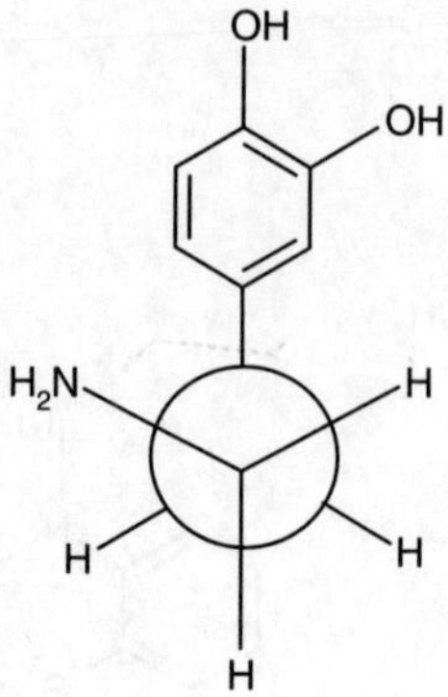

(12b)

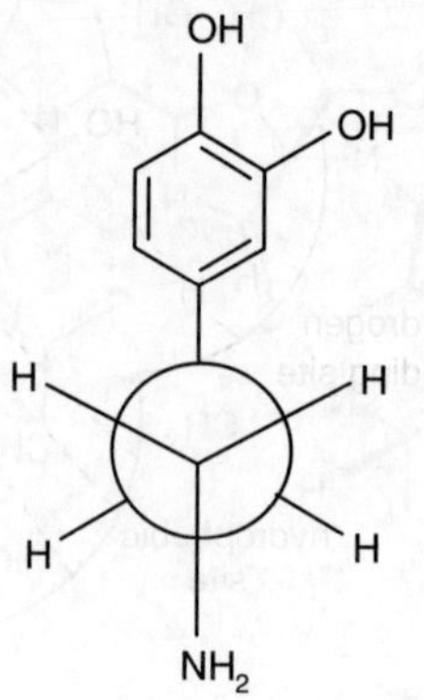

(13a)

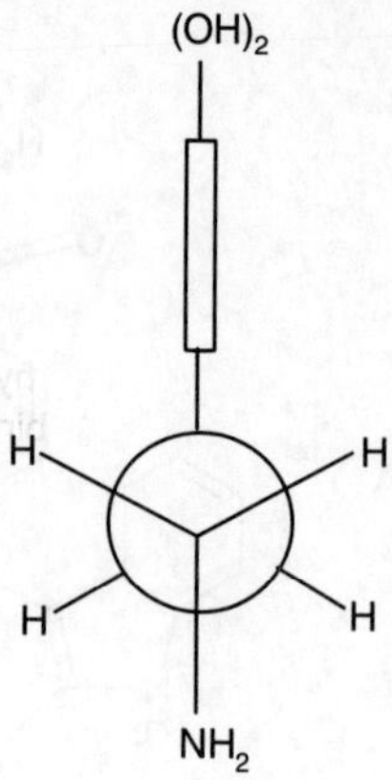

(13b)

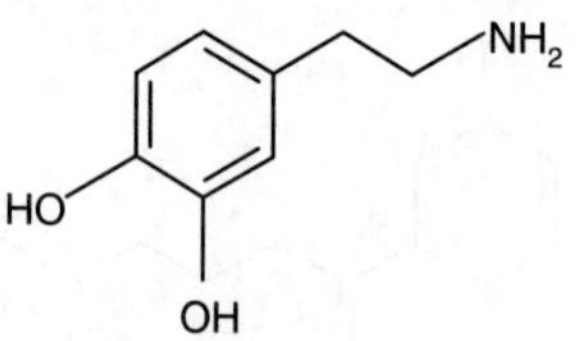

(14)

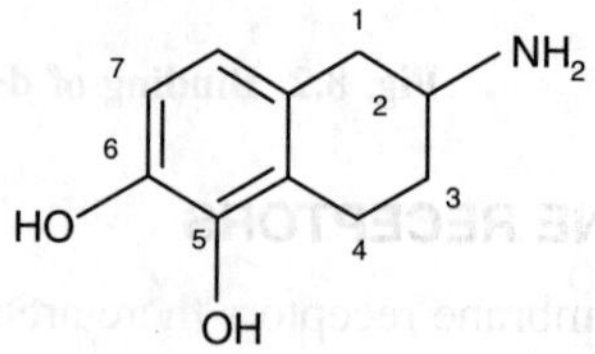

(14a)

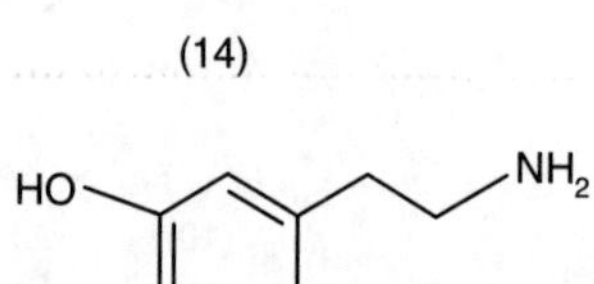

(15)

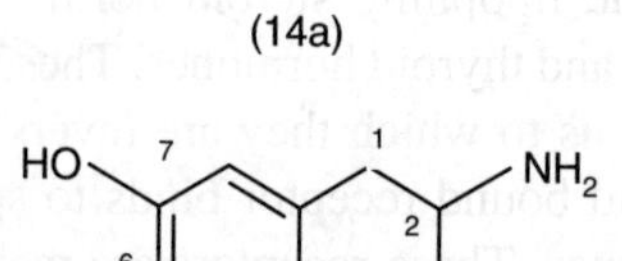

(15a)

and β-rotamer, respectively. The 2-amino-6,7-dihydroxy analog was found to be more active than 5,6-dihdroxy analog, indicating that the β-rotamer was the preferred conformation which binds to the receptor.

Number of topographical models of dopamine (1) receptors have been proposed One of these has been postulated by Seeman in 1980 (Fig. 8.2). According to this there are four sites in receptor where the dopamine (1) moiety gets bound. Two of them constitute the hydrogen binding sites through which two phenolic groups are bound. Next to this is the hydrophobic site, where the benzene moiety gets bound. After the hydrophobic site there is anionic site where the positively charged amino nitrogen gets bound. The distance between the site where *m*-phenolic group and the anionic site is about 6.5-7.8 Å (Fig. 8.2).

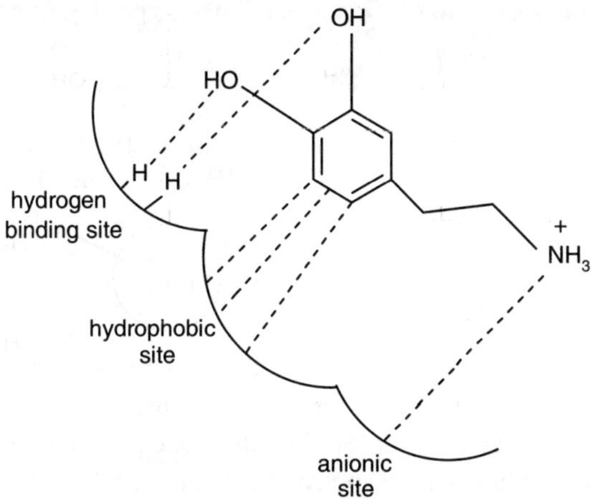

Fig. 8.2 Binding of dopamine (1) to D_2-receptor

STEROID HORMONE RECEPTORS

In addition to transmembrane receptors there are also intracellular or nuclear receptors. The ligands for these receptors include lipophilic steroid hormones such as adrenocorticoids, estrogens, progestins, androgens, vitamin D, and thyroid hormones. These hormones/ligands are carried to the receptor through blood by carrier proteins to which they are reversibly bound. After binding of the hormones/ligand to the receptor, the ligand bound receptor binds to specific DNA sequence near the gene and stimulates the transcription of genes. These receptors are mainly located in cytosol and also in the nucleus of the target cell.

All the receptors for various hormones contain three sites (Fig. 8.3), the ligand binding site, the DNA binding site and the transcription activating site. The DNA binding site in the unoccupied receptor is bound to "heat-shock protein" (hsp90) which maintains the receptor in a conformation that allows binding of ligand to it (Fig. 8.3)

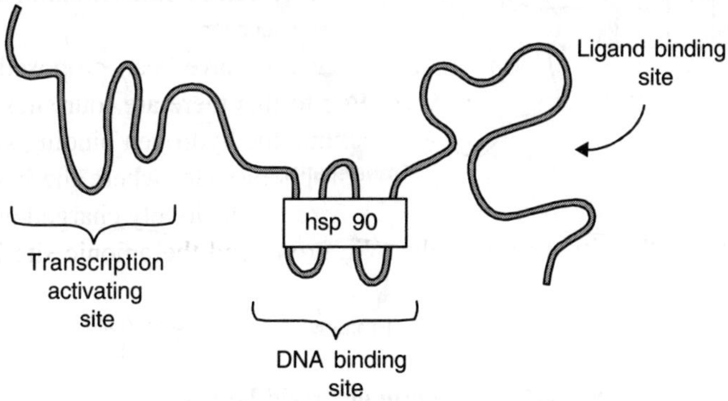

Fig. 8.3 Steroid receptor

The total number of amino acid and its sequence of various steroid hormone receptors has been deduced (Table 8.2). The nucleotide sequence of various "Hormone Responsive Element" (HRE), where the ligands bind has also been established.

Table 8.2 Number of amino acids of various steroid hormone receptors

Receptor	*Total number of Amino Acids*	*Corresponding HRE*
Estrogen (ER)	595	ERE (Estrogen Responsive Element)
Glucocorticoid (GR)	777	GRE (Glucocorticoid Responsive Element)
Androgen (AR)	905	ARE (Androgen Responsive Element)
Progesterone (PR)	934	PRE (Progestin Responsive Element)
Mineralocorticoid (MR)	984	MRE (Mineralocorticoid Responsive Element)

After the steroid molecule enters the cell, it then binds to its receptor at the same time the receptor bound hsp 90 is released (Fig. 8.4). Next, the ligand bound receptor is phosphorylated resulting in homodimerization of the receptor-ligand complex. The dimerized receptor-ligand complex then enters nucleus where it binds to region of hormone responsive element of DNA. This binding may also recruit coactivator, resulting in transcription and ultimately synthesis of protein which result in altered cellular function (Fig. 8.4).

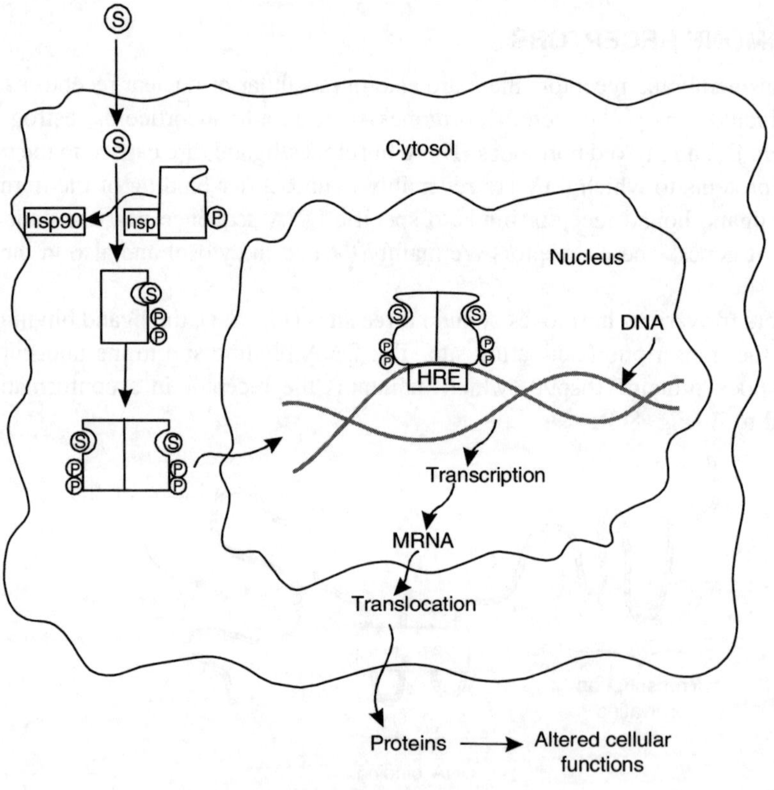

Fig. 8.4 Mechanism of steroid hormones

The basic mechanism of all the steroid hormones is as given above. Differences arise from specific cellular proteins synthesized.

FURTHER READING

1. H.B. Niznik and K.R. Jarvie in "Receptor Pharmacology and Function," M. Williams, R.A. Glennon, and P.B.M.M. Timmerman, Eds., Marcel Dekker inc., New York, 1989, p. 769.
2. I. Creese and C.M. Fraser, "Dopamine Receptors," Liss, New York, 1987.
3. A.S. Horn in "Comprehensive Medicinal Chemistry," Vol. 3, C.Hansch, Ed. in-Chief, Pergamon Press, Oxford, 2005, p. 229.
4. R.M. Evans, *Science*, **240**, 889 (1988).
5. H.P. Rang, M.M. Dale, J.M. Ritter, and P.K. Moore, "Pharmacology," 5th ed., Churchill Livingstone, London, 2003, p. 415.
6. B.L. Furman in "Drug Discovery Handbook," S. Cox Gad, Ed., Wiley Interscience, New Jersey, 2005, p. 1037.
7. T. Ojasoo, J.-P. Raynaud and J.-P. Mornon in "Comprehensive Medicinal Chemistry," Vol. 3, C. Hansch, Ed. in-Chief, Pergamon Press, Oxford, 2005, p. 1175.

9

Amino Acid Receptors

4-Aminobutyric acid (GABA, γ-aminobutyric acid, 1), glycine (2), glutamic acid (3), and aspartic acid (4) constitute the amino acid neurotransmitters in the brain. While GABA (1) and glycine (2) are

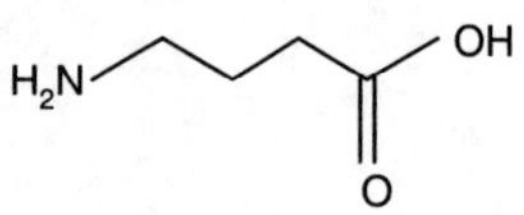

(1)

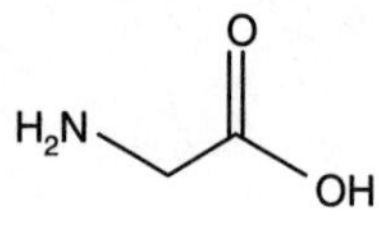

(2)

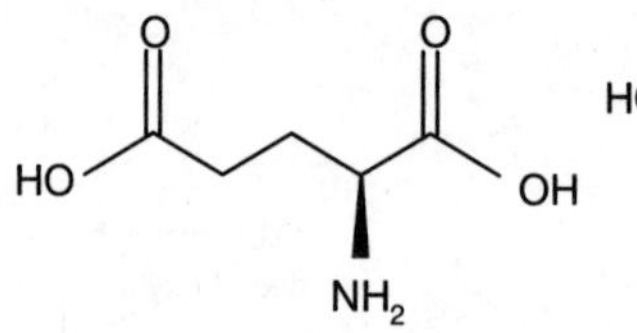

(3)

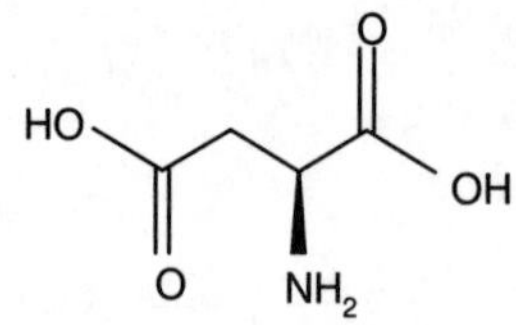

(4)

inhibitory transmitters, the glutamic acid (3) and the aspartic acid (4) constitute the excitatory neurotransmitters.

INHIBITORY AMINO ACID NEUROTRANSMITTERS

γ-Aminobutyric acid (1, GABA)

GABA (1) is a major inhibitory neurotransmitter involved in certain neurological and psychiatric diseases such as epilepsy, Huntington's Chorea and Parkinson's diseases. Analysis of brain samples from sites near the seizure foci in epileptic patients has revealed severe impairment of GABA (1) system. Low levels of GABA (1) synthesizing enzyme (*S*)-glutamate decarboxylase and reduced GABA (1) uptake capacity have been implicated in epileptic seizures. Similarly, low levels of GABA (1) and (S)-glutamate decarboxylase have also been measured in brain tissues of choreic patients. In Parkinson's disease there is imbalance between GABA (1) and dopamine (5). GABA (1) is also involved in schizophrenia and Alzheimer diseases. However, its exact role in the pathophysiology of these diseases is not yet clear.

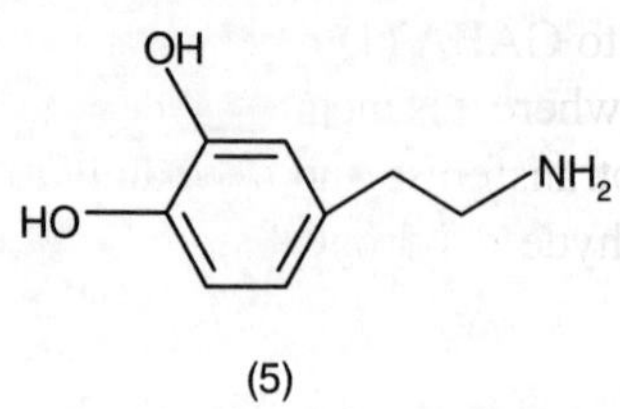

(5)

Biosynthesis and Metabolism of GABA (1)

GABA (1) is synthesized from (*S*)-glutamic acid (3) by decarboxylation. The enzyme which brings about the decarboxylation is glutamic acid decarboxylase, a pyridoxyl phosphate dependent enzyme. The glutamic acid (3) is produced by transamination of 2-oxoglutaric acid (6), an intermediate of citric acid cycle. Alternately, it is also produced by deamination of (*S*)-glutamine (7) by glutaminase. Depolarization of the presynaptic neurons results in release of GABA (1) into synaptic cleft. The

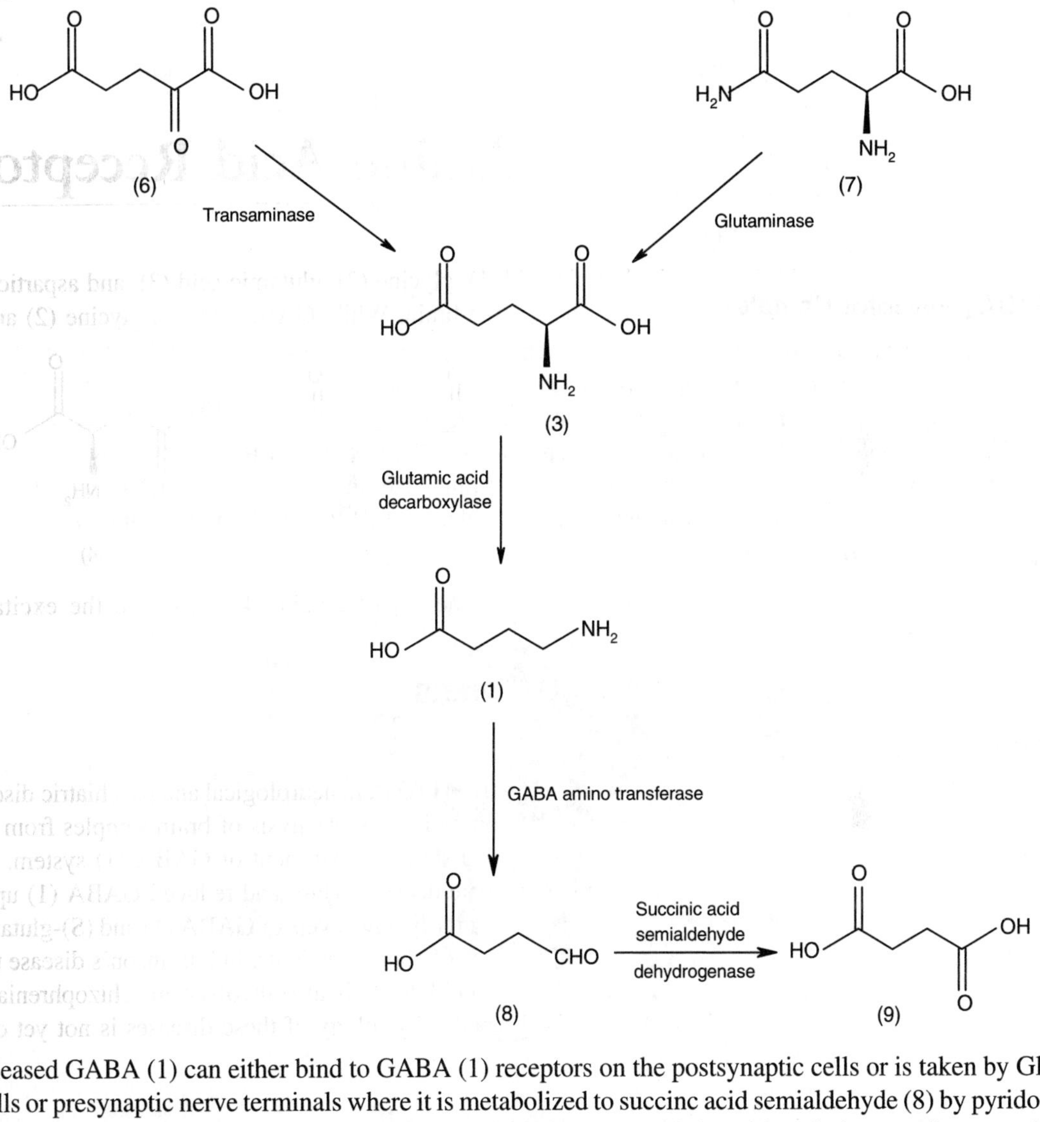

released GABA (1) can either bind to GABA (1) receptors on the postsynaptic cells or is taken by Glias cells or presynaptic nerve terminals where it is metabolized to succinc acid semialdehyde (8) by pyridoxal phosphate dependent GABA aminotransferase and ultimately to citric acid cycle intermediate, succinic acid (9) by succinic acid semialdehyde dehdrogenase.

GABA RECEPTORS

Electrophysiological and receptor binding studies have resulted in identification of two subtypes of GABA (1) receptors. These include $GABA_A$ receptor, the selective antagonist of which is bicuculline

(10) and $GABA_B$ receptor which is insensitive to bicuculline (10) and which is selectively activated by the agonist baclofen (11). The two receptors not only differ in their pharmacological profiles but also in their structures. While $GABA_A$ is a multisite chloride channel, $GABA_B$ receptors are coupled to calcium channel associated with a second messenger.

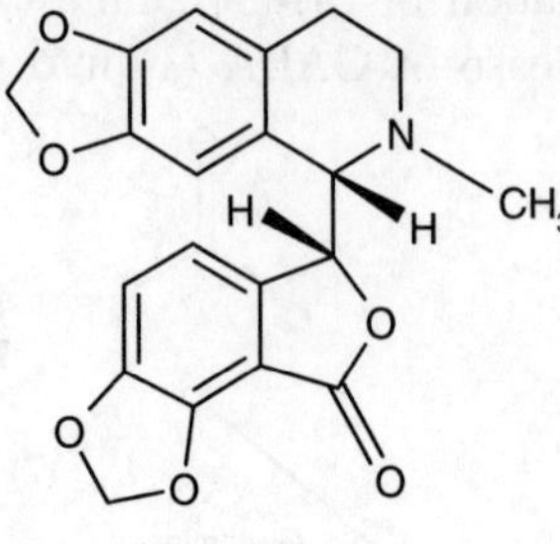

(10)

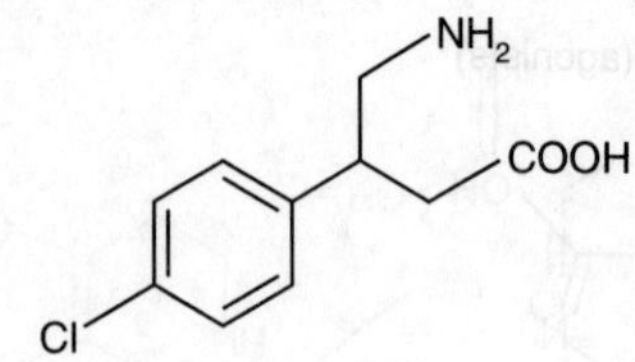

(11)

$GABA_A$ Receptor Complex

There are two $GABA_A$ receptors, the postsynaptic and presynaptic. Both are coupled to chloride ion channel. The activation of presynaptic $GABA_A$ receptor results in efflux of chloride ion and activation of postsynaptic $GABA_A$ receptor results in influx of chloride ions.

The postsynaptic $GABA_A$ receptor is a ligand gated chloride channel. It has a pentameric structure from five subunits – two of α-subunits, two of β-subunits, and one of γ-subunit, each of which in turn is composed of four membrane-spanning domains selected from multiple polypeptide classes ($\alpha_{1\text{-}6}$, $\beta_{1\text{-}3}$, $\gamma_{1\text{-}3}$, δ, ε, π, θ) (Fig. 9.1).

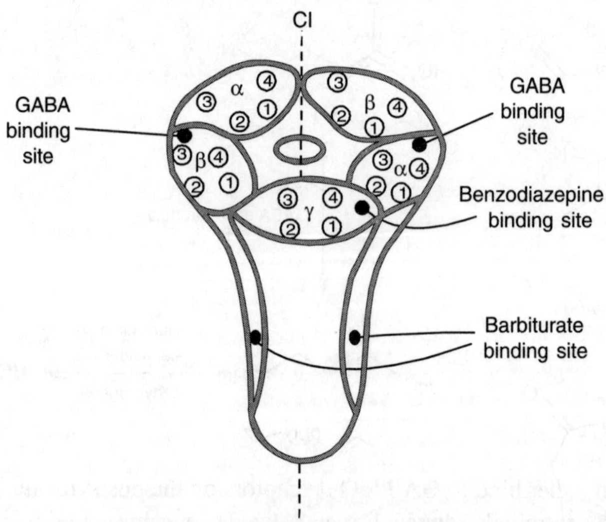

Fig. 9.1 Postsynaptic $GABA_A$ receptor

The postsynaptic $GABA_A$ receptor has multiple binding sites which include two binding sites for GABA (at α- and β-subunits), one benzodiazepine binding site (at α-γ subunits), and two barbiturate binding sites at α- and β-subunits. Binding of an agonist like GABA, benzodiazepine, or barbiturate results in change in conformation and opening of the chloride ion channel. The influx of chloride ions results in increased negativity resulting in hyperpolarization.

Binding of benzodiazepines results in increased frequency of opening of chloride channel without affecting the duration and channel conductance of chloride ions. Benzodiazepines also enhance the binding affinity of GABA receptors.

Binding of barbiturates enhances the action of GABA. However, barbiturates binding does not result in increase in frequency of chloride channel opening but duration of opening is prolonged.

Some of the $GABA_A$ receptor agonists and antagonists are listed in Figs. 9.2 and 9.3, respectively.

Direct Acting (agonists)

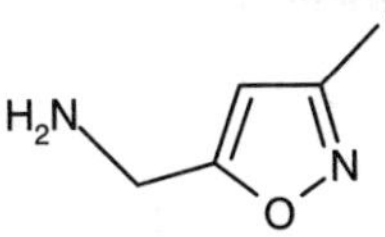

Muscimol

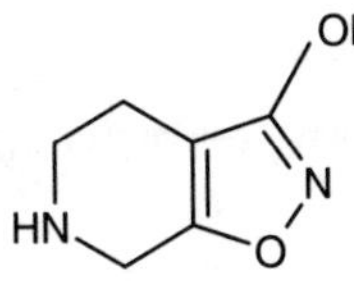

Gabaxadol

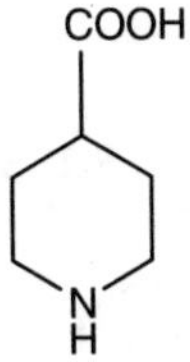

Isonipecotic acid

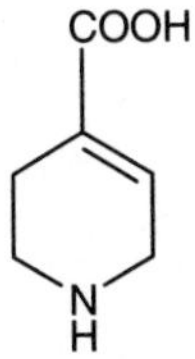

Isoguvacine

Indirectly Acting (agonists) (cause release of GABA from intracellular stores)

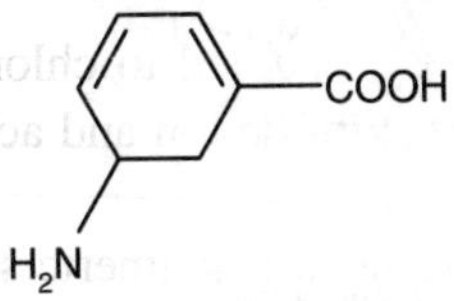

Gabaculine

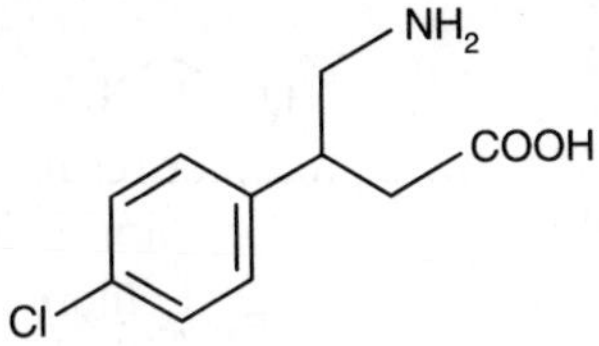

Baclofen

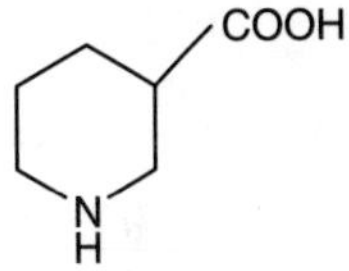

Nipecotic acid

Benzodiazepines (Potentiate the effect of GABA allosterical)

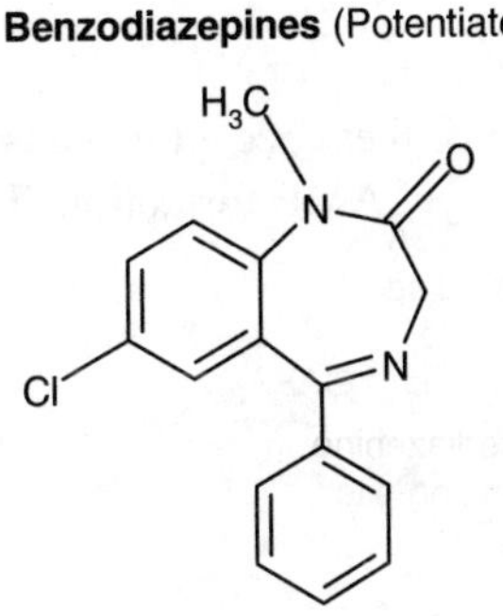

Diazepam

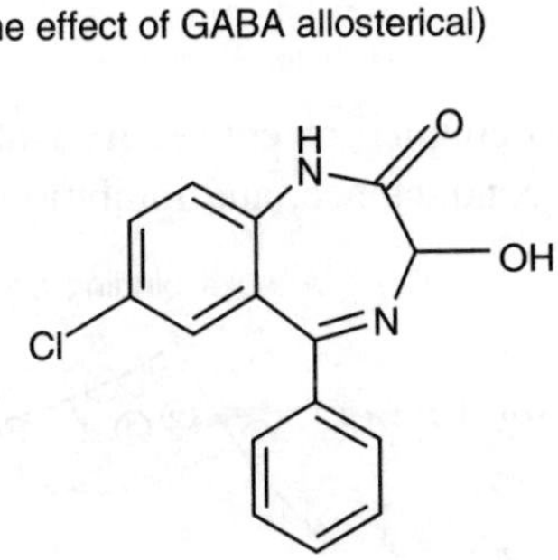

Oxazepam

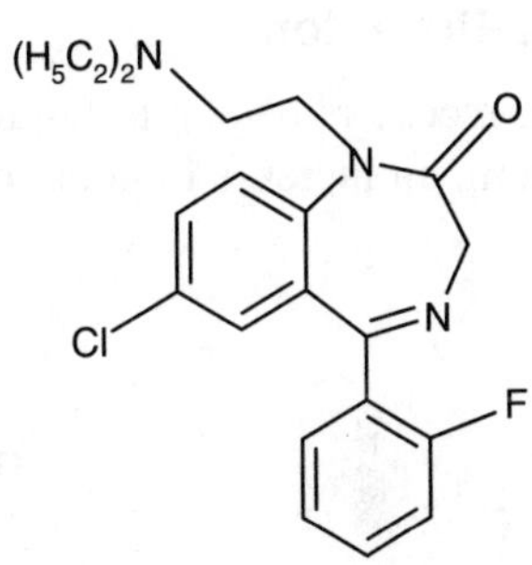

Flurazepam

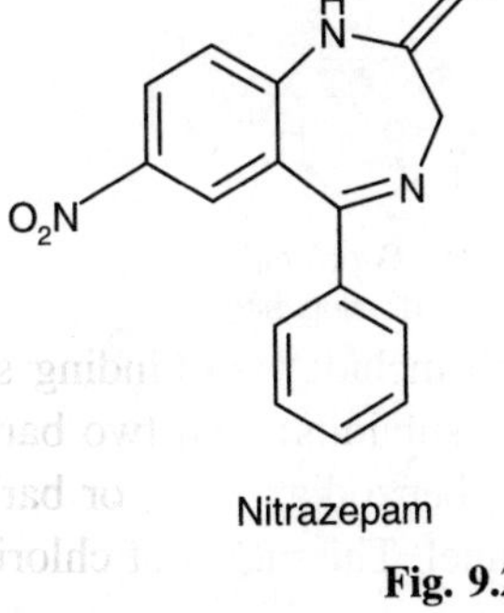

Nitrazepam

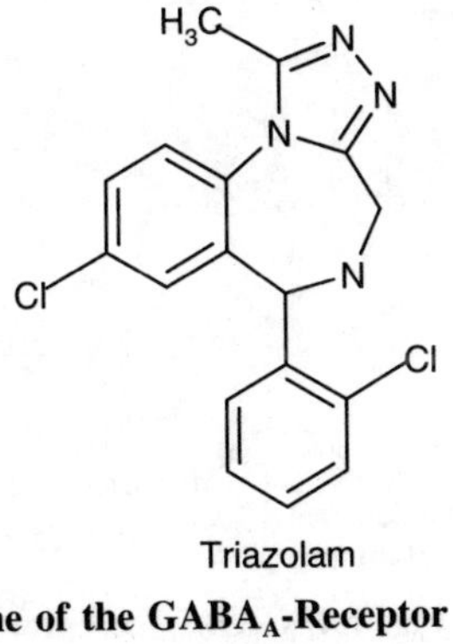

Triazolam

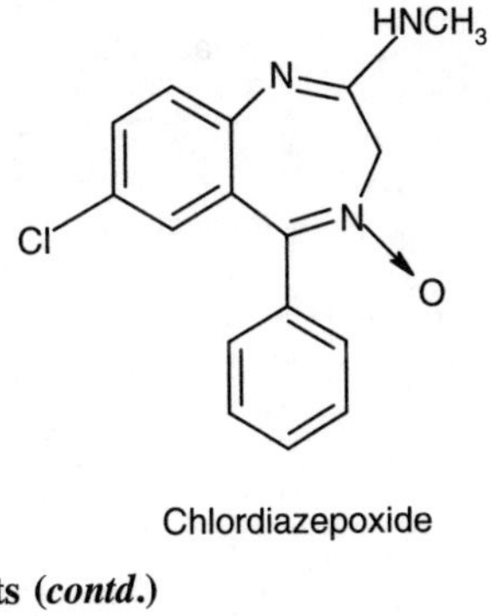

Chlordiazepoxide

Fig. 9.2 Some of the $GABA_A$-Receptor Agonists (*contd.*)

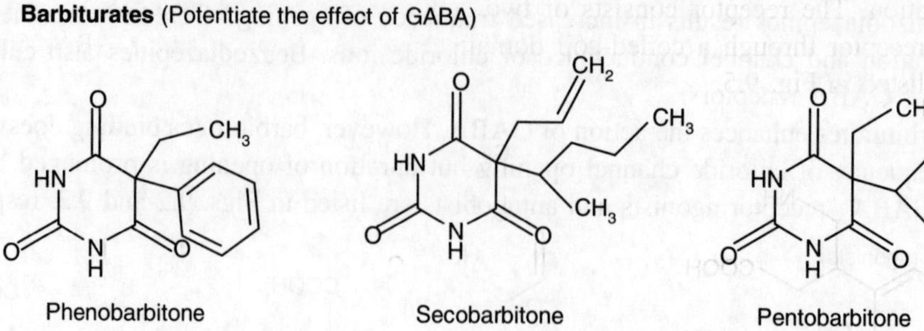

Fig. 9.2 Some of the $GABA_A$-receptor agonists

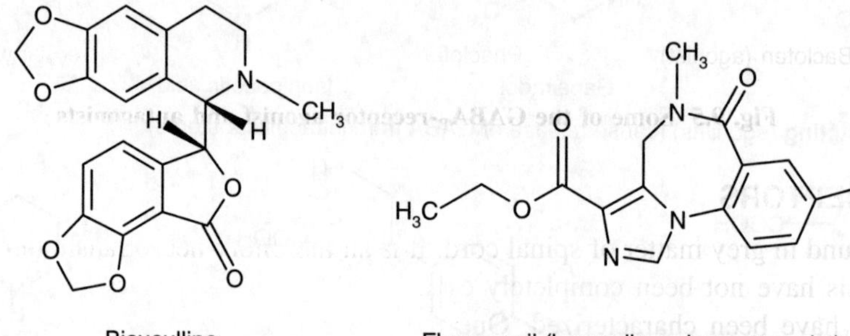

Fig. 9.3 Some of the $GABA_A$-receptor antagonists

$GABA_B$-Receptors

$GABA_B$-receptors belong to G-protein coupled receptors. Activation of these receptors cause decrease in calcium, an increase in potassium conductance, and inhibition of cyc. AMP formation. This results

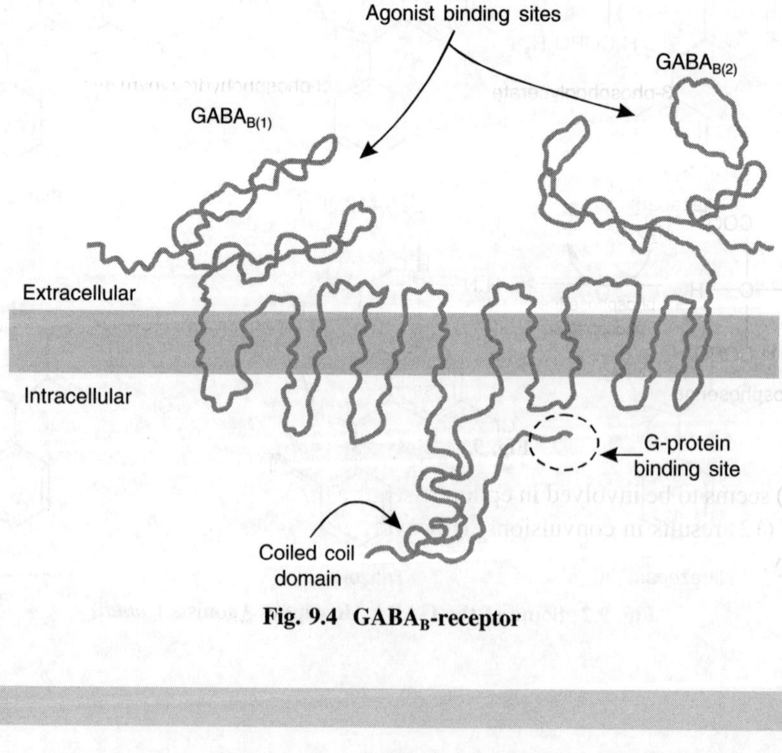

Fig. 9.4 $GABA_B$-receptor

in hyperpolarization. The receptor consists of two subtypes, $GABA_{B(1)}$ and $GABA_{B(2)}$, which form heterodimeric receptor through a coiled-coil domain (Fig. 9.4). Some of the $GABA_B$-agonists and antagonists are listed in Fig. 9.5.

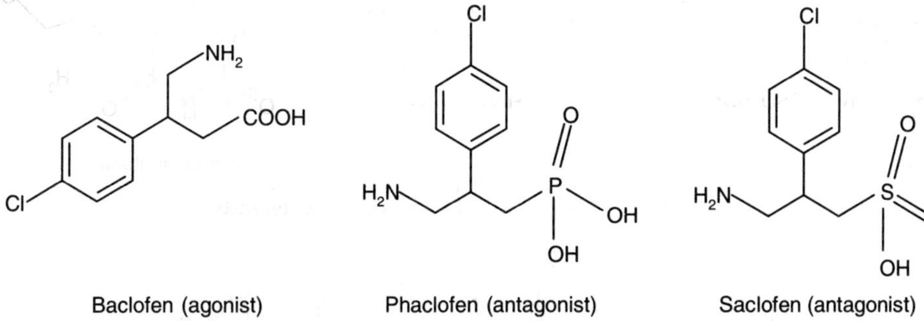

Fig. 9.5 Some of the $GABA_B$-receptor agonist and antagonists

GLYCINE RECEPTORS

Glycine (2) is found in grey matter of spinal cord. It is an inhibitory neurotransmitter. The exact details of its biosynthesis have not been completely established. However, number of reactions involved in the biosynthesis have been characterized. One route involves conversion of glucose to glycine via phosphoglycerate, hydroxypyruvate, serine, and finally to glycine (Fig. 9.6). Other route could involve conversion of hydroxypyruvate to glycoaldehyde and then to glycine (Fig. 9.7).

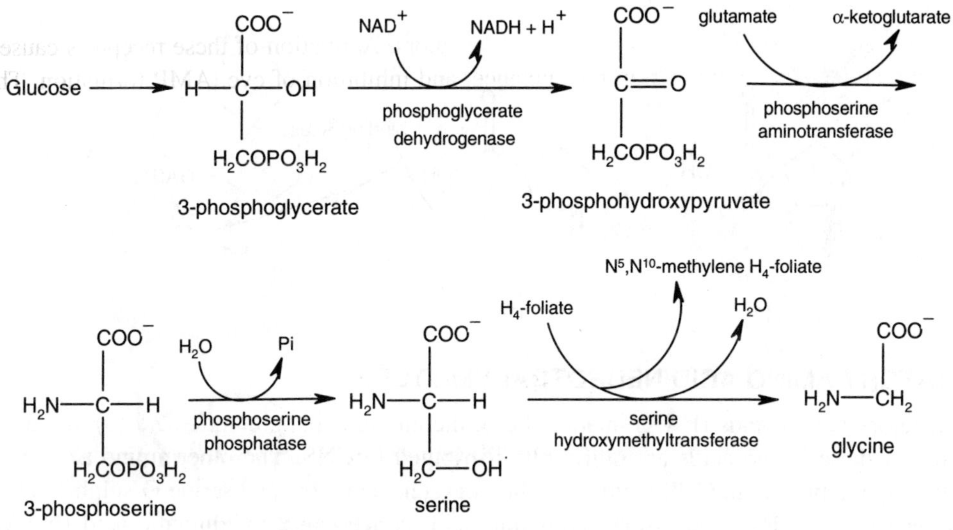

Fig. 9.6 Biosynthesis of glycine

Glycine (2) seems to be involved in epileptic seizures. The selective blockade of glycine (2) receptors by strychnine (12) results in convulsions. However, there is no conclusive proof of the role of glycine (2) in epilepsy.

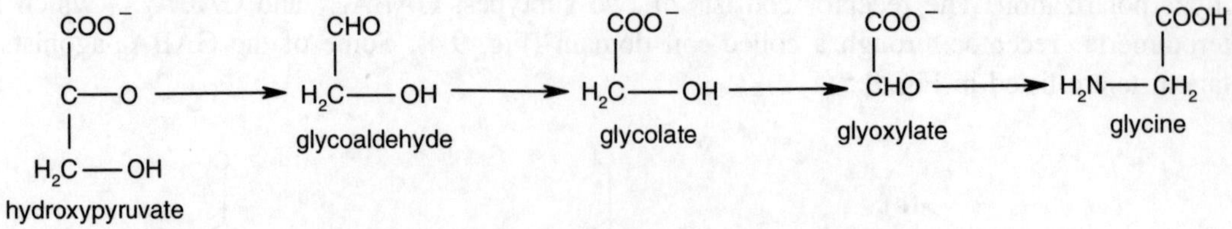

Fig. 9.7 Alternate route of biosynthesis of glycine

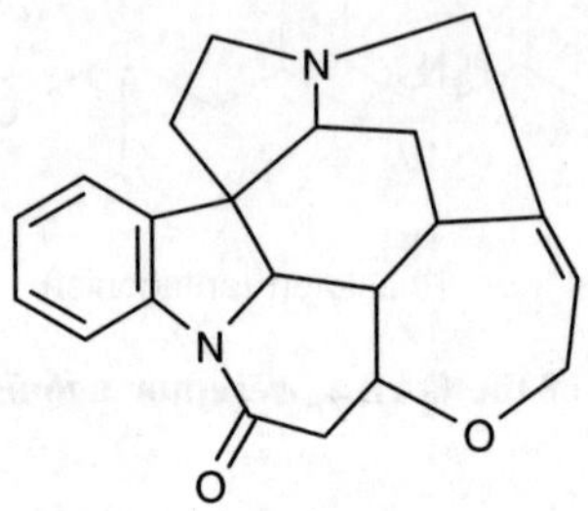

(12)

The glycine (2) receptor, like $GABA_A$-receptor, is a multimeric ligand gated chloride channel. Binding of the glycine (2) to the receptor results in opening of the chloride channel and influx of chloride ions, resulting in hyperpolarization and inhibition of synaptic response.

The 3-amino analog (13) of β-proline (14) shows neuronal depressant effect. But the action is half that of glycine (2). The depressant action of glycine (2) are blocked by strychnine (12) and diaboline (15).

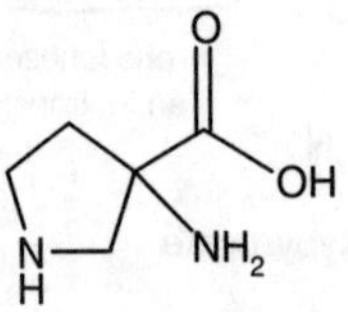

(13)

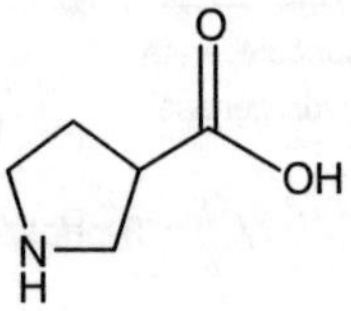

(14)

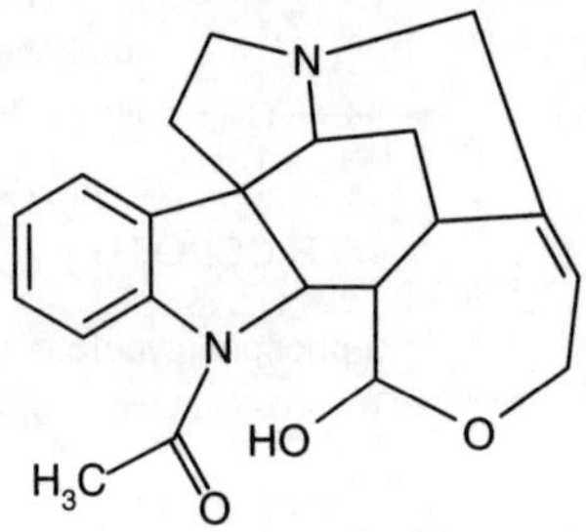

(15)

EXCITATORY AMINO ACID NEUROTRANSMITTERS

The excitatory amino acids (EAA) include the acidic amino acids glutamic acid (3) and aspartic acid (4). Both of these amino acids are uniformly distributed in CNS. The other amino acids with neuro-excitatory action present in CNS include (S)-homocysteic acid (16) and serine O-sulphate (17). The N-acetyl derivative of dipeptide, aspartylglutamic acid, N-acetylaspartylglutamic acid (NAAG, 18) is found in high concentration in brain. It binds to excitatory amino acid (EAA) receptor and excites certain types of neurons.

Glutamic acid (3) and other EAA induce epileptic form of convulsions in animals which can be prevented by the use of EAA receptor antagonists. Further, administration of EAA results in neuronal degeneration. All this and other evidences suggest that EAA are neurotoxic causing neuronal degeneration and ultimately the death of the cell.

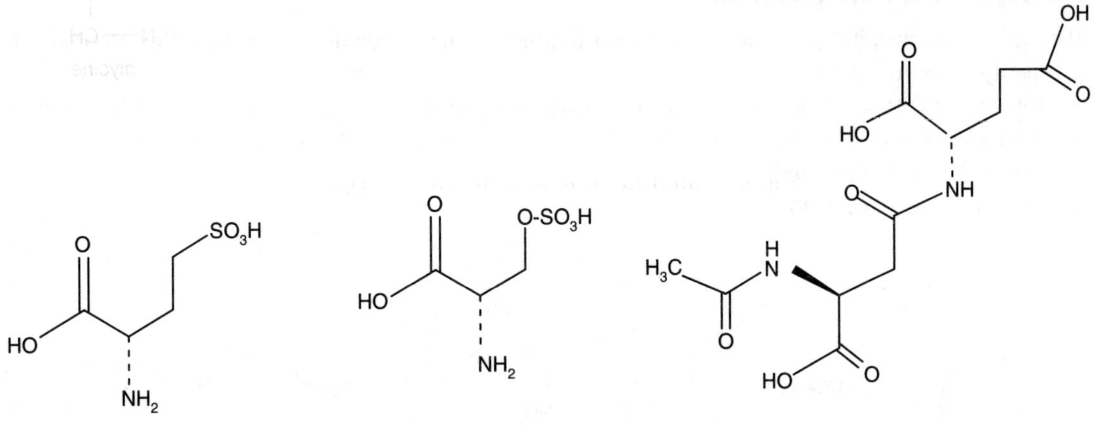

(16) (17) (18)

The main sources of glutamic acid (3) and aspartic acid (4) are α-keto-glutaric acids, and oxaloacetic acid, respectively, of the citric acid cycle (Fig. 9.8). Glutamine is another source of glutamic acid (3). Glutamic acid (3) is metabolized to glutamine and aspartic acid (4) is metabolized to oxaloacetate.

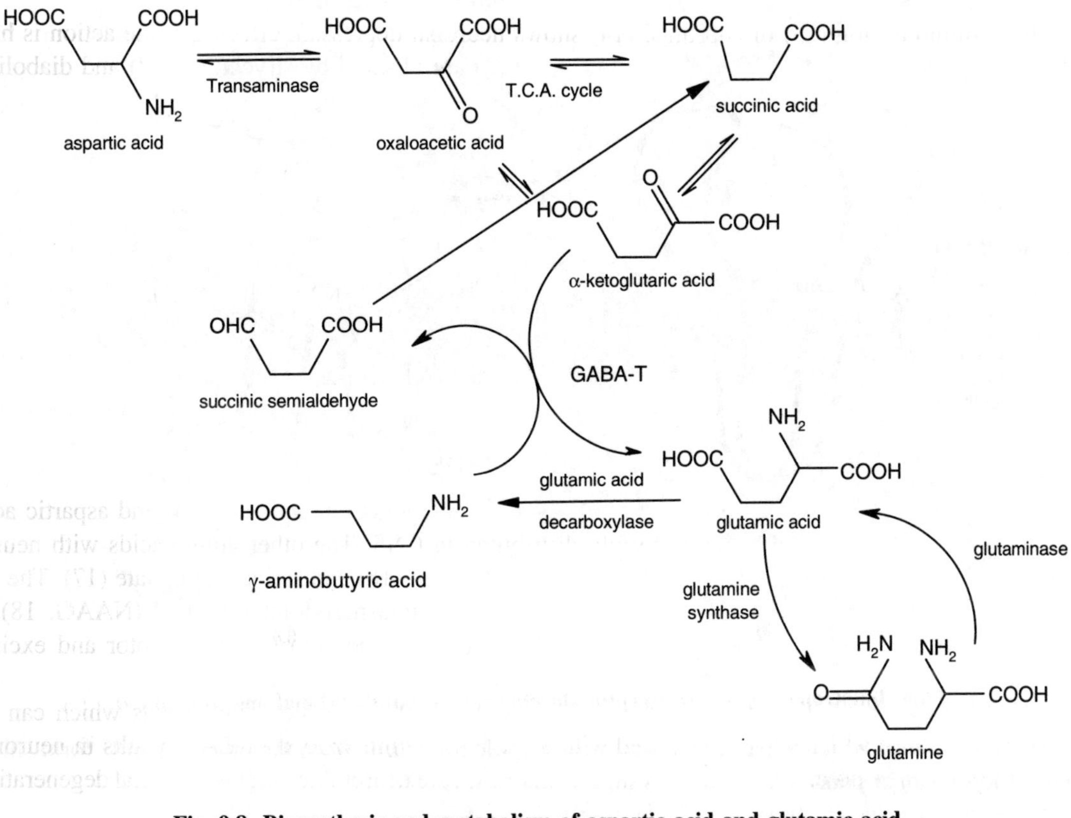

Fig. 9.8 Biosynthesis and metabolism of aspartic acid and glutamic acid

Excitatory Amino Acid Receptors

On the basis of electrophysiological and receptor binding studies, excitatory amino acid receptors have been broadly classified into:

1. Ionotropic receptors, which include N-methyl-D-aspartate (NMDA, 19), α-amino-3-hydroxy-5-methyl-4-isoxazolepropionate (AMPA, 20), and Kainite (a pyrrolidine analog obtained from sea weed, 21) receptors, and
2. Metabotropic receptors.

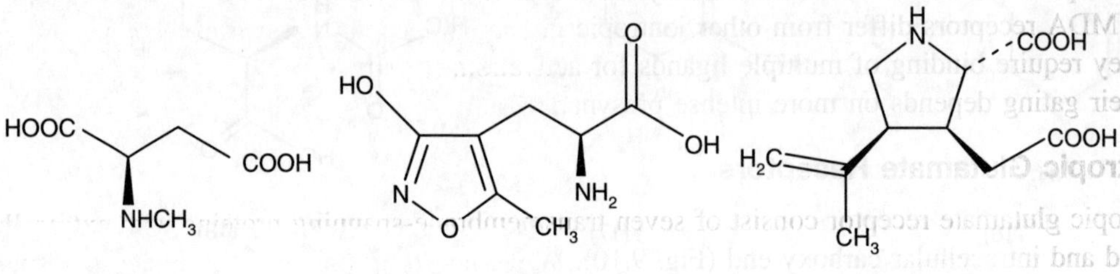

(19) (20) (21)

Both glutamate (3) and aspartate (4) probably act on all four types of receptors.

The ionotropic glutamate receptors are composed of four homomeric or heteromeric subunits (Fig. 9.9a). Each subunit has an extracellular N-terminus and spans the membrane three times (Fig. 9.9b)

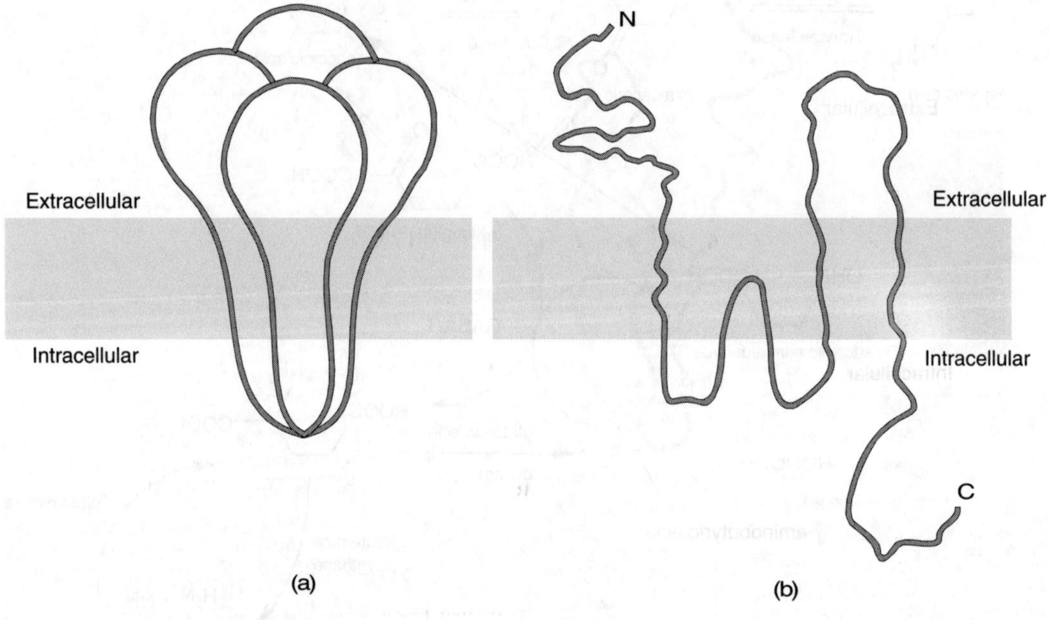

Fig. 9.9 Ionotropic glutamate receptor showing four subunits (a) and one subunit (b)

and has hair-pin turn which when juxtaposed with homologous turns from the other subunits forms the lining of ion channel pore.

NMDA-RECEPTOR

It is a heterotetramer made up of a number of subunit forms namely, GluN1, GluN2B,GluN2C, GluN2D, GluN3A, and GluN3B. Activation of NMDA receptor requires simultaneous binding of glutamate and glycine. Opening of the channel results in Na^+ and Ca^{2+} influx and K^+ efflux.

There are other sites for channel modulation on NMDA receptors and these include Zn^{2+} and Mg^{2+} sites. Binding of magnesium ion results in voltage dependent block the channel pore in the resting membrane. This blockade is relieved by depolarization which is achieved through activation of AMPA/Kainate receptors which are located at the adjascent site of the membrane.

The NMDA receptors differ from other iontropic glutamate receptors in two aspects, i.e.:

1. they require binding of multiple ligands for activation,
2. their gating depends on more intense presynaptic activity.

Metabotropic Glutamate Receptors

Metabotropic glutamate receptor consist of seven transmembrane-spanning proteins with extracellular amino end and intracellular carboxy end (Fig. 9.10). While neurotransmitter binding site is located in the extracellular region the G-protein coupling takes place in the intracellular region.

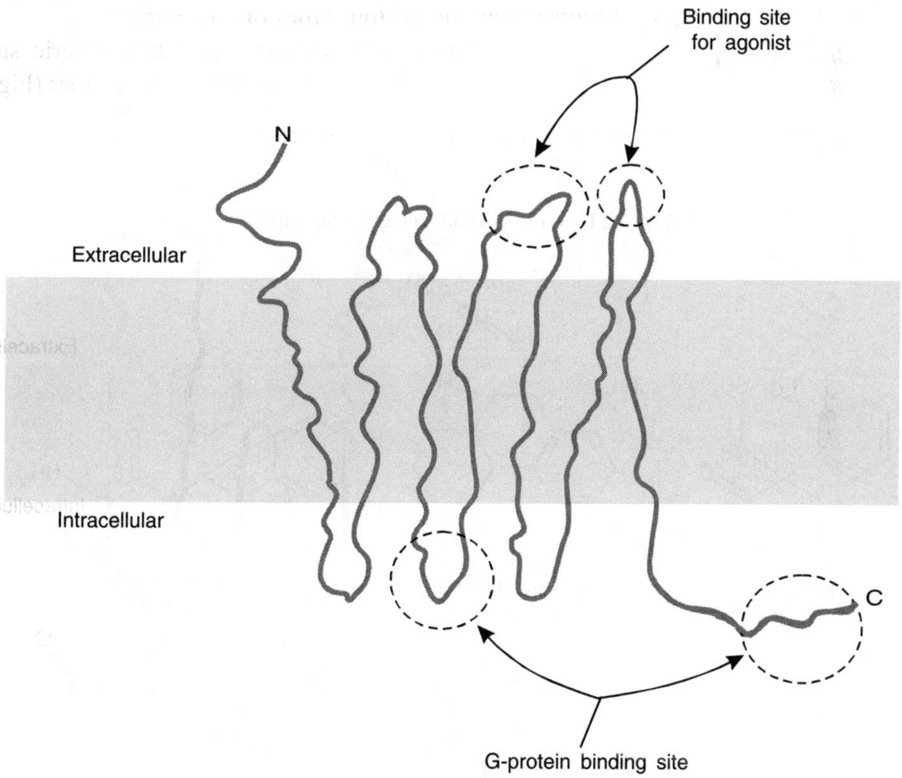

Fig. 9.10 Metabotropic glutamate receptor

At least eight subclasses of metabotropic glutamate receptors have been identified and these belong to three major classes (Table 9.1). They not only activate second messengers but also modulate the ion channels.

Table 9.1 Metabotropic glutamate receptors (MGIR)

Class	*Subtype*	*Action*
I	mGlu R_1	Activates adenylyl cyclase, increased cyc AMP
	mGlu R_5	Increases phospholipase C activity, hydrolysis of PIP_2, Increased IP_3 and DAG levels, increased Ca^{2+} levels, stimulation of PKC, inhibition of K^+ channel.
II	$mGluR_2$ $mGluR_3$	Inhibition of adenylyl cyclase, lower cyc.AMP levels, inhibition of voltage sensitive Ca^{2+} channel, activation of K^+ channel.
III	$mGluR_4$ $mGluR_6$	Inhibits adenylyl cyclase, lower cyc.AMP levels.
	$mGluR_7$ $mGuR_8$	Inhibits voltage sensitive Ca^{2+} channels.

Some of the agonists and antagonists of NMDA-, AMPA-, and KA-receptors are listed in Figs. 9.11 to 9.14.

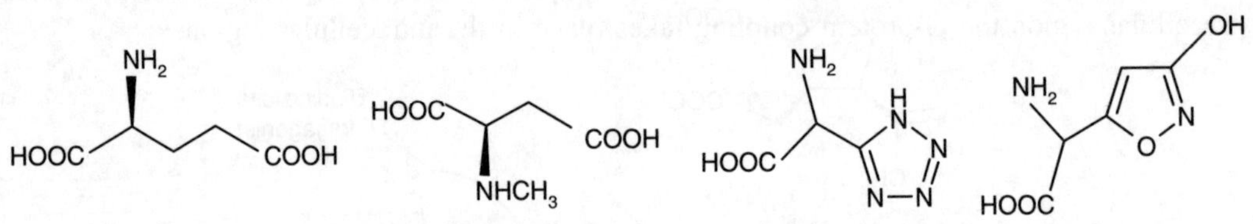

glutamic acid; N-methyl-D-aspartic acid (NMDA); Tetrazolylglycine; Ibotenic acid

Fig. 9.11 Some NMDA-receptor agonists

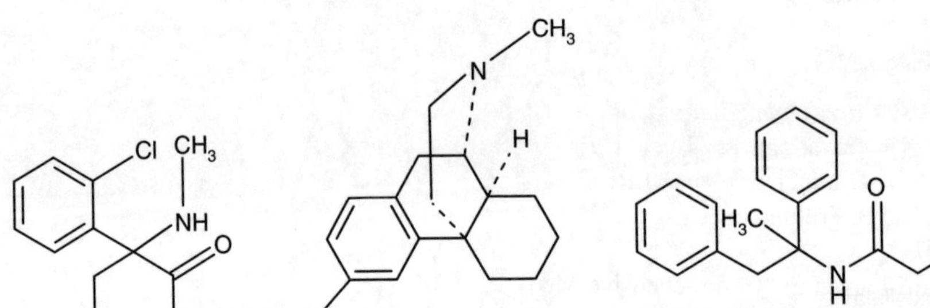

Ketamine (uncompetitive); Dextromethorphan (uncompetitive); Remacemide (uncompetitive)

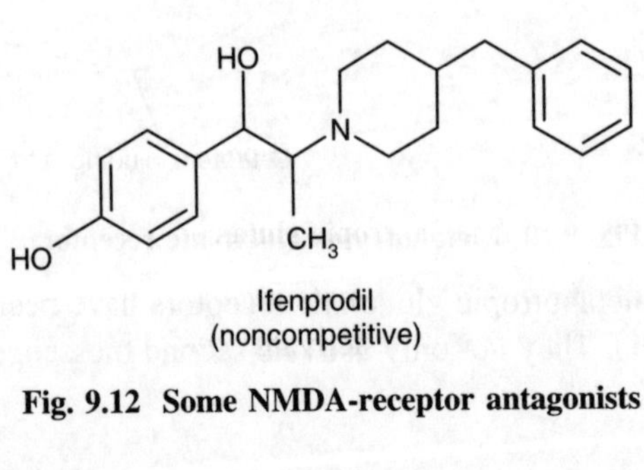

Ifenprodil (noncompetitive)

Fig. 9.12 Some NMDA-receptor antagonists

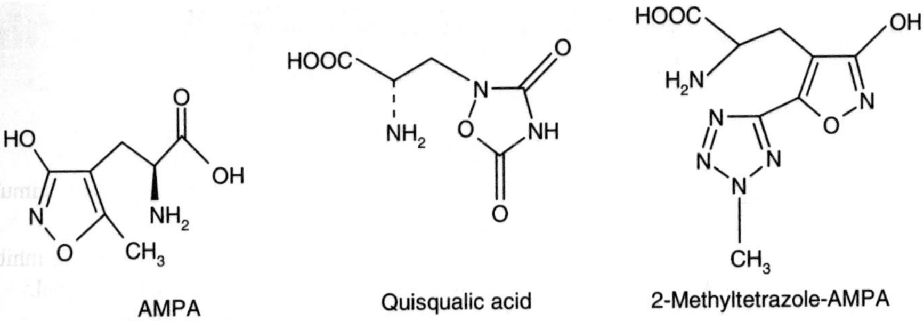

Fig. 9.13 Some AMPA-receptor agonists

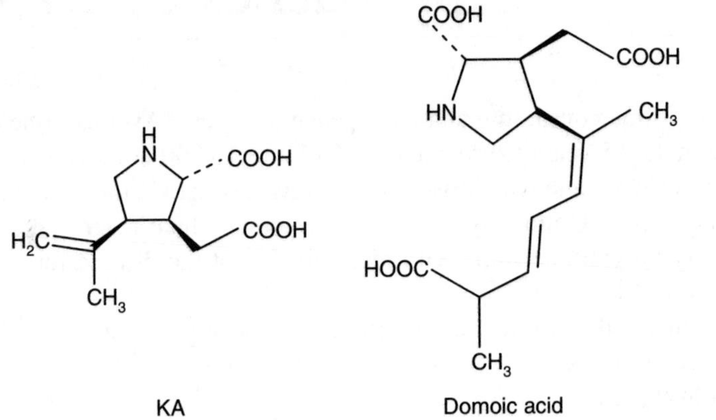

Fig. 9.14 Some KA-receptor agonists

FURTHER READING

1. N. G. Bowery, *Curr. Opin. Pharmacol.*, **6**, 37 (2006).
2. S. Ozawa, H. Kamiya, and K. Tsuzuki, *Prog. Neurobiol.*, **54**, 581 (1998).
3. U. Madsen, H. Brauner-osborne, J.R. Greenwood, T.N. Johansen, P. Krogsgaard-Larsen, T. Liljefors, M. Nielson, and B. Frolund in "Drug Discovery Handbook," S. Cox Gad, Ed., Wiley-Interscience, New Jersey, 2005, p. 797.
4. P. Krogsgaard-Larsen in "Comprehensive Medicinal Chemistry," Vol. 3, C. Hansch, Ed. in-Chief, Pergamon Press, Oxford, 2005, p. 493.

10

Approaches to Drug Design

Drug development is a time consuming and an expensive process. Average time required for a drug to reach market is about 12-15 years. Out of about 10,000 to 15,000 compounds synthesized about 500 to 600 reach animal testing stage which includes toxicity testing. Of these about 10 compounds or so reach the clnical stage level. Ultimately, it is one compound which reaches the market.

The drug discovery programme starts with identification of the disease for which the drug is to be used and this is governed by:

1. whether the current therapy for the disease is satisfactory or not,
2. commercial viability,
3. competition in the area.

Having identified the target disease, methods for in vitro tests on genetically modified cells are established. Once the methods for testing the biological activity is established, the next step involves syntheses of chemical moiety/moieties which could be the potential drug. This can be achieved through:

1. identification and modification of a "lead" compound, or
2. drug design through rational approach.

Identification and Modification of a "Lead" Compound

A "lead" is a prototype which

1. has desired biological activity coupled with reasonable amount of potency,
2. may have high toxicity,
3. does not have desired pharmacokinetic profile, i.e. absorption, distribution, metabolism, and excretion characteristics,
4. has the potential to be chemically modified so that the desired characteristics can be incorporated.

The "lead" moiety after identification is subjected to various structural changes. The synthesized compounds are then subjected to biological testing by the methods established earlier.

The purpose of modification of a "lead" compound is:

1. to improve pharmacological activity of the lead compound which may result in better therapeutic index,
2. the profit motive through patenting of a new drug or new use of an old drug. Moreover by synthesizing a new drug by modifying old drug, no matter it has same therapeutic index and use,

there are made available a selection of different drugs with similar use to the medical practitioner. This is necessary because humans vary in their sensitivities, allergies and ability to metabolize,

3. the academic interest in knowing relationship between the structure and the biological activity.

The main sources of "lead" compounds are:

1. Natural products and medicine folklore,
2. Random screening,
3. Combinatorial libraries,
4. Existing drugs.

Natural Products and Folklore Medicine as a source of "Lead"

Natural products and folklore medicine has been the richest source of drugs for various diseases. Some of the sources for these include, plants, animals, microbial, and the recently explored marine sources. The source of folklore medicine has been mainly from plants.

Prominent among plant products and folklore medicine are the analgesic morphine (1) and the antitussive codeine (2) from opium, the local anesthetic cocaine (3) from *Erythroxylon cocoa*, cardiac glycosides digitoxin (4), digoxin (5), lanatoside A (6), and lanatoside B (7) from digitalis, ouabain (8)

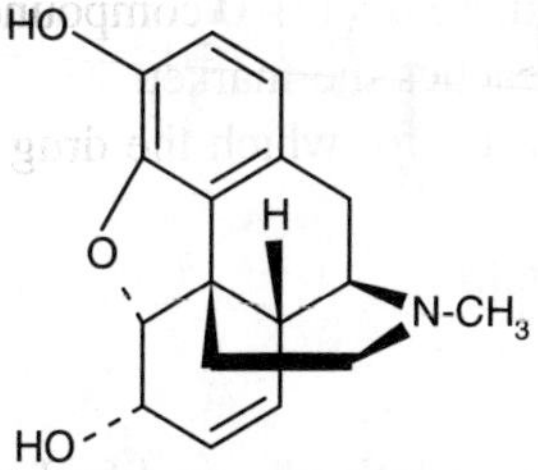

(1)

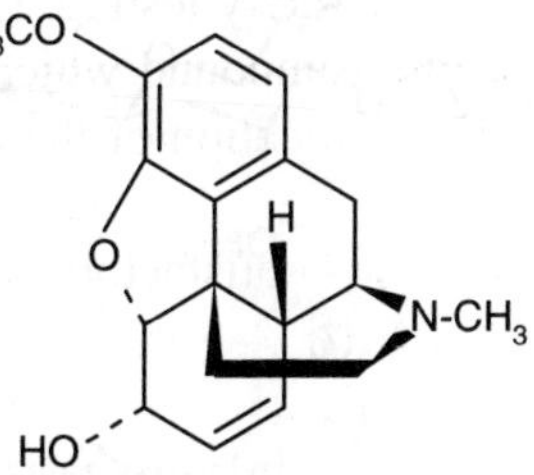

(2)

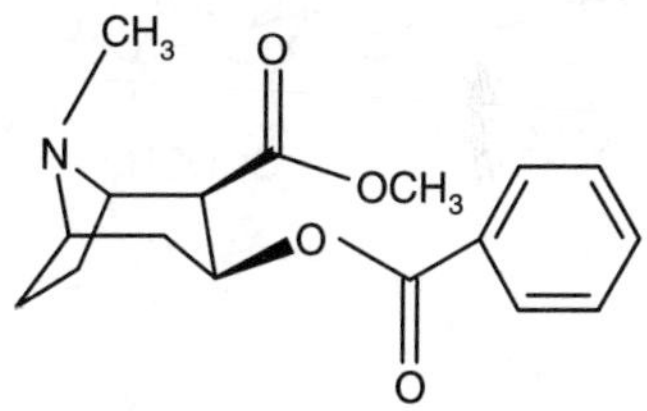

(3)

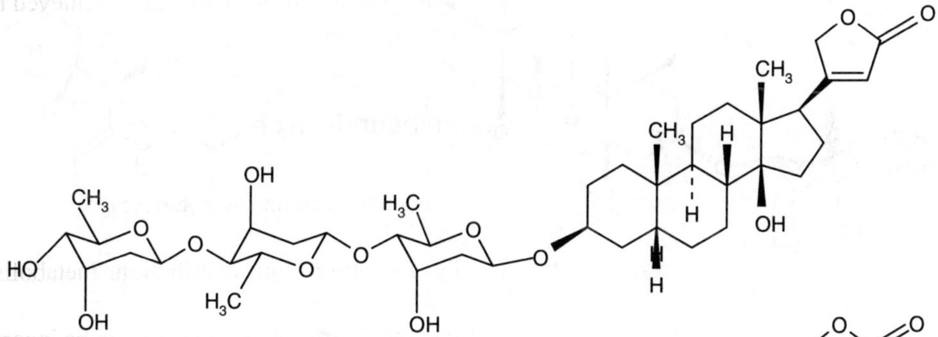

(4)

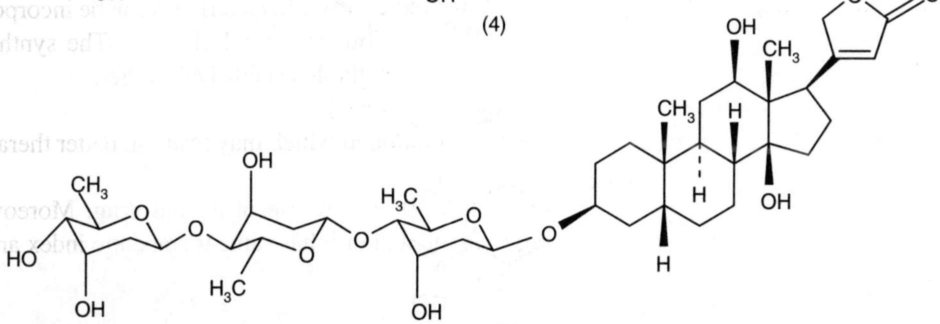

(5)

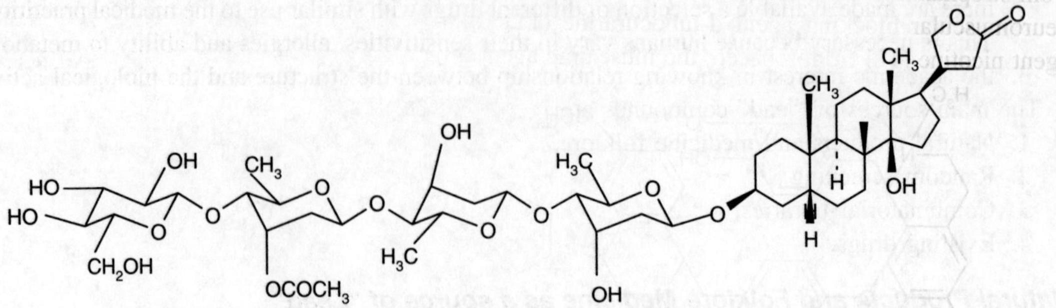

(6)

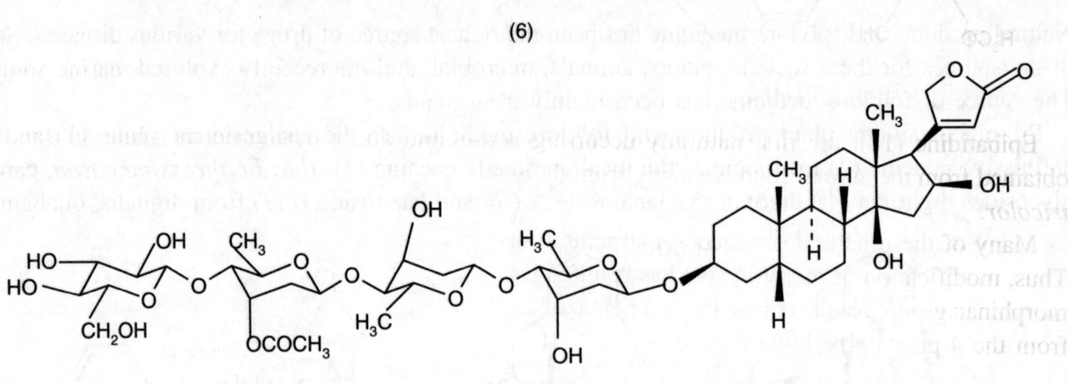

(7)

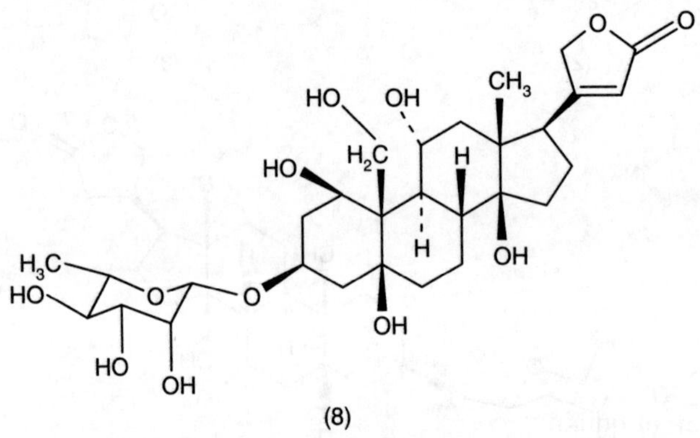

(8)

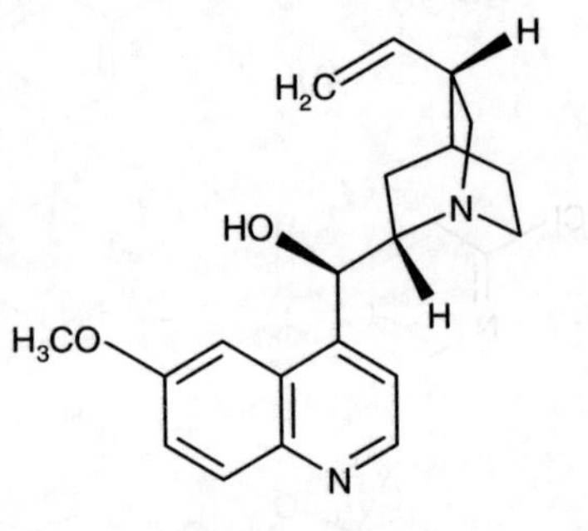

(9)

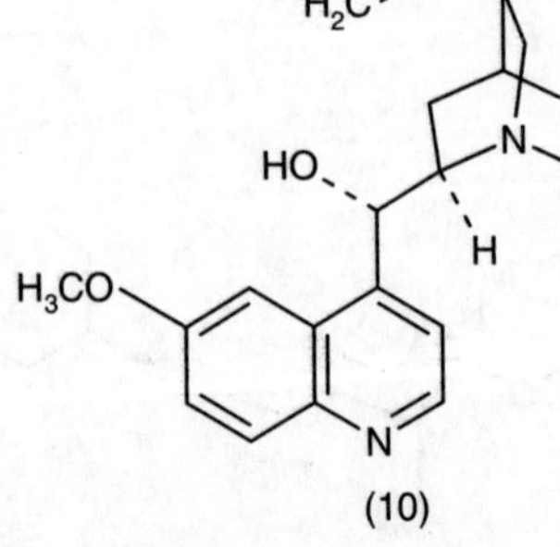

(10)

from strophanthus, the antimalarial quinine (9) and antiarrhythmic quinidine (10) from cinchona bark, neuromuscular blocking agent d-tubocurarine (11) from *Chondodendron tomentosum*, the nicotinic agent nicotine (12) from tobacco, the muscainic agent muscarine (13) from the mushroom, and so on.

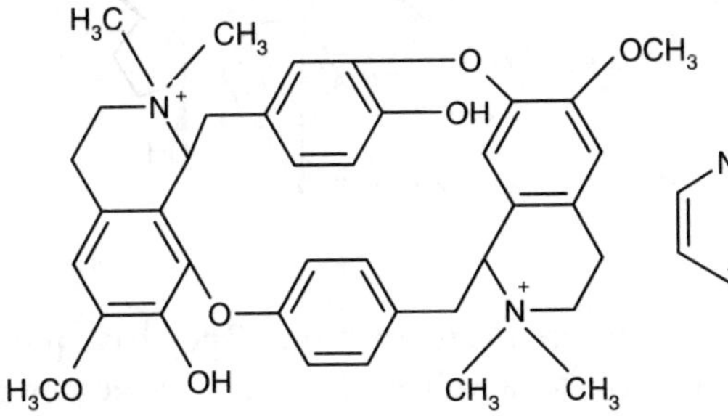

(11)

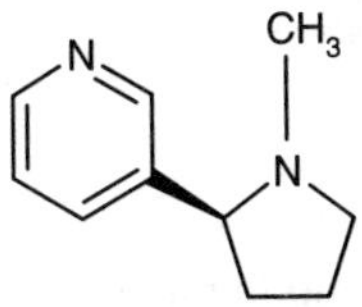

(12)

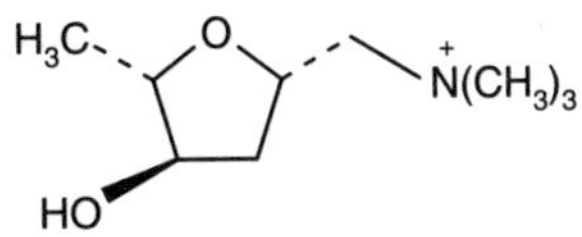

(13)

Epibatidine (14), the first naturally occurring non-opioid alkaloid, and potent analgesic has been obtained from the animal source namely from the skin extract of Ecuadorian poison frog, *Epipedobates tricolor*.

Many of these natural products on structural modifications have yielded useful therapeutic agents. Thus, modification of morphine (1) has resulted in useful analgesics such as levorphanol (15) from the morphinan group, phenazocine (16) and pentazocine (17) from the benzomorphan group, and meperidine from the 4-phenylpiperidine group.

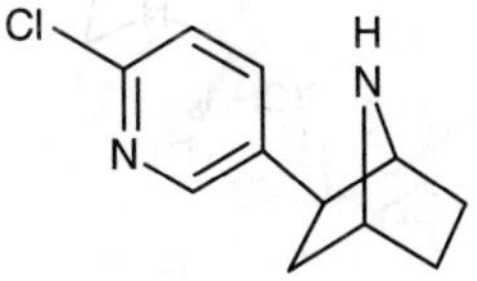

(14)

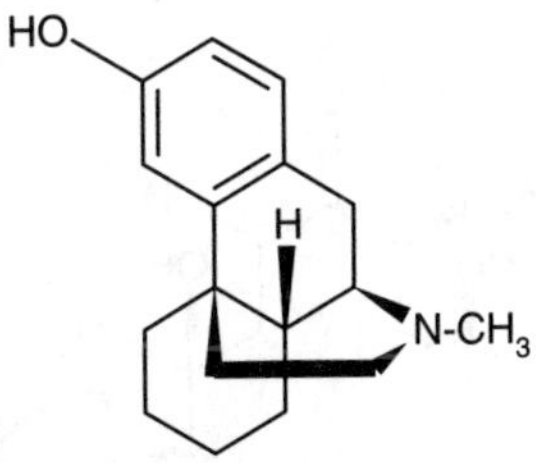

(15)

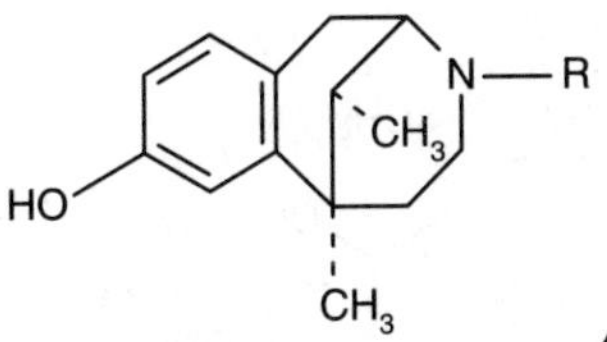

(16), R= — CH_2CH_2— 

(17), R = — $CH_2CH{=}C(CH_3)_2$

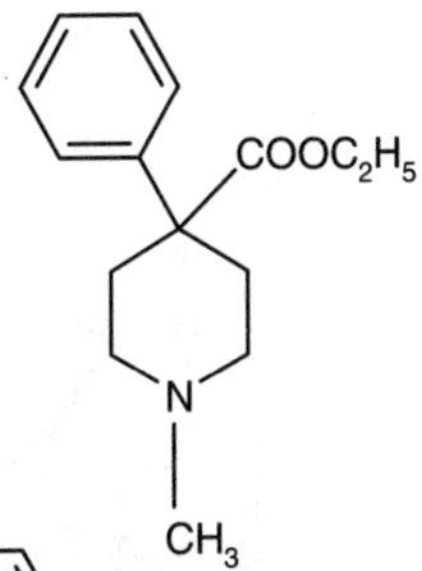

(18)

Similarly, the structural modification of quinine (9) has resulted in some of the useful antimalarials such as pamaquin (19) from 8-aminoquinoline group, chloroquin (20) from 4-aminoquinoline group,

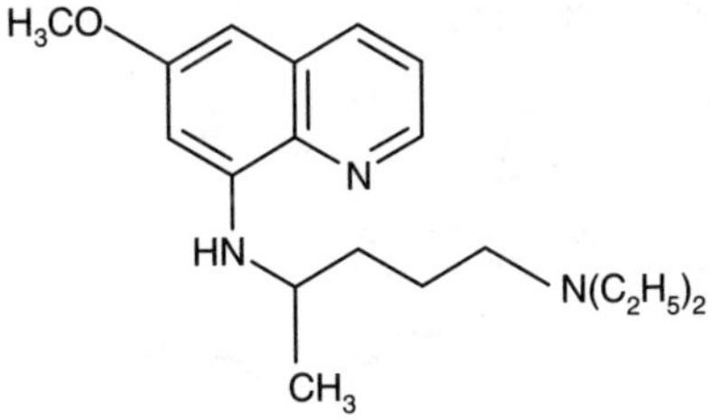

(19)

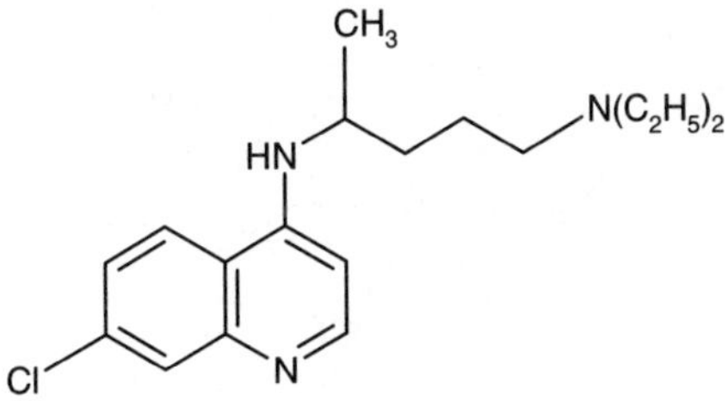

(20)

chlorguanide (21) from biguanide group and pyrimethamine (22) from 2,4-diaminopyrimidine group of antimalarials.

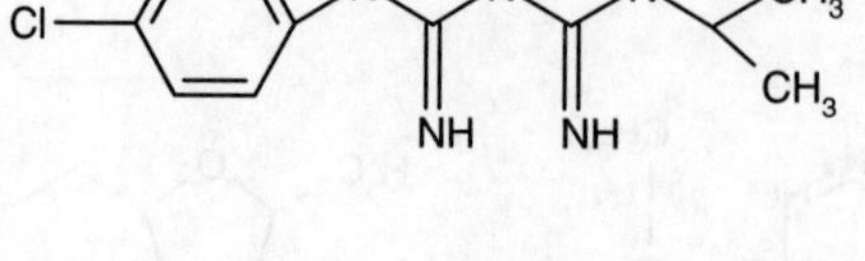

(21)

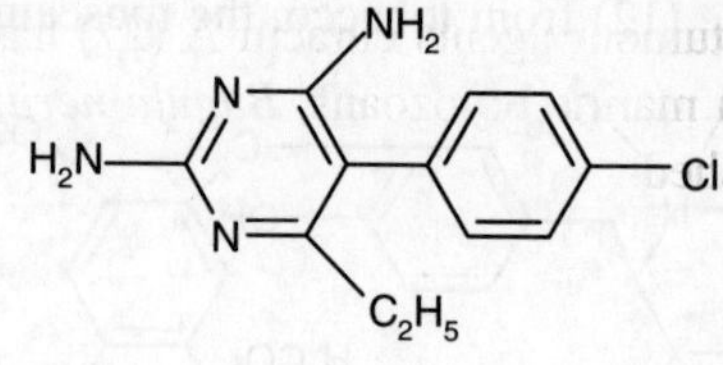

(22)

One of the important sources of chemotherapeutic agents are microorganisms. They have provided us with antibiotics such as penicillins (23), cephalosporins (24), tetracyclines (25), macrocyclic antibiotics such as erythromycins (26), etc. These antibiotics have been useful as leads for semisynthetic antibiotics with useful properties such as resistance to acids and inactivating enzymes and with broad spectrum of activity.

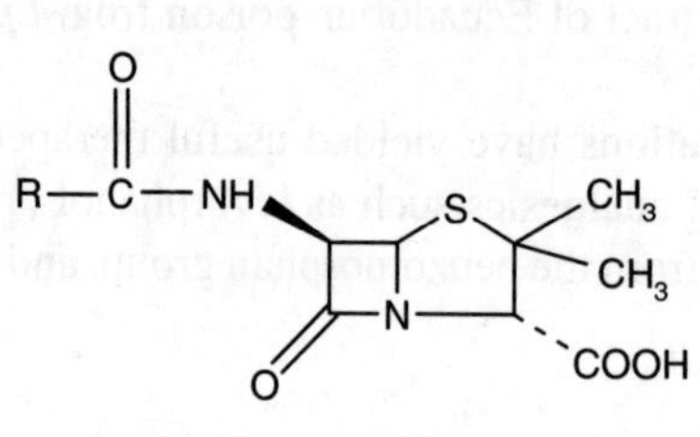

(23)

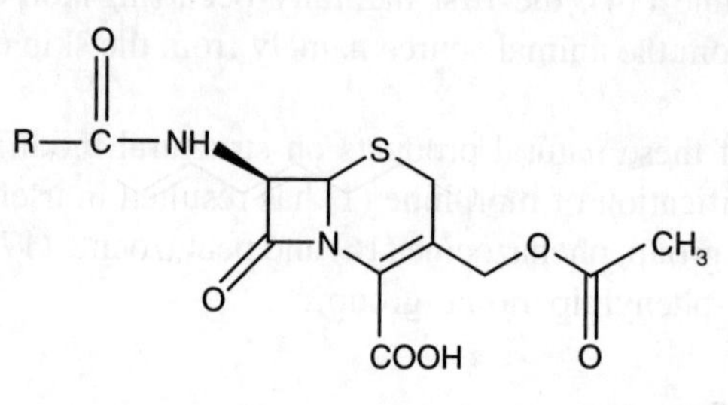

(24)

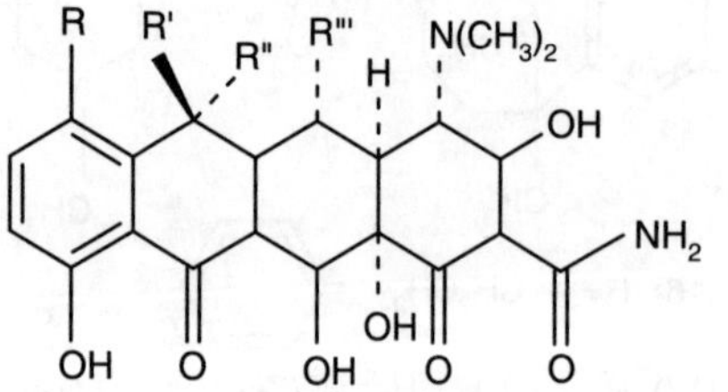

(25)

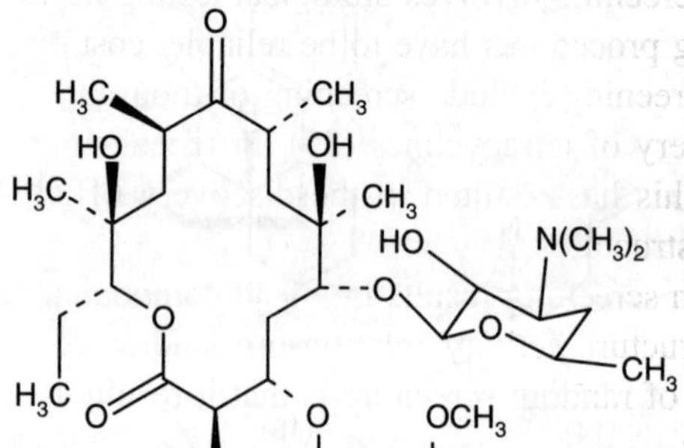

(26)

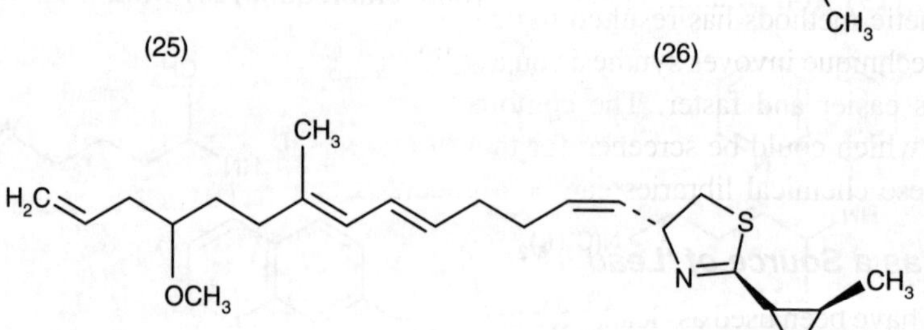

(27)

In recent times marine sources have emerged as one of the novel sources of therapeutically important moieties. Some of these have been isolated from coral, sponges, fish, and marine microorganisms. For example antitumour agents curacin A (27) has been obtained from marine cyanobacterium. Brystatins isolated from marine bryozoans, *Bugula neritina*, L. out of which the structure of brystatin 1 (28) has been established.

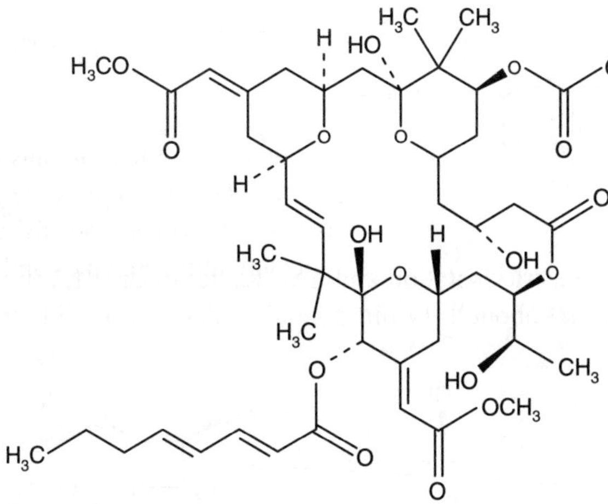

(28)

Random Screening

Random screening involves biological testing of the compounds irrespective of source on a mass scale. The testing procedures have to be reliable, cost effective and should involve automation. Examples of random screening include screening of thousands of soil samples for antibiotic activity which lead to the discovery of tetracyclines (25). In recent times, random screening has been applied for antitumor activity. This has resulted in the discovery of antitumor activity of many substances with divergent chemical structures.

Random screening results in a lead compound which after modification could lead to a better drug. Further structure-activity relationship studies could lead to discovery of a pharmacophore. Another advantage of random screening is that it results in development and perfecting of biological screening techniques.

Combinatorial Libraries

Advances in synthetic methods has resulted in combinatorial synthetic procedures, a powerful tool for new entities. The technique invoves synthesis on a solid support, as a result the isolation and purification of final product is easier and faster. The combinatorial synthetic procedures have resulted in large chemical libraries which could be screened for their biological activities by high-throughput screening methods. Thus, these chemical libraries can be a good source of leads.

Existing Drugs as a Source of 'Lead'

The existing drugs have been used as 'leads' for the development of newer drugs. The approach involves:

(a) improvement in pharmacokinetic properties such as absorption, etc.,

(b) exploitation of side effects,

(c) removal of side effects,

(d) finding a new use of old drug.

Absorption of many polar drugs has been improved by converting them into compounds which are more lipophilic and absorbed better. Thus, naproxen (29), a nonsteroidal anti-inflammatory analgesic produces gastric irritation and lower blood levels when given orally. Its dipalmitoylglycerol ester (30)

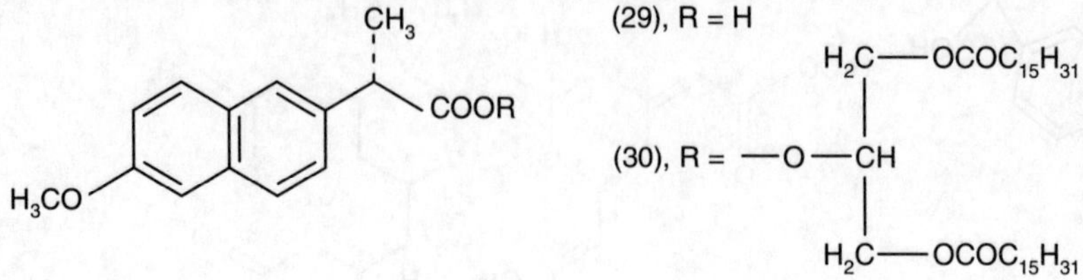

has been found to cause less gastric irritation and give higher plasma levels. Similarly, the dipivalyl ester (31) of epinephrine (32) has about 8–17 times more ocular penetrability than the parent drug (32).

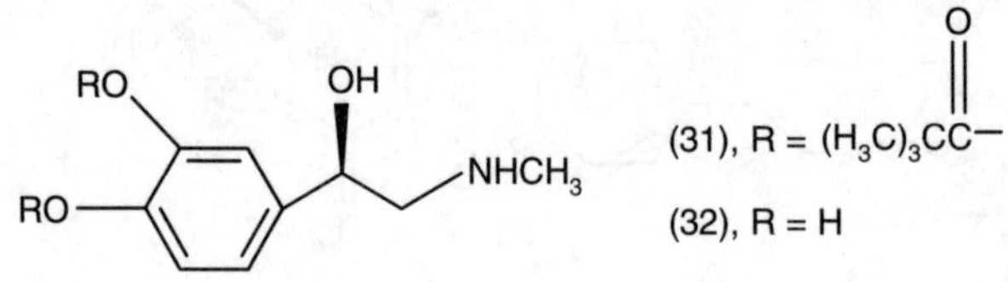

An example of exploitation of side effect is the sulphonamides. It was observed that the antibacterial activity of sulphanilamide (33) was accompanied with the diuretic effect. This resulted in development of thiazides (34) and hydrothiazides (35) which had excellent diuretic effect. Similarly, the observation that antihistaminic agent promethazine (36) had CNS depressant effect led to the development of chlorpromazine (37) as an antipsychotic agent.

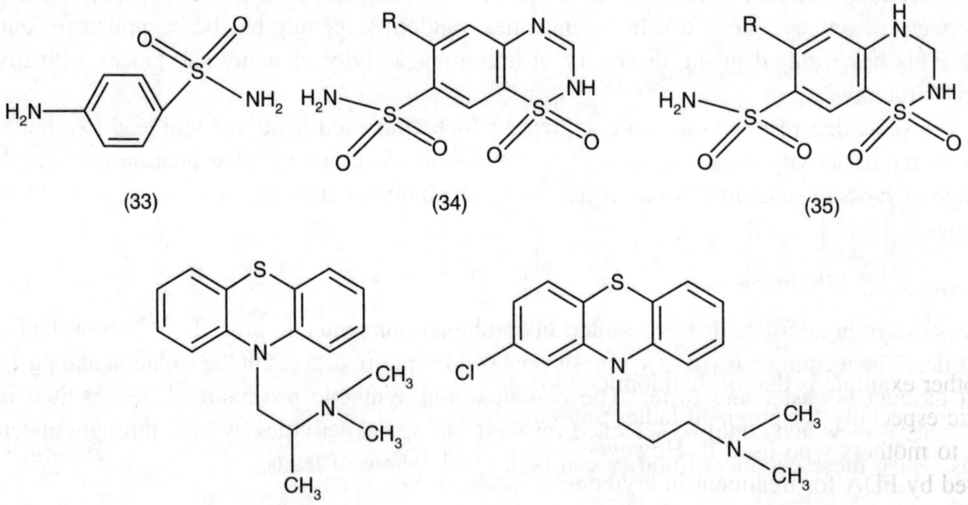

(33) (34) (35)

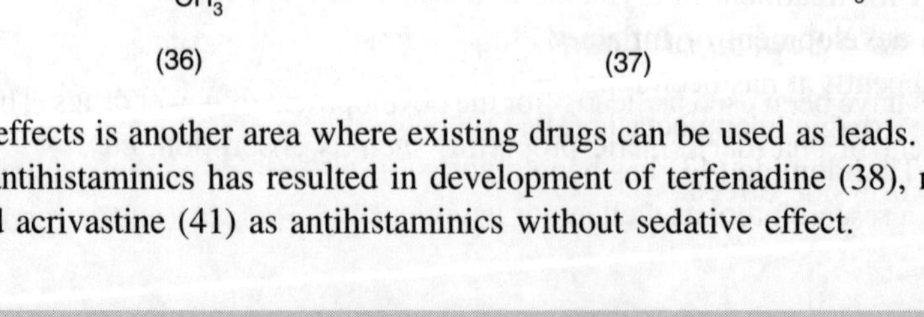

(36) (37)

Removal of side effects is another area where existing drugs can be used as leads. Thus, removal of sedative effects of antihistaminics has resulted in development of terfenadine (38), mequitazine (39), astemizole (40), and acrivastine (41) as antihistaminics without sedative effect.

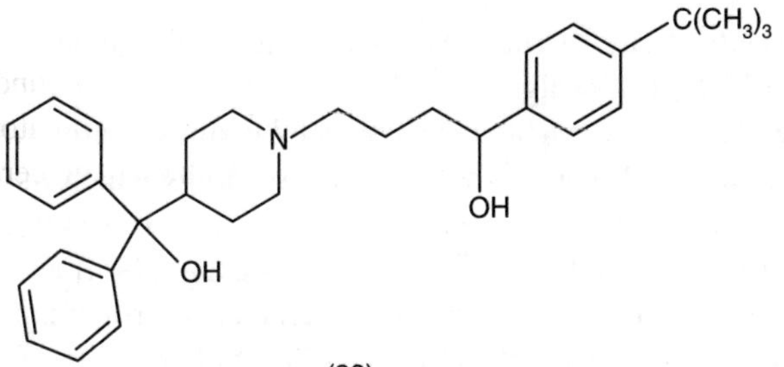

(38)

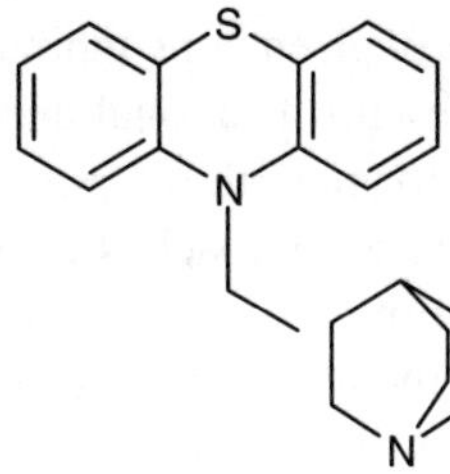

(39)

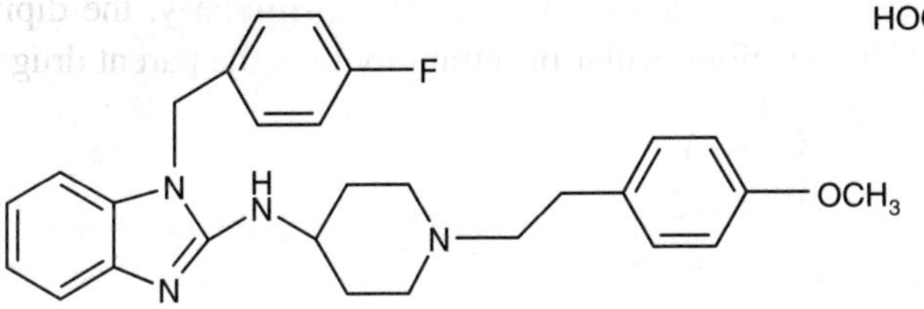

(40)

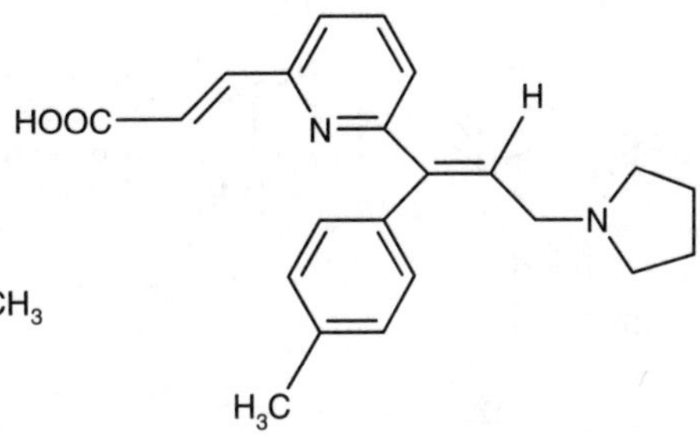

(41)

New use of an old drug has also been exploited for the development of drugs. One of the classical example is that of NSAID aspirin (42) which has found use as an antiplatelet drug for preventing the aggregation of platelets. Paracetamol (42a), another NSAID, has been recently reported to prevent heart disease. It has been also reported to prevent myeloperoxidase from producing hypochlorous acid which is responsible for damaging the tissues.

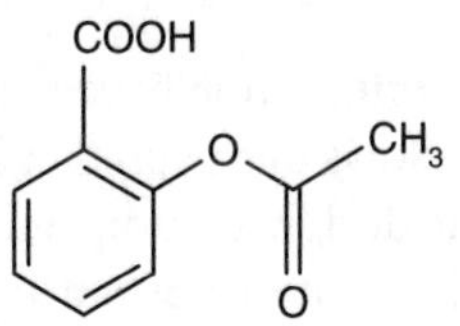

(42)

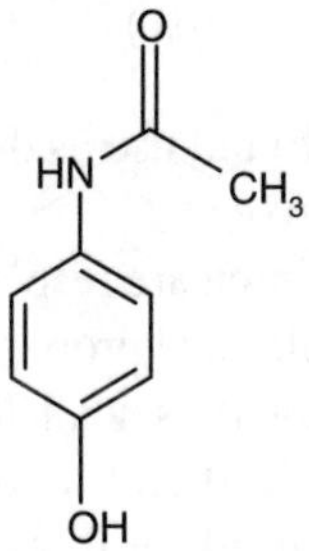

(42a)

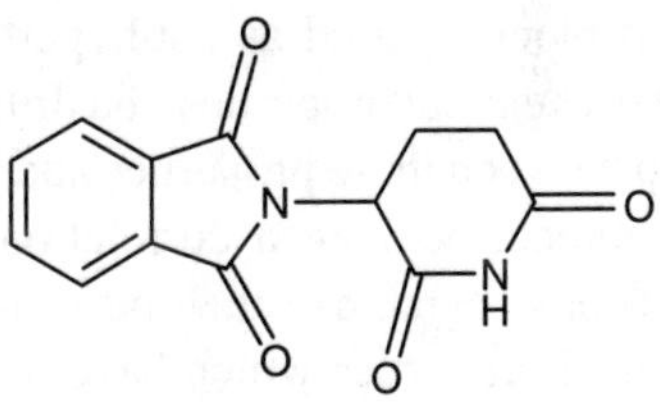

(43)

Another example is that of thalidomide (43). It was originally recommended for use as sedative and hypnotic especially for pregnant ladies and later banned because its use resulted in birth of deformed infants to mothers who used it. However, it is presently used as immunomodulator. It has also been approved by FDA for treatment in erythema nodosum leprosum (ENL), a painful condition in leprosy in which there is development of inflamed, subcutaneous nodules that disappear in a week and then reappear again. Recently it has been reported to be useful for the treatment of blood disorder known as hereditary haemmorrhagic telangiectasia (HHT). It affects one out of 5000 people. In this disease there is nose bleeding. Thalidomide (43) has been reported to repair the blood vessels. It has also been used in recent times as a research tool as well as for treatment of different cancers such as multiple myeloma.

Drug Design through Rational Approach

Drug design through enzyme inhibition, quantitative structure activity relationship studies, and molecular modeling represents a rational approach to drug design.

Design of enzyme inhibitors or design of antagonists or agonists of various neurotransmitters was one of the earliest approaches to drug design. Some of the examples of drugs which have been used as enzyme inhibitors include the antimalarial agent pyrimethamine (22), the anticancer drugs, 6-mercaptopurine (44), 6-thioguanine (45), aminopterin (46), and methotrexate (47), the antigout agent allopurinol (48), the antiprotozoal agent diaveridine (49), the antibacterial agent trimethoprim (50), and the inhibitor of angiotensin converting enzyme, captopril (51), used as antihypertensive agent.

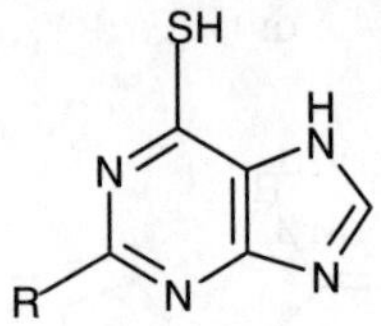

(44), R = H

(45), R = NH_2

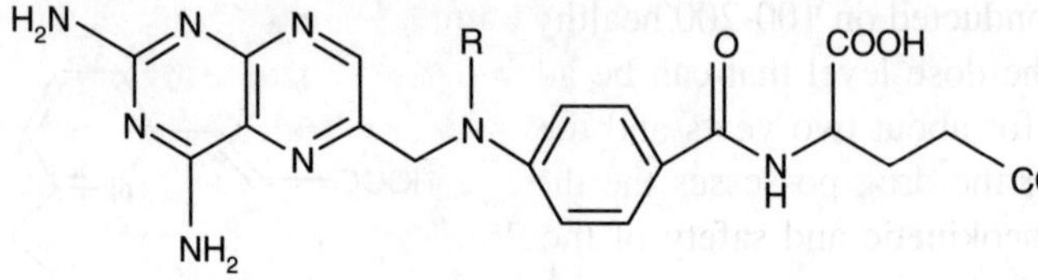

(46), R = H

(47), R = CH_3

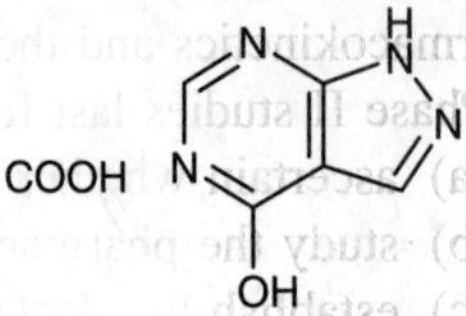

(48)

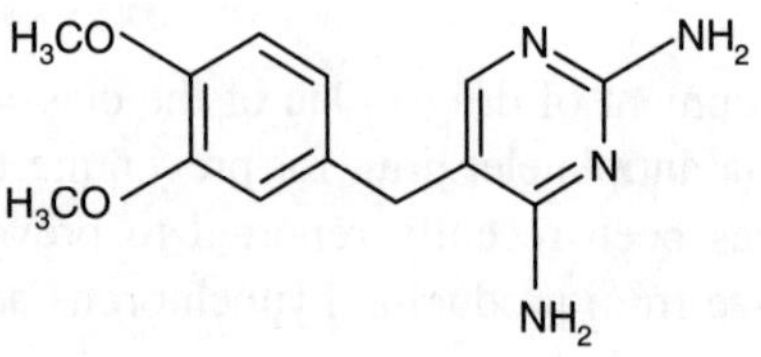

(49)

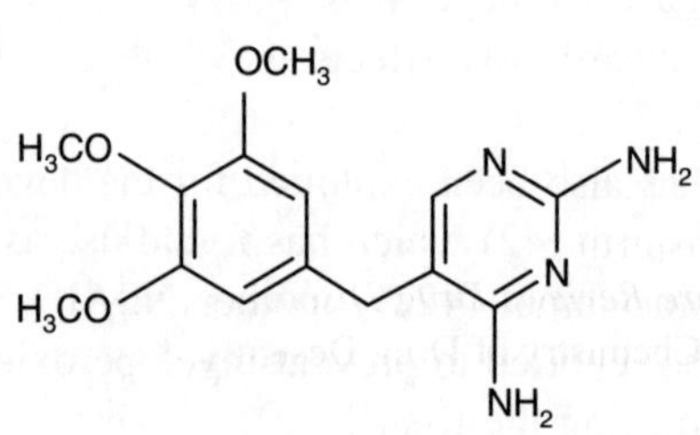

(50)

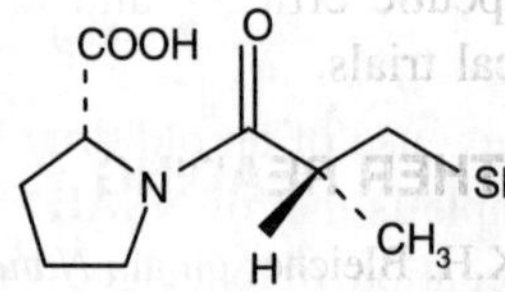

(51)

Antagonists of neurotransmitters have also found use as drugs and include antagonists of epinephrine (32) such as β-blockers used as antihypertensives.

The physico-chemical properties of a drug which are responsible for drug action have been quantified. A relationship between these properties and biological properties thus allows one to predict the biological activity of a molecule. Such a correlation can thus lead to rational design of drug molecules. The molecule, thus envisaged, can then be synthesized and its biological activity determined. The various physico-chemical properties which have been used for this purpose include, hydrophobicity, electronic factors, and steric factors.

With the advances in cell biology as well as in molecular graphics, computational techniques have been used for design of drugs. Such a technique gives a 3-dimensional visual of a receptor as well as generates various conformations of potential moiety as well as identifies the most stable conformation. Next, the most stable conformation is docked on the 3D-strucure of the receptor and the energy of potential drug-receptor combination calculated. Further, the computer may also generate various structures which can bind to the receptor. These structures could then be synthesized and tested for their biological activity.

Testing the suitability of a chemical moiety as a drug involves preclinical and clinical studies. During the preclinical studies, the drug is tested for its short term and long term toxicity including carcinogenicity.

This involves in vitro studies on genetically engineered cell culture and in vivo studies on animals. The preclinical studies also involve metabolic studies on animals. Radiolabeled drug is administered to test animals and its metabolic fate determined by analyzing the urine and blood samples of the test animals. The in vivo metabolic studies are also carried out on human volunteers during Phase I clinical trials to ascertain whether there are any differences in metabolism of drug in animals and humans.

After the preclinical and metabolic studies are successfully over, an application to appropriate authority is made for permission to carry out the clinical trials.While clinical trials are going on, studies on the formulation of drug, its stability, etc. are carried out simultaneously.

The clinical trials consist of four phases and constitute what are known as Phase I, Phase II, Phase III, and Phase IV.

Phase I studies are conducted on 100-200 healthy human volunteers to evaluate the drug's safety, its pharmacokinetics and the dose level that can be administered. It may take a year or so.

Phase II studies last for about two years and they are carried out on patients in order to:

(a) ascertain whether the drug possesses the therapeutic property which is claimed,
(b) study the pharmacokinetic and safety of the drug, and
(c) establish the dosing regimen.

Phase III studies normally take 3-6 years. During this phase the drug is tested in the same way as in Phase II but with a larger population.

If the drug has passed Phase III stage, it is put in market. However its effectiveness in terms of therapeutic efficacy and untoward side effects is still monitored. This constitutes Phase IV of the clinical trials.

FURTHER READING

1. K.H. Bleicher et. al., *Nature Reviews Drug Discovery*, **2**, 369 (2003).
2. R.B. Silverman, "Organic Chemistry of Drug Design and Drug Action," 2nd ed., Academic Press, New York, 1992.
3. J.H. Block and J.M. Beale, Eds., "Wilson and Gisvold's Text Book of Organic Medicinal and Pharmaceutical Chemistry," 11th ed., Lippincot Williams and Wilkins, New York, 2004.

11

Drug Metabolism

Drugs are mostly lipophilic in nature and unless they are eliminated, they will have extremely long half-life and would remain in body for prolonged periods resulting in increased toxicity. In order to get eliminated from body, drugs and other foreign substances commonly known as xenobiotics, have to get metabolized to water soluble compounds. In addition to making the drug more water soluble and thus amenable to elimination, metabolism of a drug usually results in an inactive metabolite, example, amphetamine (1) yields on metabolism phenylacetone (2) and phenytoin (3) yields hydroxyphenytoin (4). However, there are instances when the metabolite may be equally active or even toxic. The

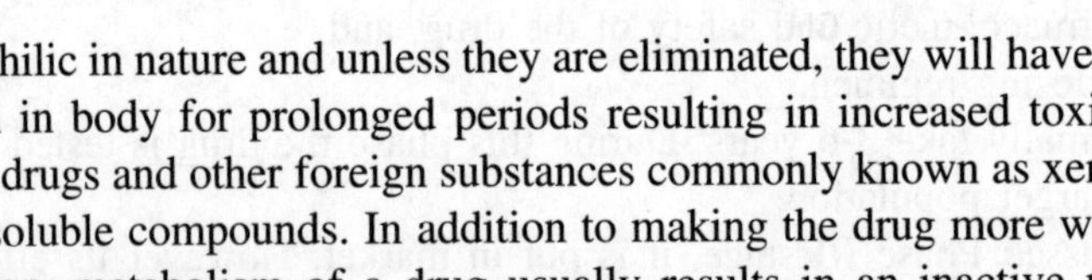

(1) (2)

(3) (4)

example of the former, i.e. where the metabolite is equally active and there is no net change in activity include the metabolite nortriptyline (5), the metabolite of amitriptyline (6), desipramine (7) the metabolite of imipramine (8). Examples where the metabolite is more active or toxic include salicylic acid (9) the metabolite of aspirin (10).

Before the drug reaches blood, orally administered drug has to pass through intestine and liver. Metabolism of drugs at these sites is known as Presystemic Metabolism or First Pass Metabolism. Presystemic metabolism usually results in lower blood levels of the drug. The enzymes which the drug

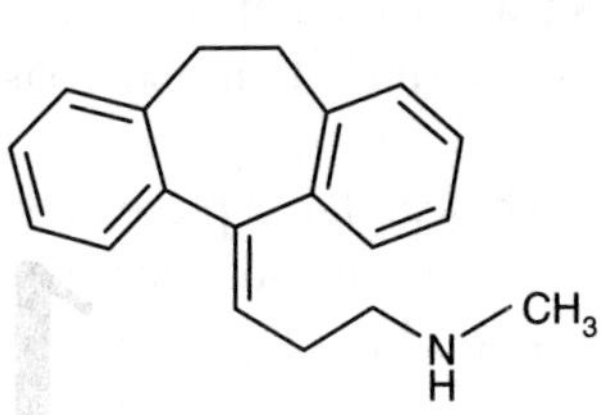
(5)

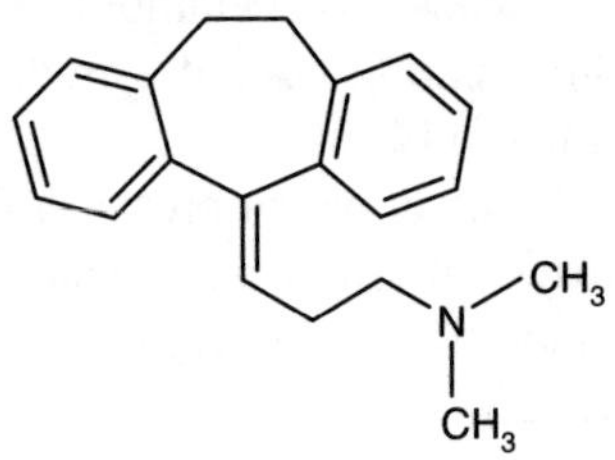
(6)

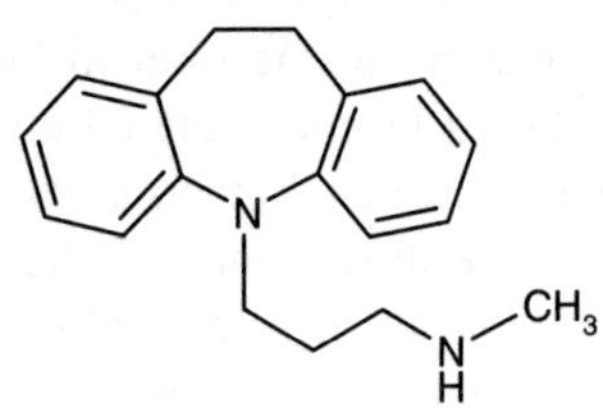
(7)

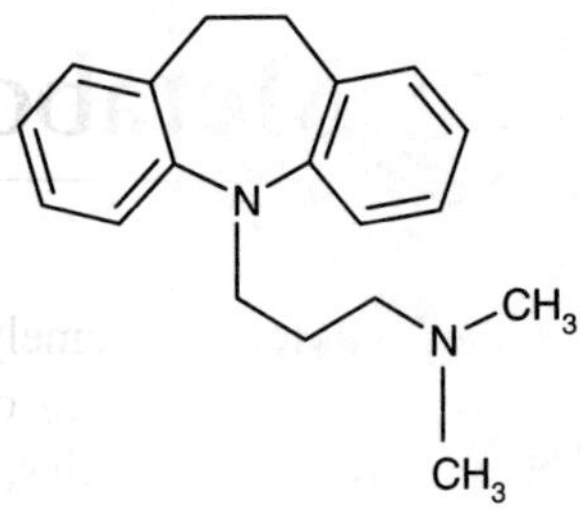
(8)

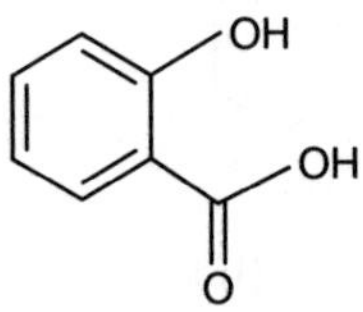
(9)

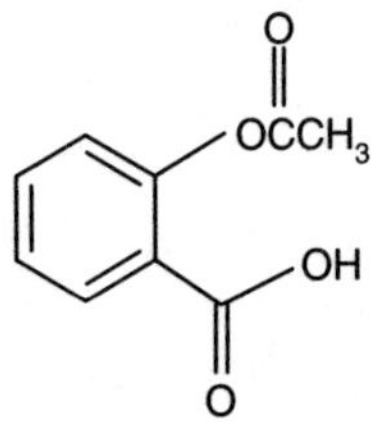
(10)

encounters in intestinal mucosa include glucouronyltransferases, glutathionetransferases, L-aromatic amino acid decarboxylases. Examples of drugs whose bioavailability is low because of presystemic first pass metabolism in intestine include albuterol (11) which when given orally is absorbed to the extent of 5% only because it is sulphated and glucouronitated. Similarly, levodopa (12) is extensively

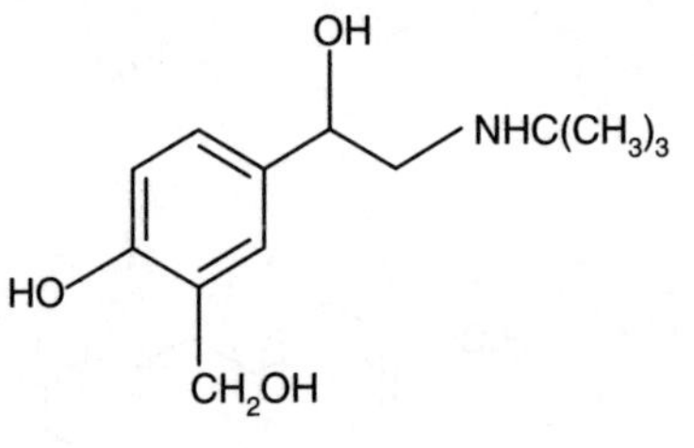
(11)

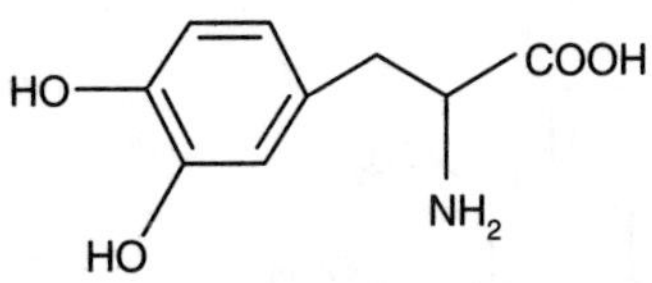
(12)

metabolized by L-aromatic amino acid decarboxylase resulting in decreased blood levels after its oral administration.

Concurrent administration of two drugs may lead to increased bioavailability of a drug. Thus, concurrent administration of paracetamol (13) with ethinyl estradiol (14) results in increased blood

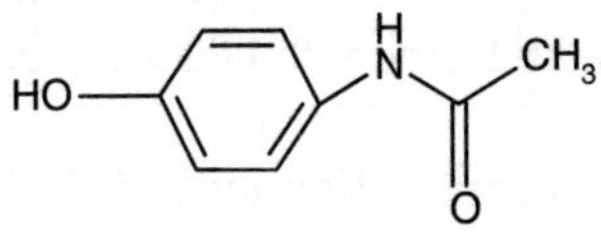
(13)

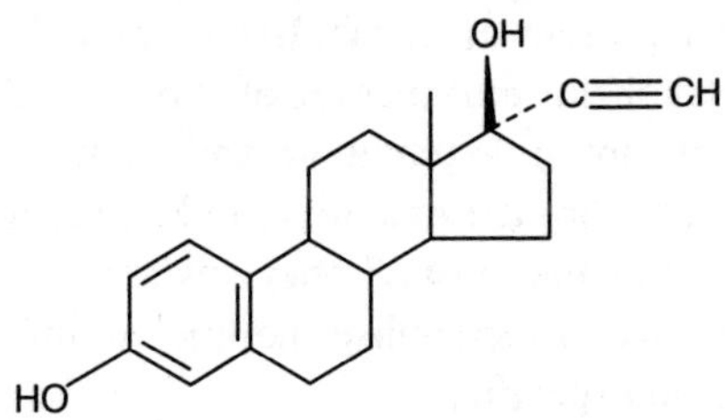
(14)

levels of ethinyl estradiol (14). This is because paracetamol (13) competes with ethinyl estradiol (14) for sulphation in intestinal mucosa thus sparing ethinyl estradiol (14) of sulphation and consequent higher blood levels of the ethinyl estradiol (14).

Next to intestinal mucosa, the other tissue in which presystemic metabolism takes place is the liver. Some of the drugs which undergo presystemic first pass metabolism in liver include alprenolol (15), isoproterenal (16), propranolol (17), morphine (18), dilitiazem (19), lidocaine (20), nifedipine (21), nitroglycerine (22), and pentoxifylline (23).

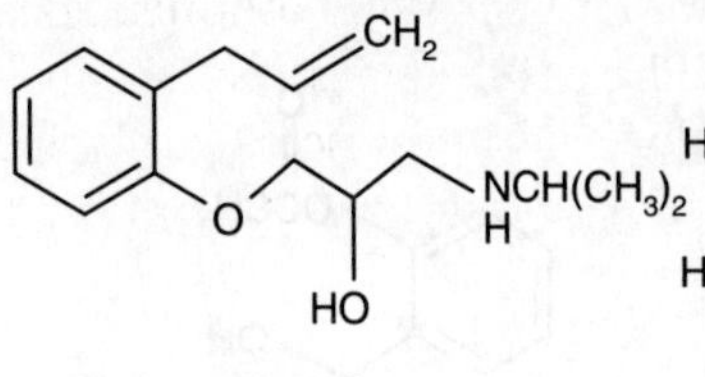

(15)

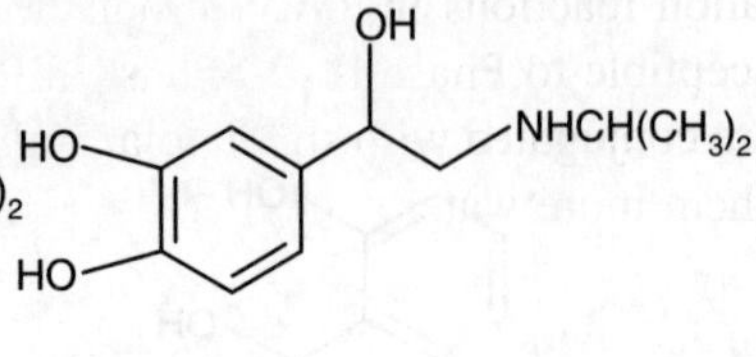

(16)

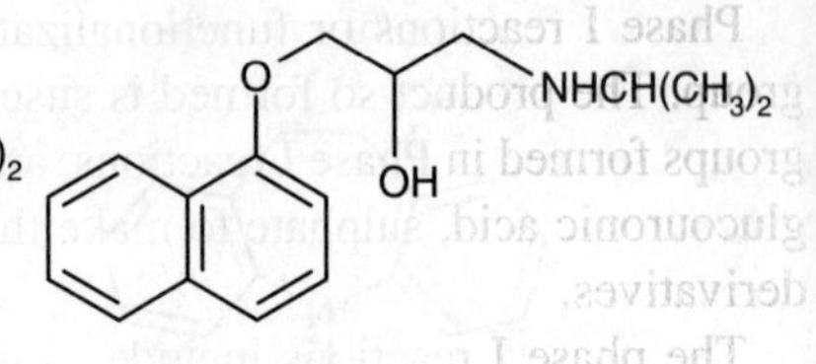

(17)

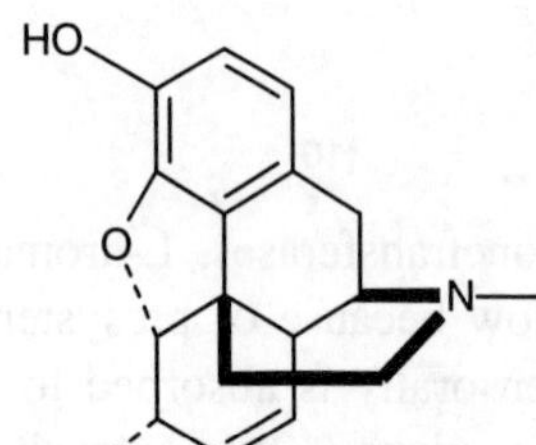

(18)

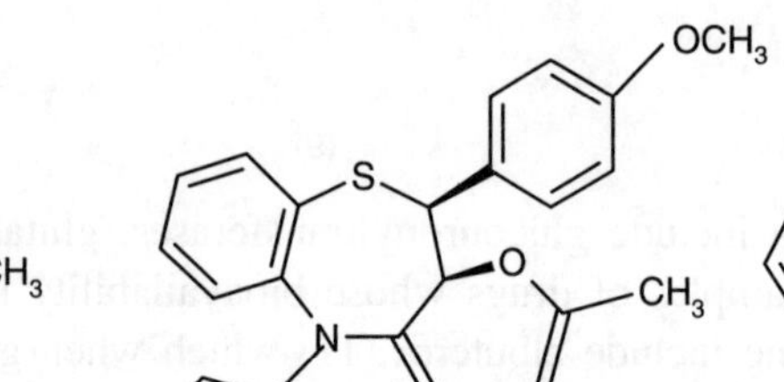

(19)

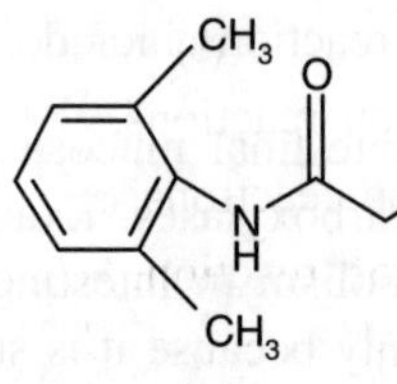

(20)

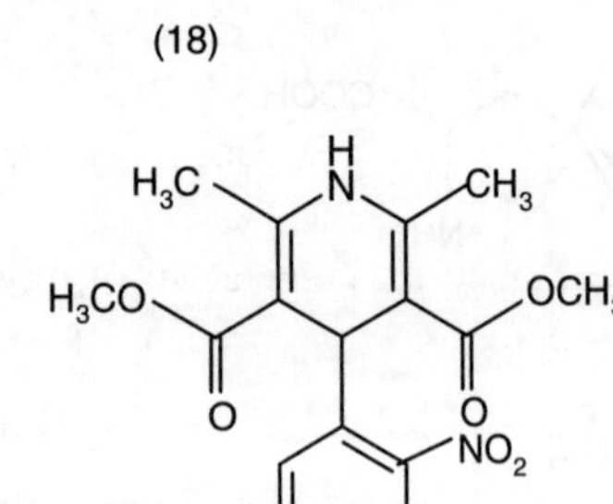

(21)

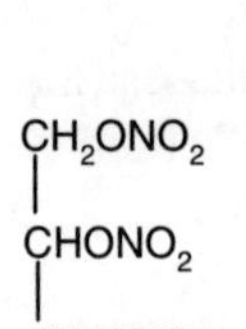

(22)

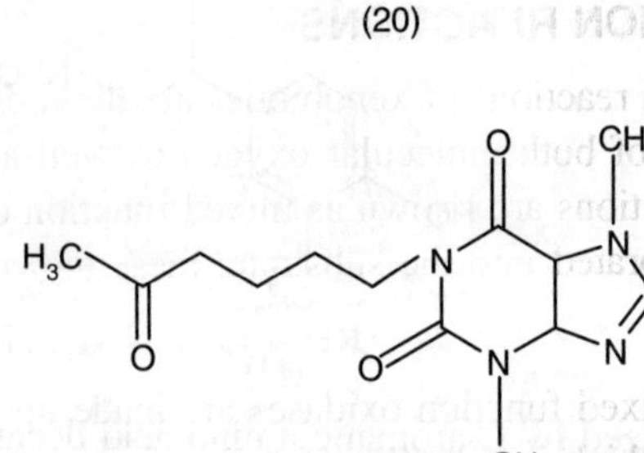

(23)

Most of the metabolism of drugs takes place in liver. The other tissues where the metabolism takes place in decreasing order of metabolizing ability include lungs, kidney, intestine, placenta, and skin.

The drug metabolizing enzymes are of two types, the microsomal and nonmicrosomal. The microsomes are attached to endoplasmic reticulum and the microsomal enzymes are responsible for metabolism of a majority of drugs through oxidative, reductive, hydrolytic and glucouronidation reactions. Some of the characteristics of microsomal enzymes are:

1. They selectively metabolise the lipid soluble drugs. In their action towards lipid soluble drugs they are non-specific.
2. The action on lipophilic drugs results in water soluble compounds.
3. The natural endogenous substances which are mostly water soluble are not prone to their action.

The non-microsomal enzymes are present in soluble form in cytoplasm and are also attached to mitochondria. They are also non-specific in nature and they usually metabolise water soluble endogenous substances as well as water soluble xenobiotics. These enzymes catalyze oxidation reaction and a number of reductive, hydrolytic and conjugation reactions.

Pathways of Drug Metabolism

Drug metabolism involves two types of reaction and these have been classified as Phase I and Phase II reactions.

Phase I reactions or functionalization reactions involve introduction or unmasking of a functional group. The product so formed is susceptible to Phase II reactions. In Phase II reactions, the functional groups formed in Phase I reactions, are conjugated with small polar endogenous substances like glycine, glucouronic acid, sulphate to make them more water soluble so that they are excreted as water soluble derivatives.

The phase I reactions include:

(a) oxidation reactions,

(b) reductive reactions, and

(c) hydrolytic reactions.

The phase II reactions include:

(a) conjugation reactions,

(b) acetylation reactions,

(c) methylation reaction.

PHASE I REACTIONS

OXIDATION REACTIONS

Oxidation reactions of xenobiotics are the most important reactions. Since these reactions take place in presence of both molecular oxygen as well as reducing agent, NADPH, the enzymes which catalyze these reactions are known as mixed function oxidases (Eq. 1). Further, since only one atom of oxygen is incorporated into the substrate, these enzymes are also known as monooxygenases.

$$RH + O_2 + NADPH + H^+ \longrightarrow ROH + NADP^+ + H_2O \quad \text{... (Eq. 1)}$$

The mixed function oxidases are made up of three components namely cytochrome P-450, a heme protein, which is actually a family of enzymes. It transfers oxygen atom to the substrate. The second component, cytochrome P-450 reductase, is a flavoprotein which is NADPH-dependent. It catalyzes the reduction of cytchrome P-450 (Fe^{+++}) to ferrous form. The third component is phosphatidylcholine which facilitates the transfer of electron from NADPH to cytochrome P-450.

The cytochrome P-450 constitutes important component of mixed function oxidases The mechanism of its action is given in Fig. 11.1. The various steps involved include:

1. The substrate (RH) binds reversibly to the enzyme CYP-450 (Fe^{3+}) **(A)** giving an enzyme substrate complex **(B)**.
2. The complex **(B)** undergoes reduction to give **(C)**, the electron being donated by NADPH.
3. The reduced CYP-450 (Fe^{2+}-HR) complex **(C)** complex binds to dioxygen to give **(D)**.
4. The oxy-CYP-450 (Fe^{2+}-RH) complex **(D)** undergoes auto-oxidation to superoxide anion **(E)**.
5. The superoxide anion **(E)** picks another electron to give peroxy complex **(F)**.

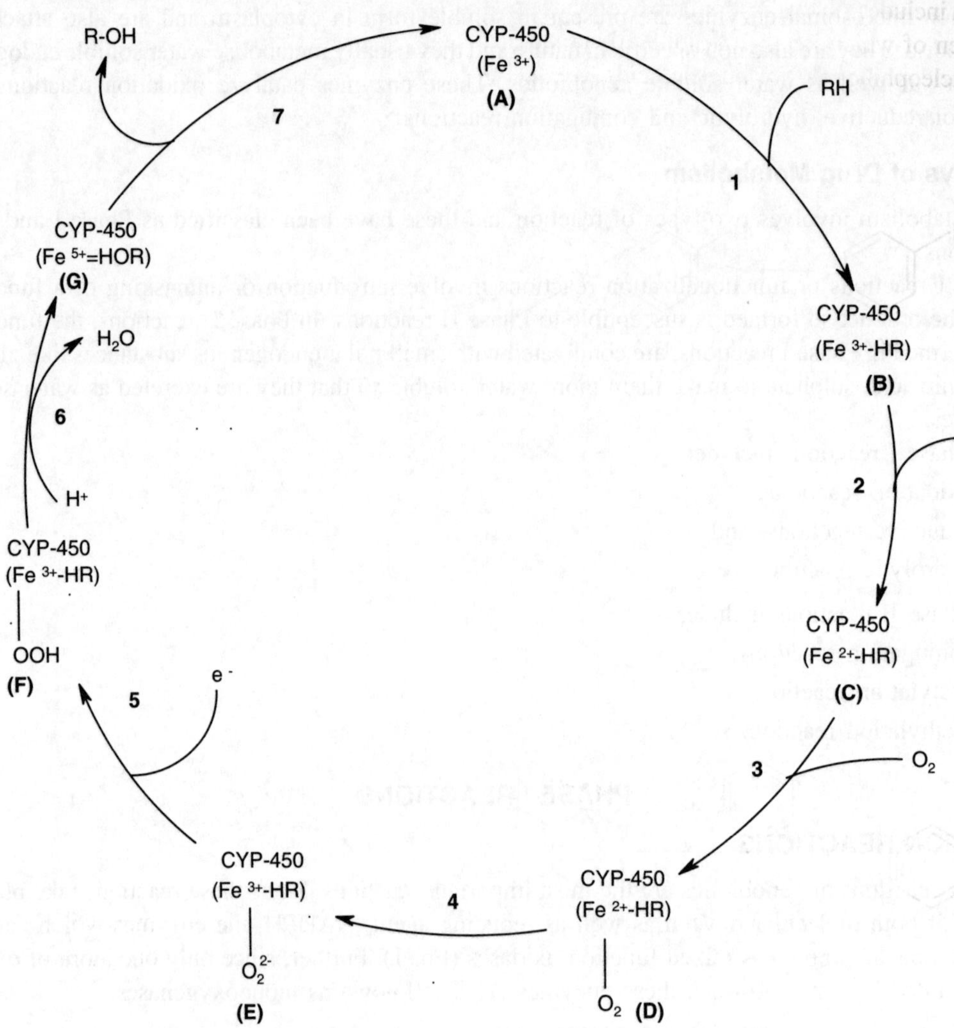

Fig. 11.1 Mechanism of cytochrome P-450 oxidation

6. The peroxy complex **(F)** loses water to give perferryl oxenoid intermediate **(G)**. The perferryl oxygen complex **(F)** is an active oxygenation species.
7. In the next step the hydrogen is abstracted by perferryl oxygen species resulting in hydroxylated substrate (ROH) and regeneration of ferric cytochrome P-450 enzyme **(A)**.

Examples of Oxidation Reactions

Oxidation of Aromatic Moieties

The aromatic (24) moieties are oxidized by cytochrome P-450 to arene oxide (25), a highly reactive electrophile, which is then converted to arenol (26). Alternately, the arene oxide (25) may be hydrolyzed by epoxide hydrase to a dihydro diol (27) which in turn may be converted to catechol (28) or the dihdro diol (27) could directly be conjugated with glutathione (SG) (29). The arene oxides (25) are highly toxic and are carcinogenic. Some of the compounds which are converted to carcinogens by metabolic oxidation include polycyclic aromatic hydrocarbons. Examples include benzo[a]pyrene (30), the ultimate carcinogen of which is (+)-7,8-diol-9,10-epoxide (31). The toxicity of these epoxides is because they attack nucleophilic sites of nucleic acids.

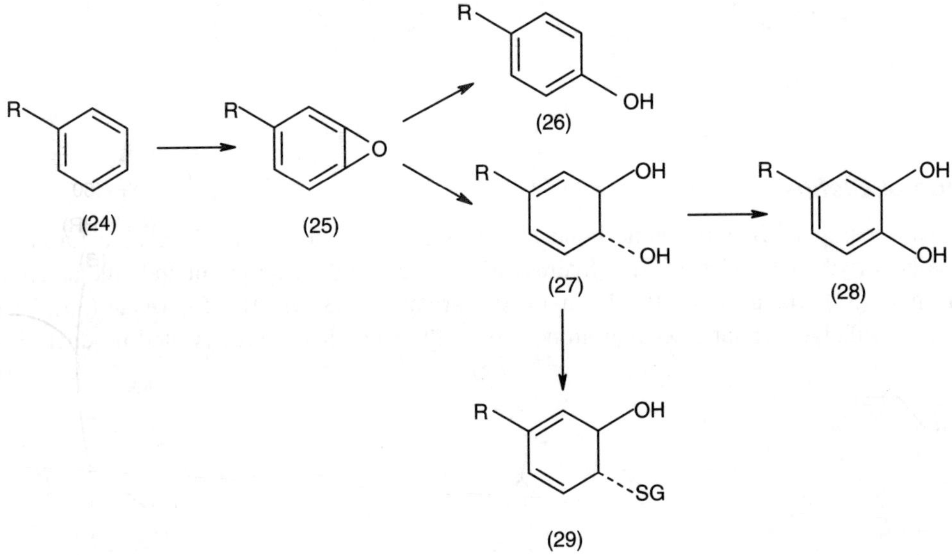

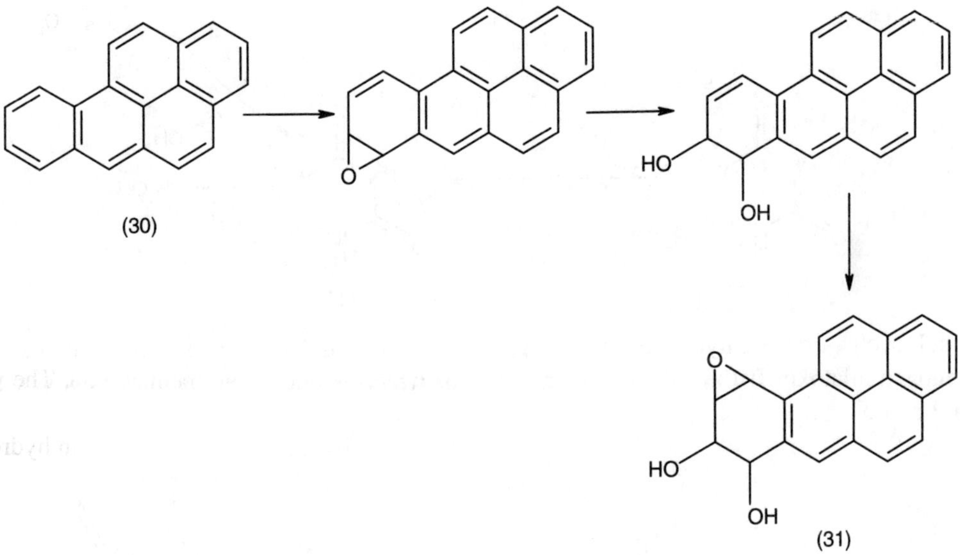

In case of substituted aromatic compounds the hydroxylation takes place at *para*-position. Examples include phenytoin (3) yielding hydroxyphenytoin (4) and propranolol (17) giving hydroxypropranolol (32). The resulting phenolic compounds (4) and (32) undergo glucouronidation. The aromatic hydroxylation usually takes place readily in electron rich or activated rings. The deactivated rings do not get hydroxylated.

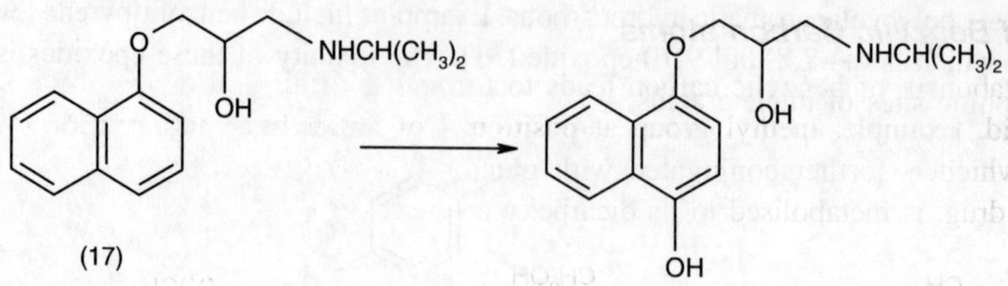

(17) (32)

Oxidation of Olefins

Like aromatic compounds, the double bond also gets hydroxylated through epoxide formation. The epoxide is next hydrated under epoxide hydrase to yield the diol. Example include the anticonvulsant carbamazepine (33) which yields 10,11-dihydroxy derivative (33) via 10,11-epoxide (35). The major metabolite of sedative hypnotic secobarbitone (36) is the side chain hydroxylated product (37).

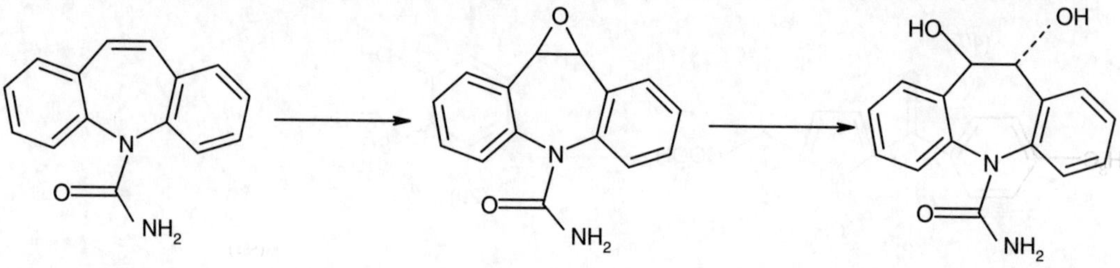

(33) (35) (34)

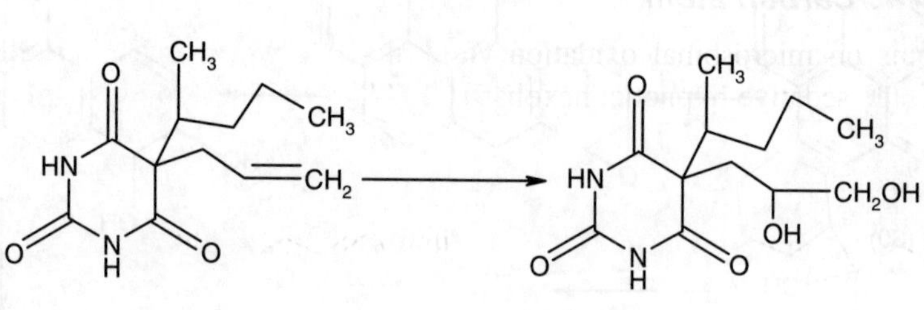

(36) (37)

Like polycyclic aromatic hydrocarbons, the epoxide of other moieties can also be toxic. Example is the carcinogen aflatoxin B (38), the carcinogenicity of which is due to formation of epoxide (39) at position 2 and 3.

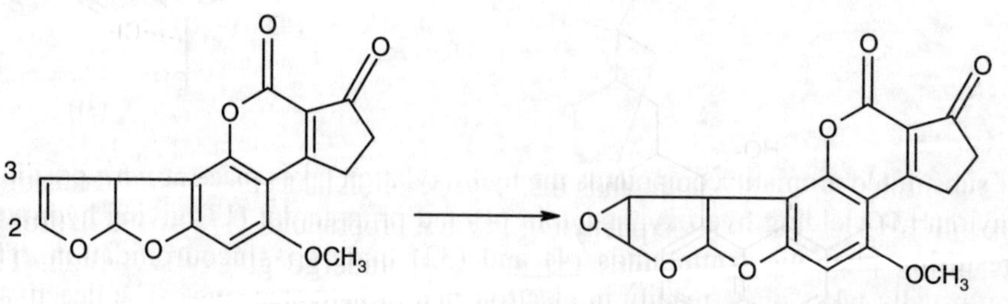

(38) (39)

Oxidation of Benzylic Carbon atoms

Oxidative metabolism of benzylic carbon leads to formation of alcohol which is further oxidized to carboxylic acid. Example, methyl group at position 4 of antidiabetic tolbutamide (40) to carboxy analog (41) which is further conjugated with glucouronic acid. Similarly, tolmetin (42), an anti-inflammatory drug, is metabolised to its dicarboxy analog (43).

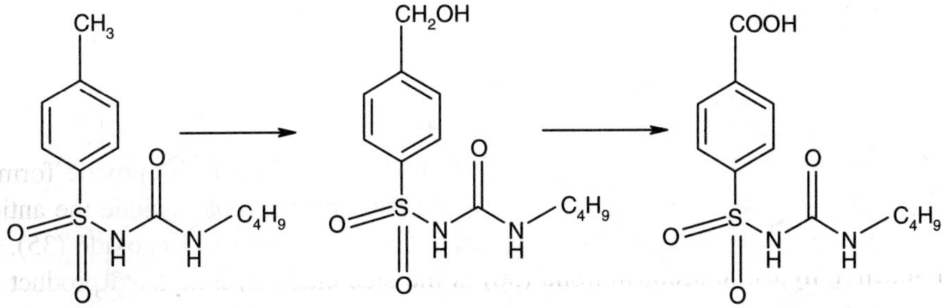

(40) (41)

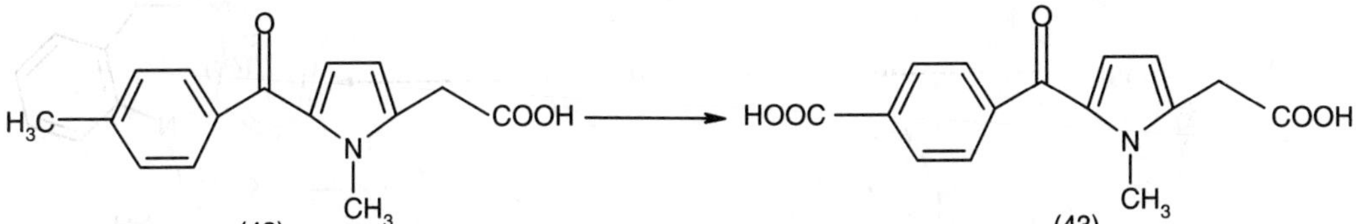

(42) (43)

Oxidation at Allylic Carbon atom

Allylic carbon atoms on microsomal oxidation yield alcohols which may be further conjugated or oxidized. Example, the sedative hypnotic, hexobarbital (44) is oxidized to hydroxyl analog (45) which

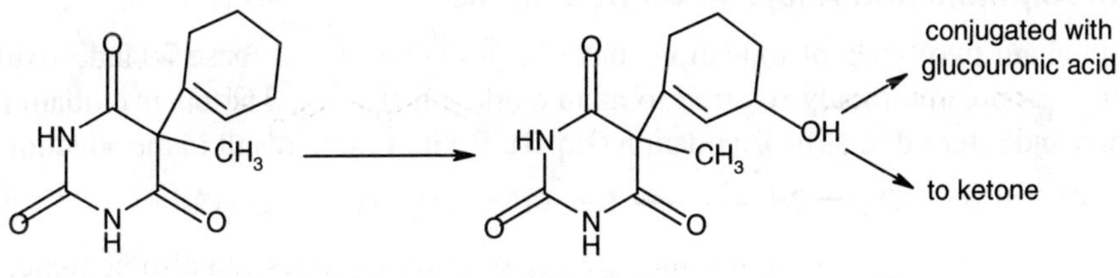

(44) (45)

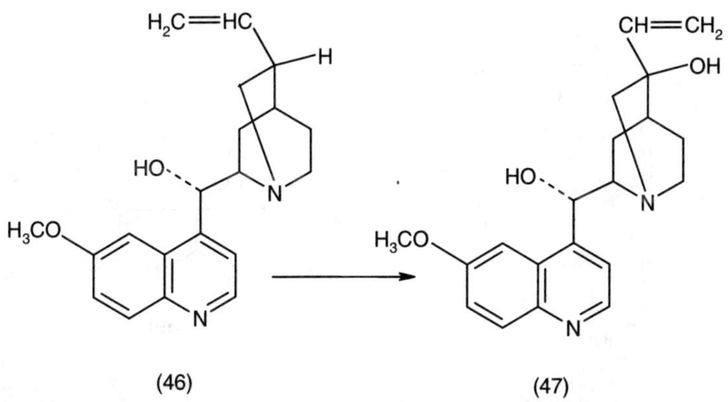

(46) (47)

may be conjugated or further oxidized. Another example is that of quinidine (46), an antiarrhythmic, which is oxidized to its hydroxy analog (47).

Oxidation at Carbon atom α- to Carbonyl and Imines

The carbon atoms α- to carbonyl or imino group are also oxidized by mixed function oxidases. Examples, metabolism of the anxiolytic diazepam (48) to oxazepam (49), and the sedative hypnotic glutethimide (50) to hydroxyglutethimide (51).

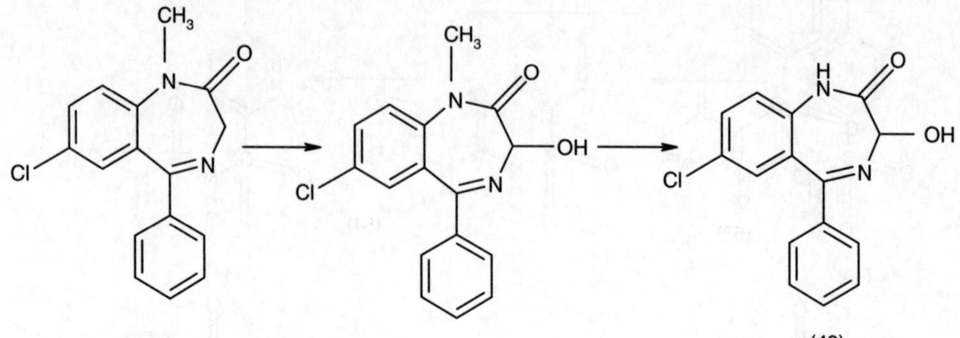

(48) (49)

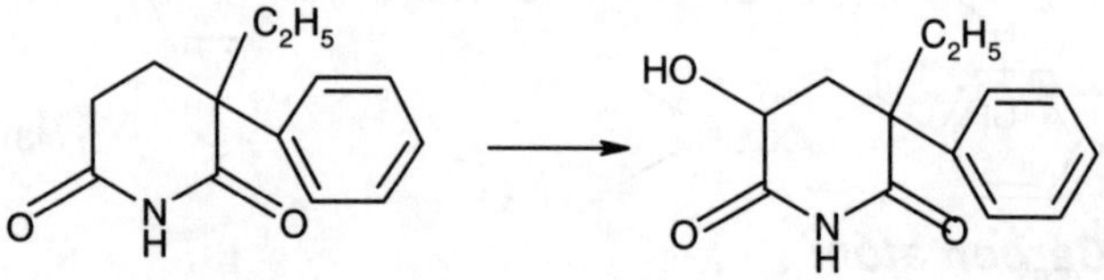

(50) (51)

Oxidation of Aliphatic and Alicyclic Carbon atoms

In an aliphatic chain two types of oxidations have been observed and these include oxidation of the terminal methyl group, commonly referred to as ω-oxidation (Eq. 2). The other oxidation at the penultimate carbon and referred to as ω-1 oxidation (Eq. 3). Both of these result in introduction of hydroxyl

$$R-CH_2-CH_2-CH_2-CH_3 \longrightarrow R-CH_2-CH_2-CH_2-CH_2OH \quad \text{... (Eq. 2)}$$

$$R-CH_2-CH_2-CH_2-CH_3 \longrightarrow R-CH_2-CH_2-\underset{\displaystyle OH}{\underset{|}{CH}}-CH_3 \quad \text{... (Eq. 3)}$$

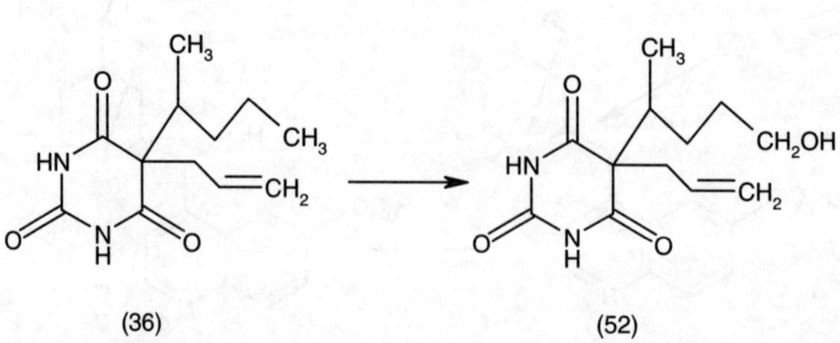

(36) (52)

groups at respective positions. The ω-1 oxidation is predominant. The oxidations at other positions are less common. Examples include oxidation of the side chain of sedative hypnotic secobarbital (36) by ω-oxidation to (52) and antidiabetic chlorpropamide(53) by ω-1 oxidation to (54). The anti-inflammatory analgesic, ibuprofen (55) may undergo ω- or ω-1 oxidation giving (56) and (57), respectively.

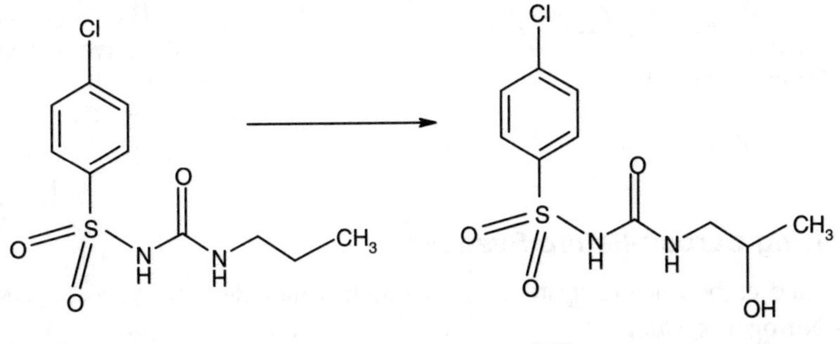

(53) (54)

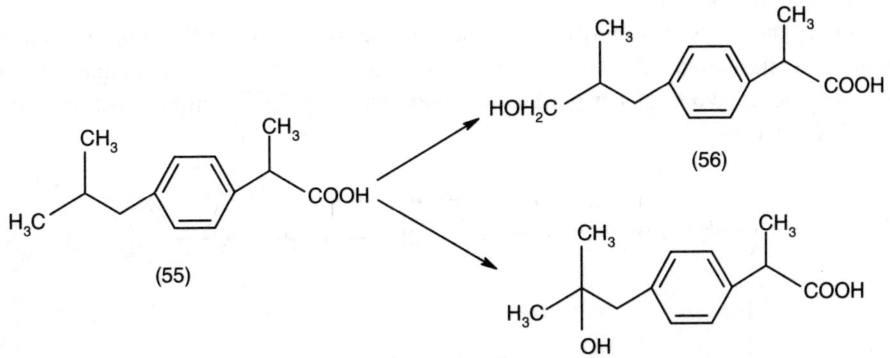

(55) (56) (57)

The alicyclic system, cyclohexyl (58), is found in many medicinal agents. This is also susceptible to oxidation at C_3 (Eq. 3) or C_4 (Eq. 4) positions and this may result in *cis*- or *trans*-isomers. Example, oxidation of antidiabetic acetohexamide (59) yields on oxidation *trans*-4-hydroxy analog (60) as the major product.

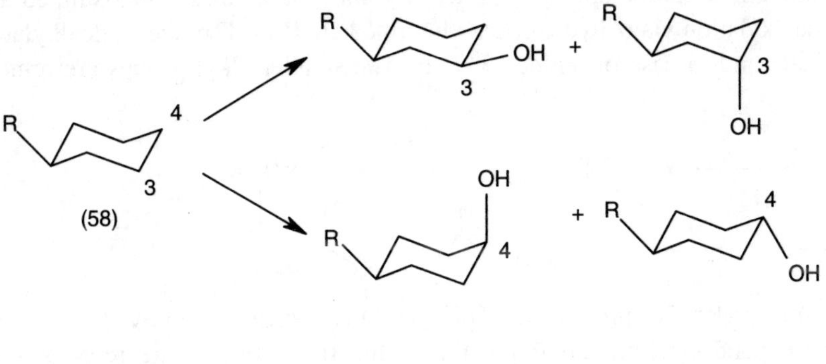

(58)

... (Eq. 3)

... (Eq. 4)

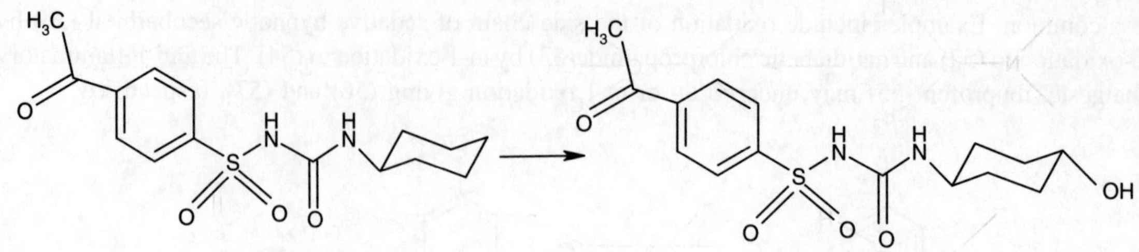

(59) (60)

Oxidation Involving Carbon-Hetero Systems

The commonly found carbon-hetero systems in medicinals include:

1. Carbon – Nitrogen system,
2. Carbon – Oxygen system, and
3. Carbon – Sulphur system.

The oxidation of these systems involve two types of oxidations. One of these involves hydroxylation of the carbon α- to the hetero atm (Eq. 5). The resulting hydroxylated intermediate is unstable and decomposes with the cleavage of carbon-hetero bond. This type of reaction constitutes N–, O–, and S– oxidative dealkylation.

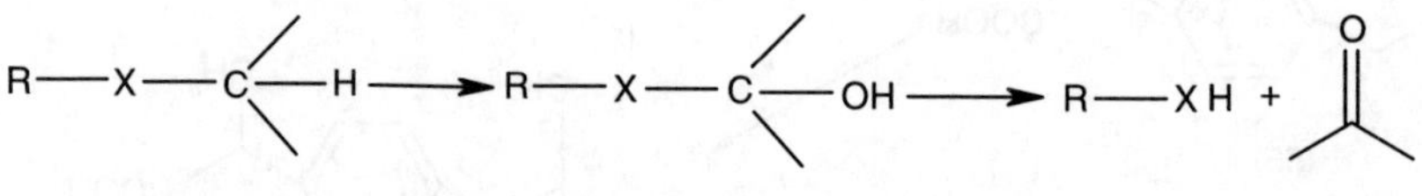

... (Eq. 5)

X = N, O, S

The second type of oxidation involves hydroxylation or oxidation of the hetero atom. This type of oxidation is usually found in case of compounds containing nitrogen or sulphur and results in N-hydroxylation or N-oxide formation. In case of sulphur compounds sulphoxide or sulphone formation may take place.

Oxidation Involving Carbon-nitrogen Systems

Secondary, tertiary aliphatic and aromatic amines, tertiary alicyclic amines, N-substituted amides and hydrazines undergo dealkylation via α-hydroxylated intermediate (61). The rate of dealkylation in case of amines is $3^0 > 2^0 > 1^0$ and in case of amides $3^0 > 2^0$. The smaller alkyl groups are removed faster

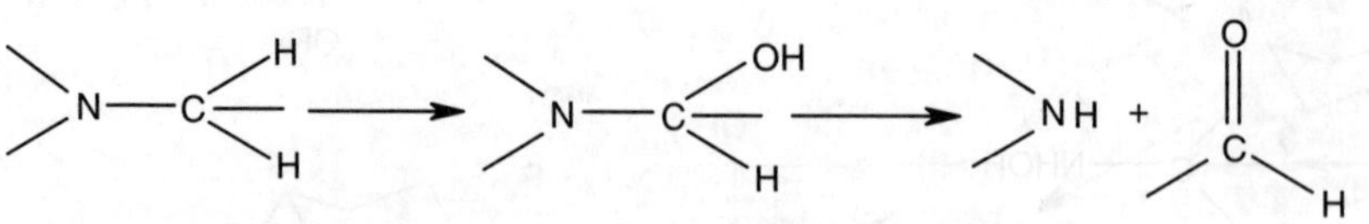

... (Eq. 6)

(61)

i.e. methyl>ethyl > *n*-propyl > *iso*-propyl etc. The *tert.*-butyl group is removed in more than one step (Fig. 11.2). The hepatic cytochromic P-450 mixed function oxidases are responsible for these oxidations.

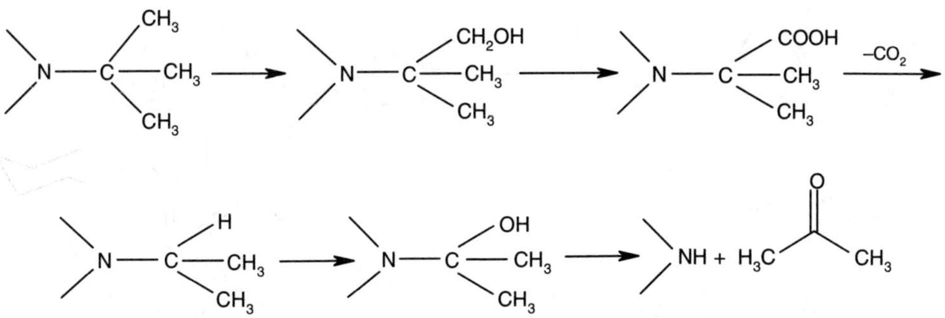

Fig. 11.2 Mechanism of oxidation of *tert*.-butyl group

The N-hydroxylations or N-oxidations are usually found in case of compounds in which the nitrogen is non-basic or less basic (Eq. 7) and (Eq. 8). The N-hydroxylation can also take place at basic nitrogen such as amines (Eq. 9). The N-hydroxylation reactions are catalysed by cytochrome P-450 and also by hepatic amine oxidases also known as N-oxidases. These enzymes are NAD^+ dependent flavoproteins and require NADPH and molecular oxygen to carry out N-oxidations.

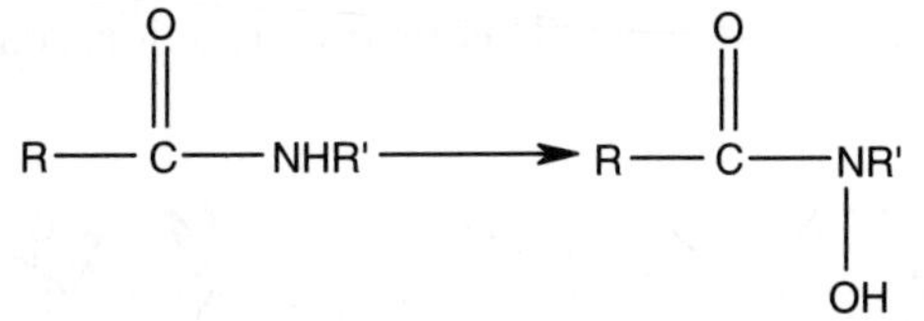

... (Eq. 7)

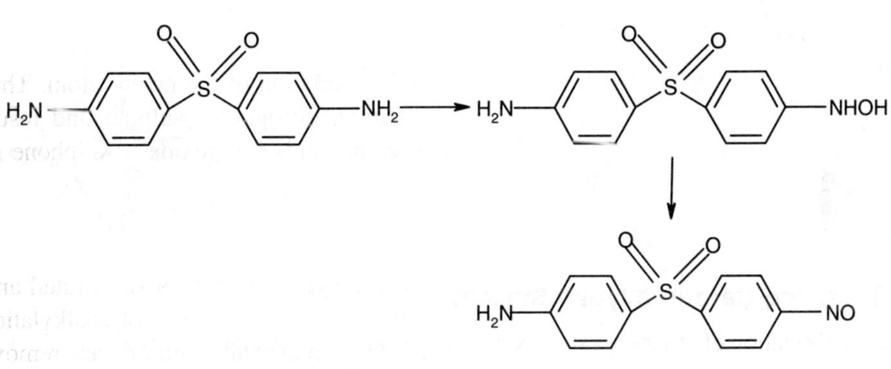

... (Eq. 8)

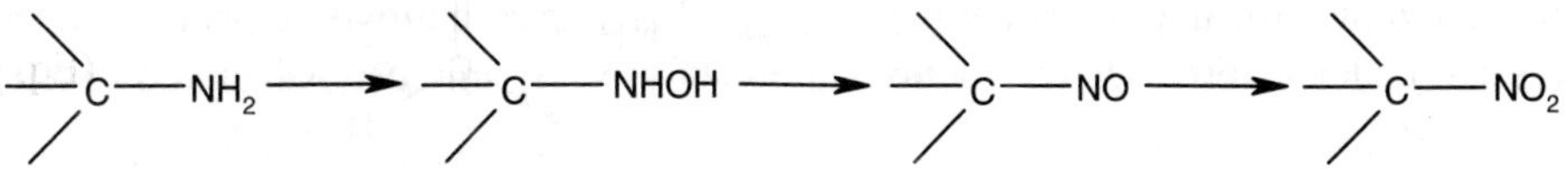

... (Eq. 9)

Examples of the above include oxidation of adrenergic drug methamphetamine (62), the anti-bacterial trimethoprim (63), the analgesic antipyretic paracetamol (13), the anorexic phentermine (64), and the antileprotic dapsone (Eq. 8).

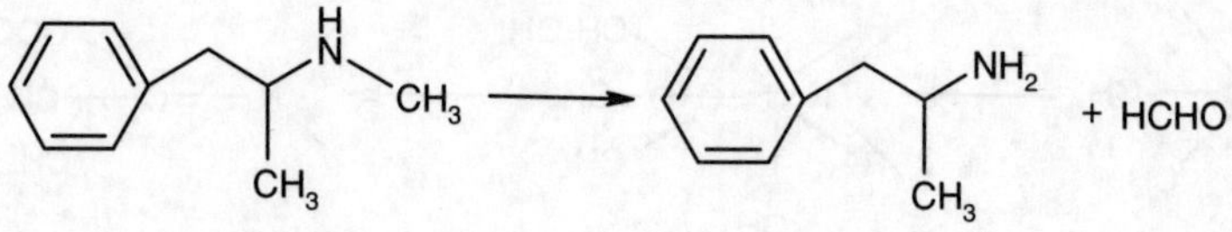

(62)

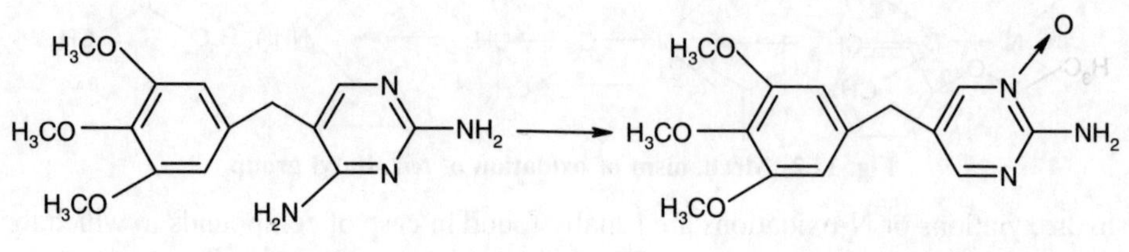

(63)

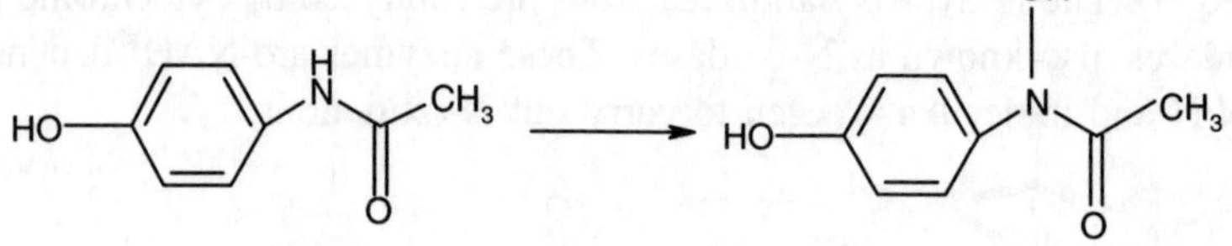

(13)

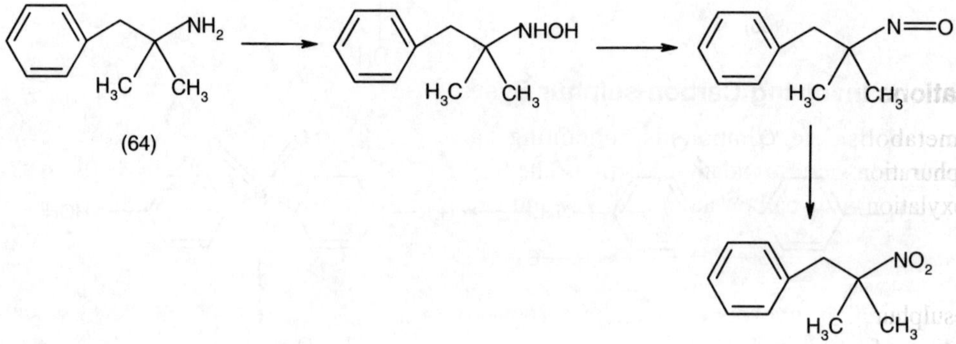

(64)

Oxidation Involving Carbon-oxygen Systems

The oxidative dealkylation of ethers or esters containing a carbon-oxygen bond involves α-hydroxylation to form hemiacetal (Eq. 10) or a hemiketal (Eq. 11), which then undergoes spontaneous C-O bond cleavage to yield dealkylated oxygen containing species such as phenol or alcohol. These undergo then conjugation reactions. Examples include oxidative metabolism of analgesic-antipyretic phenacetin (65) and analgesic-antitussive codeine (66). These reactions are catalysed by microsomal mixed function oxidases.

$$R{-}CH_2{-}O{-}CH_3 \longrightarrow \underset{\text{hemiacetal}}{R{-}\underset{\displaystyle OH}{\underset{|}{CH}}{-}O{-}CH_3} \longrightarrow R{-}CHO + HO{-}CH_3 \quad \text{... (Eq. 10)}$$

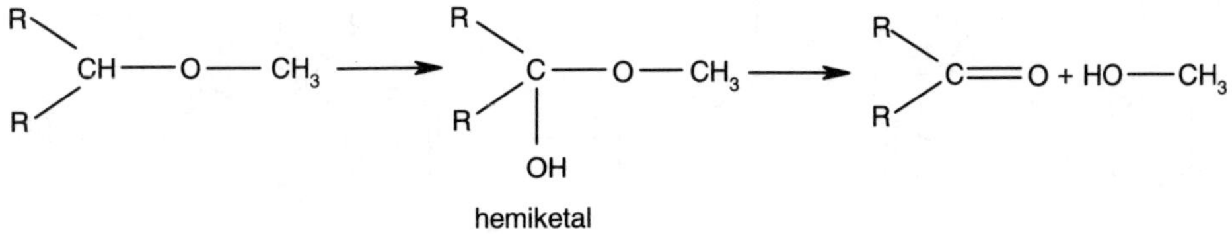

... (Eq. 11)

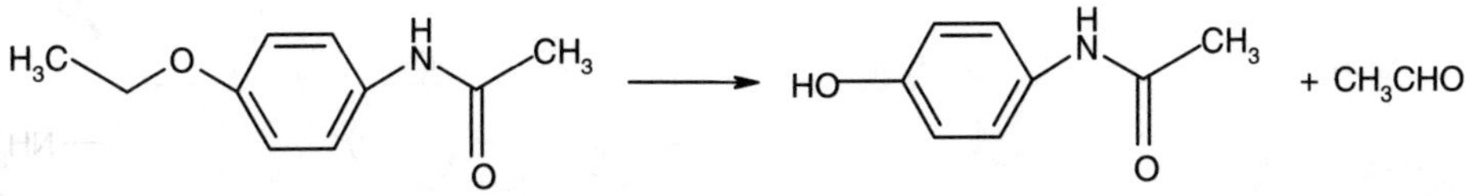

(65)

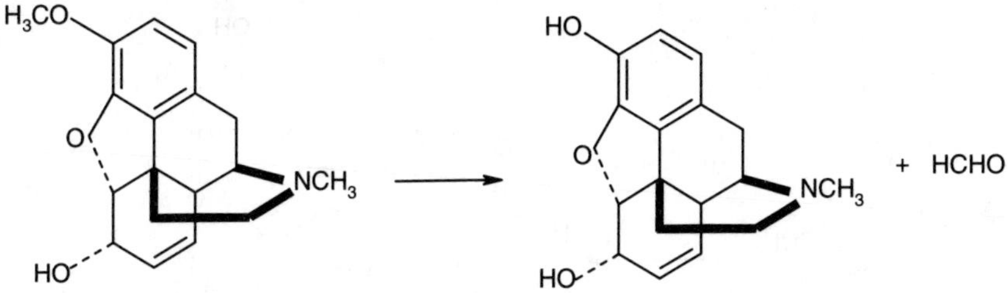

(66)

Oxidations Involving Carbon-sulphur Systems

The metabolism of compounds containing carbon-sulphur bond may involve S-dealkylation, desulphuration, and S-oxidation reaction. The S-dealkylation is similar to N-dealkylation and involves hydroxylation of α-carbon atom (Eq. 12) and dealkylation.

$$R—S—CH_3 \longrightarrow R—S—CH_2OH \longrightarrow R—SH + HCHO \qquad \text{... (Eq. 12)}$$

Desulphuration involves cleavage of carbon-sulphur bond (Eq. 13) and S-oxidation may result in formation of sulphoxide and then sulphone (Eq. 14). Examples include oxidative metabolism of antineoplastic agent, 6-methylthiopurine (67), the short acting anaesthetic, thiopental (68), and antiulcer agent cimetidine (69).

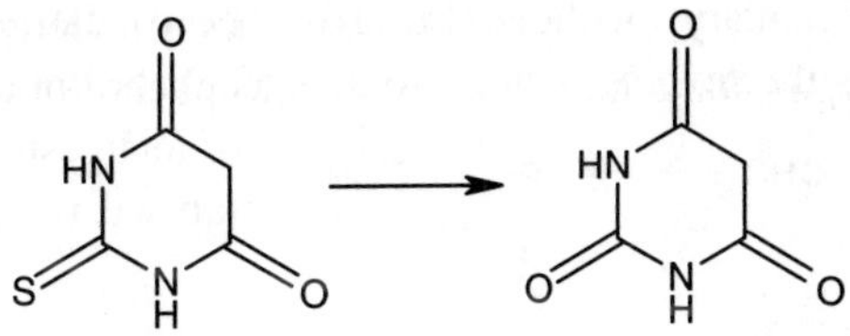

... (Eq. 13)

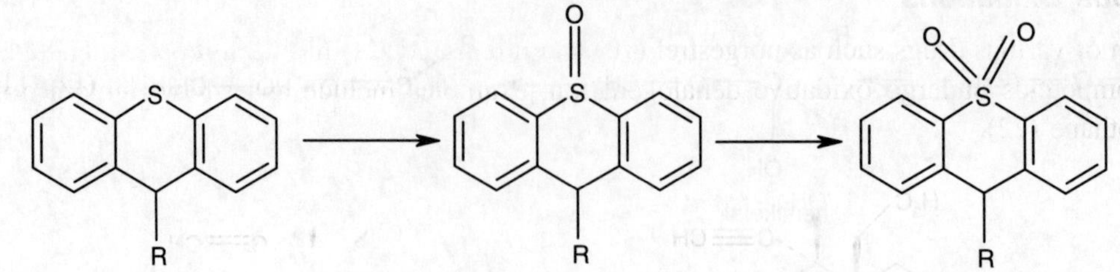

... (Eq. 14)

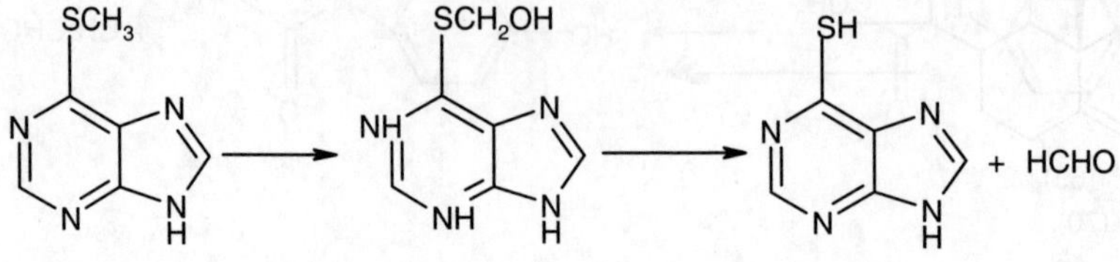

(67)

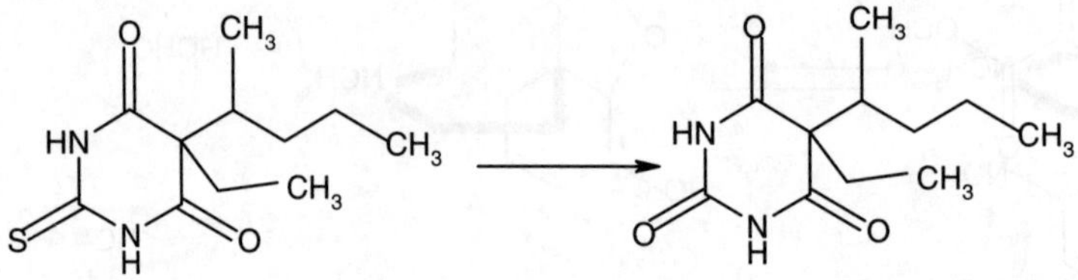

(68)

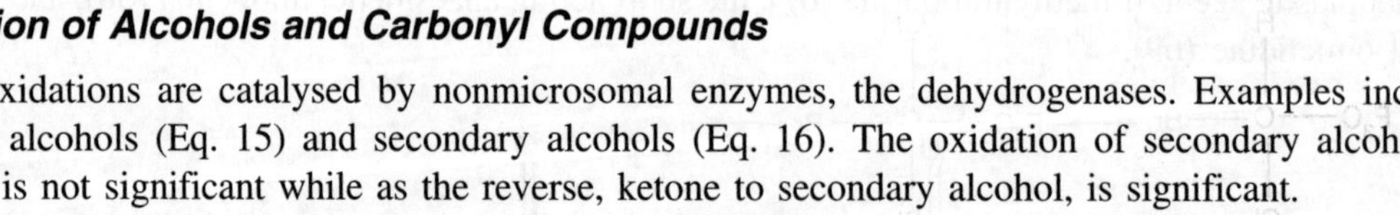

(69)

Oxidation of Alcohols and Carbonyl Compounds

These oxidations are catalysed by nonmicrosomal enzymes, the dehydrogenases. Examples include primary alcohols (Eq. 15) and secondary alcohols (Eq. 16). The oxidation of secondary alcohol to ketones is not significant while as the reverse, ketone to secondary alcohol, is significant.

$$R-CH_2OH \longrightarrow R-CHO \longrightarrow R-COOH \quad \text{... (Eq. 15)}$$

... (Eq. 16)

Miscellaneous Oxidations

Aromatization of various drugs such as norgestrel (70) and nifedipine (21) has been reported. Halogen containing compounds undergo oxidative dehalogenation, examples include anaesthetics chloroform (71) and halothane (72).

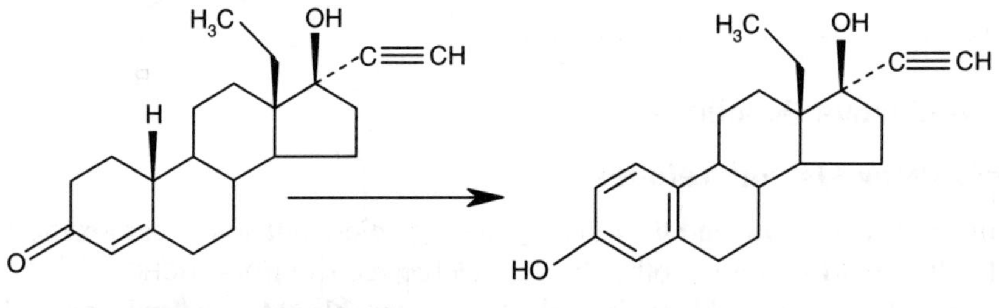

(70)

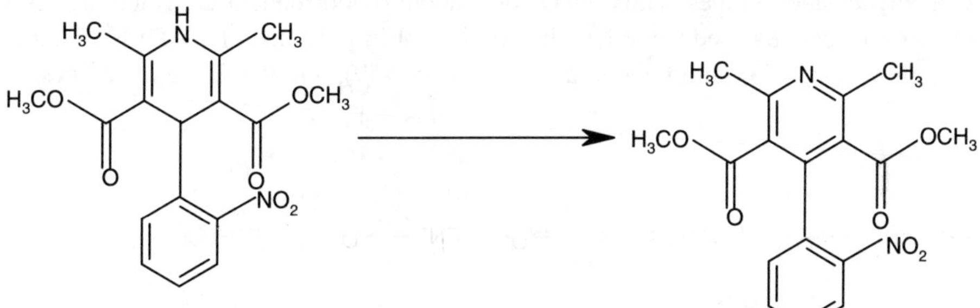

(21)

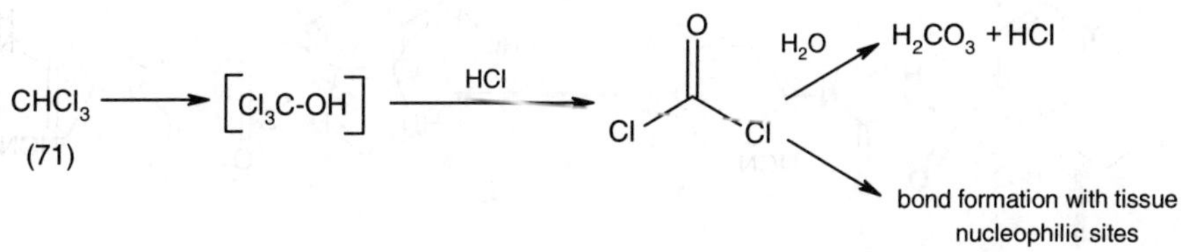

(71)

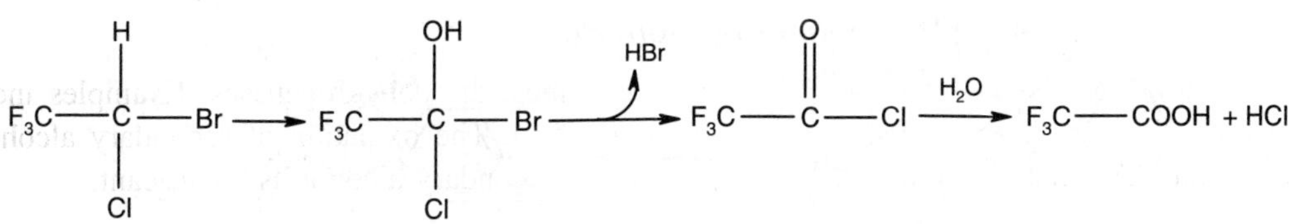

(72)

REDUCTIVE REACTIONS

Reductive reactions lead to functional groups which are polar and amenable to conjugations. Some of these include reduction of carbonyl (Eq.17), nitro (Eq. 18) and azo compounds (Eq. 19). Some of the reductive processes which are not common in drug metabolism are reduction of N-oxides to their corresponding tertiary amines and reduction of sulphoxides to sulphides.

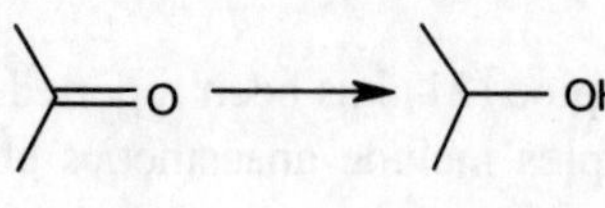 ... (Eq. 17)

$$-NO_2 \longrightarrow -NH_2 \quad \text{... (Eq. 18)}$$

$$-N{=}N- \longrightarrow -NH{-}NH- \quad \text{... (Eq. 19)}$$

Examples of Reductive Reactions

Reduction of Aldehydes and Ketones

Bioreduction of aldehydes is rare and they mainly undergo bio-oxidation to carboxylic acids. Ketones, which are difficult to oxidize, on the other hand, undergo reduction.

The enzymes which are responsible for bioreduction are soluble aldo-keto-reductases. These enzymes are mainly found in liver and kidney. Oxido-reductases that carry out both oxidation as well as reduction also reduce aldehydes and ketones. Thus NAD^+-dependent oxido-reductases which are responsible for oxidation of alcohols can also reduce aldehydes to alcohol in presence of NADPH. Examples include sedative hypnotic chloral (73), antidiabetic acetohexamide (59), and the narcotic analgesic methadone (74).

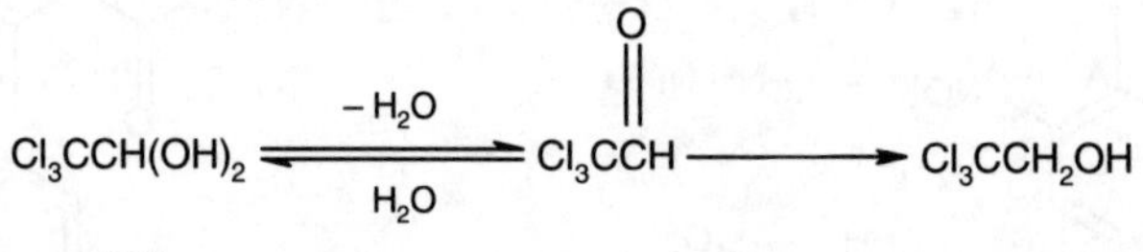

(73)

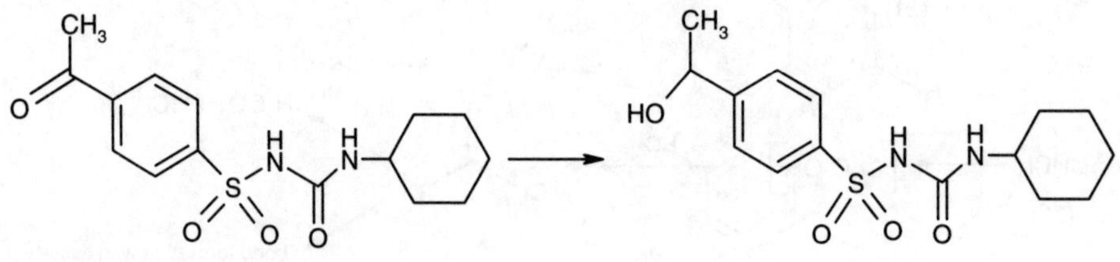

(59)

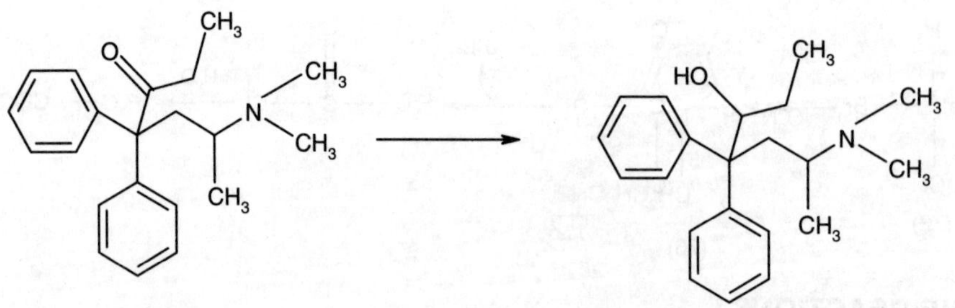

(74)

The mechanism of bioreduction is as given in (Eq. 20). Bioreduction of ketones usually results in creation of an asymmetric centre and in case of chiral ketones reduction results in diastereoisomeric alcohols.

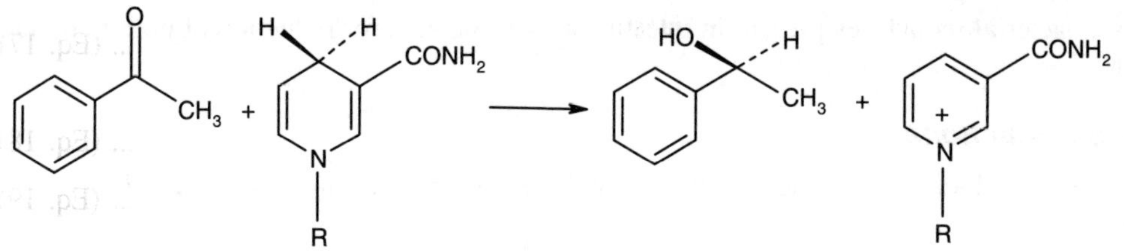

... (Eq. 20)

Reduction of Nitro and Azo Compounds

The reduction of nitro and azo compounds leads to amines. While nitro compounds are reduced via nitroso and hydroxylamine derivatives, the azo compounds are converted to hydrazo derivatives and then to amines (Eq. 21 and Eq. 22). Bioreduction of nitro compounds is catalysed by NADPH – dependent microsomal and soluble nitro reductases which are found in liver. Examples include the anti-convulsant, cloneazepam (75), the antiprotozoal, metronidazole (76), and the antibacterial, prontosil (77).

$$Ar-\overset{+}{N}(=O)\rightarrow O \longrightarrow Ar-N{=}O \longrightarrow Ar-NH-OH \longrightarrow Ar-NH_2 \quad \text{... (Eq. 21)}$$

$$Ar-N{=}N-Ar' \longrightarrow Ar-NH\,NH-Ar' \longrightarrow Ar-NH_2 + Ar'-NH_2 \quad \text{... (Eq. 22)}$$

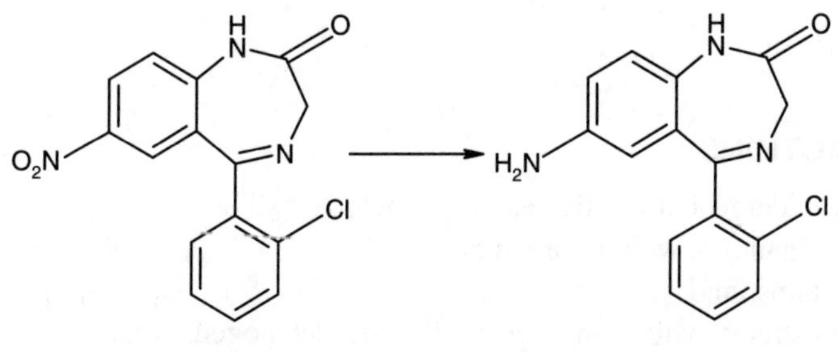

(75)

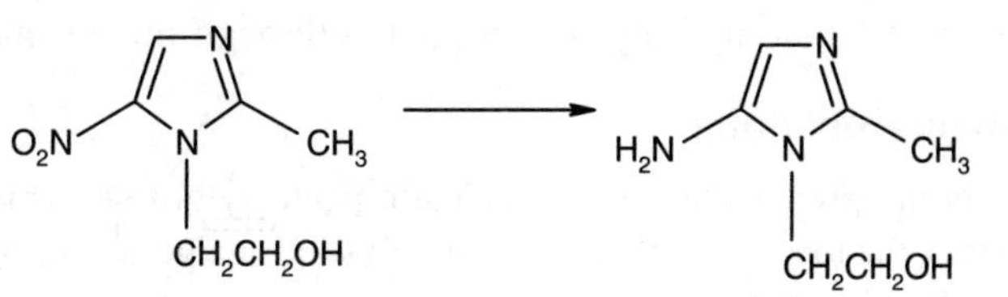

(76)

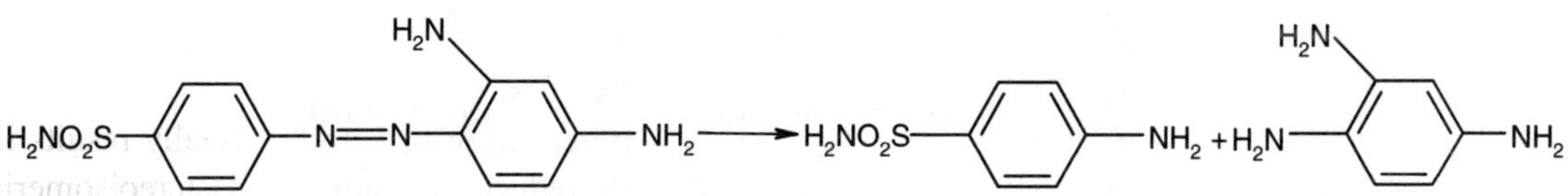

(77)

The hepatic NADPH – dependent microsomal reductases present in liver reduce azo compounds. In addition to these, bacterial reductases present in intestine are responsible for reduction of both nitro and azo compounds.

Miscellaneous Reductions

Examples from these include dimethylsulfoxide (78) and the anti-inflammatory sulindac (79).

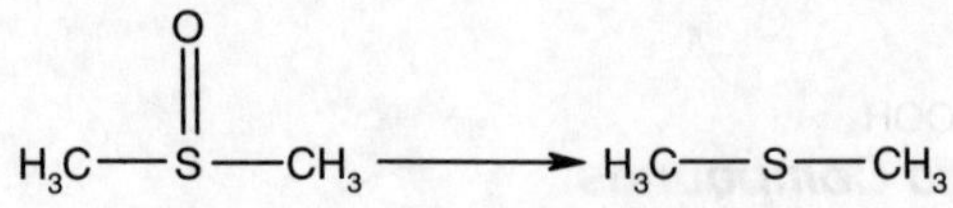

(78)

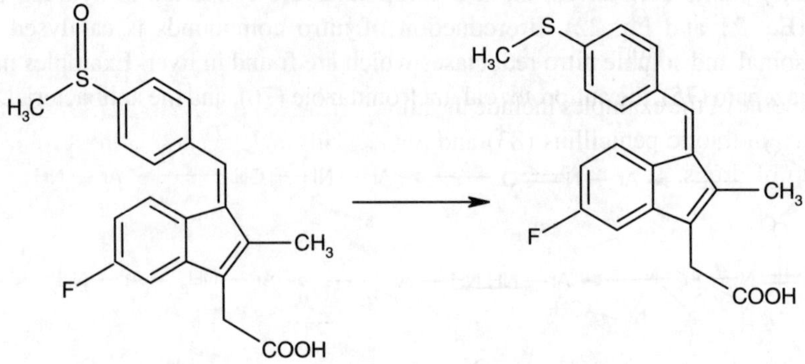

(79)

HYDROLYTIC REACTIONS

The substrates which undergo hydrolytic reactions include:

(a) esters, both inorganic as well as organic,
(b) amides and lactams, and
(c) halogenated substrates which undergo hydrolytic dehalogenations.

Hydrolysis of various substrates lead to more polar compounds which are more amenable to Phase II reactions. The enzymes responsible for hydrolysis of esters include non-specific esterases found in liver, kidney, and intestines. Amide hydrolysis is mediated through microsomal amidases.

Examples of Hydrolytic Reactions

Some of the examples among esters include the vasodilator pentaerythritoltetranitrate (80) – an inorganic ester. Among organic esters, the local anaesthetic cocaine (81) and analgesic, antipyretic anti-inflammatory aspirin (10) are some of the examples.

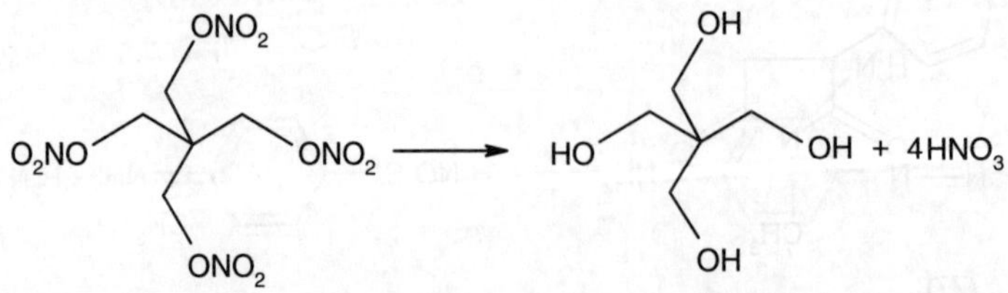

(80)

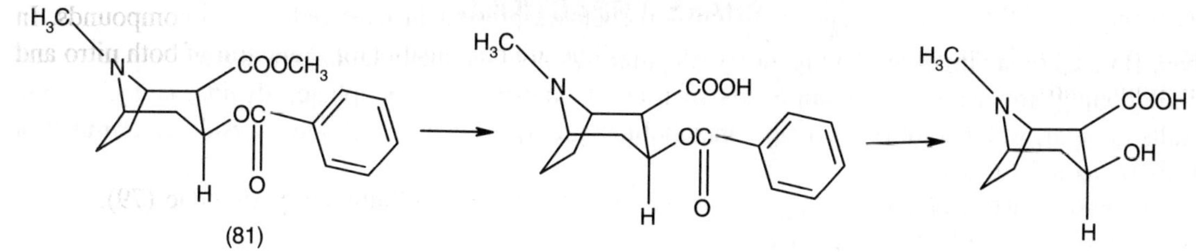

(81)

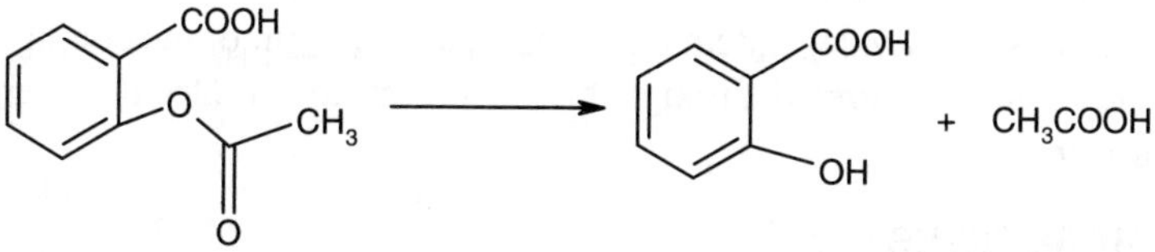

(10)

Among amides some of the examples include the antiarrhythmic procainamide (82) and local anesthetic lidocaine (20). The antibiotic penicillins (83) and anticonvulsant phensuximide (84) are the examples from lactam group of drugs.

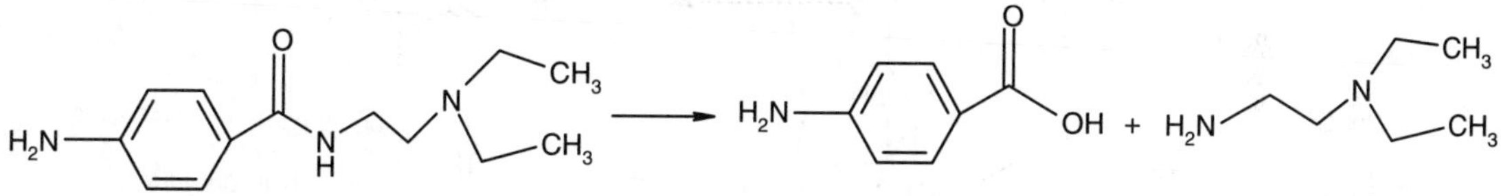

(82)

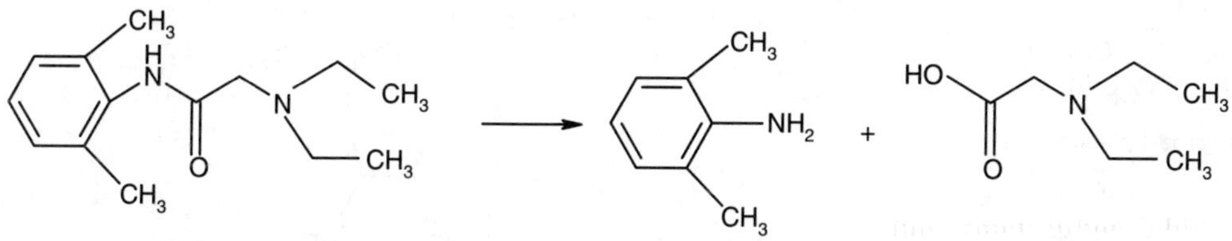

(20)

(83)

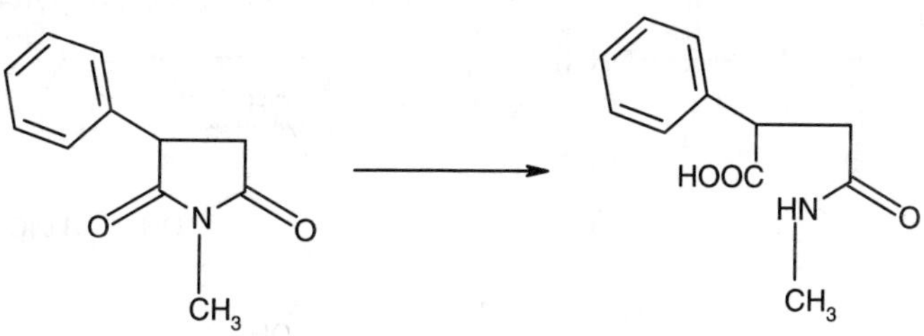

(84)

PHASE II REACTIONS

Phase II metabolism involves conjugation with polar compounds, methylation, and acetylation reactions. While conjugation with polar compounds such as glucouronic acid, sulphate, glycine, and glutamine results in polar, water soluble excretable metabolites, methylation and acetylation results in termination of pharmacological activity.

The characteristics of conjugating moieties are:

(a) they are large and highly polar,

(b) they are endogenous molecules.

The route of excretion is usually dependent on the molecular weight of the conjugate. High molecular weight conjugates are usually excreted through bile while as low molecular weight conjugates are excreted through in urine.

CONJUGATION REACTIONS

Glucouronic Acid Conjugation

This is the most common pathway for conjugation of alcohols, acids, amines, etc. This is because glucouronic acid is readily available and the enzymes required for transfer of glucouronic acid moiety

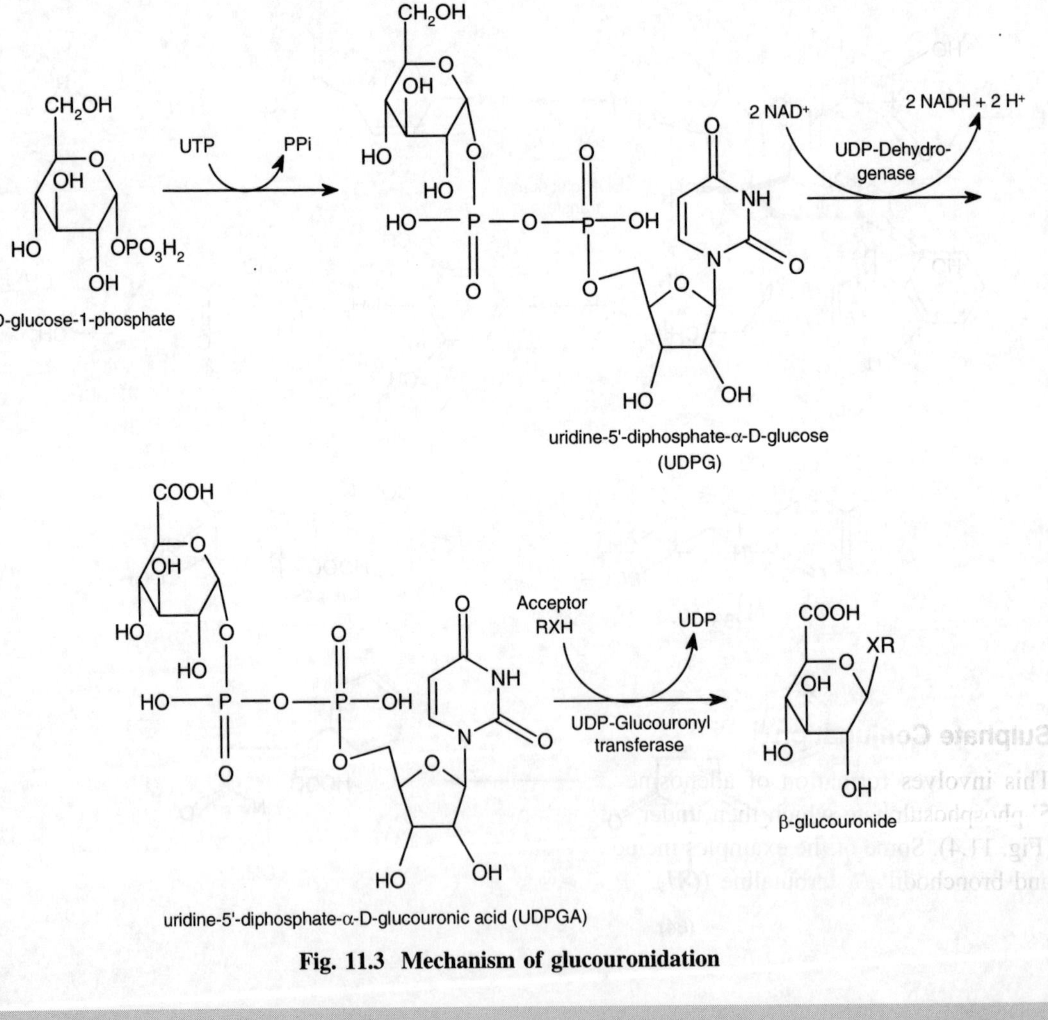

Fig. 11.3 Mechanism of glucouronidation

to phase I metabolites are available not only in liver but also in kidney, skin, intestines, lungs and in brain. The mechanism involved is given in Fig. 11.3. The glucouronide produced has β-configuration while as UDPGA has α-configuration. The inversion takes place during the enzymatic reaction involving nucleophilic displacement. Some of the examples include glucouronidation of antibacterial chloramphenicol (85) involving primary hydroxyl group, the narcotic analgesic morphine (18) involving phenolic hydroxyl group, and the antidepressant desipramine (7) involving secondary amino group.

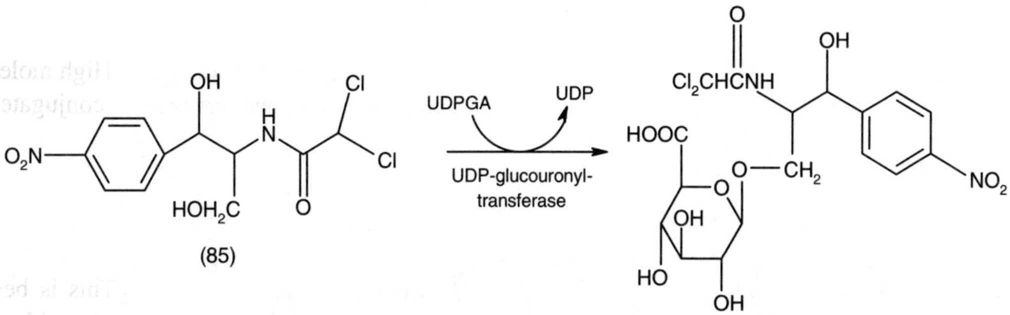

(85)

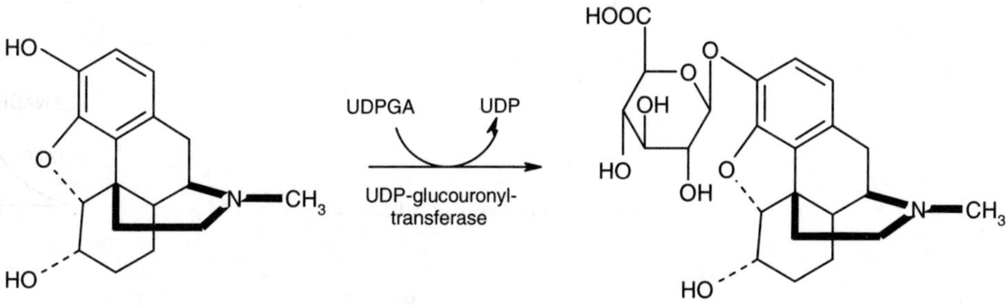

(18)

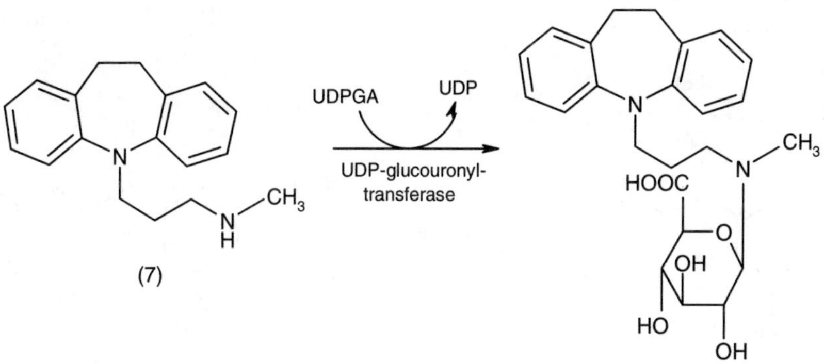

(7)

Sulphate Conjugation

This involves formation of adenosine- 5'-phosphosulphate and subsequently 3'-phosphoadenosine-5'-phosphosulphate which then under sulphotransferase transfers the sulphate moiety to the substrate (Fig. 11.4). Some of the examples include sulphate conjugation of antihypertensive α- methyldopa (86) and bronchodilator terbutaline ((87).

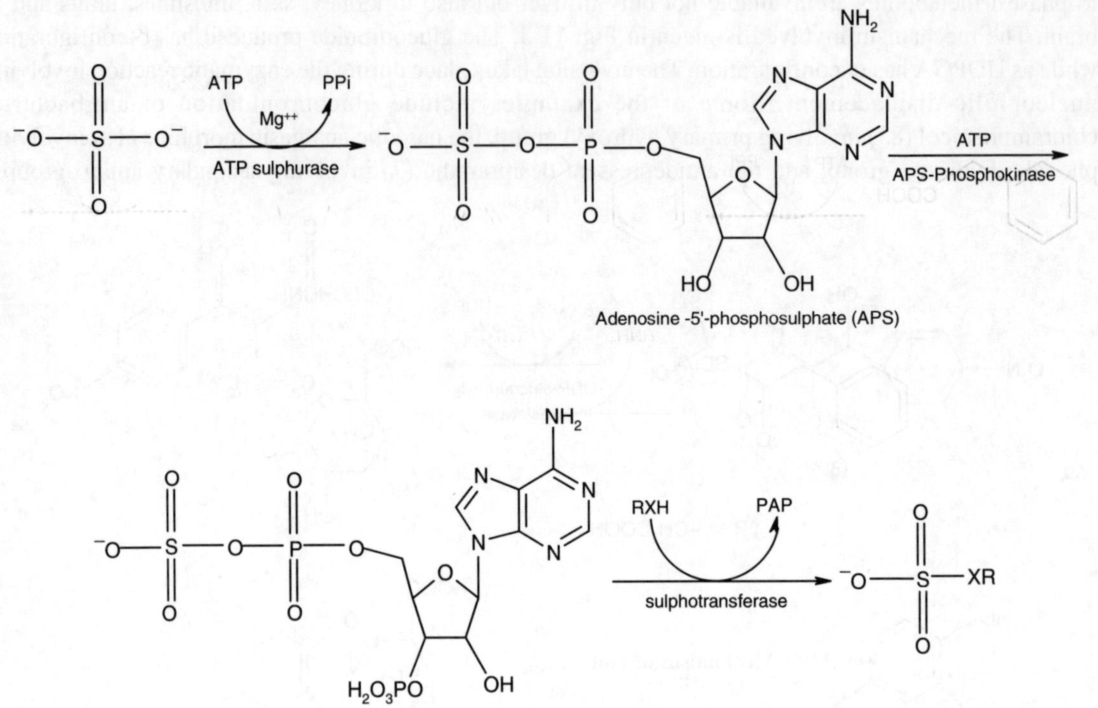

Fig. 11.4 Mechanism of sulphation

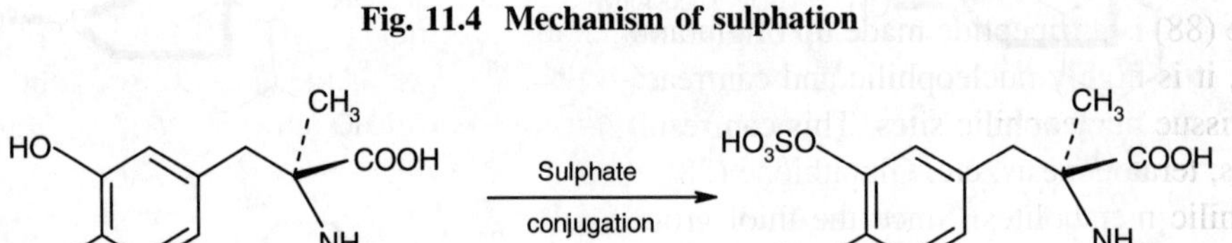

(86)

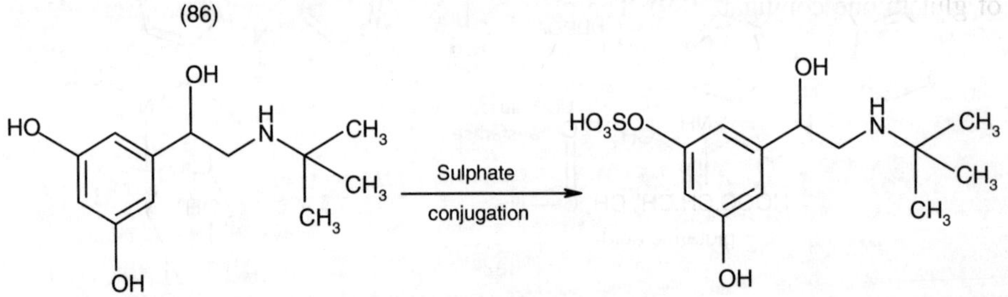

(87)

Conjugation with Glycine, Glutamine and other Amino Acids

Amino acid glycine and glutamine are used for conjugation of carboxylic acids, particularly aromatic and aralkyl acids. The conjugation involves activation of the substrate with ATP and Coenzyme A to form acyl CoA. This acyl CoA then acylates the amino group of the amino acid or glutamine.

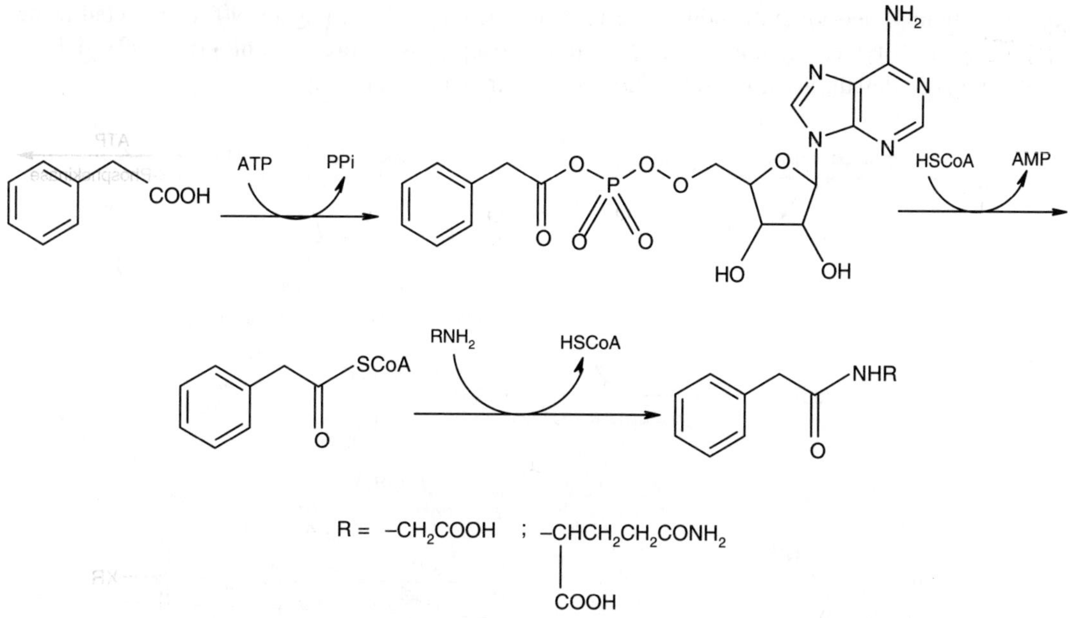

Fig. 11.5 Mechanism of conjugation with glycine and glutamine

Glutathione or Mercapturic Acid Conjugation

Glutathione (88) is a tripeptide made up of glutamic acid, cysteine, and glycine. Because of thiol group of cysteine, it is highly nucleophilic and can react with electrophilic metabolites which otherwise can react with tissue nucleophilic sites. This can result in tissue toxicity such as necrosis, carcinogenicity, mutagenesis, teratogenesis, etc. Glutathione (88), thus protects tissue nucleophilic sites from the attack of electrophilic metabolites. Since the thiol group of cysteine in glutathione (88) is highly reactive, glutathione (88) reacts directly with electrophiles without activation of glutathione (88) resulting in formation of glutathione conjugate (89). The glutathione conjugate (89) is not excreted as such. After

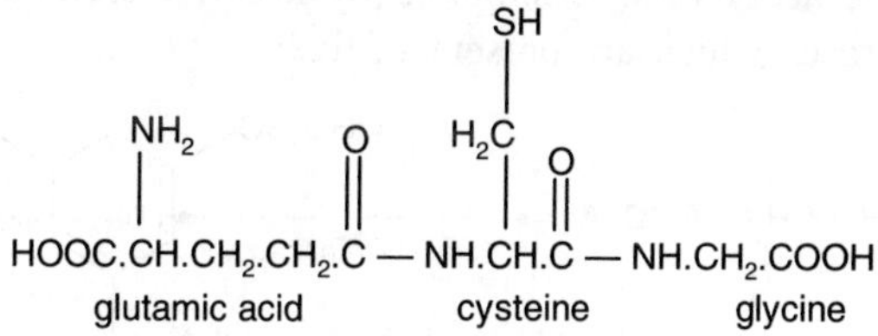

(88)

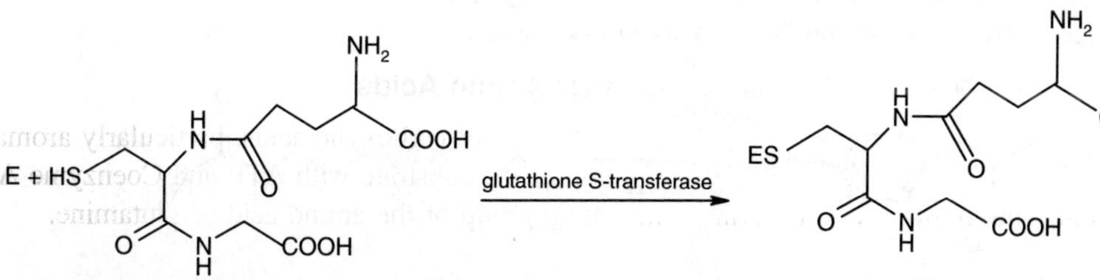

(88) (89)

removal of gltamyl and glycyl residues, the resulting mercapturic conjugate (90) is excreted as acetyl derivative (91). A typical example is that of immunosuppressive drug azathioprine (92) yielding 1-methyl-4-nitro-5-glutathionylimidazole (93) and 6-mercaptopurine (94).

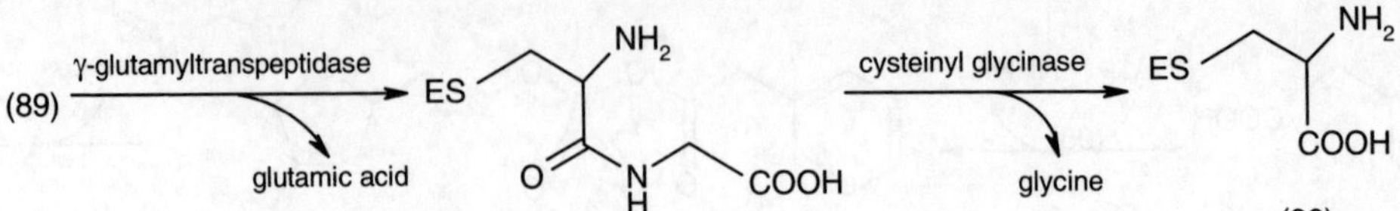

(90)

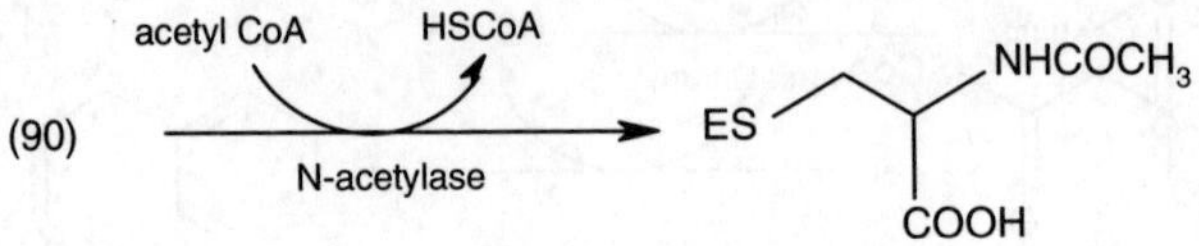

(91)

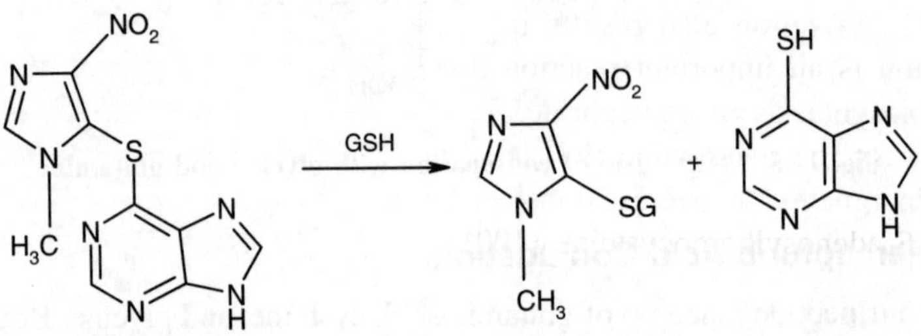

(92) (93) (94)

ACETYLATION REACTION

Acetylation reaction results in termination of a pharmacological activity. It does not result in increase in water solubility. The substrates for acetylation reactions are 1^0 amines, sulphonamides, hydrazides, etc. The acetyl group for the acetylation is supplied by acetyl CoA and transfer of acetyl group is achieved by N-acetyltransferases which are present in liver.

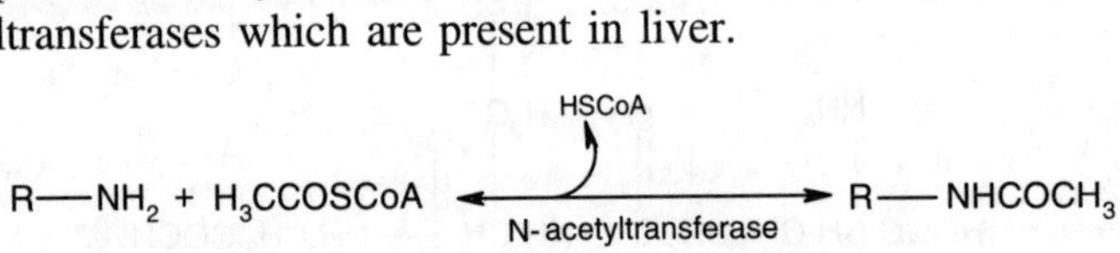

Fig. 11.6 Mechanism of acetylation

Examples include antiarrhythmic procainamide (82), antihypertensive hydralazine (95), and antibacterial sulphonamides (96) where N^1 and N^4 acetylation takes place.

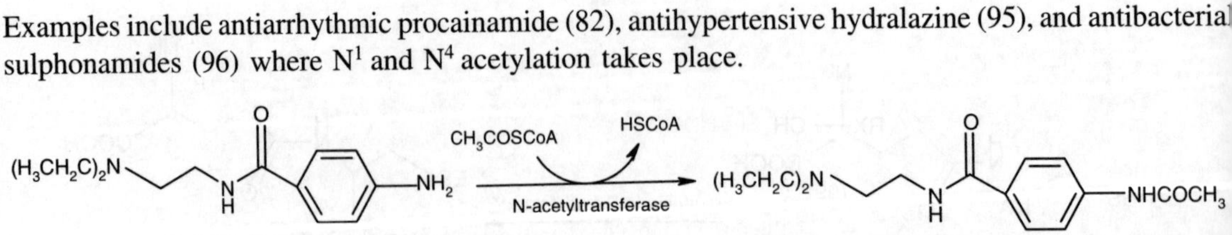

(82)

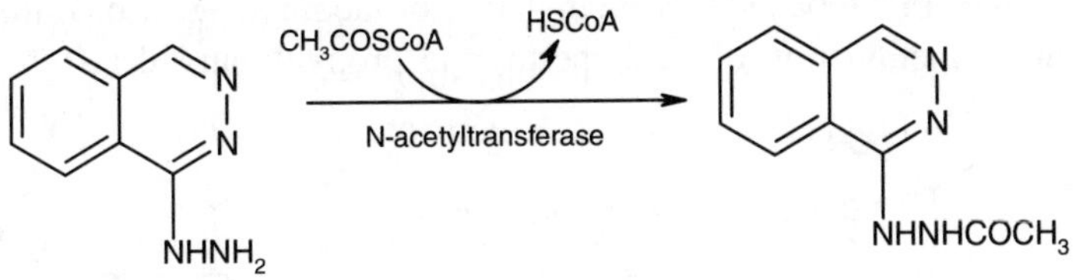

(95)

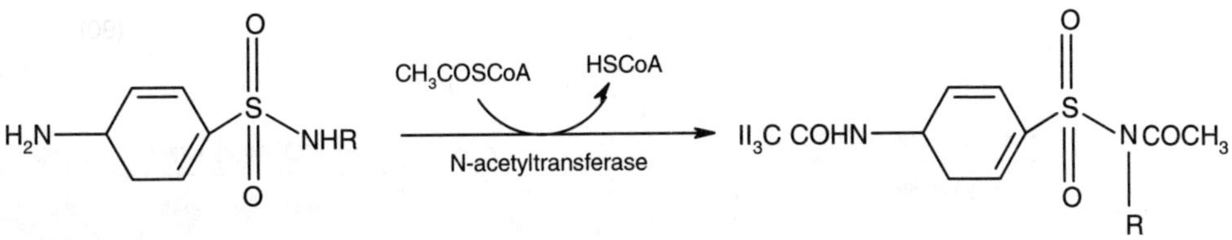

(96)

METHYLATION

Like acetylation, methylation also results in termination of pharmacological activity. However, methylation reaction is an important reaction involved in the biosynthesis of various endogenous compounds, e.g. biosynthesis of epinephrine. The methyl group of methionine (97) is used for the methylation purposes. The methionine (97) is activated through formation of S-adenosylmethionine (98) which then under methyl transferase transfers its methyl group to a substrate to yield the methylated product (99) and S-adenosylhomocysteine (100). Some of the examples include O-methylation of

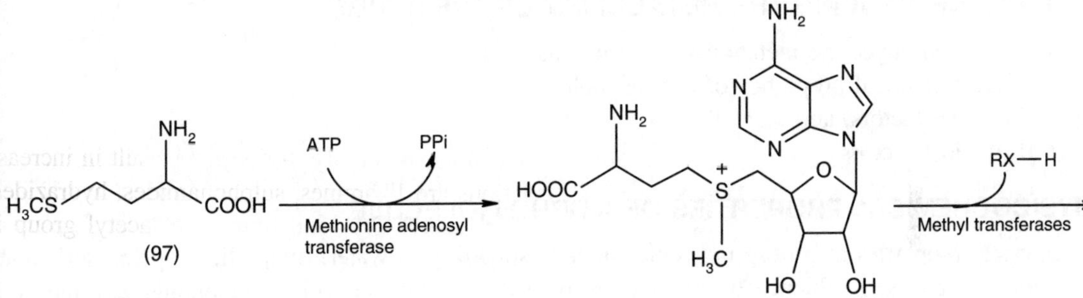

(97) (98)

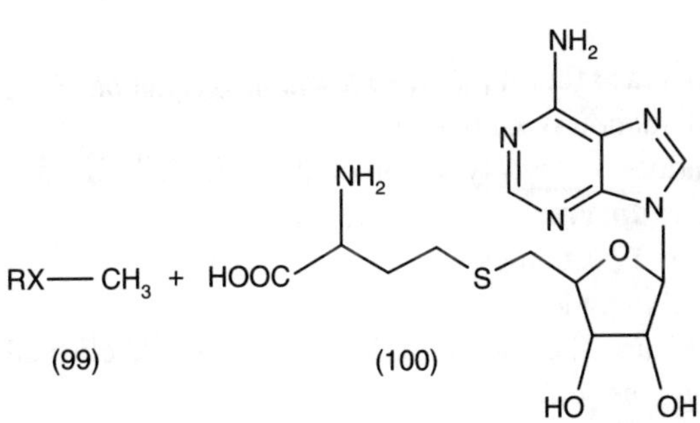

(99) (100)

antihypertensive, S(-)-α-methyldopa (86), N-methylation of nicotinic agent nicotine (101) and antiviral amantadine (102), and S-methylation of antihyperthyroid propylthiouracil (103).

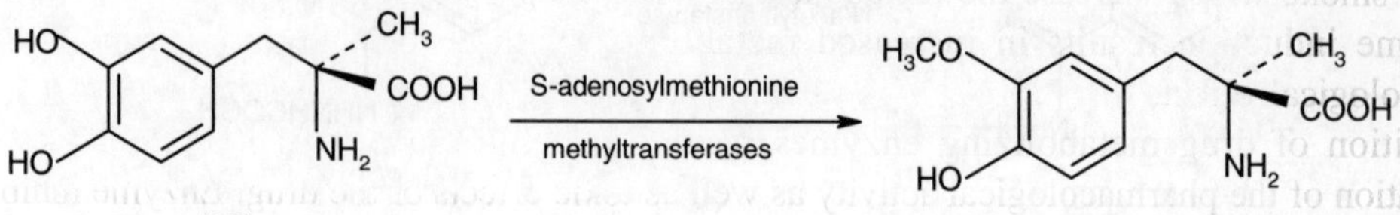

(86)

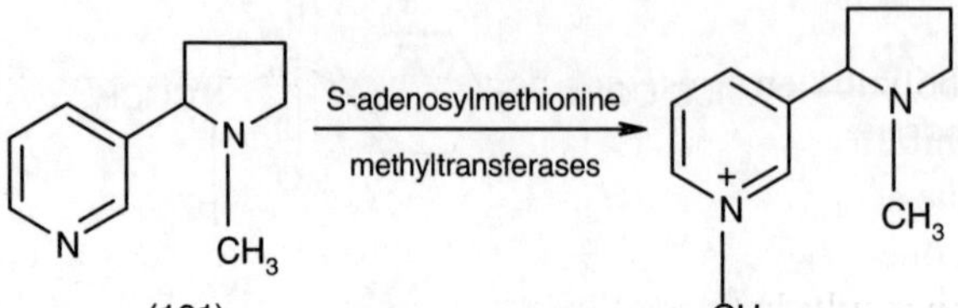

(101)

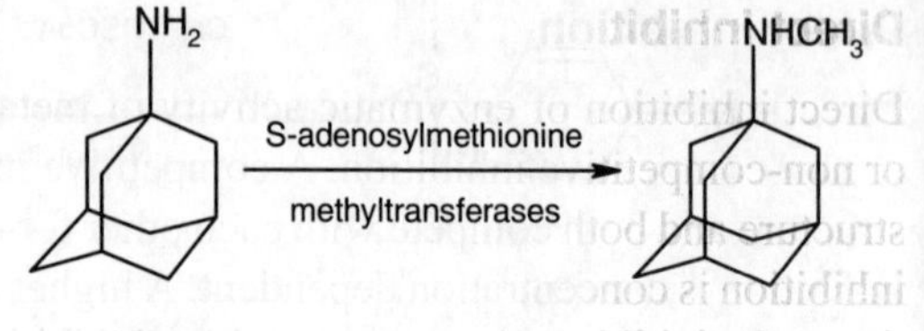

(102)

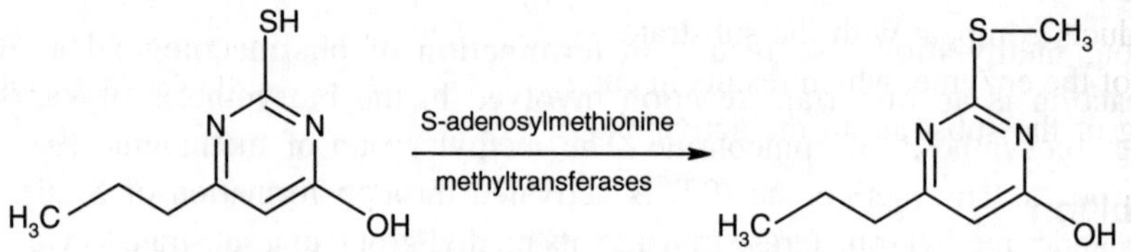

(103)

FACTORS INFLUENCING THE METABOLISM OF THE DRUGS

Factors which influence the metabolism of drugs include:

(a) Physicochemical properties of a drug molecule,
(b) Chemical factors, and
(c) Biological factors.

PHYSICOCHEMICAL PROPERTIES OF A DRUG MOLECULE

The physical properties of a drug molecule, such as solubility in water, lipophilicity, pKa, steric and electronic factors, etc, influence the interaction of a drug molecule with metabolizing enzyme and ultimately the metabolic processes

CHEMICAL FACTORS

Many chemicals or drugs increase the metabolizing capacity of some enzymes especially microsomal monooxygenases. This phenomenon is known as enzyme induction and such chemicals which increase the activity are known as inducers. Two types of inducers have been identified and include:

(a) **Phenobarbital type inducers:**

These include drugs and pesticides.

Some of the examples include:

Barbiturates : increase the metabolism of coumarins, cortisol, testosterone, oral contraceptives, etc.

Alcohol : phenobarbitone, phenytoin

Phenytoin : cortisol, oral contraceptives.

(b) **Polycyclic Hydrocarbon type Inducers:**

Examples in this category include 3-methylcholanthrene and polycyclic hydrocarbons found in cigarette smoke which increase the metabolism of some drugs

Enzyme induction results in increased metabolism of the drug and early termination of the pharmacological effect.

Inhibition of drug metabolizing enzymes results in inhibition of metabolism. This results in prolongation of the pharmacological activity as well as toxic effects of the drug. Enzyme inhibition has been found to be of two types i.e direct and indirect.

Direct inhibition

Direct inhibition of enzymatic activity of metabolizing enzymes can be achieved either by competitive or non-competitive inhibition. A competitive inhibition results when substrate and inhibitor have similar structure and both compete with each other for the active site on the metabolizing enzyme. A competitive inhibition is concentration dependent. A higher concentration of the substrate can overcome the inhibition due to the inhibitor. A non-competitive inhibition results between two structurally unrelated compounds. The interaction is not structure specific and is not reversible. Direct inhibition can also result when metabolic products compete with the substrate. A non-competitive inhibitor binds at a site other than the active site of the enzyme, which results in change in the conformation of the enzyme not favourable for the binding of the substrate to the active site of the enzyme.

Indirect inhibition

Indirect inhibition is brought about by two mechanisms.

(a) Indirect inhibition can happen due to decreased enzyme concentration, commonly known as Repression. One of the reasons for the decreased enzyme concentration is decreased synthesis of the enzyme. Examples of the drugs which decease the synthesis of enzyme include, ethionine and vitamin D.

Another reason for the decreased concentration of the enzyme is increased degradation of the enzyme. Examples of the drugs which increase the degradation of enzyme include carbon disulphide, carbon tetrachloride, etc.

(b) Altered physiology due to nutritional deficiency or hormonal imbalance also results in inhibition of enzyme synthesis.

BIOLOGICAL FACTORS

Biological factors which may result in differences in metabolism include species differences, differences in strain, sex differences, age, diet, etc.

Species differences may even result in differences in Phase I and Phase II reactions. For example, ephedrine is metabolized in humans through oxidative deamination while as in rats aromatic oxidation is the major route. Differences in Phase II metabolism may be due to presence or absence of conjugating enzymes. Example, phenol in pigs is conjugated by glucouronic acid while as in cats sulphate conjugation takes place.

Strain differences result because of genetic differences. Thus, 87% of Japanese and 95% of Eskimo are slow acylators while as among whites and blacks, there is equal percentage of slow and rapid acylators. A study of intersubject variability in drug response is known as Pharmacogenetics.

Sex related differences have been largely studied in rats. Male rats have greater metabolizing capacity than the female counterpart. Similarly in humans, it has been found that women metabolize benzodiazepines slowly than men. All these differences could be attributed due to such processes being regulated by sex hormones.

The differences due to age could be attributed to qualitative and quantitative differences in enzymes. Thus, in neonates of 2 months, microsomal enzyme system is not fully developed and many drugs are biotransformed very slowly. Children and older infants metabolize many drugs faster as compared to adults. This is because the rate of metabolism reaches maximum between 6 months and 12 years of age. This results in decreased pharmacological activity and requirement of large doses in comparision to adults.

Diet is another factor which affects the rate of metabolism. Low protein diet reduces drug metabolism while as protein rich diet increases the rate of drug metabolism. This could be attributed due to increased enzyme synthesis with rich protein diet. Similarly, dietary deficiencies in vitamin may result in decreased enzymatic activity and consequently reduced metabolism. Starvation results in decreased glucouronidation.

In addition to above, altered physiological factors such as diseased state, pregnancy, and hormonal imbalance also affect the metabolism of drugs. Examples in this category include decreased hepatic drug metabolizing enzyme during hepatic carcinoma, hepatitis, cirrhosis. Higher rate of anticonvulsant metabolism during pregnancy

Stress related changes in ACTH also influence drug biotransformation.

FURTHER READING

1. R.J. Williams, "Detoxification Mechanisms," 2nd ed., Wiley, New York, 1959.
2. B. Testa and P. Jenners, (Eds.), "Drug Metabolism: Chemical and Biochemical Aspects," Marcel Dekker, New York, 1976.
3. B. Testa and P. Jenners, (Eds.), "Concepts in Drug Metabolism," Marcel Dekker, New York, 1981.
4. J. Caldwell, *Drug Metabol. Rev.*, **13**, 745 (1982).
5. B. Testa and J. Caldwell, (Eds.), "Metabolism of Drugs and other Xenobiotics," Academic Press, London, 1995.
6. S.J. Cutler and J.H. Block in "Wilson and Gisvold's Textbook of Organic Medicinal and Pharmaceutical Chemistry," 11th ed., J.H. Block and J.M. Beale, Eds., Lippincot Williams and Wilkins, New York, 2004, p. 65.

12

Physicochemical Properties and Drug Action

For a drug molecule to show its effect, it is necessary that it reaches in sufficient concentration at the site of action and then binds to receptor/enzyme. In order to do this, the drug molecule has to pass various barriers so that it does not get stored at various sites and not get metabolically altered and reaches the site of its action in sufficient concentration. The various factors which affect the transport of the drug molecule from its site of absorption to its site of action include various physicochemical factors such as solubility, partition coefficient, diffusivity, degree of ionization, polymorphism, etc. Not only the physicochemical properties affect the availability of a drug molecule at its site of action but also the dosage form in which it is administered also has an effect on its availability.

Solubility

The term solubility usually refers to solubility in polar solvents such as water and non-polar solvents such as lipids. Accordingly, the terms hydrophilia or lipophobia refers to solubility in water and hydrophobia or lipophilia to solubility in lipids.

In a homologous series, the lower members which are more water soluble, have lower biological activity. As the length of carbon chain is increased, the lipid solubility increases along with the biological activity until it reaches a maximum. After this any increase in non-polar portion of the molecule results in lowering of the biological activity. The lower activity of lower members is due to their lower lipid solubility, a property required for absoption process. Any increase in lipid solubility results in increase in biological activity also. This increase in biological activity roughly parallels the increase in lipid solubility. However, as indicated above any further increase in lipid solubility results in fall in the biological activity. This decrease in biological activity is due to decrease in solubility in the extracellular fluid (which is polar in character) which serves as a medium of transport.

One of the parameters which reflects a relationship between the solubility in polar and non-polar solvents and biological activity is partition co-efficient between *n*-octanol/water. The *n*-octanol/water system mimics the lipid membrane/water system found in biological system. Water saturated *n*-octanol contains 2·3 M of water and approximates the polar properties of lipid layer whereas the aquous phase which does not contain n-octanol mimics the physiological aqueous compartment.

One of the classical examples illustrating the relationship of biological properties in homologous series is that of 4-*n*-alkylresorcinols (1) in which R differs. Comparision of phenol coefficients of various alkyl resorcinols against *B. typhosus* has shown that as the number of carbon atoms in R (1) is increased, the activity goes on increasing reaching a maximum when the number of carbon atoms is 6 (Fig. 12.1) After this the activity suddenly falls (Fig. 12.1).

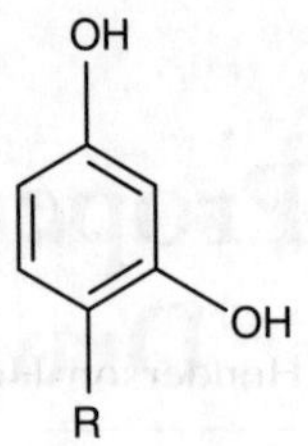

(1)

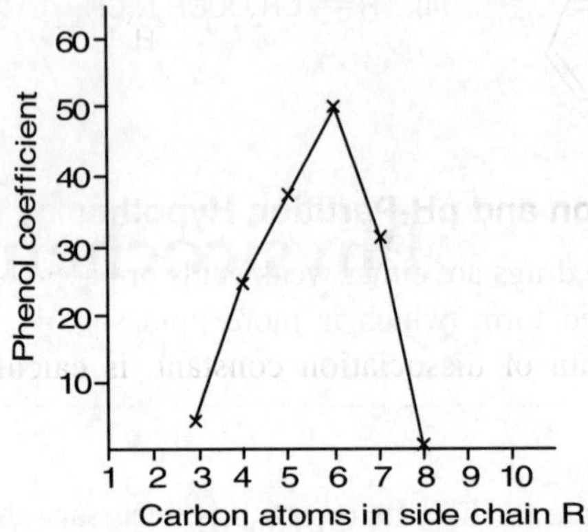

Fig. 12.1 Comparison of phenol co-efficient of various 4-*n*-alkylresorcinols (1)

A study of antibacterial activity of alcohols has shown that the antibacterial activity increases as the series is ascended from methyl to octyl. Branched chain alcohols, which are more water soluble than the primary alcohols, have lower lipid/water partition coefficient, are consequently less active as antibacterials. Thus, *n*-hexyl alcohol is twice as active as secondary hexyl alcohol as antibacterial. The higher molecular weight alcohols such as cetyl alcohol, (CH_3 $(CH_2)_{14}CH_2OH$), which has negligible water solubility, is inactive as antibacterial.

Drug Absorption

Most of the drugs are absorbed from gastrointestinal tract by passive diffusion of the unionized form across lipoidal membrane. The absorption of the drug is influenced by the dissociation constant of drug, the lipid solubility of the drug, and the pH of the medium at the absorption site. The various steps involved in the absorption of a drug from an oral dosage form say a tablet dosage form, include disintegration, dissolution and then absorption. Out of these steps, the slowest step determines the rate and extent of absorption. Frequently it is the dissolution step which is the slowest and consequently the rate determining step. Since dissolution precedes absorption, the rate of absorption of a drug is influenced by its dissolution in the medium at the absorption site. The factors that affect dissolution of a drug include its solubility, particle size, surface area, etc.

In addition to dissolution, the absorption of a drug is also affected by formation of complexes in the gastrointestinal tract which results in reduced concentration of the drug at the absorption site.

One of the examples of chemical modification of a drug to improve its absorption is phenytoin (2). It is an anticonvulsant with poor aqueous solubility. As a result it shows erratic and poor absorption on oral administration. In order to improve its solubility, esters (4-6) of 3-hydroxymethyl analog (3) have been synthesized and found to have better absorption.

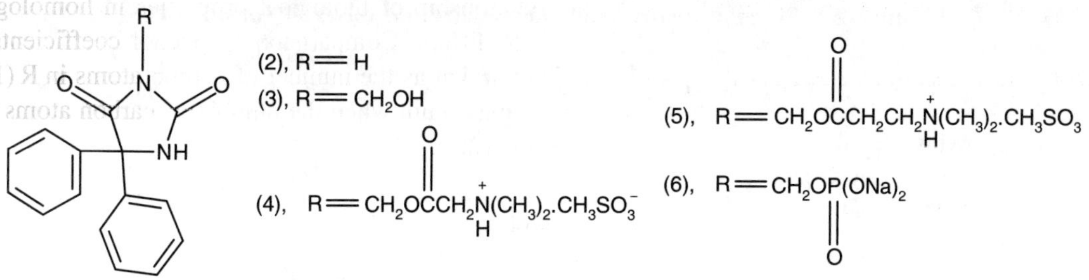

Drug Absorption and pH-Partition Hypothesis

Since most of the drugs are either weak acids or bases, their absorption from gastrointestinal tract takes place in unionized form, which is more lipid soluble species. The degree of dissociation, pKa, the negative logarithm of dissociation constant, is calculated from Henderson-Hasselbach equations (Eq. 1 and 2).

In case of acids:

$$RCOOH \longrightarrow RCOO^- + H^+$$

$$pKa = pH - \log\frac{[\text{ionized acid}]}{[\text{unionized acid}]}$$

$$= pH - \log\frac{[RCOO^-]}{[RCOOH]} \qquad \text{(Eq. 1)}$$

In case of bases:

$$RNH_3^+ \longrightarrow RNH_2 + H^+$$

$$pKa = pH - \log\frac{[\text{unionized form}]}{[\text{ionized form}]}$$

$$= pH - \log\frac{[RNH_2]}{[RNH_3^+]} \qquad \text{(Eq. 2)}$$

The antibacterial activity of benzoic, salicylic, and mandelic acids is greatest in acid media. This is because they remain largely unionzed in acid media and are thus absorbed well. After reaching the site of action they get ionized and show their antibacterial activity. A comparision of intestinal absorption of acids and bases in rat at several pH values (Table 12.1) shows that weak acids are best absorbed at low pH and weak bases at higher pH.

Minor changes in structures of closely related compounds can lead to significant changes in ionization and consequently lead to differences in biological activity. For example, barbituric acid (7) and its 5-monosubstituted (8) derivatives are inactive, while as 5, 5-disubstituted derivatives (9) are CNS depressants. This lack of CNS depressant activity of barbituric acid (pKa 4.0) and its 5-monosubstituted (8) derivatives (5-ethyl, pKa 4.4) is because they are stronger acids. They are able to achieve completely aromatic structure (7a and 8a) which can stabilize the barbiturate ion (7b and 8b) by delocalization of the extra pair of electrons. It has been found that at physiological pH barbituric acid (7) and its

Table 12.1 Percent absorbed of some acids and bases at various pH

	pKa	Percent absorbed pH 4	pH 5	pH 8
Acids				
1. 5-Nitrosalicylic acid	2.3	40	27	0
2. Salicylic acid	3.0	64	35	10
3. Benzoic acid	4.2	62	36	5
Bases				
1. Aniline	4.6	40	48	61
2. Aminopyrine	5.0	21	35	52
3. *o*-Toluidine	5.3	30	42	62
4. Quinine	8.4	9	11	54

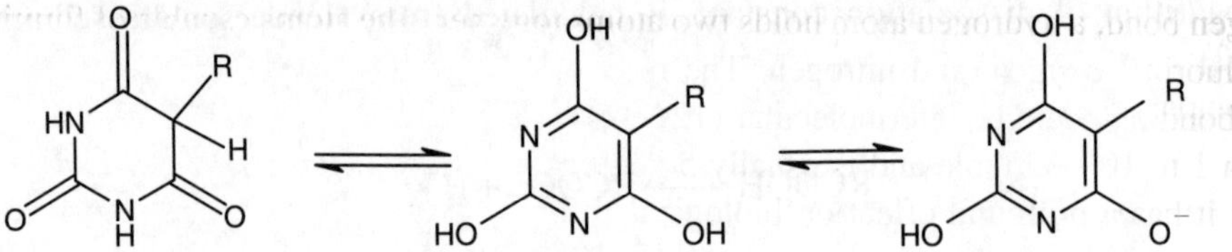

(7), R = H
(8), R = alkyl or aryl

(7a), R = H
(8a), R = alkyl or aryl

(7b), R = H
(8b), R = alkyl or aryl

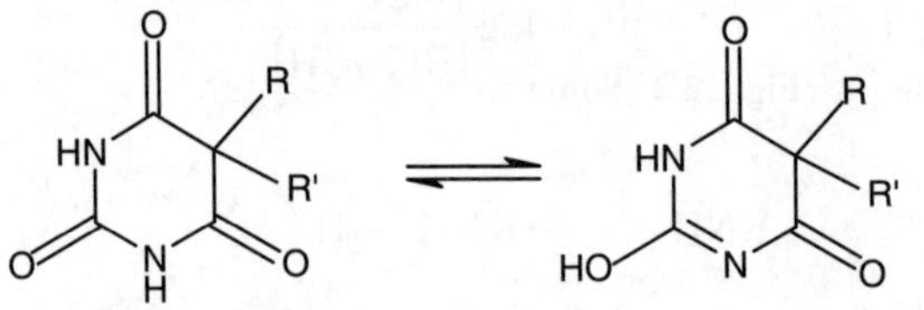

(9), R = R' = alkyl or aryl

5-monosubstituted (8) derivatives are 99.9 % in ionic form and therefore are not able to cross the blood brain barrier. In contrast, 5, 5-disubstituted barbiturates (9) cannot assume a fully aromatic structure and therefore are much weaker acids (pKa 7.0-8.5). Thus they remain largely in unionized form at physiological pH and are capable of ready passage into the lipoidal tissues of CNS.

Surface Area and Particle Size

Increase in surface area through reduction in particle size results in rapid dissolution. Higher dissolution of many poorly soluble drugs has been achieved through micronization. Thus, the absorption of spironolactone (10), a diuretic, has been increased through micronization. This has resulted in reduction of dose from 500 mg to 25 mg. Similar results have been achieved in griseofulvin (11).

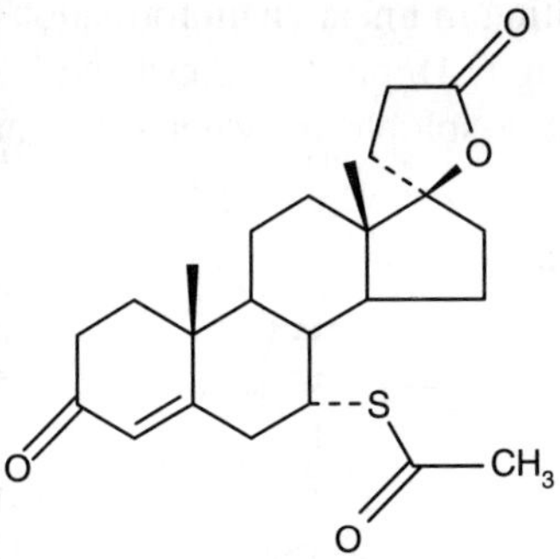

(10)

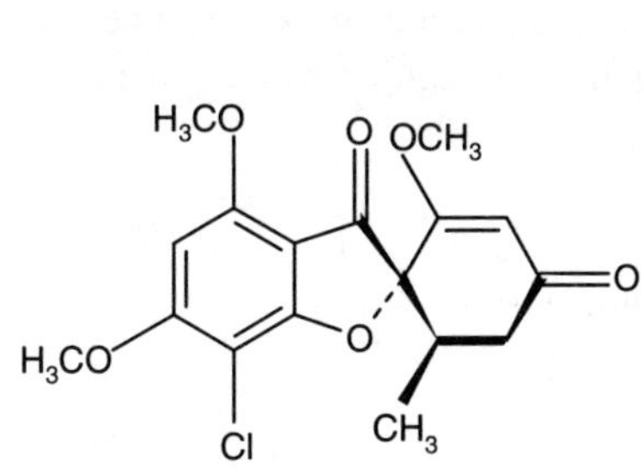

(11)

Hydrogen Bonding and Biological Activity

In a hydrogen bond, a hydrogen atom holds two atoms together. The atoms capable of forming hydrogen bond are fluorine, oxygen, and nitrogen. The most common hydrogen bonds are given in Fig. 12.2. Hydrogen bonding could be intermolecular (12) or intramolecular (13). The strength of hydrogen bond varies from 1 to 10 kcal/mole and is usually 5 kcal/mole. It is, thus, a weak bond. Even though it is a weak bond it has a profound effect on biological activity as is evident from the following examples.

O—H---O; O—H---N;

N—H---N; N—H---O;

N—H---F; F—H---F;

Fig. 12.2 Some common hydrogen bonds

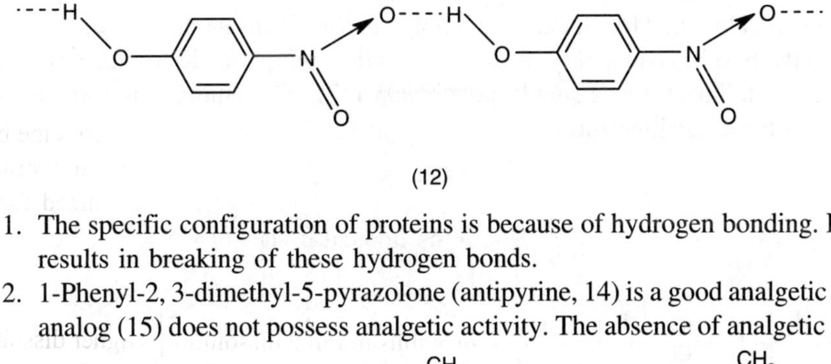

(12)

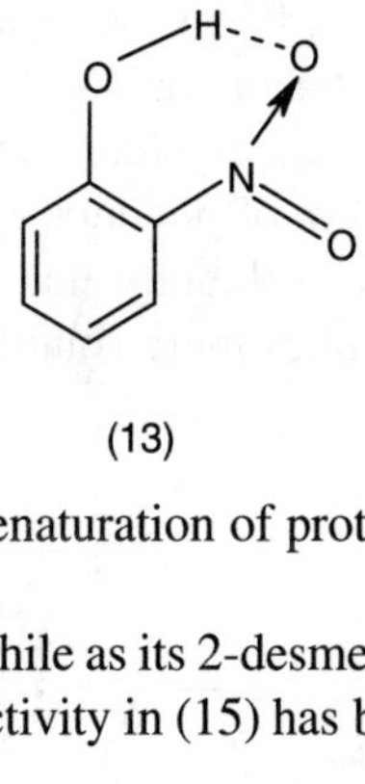

(13)

1. The specific configuration of proteins is because of hydrogen bonding. Denaturation of proteins results in breaking of these hydrogen bonds.
2. 1-Phenyl-2, 3-dimethyl-5-pyrazolone (antipyrine, 14) is a good analgetic while as its 2-desmethyl analog (15) does not possess analgetic activity. The absence of analgetic activity in (15) has been

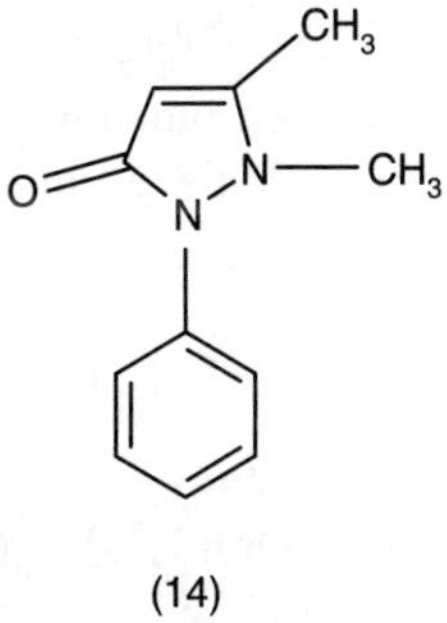

(14)

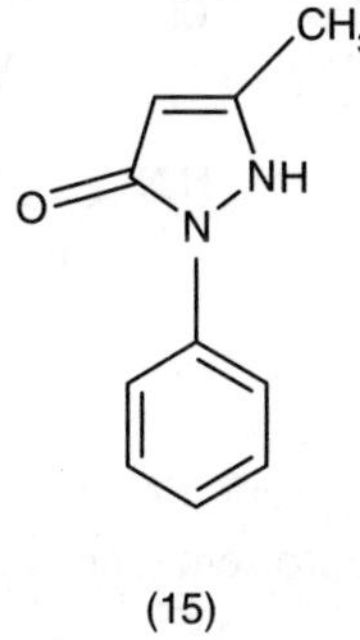

(15)

attributed to intermolecular hydrogen bonding resulting in linear chain formation (Fig. 12.3). As a result it is insoluble in water. The dimethyl analog (14), on the other hand is not capable of forming intermolecular hydrogen bonds and is more soluble in water (1:1) and an effective analgesic.

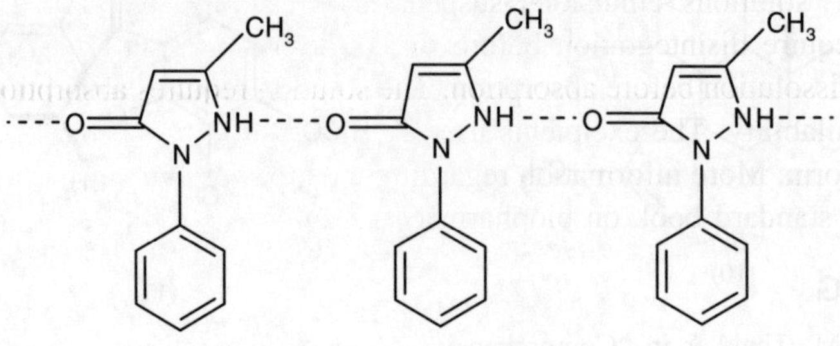

Fig. 12.3 Hydrogen bonding in case of 1-phenyl-3-methyl-5-pyrazolone

Polymorphism

A solid can exist either as amorphous powder or in crystalline form. The ability of a substance to exist in more than one crystalline form with different internal structures is known as polymorphism. Polymorphs are similar in liquid and gaseous state. The polymorphs differ in their physical properties such as solubility, melting point, density, hardness, and compression characteristics. Different polymorphs of a substance are having differing stabilities. The more stable polymorph is in lowest energy state, has highest melting point, and possesses lowest aqueous solubility. The other polymorphs are known as metastable forms. They are in higher energy state, have low melting points and possess higher water solubility. The metastable forms are, thus, preferred forms of polymorphs for the preparation of various dosage forms. Metastable forms readily go to lowest energy state, the stable form. However, when kept dry, they remain stable for long periods. One of the typical example of existence of polymorphic form is in case of chloramphenicol palmitate (16). It exists in 3 polymorphic forms namely A, B, and C. The B-form of polymorph has the best bioavailability. In some cases the amorphous form may have higher water solubility than the crystalline form, example novobiocin (17). The amorphous form is about 10-times more soluble than the crystalline form.

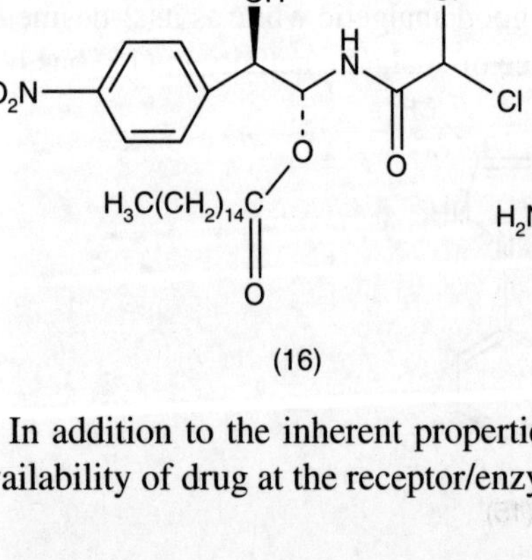

(16)

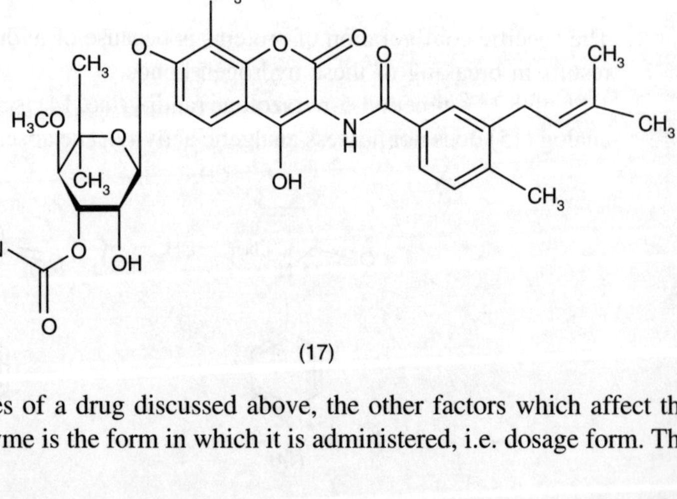

(17)

In addition to the inherent properties of a drug discussed above, the other factors which affect the availability of drug at the receptor/enzyme is the form in which it is administered, i.e. dosage form. The most common routes through which drugs are administered include, oral and parenteral. The other routes include, topical, buccal, sublingual, etc.

The various dosage forms in which the drugs are administered orally include, tablets, capsules, suspentions, emulsions, powders, solutions, etc. The relative bioavailability of these dosage forms decreases in the order: solutions>emulsions>suspentions>capsules>tablets.

While as tablets require disintegration before dissolution and absorption, capsules, powders and emulsions need only dissolution before absorption. The solution requires absorption step only, thus, the above order of bioavailability. The excipients used in formulation also affect the bioavailability of a drug from its dosage form. More information regarding the bioavailability of various dosage forms can be obtained from any standard book on biopharmaceutics.

FURTHER READING

1. S.H. Curry and K.M. Thakker in "Comprehensive Medicinal Chemistry – Biopharmaceutucs," Vol. 5, C. Hansch, Ed. in-Chief, Pergamon Press, Oxford, 2005, p. 545.
2. Han van de Waterbeemd in "Modern Methods of Drug Discovery," A. Hillisch and R. Hilgenfeld, Eds., Birkhauser Verlag, Switzerland, 2003, p. 243.
3. D.M. Brahmanker and S.B. Jaiswal, "Biopharmaceutics and Pharmacokinetics – A Treatise," Vallabh Prakashan, New Delhi, 1995.

13

Stereochemistry and Pharmacological Activity

Stereoisomers have identical constitution but differ in their configuration or arrangement of their atoms or groups and include enantiomers and geometrical isomers. Conformational isomers on the other hand result because of rotation around carbon-carbon single bond.

ENANTIOMERISM AND PHARMACOLOGICAL ACTIVITY

Instances of differences in biological activity of stereoisomers have been known since early times. Thus, Piutti reported the sweet taste of dextrorotatory asparagine (1) while as levorotatory isomer was tasteless. Similarly, out of four isomers of N-aspartylphenylalanine methyl ester, the L, L-isomer (2) is

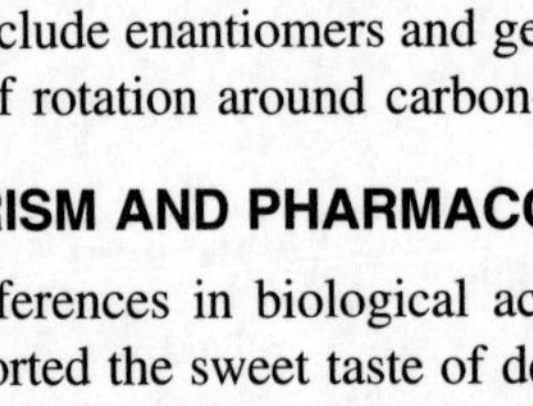

(1)

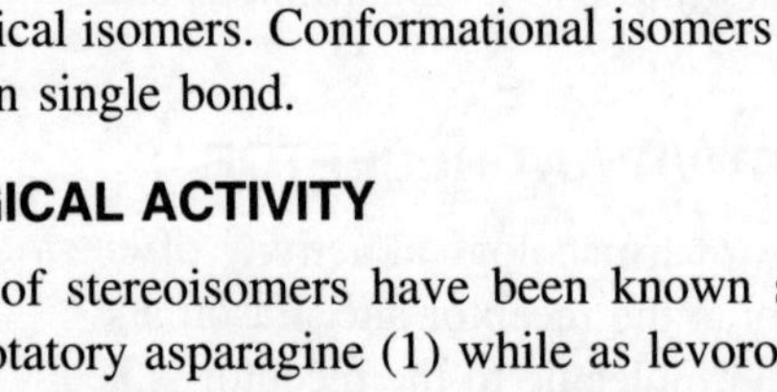

(2)

sweet and is marketed as sweetening agent, while the L, D-isomer is bitter. Examples of olefactory discrimination include limonene (3), the (R) (+)-isomer of which has an odour of orange and its enantiomer, (S) (-) smells like that of lemon.

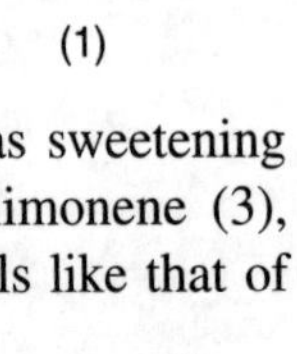

(3)

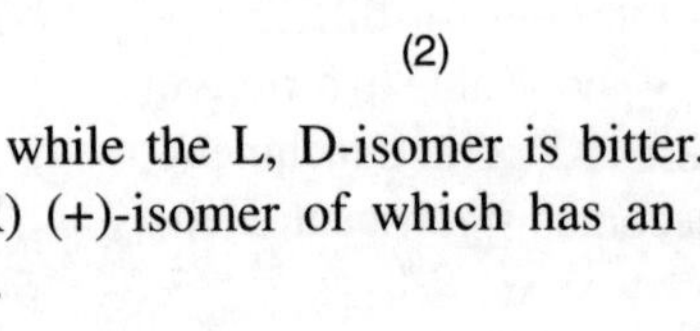

(4)

Variation in pharmacological activities have also been observed among the enantiomeric pairs. These variations could be due to differences in affinity towards receptors, stereoselectivity in pharmacokinetic parameters and stereoselectivity in metabolism. Differences in pharmacological activities among the enantiomers were not taken seriously till the thalidomide tragedy. Racemic thalidomide (4) was introduced in 1961 as a sedative and antinausea agent especially for women during early pregnancy. Unfortunately, it was observed that women using thalidomide (4) gave birth to children with limb deformities. Later investigations revealed that the (S)(-)-enantiomer was responsible for this. This tragedy could have been avoided, had the enantiomers been separated and tested separately. Following this, US Food and Drugs Act was revised. The revised Act in addition to other requirements, requires submission of information about the enantiomers of chiral substances in the new drug application. Some of the advantages of chiral drugs include:

1. they fit properly at the receptor site,
2. their use results in lowering of the dose as a result have lower toxicity,
3. there is better regulatory acceptance.

However, they are costlier to produce.

According to Ariens, the more active enantiomer of the pair is termed as *eutomer* and the corresponding less active or inactive enantiomer, a *distomer*. Ratio of more potent isomer to less potent isomer is termed as *eudismic ratio* and its logarithm as *eudismic index*. Depending on activity, a *distomer* could be *eutomer* and vice versa.

STEREOSELECTIVITY AT RECEPTOR

The differences in pharmacological activity of enantiomers could be due to differences in the binding of the enantiomers at the receptor site. Eason and Stedman postulated that for a *eutomer* a three point binding of the drug molecule to the receptor is necessary. Thus, the eutomer, CabcH has high affinity for the receptor. The atoms or groups a, b, c of drug molecule are complementary to atoms or groups a′, b′, and c′ of the receptor (Fig. 13.1). The three-point attachment hypothesis is supported by the fact that (*R*)-epinephrine (5) has higher activity than (*S*)-isomer (6) and deoxy analog, N-methyldopamine (7). The higher activity of (*R*)-epinephrine (5) is because it fits better on the receptor (Fig. 13.2). In case of (*S*)-isomer (6), the β-hydroxyl is not properly oriented (Fig. 13.3) and in case of N-methyldopamine (7), there is no hydroxyl group for interaction with the receptor (Fig. 13.4).

An ideal binding site required for differentiating the enantiomers is a 3-point site. Receptors with only two binding sites may not be able to differentiate the two enantiomers. However, affinity differences could also arise when there is 2-point attachment of a chiral drug molecule to the receptor. In such cases the role of third group becomes significant. Depending upon the orientation of the third group, it could

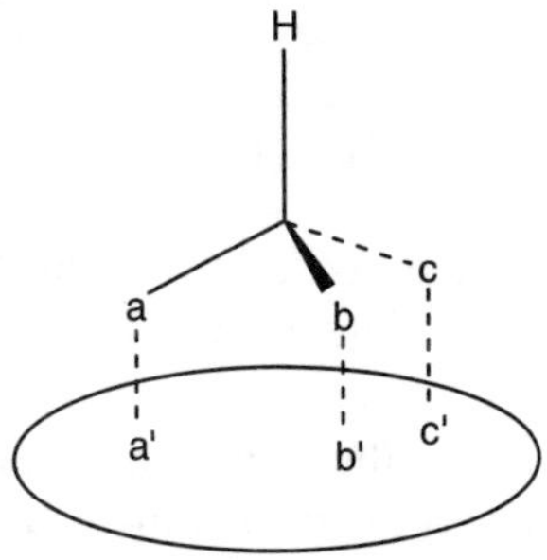

Fig. 13.1

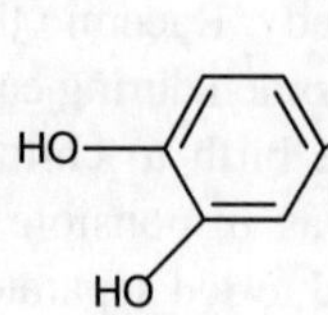

(5)

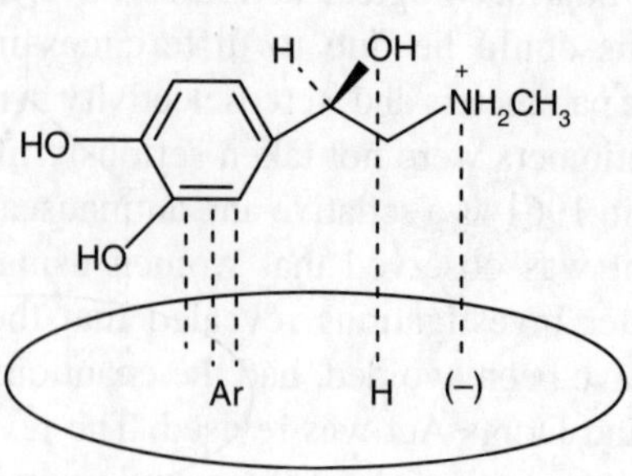

Fig. 13.2

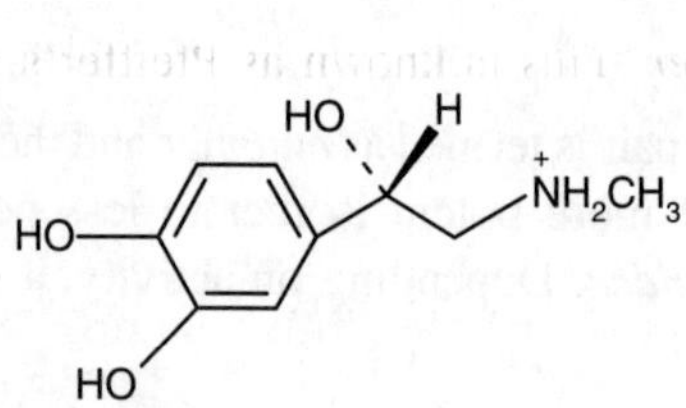

(6)

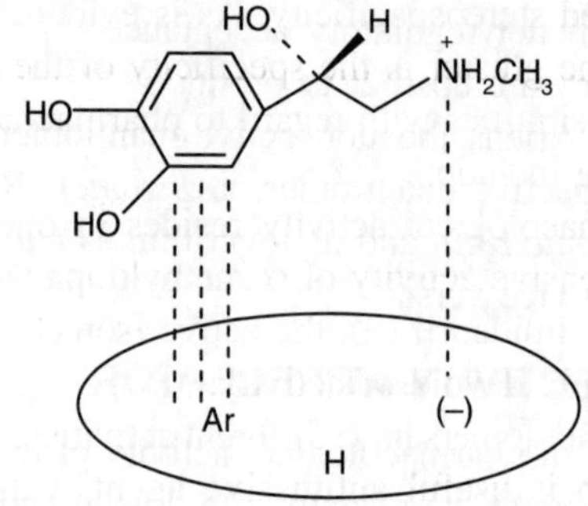

Fig. 13.3

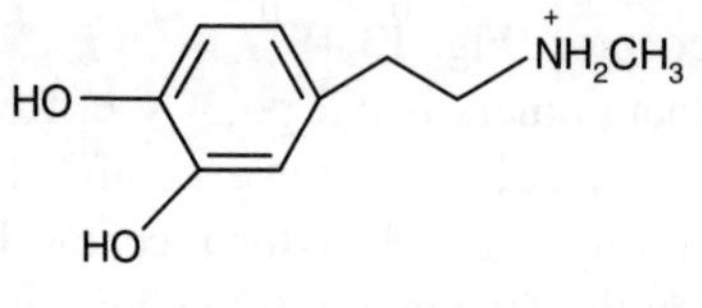

(7)

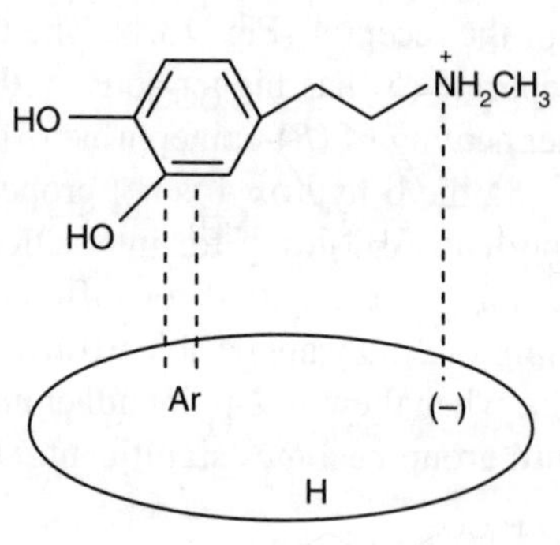

Fig. 13.4

either facilitate or hinder the proper alignment of the two groups of the drug molecule to the receptor. Two-point attachment is similar to that of 2-point attachment of achiral molecules to the receptor (Fig. 13.5).

A comparison of activity of *eutomer* with the activity of racemic mixture can be informative. Thus, if out of the two enantiomers, (*R*)–isomer is active and the activity ratio (*R/RS*) is close to 2, then the (*S*)-enantiomer is acting as a diluent. A ratio of more than 2 indicates that (*S*)-enatiomer is acting as a competitive antagonist of the (*R*)-isomer. If the activity ratio (*R/RS*) is less than 2, the (*S*)-isomer is

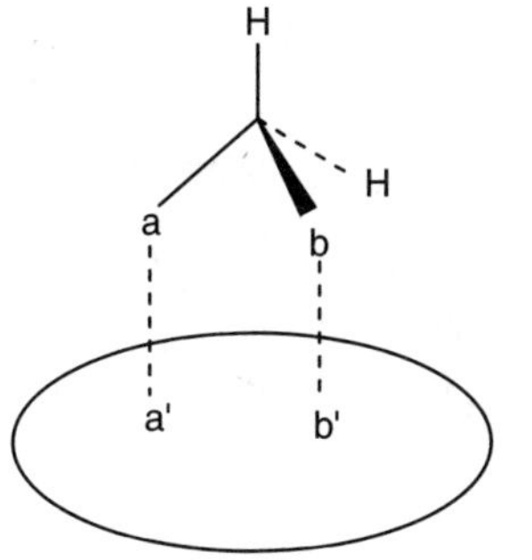

Fig. 13.5

ctive in its own right or it potentiates the activity of (*R*)-isomer. Thus, a fall of activity ratio below 2 ndicates decreased stereospecificity. As is evident, greater the difference in pharmacological activity f enantiomers, the greater is the specificity of the *eutomer*. This is known as Pfeiffer's rule.

Number of possibilities with regard to pharmacological behavior of pair of enantiomers can be there nd some of these include:

1. The pharmacological activity resides in one enantiomer and the other is inactive. Examples, antihypertensive activity of α-methyldopa (8) resides entirely in (*S*)-isomer and the (*R*)-isomer is inactive. Imidapril (9), the active isomer is (1*S*, 2*S*, 4*S*) -isomer, while (1*R*, 2*R*, 4*R*) -isomer is completely devoid of activity.
2. The two enantiomers have different activities. Examples in this category include dextromethorphan (10) which is useful antitussive agent while as its enantiomer possesses analgesic activity. Similarly, dextropropoxyphene (11) is an analgesic while as its enantiomer is antitussive.

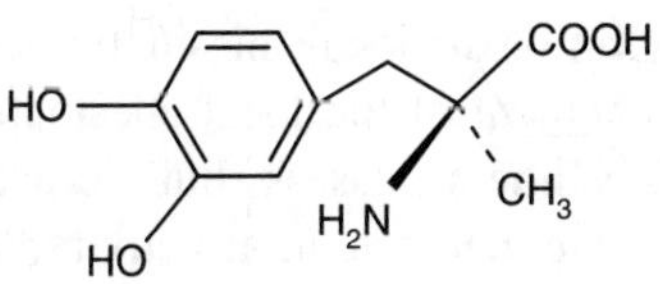

(8)

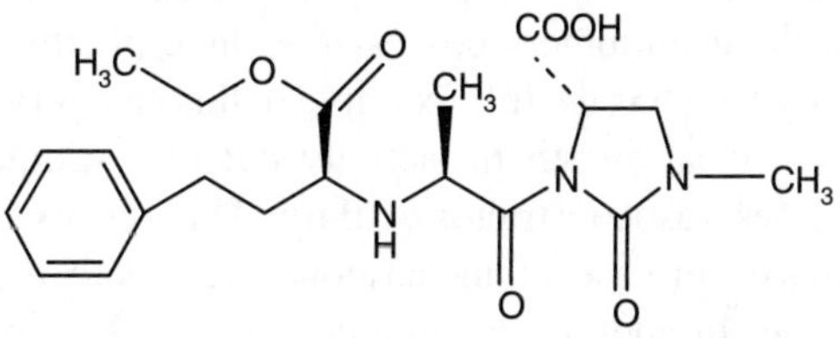

(9)

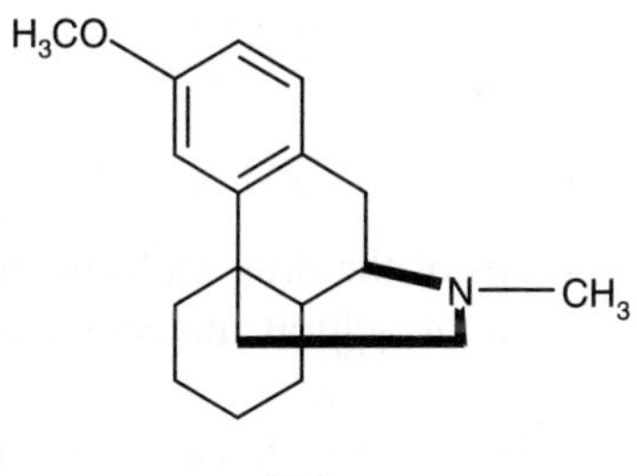

(10)

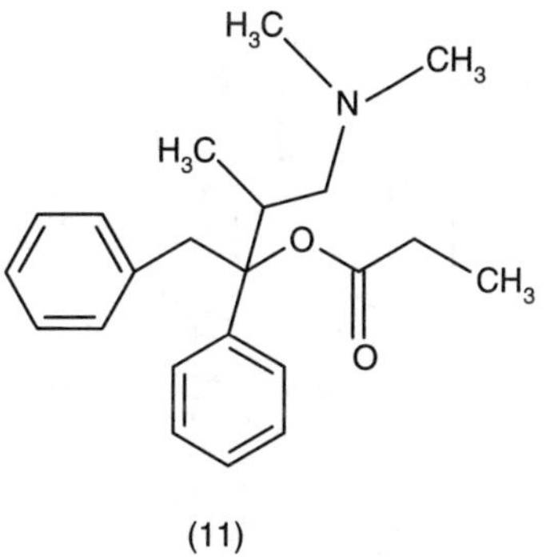

(11)

3. The pair of enantiomers have opposite action at the same receptor. Example in this category include picenadol. The (+)-3*S*, 4*R*-isomer (12) is a partial μ-receptor agonist while as its enantiomer (-)-3*R*, 4*S*-isomer is antagonist at the same site.

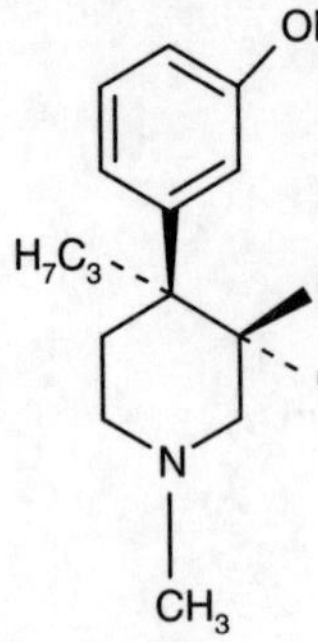

(12)

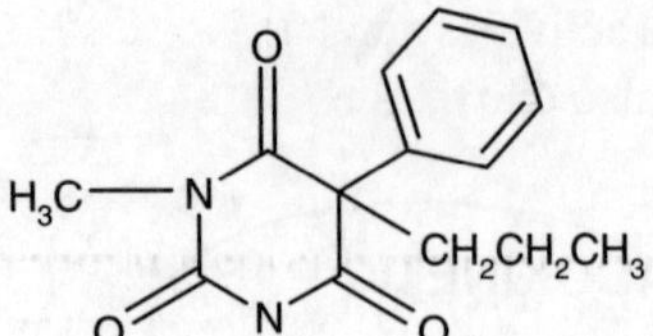

(13)

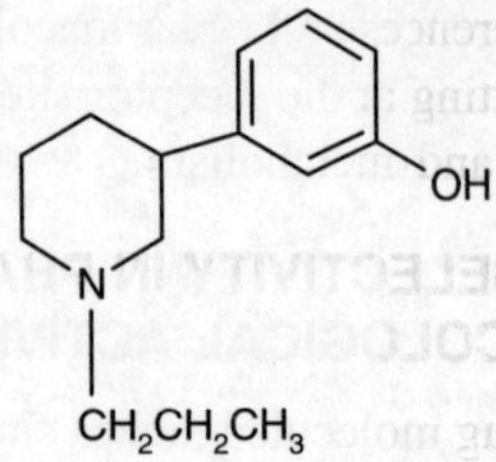

(14)

4. The enantiomers have antagonistic actions. Thus, *R*-isomer of 1-methyl-5-phenyl-5- *n*-propy barbituric acid (13) is sedative, hypnotic, narcotic (depending on dose) while as its enantiome *S*-isomer is convulsant.
5. The enantiomers may enhance the activity of one another. Example in this category is that o 3-(3-hydroxyphenyl)-N-*n*-propylpiperidine (14). The *R*-enatiomer is an agonist at both presynaptic and postsynaptic dopaminergic receptors. Its antipode, *S*-enantiomer is an agonist at presynaptic dopaminergic receptors and a blocker at postsynaptic dopaminergic receptor. Thus, when this compound is given in racemic form, the net result is increased stimulation at presynaptic dopaminergic receptors.
6. One of the enantiomer is having useful pharmacological activity and the other possesses unwantec effects. Example in this category is thalidomide (4), the *R*-isomer of which has useful sedative antinausea activity while as its enantiomer is teratogenic.
7. Both the enantiomers possess the same pharmacological activity but one of them has anothe activity which is useful. Example in this category include bupivacaine (15). Both the enantiomers possess local anesthetic activity but the *l*-isomer in addition to local anesthetic activity also possesses vasoconstrictor activity. This results in enhancement of the local anesthetic activity Similarly, in case of indacrinone (16), both *d*-, and *l*- isomers possess diuretic activity. The *d*-isomer in addition to diuretic activity also possesses uric acid retention activity, while as *l* isomer has uricosuric activity. A ratio of 1:8 (*d*:*l*) has been found to be useful as a diuretic and not the racemic mixture.

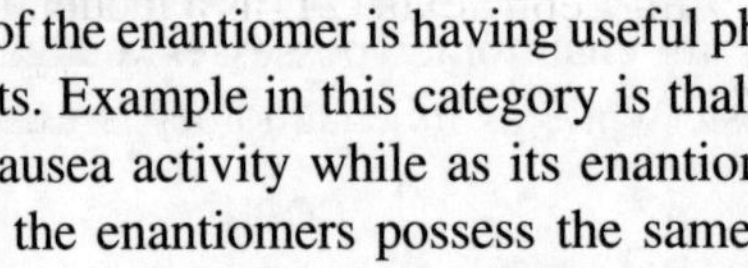

(15)

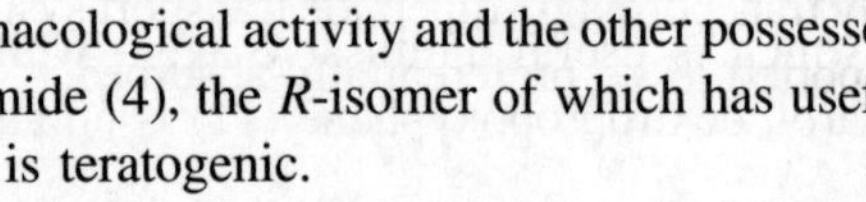

(16)

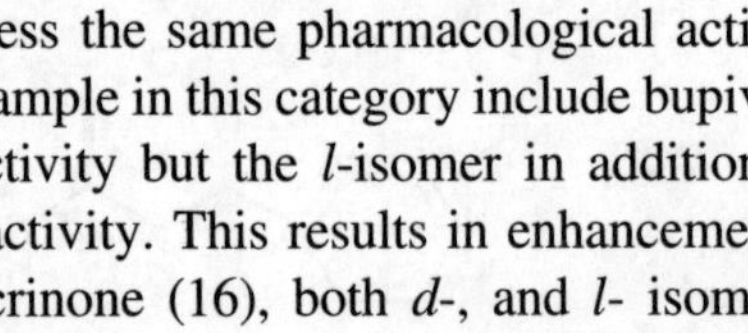

(17)

An interesting aspect of behavior of enantiomers is the conversion of one enantiomer into another in the bio-system. Thus, the *R* (-)-isomer of anti-inflammatory, ibuprofen (17), which is inactive is converted to its active *S* (+)-isomer in vivo. Ibuprofen (17) is therefore, administered as a racemic mixture.

The differences in the pharmacological activities among enantiomers can not only be due to differences in proper fitting at the receptor sites but also due to other factors such as differences in pharmacokinetic parameters and metabolism.

STEREOSELECTIVITY IN PHARMACOKINETIC PARAMETERS AND PHARMACOLOGICAL ACTIVITY

Before a drug molecule reaches site of action, it has to undergo number of processes such as absorption, transport, etc. If these steps are stereoselective, then variations in concentrations of enantiomers can result at the target site and this results in variation in pharmacological activity.

Most of the drugs are absorbed from gastrointestinal tract by passive transport – a process dependent on the physical properties, namely lipophilicity and ionization. Since enantiomers possess same physico-chemical proerties, no differences are, therefore observed among enantiomers. However, diastereoisomers such as geometrical isomers do differ in physico-chemical properties, differences in absorption of diastereoisomers are observed. Enantioselectivity, is however, observed when the transport across the membrane is mediated through active transport. Examples in this category include Dopa (18), methotrexate (19), and β-lactam antibiotics (20). L-Dopa has been reported to be selectively absorbed from rat small intestines. D-Dopa is absorbed by passive diffusion. Similarly, L-methotrexate (19) is reported to be actively transported tn preference to D-isomer. β- Lactam antibiotics have been reported to be actively transported by dipeptide transport system. Using cephalexin (21) as a model, D-cephalexin has been reported to be preferentially absorbed.

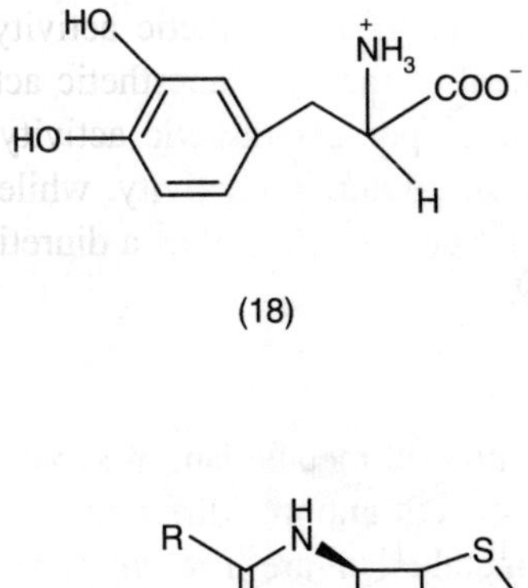

(18)

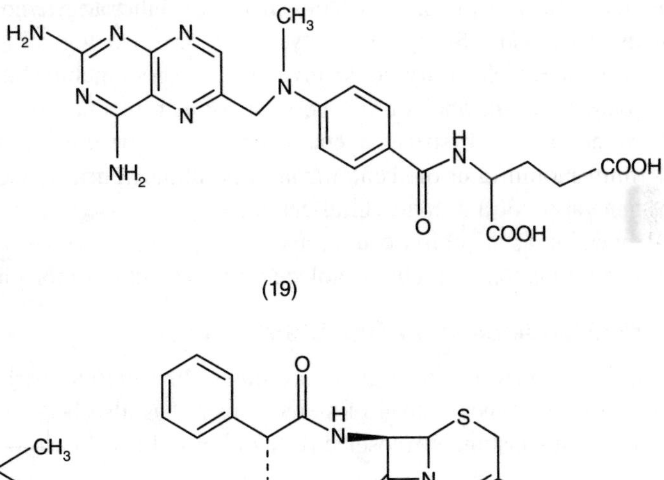

(19)

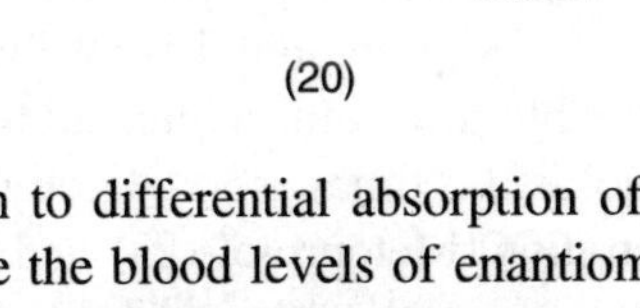

(20)

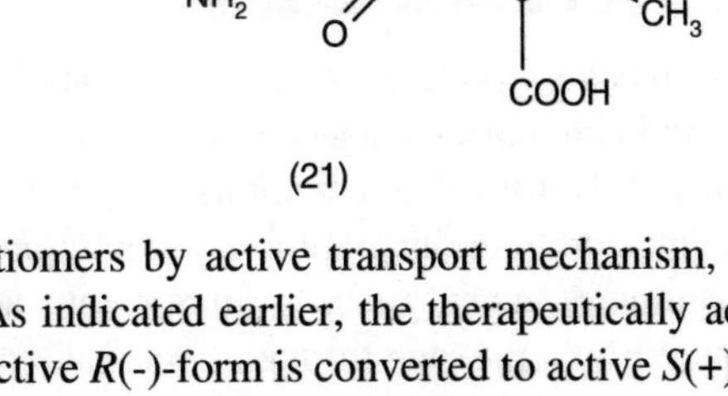

(21)

In addition to differential absorption of enantiomers by active transport mechanism, other factors also influence the blood levels of enantiomers. As indicated earlier, the therapeutically active form of ibuprofen (17) is the *S*(+)-form. However, the inactive *R*(-)-form is converted to active *S*(+)-form before absorption. Thus, the longer it remains in g. i. tract, the greater is inversion and consequently highe blood concentration of the active form.

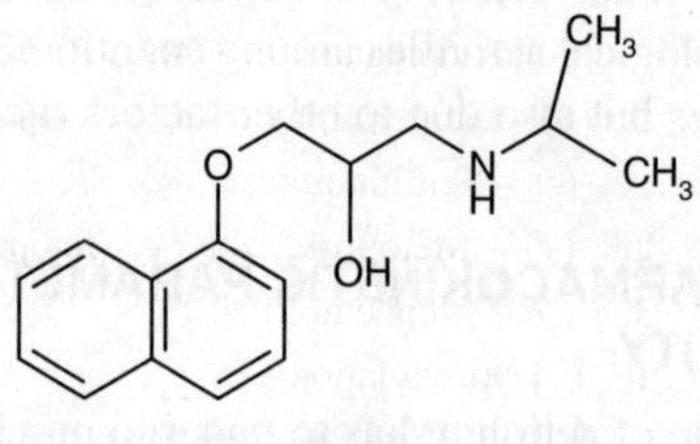

(22)

The distribution of drugs in the body is dependent on partition co-efficient and plasma and tissu binding. Since enantiomers have similar partition co-efficient characteristics, the partition into variou sites is not stereoselective. Data on tissue binding is very scarce and number of studies have bee carried out on plasma-protein binding. While acidic drugs predominantly bind to human serum albumi (HSA), the basic drugs predominantly bind at α_1-acid glucoprotein (AGP). The binding to differen proteins is stereoselective. This is illustrated by propranolol (22). While the *R*-enantiomer preferentiall binds to human serum albumin (HAS), the *S*-enantiomer binds to α_1-acid glucoprotein (AGP).

STEREOISOMERISM AND DRUG METABOLISM

Differentiation in stereoisomers is very common in metabolism of drugs. Infact this differentiation i reflected in drug disposition. The stereoselectivity is found in both Phase I as well as in Phase I metabolic reactions.

The stereoselectivity in drug metabolism can be Substrate Stereoselectivity, Product Stereoselectivity and Substrate/Product Stereoselectivity.

Substrate stereoselectivity could involve:

(a) preferential metabolism of one stereoisomer,
(b) stereoselective first pass metabolism,
(c) generation of a chiral centre from a prochiral centre,
(d) generation of a second chiral centre,
(e) inversion at the chiral centre, and
(f) transformation of a chiral molecule into an achiral molecule.

Prefrential Metabolism of One Stereoisomer

Because of asymmetry in biological molecules, the stereodifferentiation in metabolism of substrates i common. Selective metabolism of stereoisomers has also been observed amongst different species.

Examples of substrate stereoselectivity in Phase I and Phase II metabolism are listed in Table 13.1

Stereoselective First Pass Metabolism

Most of the β-blockers undergo first pass metabolism. The *R*-isomer of propranolol (22) undergoe first pass metabolism and clearance. Since the activity of racemic propranolol is attributed mainly t *S*(-)-enantiomer, therefore, this enantiomer is more bioavailable after oral administration of racemi propranolol. Thus, oral administration of racemic propranolol is 2-3 times more effective as compare to same concentration when given by intravenous administration. Metoprolol (23) and bufuralol (24 are also subject to first passage through liver. Like propranolol (22), the bioavailability of more activ

Table 13.1 Some examples of steroselective phase I and phase II metabolism

Reaction	*Examples*
(a) Deamination	(-) -Amphetamine > (+) – Amphetamine (humans)
(b) Dealkylation	1. (+) – Fenluramine > (-) – Fenfluramine (deethylation, humans)
	(-) – Fenfluramine > (+) – Fenfluramine (rats)
	2. (+) – Metoprolol > (-) – Metoprolol (O-demethylation, humans)
	3. (*R*) -Mephentoin > (*S*) – Mephentoin (demethylation, humans)
(c) Hydroxylation	1. 1′-Hydroxylation of (+)-Bufuralol > (-) -Bufuralol (humans), 4-hydroxylation of (-)-Bufuralol > (+) -Bufuralol (humans)
	2. (*R*) -Indacrinone > (*S*)-Indacrinone (monkeys)
	3. (*R*) -Mephobarbital > (S)-Mephobarbital (humans)
	4. 4-Hydroxylation of (*S*)-Mephentoin > (*R*)-Mephentoin
	5. 4-Hydroxylation of (+)-Penbutalol
	6. 4-Hydroxylation of (+)-Glutethimide as compared to side chain Hydroxylation of (-)-glutethimide
(d) Oxidation	1. Oxidative deamination of (-)-Primaquine
Examples of Phase II Metabolism	1. Glucouronidation of (*R*)-Mexiletene (humans)
	2. Glucouronidation of (*S*)-Oxazepam (monkeys)
	3. Glucouronidation of (*R*)-Oxazepam (humans)

S(-)isomer is also higher in both metoprolol (23) and bufuralol (24) after oral administration. Similar

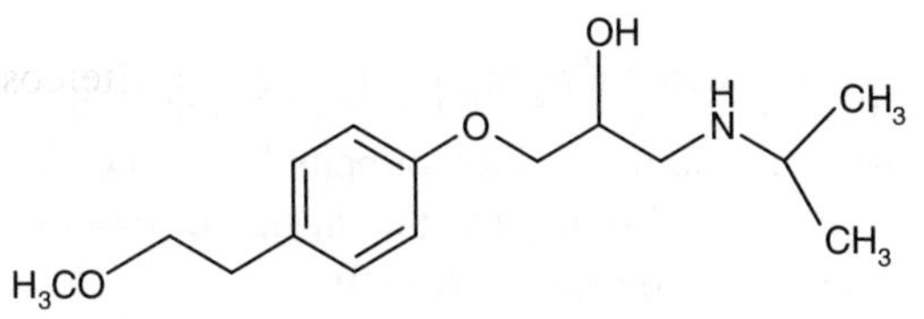

(23)

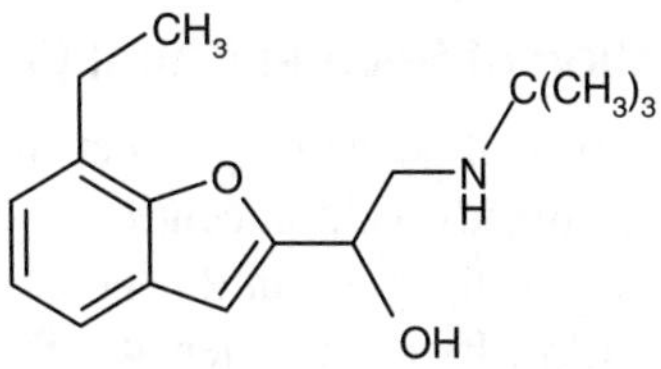

(24)

results have also been obtained in case of penbutolol (25). Thus, β-blockers like propranolol (22), metoprolol (23), bufuralol (24), and penbutolol (25) when given in racemic form orally, clearance of the inactive enantiomer is much higher because of first pass metabolism. This results in higher plasma levels of more active enantiomer. Intravenous administration of racemic form of these, on the other hand, results in lower plasma concentration, because this route of administration does not involve first pass metabolism. Xibenolol (26), on the otherhand undergoes first pass metabolism of more active isomer. This results in lower blood levels when racemic xibenolol (26) is given orally than when given intravenously.

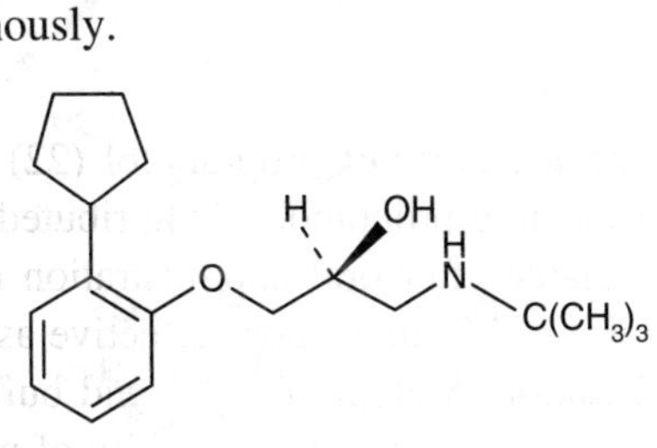

(25)

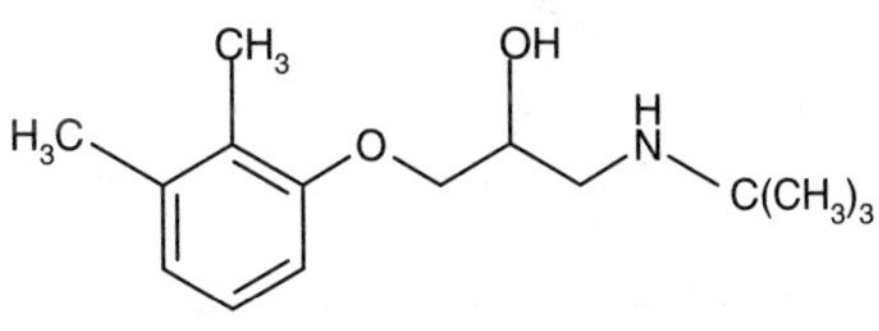

(26)

Generation of a Chiral Centre from a Prochiral Centre

This is a case of product stereoselectivity Examples include hydroxylation of phenyl ring in phenytoin (27) to yield *S*-4-hydroxyphenytoin (28) and cimitidine (29) to cimitidine sulphoxide (30).

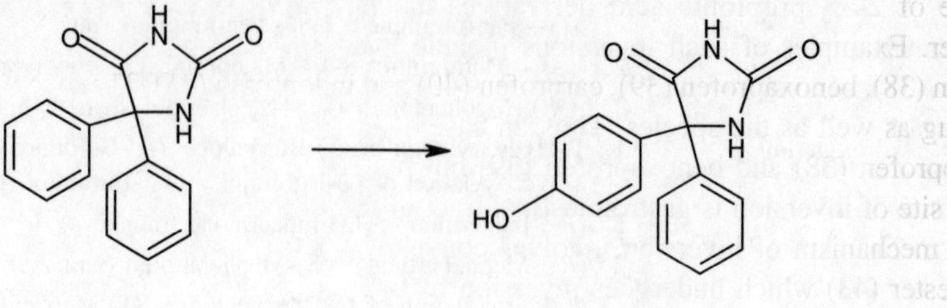

(27) (28)

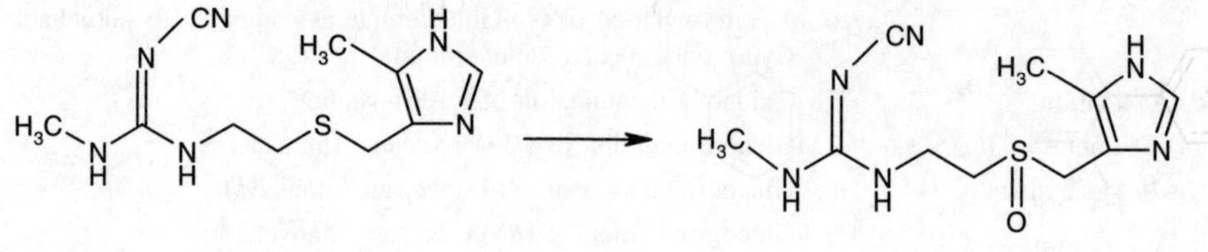

(29) (30)

Generation of Second Chiral Centre

This is a case of substrate/product stereoselectivity. A second chiral centre is introduced in a substrate which has already a chiral centre. Examples include side chain oxidation of pentobarbitone (31) to (32), reduction of keto-group in the side chain of *R*(+)-warfarin (33) to yield the diastereoisomeric alcohols (34) and (35). Its enantiomer, the *S*(-)-warfarin does not undergo the reduction.

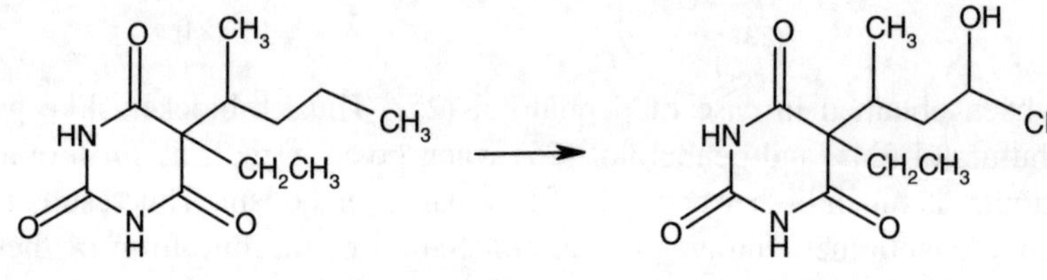

(31) (32)

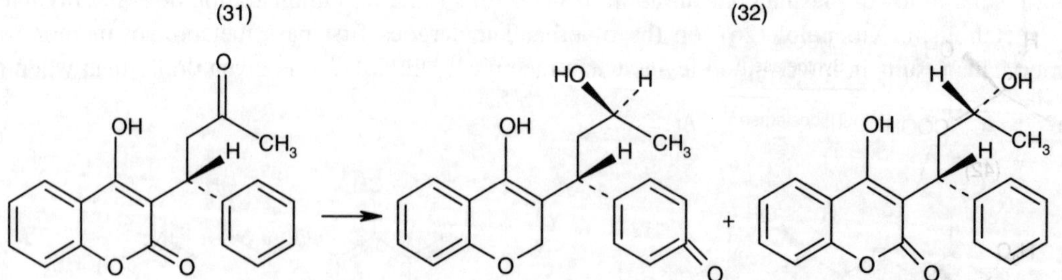

R,S-(+)-alcohol (major) *R,R*-(+)-alcohol (minor)

(33) (34) (35)

Inversion at the Chiral Centre

Another phenomenon of substrate selectivity is the inversion at chiral centre. This has been particularly observed in case of non-steroidal anti-inflammatory drugs belonging to 2-arylpropionic acid and 2-aryloxypropionic acid herbicides.

In case of 2-arylpropionic acid derivatives the inactive *R*-enantiomer is converted to active *S*-enantiomer. Examples of such inversions include ibuprofen (17), flurbiprofen (36), ketoprofen (37), fenoprofen (38), benoxaprofen (39), carprofen (40) and indoprofen (41). The extent of inversion depends on the drug as well as the species. Thus, in case of humans, the inversion is significant for ibuprofen (17), fenoprofen (38) and benoxaprofen (39) but negligible in case of carprofen (40) and indoprofen (41). The site of inversion is gastrointestinal tract in most of the species but it could be liver or kidney also. The mechanism of inversion involves conversion of *R*-enantiomer of arylpropionic acid (42) to thioCoA ester (43) which undergoes inversion by epimerase to (44) and subsequent hydrolysis of the ester to *S*-enantiomer (45).

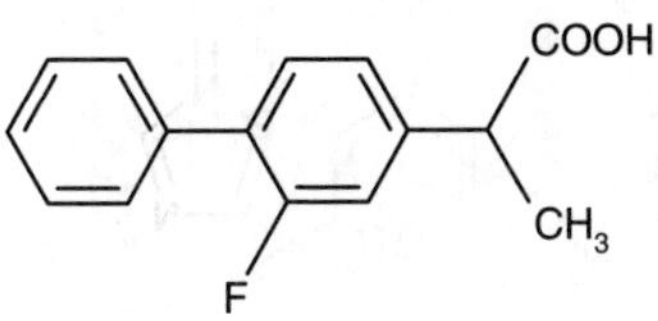

(36)

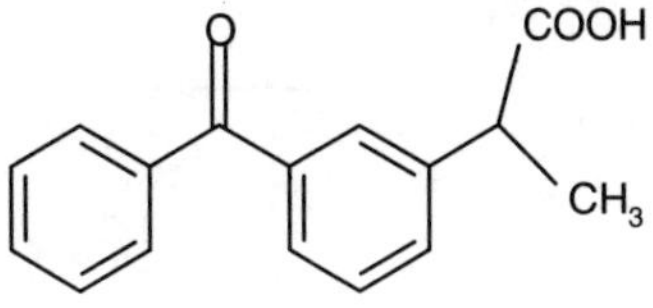

(37)

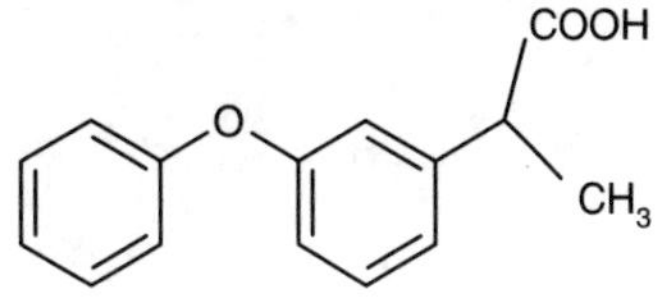

(38)

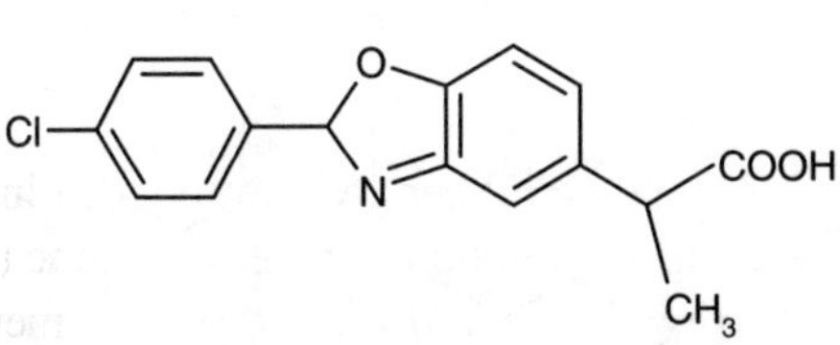

(39)

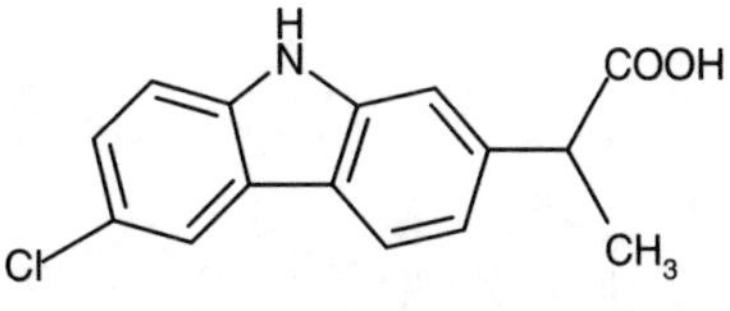

(40)

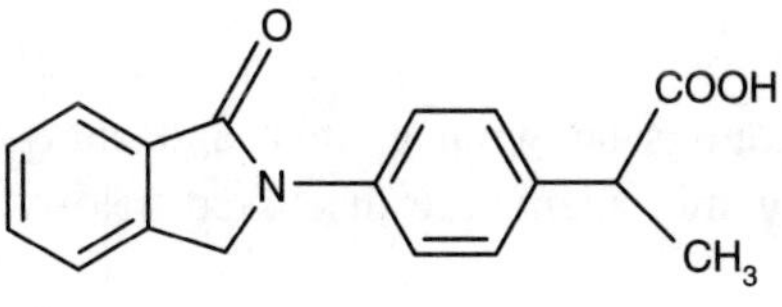

(41)

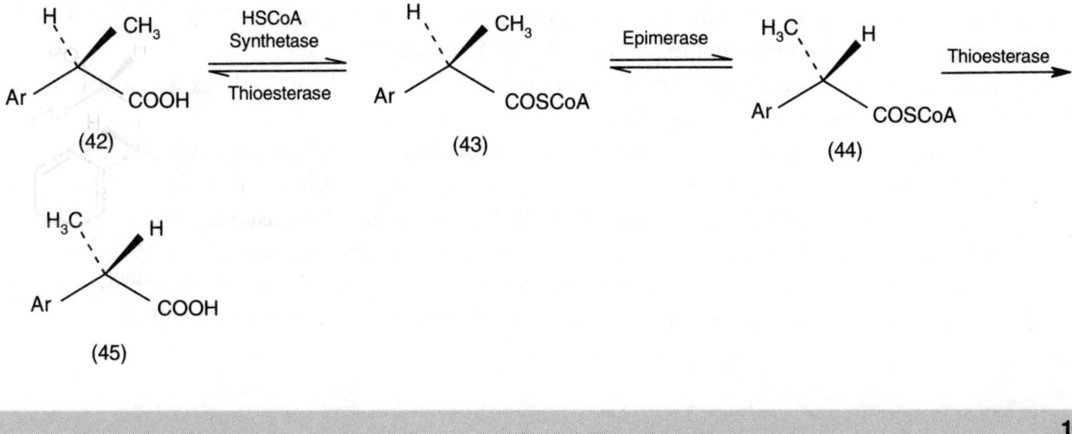

(42) (43) (44) (45)

2-Aryloxypropionic acid derivatives used as herbicides also undergo inversion, however the transformation is of *S*-enantiomer to *R*-enantiomer.

Other moieties which have been shown to undergo inversion include chiral allylic alcohols and sulphoxides.

Transformation of a Chiral Centre into an Achiral Centre

Instances of substrate undergoing metabolism at the chiral centre resulting in loss of asymmetry are also known. Examples include the calcium channel blocker nilvadipine (46) losing its asymmetry through oxidation of its dihyropyridine moiety to pyridine analog (47). Similarly the oxidation of proton pump inhibitor omeprazole (48) to its sulphone analog (49).

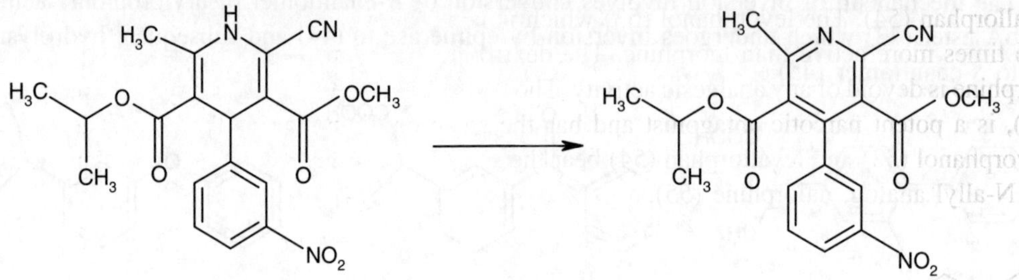

(46) (47)

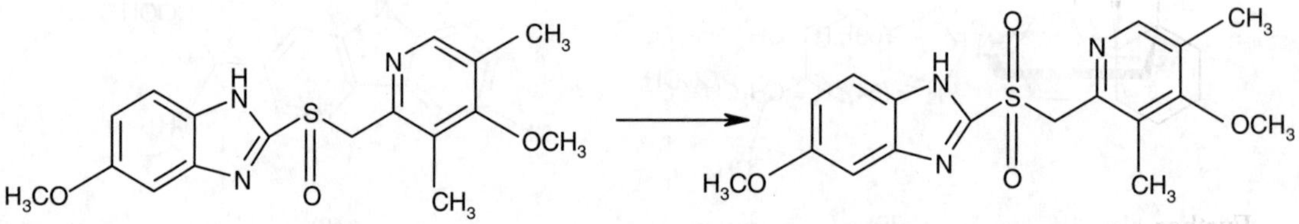

(48) (49)

Examples of various stereoisomers showing agonist and antagonistic activities and belonging to different classes of pharmacodynamic agents are discussed below.

OPIOID ANALGETICS

Morphine, Morphinans and Benzomorphans

The classical analgetic, morphine (50) has five asymmetric centres and include 5, 6, 9, 13, and 14. The absolute configurations of these centres is 5*R*, 6*S*, 9*R*, 13*S* and 14*R*.

The conformation of cycloalkene ring, which constitutes ring C is boat while as the piperidine ring, which constitutes the ring D, is in chair form.

Naturally occurring morphine is levorotatory. The synthetic dextrorotatory morphine which has inverted configurations at 5, 6, 9, 13, and 14 asymmetric centres, is devoid of analgesic activity. The hydrogen atoms at C_5, C_6, and C_{14} are all *cis*, and the bridge at C_9 and C_{13} is also *cis*. The fusion between the cycloalkene ring which is ring C and the piperidine ring constituting ring D is *trans* (e, e).

Modification of morphine (50) led to morphinans (51) which do not have ether bridge. All the members in this series which are active have same stereochemistry as in morphine (51).

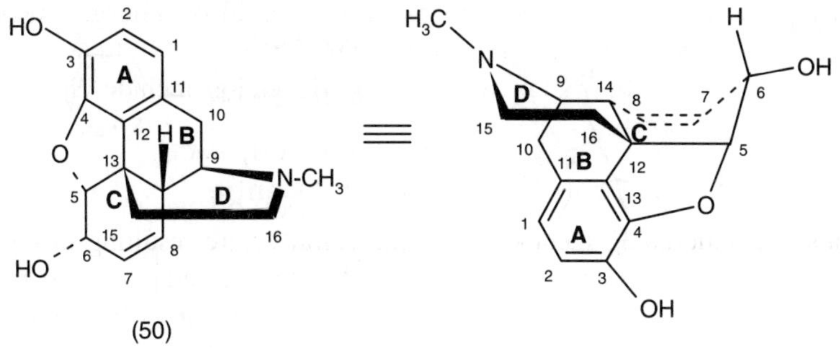

(50)

Some of the members in this series include N-methylmorphinan (52), levorphanol (53), and levallorphan (54). The levorphanol (53) which is levorotatory isomer like natural morphine is about 5 to 6 times more active than morphine. The dextrorotatory isomer, dextorphan, like the dextrorotatory morphine is devoid of any analgesic activity. The N-allyl derivative of 3-hydroxymorphinan, levallorphan (54), is a potent narcotic antagonist and has the same configuration as the agonist levorphanol (53). Levorphanol (53) and levallorphan (54) bear the same relationship as morphine (50) and its antagonist, the N-allyl analog, nalorphine (55).

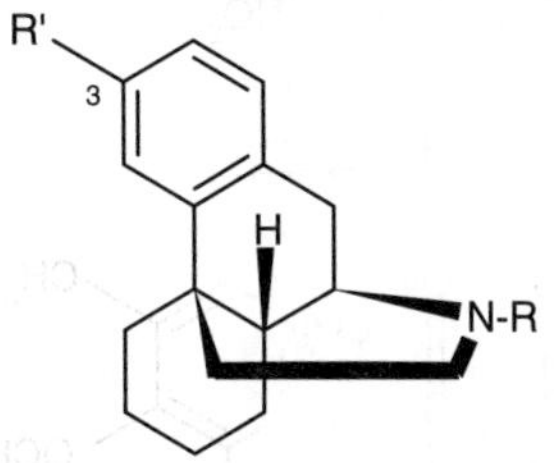

(51), R = R' = H

(52), R = CH_3, R' = H

(53), R = CH_3, R' = OH

(54), R = $CH_2CH = CH_2$, R' = OH

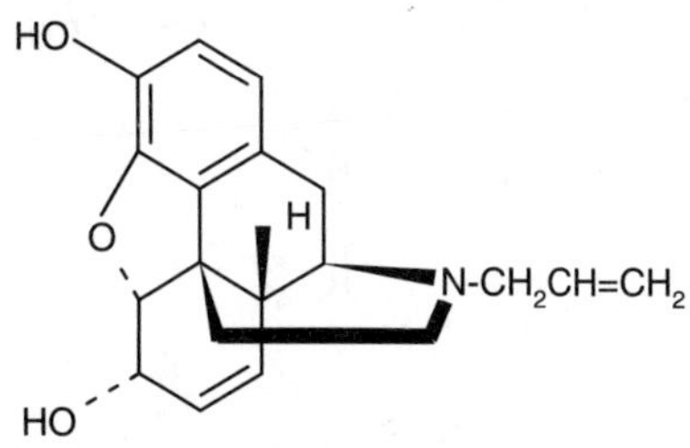

(55)

Further simplification of morphine molecule led to benzomorphans (56) in which the ring C is reduced to C_5 and C_9 substituents The two methyl groups could be *cis*- (57) or *trans*- (58). They are also

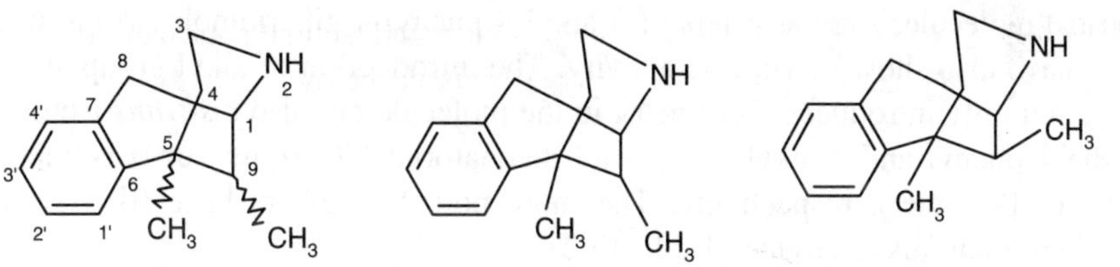

(56) (57) (58)

designated as α- and β-isomers, respectively. Some of the compounds in this series include metazocine (59), phenazocine (60), N-allylnormetazocine (61), pentazocine (62) and cyclazocine (63). The two methyl groups in all these compounds are *cis*- as is the ring junction between ring B and C in morphine (50). *N*-allylnormetazocine (61) is antagonist as levallorphan (54) and nalorphine (55). Among the two isomers the *cis*-isomers are more active than the *trans*-isomers.

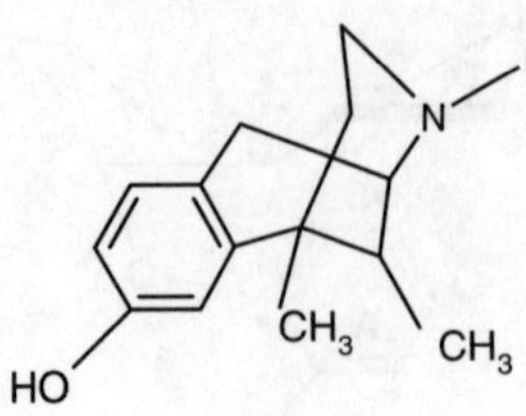

(59), R = CH_3

(60), R = CH_2CH_2—

(61), R = $CH_2CH{=}CH_2$

(62), R = $CH_2CH{=}C(CH_3)_2$

(63), R = CH_2—

Piperidine Analogs

Meperidine or pethidine (64) was the first 4-phenylpiperidine to be used as the analgesic. The other piperidines analogs include anileridine (65), diphenoxylate (66), bemidone (67), and ketobemidone (68). All of these are symmetrical molecules.

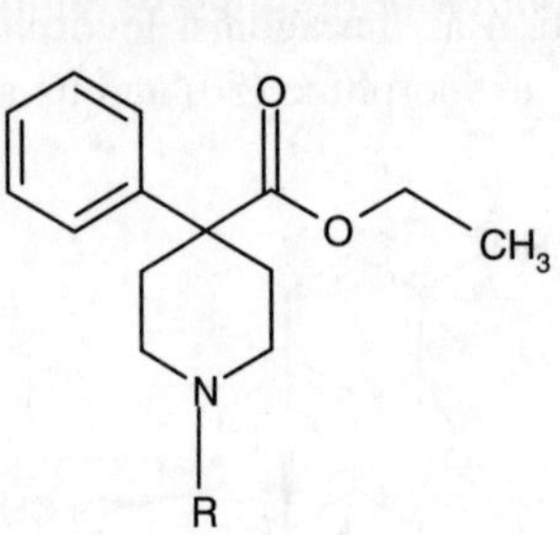

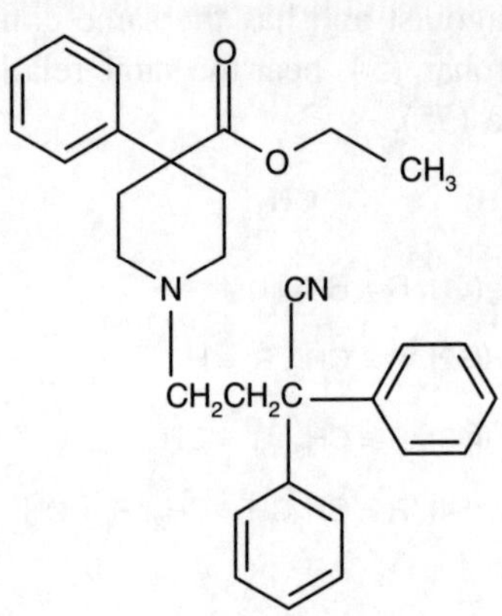

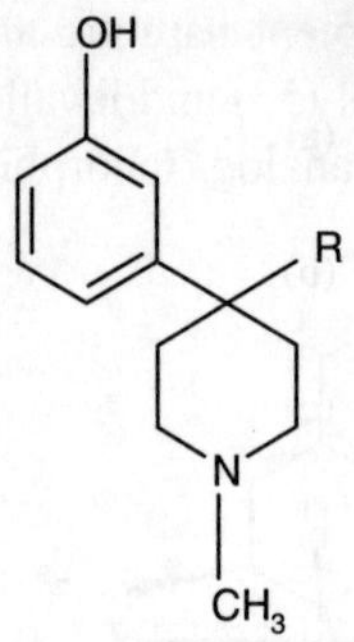

(64), R = CH_3

(65), R = CH_2CH_2— —NH_2

(66)

(67), R = $COOCH_2CH_3$

(68), R = $COCH_2CH_3$

Asymmetrical molecules such as esters of 3-alkyl-4-phenyl-4-piperidinols (69a to 69d) (*trans-* is α- and *cis-* is β-) have also shown analgesic activity. The introduction of alkyl group at position 3 of the piperidine ring not only introduces asymmetry in the molecule but also *cis-trans* isomerism depending on whether the 4-phenyl and 3-alkyl groups are diequatorial (70, *trans-*, or α-isomer) or equatorial-axial (71, *cis-* or β-isomer), respectively. The more potent members have (β) *cis*-relationship (71) between the phenyl and alkyl groups (Table 13.2).

Table 13.2 Analgesic activity of assymetrical esters of 4-piperidinols

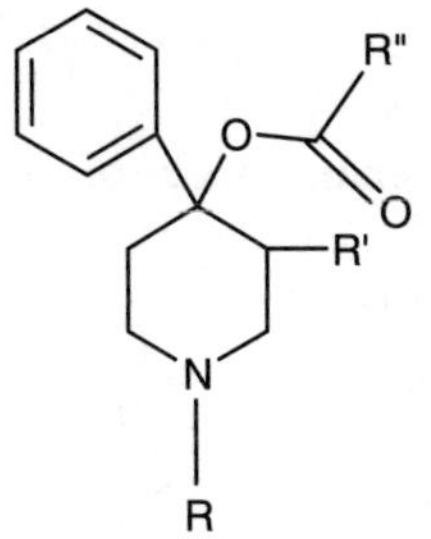

(69)

	R	*R′*	*R″*	*Form (3R′/4Ph)*	*Potency Ratio (Morphine =*	
(a)	$-(CH_2)_2C_6H_5$	CH_3	C_2H_5	α-(*trans*)	4.5	
				β-(*cis*)	22.5	
(b)	CH_3	CH_3	CH_3	α-(*trans*)	0.4	
				β-(*cis*)	2.2	
(c)	CH_3	CH_3	C_2H_5	α-(*trans*)	2.0	(α-prodin)
				β-(*cis*)	8.7	(β-prodin)
(d)	CH_3	CH_3	n-C_3H_7	α-(*trans*)	1.3	
				β-(*cis*)	2.9	

(*trans*- is α- and *cis*- is β-)

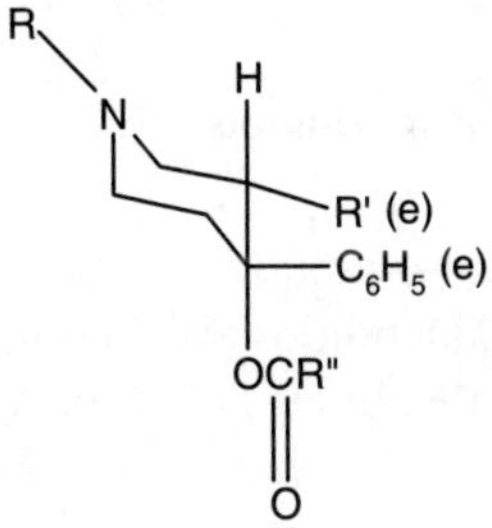

(70)

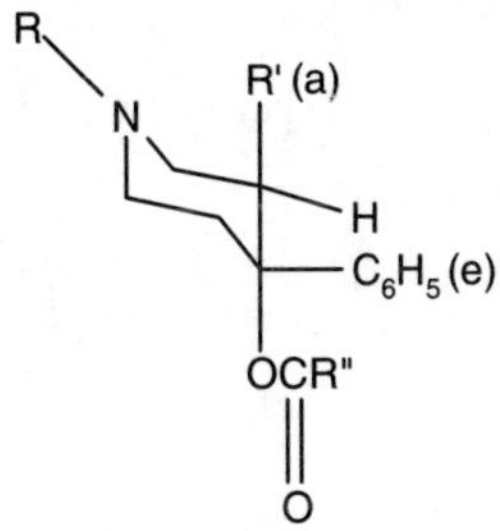

(71)

Acyclic Analgetics

Among the open chain analgetics, methadone (72) was the first potent analgetic.

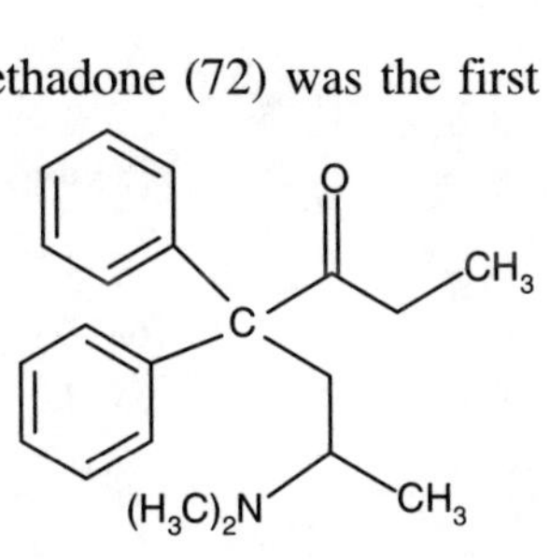

(72)

Studies on methadone (72) and other analogues have shown that excepting the ester analogue (76, Table 13.3), the *R* enantiomer is more active as an analgetic. In case of ester (76) the S-enantiomer was found to be more active.

Table 13.3 Analgetic activity of enantiomers of methadone and its other analogues

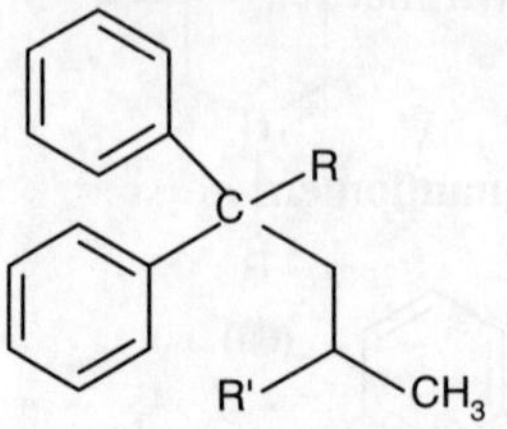

Compound No.	*R*	*R′*	*Analgetic activity of enantiomers*
(72)	$-COCH_2CH_3$	$-N(CH_3)_2$	*R* > *S*
(73)	$-COCH_2CH_3$	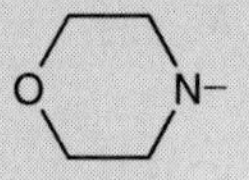	*R* > *S*
(74)	$-COCH_2CH_3$	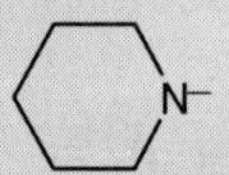	*R* > *S*
(75)	$-SO_2CH_2CH_3$	$-N(CH_3)_2$	*R* > *S*
(76)	$-COOCH_2CH_3$	$-N(CH_3)_2$	*S* > *R*

Table 13.4 Analgetic activity of methadols

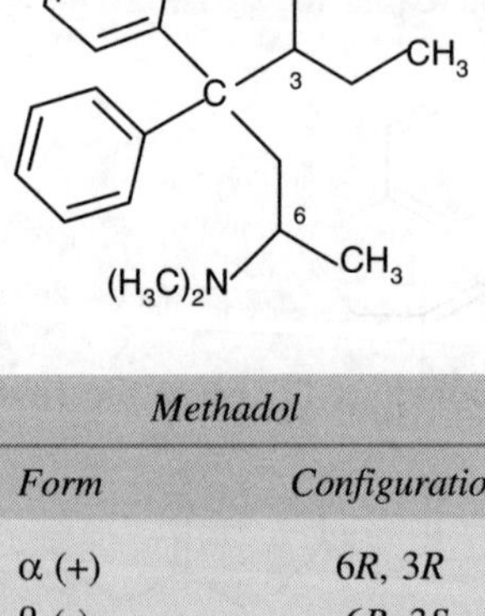

Methadone	*Methadol*		ED_{50} *(mg/kg)*
	Form	*Configuration*	
R (-)	α (+)	6*R*, 3*R*	24. 7
	β (-)	6*R*, 3*S*	7. 6
S (+)	α (-)	6*S*, 3*S*	3. 5
	β (+)	6*S*, 3*R*	63.7

Reduction of methadone (72) results in methadol which has two asymmetric centres, i.e. C_3 and C_6. The more potent methadol is derived from *S*(+)-methadone (Table 13.4) indicating that in case of methadols it is the configuration at C_3 asymmetric centre which is more important for analgetic activity than the configuration at C_6 asymmetric centre.

Shifting of methyl group from position 6 to position 5 results in isomethadone (77). Studies on various analogues (Table 13.5) have shown that it is *S*-enantiomer which is more active as analgetic than the *R*-enantiomer.

Table 13.5 Analgetic activity of enantiomers of isomethadone and its other analogues

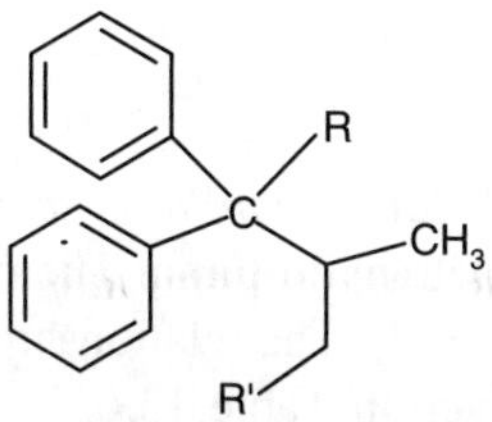

Compound No.	*R*	*R′*	*Analgetic activity of enantiomers*
(77)	$-COC_2H_5$	$-N(CH_3)_2$	*S* > *R*
(78)	$-COC_2H_5$	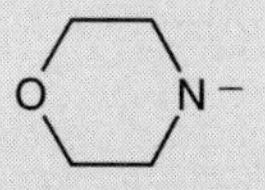	*S* > *R*
(79)	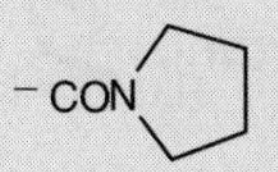	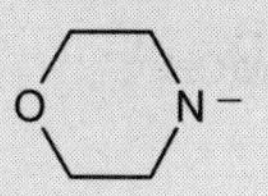	*S* > *R*

Propoxyphene (80) which is 1, 2-diphenyl-2-propionoxy-3-methyl-4-dimethylaminobutane, is an analogue of isomethadone (77). It has two asymmetric centres namely C_2 and C_3. The more active enantiomer has the same configuration at C_3 as in isomethadone (77), i.e. *S*.

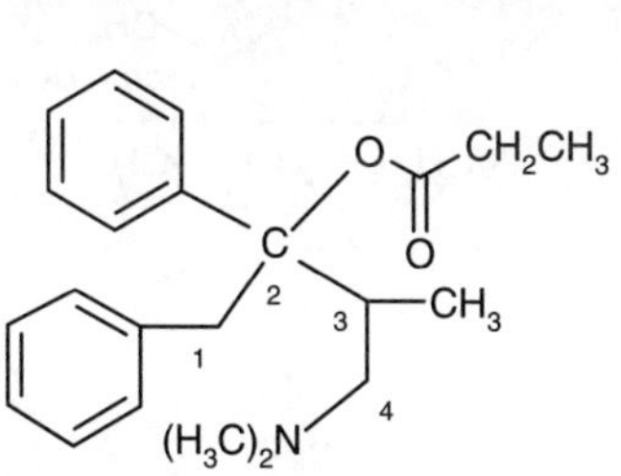

(80)

Cholinergic Agonists and Antagonists

Although acetylcholine (81) is a symmetrical molecule, but the stereochemical requirements for cholinergic activity are quite stringent. This is evidenced by the differing muscarinic activities of enantiomers of asymmetric analogs of acetylcholine (81). Thus, out of the two enantiomers of α-methyl analogs (82), the *R*(+)-enantiomer is more active (*S/R* activity ratio, 0.13) as a muscarinic agent. Similarly, among the β-methyl analogs (83), it is the *S*(+)-enantiomer which has higher muscarinc activity (*S/R* ratio, 240). The α-methyl analog (82) has more nicotinic activity as compared to β-methyl analog (83).

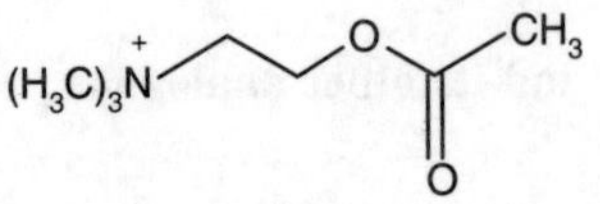

(81)

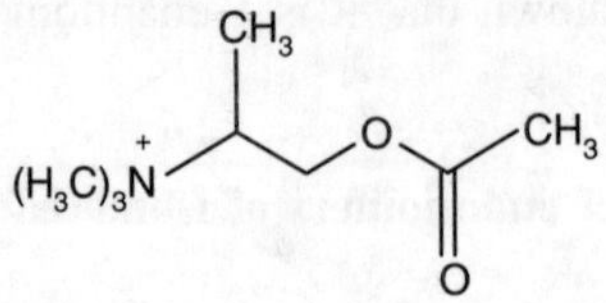

(82)

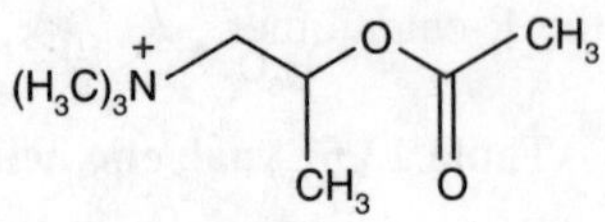

(83)

Muscarine (84), the alkaloid obtained from *Amanita muscaria,* is one of eight isomers of 2-methyl-3-hydroxy-5-trimethylammoniummethyltetrahydrofuran. The other isomers include epimuscarine (85), allomuscarine (86), and epiallomuscarine (87). The relationship between the different functional groups in these tetrahydrofuran analogues is given in Table 13.6.

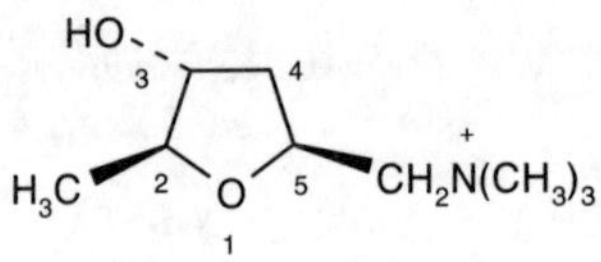

(84)

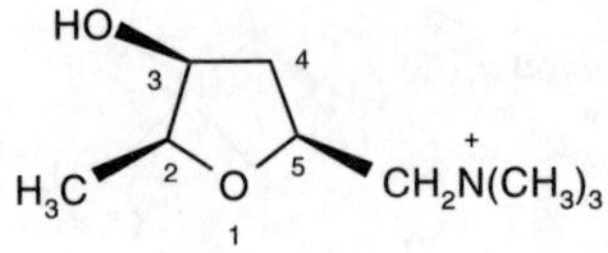

(85)

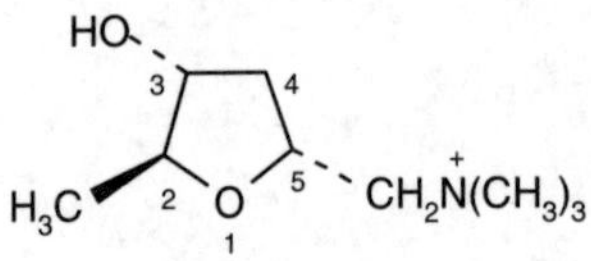

(86)

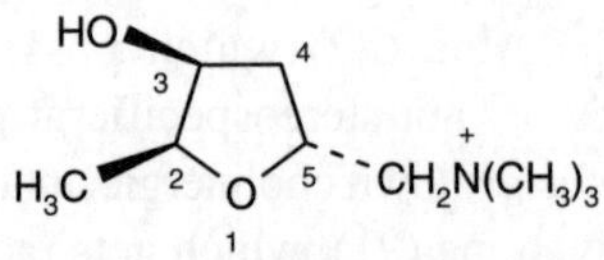

(87)

Table 13.6 Relationship of different groups in 2-trimethylammoniummethyl-4-hydroxy-5 methyl-tetrahydrofuran

Compound	*Geometric Relationship of*	
	$5\text{-}CH_2N\ (CH_3)_3/2\text{-}CH_3$	$5\text{-}CH_2N\ (CH_3)_3/3\text{-}OH$
Muscarine (84)	*cis-*	*trans-*
Epimuscarine (85)	*cis-*	*cis-*
Allomuscarine (86)	*trans-*	*cis-*
Epiallomuscarine (87)	*trans-*	*trans-*

The most active isomer, the muscarine (85) have the substituents at C_5 and C_2 *cis-* and C_5 and C_3 *trans-*. Of the various enantiomorphic forms, 2*S*, 3*R*, 5*S*, the (+) -muscarine, is highly potent. The (-) -form is several hundred times less active. The next member in the series which has higher activity is epiallomuscarine (87) which also has substituents at C_5 and C_3 *trans*. Further, as we have seen earlier, in case of β-methyl analog of acetylcholine (83) the active form has *S*-configuration as in case of active form of muscarine (84) at position 2. However, in case of mucarone (88), the ketone, derived from less active (-)-muscarine, is more active. This reversal of the activity has been attributed to different mode of binding of muscarone (88) to the receptor.

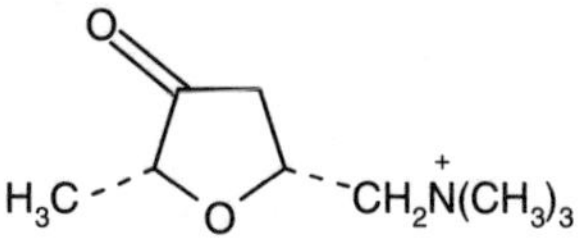

(88)

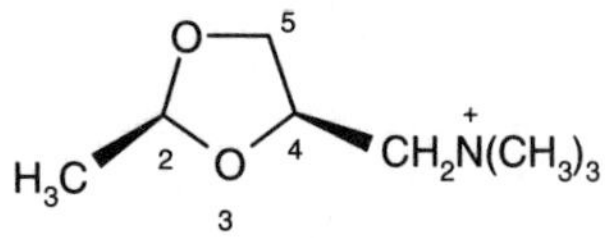

(89)

Another class of rigid compounds which show cholinergic activity are dioxolanes. Comparision of 2-methyl-4-trimethylammoniummethyl-1, 3-dioxolanes show that the *cis*-isomer (89) has maximum activity. Further, the configuration at C_4 of the more active isomer is same as in case of muscarine (84) at C_5, i.e. S.

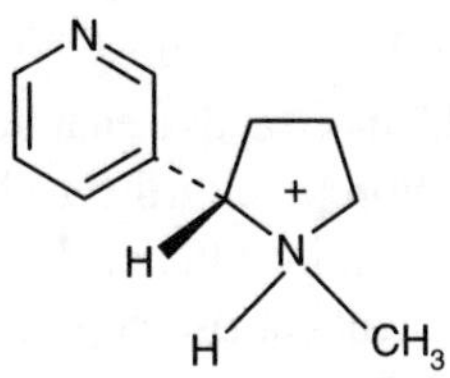

(90)

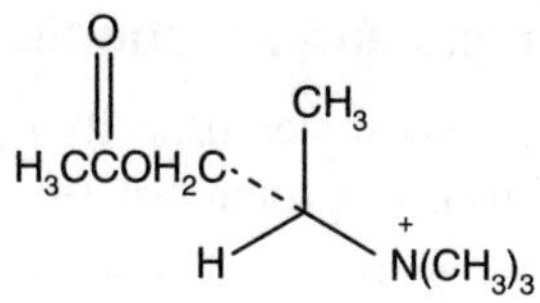

(82)

The naturally occurring nicotine (90) has S-configuration, the same configuration found in case of α-methylacetylcholine (82) which possesses most of the nicotinic activity. However, α-methyl acetylcholine (82) is not stereospecific at ganglion while as nicotine (90) is.

Atropine, the best known cholinergic antagonist, is racemic form of naturally occurring (-) hyoscyamine (91). (-) -Hyoscyamine (91), which gets racemized during isolation, is an ester of *S*- (-) tropic acid (92) with optically inactive (meso) tropine (93). The stereochemical points of interest in hyoscyamine (91) are the configuration of optically active tropic acid and the relative orientation of N-CH_3 group and the

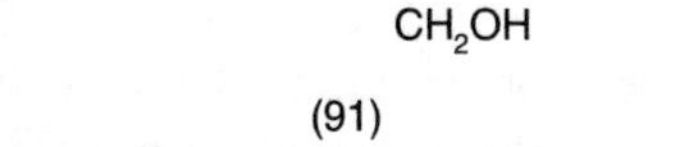

(91)

(92)

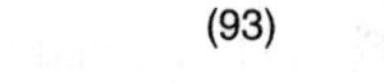

(93)

3-acyloxy group in tropine part of the ester. *S*-(-)-Hyoscyamine (92) is the pharmacologically active form of the racemic atropine. R-(+)-Hyoscyamine, an ester of R(+)-tropic acid and optically inactive tropine (93), is inactive. Same is true for *S*-(-)-hyoscine (94), which is an ester of *S*-(-)-tropic acid and optically inactive scopine. The *S*-(-)-Hyoscine is twice as active as its optical antipode, *R*-(+)-hyoscine. This indicates that for anticholinergic activity, the tropic acid should have *S*-configuration. As regards the relative orientation of the N-CH_3 and the 3-acyloxy group, they have to be *trans*- to each other. Such a configuration is necessary for the activity because the pseudotropine (95) analogs, in which the two groups are *cis*-, are inactive. The preferred conformation of the piperidine ring is chair.

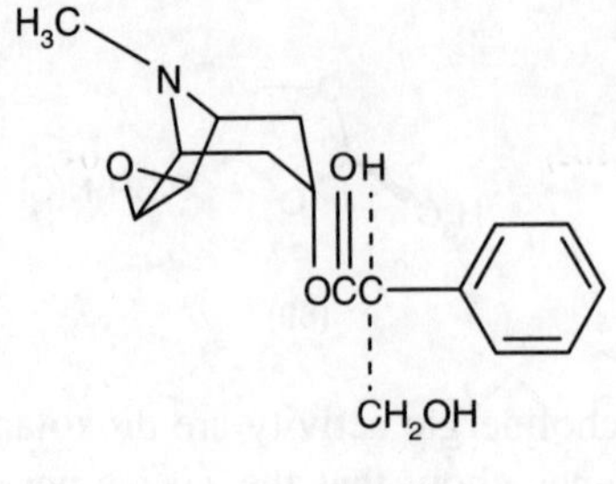

(94)

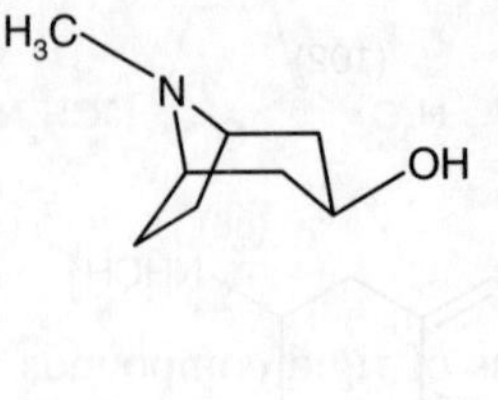

(95)

Adrenergic Agonists and Antagonists

All the catecholamines show stereospecificity. Thus, among the more active enantiomers of norepinephrine (96), epinephrine (97), isoproterenol (98) and *tert.* butyl-norepinephrine (99), compounds with *R*-configuration are more active. Same is also true for the monophenolic adrenergic compounds, synepherine (100) and phenylepherine (101). It seems that steric requirements at β-receptor are more stringent than at α-receptor. Thus, epinephrine (97) and norepinephrine (96) show *R/S* ratio of 4 and 8, respectively at the α-receptor. On the otherhand, larger ratios of 20 and 50, respectively, were noted for β-receptor. In case of isoproterenol (98) *R/S* ratio of more than 500 was observed in case of β-receptor.

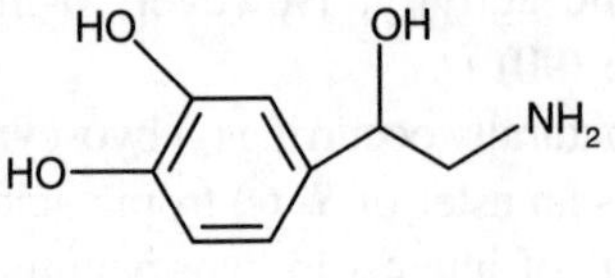

(96)

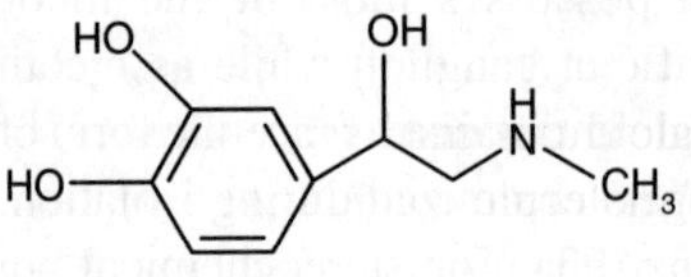

(97)

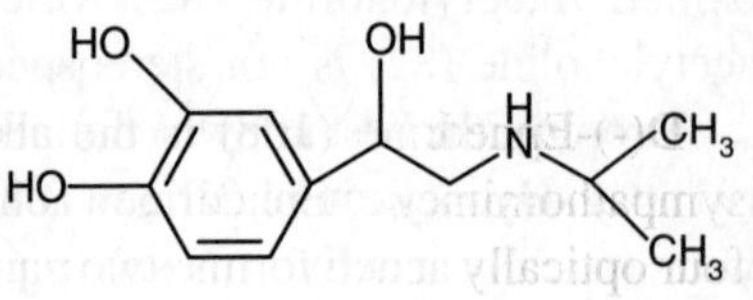

(98)

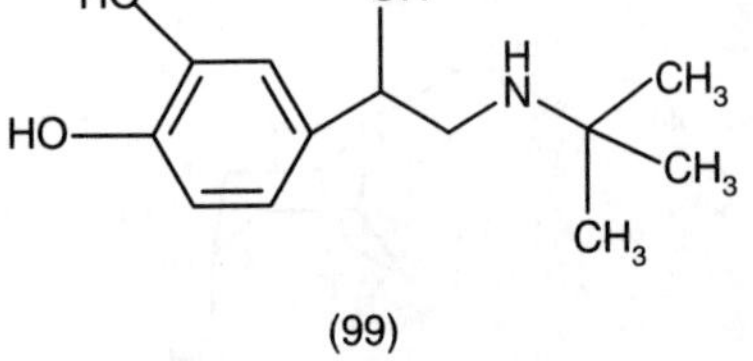

(99)

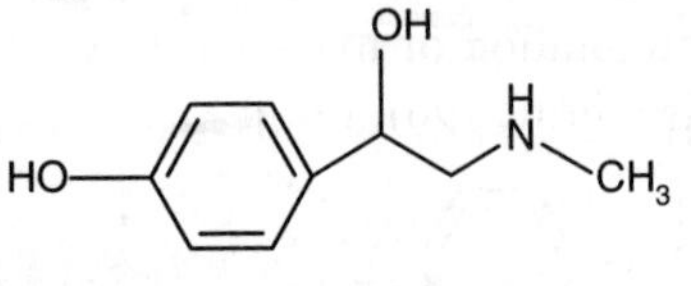

(100)

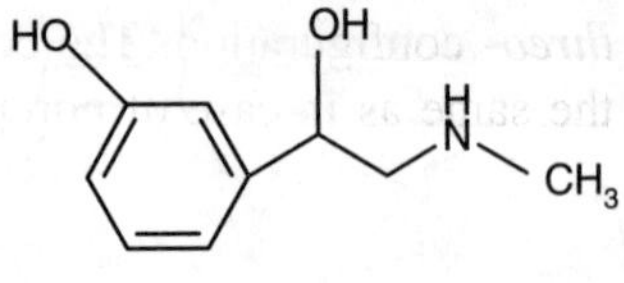

(101)

Differing stereospecificities at the two receptors have been observed in other compounds also.

According to Esson and Stedman, binding of norepinephrine (96) and epinephrine (97) to the receptor involves a three- point attachment which involves attachment at catechol moiety, β-hydroxyl group and the amino group. Sympathomimetic amines lacking a catechol moiety or a β-hydroxyl group or both of them, act indirectly. After reaching the nerve terminals, these amines are taken up into vesicles by vascular monoamine transporter where they displace norepinephrine (96) which results in increase in norepinephrine (96) concentration at the receptor. Some of these include tyramine (102), phenylpropanolamine (103), amphetamine (104), methamphetamine (105), phentermine (106), naphazoline (107), and ephedrine (108).

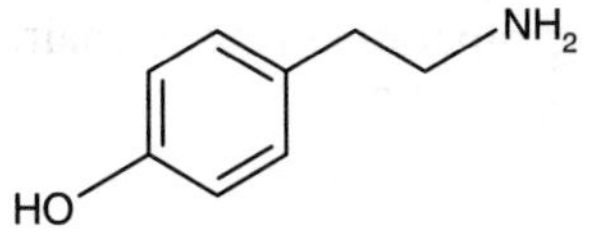

(102)

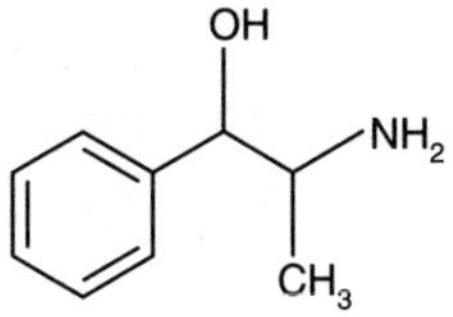

(103)

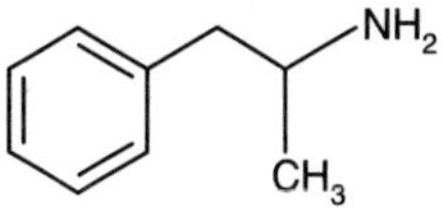

(104)

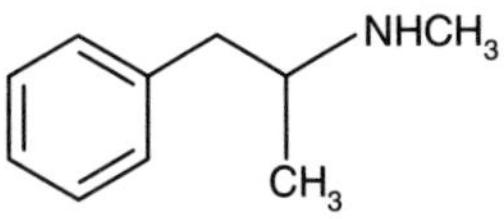

(105)

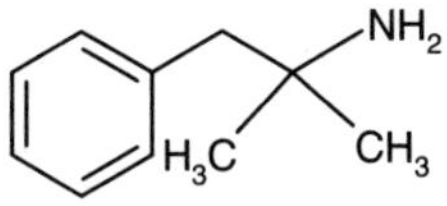

(106)

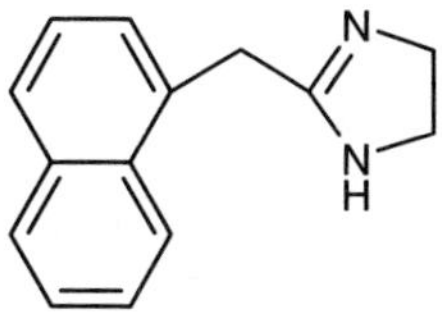

(107)

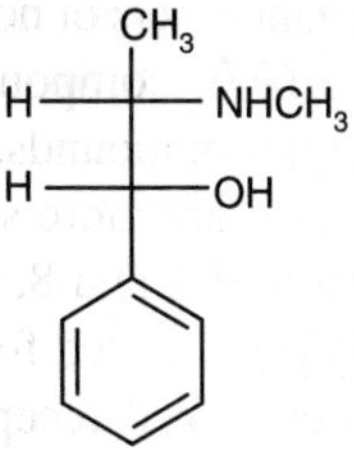

(108)

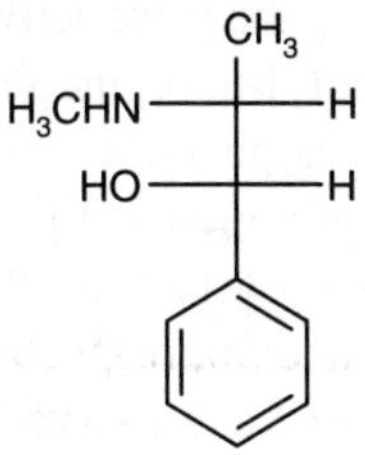

(109)

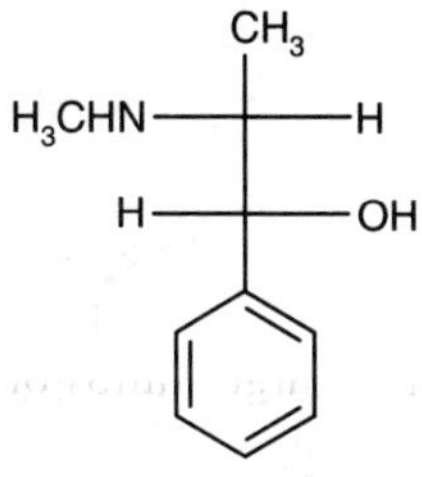

(110)

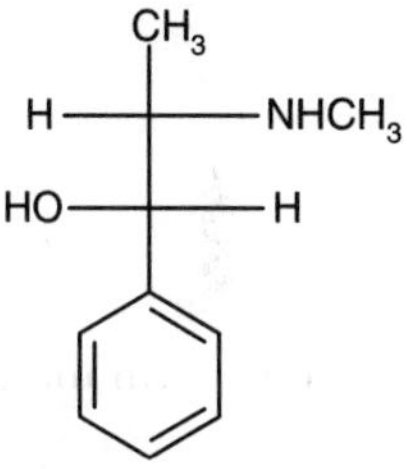

(111)

D(-)-Ephedrine (108) is the alkaloid obtained from various *Ephedra* species. It is a non-phenolic sympathomimetic. Ephedrine (108) molecule contains two dissimilar asymmetric centres and therefore four optically active forms (two pairs of enantiomers) are theoretically possible. All the four stereoisomers are known and these are D(-)-ephedrine (108), L(+)-ephedrine (109), D(-)-ψ-ephedrine (110), and L(+)-ψ-ephedrine (111) constituting the racemic mixture of ephedrine (108 and 109) and racemic mixture of ψ-ephedrine (110 and 111). While ephedrine has *erythro*-configuration the ψ-ephedrine has *threo*- configuration. The configuration of hydroxyl group at the β-carbon in D(-)-ephedrine (108) is the same as in case of norepinephrine (96), i.e. *R*.

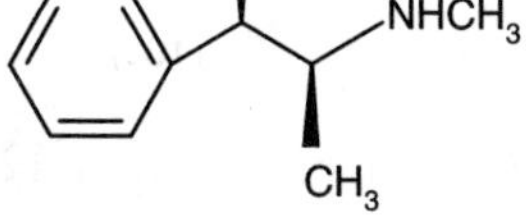

(108)

Some of the useful antihypertensive agents include β-adrenergic blocking agents such as propranolol (22), metoprolol (23), atenolol (112), nadolol (113) and acebutolol (114). Like sympathomimetic agents all the β-blockers exhibit stereospecificity. The β-blocking activity resides in *S* (-) -isomer.

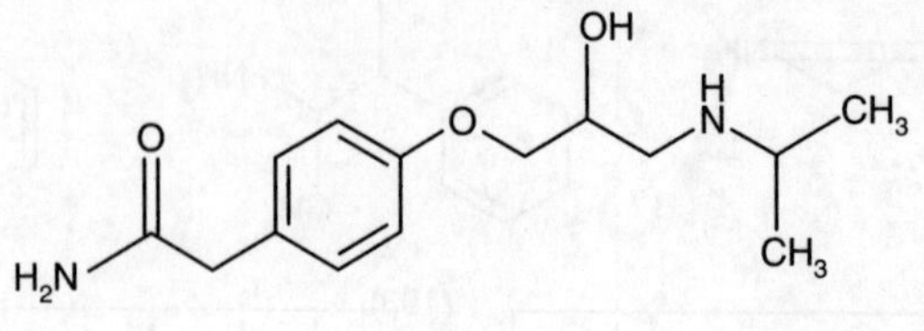

(112)

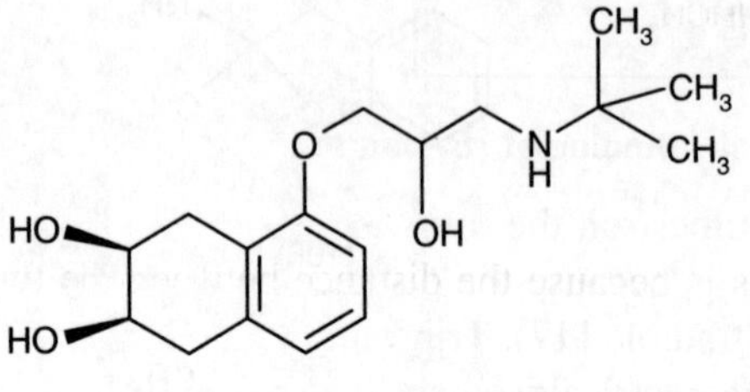

(113)

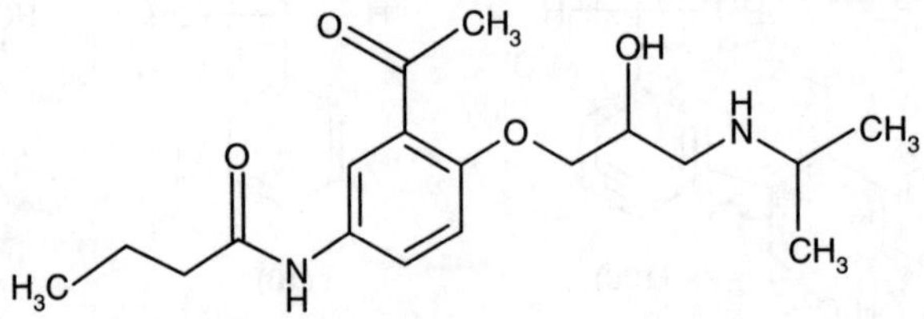

(114)

GEOMETRICAL ISOMERISM AND PHARMACOLOGICAL ACTIVITY

Geometrical isomerism results because of restriction of rotation around carbon-carbon bond. This restriction to rotation could be due to a double bond or a ring. Because of differences in physical properties, the geometrical isomers differ in distribution in various biological system resulting in differences in biological activity. Differences could also be due to differences in binding at the receptor (Figs. 13.6a and 13.6b) one fitting better than the other because of differences in the interatomic distances.

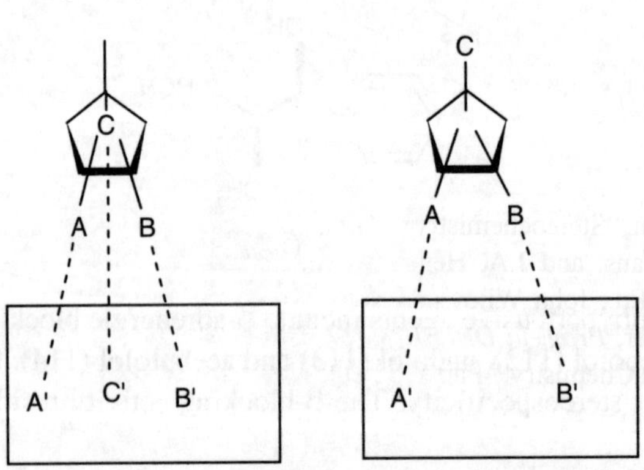

Fig. 13.6a Binding of *cis*- and *trans*-isomers

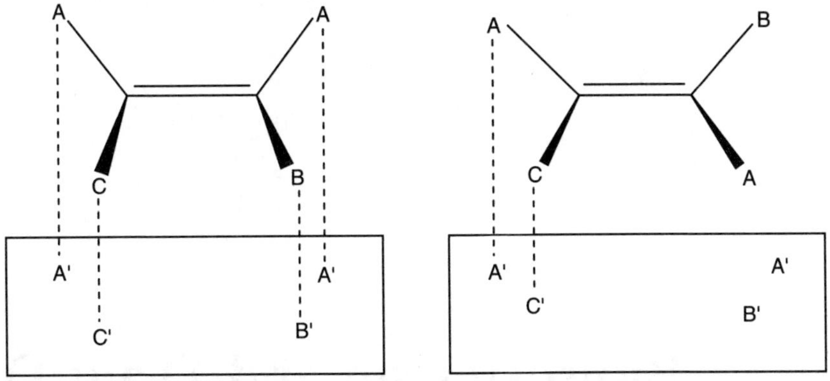

Fig. 13.6b Binding of *cis*- and *trans*-isomers to the receptors

Examples include the diethylstilbestrol, the *trans*-isomer (115) of which is about 14-times more active than the *cis*-isomer (116). This is because the distance between the two hydroxyl groups in the *trans*-isomer is same as in case of estradiol (117). Triprolidine, the H_1-receptor antagonist is another example of differences in activities of geometrical isomers. The *E*- or *trans*-isomer (118) is more active than the *Z*- or *cis* isomer (119). The distance between the two nitrogens, i.e. of pyridine and pyrrolidine being the factor for determining the activities of the two isomers.

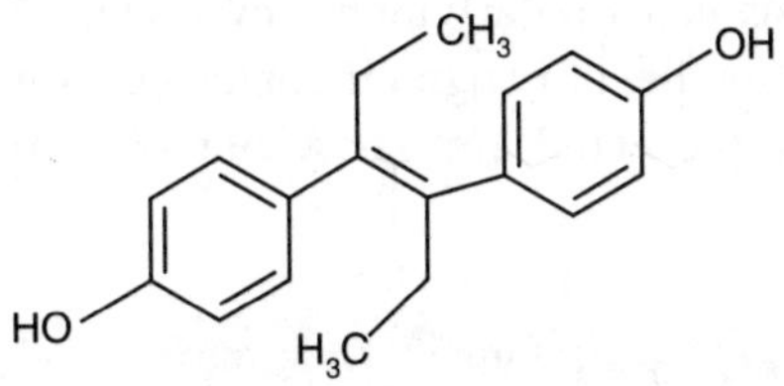

(115)

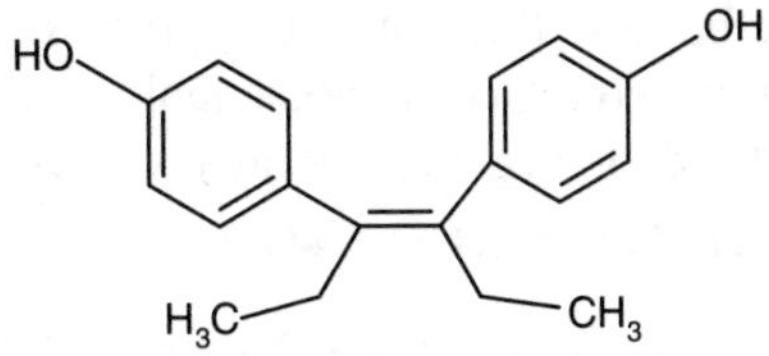

(116)

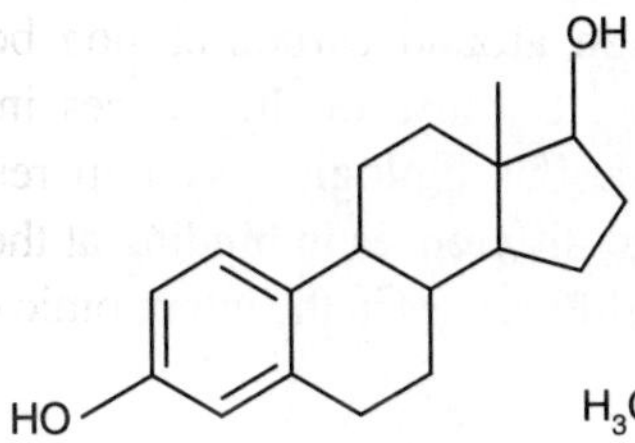

(117)

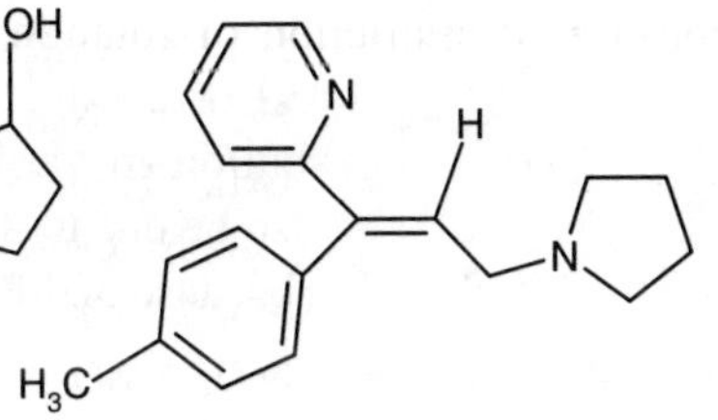

(118)

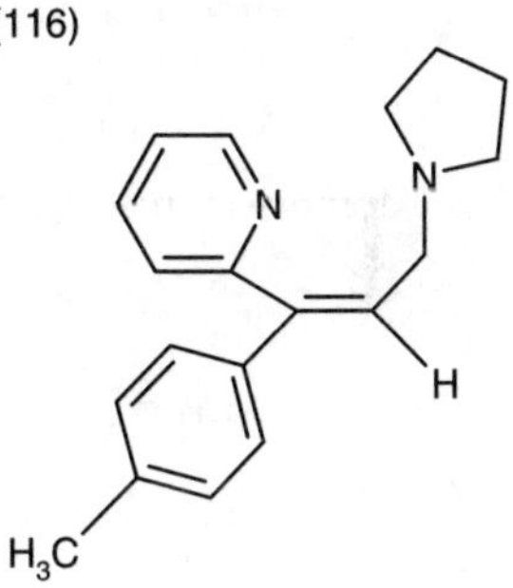

(119)

FURTHER READING

1. E.L. Eliel and S.H. Wilen, "Stereochemistry of Organic Compounds," Indian ed., Wiley India, New Delhi, 2008.
2. A.G. Draffan, G.R. Evans, and J.A. Henshilwood, in "Burger's Medicinal Chemistry and Drug Design," Vol. 1, D.J. Abraham, Ed., John Wiley and Sons, N. Y., 2003, p. 781.
3. B. Testa and J.M. Meyer, *Prog. in Drug Res.,* **32**, 249 (1988).
4. A.F. Caey in "Medicinal Chemistry," Part 1, 3rd ed., A. Burger, Ed., Wiley Interscience, New York, 1970, p. 81.

14

Bioisosterism and Drug Design

The concept of bioisosterism greatly helps in design of new moieties through isosteric replacement of atoms or groups of atoms of a lead compound. Such a replacement may also lead to compounds which are more effective, more specific, with better pharmacokinetic profile or even have antagonistic action.

The concept of isosterism goes back to Langmuir who grouped together various atoms, groups, radicals and molecules which possessed similar physical properties. These similarities in physical properties were because these atoms or group of atoms had similar number of valence electrons and were from the same column of periodic table. The original list of Langmuir contained 21 groups (Table 14.1). In the field of organic chemistry Langmuir predicted similarity between diazomethane ($H_2N{=}\overset{+}{N}{=}N$) and ketene ($H_2C{=}C{=}O$).

Table 14.1 Some groups of isosteres as proposed by Langmuir

Groups	*Isosteres*
1	H^-, He, Li^+
2	O^{2-} , F^-, Ne, Na^+, Mg^{2+}, Al^{3+}
3	S^{2-}, Cl^-, Ar, K^+, Ca^{2+}
8	N_2, CO, CN^-
9	CH_4, NH_4^+
10	CO_2, N_2O, N_3^-. CNO^-
20	MnO_4^-, CrO_4^{2-},
21	SeO_4^{2-}, AsO_4^{3-}

The concept of isosterism was further widened by Grimm, who in 1925 introduced Hydride Displacement Law. According to this law, 'Atoms anywhere upto four places in the periodic system before an inert gas, change their properties by uniting with one to four hydrogen atoms in such a manner that the resulting combination behaves like a pseudo atoms which are similar to the elements in groups one to four places, respectively, to their right'. Thus according to Grimm, the atoms and group of atoms in each vertical column of Table 14.2, represent group of isosteres. Erlenmeyer further widened Grimm's classification and according to him isosteres are "atoms, ions, and molecules in which peripheral layers of electrons are identical" (Table 14.3).

Table 14.2 Grimm's Hydride Displacement Law

C	N	O	F	Ne	Na
	CH	NH	OH	FH	–
		CH_2	NH_2	OH_2	FH_2^+
			CH_3	NH_3	OH_3^+
				CH_4	NH_4^+

Table 14.3 Isosteres with same number of peripheral electrons

Number of Peripheral Electrons				
4	**5**	**6**	**7**	**8**
N^+	P	S	Cl	ClH
P^+	As	Se	Br	BrH
S^+	Sb	Te	I	IH
As^+	–	PH	SH	SH_2
Sb^+	–	–	PH_2	PH_3

That isosteres possess similar biological activities was first demonstrated by Erlenmeyer. Thus, diazonium salts of *p*-aminodiphenylamine (1), *p*-aminodiphenylmethane (2), and *p*-aminodiphenyl ether, all showed similar antigenic activity. Similarly, the isosteric pairs (4a and 4b) and (5a and 5b) were serologically indistinguishable.

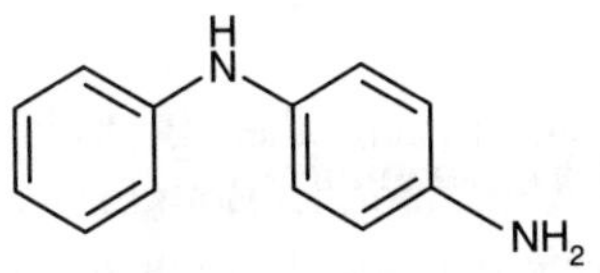

(1)

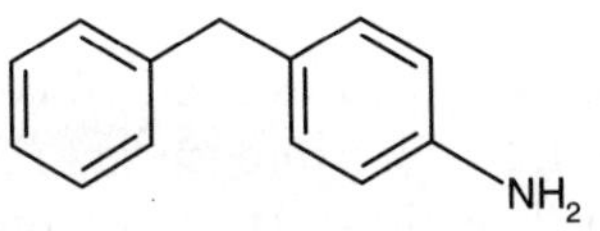

(2)

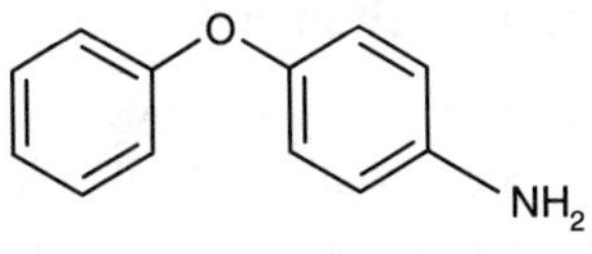

(3)

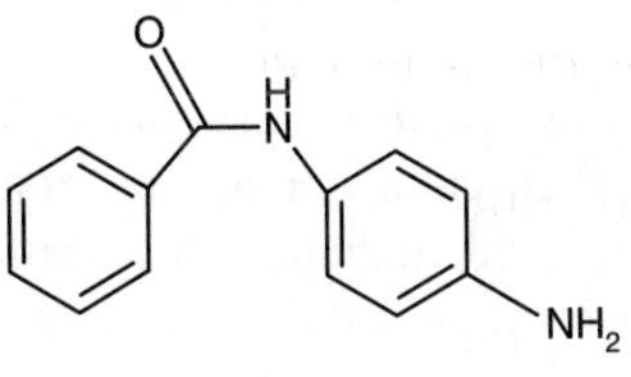

(4a)

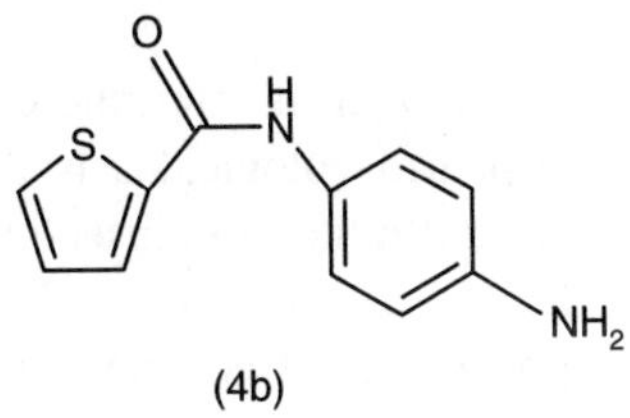

(4b)

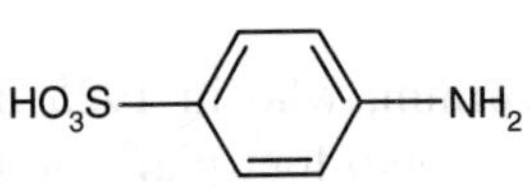

(5a)

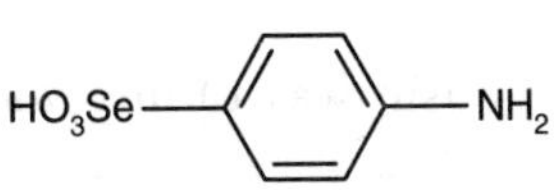

(5b)

It was Freidman who introduced the term 'Bioisosterism'. According to him 'Bioisosterism" included "compounds which fit the broadest definition for isosteres and have same type or antagonistic biological activity'. Based on this biosteres can be defined as 'groups or molecules which have physical and chemical similarities and which produce similar or antagonistic biological properties'.

Bioisosteres have been classified into (a) classical isosteres and (b) non-classical isosteres.

Classical isosteres have been further classified into:
(a) monovalent atoms and groups,
(b) divalent atoms and groups,
(c) trivalent atoms and groups,
(d) tetravalent substituted atoms, and
(e) ring equivalents.

Non-classical isosteres do not fit into steric and electronic definition of isosteres. Further, such isosteres do not possess same number of atoms (substituents) as the substituents for which they are used as replacement. They have been further classified into:
(a) exchangeable groups,
(b) ring vs acyclic structures, and
(c) reversal of groups.

CLASSICAL BIOISOSTERES – MONOVALENT ATOMS AND GROUPS

Monovalent atoms and groups which have been successfully interchanged include:
(a) hydrogen and fluorine,
(b) thiol and hydroxyl group,
(c) fluorine, hydroxyl, amino, and methyl group, an example of Grimm's Hydride Displacement Law,
(d) chloro, bromo, thiol and hydroxyl, an example of isosteres based on number of peripheral electrons.

Examples of each of these will be discussed below.

Hydrogen and Fluorine

Hydrogen and fluorine have been frequently used isosteric replacement of each other. Both the atoms have nearly same van der Waal radii, i.e. 1.2 Å for hydrogen and 1.35 Å for fluorine. Both form a stable inert bond with carbon and both are small and inert. However, fluorine is more electronegative, thus, more electron withdrawing than hydrogen. The differences in pharmacological activities between the two are due to electron withdrawing effect. This property has been also found to influence the metabolic fate of the drug.

The replacement of hydrogen by fluorine could result in similar or antagonistic activity. Thus, in β-haloalkylamines, the pharmacological activity is lost when chloro or bromo group is replaced by either fluorine or hydrogen. Similarly in insecticides related to dihalodiphenyltrihaloethanes (6), activity is encountered when X = Cl, Br, or CH_3 and Y = Cl. However, no activity is observed when X = H or F and Y = Cl. The opposite effect is found when hydrogen at position 5 of uracil (7) is replaced by

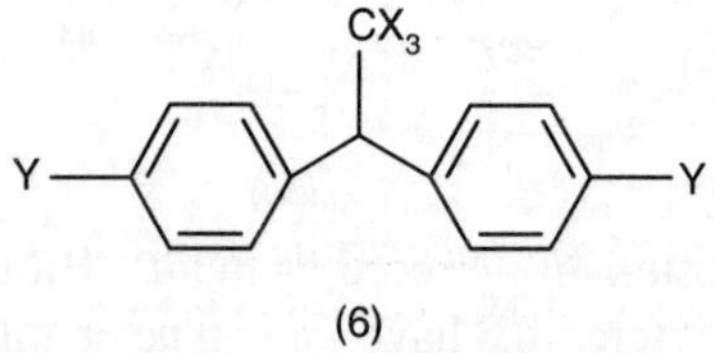

(6)

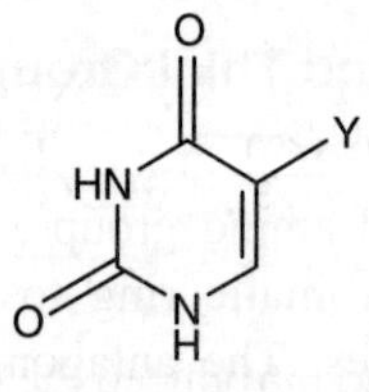

(7), Y = H
(8), Y = F

fluorine to give 5-fluorouracil (8) which is used as anticancer agent. The mechanism of which is as follows. Uracil (7) after being converted to 2'-deoxyuridylic acid (9) is converted to thymidylate (10) by thymidylate synthase in presence of 5,10-methylenetetrahydrofolic acid. The thymidylate (10) is required for the synthesis of nucleic acids. 5-Fluorouracil (8) after being converted to 5-fluoro-2'-deoxyuracil (11) acts as a competitive inhibitor of thymidylate synthase thus blocking the synthesis of thymidylate (10). This inhibitory effect of 5-fluoro analog of uracil (7) has been attributed to the inductive effect of fluorine.

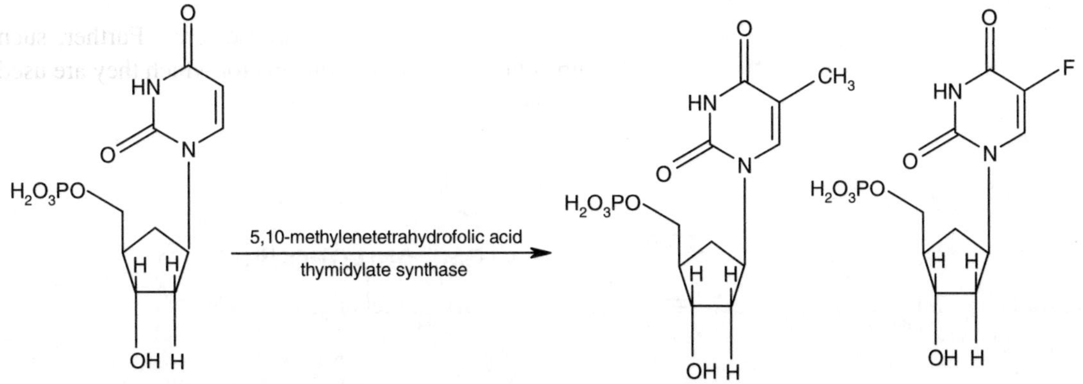

(9) (10) (11)

Replacement of hydrogen with fluorine also results in enhanced activity. Thus, the topical anti-inflammatory activity of androstane 17β-carbothionate (12a and 13a) was enhanced when hydrogens were replaced with fluorine (12b and 13b).

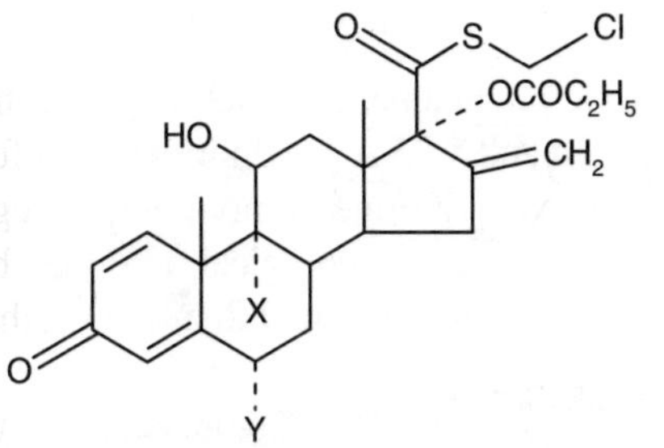

(12)

(a), X = F; Y = H

(b), X = Y = F

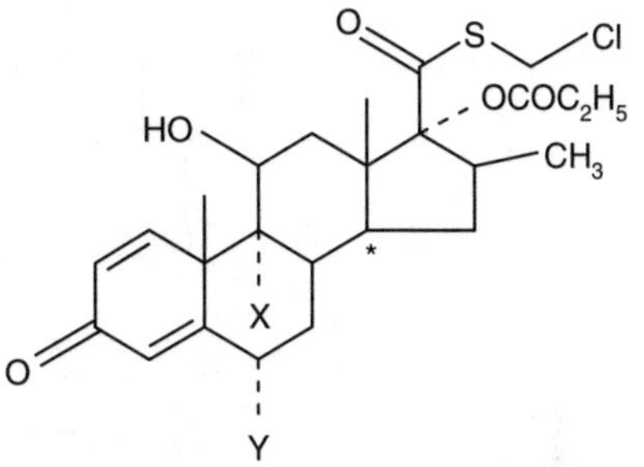

(13)

(a), X = Y = H

(b), X = F; Y = H

Hydroxyl, Amino, and Thiol Groups

Hydroxyl, amino, and thiol groups have been frequently interchanged. There are some similarities between hydroxyl and amino groups. Both donate electrons because of which they both direct the incoming group in aromatic ring to *ortho-* and *para-*positions. Both form hydrogen bonds and coordination complexes. The antagonistic activity of hydroxyl and amino groups is illustrated by pteroylglutamic acid (14) and aminopterin (15). Aminopterin (15) is inhibitor of dihydrofolic acid reductase, the enzyme required to reduce folic acid (14) to dihydrofolic acid (16) which ultimately is reduced to tetrahydrofolic acid (17).The tetrahydrofolic acid, as N^5,N^{10}-methylenetetrahydrofolic acid (18) transfers methyl group to 2'-deoxyuridylate (9) to give thymidylate (10) which is required for DNA synthesis. Thus, inhibition of dihydrofoliate (16) ultimately results in the death of the cell.

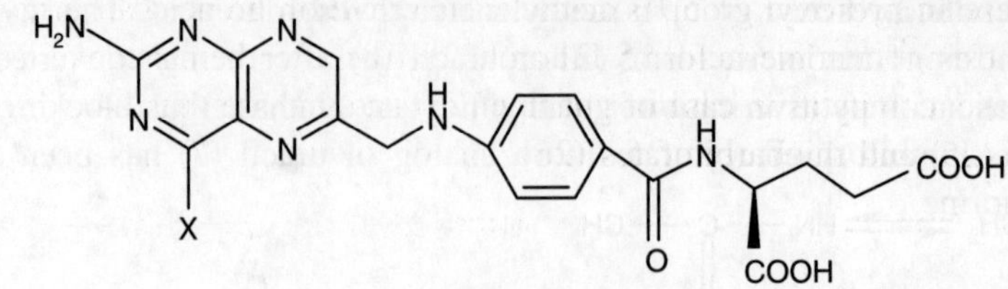

(14), X = OH

(15), X = NH_2

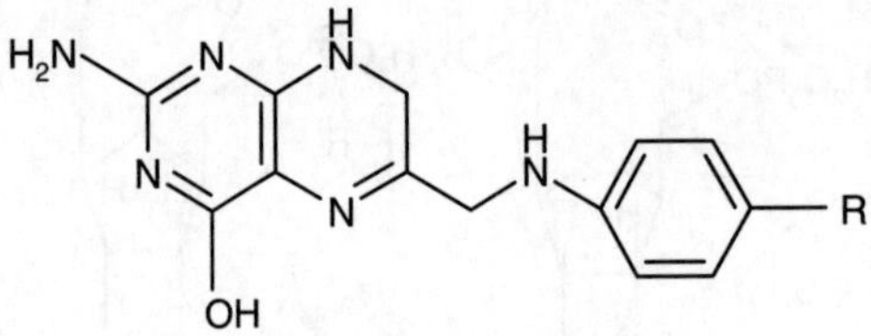

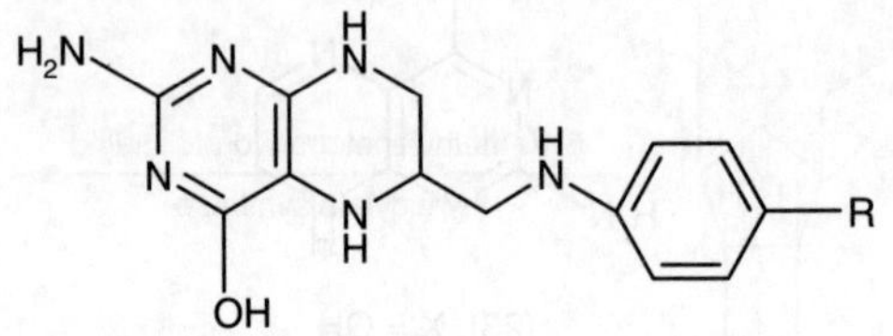

(16), R = $\overset{O}{\overset{\|}{C}}NHCH(COOH)CH_2CH_2COOH$

(17), R = $\overset{O}{\overset{\|}{C}}NHCH(COOH)CH_2CH_2COOH$

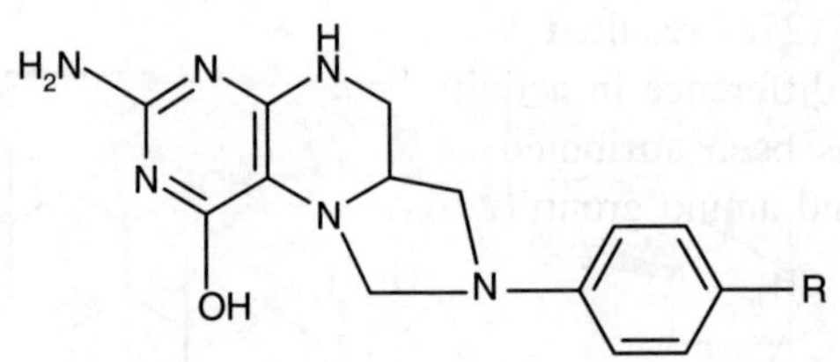

(18), R = $\overset{O}{\overset{\|}{C}}NHCH(COOH)CH_2CH_2COOH$

Other example involving interchange of hydroxyl and amino group include benzodiazepine binding activity of 9-(3-aminophenyl)methyl-6-dimethylamino-9-benzyl-9*H*-purine (19) and its 3-hydroxyl isostere (20). Not much difference was found between the two isosteres.

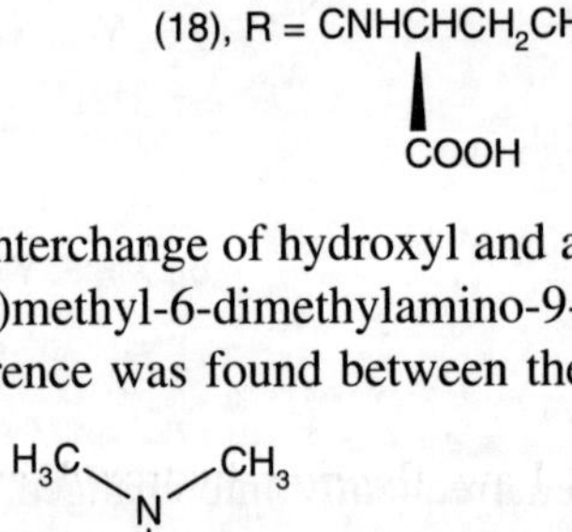

(19), R = NH_2

(20), R = OH

Thiol group like phenolic hydroxyl group is acidic in nature. Both groups can form hydrogen bonds and both can exist in different tautomeric forms (21 and 22). Isosteric interchange of hydroxyl and thiol may result in antagonistic activity as in case of guanine (23) and thioguanine (24) or similar activity as in case of barbiturates (25) and thiobarbiturates (26).

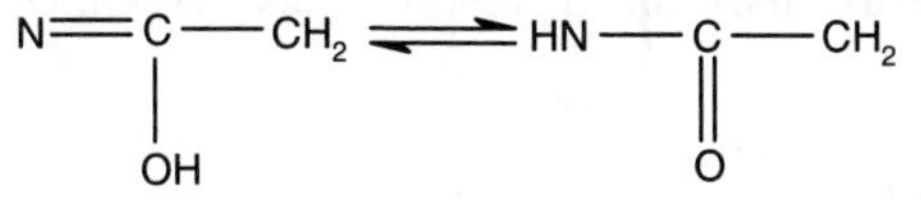

(21)

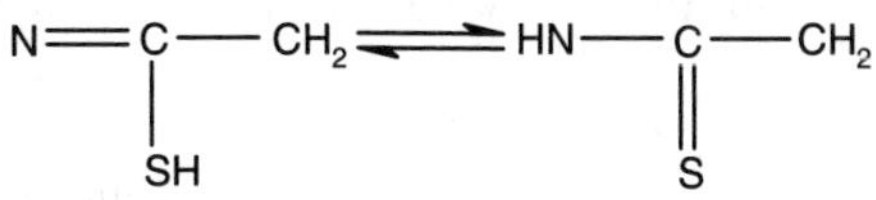

(22)

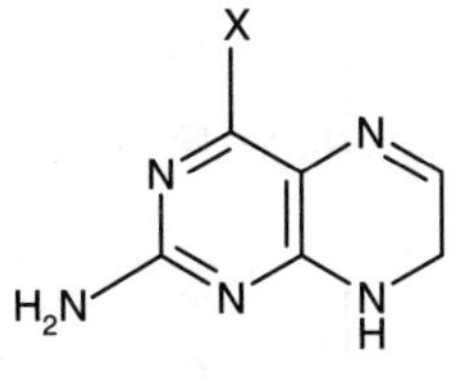

(23), X = OH

(24), X = SH

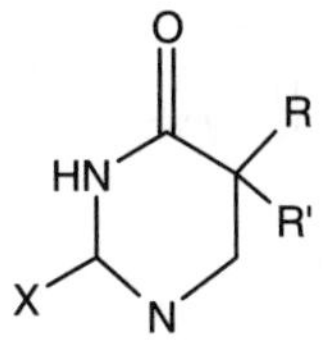

(25), X = OH

(26), X = SH

Effect of isosteric interchange of hydroxyl, amino, and thiol on the anti-inflammatory activity has been studied on thiazole analogs (27) which possess both cyclooxygenase and 5-lipoxygenase inhibitory activity. While hydroxyl (27a) and amino (27b) analogs showed similar cyclooxygenase activity the 5-lipoxygenase activity in case of amino analog (27b) was much higher than hydroxyl analog (27a). Replacement with thiol group (27c) resulted in higher potency towards both cyclooxygenase and 5-lipoxygenase activities. This difference in activity between the thiol (27) analog and the other two analogs, i.e. (27a and 27b) has been attributed to lower electronegativity of thiol group (2.32) as compared to hydroxyl (3.51) and amino group (2.61).

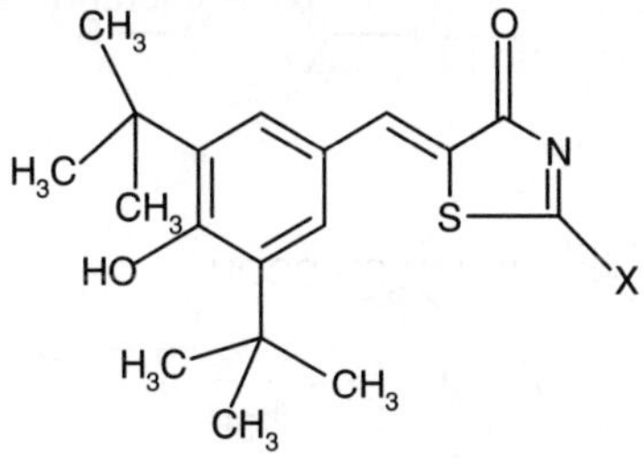

(a), X = OH

(b), X = NH_2

(c), X = SH

(27)

Fluorine, Hydroxyl, Amino and Methyl

According to Grimm's Hydride Displacement Law, fluorine, hydroxyl, amino, and methyl groups are isosteric with each other (Table 14.2). Interchange of fluorine and hydrogen and amino and hydroxyl has already been discussed earlier. Interchange of hydrogen with fluorine, hydroxyl and amino has been studied using N-[2-(mercaptomethyl)-3-phenylbutanoyl)]amino acids (28). The activity measured was the in vitro inhibition of angiotensin converting enzyme (ACE) and neutral endopeptidases (NEP) activity resulting in useful hypotensive and diuretic effect, respectively. The rating of inhibitory activity in both the cases was: H(28 a)> F(28 b)> OH (28 c)> NH_2 (28d) paralleling the van der Waal radii of hydrogen (1.20Å), fluorine (1.47Å), hydroxyl (1.53Å), and amino (1.79Å) Chloro- and methyl groups behave in similar manner, both have similar volumes,both are lipophilic and are therefore isosteric. One of the classical example where both show resemblance is the insecticide dichlorodiphenyltrichloroethane (29) and its *tert*.butyl analog (30). Both these compounds have neurotoxic properties. Since methyl substituent is subject to metabolic degradation the neurotoxic action of *tert*. butyl analog (30) does not persist for long. Thus, substitution of chloro- with methyl- results in increased metabolism and decreased half-life. The substitution by chloro- could be used to block the metabolism and thus increase the

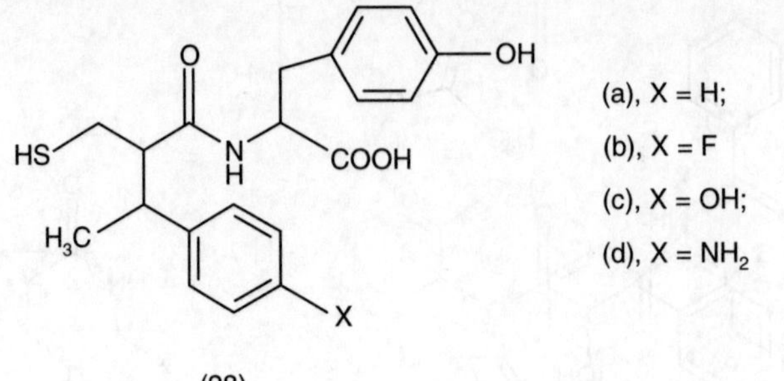

(28)

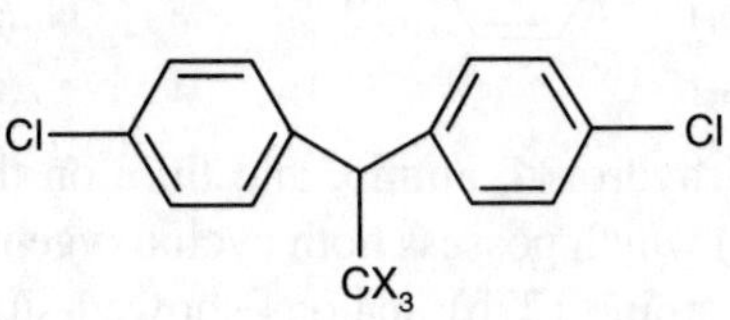

(29), X = Cl
(30), X = CH_3

duration of action. An example of this is phenobarbital (31) which is metabolized to *p*-hydroxy analog (32) and subsequently excreted as glucouronide. The 4-chlorophenyl analog (33) of phenobarbitone (31) in which the hydrogen has been replaced with chloro is metabolized slowly as compared to phenobarbitone (31) and thus its duration of action is longer.

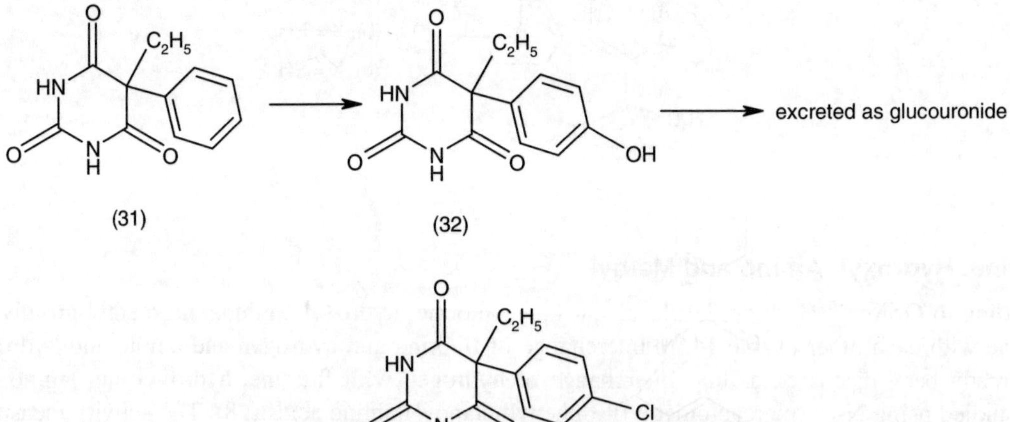

(31) (32)

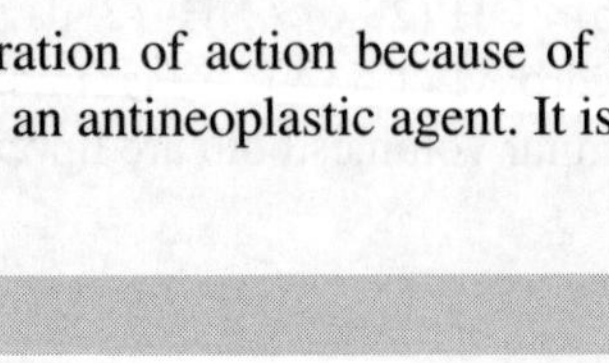

(33)

Another example of increased duration of action because of decreased metabolism using isosteric replacement is that of paclitaxel (34), an antineoplastic agent. It is metabolized to 6α-hydroxypaclitaxel

(35), which is 30-fold less active than the parent compound. Isosteric replacement of hydrogen with 6α-fluoro resulted in a compound (36) which had longer duration of action because of decreased metabolism. The 6α-bromo and chloro analogs had similar effects.

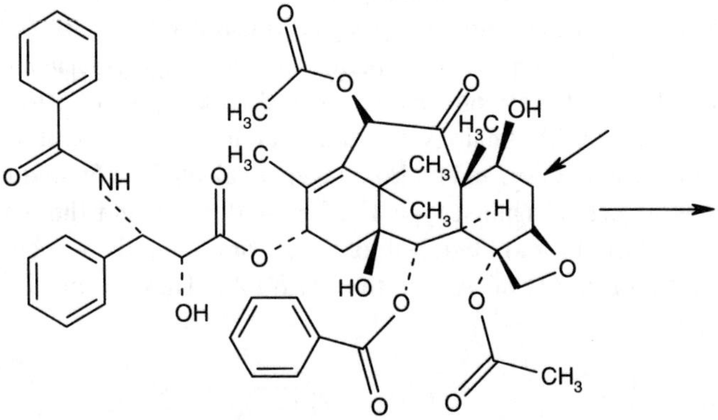

(34)

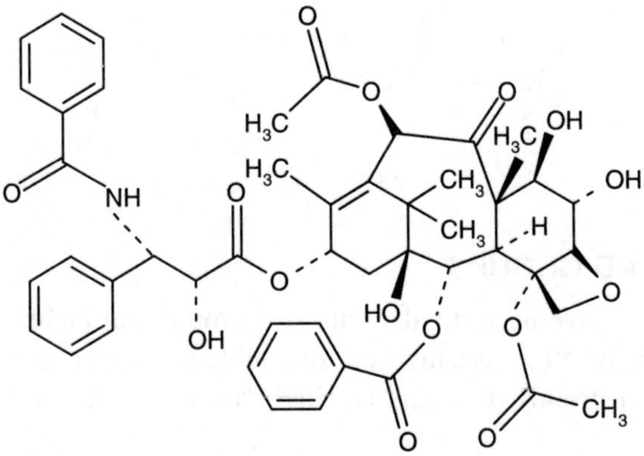

(35)

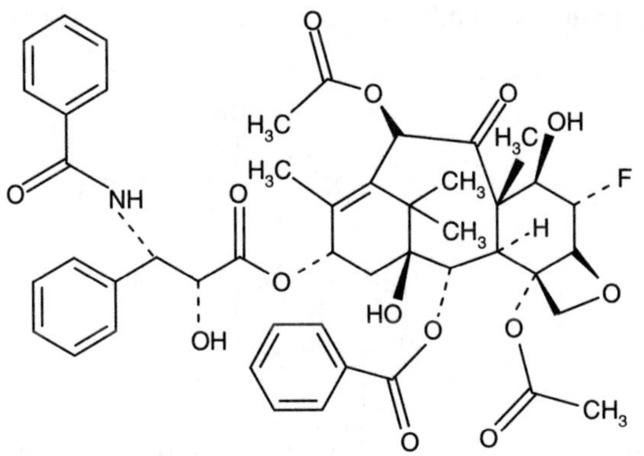

(36)

Monovalent Atoms Involving Interchange of Chloro, Bromo, Thiol and Hydroxyl Groups

The interchange of hydroxyl and thiol has already been discussed. Chloro, bromo, and thiol represent atoms and group of isosteres which have similarity in their number of peripheral electrons as enanciated by Erlenmeyer. Interchange of these atoms and groups is illustrated by design of 5α-reductase inhibitors. Dihydroteststerone (37) has been implicated in benign prostatic hyperplasia and prostratic cancer. It is produced by the action of 5α-reductase on testosterone (38). Two types of 5α-reductases are known and these include 5α-reductase I and II. Analogs of 3-oxo-4-androstene-17β-carboxamides (39) substituted at position 4 with chloro, bromo, thiol, and hydroxyl were evaluated for 5α-reductase inhibition activity. All the four analogs were active against type II of 5α-reductase and the activity was in the order: hydroxyl (39d)> chloro (39a)> bromo (39b) > thiol (39c) paralleling the van der Waal radii of hydroxyl (1.53 Å), chloro (1.73 Å), bromo (1.86 Å) and thiol (1.80 Å). These results indicate that steric factors play part in their activity.

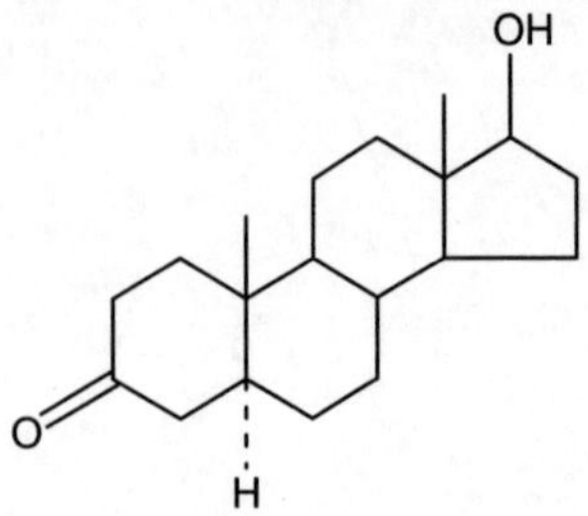

(37)

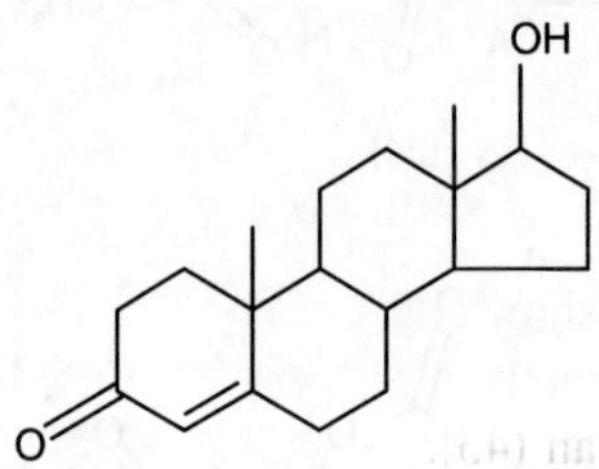

(38)

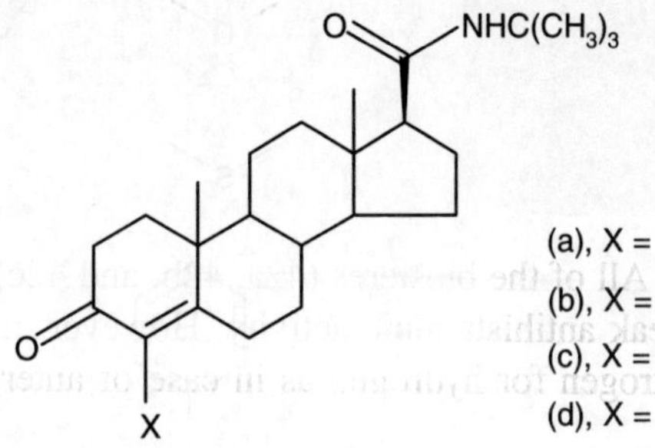

(39)

(a), X = Cl
(b), X = Br
(c), X = SH
(d), X = OH

DIVALENT ATOMS AND GROUPS

The isosteres in this class have been divided into two groups and include:

(a) isosteres in which the atoms are involved in double bond, example, C=C, C=N, C=O, and C=S,

(b) isosteres in which groups or atoms are involved in single bond and include, $-CH_2-$, -NH-, -S-, O-.

Isosteric Replacement Involving Atoms with Double Bonds

Tolrestat (40), an aldose reductase inhibitor and its oxo-isostere (41) have been found equipotent in their inhibitory activity.

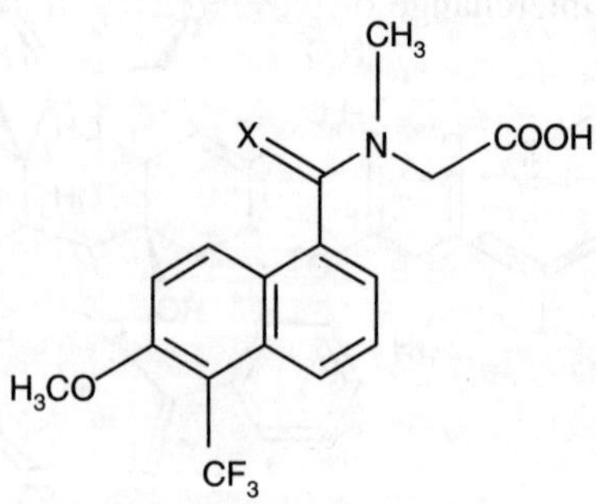

(40), X = S
(41), X = O

Isosteric Replacement in Divalent Atoms or Groups involving Single Bonds

This is a major class of isosteres and involves: –O- , -S- , -NH- , and $-CH_2-$. They have nearly similar bond angles (Table 3). One of the example of interchange of these groups is from antihistaminics of the type (42).

Table 14.3 Bond angles of some divalent atos and groups with two single bonds

Atoms and Groups	*Bond Angles*
$-O-$	108° ± 3°
$-NH-$	111° ± 2°
$-CH_2-$	111.5° ± 3°
$-S-$	112° ± 2°

All of the biosteres (42a, 42b, and 42c) show antihistaminic activity. The imino analog (42c) shows weak antihistaminic activity. However, its activity was increased when phenyl group was attached to nitrogen for hydrogen as in case of antergan (43).

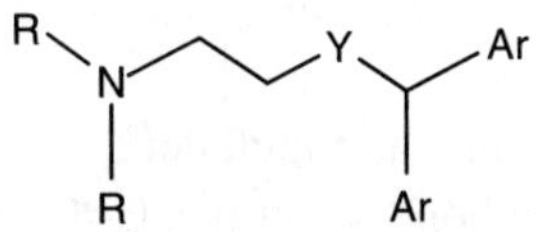

(42)

(a), Y = CH_2 ; (b), Y = O ;

(c), Y = NH

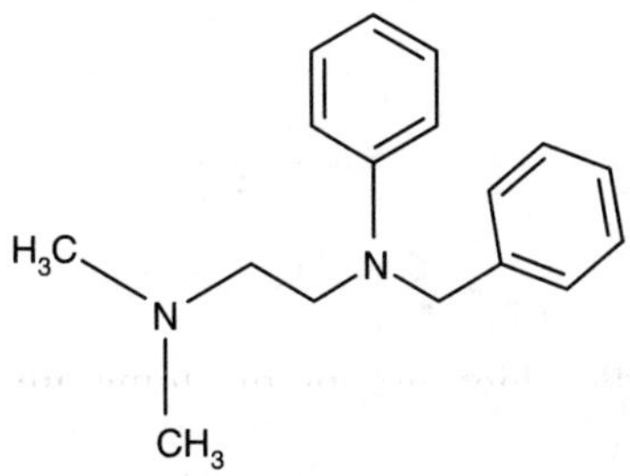

(43)

Presence of these atoms near carbonyl group results in esters (44a), thioesters (44b), amides (44c), and ketone (44d). Examples of interchange of these functional groups are found in various classes of drugs as given below.

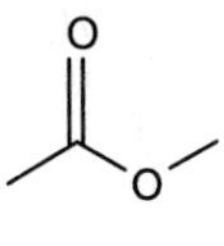

(44a)

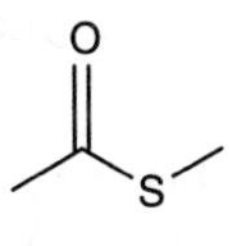

(44b)

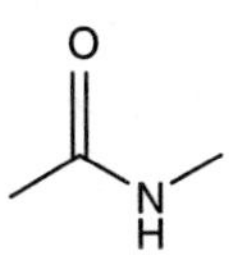

(44c)

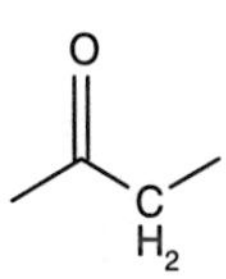

(44d)

Local anesthetics – Procaine (45a) and Thiocaine(45b):

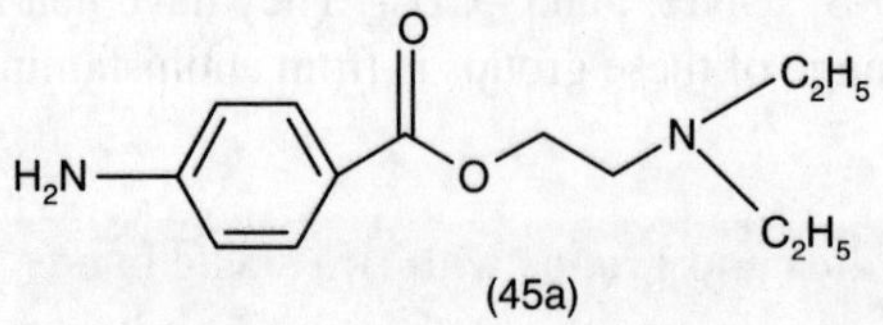

(45a)

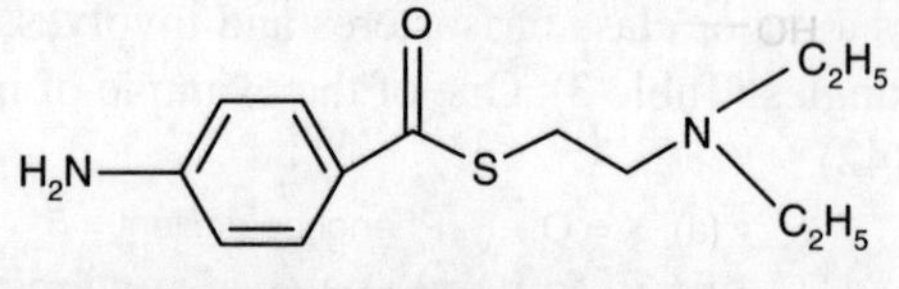

(45b)

Antispasmodics – Adiphenine (46a), its Amide (46b) and Thioloester (46c).

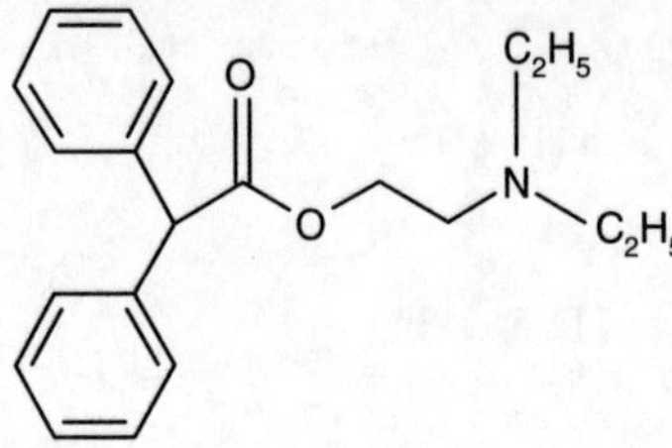

(46a)

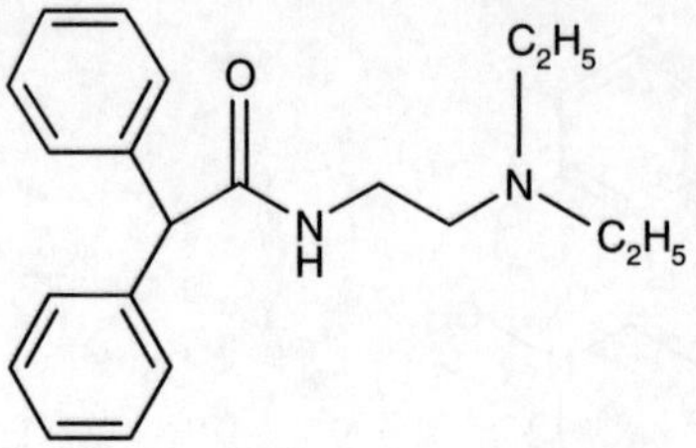

(46b)

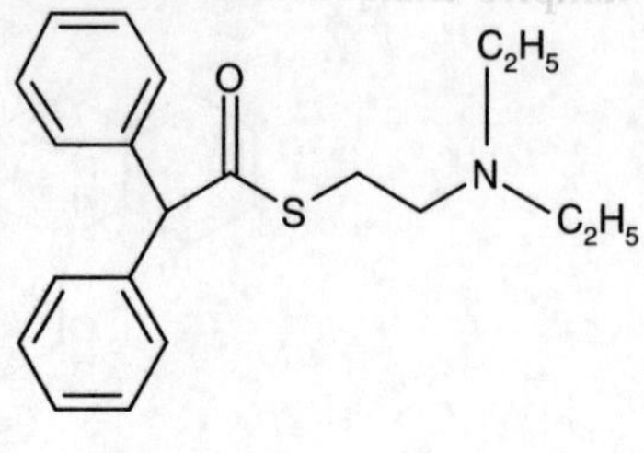

(46c)

The ester (46a) is more potent than the amide (46b) and thioloester (46c).

Analgesics – Meperidine (47a) and its keto isostere (47b), both have similar activity. Another example from analgesics is of bemidone (48a) and ketobemidone (48b).

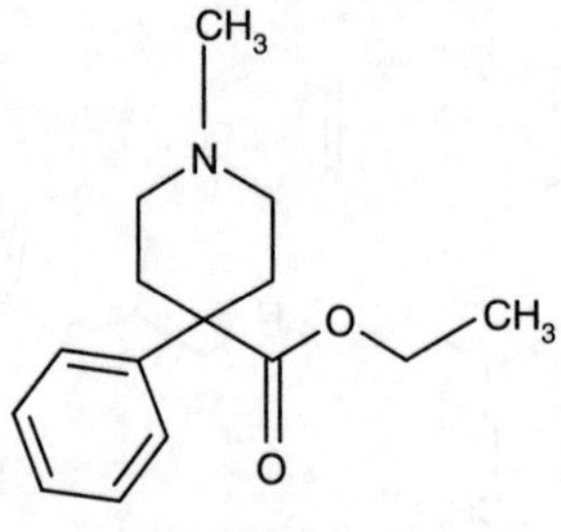

(47a)

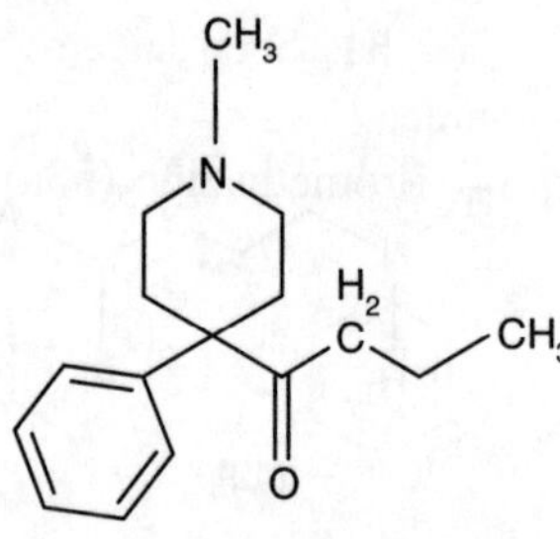

(47b)

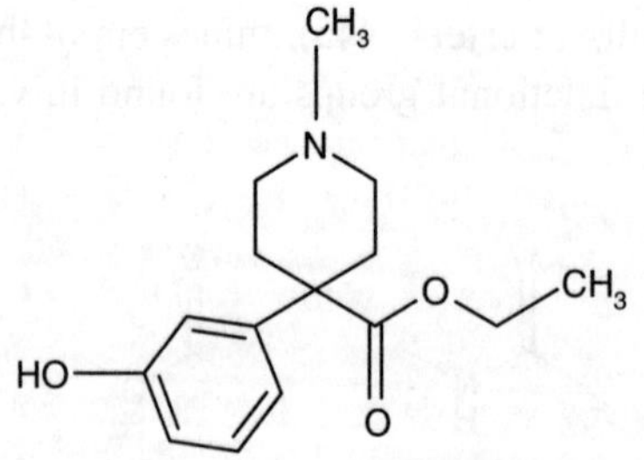

(48a)

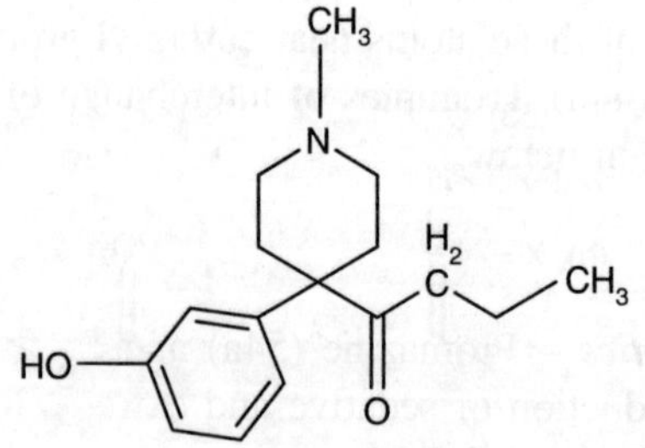

(48b)

Replacement of oxygen with $-CH_2-$ has been carried out in other cases also with good results.

Examples:

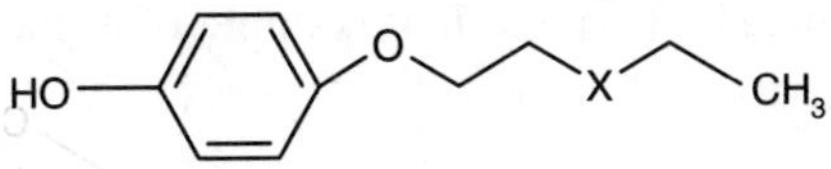

(49)

(a), X = O, Phenol coefficient = 5

(b), X = CH_2, Phenol coefficient = 30

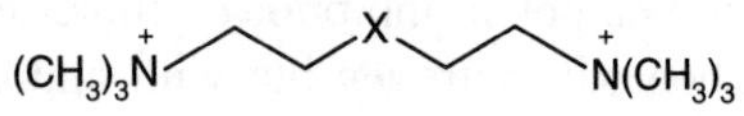

(50)

(a), X = O Ganglionic blocking activity = 10%

(b), X = CH_2 Ganglionic blocking activity = 100%

Interchange of sulphur, oxygen, -NH-, and -CH_2- in heterocyclic rings usually results in similar activities, examples tranqullizers (51) and antidepressants (52).

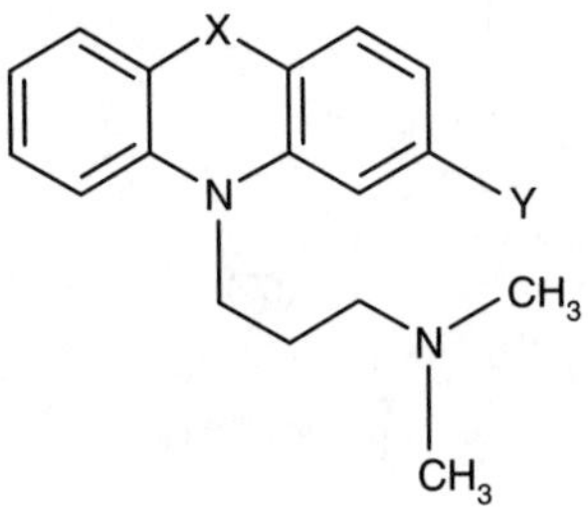

(51), X = S or O; Y = Cl or CF_3

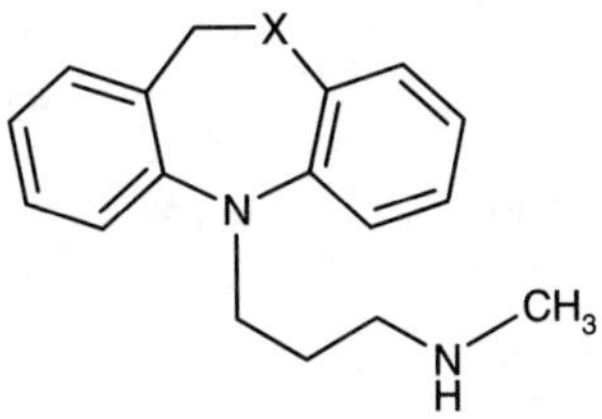

(52), X = CH_2, S, or NH

Trivalent Atoms and Groups

Trivalent group =CH- has been successfully interchanged with trivalent atom =N-. Examples from various classes include:

Antihistaminics – Promethazine (53a) and Isothipendyl (53b)

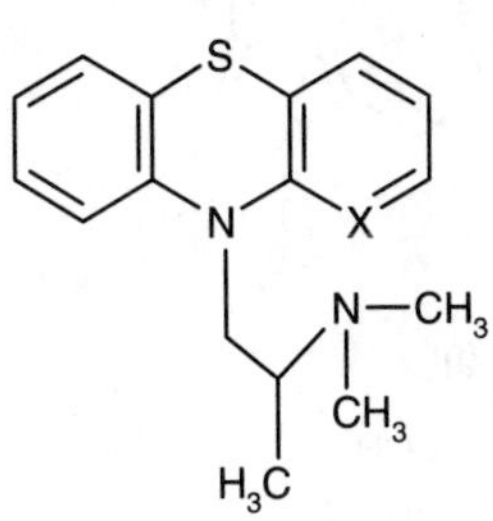

(53)

(a), X = CH

(b), X = N

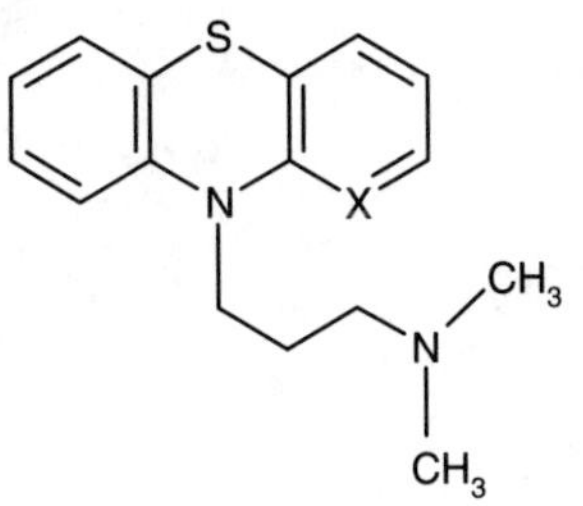

(54)

(a), X = CH

(b), X = N

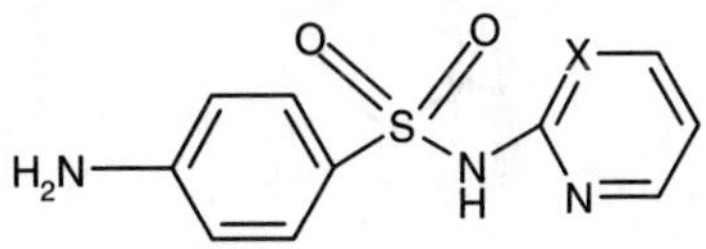

(55)

(a), X = CH

(b), X = N

Neuroleptics – Promazine (54a) and Prothipendyl (54b).Change from carbon isostere to nitrogen results in reduction of sedative and extrapyramidal effects.

Sulpha Drugs – Sulphapyridine (55a) and Sulphadiazine (55b).

Antipyretics – Aminopyrine (56a) and its isostere (56b) are equally effective as antipyretics.It is an example of effective interchange of extra-annular tertiary amino nitrogen with carbon with same activity.

Steroids – Cholesterol (57a) and its nitrogen isostere (57b) is an example from steroidal drugs. The nitrogen isostere is a potent inhibitor of cholesterol synthesis. It is another example of replacement of extrannular carbon with nitrogen but with opposite activity.

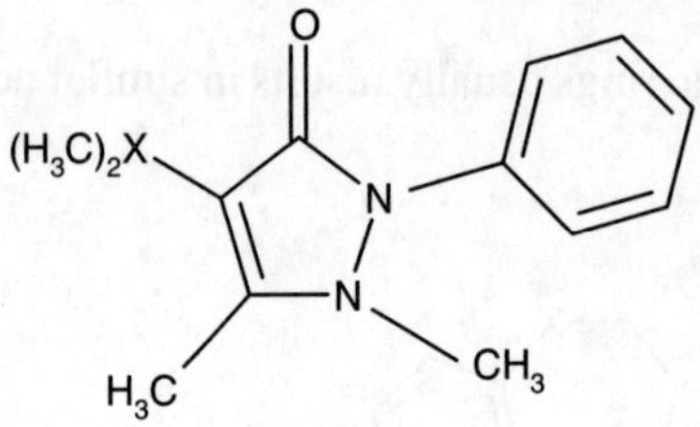

(56)

(a), X = N

(b), X = CH

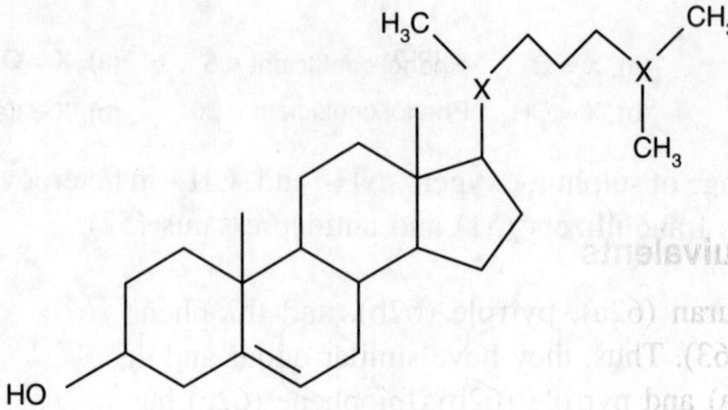

(57)

(a), X = CH

(b), X = N

Antibacterials – Norfloxacin (58a) and enoxacin (58b).

Miotic – Pilocarpine (59a) and its oxazolidinone (59b) isostere. The nitrogen isostere (59b) has a longer duration of action than the carbon isostere (59a).

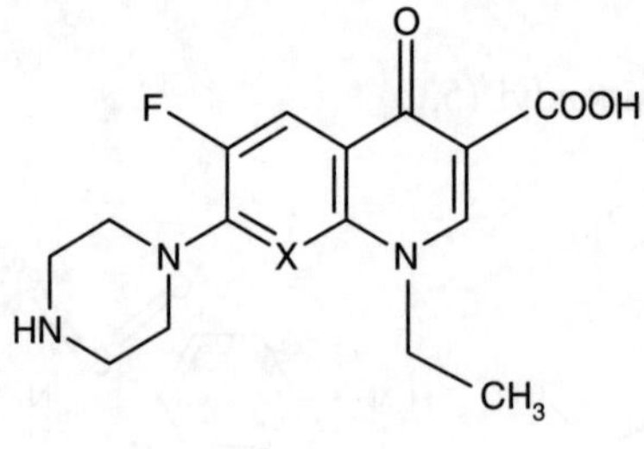

(58)

(a), X = CH

(b), X = N

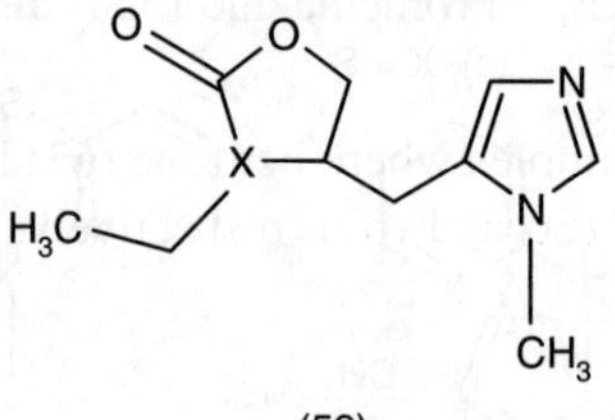

(59)

(a), X = CH

(b), X = N

Tetrasubstituted Atoms

The tetrasubstituted atoms and include: $=C=$, $=\overset{+}{P}=$, $=\overset{+}{As}=$ and $=\overset{+}{Sb}=$

Tetrasubstituted carbon and tetrasubstituted nitrogens are not equivalent because the nitrogen carries a positive charge. However some resemblance has been observed. Thus, the carbon isostere (60) of acetylcholine (61a) is hydrolyzed by cholinesterase of human erythrocytes at about half the rate at which acetycholine (61) is hydrolyzed. The phosphonium (61b), arsonium (61c), and stibonium (61d) isosteres are more akin to nitrogen isostere, acetylcholine (61a). However they are more toxic.

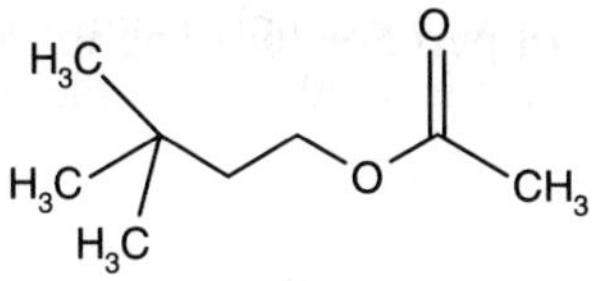

(60)

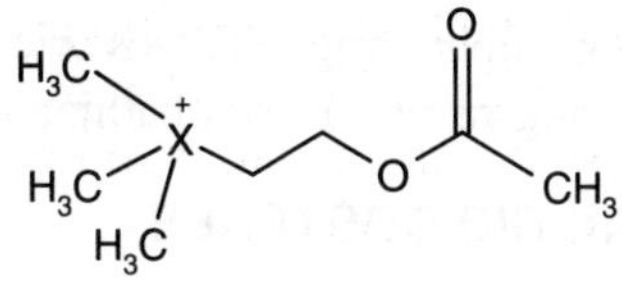

(61)

(a), X = N ; (c), X = As
(b), X = P ; (d), X = Sb

Ring Equivalents

Among furan (62a), pyrrole (62b), and thiophene (62c), thiophene (62c) has great similarity with benzene (63). Thus, they have similar odour and nearly same boiling point. Moreover as compared to furan (62a) and pyrrole (62b), thiophene (62c) has more aromatic character and therefore, resembles benzene (63) much more. These similarities have also been observed in biological activities. Thus, benzene (63) ring, which is the commonest ring in many classes of drugs, has been interchanged with thiophene (62c). Similarly, pyridine (64) and benzene (63) and pyridine (64) and thiazole (65) rings are also bioisosteric.

(62)

(63)

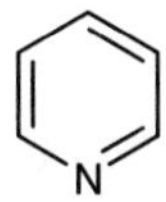

(64)

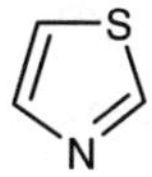

(65)

(a), X = O
(b), X = NH
(c), X = S

Some of the examples where benzene (63) has been replaced by thiophene (62c) ring include 2- and 3- thienyl analogs (66 and (67), respectively, of tripelennamine (68).

(66)

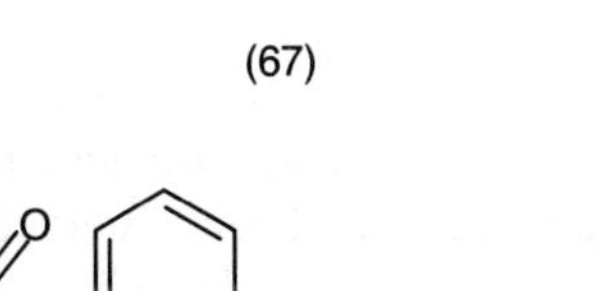

(67)

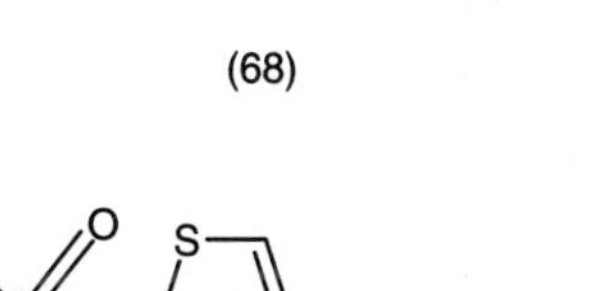

(68)

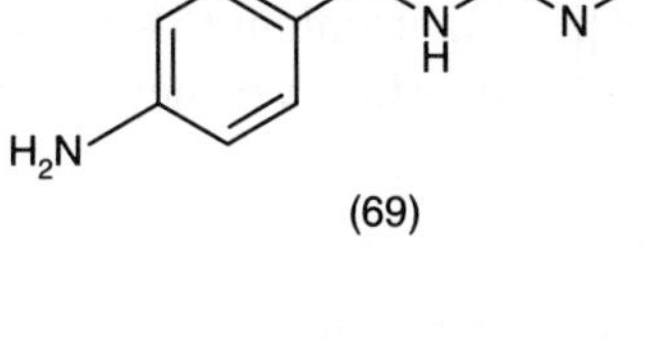

(69)

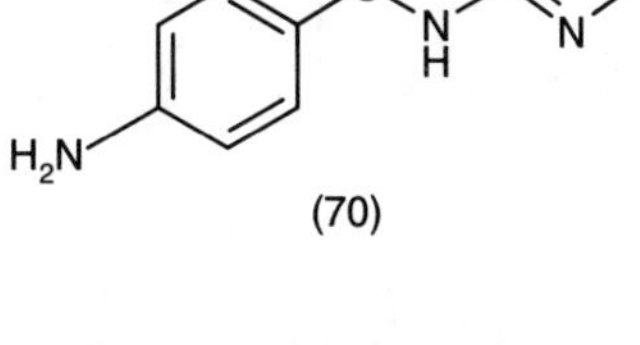

(70)

Similarly, among sulpha drugs the isosteric replacement of pyridine (64) ring in sulphapyridine (69) with thiazole (65) ring results in sulphathiazole (70).

NON-CLASSICAL BIOISOSTERES

Non-classical bioisosteres are groups that are structurally similar but do not fit in the definition of classical bioisosteres. These isosteres possess similar biological activities because of similarities in some physicochemical properties of molecule or functional group.

Exchangeable Groups

The examples in this class include carboxylic and sulphonic acid analogs, such as niacin (71) and pyridine 3-sulphonic acid (72) and pantothenic acid (73) and its sulphonic acid analog (74).

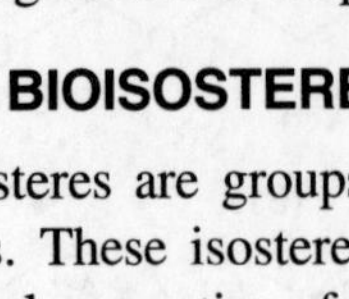

(71)

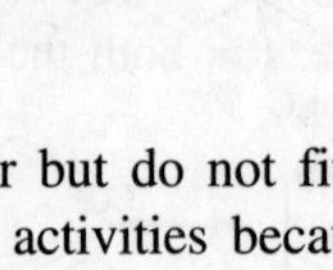

(72)

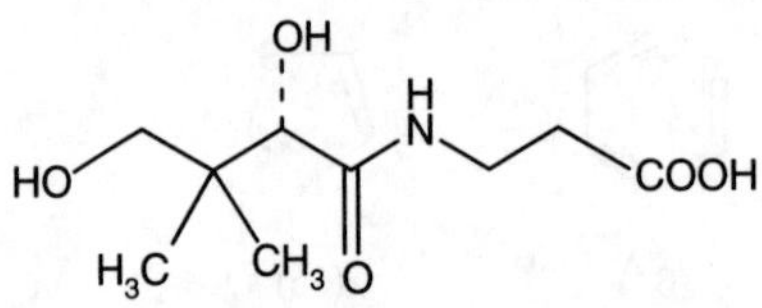

(73)

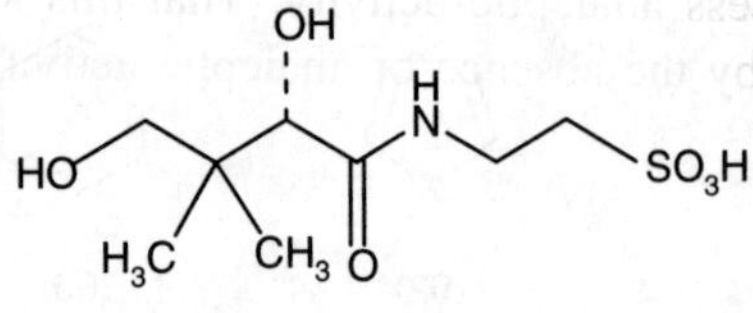

(74)

The polarity of sulphonamide group is comparable to that of carboxylic acid group. This is the case of sulphanilamide (75) and *p*-aminobenzoic acid (76) which show antagonistic biological activity.

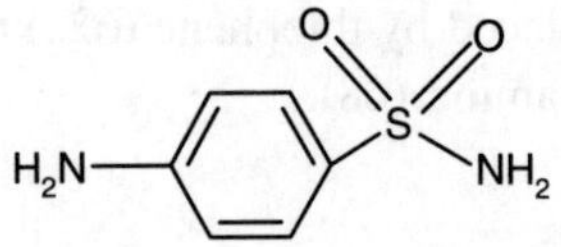

(75)

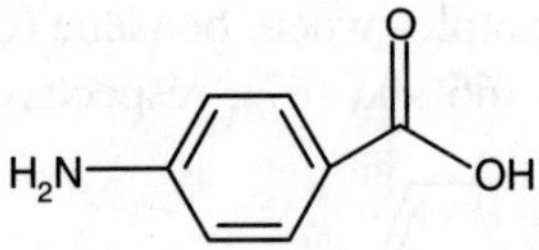

(76)

Among analgetics, the carbonyl group has been interchanged with sulphone group. Examples include meperidine (47a) and its sulphone analog (77) both of which show analgetic activity. Similarly, both

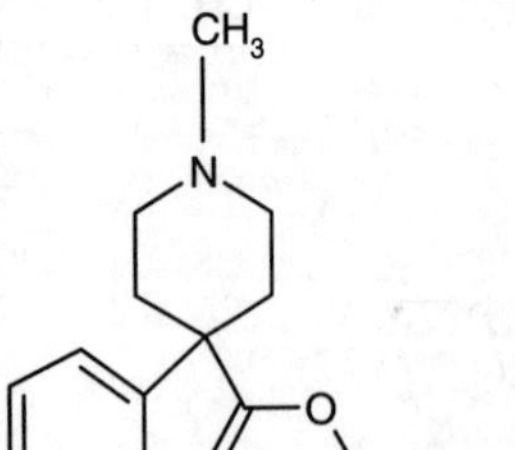

(47a)

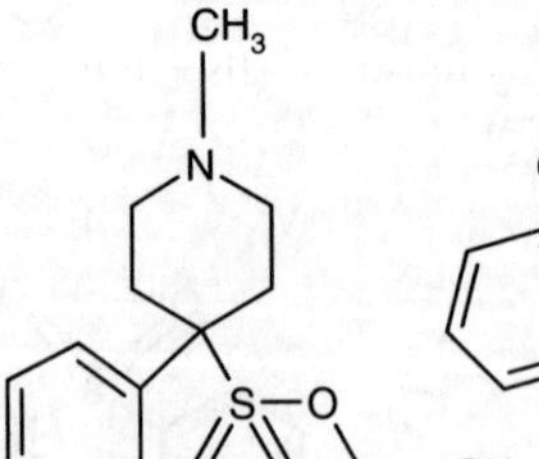

(77)

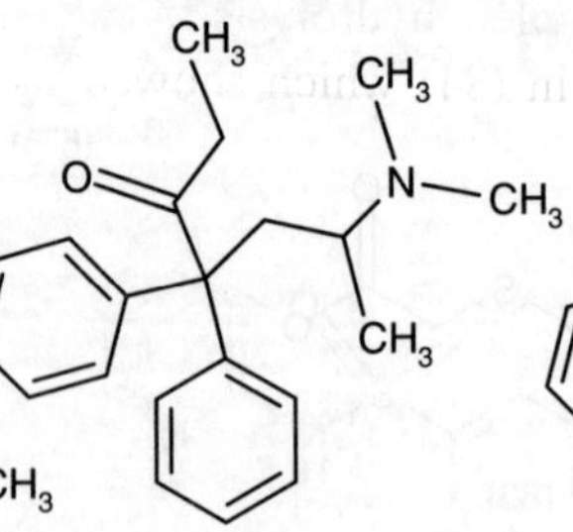

(78)

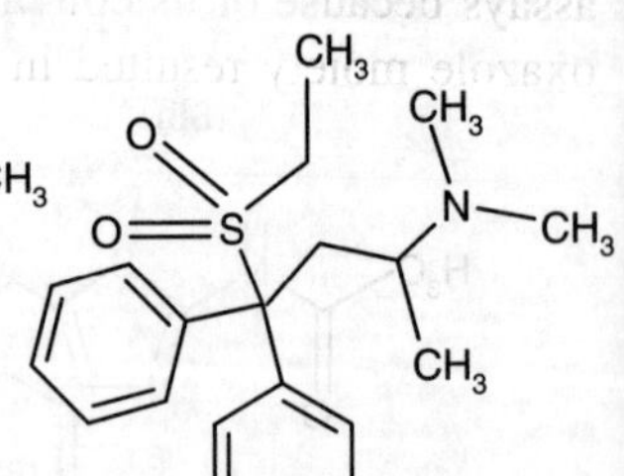

(79)

methadone (78) and its sulphone analog (79) show analgetic activity. However, the sulphone analogs in both the cases show lower analgetic activity.

An interesting example is that of pyridine and nitrobenzene. A comparision of resonance structures shows that polar effects in both the rings are similar (Fig. 14.1).

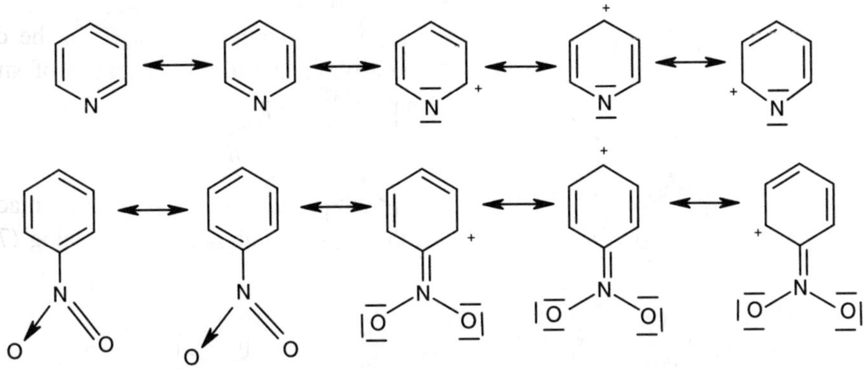

Fig. 14.1

An example of this is in the nikethamide (80) and diethylamide of *m*-nitrobenzoic acid (81), both of which possess analeptic activity. That this similarity in biological activity is due to polar effect is confirmed by the absence of analeptic activity in diethylamide of *p*-nitrobenzoic acid (82).

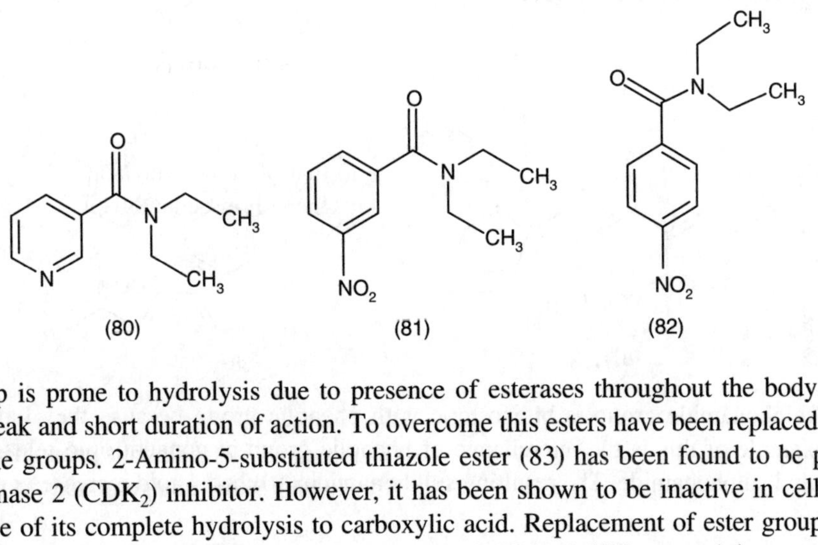

(80) (81) (82)

Ester group is prone to hydrolysis due to presence of esterases throughout the body. As a result, esters have weak and short duration of action. To overcome this esters have been replaced with oxazole and oxadiazole groups. 2-Amino-5-substituted thiazole ester (83) has been found to be potent cyclin-dependent Kinase 2 (CDK_2) inhibitor. However, it has been shown to be inactive in cell proliferation assays because of its complete hydrolysis to carboxylic acid. Replacement of ester group of (83) with oxazole moiety resulted in (84) which showed increased CDK_2 inhibitory activity as well as potent

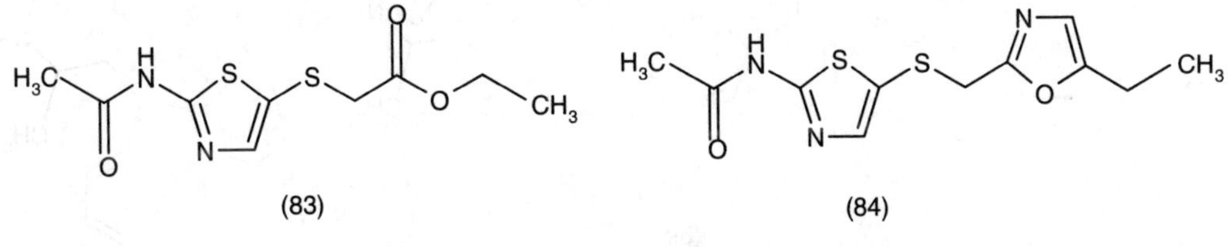

(83) (84)

antiproliferative activity. Stability of esters towards metabolic hydrolysis has also been achieved by replacing the ester group with oxadiazole moiety. The piperidine analog (85) is a dopamine transporter.

In an effort to increase its duration of action the ester moiety of (85) was replaced with oxadiazole moiety. The resultant analog (86) had similar affinities towards dopamine and norepinephrine as that of ester analog (85). Further its duration of action was twice that of the ester analog (85).

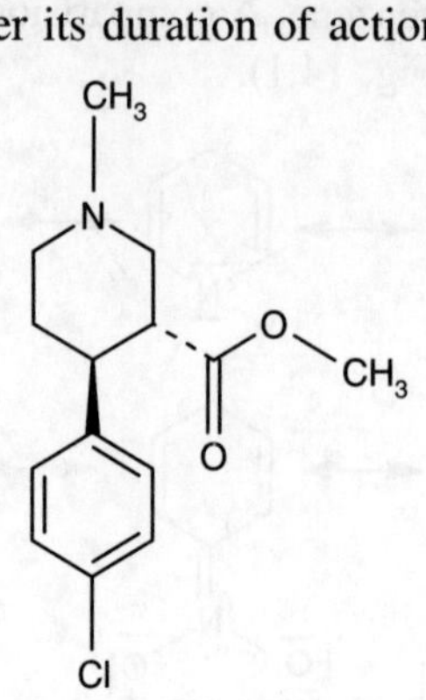

(85)

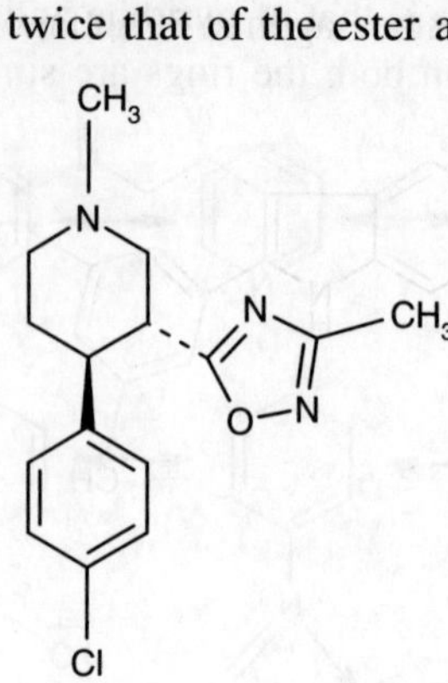

(86)

Amide function has been replaced by pyrrole, oxazole and thiazole moieties. Thus, replacement of amide function in antipsychotic, sultopride (87), by pyrrole led to (88). In addition to similar selectivity towards dopamine D_3 receptor as that of sultopride (87), the pyrrole analog (88) had also modest selectivity towards dopamine D_2 receptor.

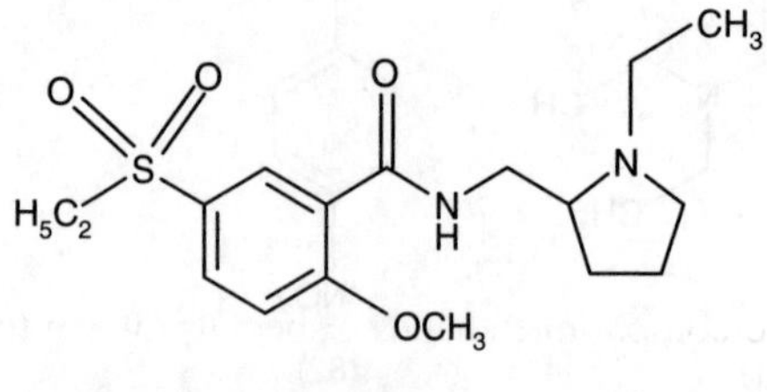

(87)

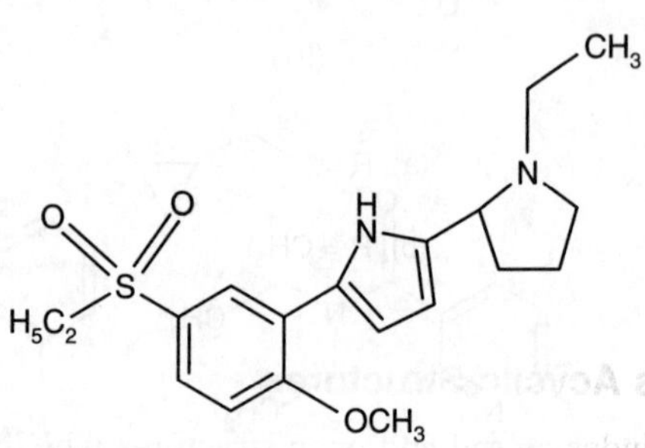

(88)

The alkylsulphonamide group is bioisosteric with phenolic group because they have similar pKa values. An example of this is the interchange of phenolic group in gonadotropin releasing antagonist (89) with methyl sulphonamide. The resulting sulphonamide (90) had 4-fold increase in binding affinity

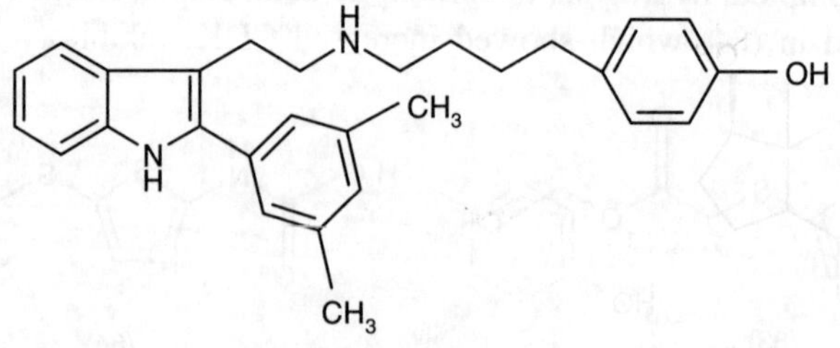

(89)

as compared to parent compound (89). However, interchange of these groups in opioid antagonists naltrexone (91a) and opioid agonist oxymorphone (91b) resulted in alkylsulphonamides (92a and 92b) which were devoid of either agonist or antagonistic activity, indicating such an interchange is not suitable for this series.

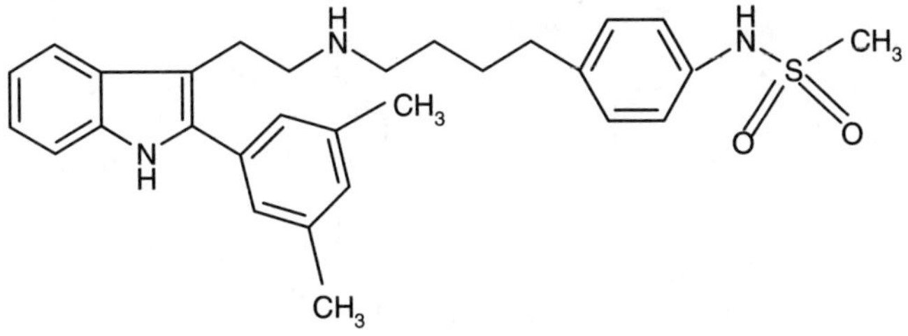

(90)

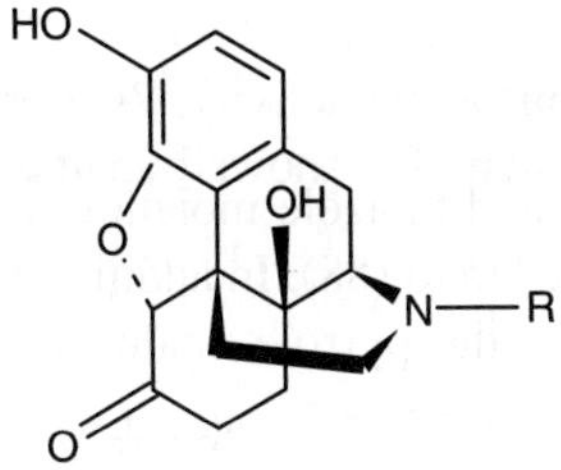

(91)

(a), R = 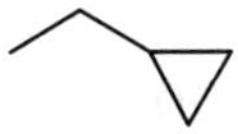

(b), R = CH_3

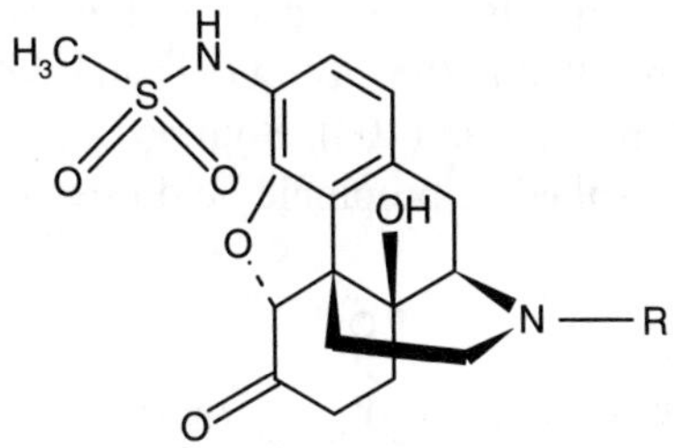

(92)

(a), R = 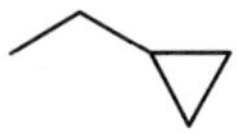

(b), R = CH_3

Ring Vs Acyclic Structures

This includes closed and open structures which have comparable shapes, especially when the shape of open analog is held by rigid structures. Among the best known example is the natural estrogen, estradiol (93) and its synthetic cogner diethylstilbestrol (94). The synthetic analog (94) is as active as the natural hormone (93). The central double bond in (94) holds the groups in *trans*-position. The *cis*-analog (94a) is only 1/4th as active as the *trans*-analog (94). Similarly, among the antihistaminics, the terminal diethylamino portion of diphenhydramine (95) has been interchanged with pyrrolidine moiety (96). The pyrrolidine analog (96) has been found to be several times more active than the open chain analog (95).

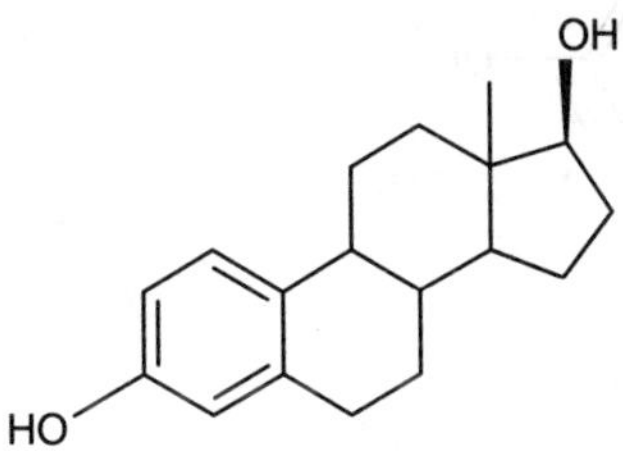

(93)

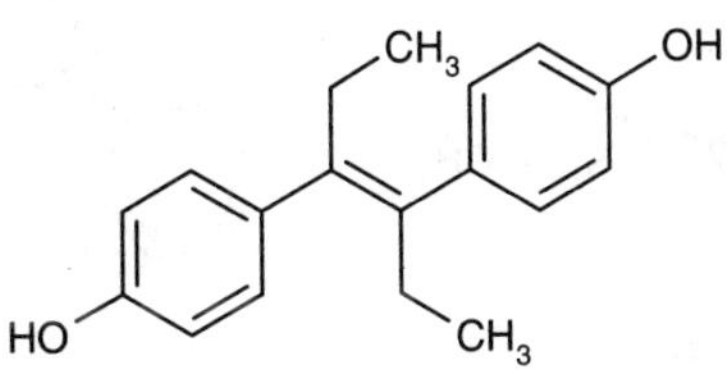

(94)

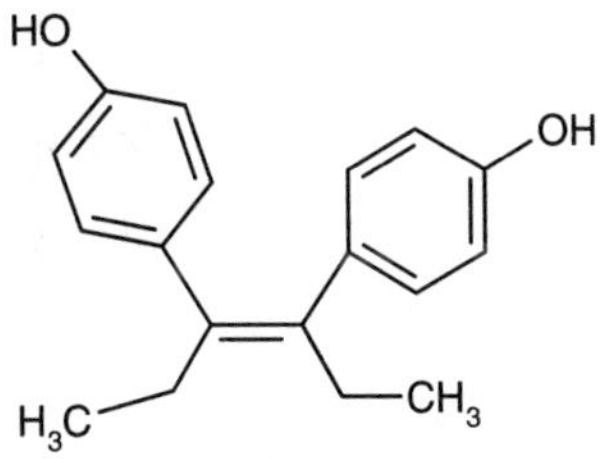

(94a)

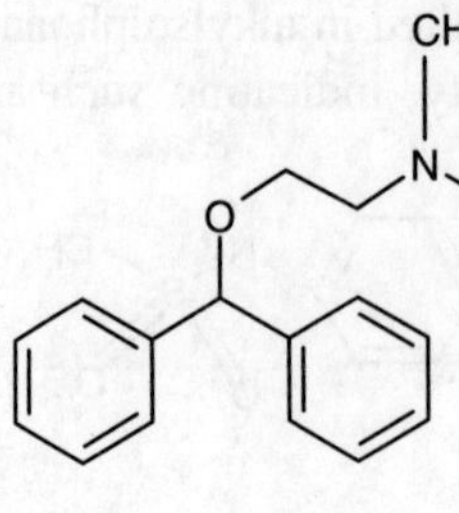

(95)

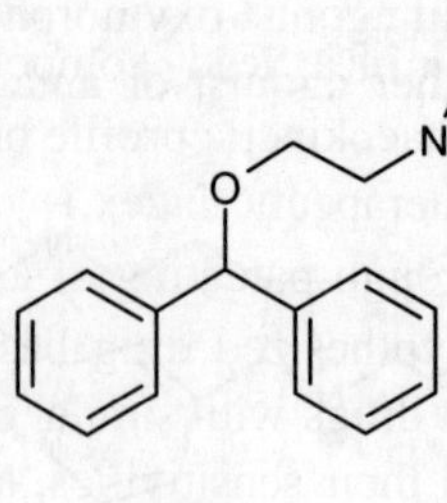

(96)

Reversal of Groups

Reversal of groups has also resulted in analogous activity. Thus, the reversal of ester group in the betaine ester (97) resulted in (98). Both (97) and (98) showed muscarinic activity. Similarly reversal of ester group in (99) resulted in (100). Both possessed antispasmodic activity. Reversal of ester group in meperidine (47a) resulted in propionic acid ester (101) which also showed analgetic activity.

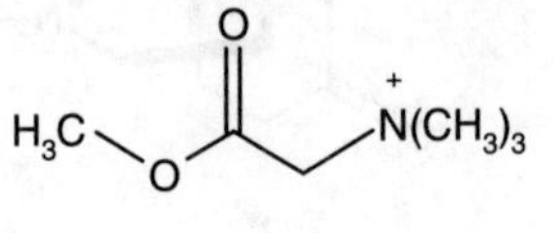

(97)

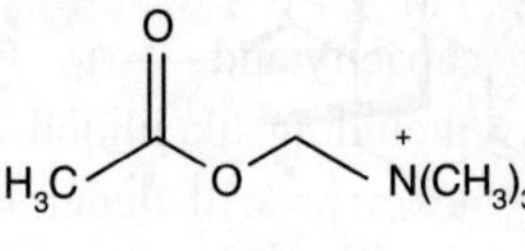

(98)

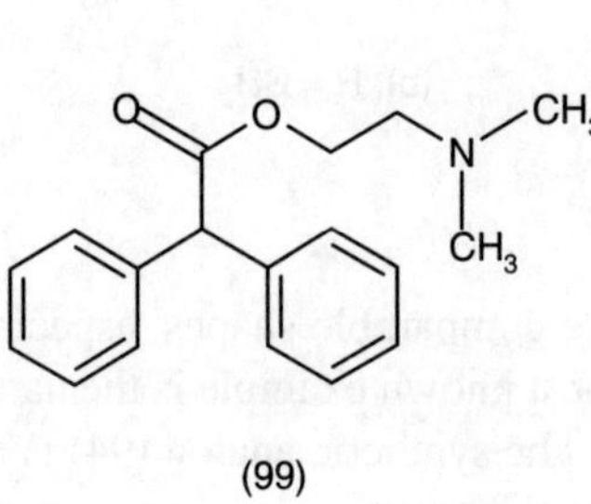

(99)

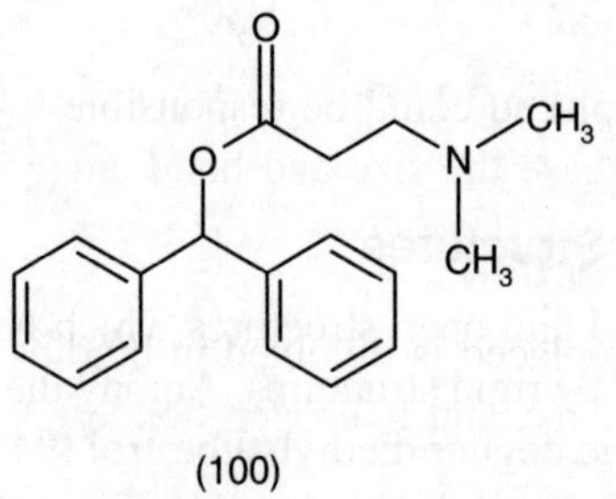

(100)

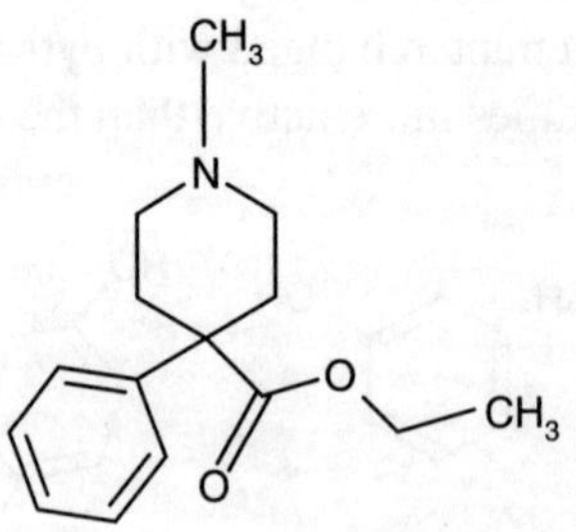

(47a)

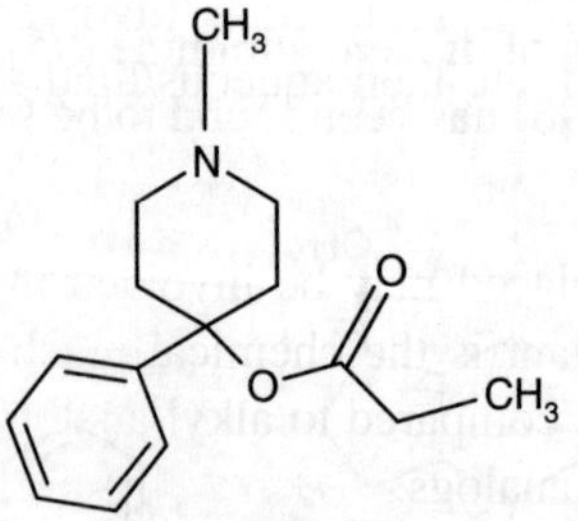

(101)

THEORETICAL ASPECTS OF BIOISOSTERIC CHANGES

The purpose of modification of a 'lead' compound is

1. to improve the pharmacokinetic profile or pharmacological activity of a 'lead' compound which may lead to better therapeutic index,
2. the profit motive through patenting of a new drug,
3. even if the newly synthesized drug has similar therapeutic effect, there is made available a selection of different drugs with similar use to the physician. This is necessary because humans vary considerably in their sensitivities, allergies, and ability to metabolise a compound.
4. Academic interest in knowing the relationship between the structure and biological activity.

The modification of a 'lead' compound is greatly aided by use of the concept of bioisosterism. The parameters usually considered for replacement of groups or atoms include:

(a) size of atoms/groups,
(b) bond angles including hybridization,
(c) electronic distribution including polarisability, inductive effect, dipole moment, etc
(d) lipophilicity and hydrophilicity,
(e) pKa,
(f) hydrogen bonding capacity,and
(g) chemical reactivity including likelihood of metabolism.

The usefulness of replacement will depend upon which of these parameters are important for pharmacological activity and which bioisostere can best mimic.

The groups in the molecule being modified could have one or more of the following roles;

(a) Structural

The moiety being replaced could be responsible for holding the structure of a molecule in a particular geometry. In such a case the size and bond angle could be important.

(b) Receptor Interaction

If the moiety to be replaced is involved in binding to the receptor then size, shape, electronic factors, pKa, chemical reactivity, and hydrogen bonding will be important.

(c) Pharmacokinetics

In case the moiety to be replaced is involved in pharmacokinetic parameters such as absorption, distribution, excretion, etc then aqueous/lipid solubility, pKa, hydrogen bonding will be important.

(d) Metabolism

The moiety to be replaced may be involved in blocking/aiding metabolism. In such a case the factor which will be important is the chemical reactivity. For example halogen analogs of benzene are not metabolized easily as compared to alkyl analogs. Thus, alkyl analogs have shorter biological half lives as compared to halo analogs.

It is not possible to have completely identical properties between a lead compound and its bioisostere. However, the aim of the bioisosteric change is to have improved potency, selectivity, better absorption, longer duration of action, and lower toxicity. If the bioisosteric replacement results in some property being changed and some other important property getting affected, the affected property could then be rectified by making changes in other part of the molecule. Thus, if by making a bioisosteric change, the lipophilicity is affected, this may affect its absorption, transport and therby its potency. The lipophilicity in such a bioisostere could be regained by making further changes in other part of the molecule.

Thorenber has formulated the following mathematical equation given below.

$$\text{Log } 1/c = A(\pi) + B(\sigma) + C(Es) \quad \text{... (Eq. 1)}$$

Where, c is the concentration of drug required to achieve a given effect,

Hansch's π represents the lipophilic character,

Hammet σ denotes the electronic parameters,

Taft's Es denotes the steric parameters, and

A, B and C are the constants.

Thus, if B and C were zero, then the potency would be a function of lipophilicity. In such a case, groups with same π value would be bioisosteric. However if the three constants are all significant, then there would be limited range of bioisosteric groups available. Further, the desired activity of a compound could be represented by (Eq.1) and the undesirable or side effects by (Eq. 2)

$$\text{Log } 1/c = D(\pi) + E(\sigma) + F(Es) \quad \text{... (Eq. 2)}$$

If A = D, B = E, and C = F, then in that case there would be no selectivity. On the other hand if $C << F$, then Es is not important for the desired activity. Accordingly, π and σ could be optimized while reducing the value of Es. This would result in reduction of side effects. Thus, the increase in selectivity could be achieved by varying the unimportant parameters.

From the above it is clear that bioisosteric parameters are useful in searching for potency, selectivity, absorption, and duration of action.

FURTHER READING

1. V.B. Schatz in "Medicinal Chemistry," 2nd ed., A. Burger, Ed., Interscience Publishers Inc., New York, 1960, p. 72.
2. C.W. Thornber, *Chem. Soc. Rev.*, **8**, 563 (1979).
3. R.C. Allen, *Ann. Repts. Med. Chem.*, **21**, 283 (1986).
4. G.A. Patani and E.J. Lavoie, *Chem. Rev.*, **96**, 3147 (1996).
5. X. Chen and W. Wang, *Ann. Rept. Med. Chem.*, **38**, 333 (2003).
6. L.M. Lima and E.J. Barreiro, *Curr. Med. Chem.*, **12**, 23 (2005).

15

Enzyme Inhibition as a Tool for Drug Design

All the biochemical processes lead to formation of substances which are known as metabolites. However, there are some substances which cannot be synthesized by the cell and these have to be provided from outside. These substances are known as essential metabolites. Both metabolites and essential metabolites are involved in the maintenance and formation of cell. Since the biochemical processes involve enzymes, inhibition of an enzyme could lead to a conditioned deficiency of a metabolite which could result in death of a cell. The inhibition of an enzyme, thus, becomes a rational way of designing drugs such as chemotherapeutic agents or for metabolic diseases. Enzyme inhibitors have also been used for producing experimental animal models of genetic diseases.

Before an account of enzyme inhibition is given, a brief introduction to the study of enzyme kinetics is given.

Michaelis-Menton Equation

An enzymatic reaction involves formation of enzyme-substrate complex (*ES*) between an enzyme (*E*) and the substrate (S) with subsequent formation and release of product (Eq. 1). The rate of enzyme catalyzed reaction is affected by the substrate concentration.

$$E + S \underset{k_{-1}}{\overset{k_1}{\rightleftharpoons}} ES \underset{k_{-2}}{\overset{k_2}{\rightleftharpoons}} E + P \qquad \text{... (Eq. 1)}$$

Since the substrate concentration varies during the course of reaction, because of formation of product, it is difficult to determine the effect of substrate concentration on the rate of enzymatic reaction. One approach is to measure the initial rate or initial velocity, V_o, when the substrate concentration is large. During this period the concentration of enzyme-substrate complex (*ES*) (Eq. 1) builds up. This is known as presteady state. Afterwards changes in substrate concentration have negligible effect on the rate because the enzyme is completely saturated and is in form of enzyme-substrate complex (*ES*) (Eq. 1). This is known as steady state. In the next step enzyme-substrate complex (*ES*) breaks down to enzyme and product (Eq. 1). This reaction is slower, so the overall rate of reaction (Eq. 1) is governed by this breakdown of enzyme-substrate complex (*ES*) to enzyme (*E*) and the product (*P*) (Eq. 1).

Suppose the initial concentration of the enzyme is E_T. After the addition of substrate, $E_T = [E] + [ES]$. Since the overall rate is governed by the breakdown of of ES and formation of product P, therefore, initial rate V_o will be (Eq. 2):

$$V_0 = k_2[ES] \qquad \text{... (Eq. 2)}$$

The rate of formation of enzyme-substrate complex, (*ES*), is given by k_1 [*E*] [*S*] (Eq. 1). Further, since enzyme-substrate complex, *ES*, is used in the formation of *E* + *S* and *E* + *P* (Eq. 1), therefore, the breakdown of enzyme-substrate complex, *ES*, is given by $k_{-1}[ES] + k_2[ES]$. At equilibrium the formation and breakdown of enzyme-substrate complex are equal (Eq. 3).

$$k_1[E][S] = (k_2 + k_{-1})[ES] \qquad \text{... (Eq. 3)}$$

or

$$\frac{[E][S]}{[ES]} = \frac{k_2 + k_{-1}}{k_1} = K_m \qquad \text{... (Eq. 4)}$$

K_m is designated as Michaelis constant. Substituting (E_T – [*ES*]) for [*E*], we have

$$\frac{(E_T - [ES])[S]}{[ES]} = K_m \text{ or } [ES] = \frac{E_T[S]}{[S] + K_m} \qquad \text{... (Eq. 5)}$$

Substituting this in (Eq. 2) gives

$$V_0 = \frac{k_2 E_T[S]}{[S] + K_m} \qquad \text{... (Eq. 6)}$$

When whole of the enzyme, E_T, is in form of *ES*, then the maximum velocity, V_{max}, becomes equivalent to k_2E_T, and (Eq. 6) becomes,

$$V_0 = \frac{V_{max}[S]}{[S] + K_m} \qquad \text{... (Eq. 7)}$$

This is known as Michaelis-Menton equation, the rate equation for one substrate enzyme catalyzed reaction. The effect of substrate concentration on the rate of enzymatic reaction is given by the Fig. 15.1.

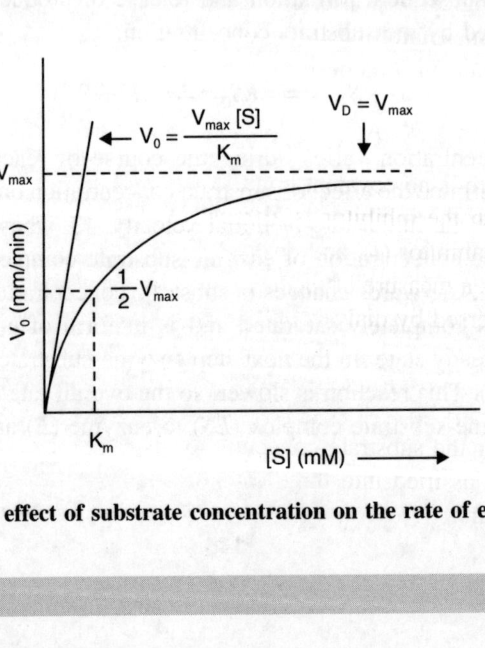

Fig. 15.1 The effect of substrate concentration on the rate of enzyme action

The Michaelis-Menton equation (Eq. 7) gives a quantitative relationship between initial velocity, V_o, the maximum initial velocity, V_{max}, and initial substrate concentration, [S], all of which are related to Michaelis constant K_m.

At low concentration of substrate, $K_m >> [S]$, the [S] in the denominator of (Eq. 7) becomes insignificant. The (Eq. 7) is accordingly reduced to (Eq. 8). The relationship between V_o and [S] is linear.

$$V_0 = \frac{V_{max}[S]}{K_m} \qquad \text{... (Eq. 8)}$$

At high concentration of substrate, when $[S] >> K_m$, the K_m in the denominator of (Eq.7) becomes insignificant and the (Eq. 7 is reduced to (Eq. 9). This is a plateau region of Fig. 15.1.

$$V_0 = V_{max} \qquad \text{... (Eq. 9)}$$

When V_0 is exactly one-half of V_{max}, the Michaelis-Menton equation (Eq.7) becomes

$$\frac{V_{max}}{2} = \frac{V_{max}[S]}{[S] + K_m} \qquad \text{... (Eq. 10)}$$

dividing by V_{max}, we get

$$1/2 = \frac{[S]}{[S] + K_m} \qquad \text{... (Eq. 11)}$$

solving for K_m, we get

$$K_m + [S] = 2[S]$$

or

$$K_m = [S] \qquad \text{... (Eq. 12)}$$

Thus, K_m is equivalent to substrate concentration when $V_o = 1/2\ V_{max}$.

ENZYME INHIBITION

Enzyme inhibition can be reversible or irreversible. A reversible or partial inhibition of an enzyme could lead to a desired biological response. Irreversible enzyme inhibition on the other hand would lead to death. Irreversible enzyme inhibition in host is, thus, undesireable while as if inhibition involves enzyme in an invading organism, it is desirable.

Reversible Inhibition

In reversible inhibition there is no covalent bond formation between the enzyme and inhibitor and the association of enzyme with the inhibitor is a transient. This type of inhibition involves equilibrium between the enzyme (*E*), inhibitor (*I*), and enzyme-inhibitor (*E.I*) complex (Eq. 11). The equilibrium dissociation constant, k_{-1} is a measure of the affinity of inhibitor with the enzyme. Since the inhibition is reversible, it can be reversed by dialysis and gel filtration.

$$E + I \underset{k_{-1}}{\overset{k_1}{\rightleftharpoons}} EI \qquad \text{... (Eq. 13)}$$

On the basis of whether the substrate concentration is able to alter the rate of reaction, reversible inhibitors can be further classified into three categories. These include competitive, noncompetitive, and uncompetitive inhibitors.

Competitive Inhibition

In competitive inhibition, the inhibitor (*I*) may or may not be structurally related to substrate (*S*). Further, the inhibitor (*I*) may combine with the enzyme (*E*) at the active site or near it. In competitive inhibition there is formation of enzyme-substrate (*ES*, Eq. 1) and enzyme-inhibitor (*EI*, Eq. 13) complexes but no enzyme-inhibitor-substrate (*EIS*) complex. Thus, high concentration of substrate can overcome the inhibition caused by the inhibitor by causing the reaction sequence to be in favour of formation of (*ES*) and subsequently (*EP*) and then (*P*).

The kinetics of competitive inhibition is given by the Eq. 14. The apparent K_m is increased and there is no change in the V_{max} value (Fig. 15.2).

$$V = \frac{[S]V_{max}}{[S] + K_m\left(1 + \frac{[I]}{K_i}\right)} \qquad \text{... (Eq. 14)}$$

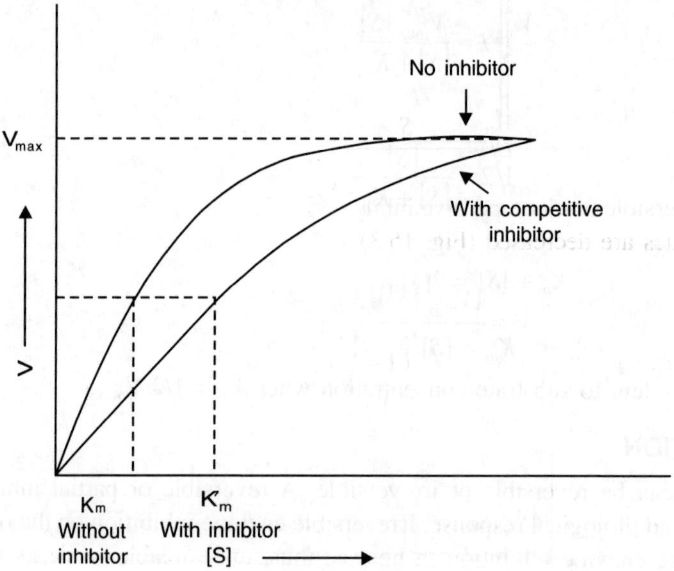

Fig. 15.2 Competitive inhibition

It is just possible that product of a metabolic reaction which is obtained after one or more steps can act as an inhibitor of the enzyme. This is known as feedback inhibition. Feedback inhibition is of competitive type. Further, in feedback inhibition, it is often the first enzyme unique to the specific pathway that is inhibited. Moreover, when a cell makes two or more isoenzymes, one of them may be inhibited by a particular product.

All the reversible competitive inhibitors do not inhibit the enzyme instantaneously. Reversible inhibitors could also be slow-, tight-, and slow-tight-binding. In case of slow binding inhibitors, the establishment of equilibrium between the enzyme and inhibitors takes considerable time, which is due to slow dissociation of enzyme-inhibitor complex but the formation of complex may be slow or fast.

In case of tight-binding inhibitors, the inhibitor binds tightly to the enzyme resulting in lower concentration of inhibitor molecule. Often tight-binding inhibitors have slow onset of action and are, therefore, also termed as slow-tight-binding inhibitors. As in case of rapid reversible inhibitors, larger concentration of inhibitor than enzyme is also required in case of slow-binding inhibitors.While as tight-binding and slow-tight-binding inhibitors are effective at concentrations comparable to enzyme concentration.

Non-competitive Inhibition

In a non-competitive inhibition, a complex of enzyme with substrate and inhibitor is formed (*ESI*). This complex formation can take place in two ways, i.e. either inhibitor (*I*) combines with enzyme-substrate (*ES*) complex or substrate (*S*) can complex with enzyme-inhibitor (*EI*) complex (Eq. 15). The binding of the inhibitor (*I*) to the enzyme does not take place at the active site but at the allosteric site. This results in distortion of the structure of enzyme and consequent inhibition of enzyme. This type of inhibition is not reversed by high substrate concentration.

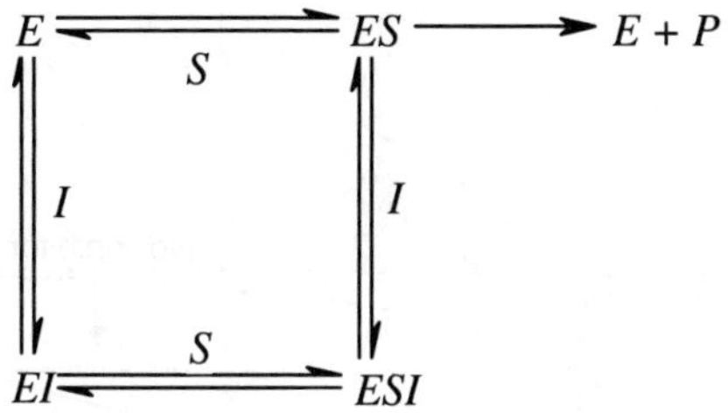

... (Eq. 15)

The kinetics of reversible non-competitive inhibition is given by the Eq. 16. While there is no change in K_m value, V_{max} values are decreased (Fig. 15.3).

$$V = \frac{\left(V_{max}[S]\right)\left(K_{max} + [S]\right)}{\left(1 + \frac{[I]}{K_i}\right)} \quad \text{... (Eq. 16)}$$

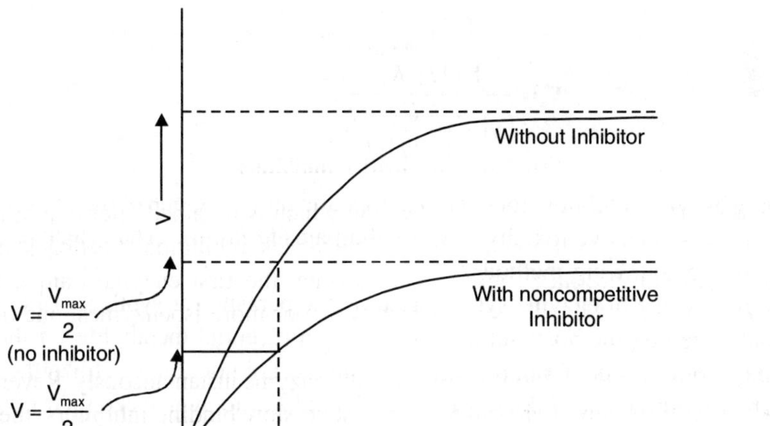

Fig. 15.3 Non-competitive inhibition

Uncompetitive Inhibition

In reversible uncompetitive inhibition, the inhibitor (*I*) binds to the enzyme-substrate complex (ES) and not to the enzyme (*E*) itself (Eq. 17). This type of inhibition is also not reversed with large concentration of substrate (*S*). The kinetics of the reaction is given by the Eq. 18. Both apparent K_m as well as V_{max} values are decreased (Fig. 15.4).

$$\begin{array}{c} E \rightleftharpoons ES \rightleftharpoons ESI \\ \downarrow \\ E + P \end{array} \qquad \text{... (Eq. 17)}$$

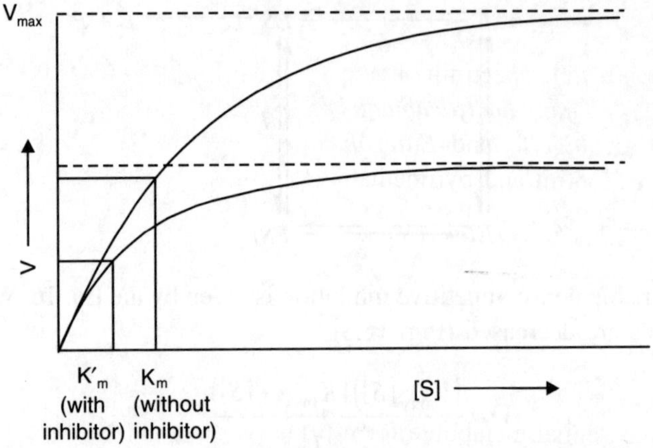

Fig. 15.4 Uncompetitive inhibition

$$V = \frac{\dfrac{[S]V_{max}}{1+[I]/K_i}}{[S] + \dfrac{K_M}{1+[I]/K_i}} \qquad \text{... (Eq. 18)}$$

While designing enzyme inhibitors for chemotherapeutic purposes, one of the important consideration is that it should possess selective toxicity towards the parasite *in vivo*. The selective toxicity could be achieved by any of the following methods:

1. Blockade of any one of enzyme system used by the parasite for synthesis of a metabolite which is not synthesized by the host and thus becomes an essential metabolite for the host and has to be provided from outside. Example, microorganisms are not able to utilize the pre-formed folic acid for their requirement of dihydrofolic acid and have to synthesize their own requirement of dihydrofolic acid. The humans, on the other hand require preformed folic acid for the synthesis of dihdrofolic acid. Thus, any one of the enzyme involved in the synthesis of dihydrofolic acid in parasites can be blocked in order to achieve selective toxicity, example sulphonamides.
2. The host may be able to detoxify the enzyme inhibitor by the enzyme/s which are not available in case of parasite, example 6-mercaptopurine.

3. The invading cell may enzymatically convert the enzyme inhibitor to an effective inhibitor of enzyme/s of the invading cell but the host may not.
4. The structure of same enzyme in host and parasite may differ and these differences could result in selective toxicity towards the enzyme of parasite, example, trimethoprim.
5. The inhibitor may require enzyme system which would facilitate its entry into the cell. Such an enzyme system may be present in the invading cell but not in the host cell. This would facilitate the entry of the inhibitor into the invading cell.
6. There could be other methods to achieving the selective toxicity.

Below are given some examples from various classes of drugs where the metabolite antagonism is the mechanism of their action.

Chemotherapeutic Agents

Sulphonamides

Sulphonamides (1) have a wide spectrum of activity. This includes activity against gram +ve and gram –ve bacteria, *Nocardia*, *Chlamydia trachomatis*, some protozoa, enteric bacteria such as *E.coli* and *Klebsiella*, *Salmonella*, *Shigella* and *Enterobacteria* species. Sulphonamides are usually used in combination with trimethoprim and pyrimethamine.

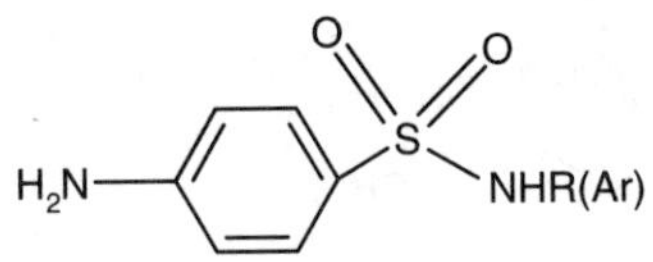

(1)

Folic acid (2) is an essential metabolite for mammals. It is reduced to dihdrofolic acid (3) and then to tetrahydrofolic acid (4) by folic acid reductases. Tetrahydrofolic acid (4) is converted to N^5-formyltetrahydrofolic acid, N^{10}-formyltetrahydrofolic acid, N^5-hydroxymethyltetrahydrofolic acid, N^5-methyltetrahydrofolic acid, and N^5,N^{10}-methylenetetrahydrfolic acid, these act as cofactors for various enzymes involved in one carbon transfer in the synthesis of purines and pyrimidines and ultimately the nucleic acids. Folic acid (2) is not an essential metabolite of microorganisms. They synthesize their own requirement of dihydrofolic acid (3). Condensation of dihyropteridine-pyrophosphate (5) and *p*-aminobenzoic acid (PABA, 6) in presence dihydropteroate synthase yields dihydropteroic acid (7) which on condensation with glutamate in presence of ATP and Mg^{++} and dihydrfoliate synthase yields dihydrofoliate (3). The enzyme dihydropteroate synthase is inhibited by the sulphonamides (1). As a result the synthesis of dihydropteroic acid is blocked and this results in blockade of subsequent steps resulting ultimately in the blockade of synthesis of nucleic acids.

The microorganism is not able to utilize the folic acid (2) available in the blood of the host. This is because the folic acid (2) exists as dianion at physiological pH and it requires active transport system to enter the microbial cell. Micoorganisms which are susceptible to sulphonamides do not possess such active transport system and therefore, cannot utilize the folic acid (2) available in the host. Microorganisms, such as *Strptococcus faecalis,* which possesses such an active transport system, is resistant to sulphonamides.

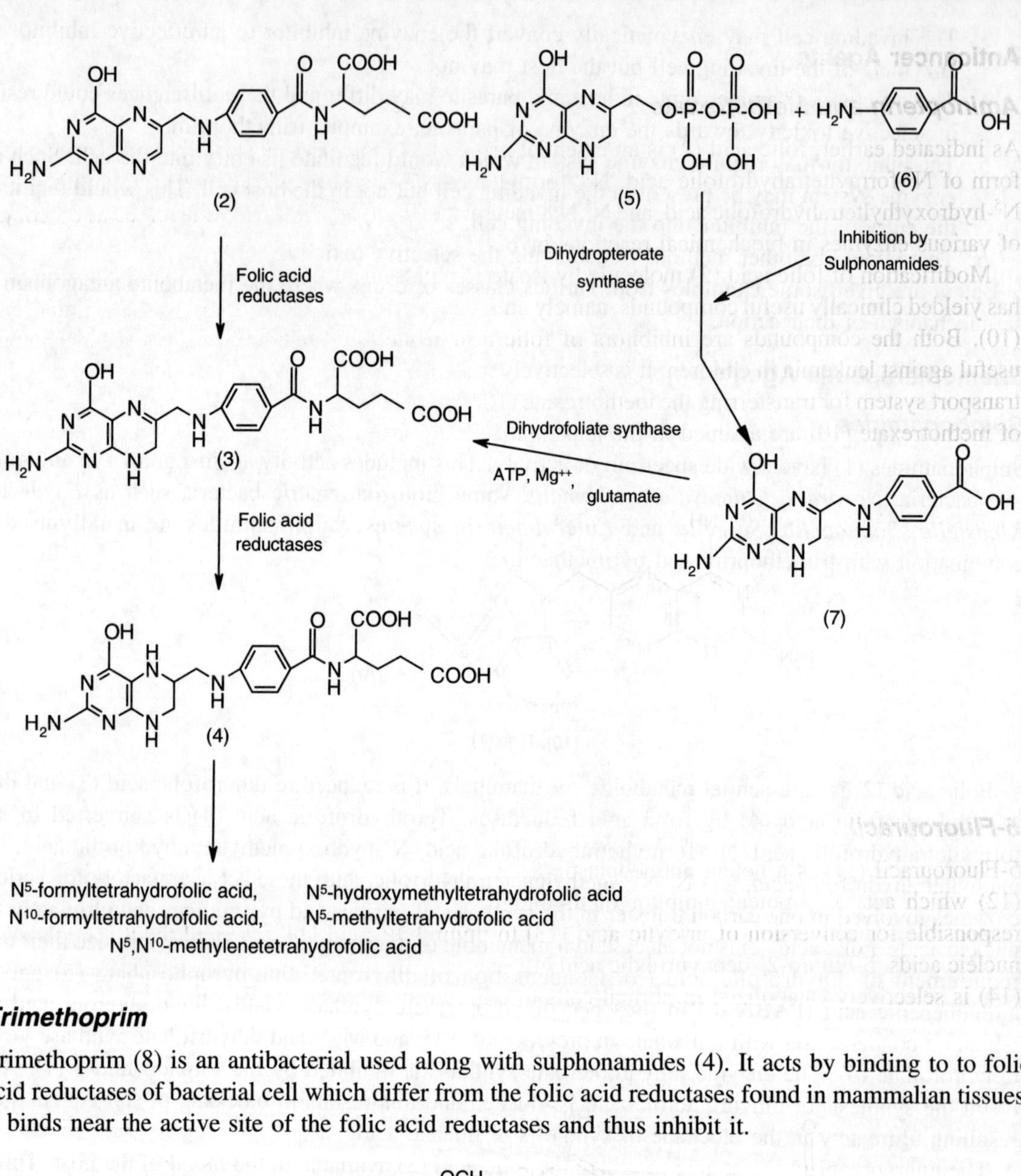

Trimethoprim

Trimethoprim (8) is an antibacterial used along with sulphonamides (4). It acts by binding to to folic acid reductases of bacterial cell which differ from the folic acid reductases found in mammalian tissues. It binds near the active site of the folic acid reductases and thus inhibit it.

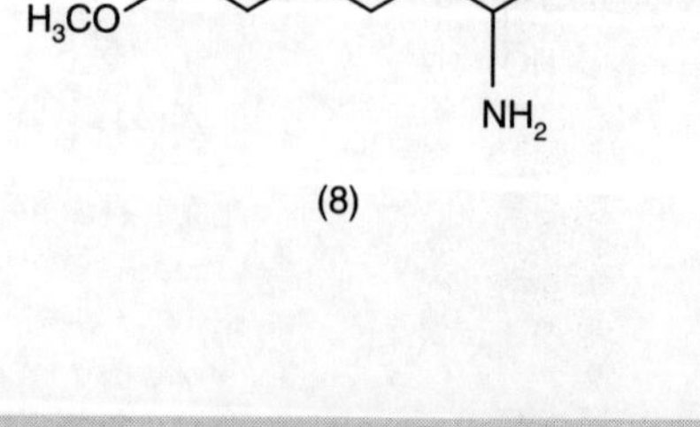

(8)

Anticancer Agents

Aminopterin and Methotrexate

As indicated earlier, folic acid (2) is an essential metabolite for mammals. Tetrahydrofolic acid (4), in form of N^5-formyltetrahydrofolic acid, N^{10}-formyltetrahydrofolic acid, N^5-methyltetrahydrofolic acid, N^5-hydroxythyltetrahydrofolic acid, and N^5,N^{10}-methylenetetrahydrofolic acid, is involved as co-enzyme of various enzymes in biochemical reactions involving transfer and utilization of one carbon transfer.

Modification of folic acid (2) molecule by isosteric replacement of hydroxyl group by amino group has yielded clinically useful compounds, namely aminopterin (9) and its N^{10}-methyl analog, methotrexate (10). Both the compounds are inhibitors of folic acid reductase. Methotrexate (10) has been found useful against leukemia in children. It is selectively toxic to leukemic cells which possess a super-active transport system for transferring the methotrexate (10) to leukemic cells. As a result higher concentration of methotrexate (10) are attained in the leukemic cells which result in its death.

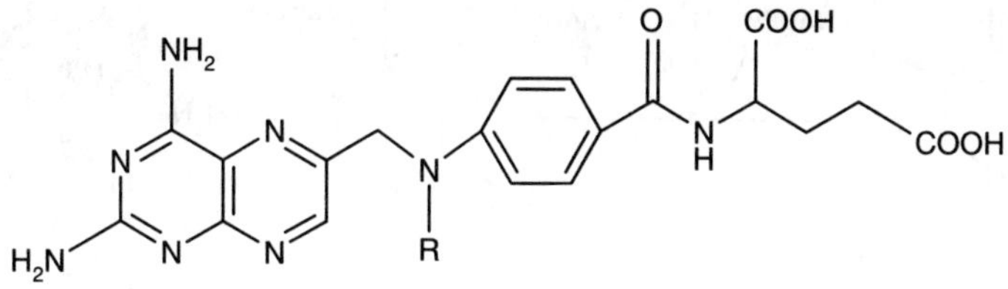

(9), R = H

(10), R = CH_3

5-Fluorouracil

5-Fluorouracil (11) is a potent antineoplastic agent. It is converted to 5-fluoro-2'-deoxyuridylic acid (12) which acts as a potent inhibitor of thymidylate synthase. Thymidylate synthase is an enzyme responsible for conversion of uridylic acid (13) to thymidylic acid (14) required for the synthesis of nucleic acids. 5-Fluoro-2'-deoxyuridylic acid (12) causes "thymine less death" of a cell. 5-Fluorouracil (14) is selectively catabolized in normal cells to α-fluoro-β-aminopropionic acid (15).

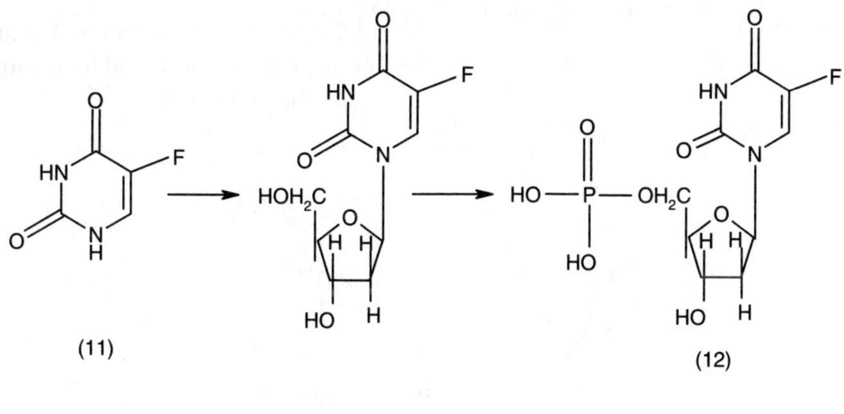

(11)

(12)

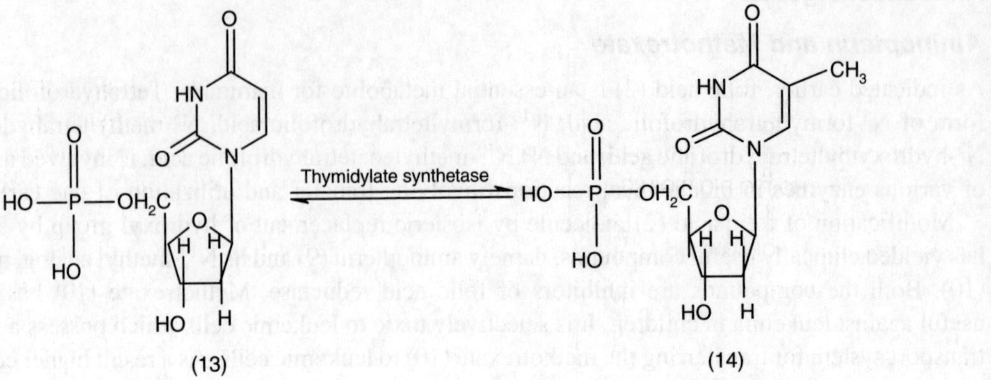

(13) (14)

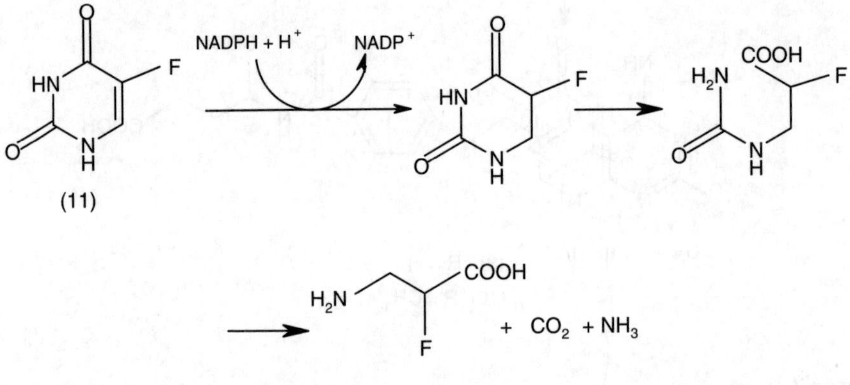

(11)

(15)

Antiviral Agents

Zidovudine

Zidovudine or azidothymidine (AZT, 16) is an azido analog of thymidine (17) in which the 3′-hydroxyl group of the deoxy ribose has been replaced with azido group.

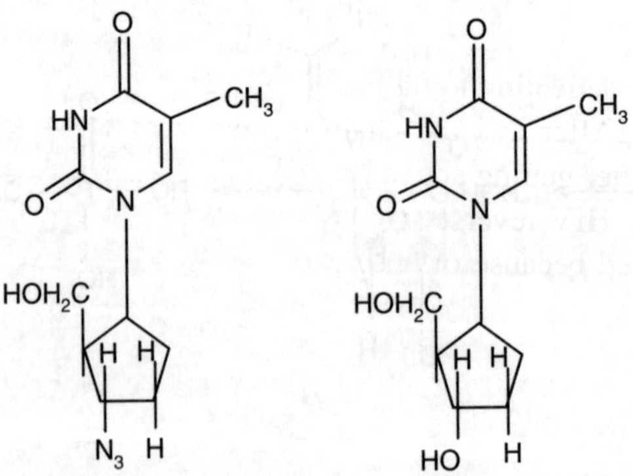

(16) (17)

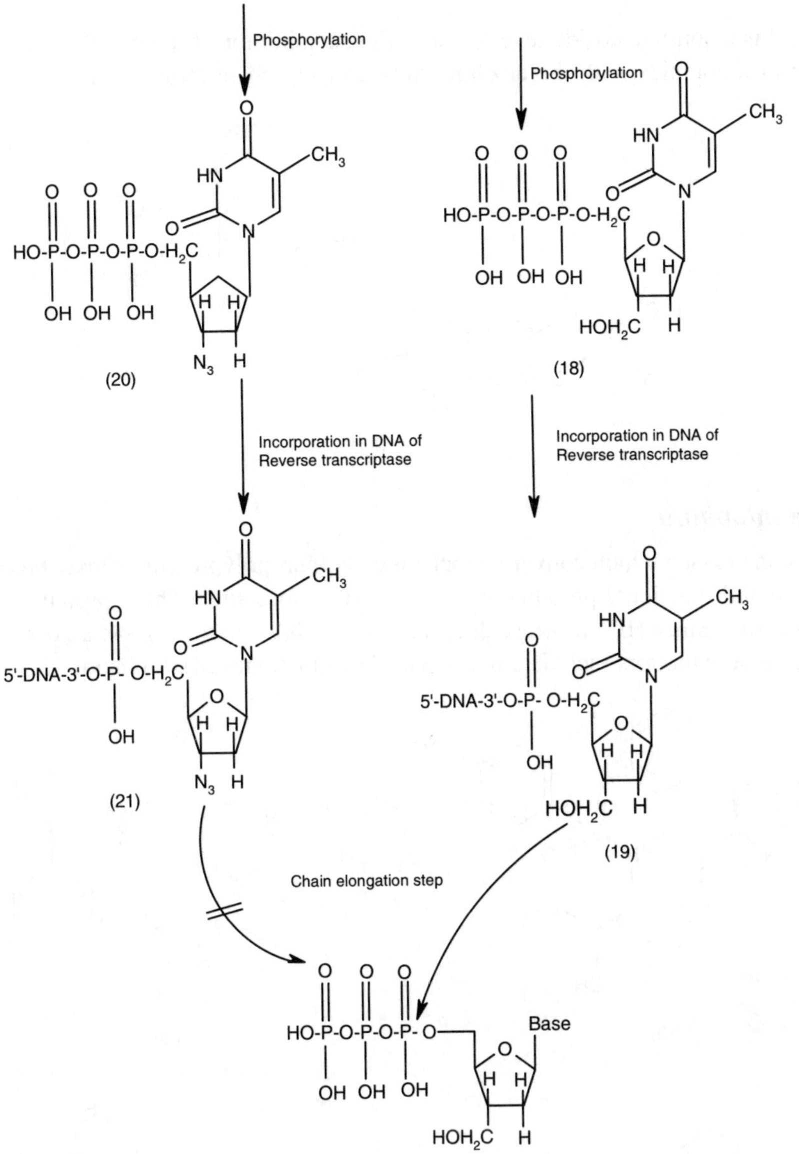

Thymidine (17) after its activation to thymidine triphosphate (18) is incorporated into DNA (19) by HIV-reverse transcriptase. After this the chain extension of DNA takes place through deoxyribose portion. Zidovudine (16) after getting activated through its triphosphate (20), competes with thymidine triphosphate for uptake by HIV-reverse trancriptase into DNA. Once incorporated into DNA further chain extension is prevented because of absence of 3'-hydroxy group on deoxyribose.

Delaviridine

Delaviridine (22) is a non-nucleoside reverse transcriptase inhibitor. It inhibits the reverse transcriptase after formation of a complex with the enzyme, thus, causing chain termination.

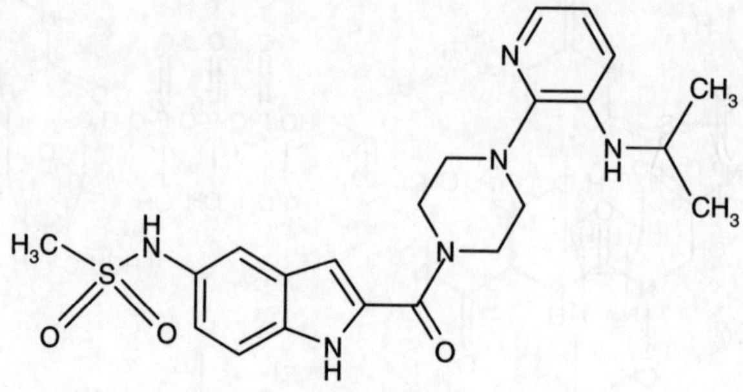

(22)

HIV-Protease Inhibitors

HIV-protease is an enzyme which converts biochemically inert polyproteins transcribed by mRNA into various structural and functional proteins by cleavage at various sites. These proteins are mature viral particles and infective. Since HIV-protease does not occur in host, so these proteases are the best targets. Examples of protease inhibitors include amprenavir (23), indinavir (24), lopinavir (25), nelfinavir (26),

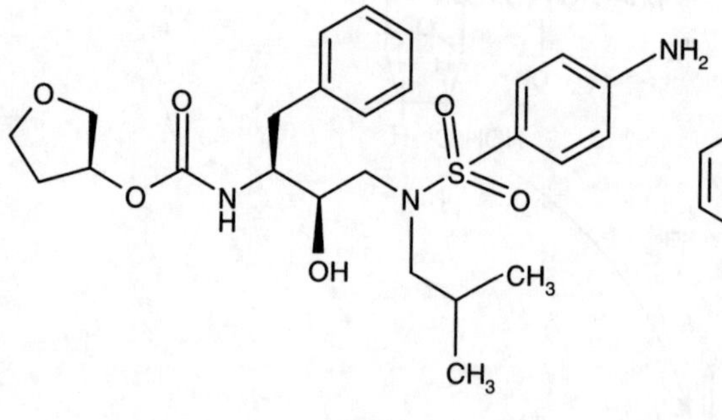

(23)

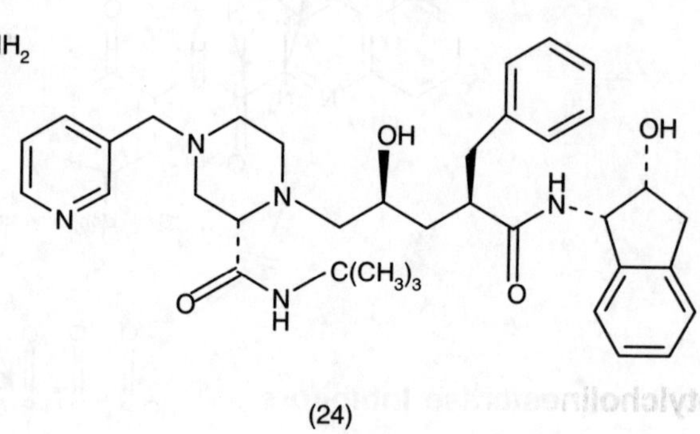

(24)

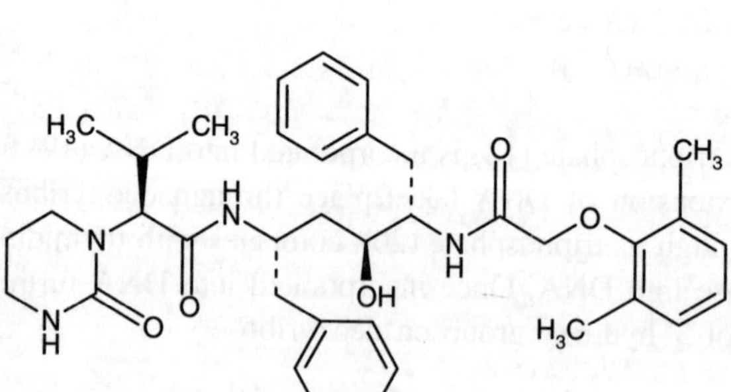

(25)

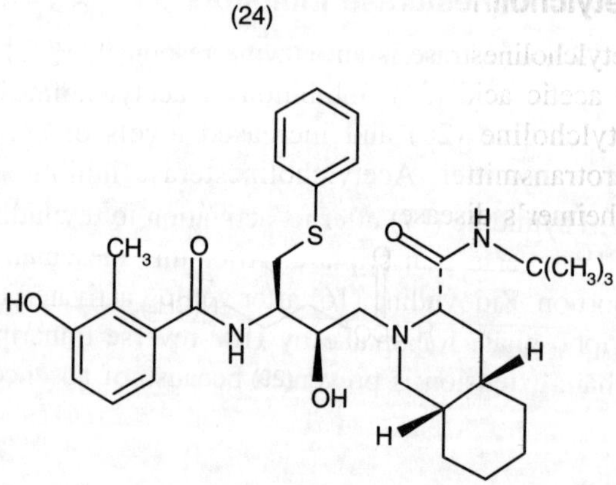

(26)

ritonavir (27), and saquinavir (28). HIV-protease inhibitors act by binding at the site of peptide chain where cleavage occurs and thus prevent the cleavage of inactive polypeptide chain. They are used in combination with reverse transcriptase inhibitors.

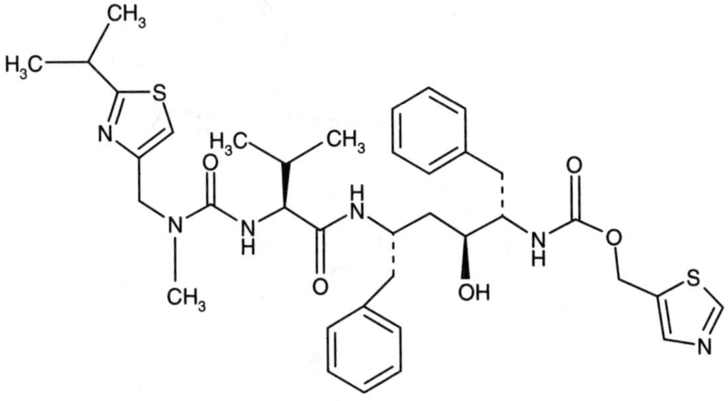

(27)

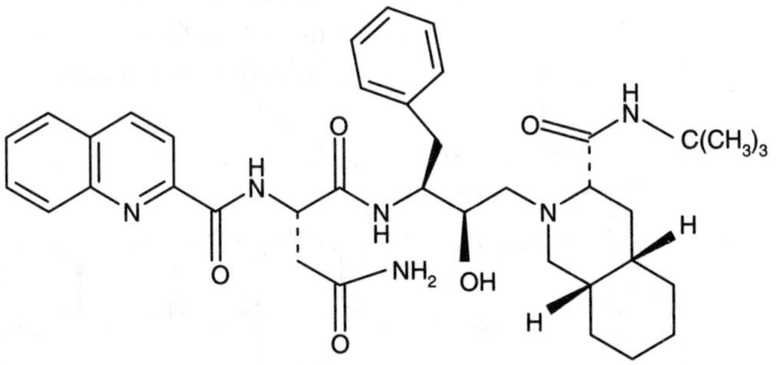

(28)

Acetylcholinesterase Inhibitors

Acetylcholinestrase is an enzyme responsible for the hydrolysis of acetylcholine (29) to choline (30) and acetic acid (31). Inhibition of acetylcholinesterase thus results in conservation of endogenous acetylcholine (29) and increased levels of acetylcholine (29) lead to prolonged action of the neurotransmitter. Acetylcholinesterase inhibitors are used in myasthenia gravis, glaucoma, and Alzheimer's disease.

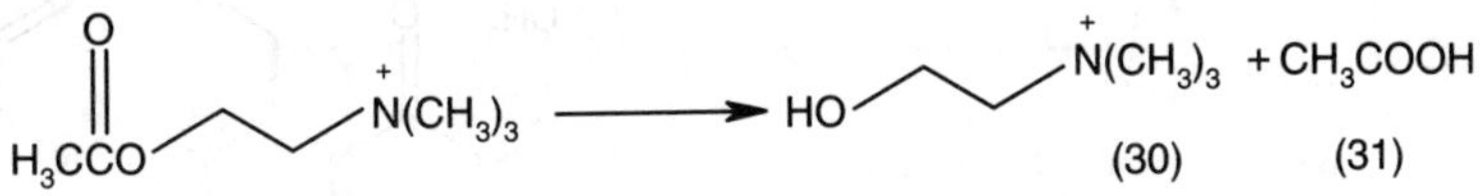

(29) (30) (31)

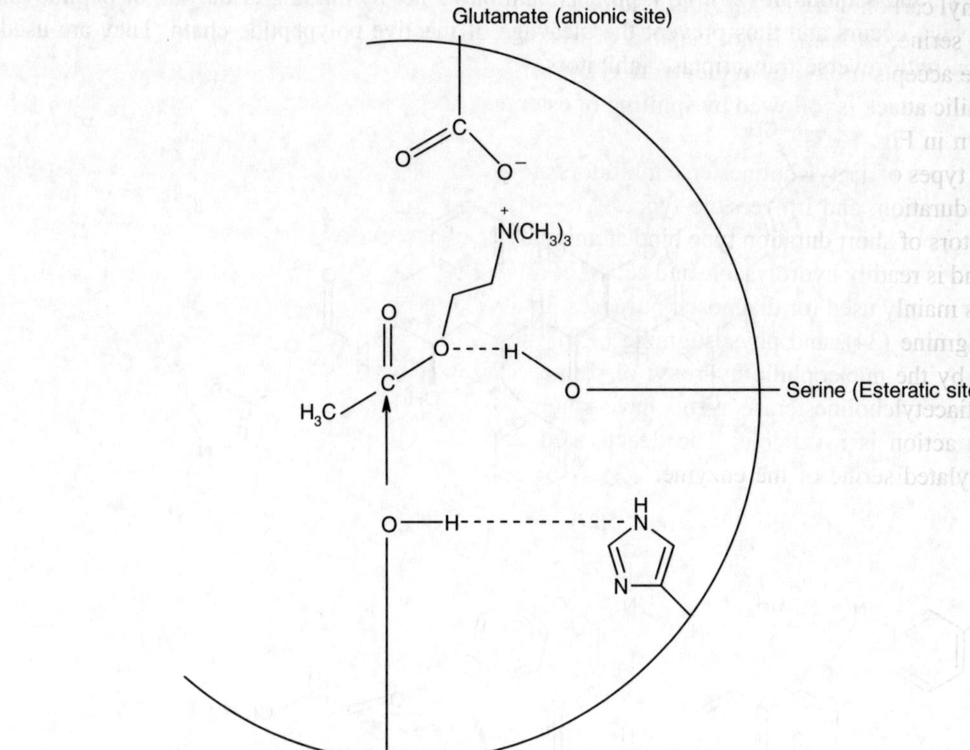

Fig. 15.5 Mechanism of binding and hydrolysis of acetylcholine at acetylcholinesterase receptor

The active site of the acetylcholinesterase is composed of an anionic and an esteratic site. The anonic site is believed to be the ω-carboxylic group of aminodicarboxylic acid. Both aspartic acid and glutamic acid have been isolated from the site. At the esteratic site, the oxygen of the acyloxy group is believed to bind with the hydroxyl of the serine through hydrogen bonding. For hydrolysis, nucelophilic attack on carbonyl carbon is necessary. It is assumed that hydroxyl of serine is involved in this. Since hydroxyl group of serine, as such, is not capable of hydrolyzing the ester, it gets activated by imidazole. The imidazole accepts proton from the hydroxyl of serine, the alkoxy group then acts as a nucleophile. The nucleophilic attack is followed by splitting of ester and liberation of choline. The various steps involved are shown in Fig. 15.5.

Three types of acetylcholinesterse inhibitors are known and these include inhibitors of short duration, medium duration, and irreversible type.

Inhibitors of short duration type bind at anionic site of acetylcholinesterase (Fig. 15.5). The resulting ionic bond is readily hydrolysable and action of drug is of short duration. Example include edrophonium (32). It is mainly used for diagnostic purposes. Inhibitors of medium duration include neostigmine (33), pyridostigmine (34), and physostigmine (35). They bind at anionic site and the carbamoyl carbon is attacked by the nucleophilic hydroxyl of serine. Since carbamoyl esters are hydrolyzed slowly, all of these antiacetylcholinesterase agents have longer duration than the edrophonium (32), but at the same time the action is reversible. The deactivated acetylcholinesterase is reactivated by hydrolysis of carbamoylated serine of the enzyme.

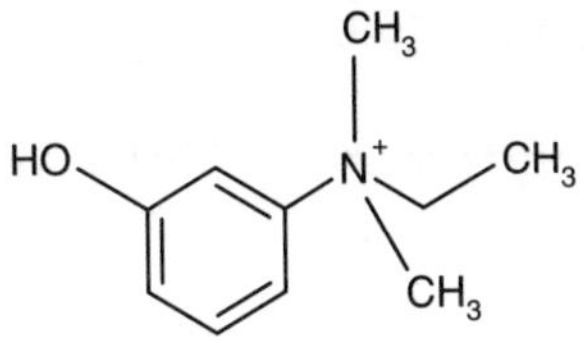

(32)

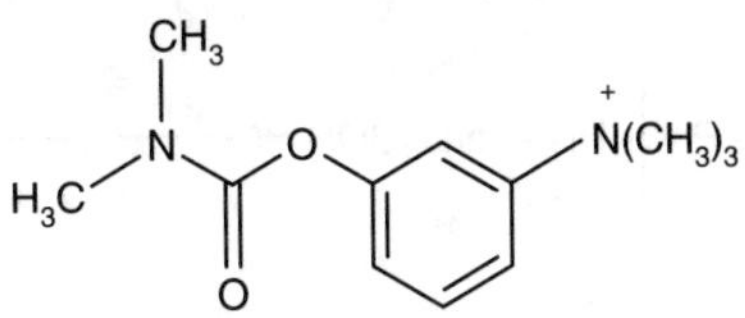

(33)

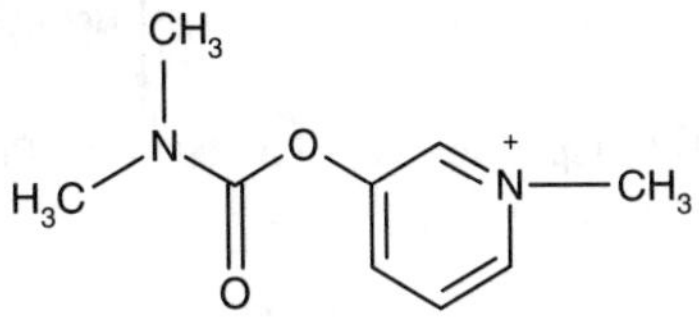

(34)

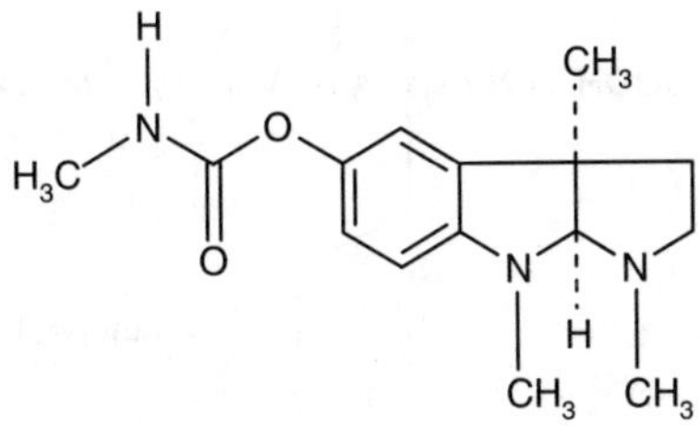

(35)

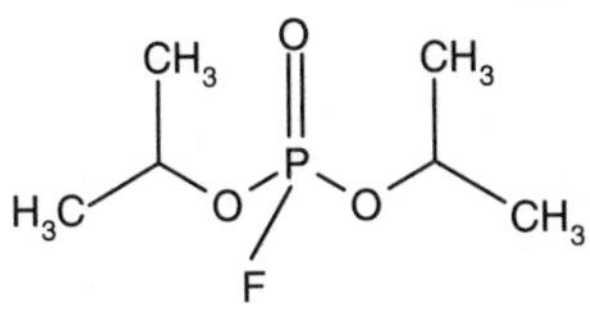

(36)

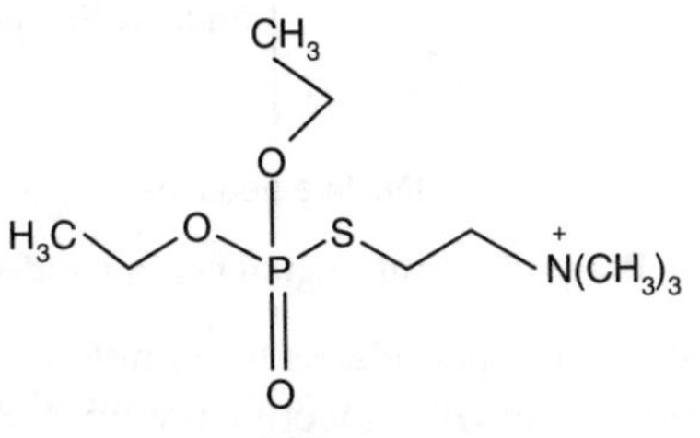

(37)

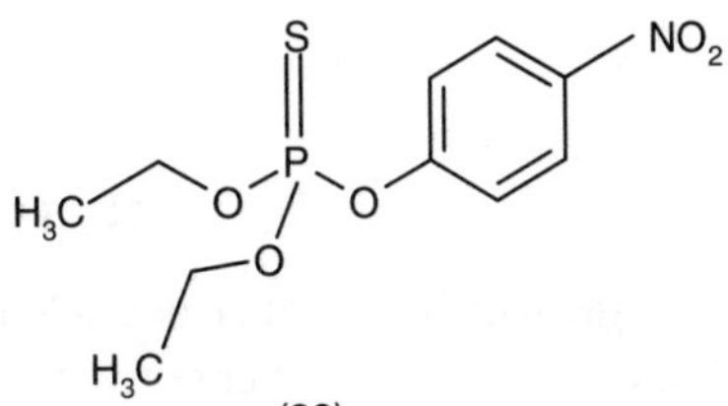

(38)

The irreversible enzyme inhibitors include isoflurophate (36), ecothiophate (37), and parathion (38). Excepting ecothiophate (37) none of them have cationic site. They interact with the esteratic site of the enzyme (Fig. 15.4). These compounds phosphorylate the serine hydroxyl of the enzyme after the labile group such as fluorine or organic moiety is released. These compounds are mainly used as insecticides in agricultural practice.

Angiotensin Converting Enzyme Inhibitors

Renin-angiotensin system is important for long term regulation of blood pressure and operates through kidneys.

Renin, a proteolytic enzyme, is secreted in response to:

1. decreased level of sodium in distal tubule,
2. decreased renal profusion pressure, and
3. β-adrenoreceptor agonists.

After its release, renin acts on angiotensinogen – an α_2-globulin with 452 amino acids, giving angiotensin I, a decapeptide. This is then cleaved by angiotensin converting enzyme(ACE) to an octapeptide, angiotensin II (Fig. 15.6).

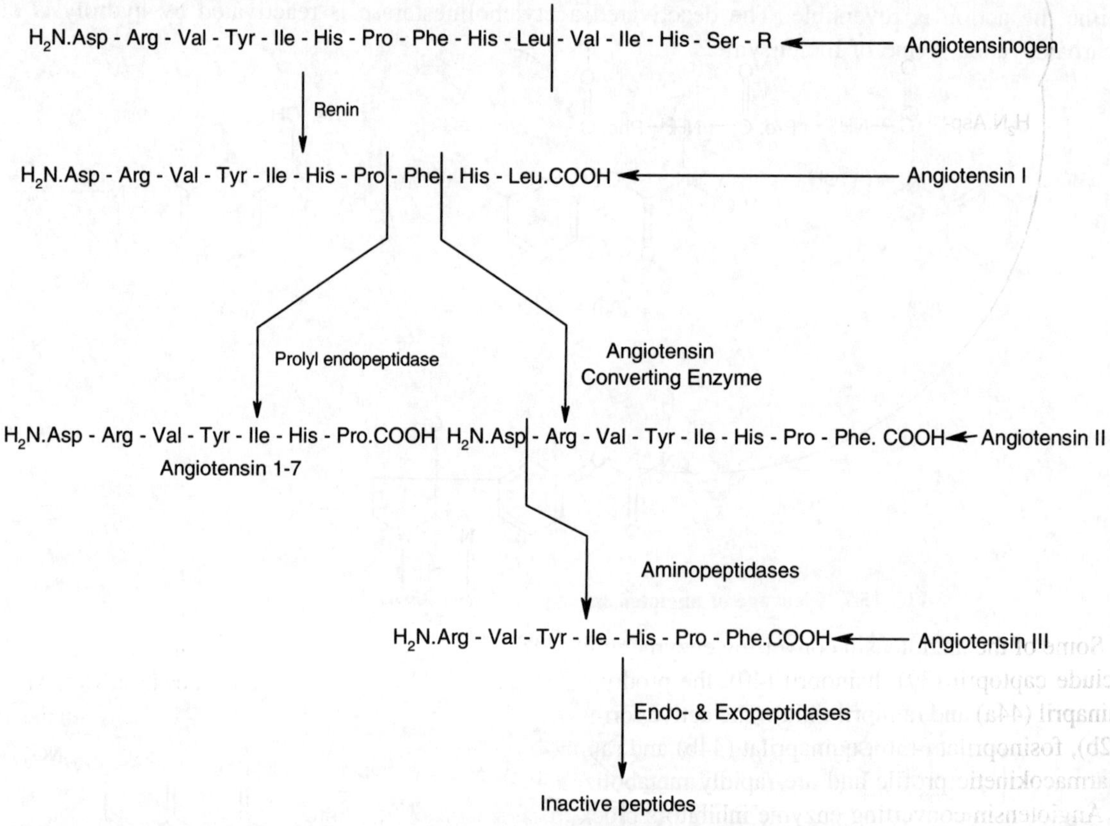

Fig. 15.6 Biosynthesis of angiotensin peptides

Angiotensin II is further degraded by aminopeptidases to angiotensin III, a heptapeptide. The Exo- and Endopeptidases further convert angiotensin III to inactive peptides. Angiotensin I is also cleaved by prolyl-endopeptidases to angiotensin 1-7, a heptapeptide (Fig. 15.6).

Angiotensin converting enzyme has a cationic site to which carboxylate of leucine (Leu) is bound and a zinc ion that polarizes the carbonyl group of phenylalanine (Phe) to make it susceptible to hydrolysis by the carboxylate of glutamate (Fig. 15.7).

Binding of Angiotensin II to Angiotensin II subtype 1 receptor results in:

1. Vasoconstriction, which may be direct or indirect via increased norepinephrine release from sympathetic nerves,
2. Salt retention due to aldosterone secretion and tubular Na^+ reabsorption.

All these effects result in increased blood pressure.

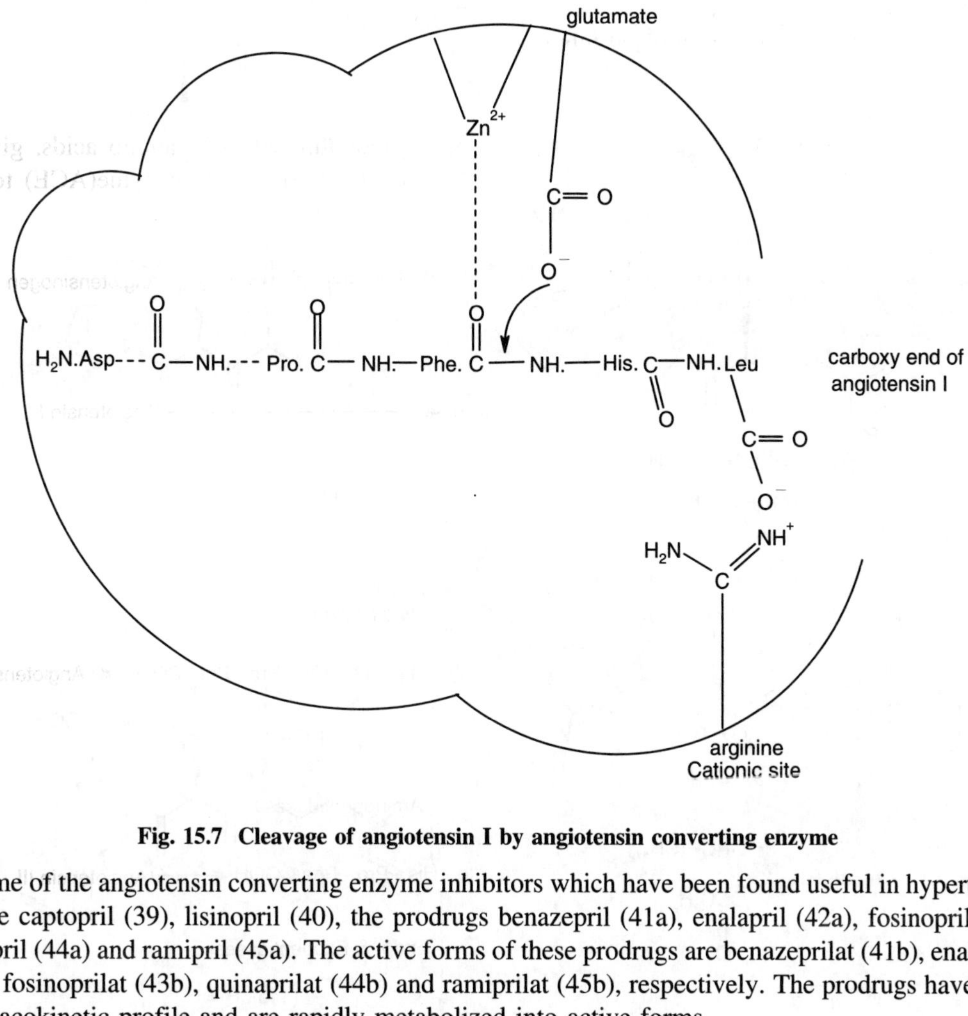

Fig. 15.7 Cleavage of angiotensin I by angiotensin converting enzyme

Some of the angiotensin converting enzyme inhibitors which have been found useful in hypertension include captopril (39), lisinopril (40), the prodrugs benazepril (41a), enalapril (42a), fosinopril (43a), quinapril (44a) and ramipril (45a). The active forms of these prodrugs are benazeprilat (41b), enalaprilat (42b), fosinoprilat (43b), quinaprilat (44b) and ramiprilat (45b), respectively. The prodrugs have better pharmacokinetic profile and are rapidly metabolized into active forms.

Angiotensin converting enzyme inhibitors block the formation of angiotensin II from angiotensin I. Further, these inhibitors also increase the bradykinin levels which result in stimulation of prostaglandin biosynthesis which contributes to overall action of angiotensin converting enzyme inhibitors. Decreased angiotensin II levels result in rebound effect resulting in increased release of renin and formation of angiotensin I. Since angiotensin converting enzyme is inhibited, angiotensin I is converted by prolyl endopeptidases to inactive angiotensin 1-7 (Fig. 15.6).

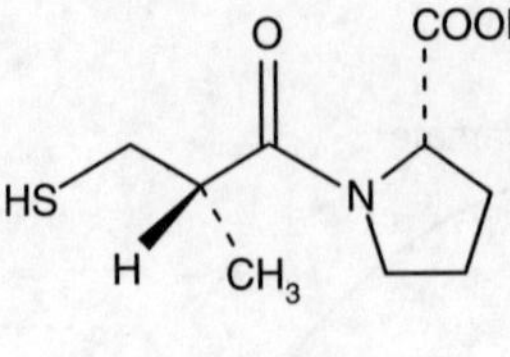

(39)

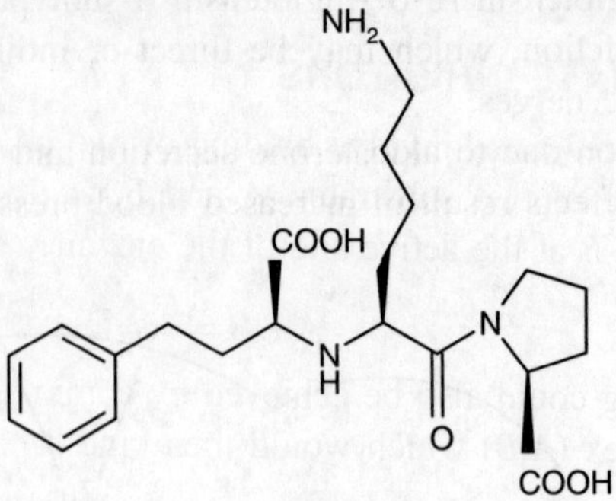

(40)

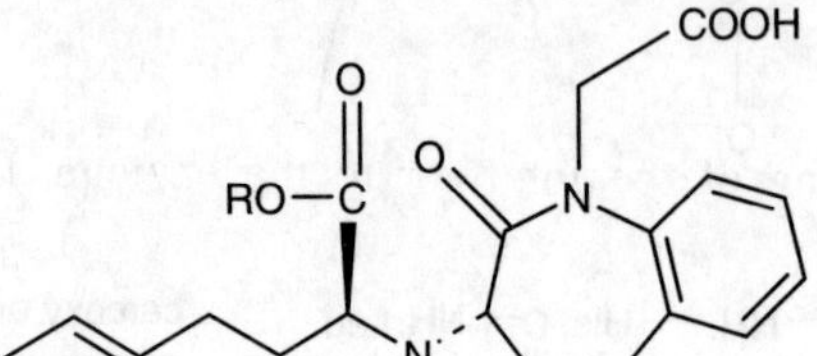

(41a), R = $-C_2H_5$

(41b), R = H

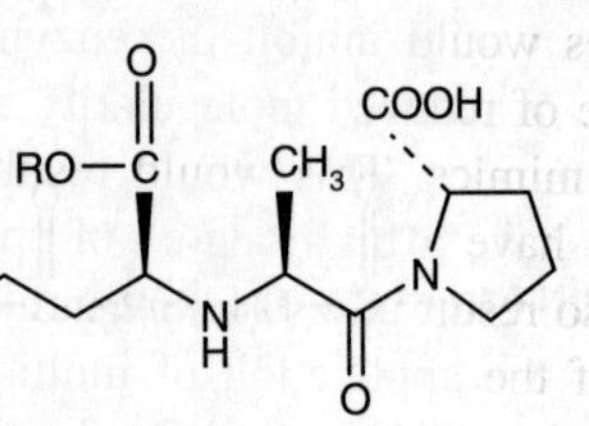

(42a), R = $-C_2H_5$

(42b), R = H

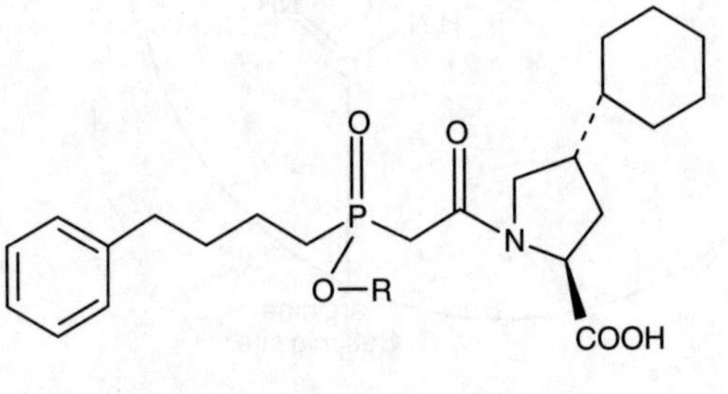

(43a), R =

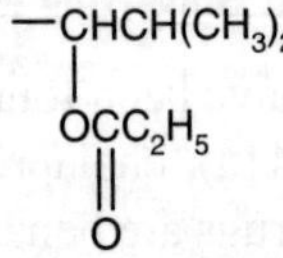

(43b), R = H

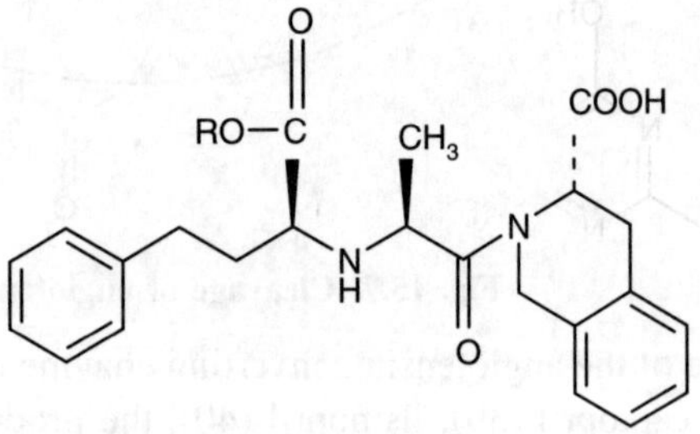

(44a), R = $-C_2H_5$

(44b), R = H

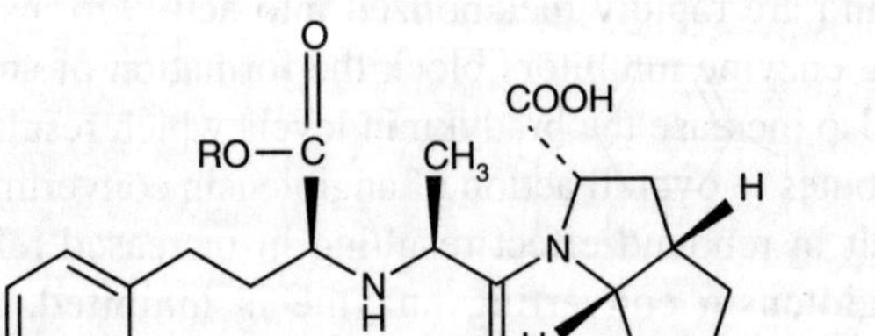

(45a), R = $-C_2H_5$

(45b), R = H

MULTISUBSTRATE INHIBITORS

Some enzymatic reactions involve binding of two or more substrates at the active site of the enzyme. Thus, complexing of two substrates, *A* and *B*, at the active site could be achieved by simultaneous binding of *A* and *B* at the active site of the enzyme (*E*) (Eq. 9).

$$A + B \overset{E}{\rightleftharpoons} E.A.B \longrightarrow E + P \qquad \text{... (Eq. 9)}$$

Such a binding could also be achieved by coming together of the two substrates, *A* and *B*, to form a reactive complex (*A.B*) which would then bind to the the enzyme (Eq. 10).

$$A + B \rightleftharpoons A.B \overset{E}{\rightleftharpoons} E.A.B \longrightarrow E + P \qquad \text{... (Eq. 10)}$$

Based on this, inhibitors could be designed which would mimic *A.B* complex. Binding of such substances would inhibit the enzyme. The inhibitor, being a single molecule would have entropic advantage of reduced molecularity and also the advantage of having characteristics of two molecules which it mimics. This would result in tight binding of the inhibitor to the enzyme. Further, such inhibitors have a high degree of specificity. Combination of two or more structure in one structure would also result in a structure unlikely to bind to an enzyme which utilize one or the other substrate.

One of the application of multisubstrate inhibition has been in the inhibition of *de novo* purine biosynthesis which is used for the development of antineoplastic agents. through inhibition of purine biosynthesis. Glycinamide ribonucleotide transformylase (GAR TFase) is an enzyme which transfers formyl group from N^{10}-formyltetrahydrfolate (46) to glycinamide ribonucleotide (47). The resulting N-formylglycinamide ribonucleotide (48) is an important metabolite in the synthesis of purines. Inhibitors have been developed for inhibition of GAR TFase and include thioesters (49) and (50). Both of these inhibitors combine the features of N^{10}-formyltetrahydrofolate (46) and glycinamide nucleotide (47).

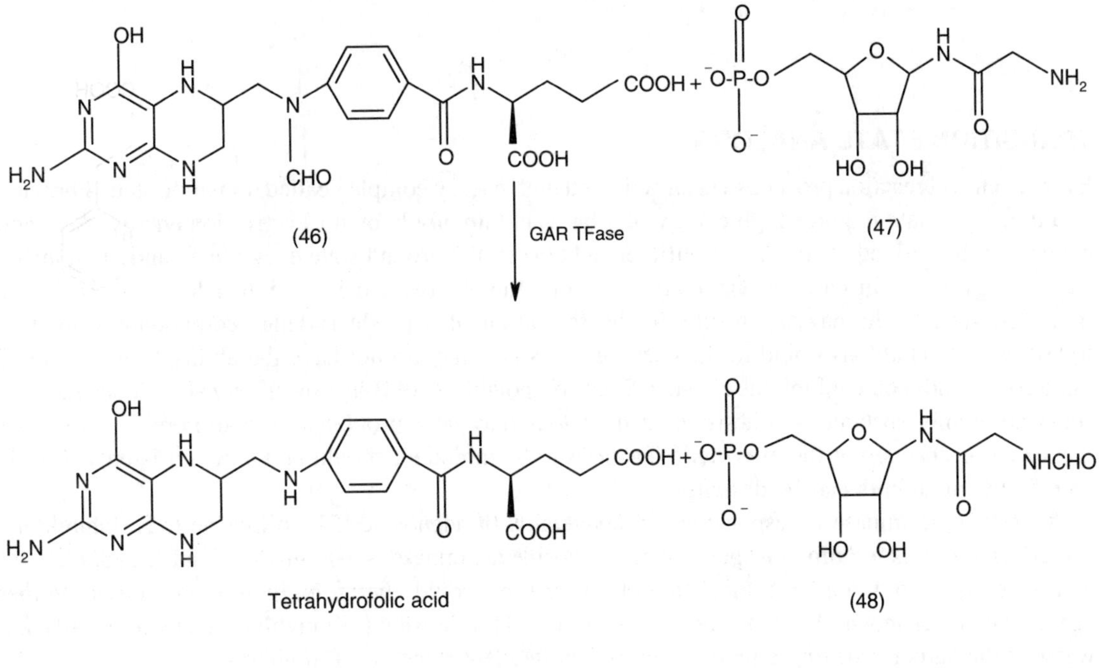

(46) (47)

Tetrahydrofolic acid (48)

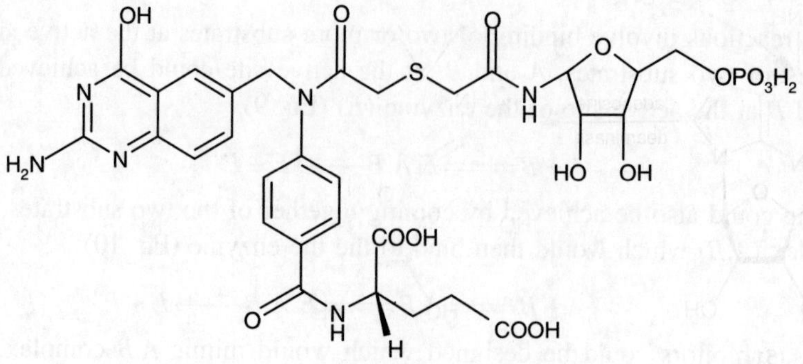

(49)

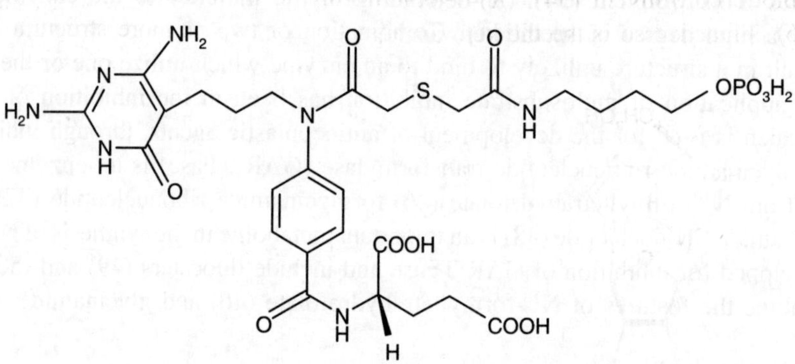

(50)

TRANSITION STATE ANALOGS

Every chemical reaction proceeds via an activated high energy complex called transition state. Formation of a transition state requires high energy or what is commonly known as activation energy. Activation energy can be defined as the energy difference between the ground state enegy level and the transition state energy level. In case of enzymatic reactions this energy barrier is much low. Binding of the transition state to the enzyme results in the formation of a product. Thus, compounds resembling transition state could also bind to the enzyme and since they do not have the ability to form product, these compounds could inhibit the enzyme. Such compounds would have specificity also. Since transition states are highly unstable, synthesis of such analogs may pose problems. Furthermore, it is necessary that exact mechanism of the enzymatic reactions to be inhibited, should be known. It is only then that an effective inhibitors can be designed.

Adenosine deaminase is responsible for conversion of adenosine (51) to inosine (52). Inhibition of this enzyme results in immunosuppression. Adenosine deaminase is also involved in the degradation of anticancer and antiviral agents. Inhibition of this enzyme could, therefore, prolong the activity of these agents. The mechanism of conversion of adenosine (51) to inosine (52) involves nucleophilic attack by water at the carbon carrying amino group and subsequent removal of ammonia.

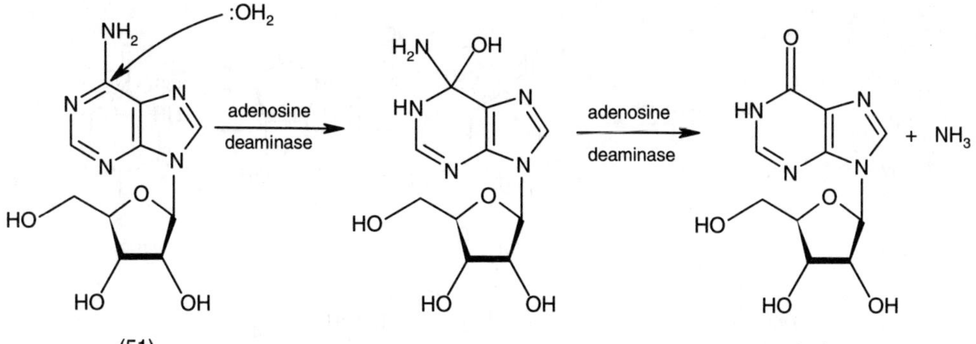

(51) (52)

Some of the adenosine deaminase inhibitors are 1,6-dihydro-6-hydroxymethyl purine ribonucleoside (53), the antibiotic coformycin (54), (*R*)-deoxycoformycin or pentostatin (55). The (*S*)-isomer of pentostatin (56) is inactive so is the the keto analog (57).

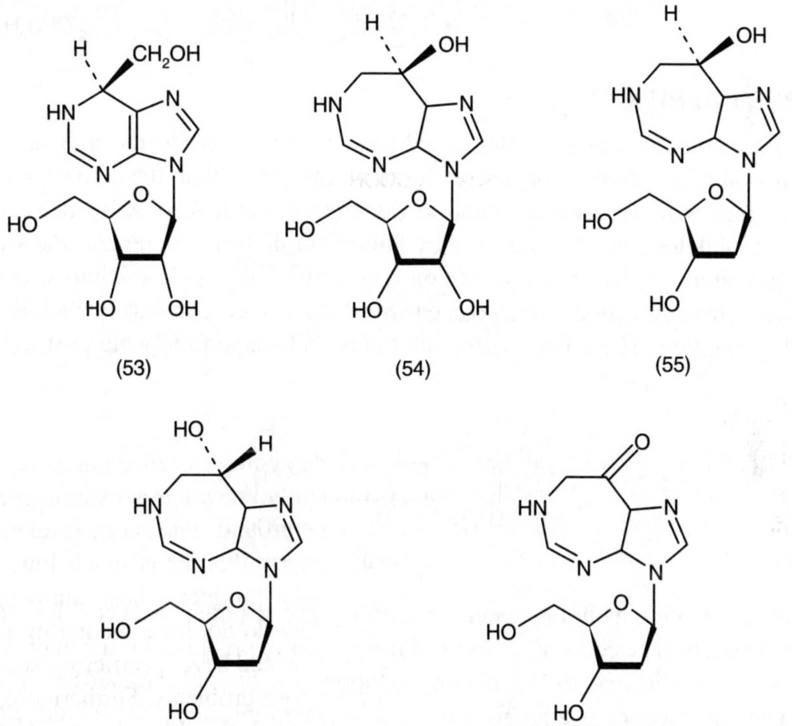

(53) (54) (55) (56) (57)

Transition state analogs have also been used as antineoplastic agents. One of the target has been the enzyme dihydroortase. In the biosynthesis of pyrimidines, dihydroorotase catalyses the conversion of carbamyl aspartate (58) to dihydroortate (59) via the transition state (60). The inhibitor (61), the boron containing analog of ethyl ester of carbamyl aspartate, rearranges to a stable tetrahedral boronic acid derivative (62) at pH 6-8 and binds to dihydroorotase with affinity which is 10-fold greater than that of carbamyl aspartate.

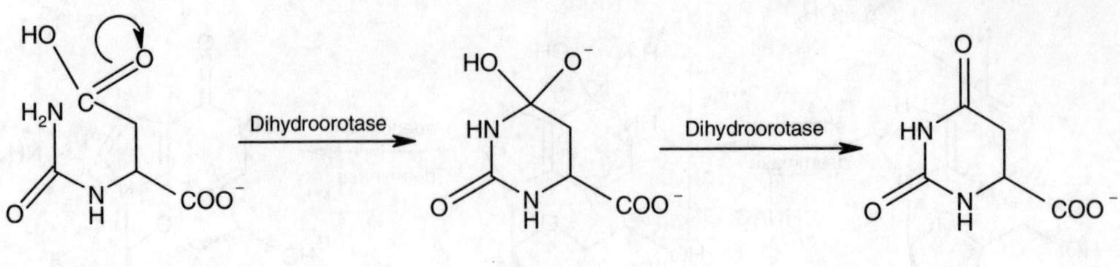

(58) (60) (59)

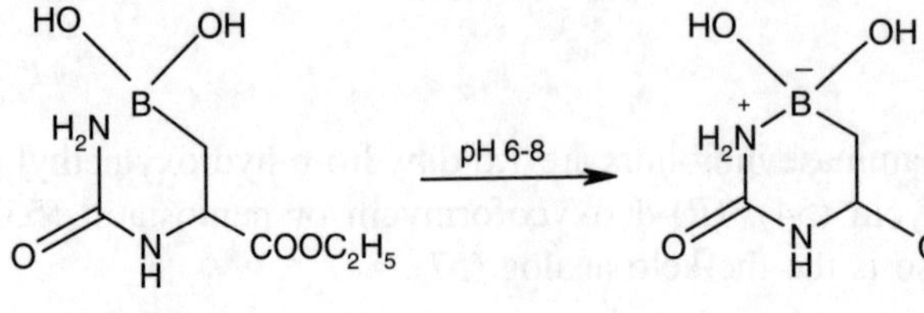

(61) (62)

IRREVERSIBLE INHIBITION

The irreversible inhibition involves covalent bond formation between the the enzyme and the inhibitor. This bond formation takes place at the active site or at sites other than the active site. Since there is a covalent bond formation in irreversible inhibitors, its effect is not reversible by increasing the substrate concentration and inhibitor cannot be released by dilution or dialysis. As regards the kinetics, the effect of irreversible inhibitors is similar to that of non-competitive reversible inhibitors, described earlier.

One example of irreversible inhibition has been already discussed under acetylcholinesterase inhibitors under reversible inhibition. These irreversible inhibitors include isoflurophate (36), echothiophate (37) and parathion (38).

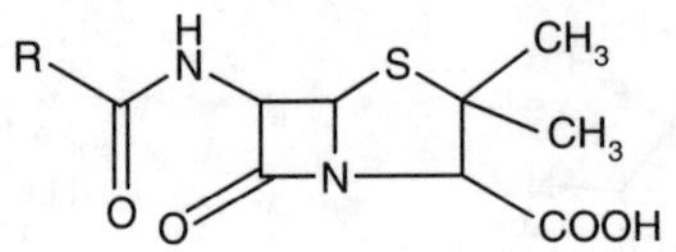

(63)

The β-lactam antibiotics including penicillins (63) have a potent irreversible bactericidal action against growing bacteria. The cell wall of most of the gram +ve organisms is a complex structure made-up of variety of polymeric materials including lipoproteins, lipopolysaccharides, teichoic acid, and mucopeptide. The mucopeptide is a highly cross linked giant molecule that provides rigidity to the cell wall. This cross-linked structure is called murein sacculus (Fig. 15.8). The mucopeptide consists of alternating units of D-N-acetylglucosamine (NAG) and N-acetylmuramic acid (NAMA). The carboxyl of NAMA is attached to polypeptide chain which varies with bacterial species. In case of *S. aureus* this chain consists of L-alanine (L.Ala), D-glutamic acid (D.Glu), L-lysine (L.Lys), and D-alanine (D.Ala). The glutamic acid is linked through its γ-carboxyl to the α-amino of L-lysine.

The murein strands are cross-linked by bridges of 5-glycine units to form murein sacculus (Fig. 8). These bridges link the ε-amino of L-lysine with carboxyl terminal of D-alanine. This cross-linking is carried out by transpeptidases.

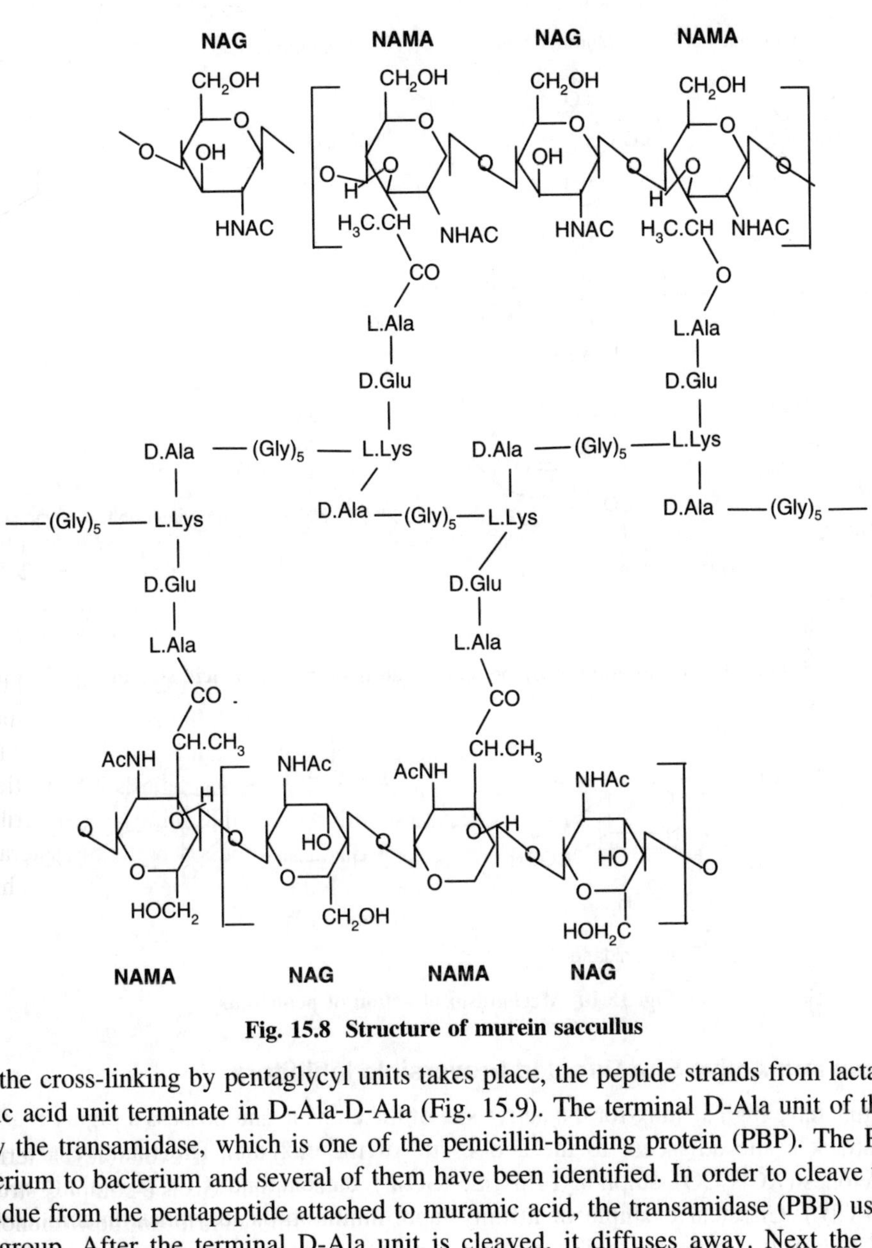

Fig. 15.8 Structure of murein sacculus

Before the cross-linking by pentaglycyl units takes place, the peptide strands from lactate carboxyl of muramic acid unit terminate in D-Ala-D-Ala (Fig. 15.9). The terminal D-Ala unit of this strand is cleaved by the transamidase, which is one of the penicillin-binding protein (PBP). The PBP's differ from bacterium to bacterium and several of them have been identified. In order to cleave the terminal D-Ala residue from the pentapeptide attached to muramic acid, the transamidase (PBP) uses its serine hydroxyl group. After the terminal D-Ala unit is cleaved, it diffuses away. Next the tetrapeptide is attached by the pentaglycyl unit in presence of transpeptidase to cross-link the different strands (Fig. 15.9).

The penicillins (63) and other β-lactam antibiotics act by acylating the serine-OH group of the transamidases (PBP). This acylation is irreversible as a result the terminal D-Ala unit of the pentapeptide strand is not cleaved and consequently the cross linking does not take place. This results in lysis (Fig. 15.10).

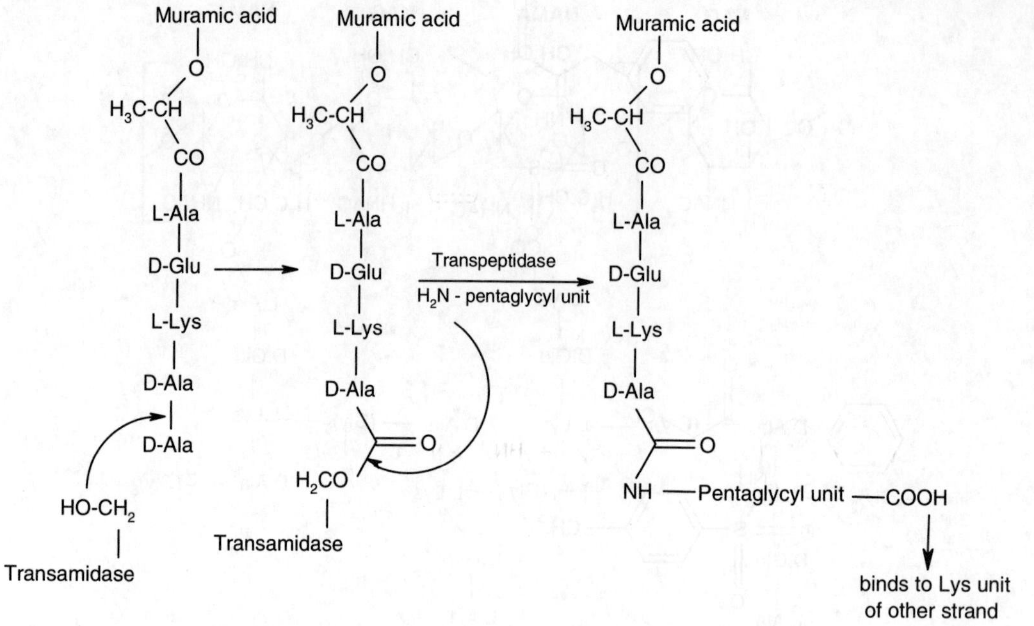

Fig. 15.9 Cross-linking by pentaglcyl units of muramic acid strands

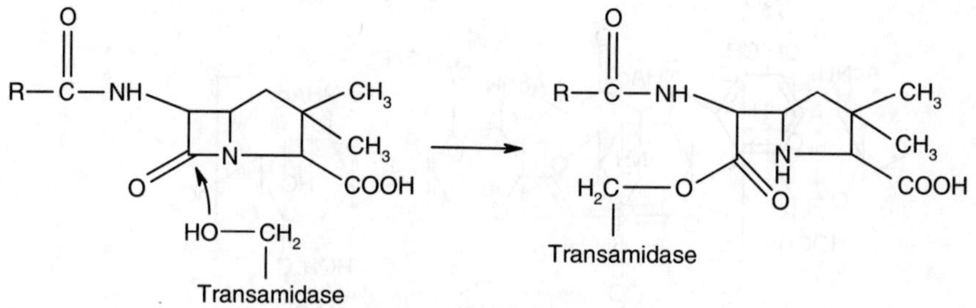

Fig. 15.10 Mechanism of action of penicillins

Affinity Label and Active Site Directed Irreversible Inhibitors

These inhibitors have high affinity for the active site of the enzyme and possess a highly reactive group which can attack a site adjascent to the active site of the enzyme. The reactive groups include halomethylketones (XCH_2CO), sulphonyl fluoride (SO_2F), diazoketone ($COCH_2N_2$), nitrogen mustard ($HN(CH_2CH_2Cl)_2$). Classical example of affinity label inhibitors is tosylphenylalaninechloromethyl ketone (TPCK, 64). It is a potent inhibitor of chymotrypsin. Chymotrypsin has selectivity for amino acid residues such as phenylalanine, tyrosin, etc. TPCK (64), besides containing phenylalanine residue also contains a halomethyl residue. After binding to the active site of the chymotrypsin, the halomethyl residue attacks the nitrogen of the histidyl residue of chymotrypsin thereby inactivating the enzyme (Fig. 15.11).

One of the uses of aspirin (65) is as antiplatelet aggregation drug. Cyclooxygenase 1 is an enzyme which is present in platelets. It converts arachidonic acid (66) into cyclic endoperoxide precursors, PGG_2 (67) and PGH_2 (68). These are then converted to thromboxane A_2 (69). Thromboxane A_2 (69) is a potent vasoconstrictor and platelet aggregation inducer. Aspirin (63) irreversibly acylates the hydroxyl

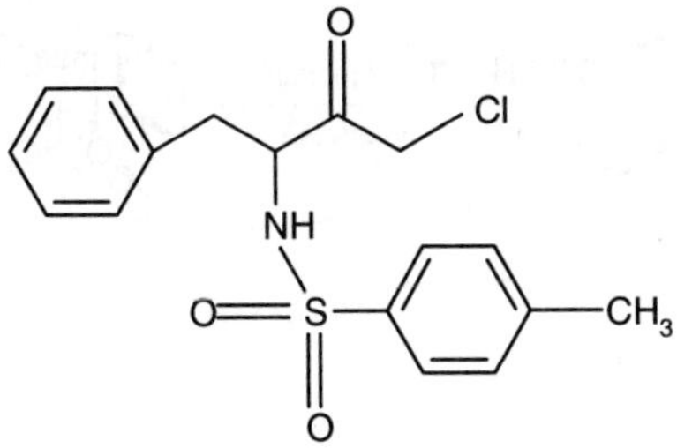

(64)

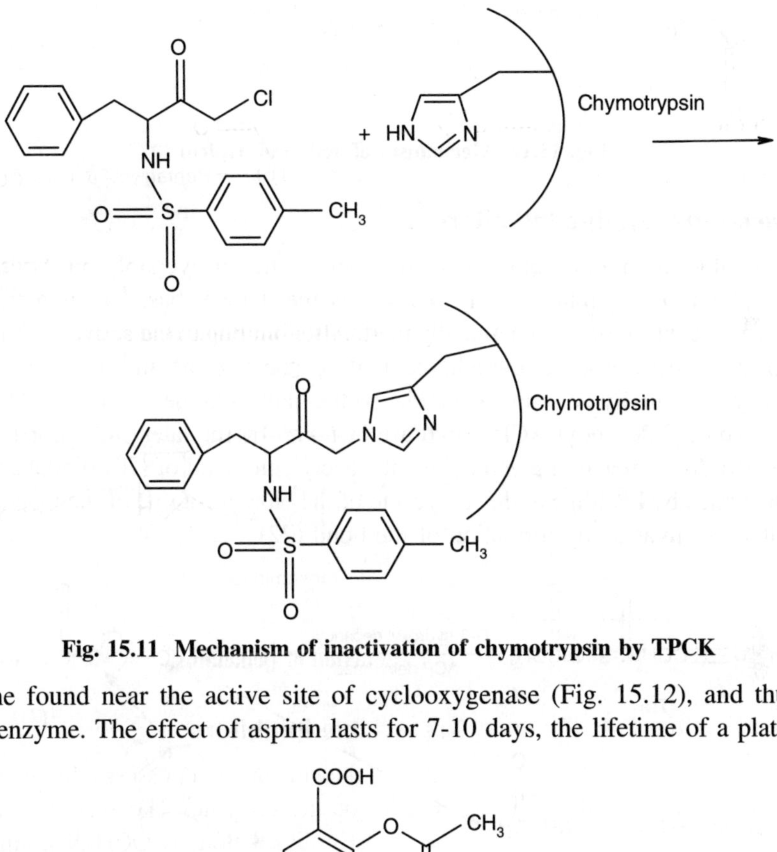

Fig. 15.11 Mechanism of inactivation of chymotrypsin by TPCK

groups of serine found near the active site of cyclooxygenase (Fig. 15.12), and thus permanently inactivates the enzyme. The effect of aspirin lasts for 7-10 days, the lifetime of a platelets.

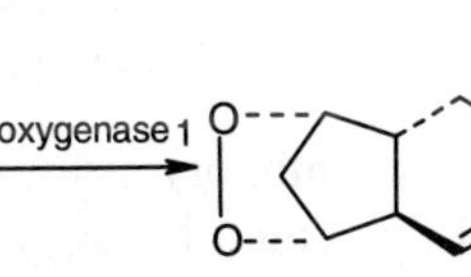

(65)

(66)

(67)

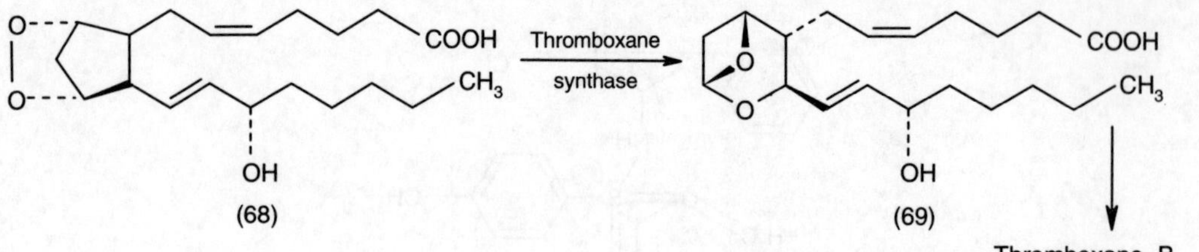

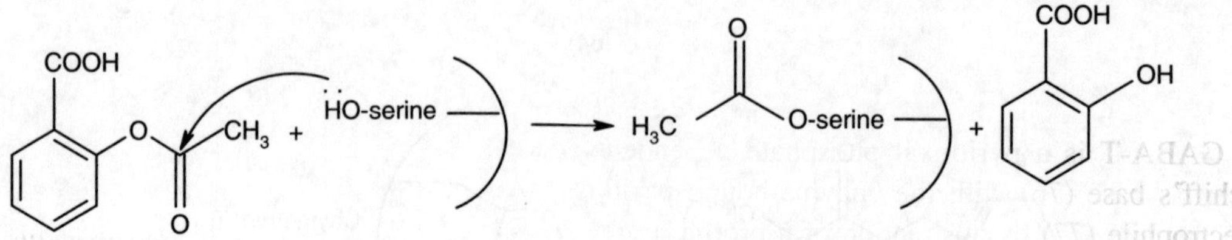

Fig. 15.12 Mechanism of action of aspirin

Mechanism based Irreversible Inhibitors

Some of the irreversible inhibitors require activation before they irreversibly bind to the enzyme and thereby inactivate them. These inhibitors are known as mechanism based inhibitors, k_{cat} inhibitors, suicide substrates. These inhibitors are chemically inert. After binding to the active site they are activated by a nucleophilic attack by a group at the adjascent site of the enzyme and this results in irreversible inhibition. The enzyme virtually commits a suicide, so the name suicide substrates. An example is the inhibition of D-3-hydroxyl decanoyl ACP dehydrase of *E.coli* by the latent inhibitor D-3-decynoyl-N-acetyl cystamine (70). In the reaction given below, the acetylenic bond of (70) is converted to an allene (71). Nucleophilic attack by histidine at the active site of the enzyme at one of the reactive double bond leads to irreversible inactivation by formation of the bond (72).

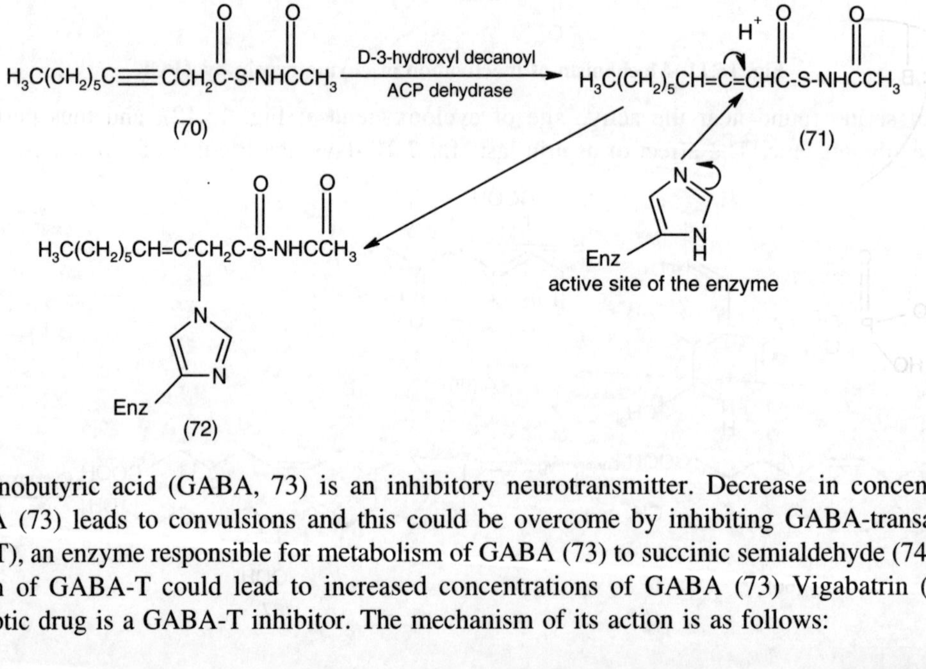

γ-Aminobutyric acid (GABA, 73) is an inhibitory neurotransmitter. Decrease in concentrations of GABA (73) leads to convulsions and this could be overcome by inhibiting GABA-transaminase (GABA-T), an enzyme responsible for metabolism of GABA (73) to succinic semialdehyde (74). Thus, inhibition of GABA-T could lead to increased concentrations of GABA (73) Vigabatrin (75), an antiepileptic drug is a GABA-T inhibitor. The mechanism of its action is as follows:

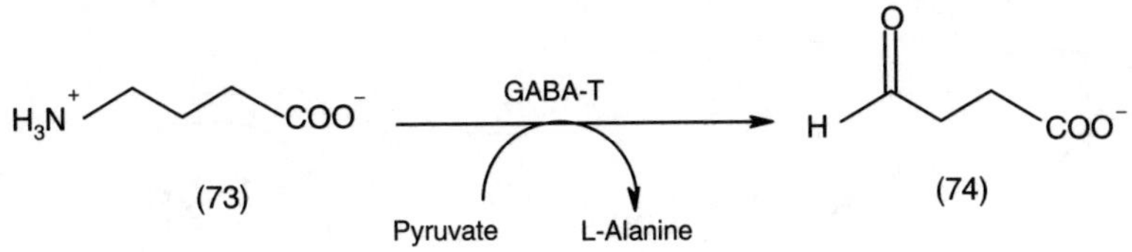

(73) (74)

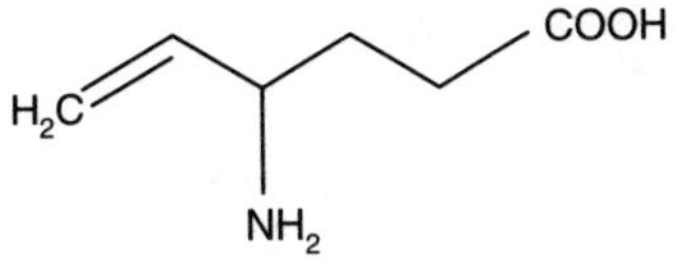

(75)

GABA-T is a pyridoxal phosphate dependent enzyme. In the first step, there is formation of a Schiff's base (76) with the enzyme-bound pyridoxal phosphate followed by formation of a reactive electrophile (77) by abstraction of a proton by the base at the active site of the enzyme. This is then attacked by the adjacent nucleophile resulting in formation of covalent bond (78) and enzyme inactivation.

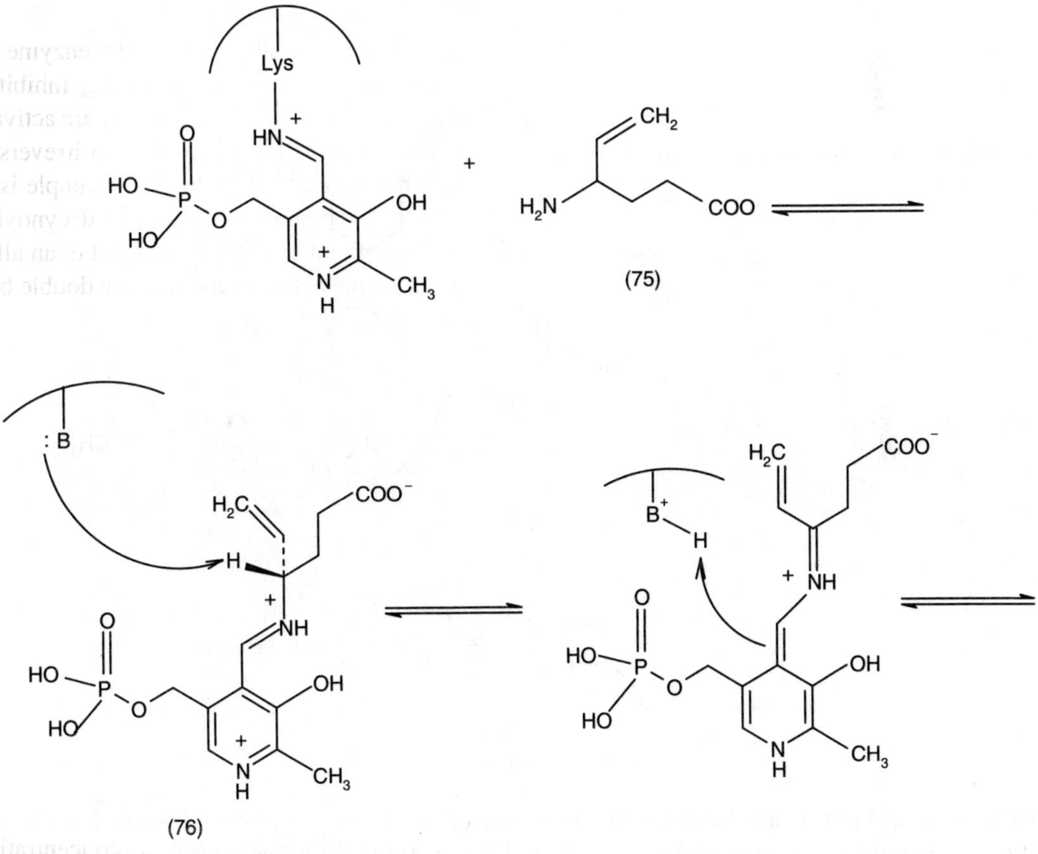

(75)

(76)

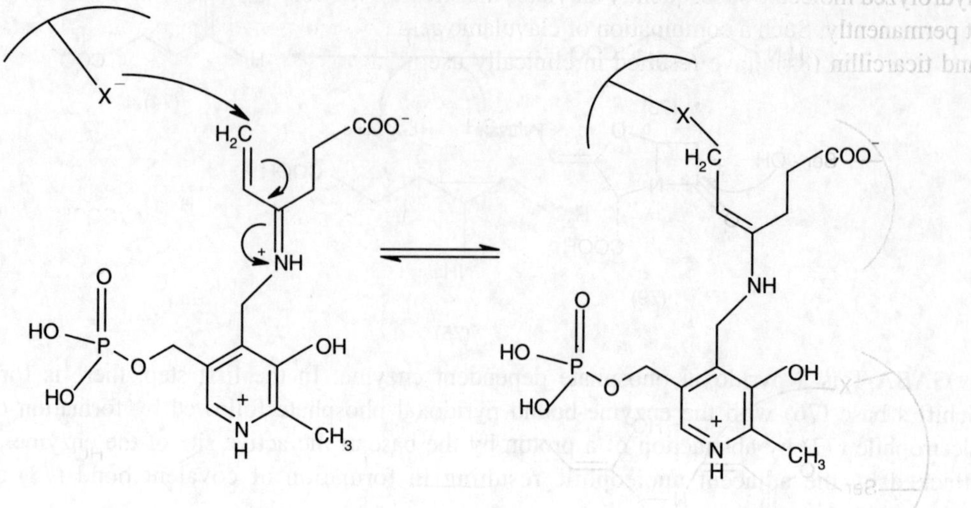

(77)

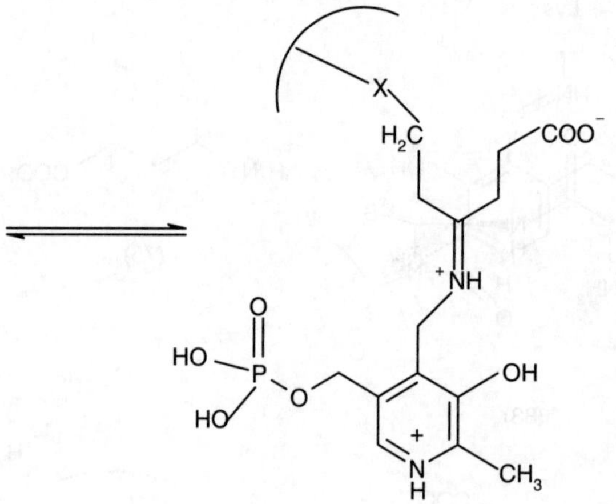

(78)

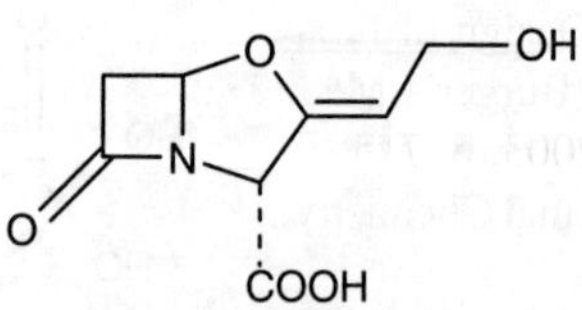

(79)

Clavulanic acid (79) is a β-lactam antibiotic produced by *Streptomyces clavuligerus*. It has a weak antibiotic action but is a potent inhibitor of bacterial β-lactamase. β-Lactamase is a serine protease and can hydrolyze β-lactam ring of antibiotics like penicillins.When given in combination with penicillins, clavulanic acid (79) is preferentially taken up by β-lactamases and hydrolyzed to (80) and (81). The hydrolyzed molecule subsequently alkylates the site near the active site of β-lactamase, thus inactivating it permanently. Such a combination of clavulanic acid (79) and penicillins, particularly amoxicillin (83) and ticarcillin (84), have resulted in clinically useful agents.

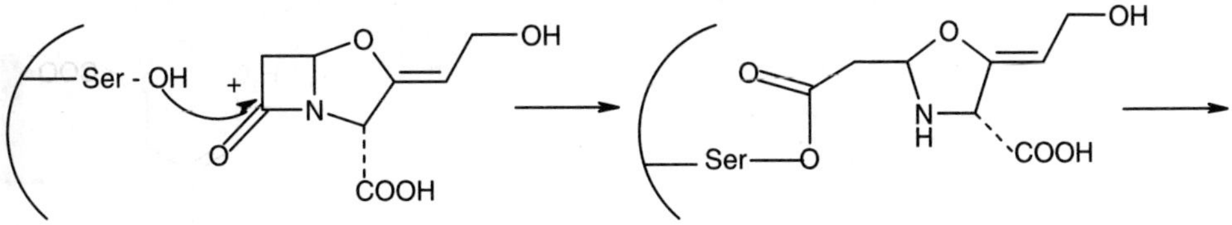

(79) (80)

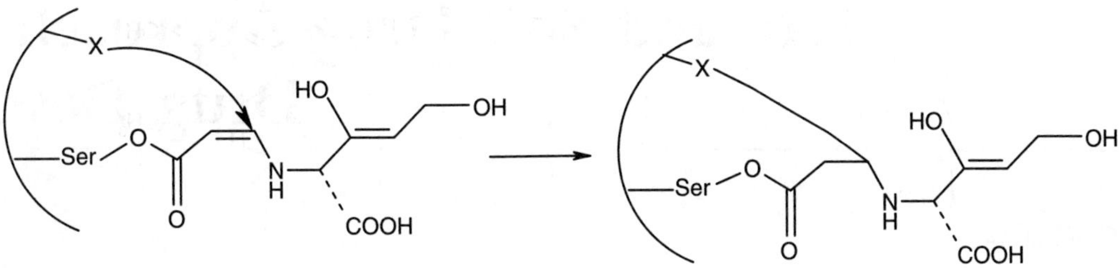

(81) (82)

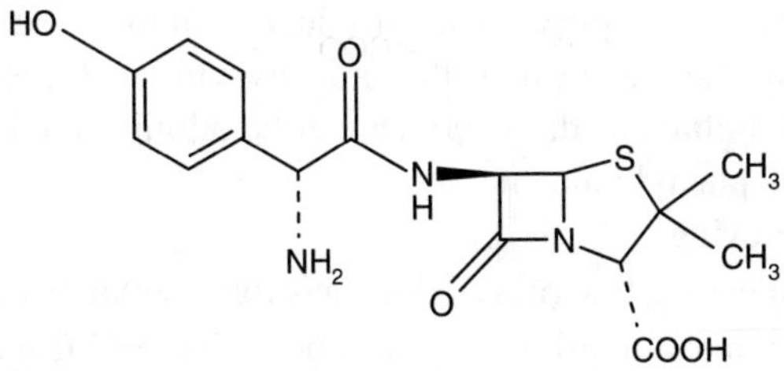

(83)

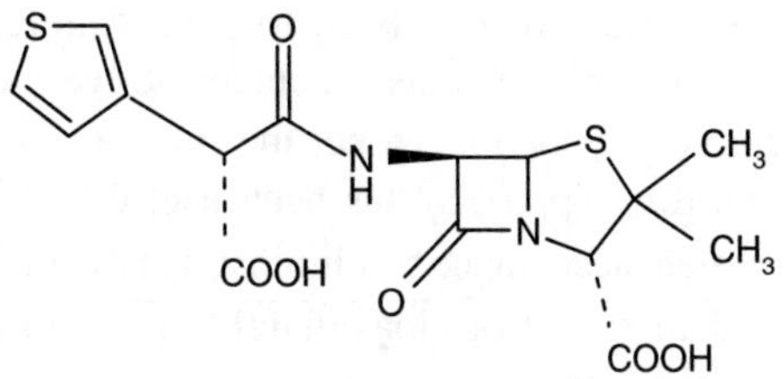

(84)

FURTHER READING

1. M.I. Page, Ed., "Chemistry of Enzyme Action," Elsevier, Amesterdam, 1984.
2. M.I. Page and A. Williams, Eds., 'Enzyme Mechanisms," Royal Society of Chemistry, London, 1987.
3. M. Sandler and H.J. Smith, Eds., "Design of Enzyme Inhibitors," Oxford University Press, Oxford, 1989.
4. M.J. Meheish and G.L. Kenyon in 'Burger's Medicinal Chemistry,' 6th ed., Vol. 1, D.J. Abraham, Ed., John Wiley and Sons Inc., New Jersey, 2003, p. 715.
5. M.I. Page in "Comprehensive Medicinal Chemistry," Vol. 2, C. Hansch, Ed. in-Chief, Pergamon Press, Oxford, 2005, p. 61.

16

Pro- and Soft Drug Approach to Drug Design

PRODRUGS

The undesirable properties in a lead compound can be overcome by pharmaceutical formulation or change in the route of administration. However, where such methods fail, the method of designing reversible derivatives or prodrug approach is resorted to. A prodrug can be defined as 'pharmacologically inactive reversible derivative of a known active drug which upon introduction into an appropriate biological system reverts back to parent molecule/active form of the drug by virtue of chemical or enzymatic action'. This also includes active metabolites of drugs which can be administered directly, for example oxyphenbutazone, the metabolite of phenylbutazone.

The prodrug approach has been useful in achieving:

1. patient acceptance by eliminating pain on injection, bitterness, odour, gastrointestinal irritation, etc,
2. enhancement of bioavailability through changes in absorption, transport, tissue distribution and metabolism,
3. enhancement of stability of the drug, and
4. improvement of drug formulation.

Characteristics of a Prodrug

1. It should be pharmacologically inactive for example acetylsalicylic acid (1) is not a prodrug of salicylic acid (2) because acetylsalicylic acid is itself more potent than salicylic acid (2). On the

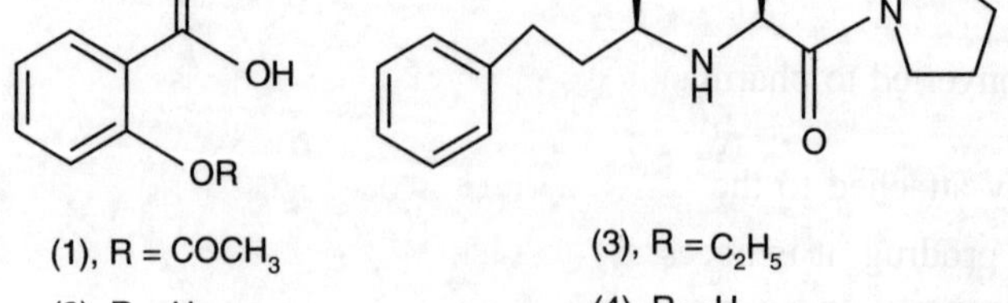

(1), R = $COCH_3$

(2), R = H

(3), R = C_2H_5

(4), R = H

other hand enalapril (3) the inactive ethyl ester of enalaprilat (4) is a prodrug because it is hydrolyzed to enalaprilat (4), the active form of the drug.

2. It should get converted to active form of the drug readily and should not get metabolized to other products. Example, L-dopa (5) is not a prodrug of dopamine(6) because most of L-dopa is metabolized to other products such as 3-methoxy derivative (7), 3,4-dihydroxyphenylacetic acid (8), and homovanilic acid (9). Inositol hexanicotinate (10), on the otherhand, is a true pro-drug because it is hydrolyzed to vasodilator nicotinic acid (11) without any metabolism prior to ester hydrolysis.

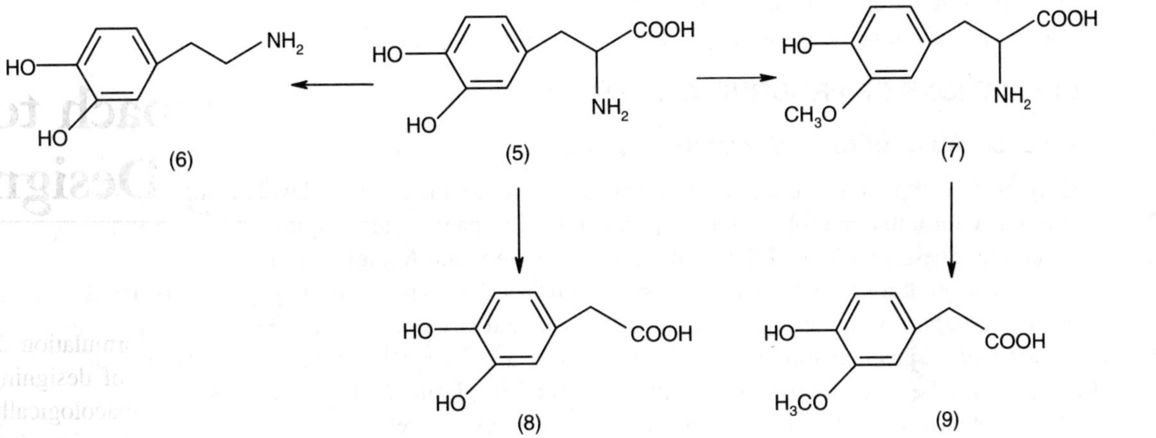

(6) (5) (7) (8) (9)

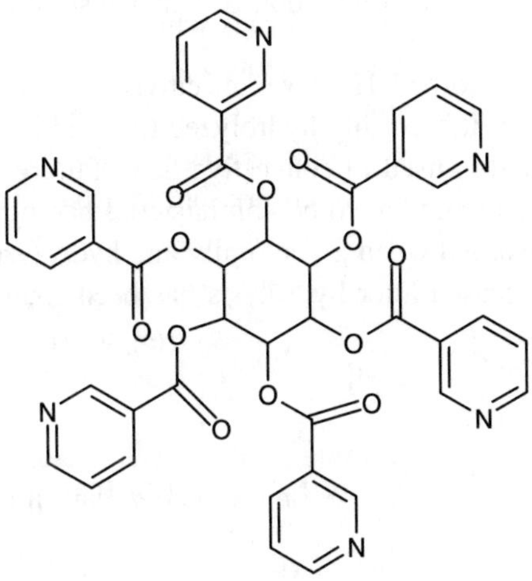

(10)

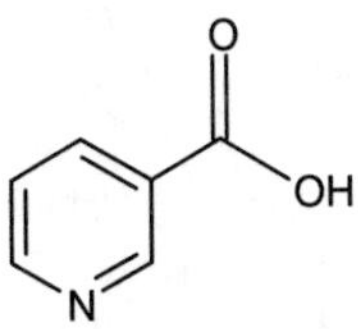

(11)

3. It should be converted to pharmacologically active form of the drug after being absorbed in the blood.
4. The pro-moiety attached to the active form of drug should be non-toxic.

While designing a prodrug, it is necessary to identify the functional group whose modification can lead to the desired property and a reversible derivative. Generally molecules containing alcoholic, amino, thiol, carboxylic and ketonic groups have been derivatized. The derivatization should normally involve not more than one or two steps and the prodrug should be obtainable in pure form or be readily purifiable.

The pro-moiety attached to the parent drug should be nontoxic. The prodrug should be chemically stable and should not interact with the excipients when formulated in various dosage forms. It should not give rise to formulation problems such as polymorphism, degradation in liquid dosage forms, caking etc. While designing a prodrug, the conditions under which the parent moiety is regenerated in vivo should be known. This is particularly true for the enzyme system required for activation of prodrug into a drug. The most frequently used enzyme systems include esterases, amidases, phosphatases, oxido-reductases, transferases, and lipases.

Below are given some of the applications of prodrug approach.

APPLICATIONS OF PRODRUG APPROACH

Increased Absorption and Aqueous Solubility

Highly polar compounds are not well absorbed as a result lower blood levels result.

Similarly formulation problems are encountered with many water insoluble drugs. Prodrug approach to overcome these problems utilizes conversion to esters and Mannich bases.

Ester type prodrugs form the largest class of prodrugs. This type of prodrugs possess better absorption, increased duration of action, masking of bitter taste and sustained release. Ester type of prodrugs can be made from drugs containing a carboxylic acid or a hydroxyl functional group. Hydrolysis of ester function can take place by esterases which are found in plasma and other tissues.

Esters of alcoholic function can be made with alkyl or aryl carboxylic acids. Esters with alkyl carbonates result in lower gastric irritation. Hemiesters of alcohols prepared with dicarboxylic acids result in increased water solubility which helps in formulation of water insoluble drugs. Some of the examples given below illustrate this.

Enalaprilat (4), the active form is not well absorbed. However, its ethyl ester, enalapril (3), is absorbed better because of its lipophillic ester function. It is readily hydrolyzed to its active form enalaprilat (4). Candoxatrilat (12) is a protease inhibitor and is used in congestive heart failure. Because of its polar character, it is not absorbed when given orally and has to be administered parentrally. However, its 5-indanyl ester, candoxatril (13) is readily absorbed when given orally and hydrolyzed to the parent drug candoxatrilat (12). The 5-indanyl moiety released after hydrolysis has been found to be non toxic.

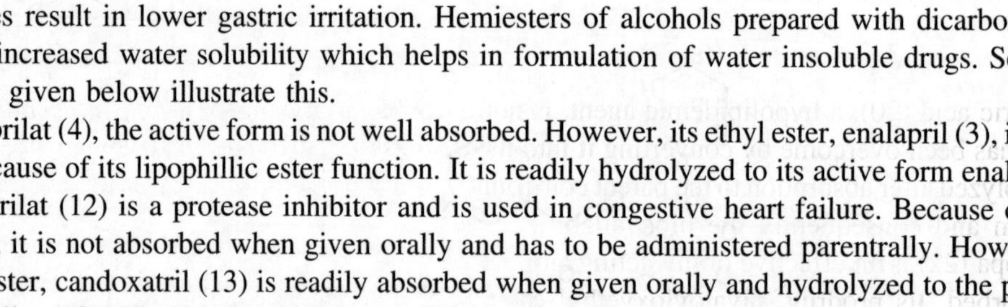

In case of β-lactam antibiotics there is a problem of absorption because of their polar character. Thus, ampicillin (14) when given orally is absorbed to the extent of 30-40% only. This not only results in decreased blood levels but also in destruction of useful intestinal flora of the host. On the other hand simple esters like methyl, ethyl, propyl, etc. of β-lactam antibiotics are not hydrolyzed easily because of steric hinderance. In such cases double esters have been found to be suitable. Some of the examples of the esters of ampicillin (14) include pivampicillin (15), bacampicillin (16), and talampicillin (17). Among cephalosporins, cefpodoxime proxetil (18) and cefuroxime axetil (19) are some of the examples.

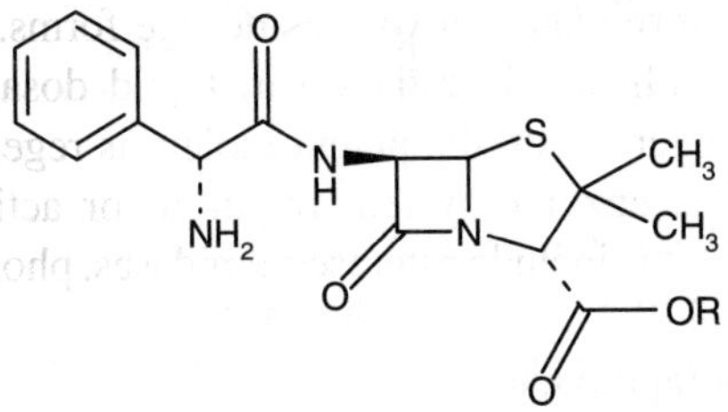

(14), R = H; (15), R =

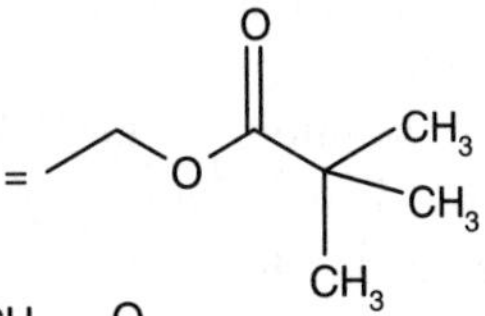

(16), R =

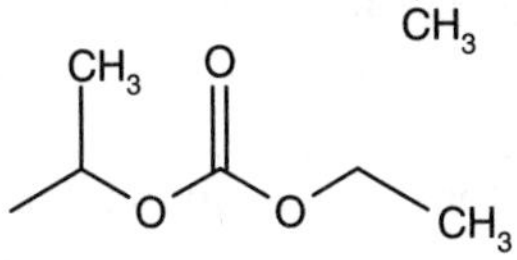

(17), R =

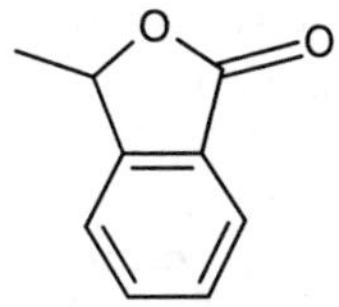

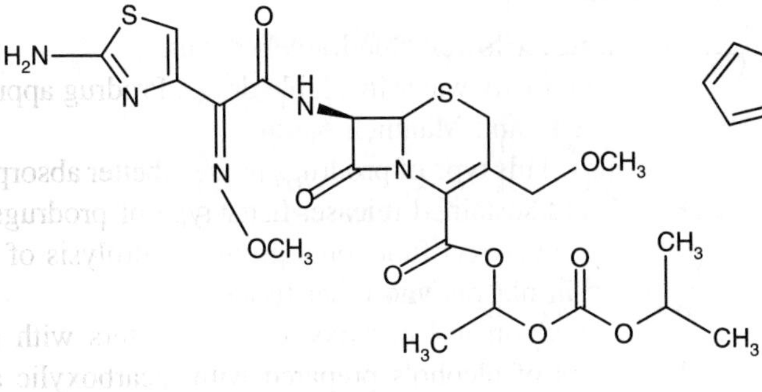

(18)

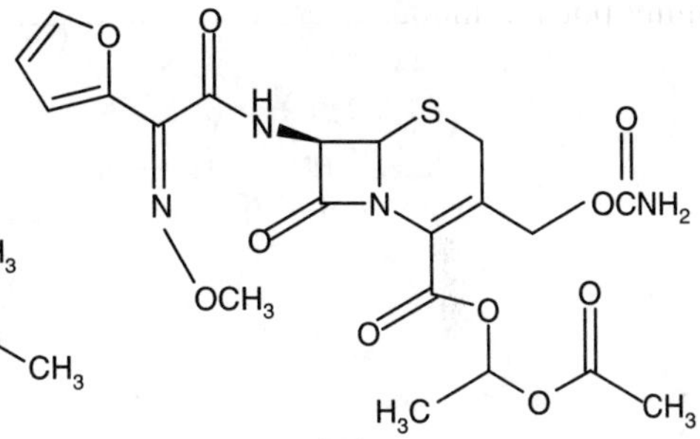

(19)

Clofibric acid (20), a hypolipidemic agent, is not absorbed well because of its polar character. This problem has been overcome by converting it into its ethyl ester, clofibrate (21), which is well absorbed and hydrolyzed after absorption to the parent compound clofibric acid (20). Another example of increasing absorption and consequently the bioavailability through esterfication is of α-methyldopa (22). α-Methyldopa (22) is an effective orally acting antihypertensive but because of its polar character it is not well absorbed. Its prodrug, pivaloyloxyethyl ester (23) is well absorbed from gastrointestinal tract because of its lipophilic character.

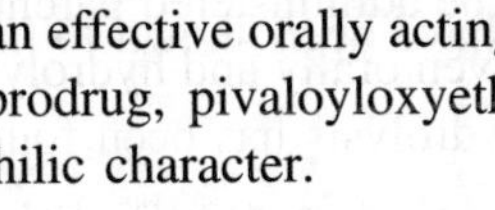

(20), R = H

(21), R = CH_2CH_3

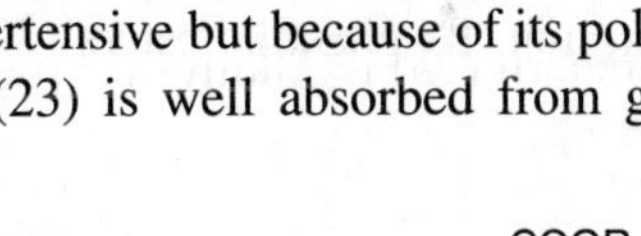

(22), R = H

(23) R =

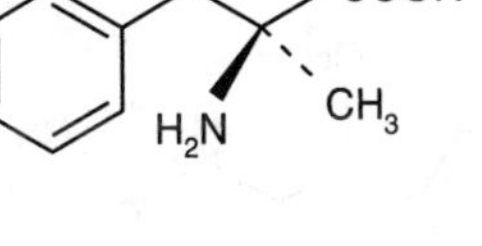

Esterfication as a means of preparing prodrug has also been used for increasing the water solubility of water insoluble drugs and thus facilitate their formulation in parentral dosage form. The water solubility of chloramphenicol (24) is poor, its sodium hemisuccinate (25) ester is water soluble and is used for preparation of parentral formulation. Further, by increasing the water solubility of chloramphenicol (24), it is not precipitated at the sight of injection and there is no pain at the site of injection.

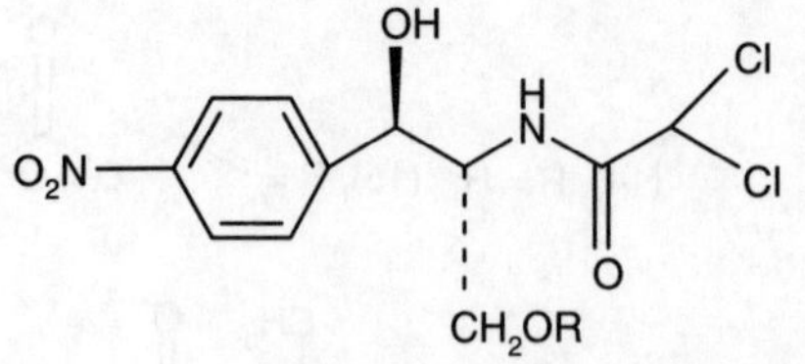

(24), R = H

(25), R = 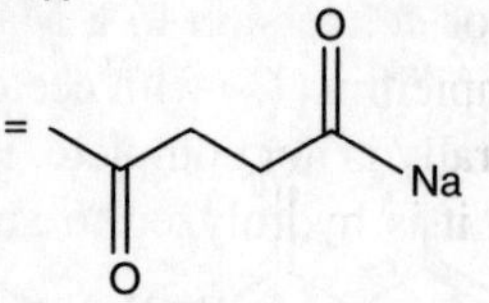

Phenytoin (26), an antiepileptic drug, is highly water insoluble drug. As a result it shows erratic and poor absorption upon oral administration. In order to improve its absorption it has been converted to hydroxymethyl derivative (27). Esters (28-30) of hydroxymethyl derivative (27) have been found to have better absorption.

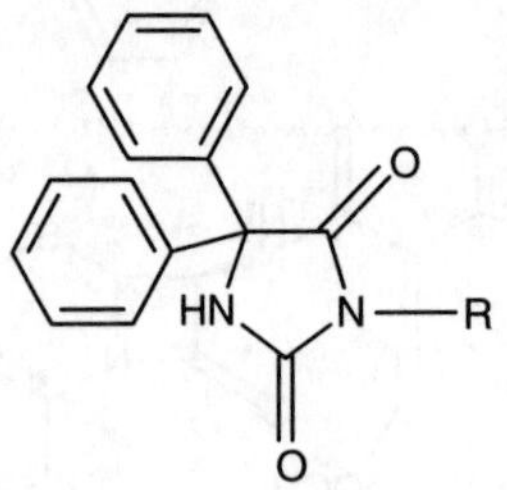

(26), R = H

(27), R = CH_2OH

(28), R = 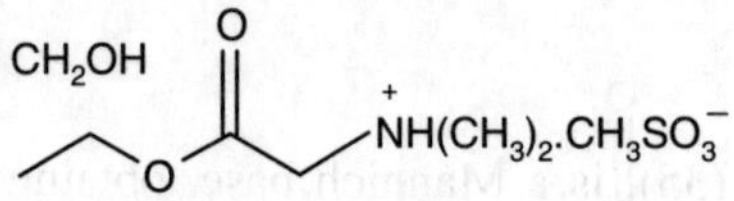

(29), R = 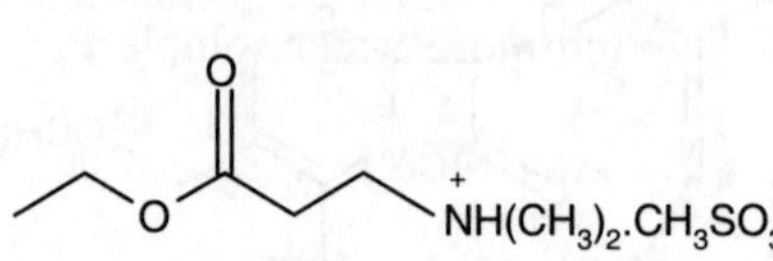

(30), R = 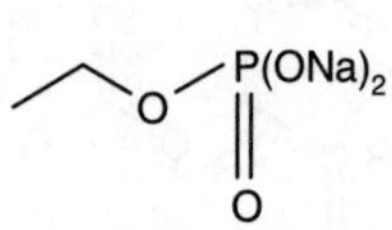

Another problem overcome through prodrug approach is the first-pass metabolism. It is known that phenolic compounds undergo first-pass metabolism through conjugation with sulphuric acid and glucouronic acid. As a result there is slow and incomplete absorption of such compounds from gastrointestinal tract. To avoid this esters of phenol have been prepared. Terbutaline (31), a bronchodilator, is an example of this category of drugs. It undergoes extensive first-pass metabolism as a result there is incomplete absorption. Its phenolic esters (32 and 33) have been shown to have better absorption.

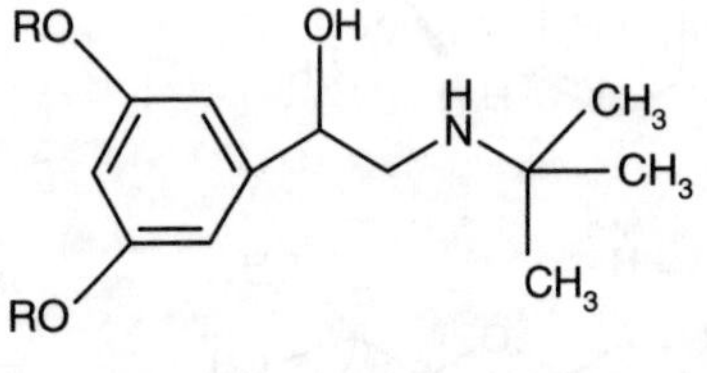

(31), R = H

(32), R = 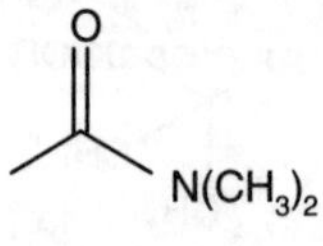

(33), R = 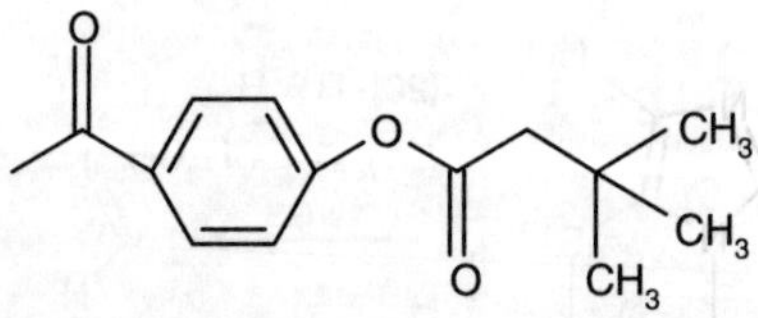

Amides as derivatives of amines are not good candidates as prodrugs. This is because amides are not as easily hydrolyzed as esters. Secondly amidases, the enzymes responsible for hydrolysis of amides, are rare. Since peptidases are available, amines have been converted to a peptide linkage. This way their absorption is also facilitated through amino acid transporters. Further, after absorption the peptide linkage is hydrolyzed by peptidases. Another approach to the derivatization of amines is through reaction with acetone or conversion to a Mannich base. An example of this is hetacillin (34) which is formed by treating ampicillin (14) with acetone. Because of its polar character, the absorption of ampicillin (14) when given orally is not complete. Hetacillin is much more lipophilic and its absorption is better. After its absorption it is hydrolyzed to ampicillin (14) and acetone in plasma.

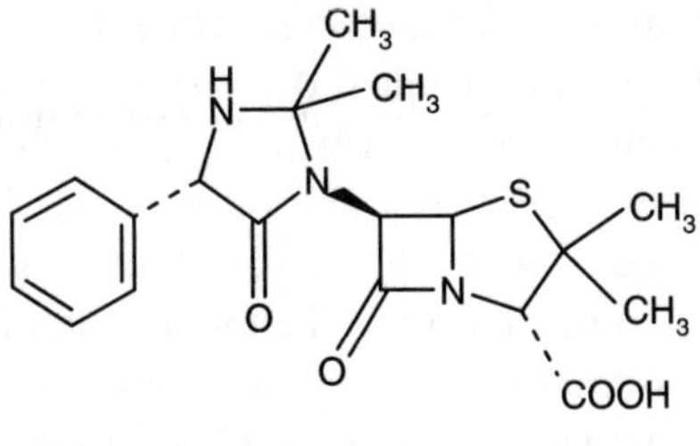

(34)

Rolitetracycline (35), is a Mannich base, obtained by treating tetracycline (36) with formaldehyde and pyrrolidine. It is much more water soluble than tetracycline (36).

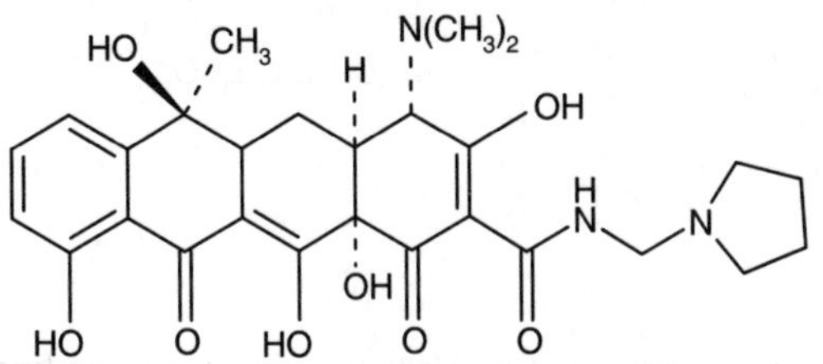

(35)

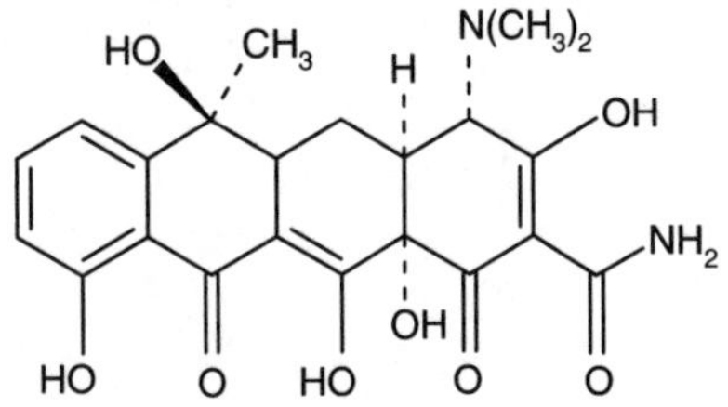

(36)

Prodrug Approach for Prolongation of Activity

Azathioprine (37) is an example of this class of prodrugs. Azathioprine (37) is a prodrug of 6-mercaptopurine (38) which is used for suppressing the immune response during tissue grafting. If given as such, 6-mercaptopurine (38) is eliminated very fast. Azathioprine (37) is slowly converted to 6-mercaptopurine (38) by the action of glutathione (GS) in the body through its adduct (39). Thus there is a sustained release of 6-mercaptopurine (38) over a period of time and the donor is protected from immune reaction.

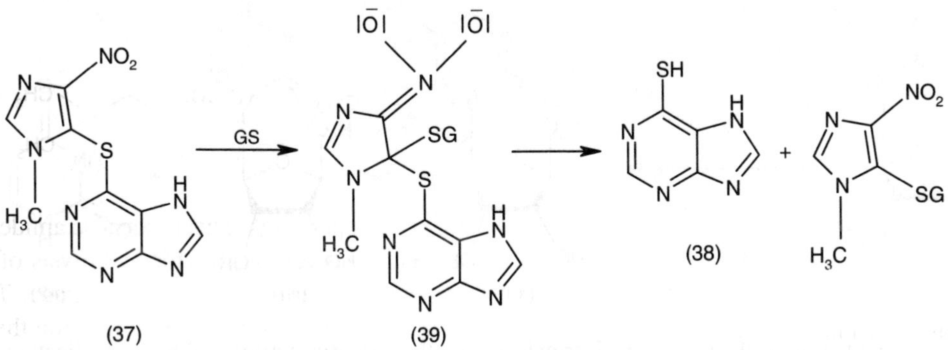

(37) (39) (38)

GS = glutathione

Site Specific Chemical Delivery System

Site specific delivery of drugs or drug targeting has several advantages. By targeting the drug molecule at the site of action, the dose of the drug is reduced, moreover other sites or organs are not affected. This results in overall reduction in toxicity. Various approaches have been used for drug targeting. One approach is to tag the molecule with a carrier molecule which has affinity for that site, for example, liposomes. Another approach is the use of chemical delivery system which was enunciated by Bodor and his colleagues. According to them there could be two approaches to drug targeting:

1. synthesize a prodrug which is selectively transported to the desired site, and
2. synthesize a prodrug which has a wide spread distribution but is converted to the active drug only at the desired site. This could be achieved either due to pH and/ higher activity of enzyme, responsible for converting prodrug to drug, at the desired or target tissue.

Methenamine (40) or hexamethyltetramine is an example of chemical delivery system using the first type of approach. It is used as urinary antiseptic. Its antiseptic action is due to formation of formaldehyde after hydrolysis. It is administered in enteric capsules so that it is not hydrolyzed in stomach. After passing from stomach, it is absorbed from intestines and excreted in urine where due to acidic pH it gets hydrolyzed to formaldehyde and ammonia and acts as antiseptic.

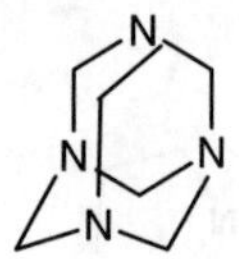

(40)

Because of higher rate of growth of tumor cells, they also contain higher concentration of enzymes. One of the approaches of chemical delivery system is to exploit these differences in enzyme concentrations between the normal and cancerous tissues.

Capecitabine (41), an anticancer prodrug utilizes the above approach for delivery of 5-fluorouracil (42). The esterases of the liver convert it to (43) and the other enzymes which convert (43) to 5-fluorouracil (42) via (44) are present in higher concentration in tumor cells.

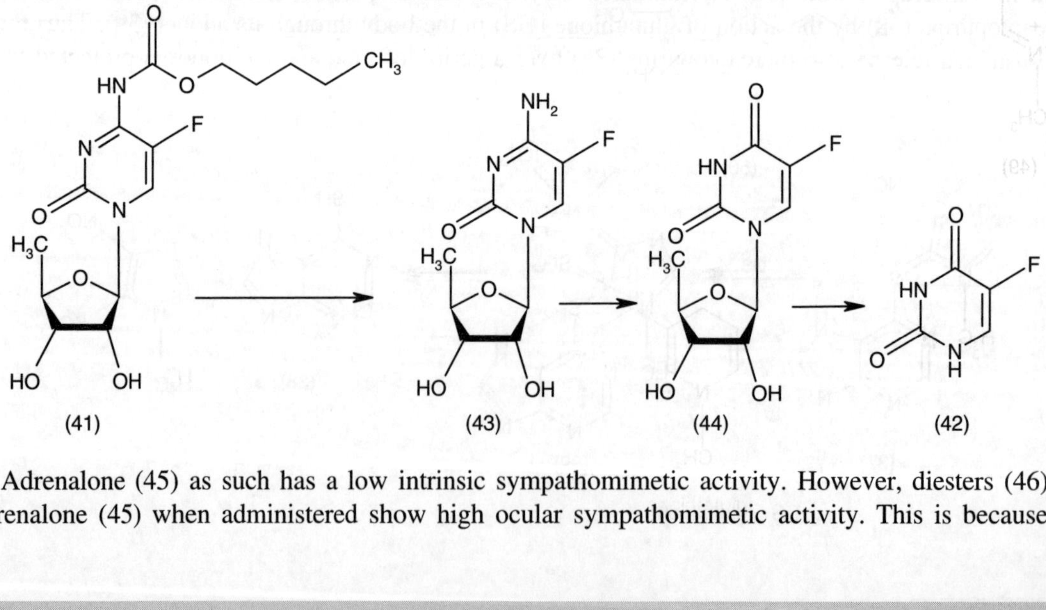

(41) (43) (44) (42)

Adrenalone (45) as such has a low intrinsic sympathomimetic activity. However, diesters (46) of adrenalone (45) when administered show high ocular sympathomimetic activity. This is because of higher ocular concentration of reductases which reduce the adrenalone diester (46) to the hydroxyl diester (47) and finally the esterases hydrolyse the diester (47) to adrenaline ((48).

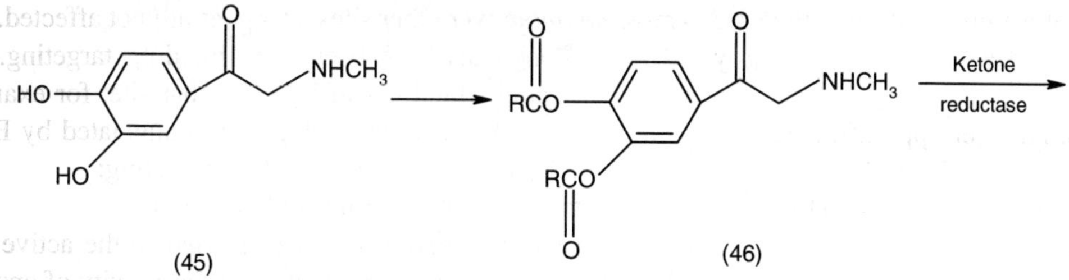

(45) (46)

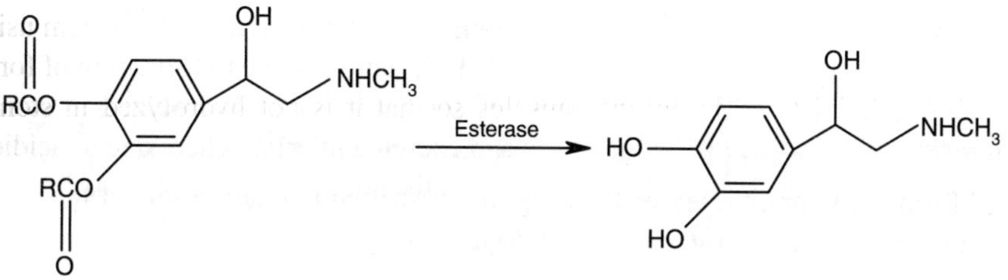

(47) (48)

A chemical delivery approach for delivery of drugs to the brain has been developed by Bodor and his coworkers. It uses trigonelline (49) as a carrier moiety for this purpose. A drug, say dopamine (50), to be delivered to the brain is first of all tagged with trigonelline (49). The amide (51) is then reduced to give the dihydro-analog (52). The reduced (52) form after administration gets distributed in the body including in the brain. In the body it gets oxidized and then gets excreted because of its ionic character.On the otherhand, in brain, it gets oxidized but cannot get excreted because of its ionic character.

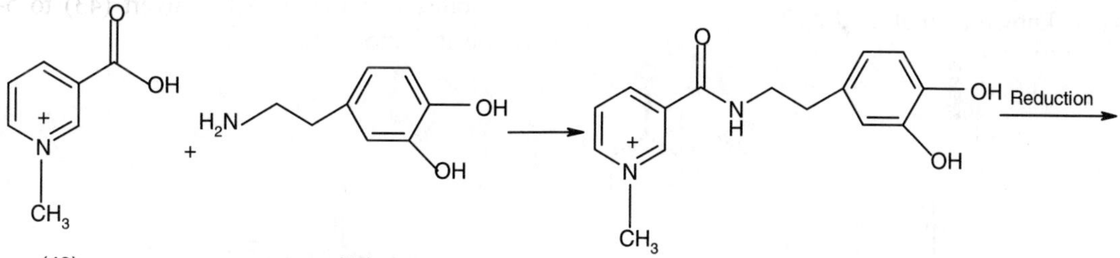

(49) (50) (51)

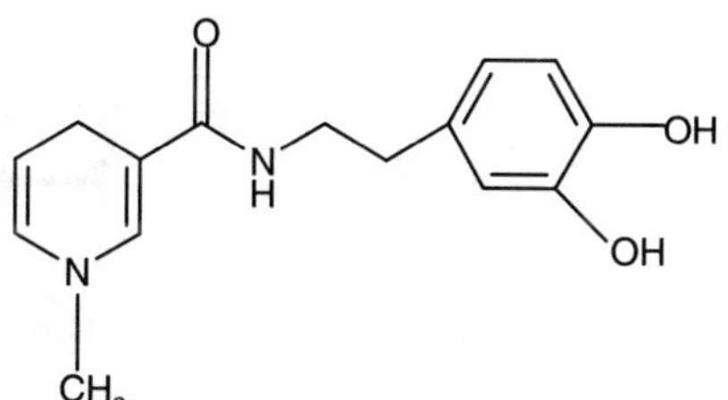

(52)

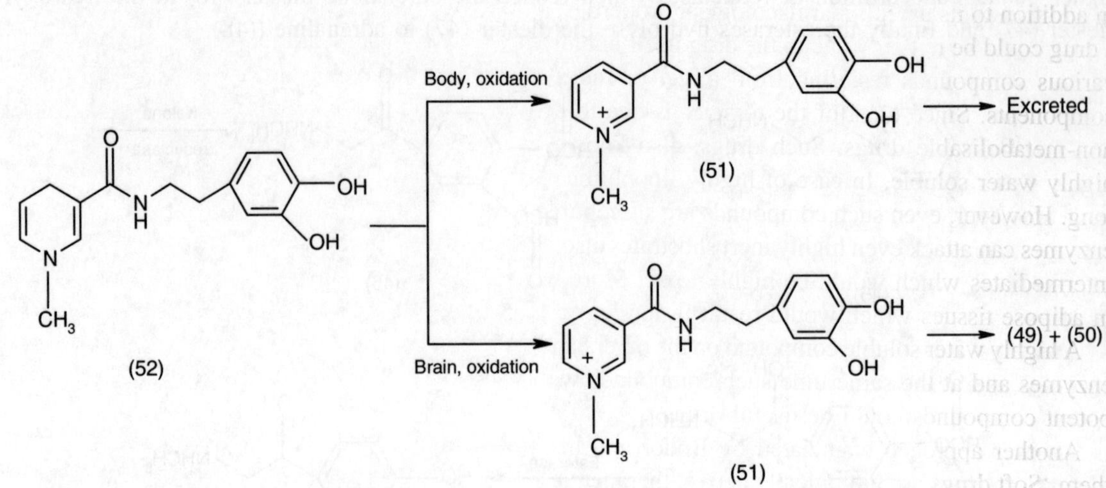

The oxidized form in the brain releases the drug in a sustained manner. Some of the drugs delivered by this method include dopamine (46) and phenytoin (26).

Mutual Prodrugs

Mutual prodrugs are the prodrugs in which the promoiety after getting detached from the active drug also show activity, example estramustine (53a) in which normustine (54) has been tagged with estradiol (55). The 17β-phosphate ester (53b) of estramustine (53a) after administration, gets concentrated in prostrate and is hydrolyzed to normustine (54), 17β-estradiol (55), carbon dioxide, and sodium phosphate. The normustine (54) acts as an alkylating agent destroying the cancerous tissues while as 17β-estradiol (55) which has an antiandrogenic effect slows down the growth of cancerous tissues. Since both normustine (54) and 17β-estradiol possess activity, therefore 17β-phosphate ester (53b) of estramustine (53a) is known as mutual drug.

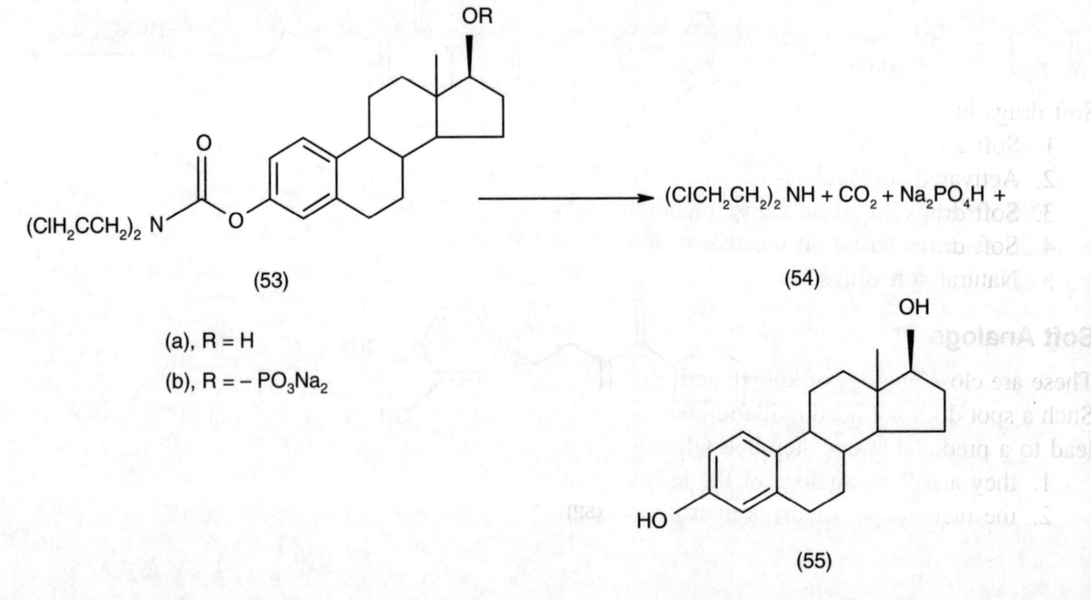

HARD AND SOFT DRUGS

In addition to its useful pharmacological properties, a drug also possesses toxic actions. The toxicity of a drug could be not only due to the drug itself but also due to its metabolites, reactive intermediates, and various compounds resulting from direct or indirect interaction of the drug molecule with the cell components. Since most of the toxicity is due to activated metabolites, Ariens suggested design of a non-metabolisable drugs. Such drugs, also known as "Hard Drugs", could be highly lipophillic or highly water soluble. In case of highly lipophillic drugs the elimination half-life would be extremely long. However, even such compounds are susceptible to oxidation by cytochrome P-450, because these enzymes can attack even highly inert substrates also. Further, such substrates would yield highly reactive intermediates which would be highly toxic. Moreover, such lipophillic compounds would accumulate in adipose tissues which would result in long term toxicity.

A highly water soluble compound on the other hand would lack the substrate properties to metabolizing enzymes and at the same time such compounds would have extremely short half-life and only highly potent compounds could be useful drugs.

Another approach enunciated by Bodor and his colleagues is that of "Soft Drugs". According to them 'Soft drugs are biologically active, therapeutically useful compounds characterized by predictable and controllable in vivo metabolism to non-toxic moieties after they achieve their therapeutic role'. Further, according to these workers, 'in order to achieve predictable and controllable metabolism, it is necessary that the oxidative metabolism should be avoided and metabolism should involve only hydrolytic cleavage'. Thus, a soft drug after its administration would show a pharmacological response and then get eliminated from the body either directly or as an inactive metabolite (Fig. 16.1). Such an approach would improve therapeutic efficacy/index by eliminating the formation of reactive intermediates.

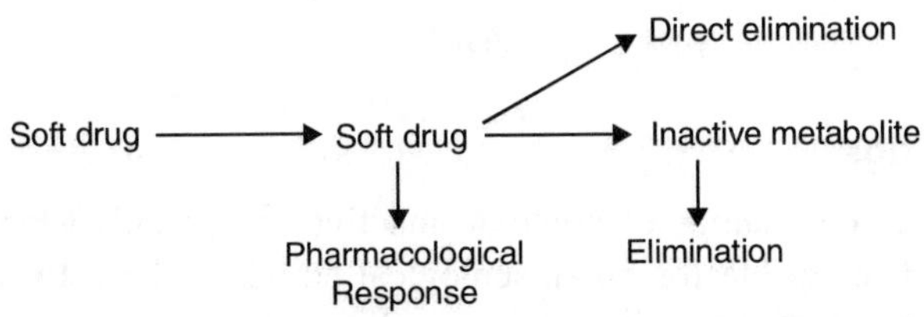

Fig. 16.1 Steps involved in soft drug after administration

Soft drugs have been classified as follows:

1. Soft analogs.
2. Activated soft analogs
3. Soft drugs based on active metabolite approach.
4. Soft drugs based on inactive metabolite approach.
5. Natural soft drugs.

Soft Analogs

These are close analogs of known active drugs in which there is built in a metabolically sensitive spot. Such a spot does not need oxidation but can be hydrolyzed and metabolism at the sensitive spot would lead to a predictable one step detoxification. The characteristics of a soft analogs are :

1. they are close analogs of the lead cmpounds in which is built a metabolically sensitive spot,
2. the metabolism involves hydrolytic and not an oxidative or conjugative step,

3. the drug undergoes metabolism after it shows pharmacological response,
4. the built-in metabolism is the only metabolism which the soft analog undergoes,
5. the metabolic products are non-toxic and have no pharmacological activity.

One of the examples of the soft analogs is that of analogs of cetylpyridinium chloride (56). It is quaternary antimicrobial agent. Its isostere (57) has the same number of atoms attached to nitrogen

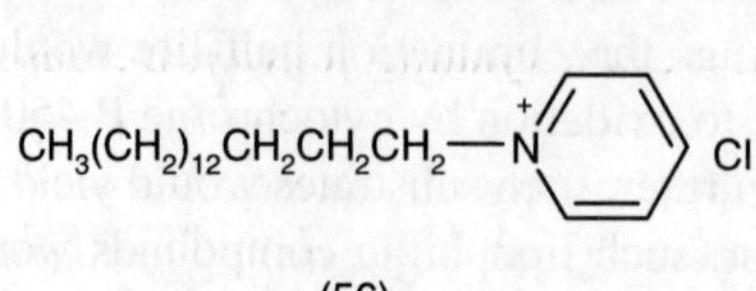

(56)

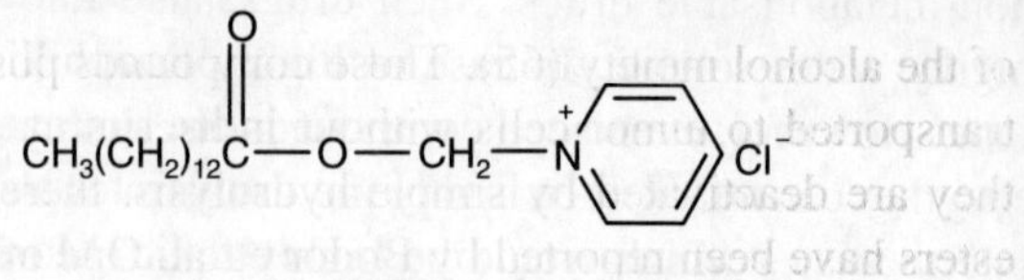

(57)

This soft analog (57) as well as other analogs (58-60) have shown good antimicrobial activity. Unlik cetylpyridinium chloride (56) all of these analogs are detoxified easily by one step hydrolytic cleavage

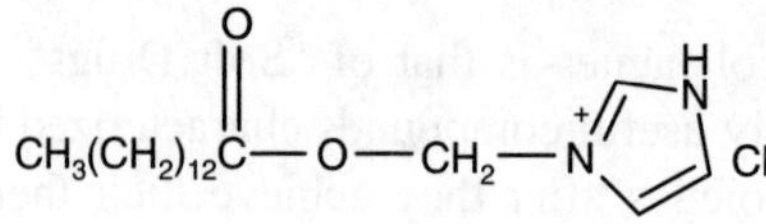

(58)

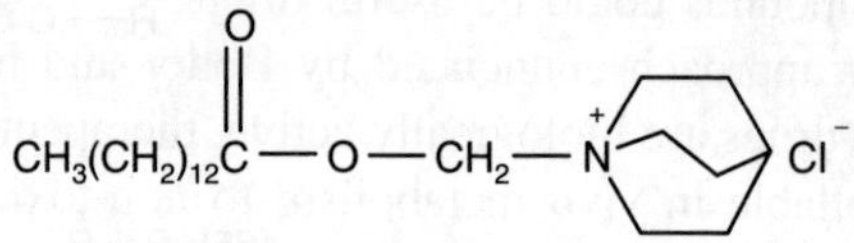

(59)

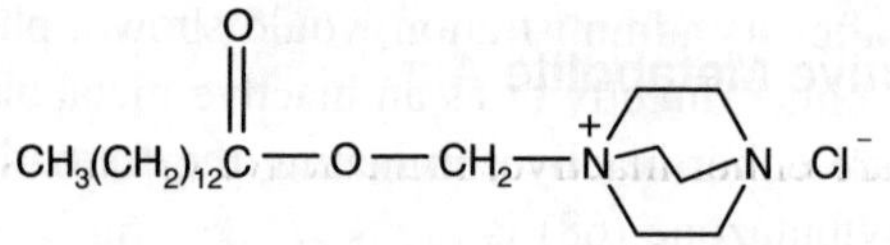

(60)

Activated Soft Analogs

This class of soft drugs are analogs of nontoxic inactive compounds which have been activated b introducing structures responsible for pharmacological activity. The activated drug after exerting it pharmacological activity loses the active moiety and reverts back to the original non-toxic inactiv compound.

N-Chloramines (61) are known to possess antimicrobial activity. However they are unstable an accordingly they can neither be formulated nor can be stored for long periods. The mechanism of thei decomposition is α,β-dehydrohalogenation. Thus, highly stable chloramines can be obtained if they d not contain a hydrogen atom at α-carbon atom. Some of the examples of these chloramines are (62) t (64). Their mechanism of antibacterial action involves formation of chloronium ion (Fig. 16.2).

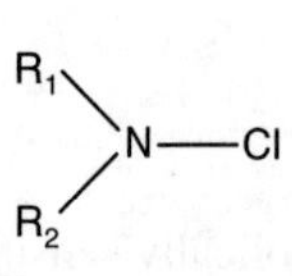

(61)

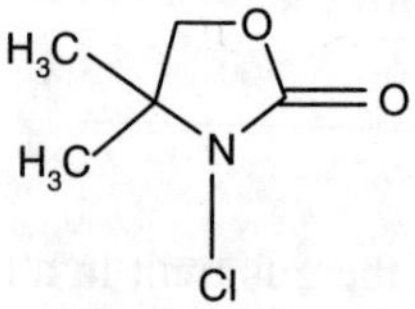

(62)

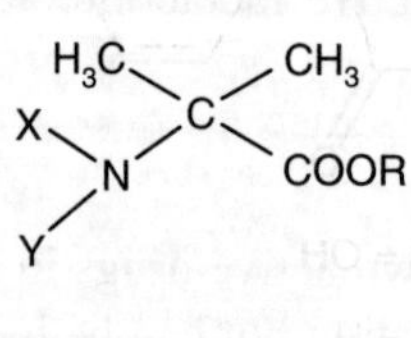

(63), X = Cl
Y = H or Cl
R = alkyl

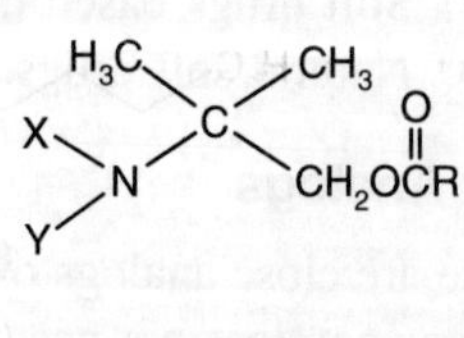

(64), X = Cl
Y = H or Cl
R = alkyl or aryl

Another example of activated soft analogs is the soft alkylating agents. These compounds are alkan esters of aliphatic and aromatic acids which have been activated by introduction of halogen at α- carbo

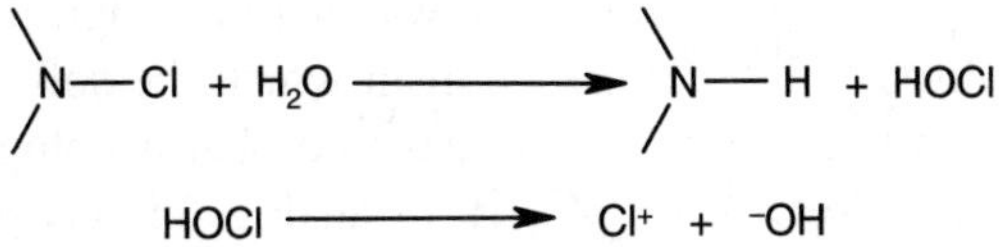

Fig. 16.2 Mechanism of chloramine action

of the alcohol moiety (65). These compounds possess weak alkylating activity. Because of this they are transported to tumor cells without indiscriminate alkylation, resulting in lower toxicity Further, since they are deactivated by simple hydrolysis, therefore, overall toxicity is much lower. Number of such esters have been reported by Bodor et. al. One of the compounds chloromethyl hexanoate (66) has been reported to be active against P-388 leukemia.

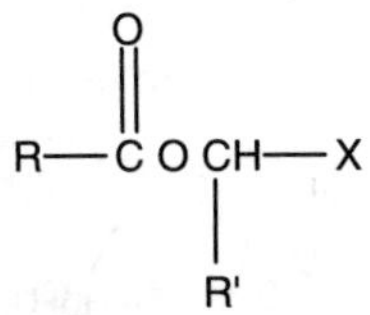

(65), R = R' = alkyl; X = halogen

(66), R = $CH_3(CH_2)_4$, R' = H; X = Cl

Soft Drugs Based on Active Metabolite Approach

Metabolites of many drugs are either inactive, more active or have similar activity. Oxyphenbutazone (67), the metabolite of phenylbutazone (68) is more active. Similarly, the 4′-hydroxypropranolol (69) is an active metabolite of propranolol (70). According to this concept, whenever oxidative metabolic step results in highly reactive intermediate or a pharmacologically active species, if the pharmacokinetic parameters permit, the drug of choice should be active metabolite which is in highest oxidized state. Another example is that of bufuralol (71), a β-blocker. The half-life of bufuralol (71) is 4 hr., while the half-lives of its metabolites (72) to (74) are 7, 12, and 4 hr, respectively. All the metabolites are active. Since metabolites (72) and (73) have higher half-lives, therefore they are better β-blockers as compared to bufuralol (71). This approach can be extended to metabolites of other drugs.

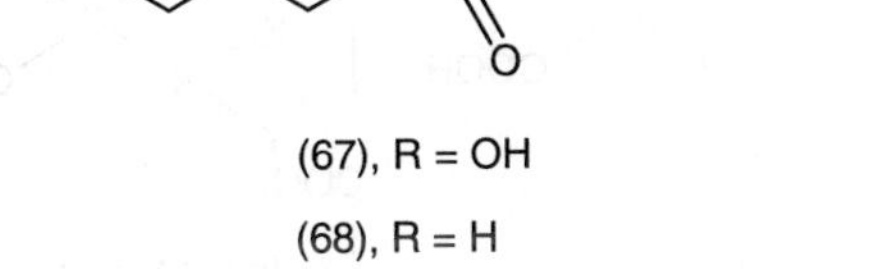

(67), R = OH

(68), R = H

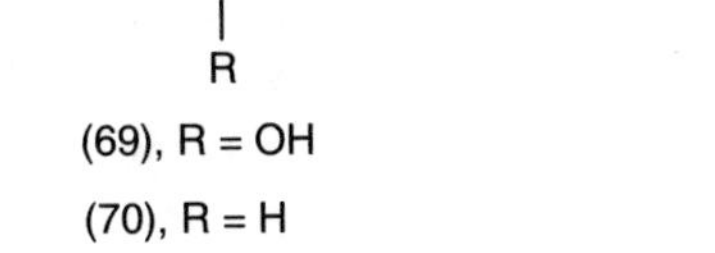

(69), R = OH

(70), R = H

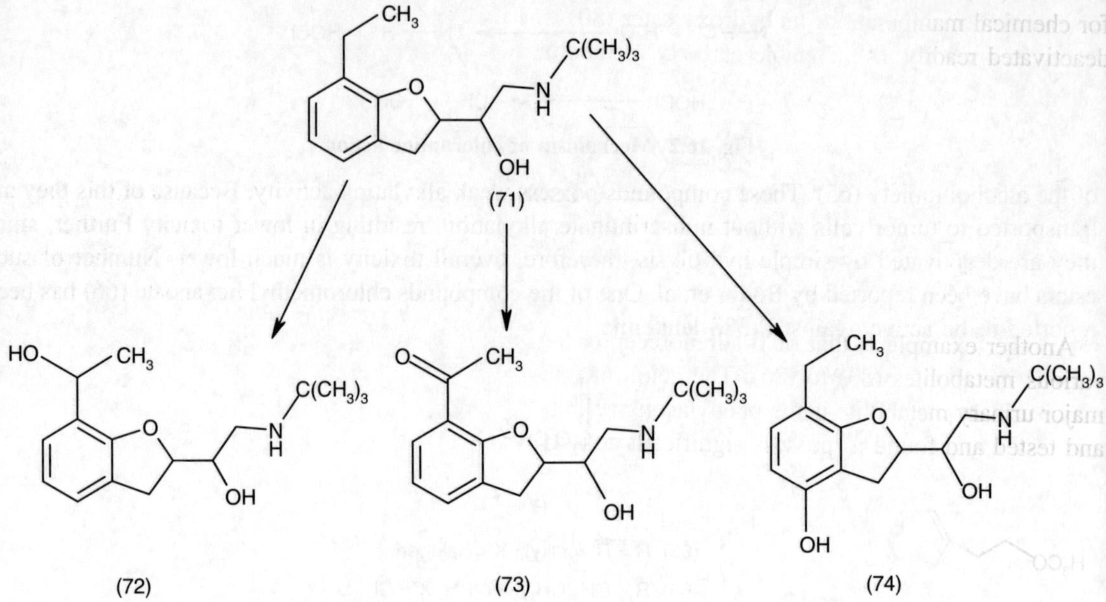

Soft Drugs Based on Inactive Metabolite Approach

This approach utilizes the inactive metabolite for the design of an active soft drug. An example of this is the molecular modification of dichlorodiphenyltrichloroethane (DDT, 75). The various metabolites of

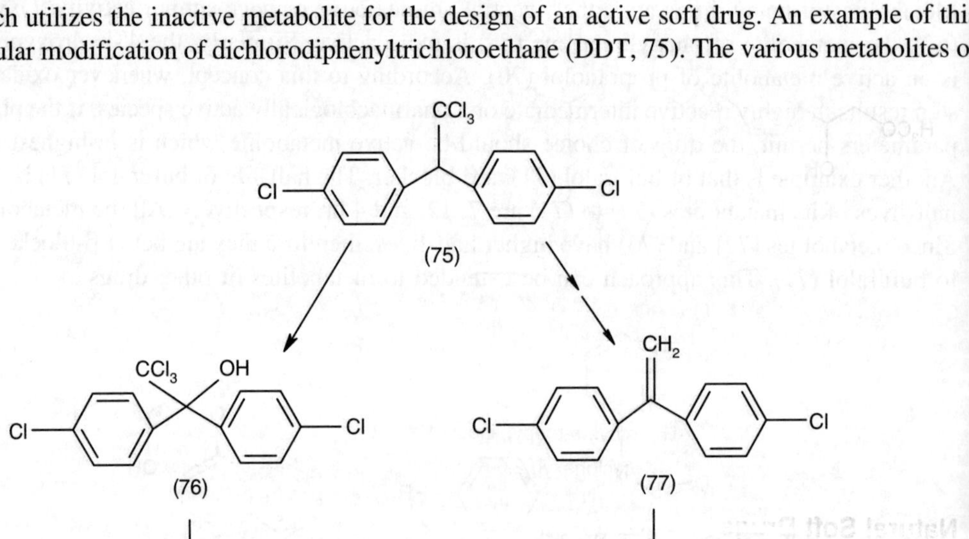

DDT are (76) to (79). Out of the various metabolites, the carboxy metabolite (79) is inactive and is ideal for chemical manipulation. Its hydroxy ester (80) was found to have good activity. Further, since it is deactivated readily to excretable carboxy metabolite (81), it has lower toxicity and carcinogenicity.

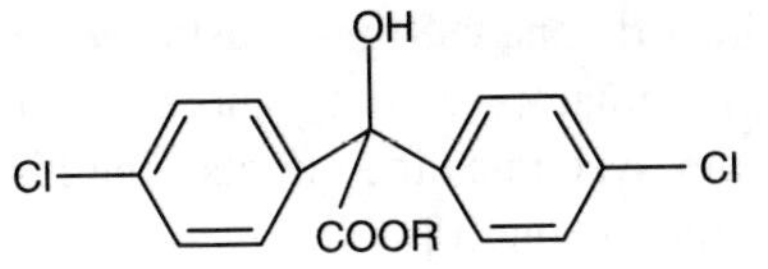

(80), R = alkyl

(81), R = H

Another example is that of β-adrenoreceptor antagonist, metoprolol (82). On metabolism it yields various metabolites (83) to (86). The acidic metabolites (85) and (86) are inactive. Out of these the major urinary metabolite is the phenylacetic acid metabolite (86). Various esters of (87) were prepared and tested and found to possess significant activity.

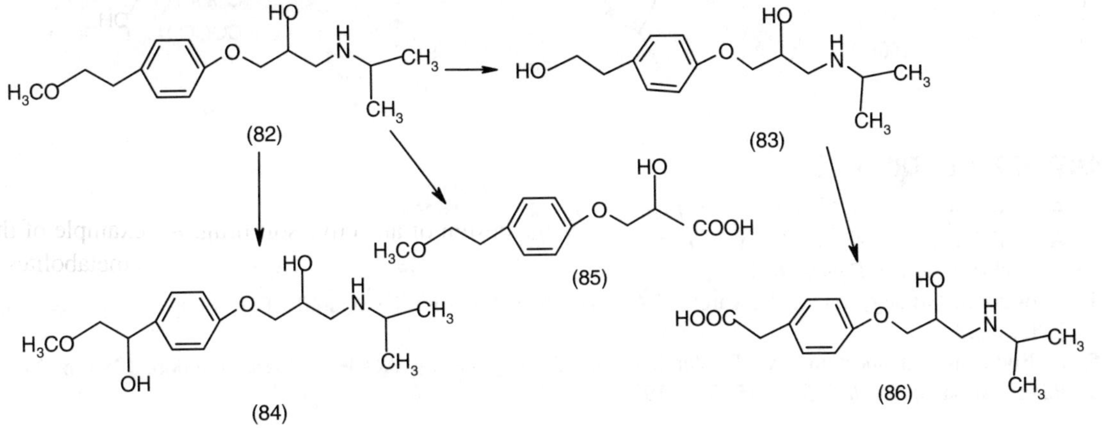

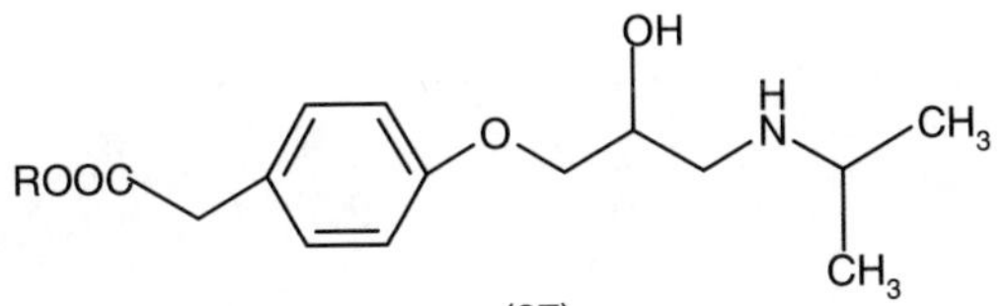

(87)

R = ethyl, *n*-propyl, isopropyl, *n*-butyl, benzyl cyclohexyl, 2,6-dimethylcyclohexyl, 3,3,5,5-tetramethyl.

Natural Soft Drugs

Endogenous substances such as steroidal hormones like testosterone, progesterone, hydrocortisone and neurotransmitters like acetylcholine, adrenaline, dopamine can all be considered as soft drugs. They are metabolized without going through reactive intermediates. Thus, their metabolism is more predictable and when used in concentrations close to their normal levels in body, they do not cause toxicity. However, they cannot be used as drugs because their metabolism is fast and they cannot be transported to the site of action efficiently. This could be overcome by designing chemical delivery approach for these natural soft drugs.

Hydrocortisone (88), the endogenous glucocorticoid, when used topically results in higher than normal in vivo levels, resulting in toxicity such as dermal atrophy, thymus involution, etc. Bodor et al have overcome this problem by reporting the synthesis of 3-spirothiazolidine derivatives(89) which accumulate in skin and release hydrocortisone (88) in a sustained manner. Some of these compounds (89) were tested for topical anti-inflammatory activity and found to be 6-8 times more active than hydrocortisone (88) acetate with lower systemic side effects. The higher and longer duration of action was due to sustained release of hydrocortisone (88).

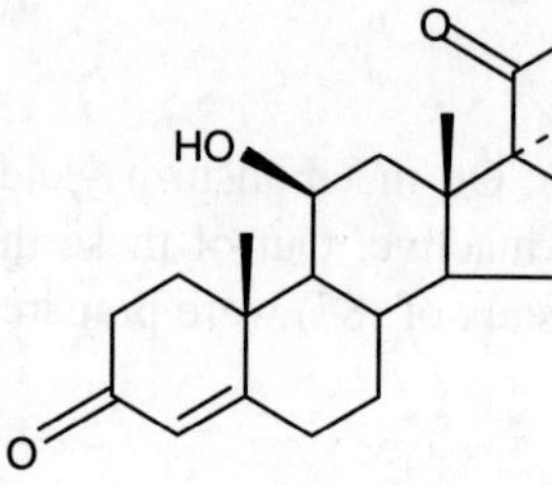

(88)

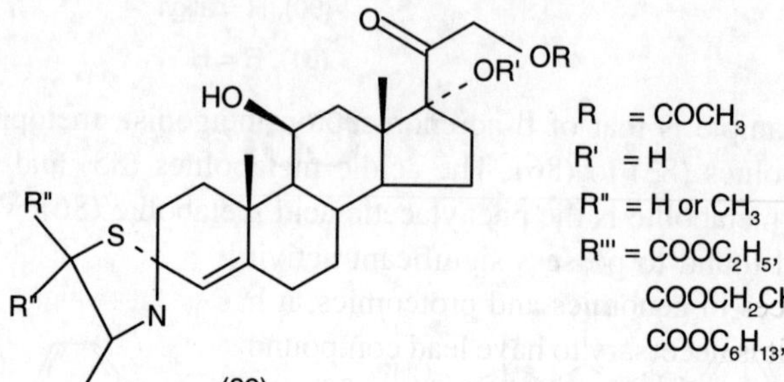

(89)

FURTHER READING

1. A.A. Sinkula and S.H. Yalkowsky, *J. Pharm. Sci.*, **64**, 181 (1975).
2. A.A. Sinkula, *Ann. Repts. Med. Chem.*, **10**, 306 (1975).
3. N. Bodor, *Drugs of Future*, **6**, 165 (1981).
4. N. Bodor in "Strategy in Drug Research," J.A.K. Buisman, Ed., Elsevier Scientific Publishing Co., Amsterdam, 1982, p. 137.
5. N. Bodor in "Advances in Drug Research," Vol. 13, B. Testa, Ed.,Academic Press, London, 1984, p. 255.
6. P.D. Sharma, *J. Sci. Ind. Res.*, **45**, 534 (1986).

17

Combinatorial Synthesis

With the advances in genomics and proteomics, it has been possible to identify newer targets for drug action. For this it is necessary to have lead compounds which can interact with the targets. Combinatorial synthesis provide such leads for discovery of drugs for newer targets. Combinatorial synthesis can be defined as "parallel synthesis of all possible combinations of substituents or components in a synthetic experiment resulting in synthesis of large number of compounds". Thus, combinatorial synthesis not only results in the synthesis of large number of compounds but it also cuts down on the expenses and time taken for a discovery of a new drug entity.

Combinatorial synthesis is based on solid phase synthesis of peptides introduced by Merrifield in 1963. By this method peptides could be synthesized on a solid support or resin. The whole process could also be automated.

The solid phase peptide synthesis (SPPS) involves tagging of C-terminal end of a N^{α}-protected amino acid with a resin/solid polymer. Next, the N^{α}-protected amino acid tagged with resin/polymer is deprotected and coupled with N^{α}-protected amino acid. The process (Fig. 17.1) can be continued till the desired peptide is obtained. At the end, the peptide is deprotected, purified, and cleaved from the polymer.

During the synthesis, the growing polypeptide chain remains attached to insoluble polymer. At the end, the polymer bound peptide chain is removed by filtration and soluble reagents removed from the chain by simple washing. This results in better yields and purity. After purification the polymer can be removed by a suitable deprotecting agent. In addition to easy removal and purification of the product, another advantage of the solid phase synthesis is that excess reagent can be used so that the reaction goes to completion. The excess reagent can be removed by filtration. Further the polymeric material after regeneration can be reused. The process can also be automated.

Since isolation and purification consume lot of time, solid phase synthesis reduces this and large number of compounds can be synthesized in a short period of time.

The requirements for a solid phase synthesis is a cross-linked insoluble polymeric material to which is attached a **linker** or **anchor** which has a functional group which can react with substrate to form a linkage.

The polymeric material used by Merrifield was polystyrene bead in which styrene is partially crosslinked with 1% divinylbenzene. Since polystyrene are hydrophobic and growing peptide chain is

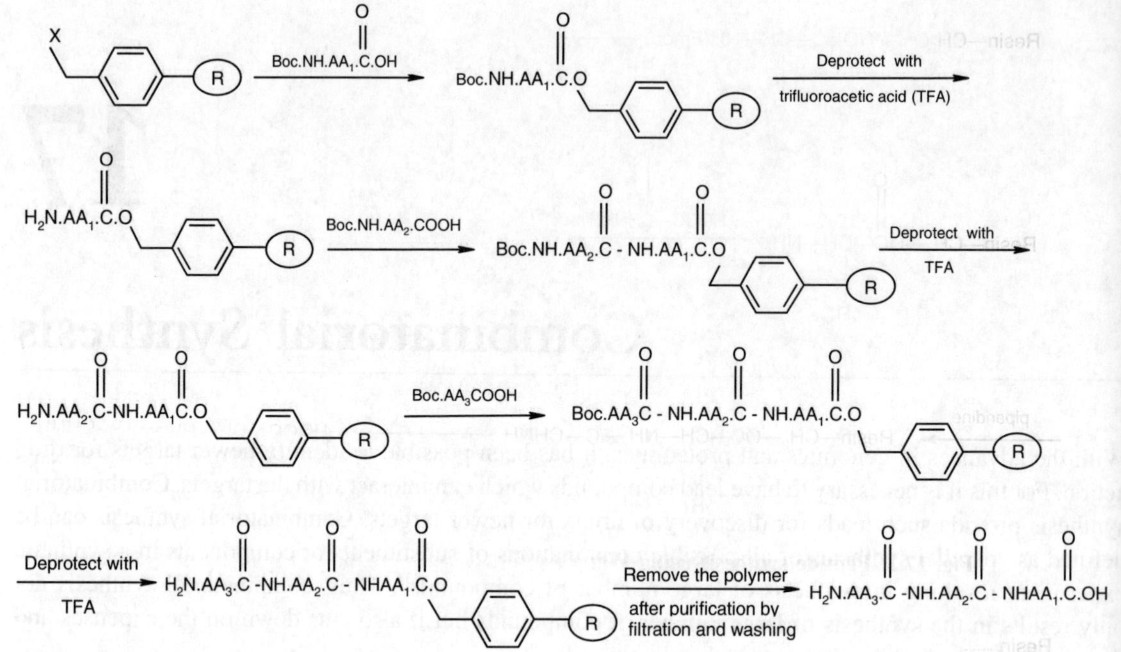

Fig. 17.1 Solid phase peptide synthesis, (R) = resin; x = reactive group of linker; Boc = *tert.* butyloxycarbonyl; AA_1, AA_2, AA_3 = amino acids 1, 2 and 3

hydrophilic, it does not get solvated. This results in folding of the peptide chain and formation of hydrogen bonds. As a result the amino acids added to the reaction vessel do not have access to the end of the chain. To overcome this more polar polymers have been developed and these include Sheppard's polyamide resin, Tentagel resin which is 80% polyethylene glycol grafted to cross-linked polystyrene. These polymeric materials are capable of swelling which results in unfolding of the polymeric chain, thus exposure to solvent and reagents.

The polymeric material should contain a reactive group which would form a bond with substrate. This bond should be quite stable to the reagents and chemicals used during the synthesis and be removable at the end of reaction. The linker/anchor used by Merrifield was chloromethyl (1) group which formed an ester linkage (2) with the carboxyl group of the N-protected amino acid (3). The other anchors/linkers include Wang resin and Rink resin which contain a hydroxymethyl and amino group, respectively. These groups react with the carboxyl group of substrate (Figs 17.2 and 17.3).

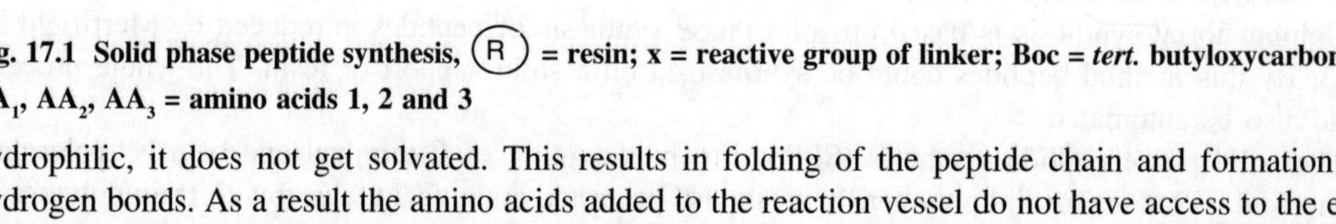

(R) = Resin; Boc = *tert.* butyloxycarbonyl

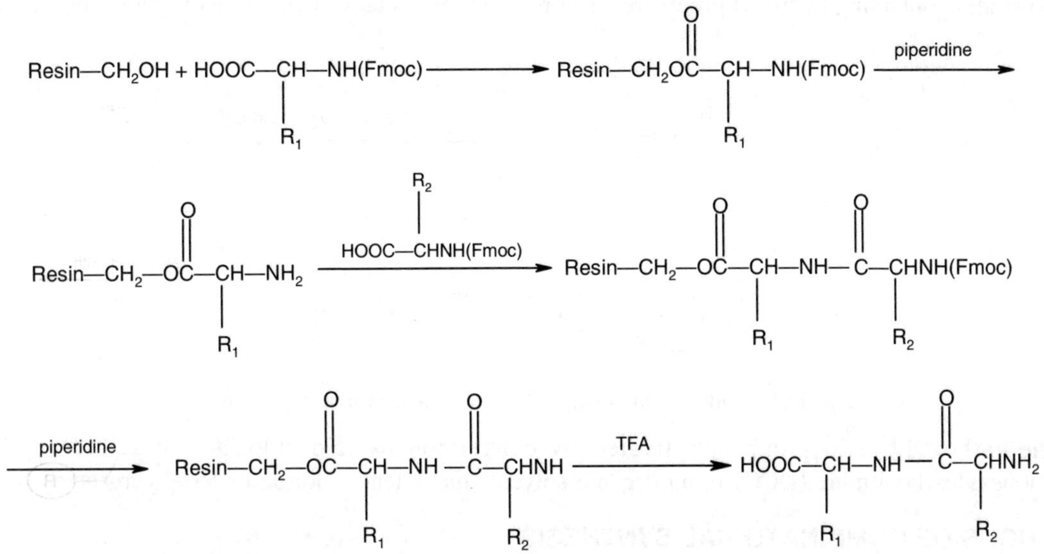

Fig. 17.2 Peptide synthesis using Wang's resin (Fmoc = 9-fluorenylmethoxycarbonyl)

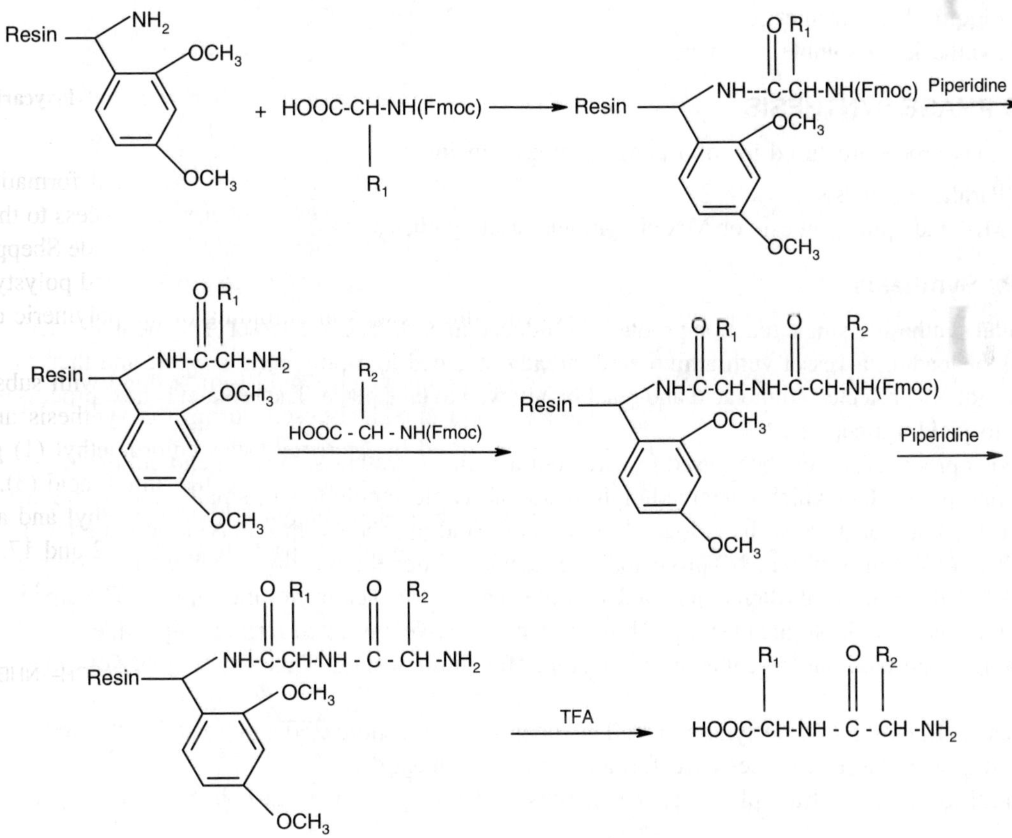

Fig. 17.3 Peptide synthesis using rink resin (Fmoc = 9-fluorenylmethoxycarbonyl)

Substrates containing hydroxyl group are anchored with resins tagged with dihydropyran (Fig. 17.4).

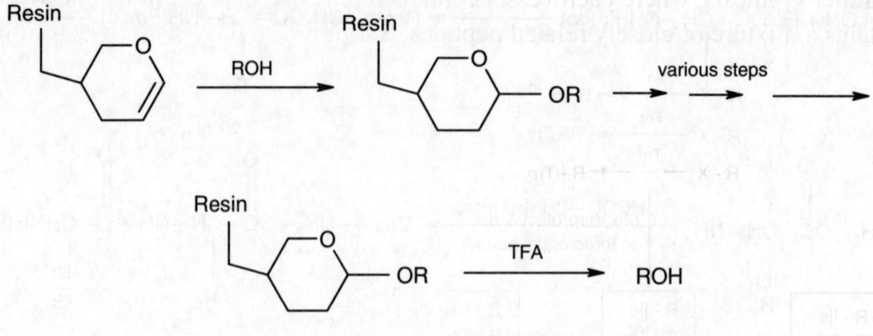

Fig. 17.4 Synthesis involving dihydopyran-functionalised resin

The carboxylic acid group is activated by conversion to acid chloride, acid azide or by dicyclohexylcarbodiimide (DCC) in an organic solvent (methylene chloride or tetrahydrofuran).

METHODS OF COMBINATORIAL SYNTHESIS

The various methods used in combinatorial are:

(a) Solid phase synthesis,
(b) Liquid phase synthesis,
(c) Synthesis on soluble polymers.

SOLID PHASE SYNTHESIS

The various procedures used in solid phase synthesis include:

(a) Parallel synthesis
(b) Mix and split synthesis or Mixed combinatorial synthesis

Parallel Synthesis

In parallel synthesis a single reaction product is produced in each reaction vessel. The method essentially consists of loading a vessel with amino acid already attached to a polymeric support and then this is treated with N^{α}-protected amino acid and reaction allowed to take place. The product is next processesed further to yield a dipeptide.

Various procedures have been used to carry out a parallel synthesis. Geysen and colleagues used a plastic microtiter plate which contained eight rows and tweleve columns of small wells giving a total of 96 wells. Each of these wells is loaded with amino acid attached with a polymeric material. These are then treated with different N^{α}-protected amino acids. After the reaction is allowed to complete, a library of 96 dipeptides are filtered, purified, deprotected, and cleaved from solid support. The dipeptides are next subjected to biological testing. Those which are active are tested further. Dipeptides which are inactive in a particular biological activity are stored for future testing. This way a library of dipeptides is created.

In case a tripeptide is to be synthesized. The dipeptides are deprotected and treated with another N^{α}-protected amino acid and processesed further to yield a tripeptide.

In addition to microtiter plate, tea bags, pins and lollypops have also been used in parallel synthesis.

Mix and Split Synthesis

Compared to parallel synthesis, where each vessel contained only one peptide, in mix and split method, each vessel contains a mixture of closely related peptides. Starting with three amino acids, mix and split

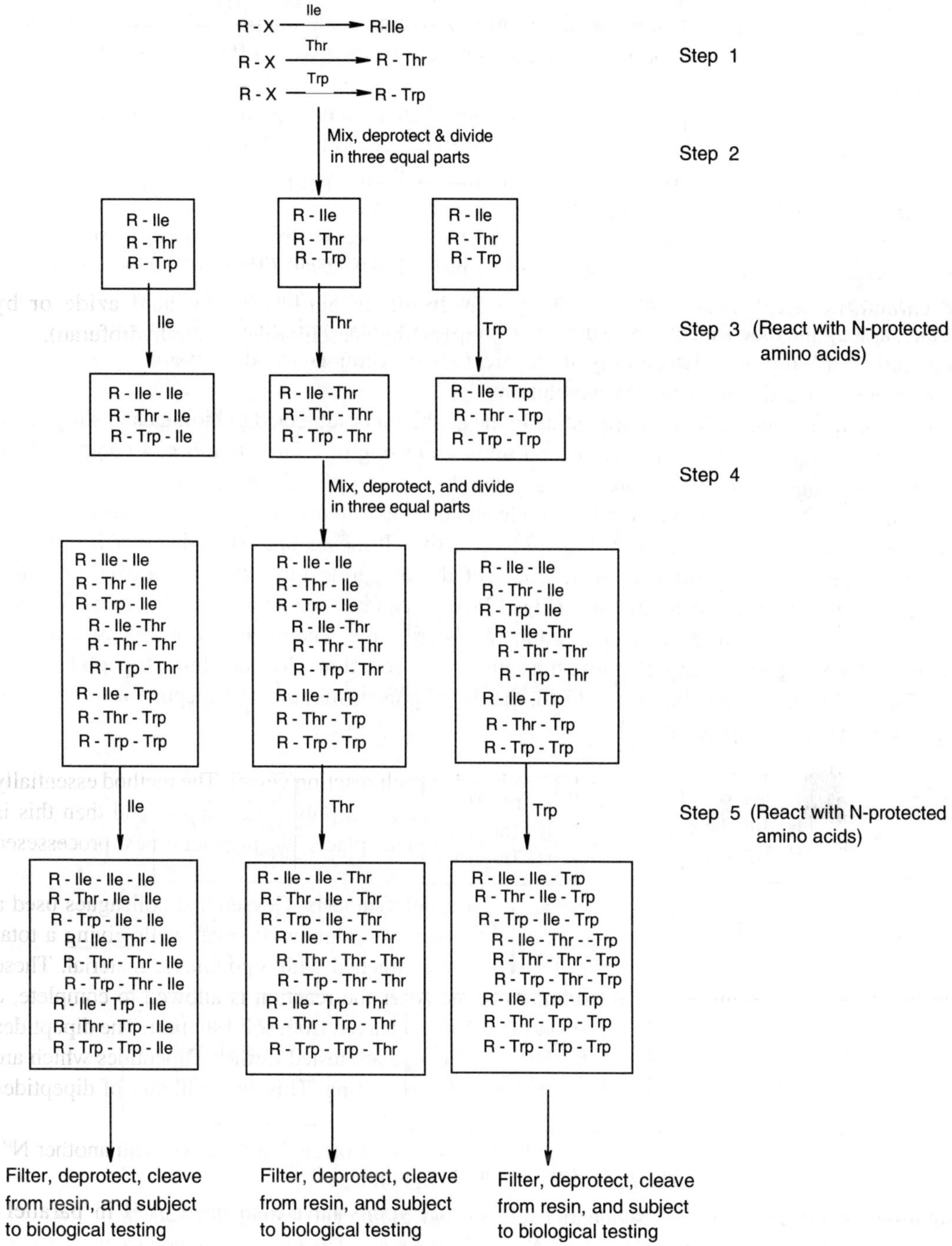

Fig. 17.5 Mix and split method of combinatorial synthesis

method is illustrated by an example given in Fig. 17.5 and consists essentially of the following steps:

1. In the first step the N^{α}-protected amino acids are linked with the resin through a linker (Fig. 17.5).
2. Next, all the resin bound amino acids are mixed, deprotected, and divided into 3 equal portion.
3. The different portions of the mixed amino acids are reacted with different N^{α}-protected amino acids to yield dipeptides.
4. The various portions of polymer bound dipeptides are mixed, deprotected, and divided again in 3 portions giving nine dipeptides into each of the three portions (Fig. 17.5).
5. Next each of the portions is reacted with each of the amino acids resulting in a total of 27 tripeptides in the 3 lots of 9 tripeptides each (Fig. 17.5).

The 27 tripeptides (Fig. 17.5) are filtered, deprotected, and cleaved from the solid support. Next, the three individual lots of tripeptides are subjected to biological testing. Once an individual lot of the mixture of tripeptides has been identified to be biologically active, the next thing is to identify the tripeptide, among the nine tripeptides, which is responsible for the biological activity. This is known as deconvoluting the mixture. Essentially there are two procedures for deconvoluting and include Micromanipulation and Recursive Deconvolution.

In micromanipulation, each of the tripeptide in the active lot is subjected to biological testing and the tripeptide identified. As is evident, this method involves testing of a large number of compounds and is not therefore, suitable when mixtures of large number of compounds are involved.

The Recursive Deconvolution method is simple and does not involve much of time and work. Let us assume that out of three lots, lot no. 2 (Fig. 17.5) is active. It means that tripeptide which is active is having threonine at the N-terminus. Next, 3 lots of the dipeptide mixtures, synthesized and stored earlier, are taken and linked with threonine (Fig. 17.6). As can be seen from Fig. 17.6, in each of these three lots of tripeptide mixtures 2nd and 3rd amino acids are same. The three lots of tripeptide mixtures are subjected to biological testing. Suppose the activity was found in a lot containing tripeptides having Ile and Thr in 2nd and 3rd position (Fig. 17.6), the 3-component mixture of tripeptide are synthesized and tested individually and identified.

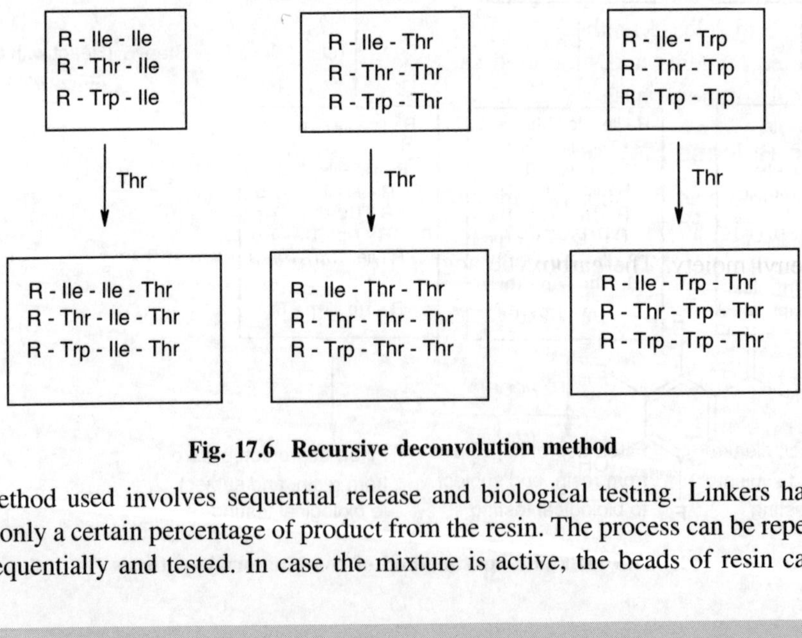

Fig. 17.6 Recursive deconvolution method

Another method used involves sequential release and biological testing. Linkers have been made which release only a certain percentage of product from the resin. The process can be repeated, releasing the product sequentially and tested. In case the mixture is active, the beads of resin can be split into smaller mixtures. Each of the mixtures can then be subjected to release and testing. Finally that mixture which has shown activity is subjected to release and testing individually and the active component identified.

Protecting Groups

While carrying out solid phase synthesis, it is necessary to protect some functional groups which are not involved in the synthesis. Such groups have to be stable towards reagents used during synthesis Some of these are *tert*.butyloxycarbonyl group (Boc, 4).

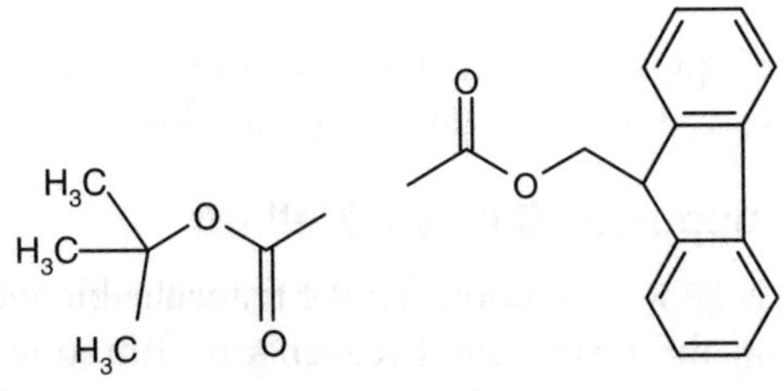

(4) (5)

This group is used for protecting amino group and can be removed by trifluoroacetic acid (TFA). TFA does not affect the bond between the linker and the amino acid. However, the linker can be removed from the peptide chain by hydrofluoric acid (HF). Another amino protecting group is 9-fluorenylmthoxycarbonyl (Fmoc, 5). It can be removed by piperidine.

In addition to amino group, there may be present other groups also which need protection. When using Boc, benzyl group is usually used for the protection of other groups. Benzyl group is not affected by TFA, but HF removes it. *tert*. Butyl group has also been used to protect groups other than amino group. This can also be removed with acid when the resin portion is being cleaved.

LIQUID PHASE SYNTHESIS

Some of the methods used in liquid phase synthesis include:

1. Capture and release method,
2. Supported reagents and supported catalyst method, and
3. Classical solution phase solution.

Capture and Release Method

This involves capture of the substrate in the first step and then reaction with a reagent and release in the second step (Fig. 17.7). An example of this is the synthesis of amide libraries using resin bound tetrafluorophenyl moiety. The carboxylic acid is first activated with the resin bound tetraflurophenyl

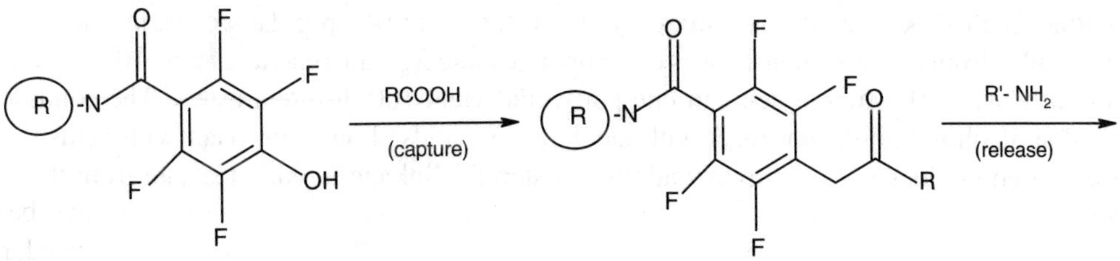

Fig. 17.7 Capture and release method (*Contd.*)

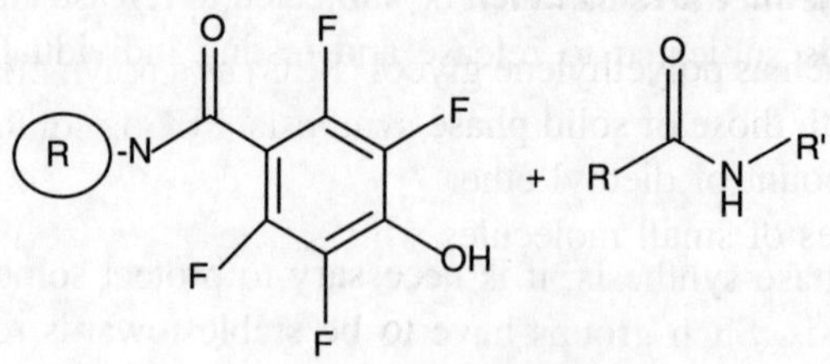

Fig. 17.7 Capture and release method, (R) = resin (*Contd.*)

moiety. This is known as a the capture step. Next, it is allowed to react with nucleophilic amine to give the amide which is then released, this is known as release step.

Supported Reagent and Supported Catalyst Method

In this approach, the substrate is kept in solution and the reagents are bound to resin. The product which is in solution is separated from the resin bound reagents by filtration and the product isolated from solution (Fig. 17.8).

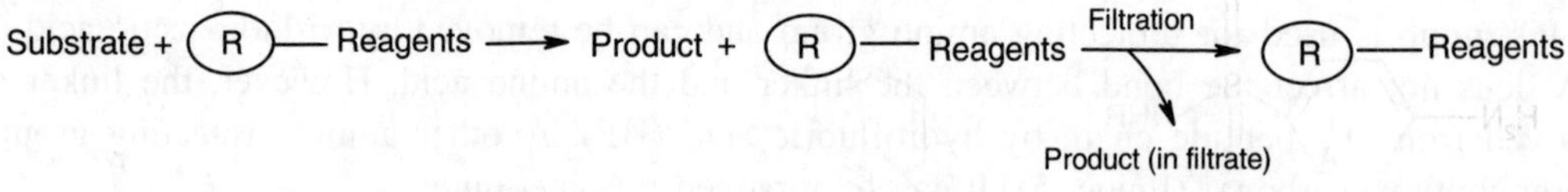

Fig. 17.8 Supported reagent and supported catalyst method, (R) = resin

This method gives better yields and has better selectivity. The reaction can be carried out on a large scale, say 100 mg or so.

The crude cleavage products can be purified by liquid chromatography. In addition, scavenger resins, solid phase extraction, solid supported liquid-liquid extraction have also been used.

Scavanger resins are designed to selectively trap side products according to their reactivity and can be acidic, basic, nucleophilic, electrophilic and so on. This technique has been found useful in removing acids (with basic resins), bases (with acidic resins), aldehydes (with tosylhydrazine resins), nucleophiles (with electrophiles), so on.

Classical Solution Phase Synthesis

Classical solution phase synthesis requires that the yields should be high without the formation of side products.

Indiviual substances can be synthesized by fast parallel synthesis, i.e. *n*-number of substances synthesized in *n*-reaction vessels using method of parallel synthesis.

Another method is to synthesize mixtures of substances in one pot. However, in one reaction step, two molecules from two different classes of compounds undergo the reaction.Thus, 10 different alcohols when treated with 10 different acids in one pot would yield 100 different esters. The condition in this case is that alcohols should not react with alcohols and acids should not react with acids.

This procedure does not require any additional step for linkage to and cleavage from the polymeric support.

SYNTHESIS ON SOLUBLE POLYMERS

Use of soluble polymers such as polyethylene glycol (PEG) as a polymeric support combines advantages of synthesis in solution with those of solid phase synthesis. PEG is soluble in many solvents but can be precipitated with large amount of diethyl ether.

Some of the varied types of small molecules which have been synthesized by solid phase synthesis are given in Fig. 17.9.

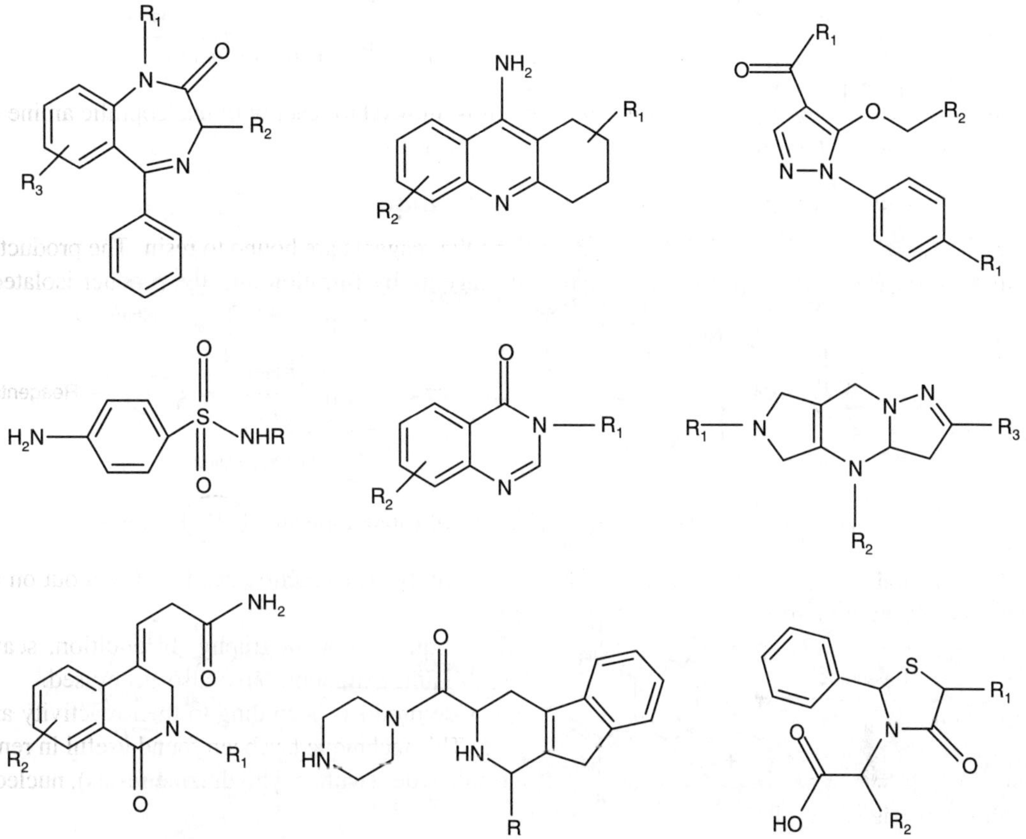

Fig. 17.9 Some of the small molecules synthesized by solid phase synthesis

EXAMPLES OF COMBINATORIAL SYNTHESIS

In addition to synthesis of polypeptides, combinatorial libraries, using solid phase synthesis, have also been developed for heterocyclic moieties. Some of these include, benzodiazepines (Figs. 17.10 and 17.11), quinazolinones (Fig. 17.12), imidazoles (Fig. 17.13), hydantoins (Fig. 17.14), piprazines (Fig. 17.15), etc.

SOLID PHASE SYNTHESIS

Benzodiazepines

One of the earliest examples was the synthesis of benzodiazepines. It starts with (6, Fig. 17.10). The limitation of this method is that the starting material has a phenolic or carboxylic group to allow the attachment of the resin. As a result final product also contains either of these groups. In an alternative method, a substituted amino acid (7, Fig. 17.11) is tagged with the resin and then condensed with an imine (8, Fig. 17.11). The resulting product is then cyclized after removal of the resin with TFA.

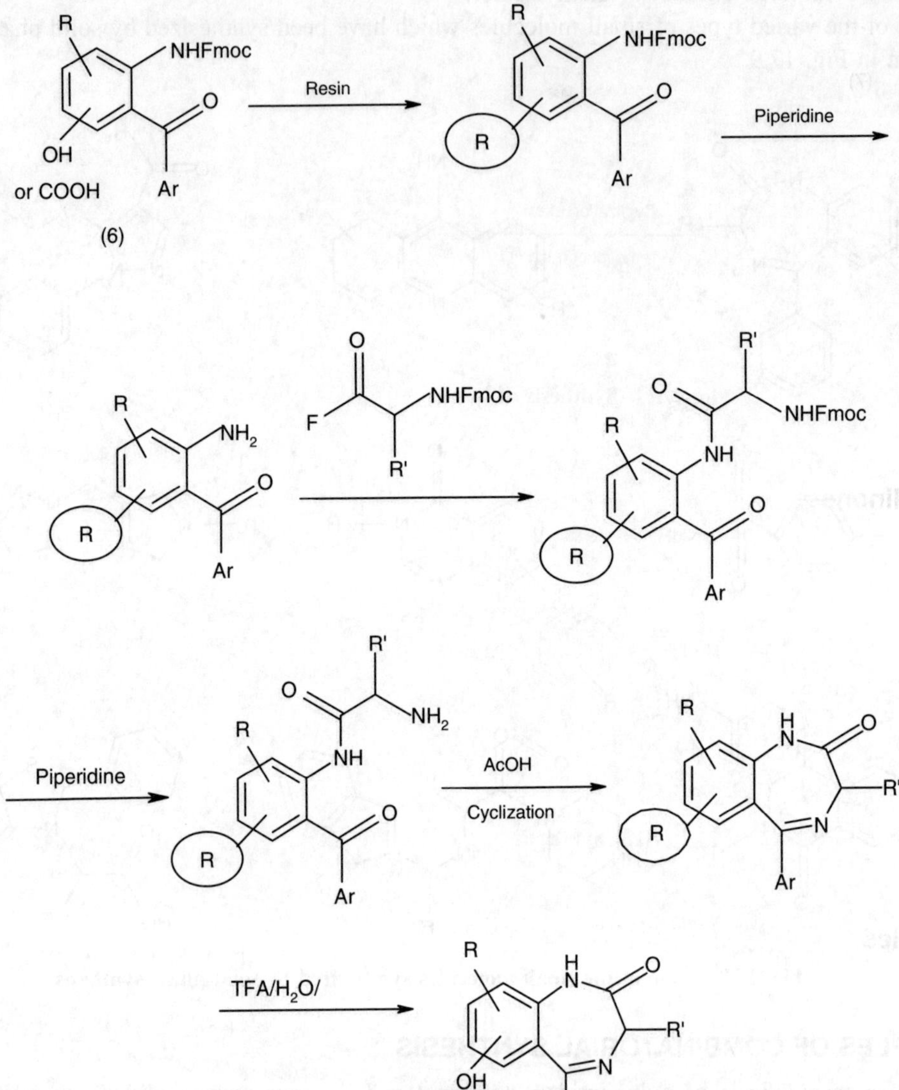

Fig. 17.10 Synthesis of benzodiazepine, (R) = resin; Fmoc = 9-fluorenylmethoxycarbonyl

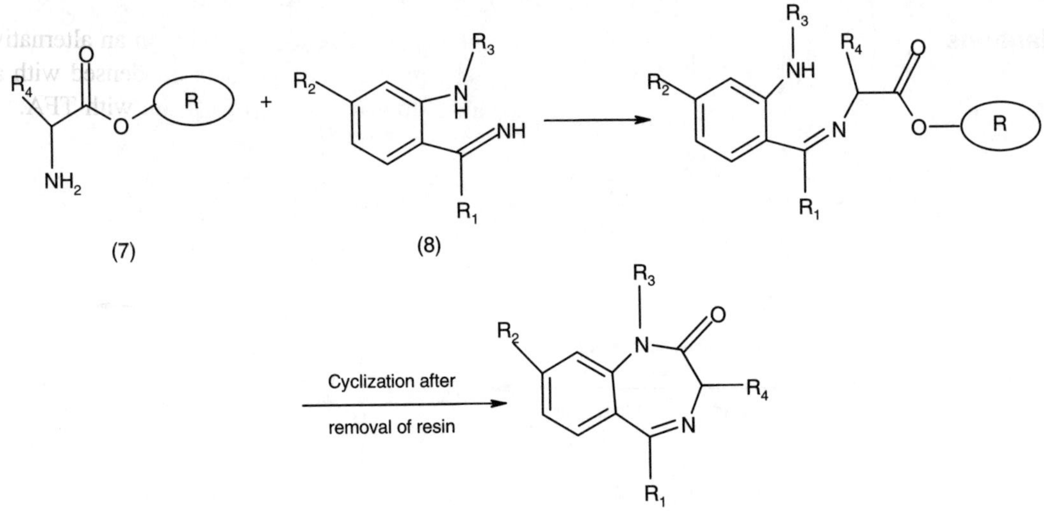

Fig. 17.11 Synthesis of benzodiazepine, (R) = resin

Quinazolinones

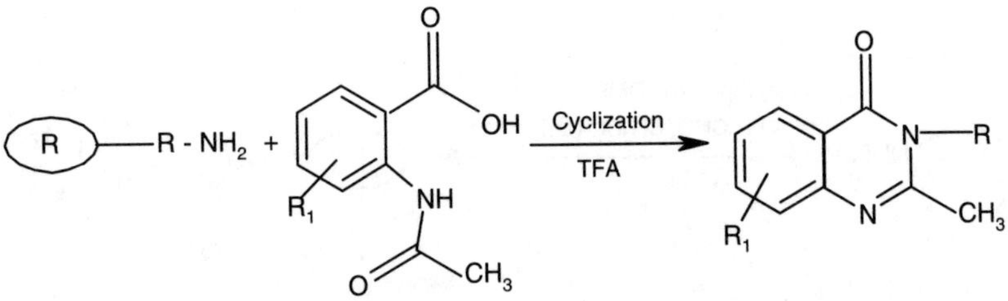

Fig. 17.12 Synthesis of quinazolinones, (R) = resin

Imidazoles

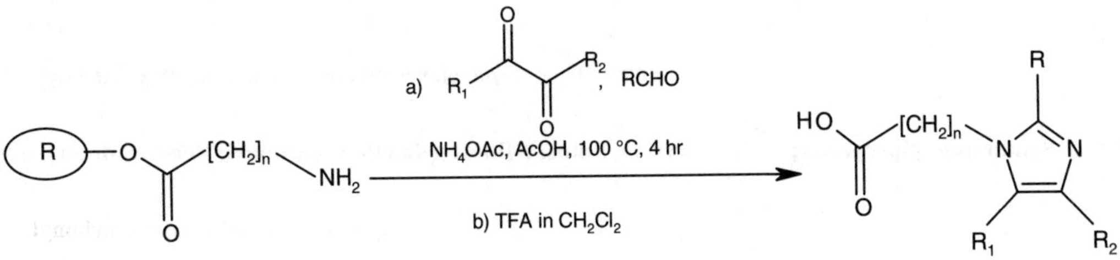

Fig. 17.13 Synthesis of imidazoles, (R) = resin

Hydantoins

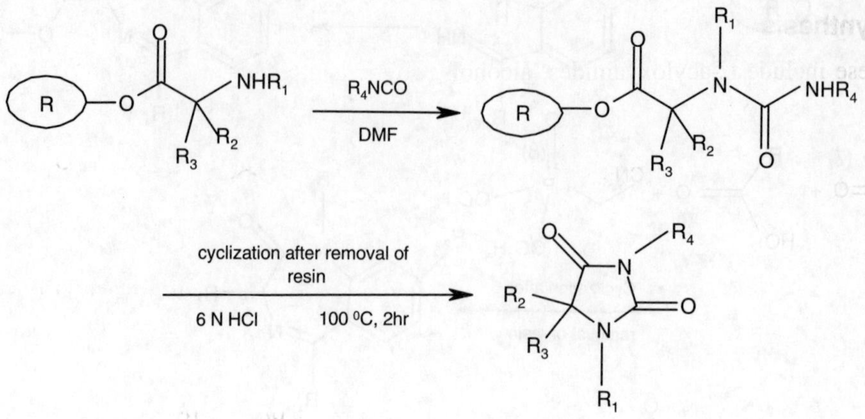

Fig. 17.14 Synthesis of hydantoins, (R) = resin

Piperazines

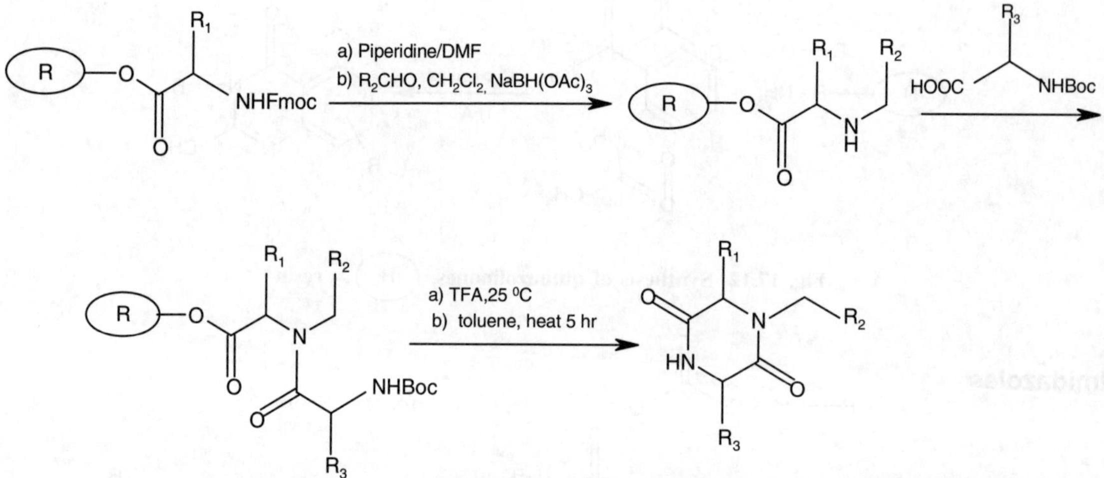

Fmoc, 9-fluorenylmethoxycarbonyl; Boc, *tert.*butoxycarbonyl

Fig. 17.15 Synthesis of piperazines; (R) = resin, Fmoc, 9-fluorenylmethoxycarbonyl; Boc *tert.* butoxycarbonyl

CLASSICAL SOLUTION PHASE SYNTHESIS

Parallel Synthesis

Some of these include α-acyloxyamides, alcohols, esters, and heterocycles (Fig. 17.16a and 17.16b)

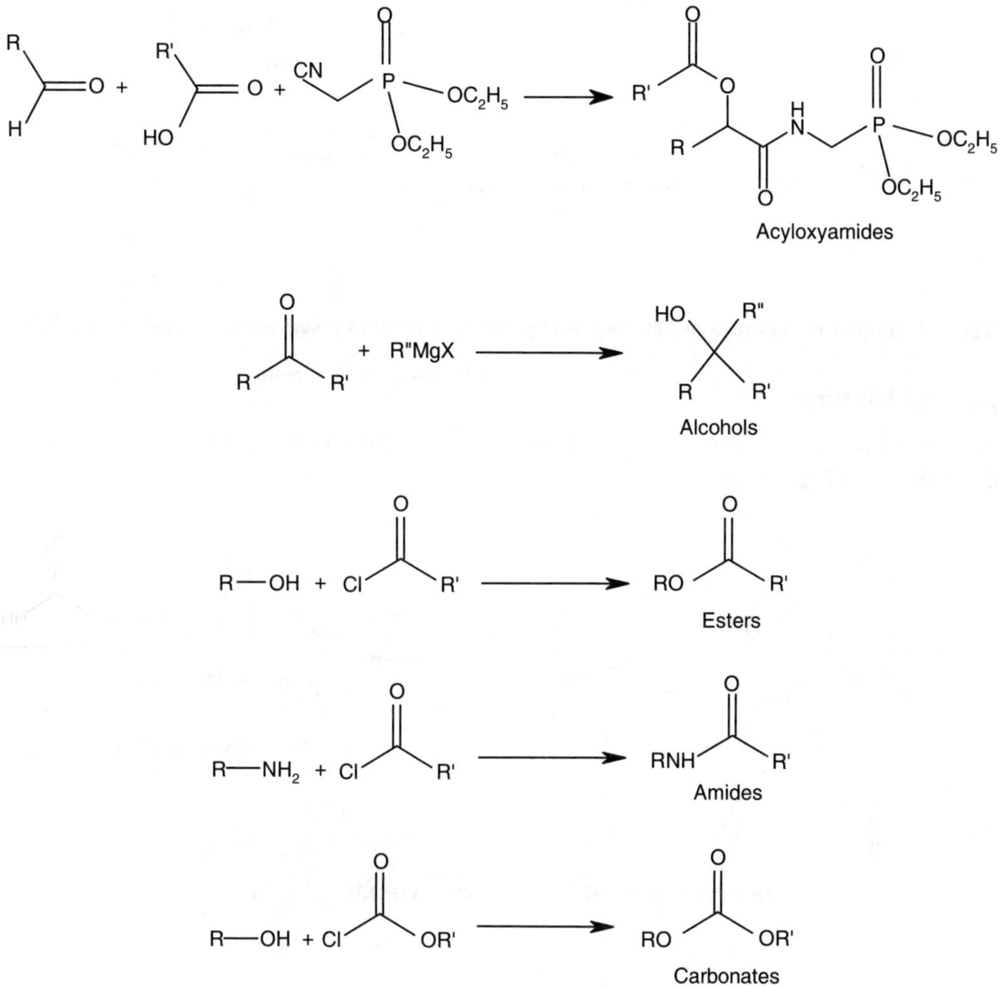

Fig. 17.16a Examples of synthesis of open chain compounds by classical solution phase synthesis using parallel synthesis

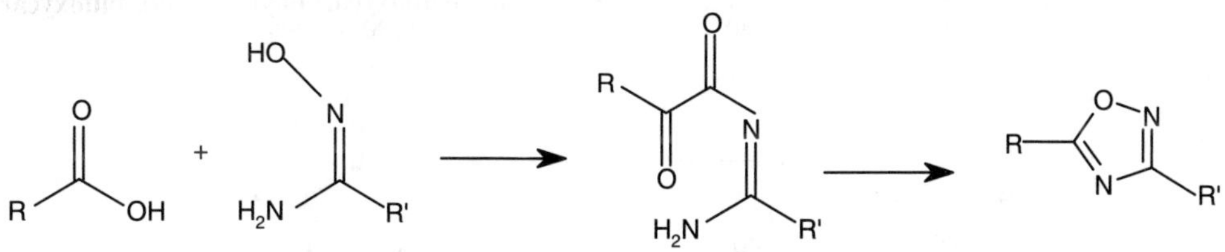

Fig. 17.16b Examples of synthesis of heterocycles by classical solution phase using parallel synthesis (*Contd...*)

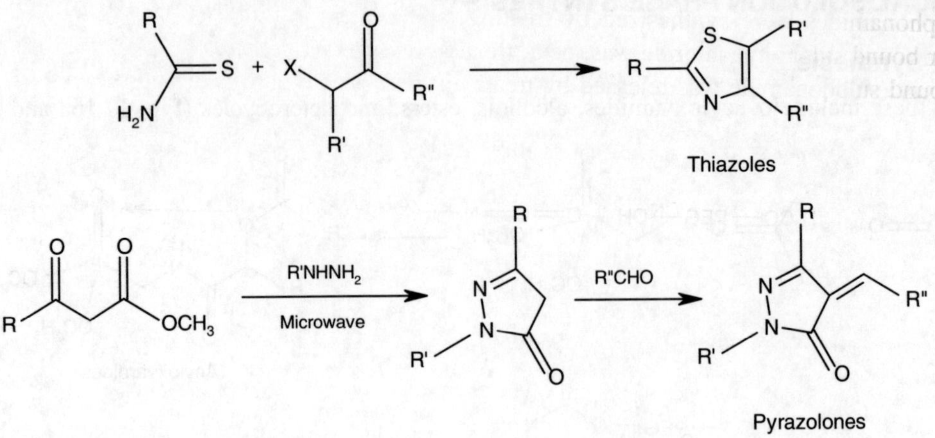

Fig. 17.16(b) Examples of synthesis of heterocycles by classical solution phase using parallel synthesis (*Contd...*)

Synthesis of Mixtures

Some of the examples of synthesis of mixtures using classical solution phase synthesis by one pot method are given in Fig. 17.17.

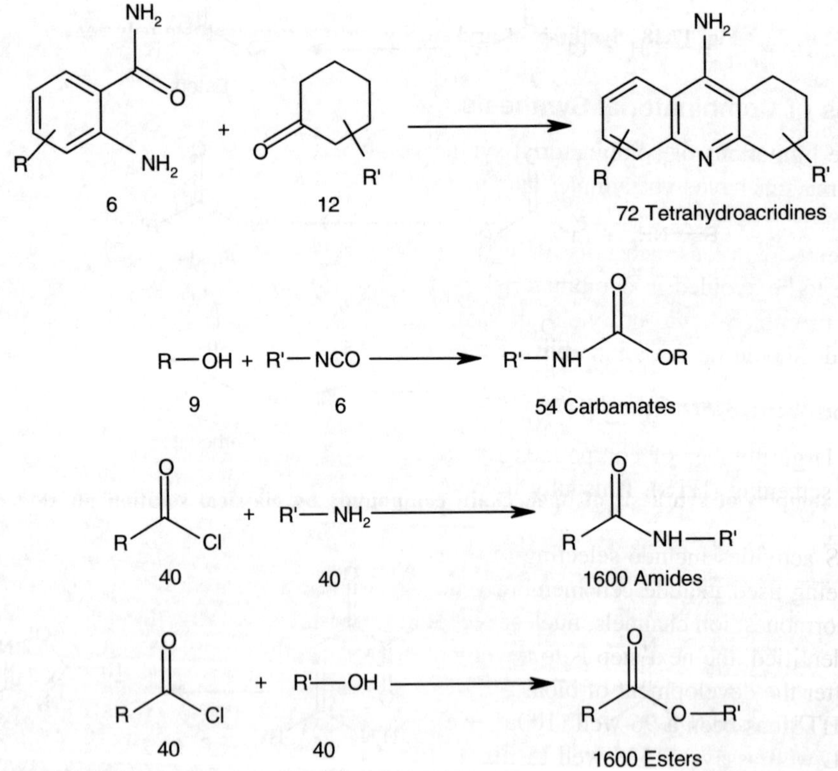

Fig. 17.17 Examples of classical solution phase synthesis using one pot synthesis of mixtures

Synthesis on Solid Polymers

Arylsulphonamides were synthesized by treating isocyanate (9) with PEG monomethyl ether. The polymer bound sulphonyl shloride was, next, treated with amines to give various sulphonamides. The PEG bound sulphonamide was released by treatment with 0.5 sodium hydroxide (Fig. 17.18).

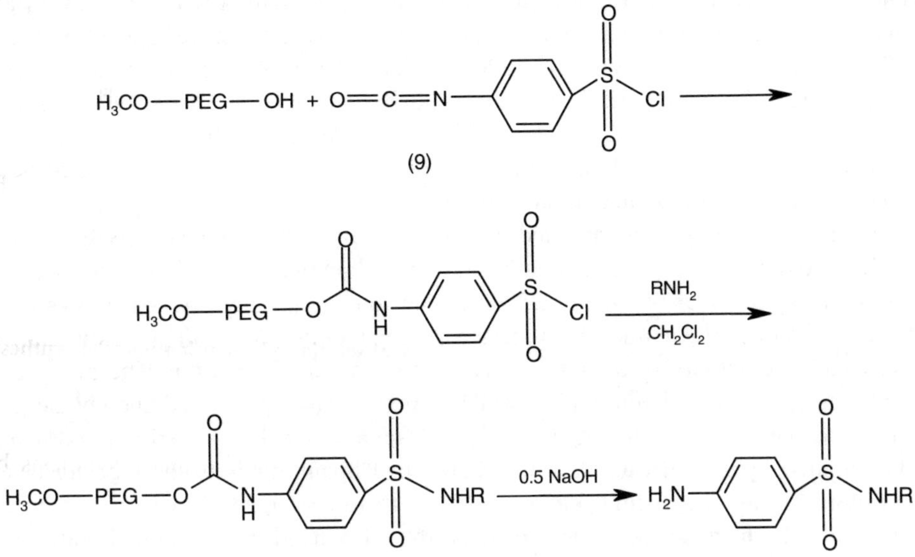

Fig. 17.18 Synthesis of aryl sulphonamides using soluble polymer

Limitations of Combinatorial Synthesis

Some of the limitations of combinatorial synthesis include:

1. The reactins have to be simpler than many reactions that can be performed by classical synthetic methods.
2. Extreme conditions such as use of higher temperatures, pressure, caustic reagents, inert atmosphere have to be avoided in combinatorial synthesis.
3. The reactions should not yield alternative products.
4. Yields should be 80% and above which can be achieved through the use of excess reagents.

High Throughput Screening (HTS)

Testing of large number of compounds for large number of biological activities is known as high throughput screening (HTS). It usually involves automation, robotics, and miniaturization of in vitro tests.

The HTS activities include selecting of a target and measurement of activity. The various targets currently being used include cell membrane coupled receptors (mostly G-protein coupled receptors), enzymes, hormones, ion channels, nuclear receptors, and DNA. Once the target for a particular activity has been identified, the next step is to develop a bioassay that can give a readout about the biological activity. After the development of bioassay, the compounds are assayed for that activity. The standard layout for HTS has been a 96-well (100μL well assays) microtiter plate. Denser formats such as 384-well (25 μL well assays), 1536-well (5 μL well assays), and 3456-well (2 μL well assays) microtiter plates are also being used.

Broadly the HTS assays fall in two categories and include non-radiometric and radiometric assays. The non-radiometric assays use absorbance, fluorescence, and luminescence spectroscopy as the analytical tool for measuring the activity. Enzyme assays are usually run at or below the K_m value of the substrate.

The radiometric assays include filtration and scintillation proximity assay (SPA). In filtration assays the substance is tagged with a radiolabeled ligand by a bond which can be cleaved by the enzyme to be tested. The bonded substrate, enzyme, and the inhibitor, the activity of which on the enzyme has to be tested, are mixed. After sometime, the mixture is filtered on a special filter paper that can capture the radiolabeled ligand. If the enzyme is not inhibited it will split the radiolabeled ligand from the substrate and while filtering it will be retained on filter. A scintillation fluid is added and the radioactivity of filter measured. Depending on the amount of radioactivity measured the degree of inhibition can be calculated. If on the other hand the enzyme is inhibited, no radioactivity will be retained on the filter.

Scintillation proximity assays (SPA) are also known as homogenous radioisotope assays. The basic principle of this assay involves binding of a plastic bead containing fluor and coated with lectin (known as SPA bead) to carbohydrate extracellular surface of a membrane. Accordingly, membrane containing receptor on which the activity of a substrate has to be measured are taken. The procedure involves adding four components in a microtiter plate well and these include SPA bead, membrane, radiolabeled ligand and the compound under investigation. After a suitable incubation period to allow equilibrium to occur the emitted light is measured. If the radioactive ligand binds to the receptor-bead complex during the isotopic decay, it will emit β-rays and excite the embedded fluor which is in its vicinity and light will be emitted which can be measured. If on the other hand the compound under investigation binds to the receptor, the radiolabeled ligand will be away from the embedded fluor and thus will not be able to excite it. Thus, in a screen designed to find the receptor antagonist, a reduction in light is proportional to the activity of the compound under investigation. If the compound is full antagonist, no light will be emitted.

Number of ways have been developed to measure the activity in HTS assays and the results are qualitative or semiqualitative but not precise. However, method has to be reproducible.

FURTHER READING

1. N.K. Terret, "Combinatorial Chemistry," Oxford University Press, Oxford, 1998.
2. S.V. Ley, I.R. Baxendale, R.N. Bream, P.S. Jackson, A.G. Leach, D.A. Longbottom, M. Nesi, J.S. Scott, R.I. Storer, and S.J. Taylor, *J. Chem. Soc., Perkin. Trans. I*, 3815 (2000).
3. A. Beck-Sickinger and P. Webey, 'Combinatorial Strategies in Biology and Chemistry," John Wiley & Sons, 2002.
4. O. Ramstrom and J.M. Leh, *Nature Reviews Drug Discovery*, **1**, 26 (2002).
5. H.M. Greysen et. al, *Nature Reviews Drug Discovery*, **2**, 22 (2003).
6. L.A. Mischer and A. Dutta in "Burger's Medicinal Chemistry and Drug Discovery," 6th ed., Vol. 2, D.J. Abraham, Ed., Wiley Interscience, New Jersey, 2003, p. 1.
7. F. Balkenhohl, C. von dem Bussche-Huennefeld, A. Lansky, and C. Zechel, *Angew. Chem. Int. Ed. Eng.*, **35**, 2288 (1996).

18

Quantitative Structure Activity Relationships

Swastika Ganguly*

The design of a new chemical entity targeted at a specific biological activity is a challenging task. For acting effectively at the molecular target a rigorous task of optimization is needed. A good drug should not only have a high and selective affinity for the target but also have appropriate pharmacokinetic and biopharmaceutic properties.

Biological properties of chemical compounds depend in a very sensitive way on their chemical structure. The understanding of such relationships have given rise to the so called structure activity relationships (SAR) which is one of the principal objective of medicinal chemistry and is also the heart of modern computer aided drug design (CADD). Structure Activity Relationship (SAR) is a qualitative expression whereas the same structure activity relationship when set in mathematical terms by applying numbers to describe three important parameters, activity, structure and most importantly, property results in coining of the term Quantitative Strucure Activity Relationship (QSAR).

QSAR dates back to the 19th century. In 1863, A. F. A. Cros at the University of Strasbourg observed that toxicity of alcohols to mammals increased as the water solubility of the alcohols decreased. In the 1890's, Hans Horst Meyer of the University of Marburg and Charles Ernest Overton of the University of Zurich,working independently, noted that the toxicity of organic compounds depended on their lipophilicity. Overton, in particular found a systematic increase in narcotic potency with increasing chain length in groups of related compounds and he was able to correlate one physical property, the partition coefficient, with this increase. Overton's work was followed by other investigators and in 1904 Traube found a linear relation between narcosis and surface tension, and in 1912 Seidell measured both the solubility and partition coefficient of thymol in the hope that it might assist him in understanding how thymol exerts its action against hookworm. In 1939, Fergusson formulated a concept linking narcotic activity, partition coefficient and thermodynamics known as Fergusson's principle, which said that, when in a state of equilibrium, simple thermodynamic principles could be applied to drug activities, and so the important parameter to consider for the correlation of narcotic activities was the relative saturation of the substance in applied phase.

* Associate Professor, Department of Pharm. Sciences, Birla Institute of Technology, P.O. Mesra 835215, Ranchi (India).

A further insight into the history of QSAR is beyond the scope of this book and interested readers may refer to excellent review related to the history of QSAR.

Quantitative Structure Activity Relationship or QSAR can be defined as the quantitative correlation of biological activity with physicochemical properties, (Eq. 1).

$$\text{Biological Activity} = f\,(\text{physicochemical parameter}) \quad \text{... (Eq. 1)}$$

The use of this quantitative correlation analysis lies in:

1. its ability to develop quantitative structure-activity relationships,
2. predicting the properties and activities of untested molecules,
3. optimizing the properties of a lead compound,
4. comparing different QSAR models statistically,
5. generating hypotheses about the characteristics of a receptor binding site,
6. validating models of receptor binding sites, and
7. prioritizing compounds for synthesis or screening.

Among all these, the predictive ability is the most exciting aspect of QSAR but has not proved to be the most useful feature every time.

PHYSICOCHEMICAL PROPERTIES

From the historical perspectives of QSAR, the biological activity is a function of physicochemical properties. Physicochemical properties essentially refer to any structural, physical and chemical property of a drug. Physicochemical properties are often called "descriptors". Though a number of physicochemical parameters have been studied by the QSAR approach, the most important and commonly studied are hydrophobic, electronic and steric. These properties can be quantified relatively easily.

Hydrophobicity

The term "hydrophobic" means "water fearing", from the Greek words 'hydro', water, and 'phobo', fear. Hydrophobicity may be defined as the tendency of organic molecules to partition away from water into some less polar medium. Hydrophobicity is frequently discussed literally in oil and water terms but actual drug (and other) molecules are not like that at all. Hydrophobicity governs numerous and different biological processes, such as, for example, transport, distribution, and metabolism of biological molecules molecular recognition; and protein folding. How hydrophobicity of a drug plays a part in its ability to reach its site of action, it is necessary to have a brief insight into the structure of a cell.

All cells in human body contain a cell membrane which encloses the contents of the cell, the cytoplasm. The cell membrane consists of two identifiable layers, and each layer is made up of an ordered row of glycerophospholipid molecules such as phosphatidylcholine (lecithin), which comprises the outer layer of the membrane whereas the inner layer is made up of phosphatidylethanolamine phosphatidylserine, and phosphatidylinositol.

In the cell membrane, the two layers of phospholipids are arranged in such a way that the hydrophobic tails point to each other and form a fatty, hydrophobic centre, while the ionic head groups are placed at the inner and outer surfaces of the cell membrane. Thus, the ionic hydrophilic head groups can interact with the aqueous media inside and outside the cell, while the hydrophobic tails are kept away from the aqueous environments. The overall objective of this kind of stable structure is to construct a fatty barrier between the cell's interior and its surroundings.

The brief outline of the structure of the cell membrane shows us the importance of the hydrophobic character of a drug and how crucial it is to the passage of the drug molecule into the cell membranes. For a drug to reach the site of action, it must be able to interact with two different environments, one being the lipophilic membrane and the other being the aqueous phase such as the cytoplasm. Any change in the substituents on a drug molecule, therefore, will have significant effect on its hydrophobicity and certainly on its biological activity. A means of predicting it quantitatively is therefore important to the medicinal chemist.

Partition coefficient (P)

Hansch proposed a model for a membrane by which the lipophilicities could be determined. 1-Octanol (1) has a long saturated alkyl chain, a hydroxyl group for hydrogen bonding, and it dissolves water to the extent of 2.3 M (saturation). This combination gives 1- octanol (1) properties, which are very close to that of natural membranes and macromolecules. 1-octanol (1), could, therefore simulate the lipid membrane relative to water, which could simulate the aqueous phase or cytoplasm.

(1)

The relative distribution between the two phases is known as partition coefficient and is represented by (Eq. 2).

$$P_A = \frac{\text{Concentration of drug in octanol}}{\text{Concentration of drug in aqueous phase}} \quad \text{... (Eq. 2)}$$

Thus, the partition coefficient P is the quotient of two concentrations and is normally calculated in the form of its logarithm to base 10 (log P), because P ranges from 10^{-4} to 10^8.

Hydrophobic compounds have a high P_A value, whereas hydrophilic compounds have a low P_A value.

By variation of substituents on a lead compound a number of analogs can be obtained which will have different hydrophobicities, the log P being different for each of the analogs. The partition coefficient of each analog can now be correlated with the biological activity of each analog. A graph may then be drawn correlating the log P and the biological activity, represented by log ($1/C$),where C is the concentration of drug required to achieve a defined level of biological activity ($1/C$ is used because the more active drug will be able to carry out the defined biological activity at a lower concentration). A straight line graph can be obtained, in studies where the range of log P values is restricted to a narrow range, which can be represented by (Eq. 3).

$$\log 1/C = k_1 \log P + k_2 \quad \text{... (Eq. 3)}$$

Generally, it has been found that increasing hydrophobicity of a lead compound results in increase in biological activity. This correlation, shows the fact that drugs have to cross hydrophobic barriers like cell membrane or blood brain barriers to reach their target receptor. The interaction of the drug molecule with the receptor may also be governed by hydrophobic forces, because the binding site in the receptor is usually hydrophobic. Increasing the hydrophobicity results in a drug which is poorly soluble in aqueous phase. This may lead to difficulties in administration through oral route. Further, a poorly soluble drug may also get "trapped" in the fat depots and may never reach the target site. Hydrophobic drugs are also more susceptible to metabolism and elimination. This requires that a state of optimum hydrophobicity be achieved. Studies have shown that in a series of related structures, an increase in activity corresponds to an increase in partition coefficient until a maximum activity is obtained. After this, the activity decreases even though the partition coefficient increases. Accordingly, there has to be an optimum partition coefficient for a biological activity. This results in a parabolic curve instead of a straight line (Fig. 18.1, Colour Plate 1). The parabolic curve can be represented by the (Eq. 4):

$$\log 1/C = -k_1 (\log P)^2 + k_2 \log P + k_3 \quad \text{... (Eq. 4)}$$

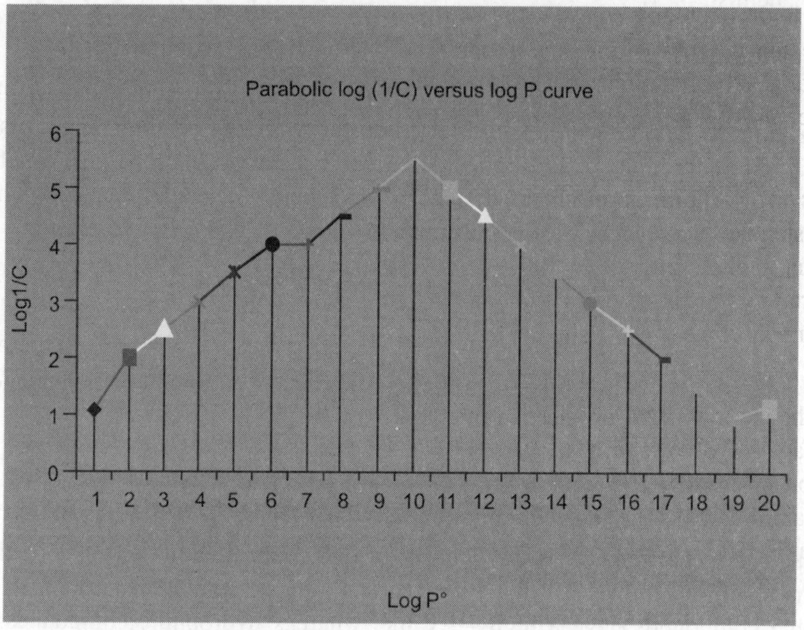

Fig. 18.1 The parabolic curve representing optimum log *P*

When P is small, the log $(P)^2$ term is very small compared to log P term and hence can be ignored. This represents the first part of the curve. When P is large the log $(P)^2$ term becomes much more significant and it dominates the log P term. This represents the last part of the graph.

Measurement of log P

The basic procedure for obtaining a partition coefficient is to shake a weighed amount of a substance in a flask containing measured amounts of water saturated octanol and octanol saturated water. The aqueous phase may be buffered with a phosphate buffer of pH 7. 4 so as to mimic the physiological pH. The amount of substance dissolved in one or both the phases is determined by an appropriate analytical technique and the partition coefficient is calculated from Eq 2. This is known as the "shake flask"method. Though the 1-octanol-water system is often taken as the reference or standard for partition coefficients, other partitioning systems may also be used. A 'critical quartet' of solvent systems for measurement of lipophillicity has been recommended. It was suggested that any biological membrane can be modeled by one of the four solvents: alkane (inert), octanol (amphiprotic), chloroform as a proton donor, and propylene glycol dipelargonate as a proton acceptor. Previously partition coefficient was measured by the tedious "shake flask" method, but now the lipophillicities of a series of molecules are often measured by RP-HPLC or centrifugal partition chromatography, and more recently by high throughput shake plate approaches.

Experimental measurements of log P is often time-consuming and difficult. However, in recent times, several methods have been developed by which log P can be predicted and these include:

1. substituent hydrophobicity constant,

2. fragment method,
3. method based on atomic contribution and or surface area,
4. method based on molecular properties, and
5. method based on solvated chromatic parameters.

Substituent hydrophobicity constant (π) is a measure of hydrophobicity of a substituent relative to hydrogen. The substituent hydrophobicity constant (π) can be obtained by measuring the partition coefficient of a standard compound such as benzene with and without the substituent *x*. The hydrophobicity constant of the substituent (π_x) is given by the Eq. 5.

$$\pi_x = \log P_x - \log P_H \qquad \text{... (Eq. 5)}$$

where P_x is the partition co-efficient of standard substance with substituent *x* and P_H is partition coefficient of standard substance without substituent.

The fragment method reported by Rekker and Mannhold calculates the log *P* as sum of the fragment values plus certain correction factors. Using a large data base, these determined the average contribution of simple fragments. The log *P* value of the molecule could then be calculated by the (Eq. 6).

$$\text{Log } P = \Sigma\, anfn + \Sigma\, bmFm \qquad \text{... (Eq. 6)}$$

where *a* is the number of occurrences of the fragments *f* of type *n*, while *b* is the number occurrences of correction factor *F* of type *m*. Hansch and Leo in collaboration with Chou and Jurs have developed the first version of computer programme, CLOGP, for calculation of log *P* from structural formula. CLOGP programme breaks the molecule into fragments and sums these constant fragment values and structure-dependent correction values taken from Hansch and Leo's database, to predict the log P values of several organic molecules. The division of the molecule into various fragments is done by the programme on the basis of some set rules which are not alterable by the user. The current version of this programme, CLOGP-3, is now used by industry for calculation of the log *P* values.

The method based on atomic contribution and/or surface area use atomic fragments and surface area data to predict hydrophobicity. The contribution of each atom to a molecule, in terms of hydrophobicity, can be evaluated by multiplying the corresponding atomic parameter by the degree of exposure to the surrounding solvent. The exposure degree is typically represented by the solvent-accessible surface area (SASA). The first promoters of this method were Broto and his colleagues, who developed a 222 descriptors set, made by combinations of up to four atoms with specific bonding pathways up to four in length, reaching a precision of about 0. 4 log units.

The method based on molecular properties was developed by Bodor. The method computes log *P* as a function of different calculated molecular properties, like conformations, ionization, hydration, ionpair formation, keto-enol tautomerism, intramolecular and intermolecular H-bond formation, folding, etc.

The fifth log *P* determination method, based on solvatochromic comparisons, was proposed by Kamlet and coworkers and constitutes, once more, a molecular properties methodology. Log *P* can be calculated through the (Eq. 7)

$$\log P_{\text{oct}} = a\,V + b\,\pi^* + c\,\hat{a}_H + d\,\acute{a}_H + e \qquad \text{... (Eq. 7)}$$

V is a solute volume term, π^* is a polarity/polarizability solute term, $\hat{a}_H$ is an independent measure of solute hydrogen-bond acceptor strength, $\acute{a}_H$ the corresponding hydrogen-bond donor strength, while *e* is the intercept. π^*, $\hat{a}_H$, and $\acute{a}_H$ represent solvatochromic parameters obtained by averaging multiple normalized solvent effects on a variety of properties, involving many different types of indicators.

In recent times a computerized program termed as "HINT" namely 'Hydropathic Interactions' has been developed from log *P* o/w and is a module integrated in the SYBYL package and has been well used with 3DQSAR modules like ComFA with certain success.

Electronic Effects

The electronic effects of various substituents have an effect on ionization or the polarity of a drug and this effect on ionization affects the passage of drug through cell membrane and can determine as to how strongly the drug binds to the receptor.

Hammett Substitution Constant

Hammett substitution constant (σ) is a measure of electron-withdrawing or electron-donating capacity of a substituent on an aromatic ring. Thus, the ionization of weak acid, benzoic acid (2) can be represented by (Eq. 8). At equilibrium the relative proportions of various species is given by (Eq. 9). The subscript

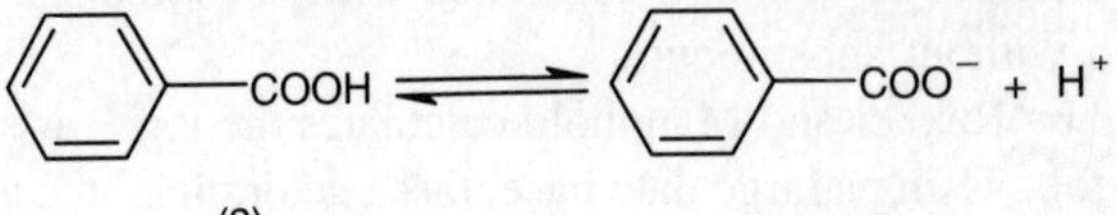

(2)

... (Eq. 8)

$$K_H = \frac{[\mathrm{PhCOO}^-]}{[\mathrm{PhCOOH}]} \qquad \text{... (Eq. 9)}$$

H indicates that there are no substituents on aromatic ring. In presence of a substituent in the aromatic ring, the value of equilibrium constant, *K*, will change. Thus, in presence of an electron withdrawing group (*X*) at *meta*- or *para*-position the equilibrium will be more towards right (Eq. 9) and in presence

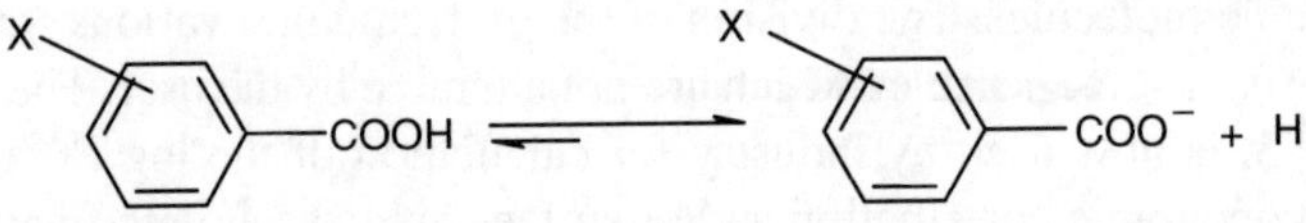

... (Eq. 9)

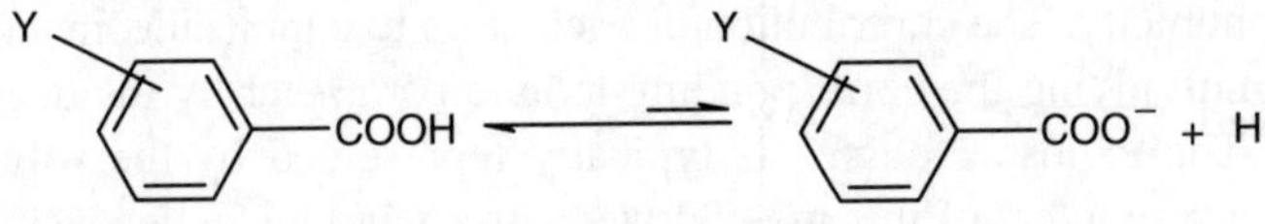

... (Eq. 10)

of an electron donating group (Y) at *meta*- or *para*-position the equilibrium will be more towards lef (Eq. 10). The Hammett substituent constant for substituent X and Y can then be represented by the (Eq 11) and (Eq. 12). Thus, in case of

$$\sigma_X = \log (K_X/K_H) \text{ or } \log K_X - \log K_H \qquad \text{... (Eq. 11)}$$

$$\sigma_Y = \log (K_Y/K_H) \text{ or } \log K_Y - \log K_H \qquad \text{... (Eq. 12)}$$

electron-withdrawing group (*X*), the log K_X being much larger than log K_H, the σ value will be positive while as in case of electron donating group (*Y*), the log K_Y will be much smaller than log K_H, the σ wil be negative.

The Hammett substituent constant takes into consideration both resonance and inductive effects o *meta-/para*-substituents on benzoic acid (2). The Hammett substituent constant cannot be calculated fo *ortho*-substituents because in addition to resonance and inductive effects, steric effects also play a par with such substituents.

Steric Effects

The interaction of a drug with a receptor requires that both approach each other and this approach coul be affected by the size and shape of the molecules involved. Thus, a bulkier group may block the dru molecule from binding to the active site. Similarly, a group which is very small in size, may not fit at the active site properly. For a proper fitting, it is therefore necessary that the sizes of the drug molecule and the shape of the receptor site are complimentary to each other. Since acid and base catalyzed hydrolysis of an ester (Figs. 18.2 and 18.3) involves a tetrahedral transition state, ester hydrolysis has been used to quantify the steric parameter. Thus, esters with bulky substituents (*X*) will get hydrolysed slowly as compared to substituents (*X*) which are smaller in bulk. With this background Taft Steric Factor (*Es*) has been used to quantify the steric features of the substituent, where, k_x is the rate of hydrolysis of aliphatic esters with substituent

$$Es = \log k_x - \log k_o \qquad \text{... (Eq. 13)}$$

X and k_o is the reference ester without the substituent *x*

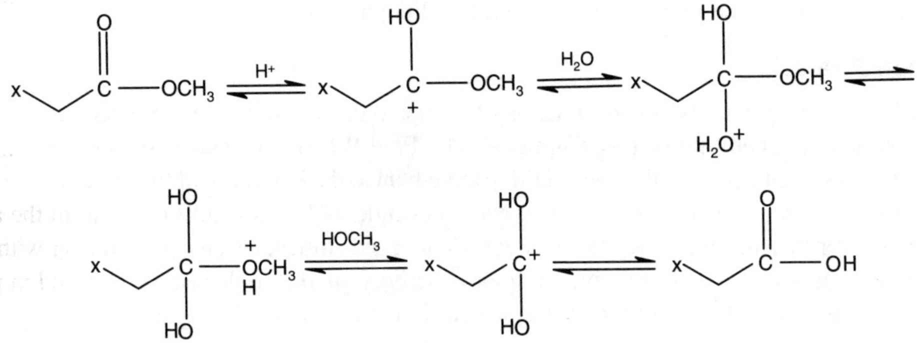

Fig. 18.2 Acid catalyzed hydrolysis of an ester

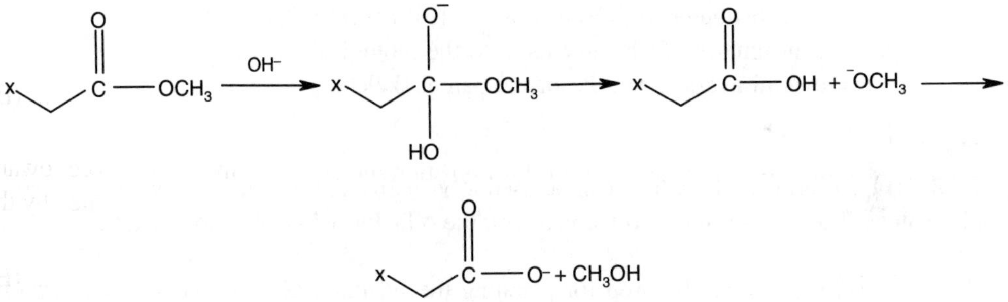

Fig. 18.3 Base catalyzed hydrolysis of an ester

The STERIMOL set of parameters was introduced by Verloop in 1976. This calculates steric substituent values known as Verloop steric parameters from standard bond angles, van der Waals radii, bond lengths, and possible conformations for the substituent. However, whereas Es is difficult to measure, the Verloop steric parameter can be measured for any substituent.

Other physicochemical parameters are H-bonding, conformation, dipole moments, inter-atomic distances which are all difficult to quantify and therefore have a limited use. A various number of software are available in the market, among this DRAGON is quite popular and calculates 1,481 molecular descriptors, distributed in 18 blocks. Each molecule has to be represented by 3D geometrical coordinates, including hydrogen. The maximum number of atoms (hydrogen atoms included) is 150. Calculations are quite fast; however, several condensed or adjacent rings can slow down the calculations.

CORRELATION OF PHYSICOCHEMICAL PARAMETERS WITH BIOLOGICAL ACTIVITY

Hansch Approach

Hansch equation (Eq. 14) correlates the biological activity with three most commonly used physicochemical parameters namely partition coefficient or substituent hydrophobicity constant, electronic and steric factors. When P values are spread over a large range (Eq. 14) becomes (Eq. 15).

$$\log 1/C = k_1 \log P + k_2\sigma + k_3\,Es + k_4 \quad \text{... (Eq. 14)}$$

$$\log 1/C = -k_1 (\log P)^2 + k_2 (\log P) + k_3\sigma + k_4\,Es + k_5 \quad \text{... (Eq. 15)}$$

C is the molar concentration that evokes a standard biological activity (reciprocal of the concentration is taken because it is desirable that greater activity is achieved at a minimum dose), and the negative sign for $(\log P)^2$ signifies the requirement of optimum lipophillicity.

Free Wilson Analysis

The Free Wilson Analysis is useful for a series of compounds which have a common structure with variable substituents, usually known as fragments. The Free Wilson analysis assumes that the parent structure and each substituent contribute an additive increment to the logarithm of the biological response. The increment from each substituent is constant and independent of interactions of substituents in other positions. It means that the introduction of any particular substituent at any particular position in a molecule will always change the relative biological activity of the molecule by the same amount, independent of whatever other substituents are present in the molecule. An equation can be drawn up such as

$$BA = \Sigma\, a_i x_i + m \quad \text{... (Eq. 16)}$$

where BA = biological activity,

x_i = ith substituent (if present value = 1, if absent value = 0)

a_i = contribution of ith substituent to the biological activity

μ = overall average activity of the parent skeleton

The Craig Plot

The Craig plot (Fig. 18.4) is a plot which can be used to visualize the properties of various substituents viz. π and σ values. The *y* axis is taken as the value for the σ factor, while the *x* axis is taken as the value for π factor.

The Craig plot (Fig. 18.4) can be used for planning the selection of substituents used in a QSAR study. It also shows which substituents have a positive parameter and which substituents have a negative parameter.

The Topliss Operational Schemes

When synthesis of large number of compounds are difficult but biological testing of the compounds is easily possible, an approach known as the Topliss scheme, also called as the **"Topliss decision Tree"** can be used for the synthesis of only the most active compounds instead of arbitrary synthesis of a huge number of compounds. This is actually a flow diagram of substituents which has been conjured up by considering the hydrophobic and electronic properties of the substituents. Topliss schemes are of two types, one is for aromatic substituents and the other for aliphatic side chain substituents.

Here L refers to Low activity, E refers to Equal activity and M refers to More activity of the synthesized compounds. In the Topliss scheme for aromatic substituents (Fig. 18.5) it is hypothetized

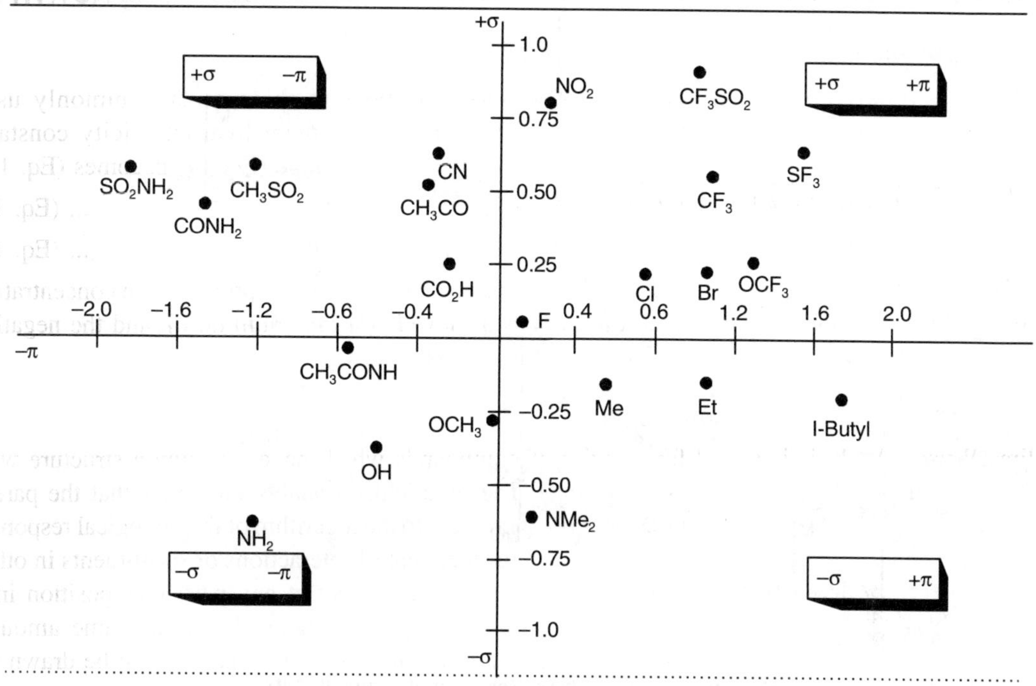

Fig. 18.4 The Craig plot of π and σ parameters
(*Source:* Introduction to Medicinal Chemistry by G. L. Patrick, 2nd ed., Oxford University Press, p. 274.)

that the lead compound contains a monosubstituted aromatic ring which has been evaluated for its biological activity. The first analogue is the 4-chloro derivative, which is more hydrophobic and electron withdrawing than hydrogen. π and σ are therefore positive. The chloro analogue is then synthesized and its biological potency is measured. Depending on the activity of the analoguc which may be less (L), equal (E), or more (M), it is decided which analogue is to be synthesized next. For example, if the biological activity increases,it implies that π and σ are contributing positively to biological activity and therefore compounds will be synthesized with further positive hydrophobic and σ values, that is, according to the (M) branch, in this case the 3,4-dichloro-substituted analogue. If experimental values agree with this fact, then substituents are incorporated further such that there is again increase of the π and σ values. If, however the 4-chloro analog is as potent as the parent compound then the (E) branch is to be followed. In case the 4-chloro analogue exhibits less activity than its parent molecule from which it has been derived, it implies that π and/or σ are negatively contributing to the biological activity and therefore, the (L) branch is to be followed for further synthesis.

The Topliss scheme for aliphatic substituents (Fig. 18.6) also works in the same way and has been designed keeping the hydrophobic and electronic parameters in mind. However, the steric parameters are not taken into consideration and the substituents have been incorporated such that there is not much steric difference among them.

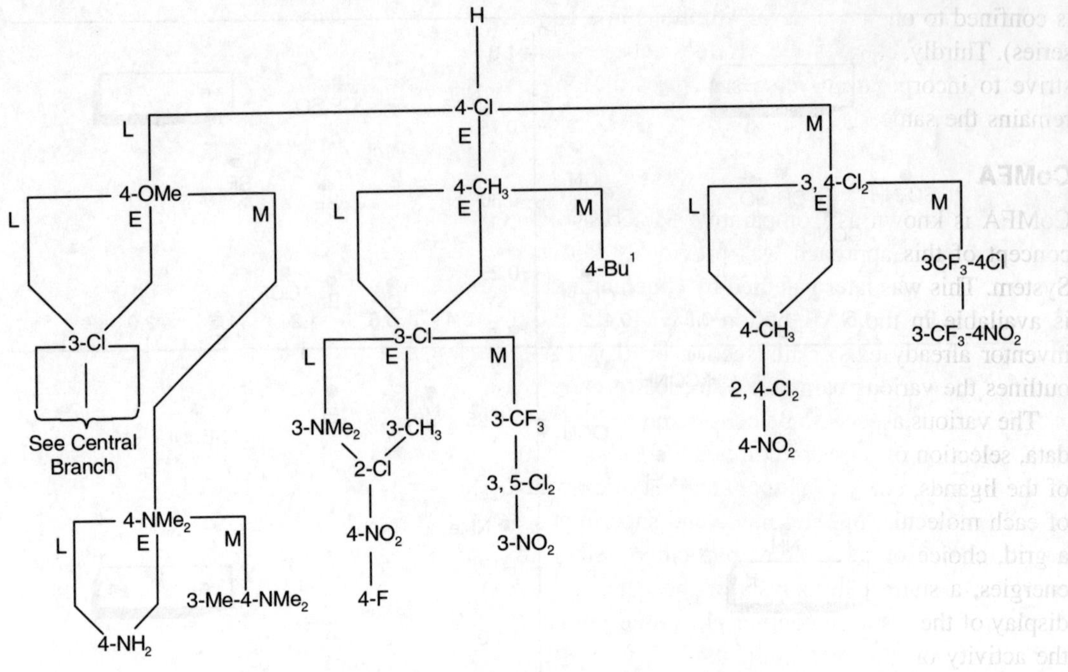

Fig. 18.5 Topliss scheme for aromatic substituents
(*Source:* Introduction to Medical Chemistry by G.L. Patrick, 2nd ed., Oxford University Press, p. 276.)

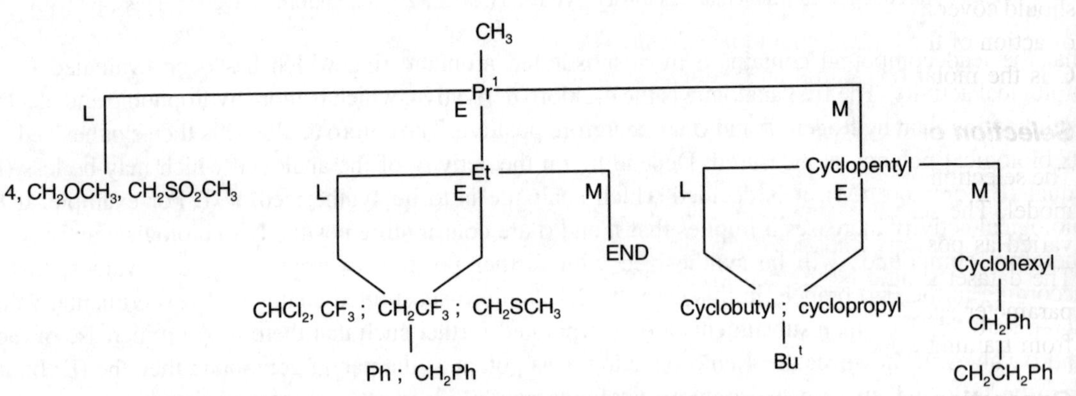

Fig 18.6 Topliss scheme for aliphatic substituents
(*Source:* Introduction to Medical Chemistry by G.L. Patrick, 2nd ed., Oxford University Press, p. 276.)

COMPUTERIZED METHODS OF QSAR

Computer based methods of QSAR consist of Three dimensional Quantitative Structure Activity Relationships and the most popular approaches have been ComFA and ComSIA. The question arises what are the real advantages of 3 D QSAR? In case of classical QSAR certain physicochemical parameters may be missing and may also be difficult to incorporate. Secondly, the parameters considered may not be sufficient to describe drug receptor interactions. A serious disadvantage of classical QSAR is that it is confined to one or more substitutions in a common reference structure (works best with congeneric series). Thirdly, classical QSAR does not consider 3D structures of the molecules. 3D QSAR approaches strive to incorporate diverse structures as long as the mechanism of action at the molecular level remains the same.

CoMFA

CoMFA is known as Comparative Molecular Field Analysis and has been developed at Tripos. The concept of this approach was previously known as Dynamic Lattice Oriented Molecular Modeling System. This was later patented by Craemer and Wold in the name of CoMFA in 1988 and the module is available in the SAR option of SYBYL. Extensive reviews and numbers of publications of the inventor already exist. This section on CoMFA deals briefly on the various aspects of CoMFA and outlines the various parameters needed to carry out a CoMFA analysis successfully.

The various aspects to be considered for a CoMFA analysis include the need for authentic biological data, selection of series of compounds and design of training and test series, generation of 3D structure of the ligands, conformational analysis of each molecule, establishment of the bioactive conformation of each molecule, binding mode and superimposition of the molecules, position of the lattice point in a grid, choice of force fields particularly steric and electrostatic fields, calculation of the interaction energies, a statistical analysis of the data generated and the establishment of the 3D-QSAR model, display of the result in contour plots, interpretation of these contour plots and design and prediction of the activity of unknown compounds.

Biological Data

The biological data for a CoMFA analysis should be authentic, obtained from a single source and should cover as large a range as possible. Though the ligands may be of diverse structures the mechanism of action of the ligands should be similar. The biological activity should be measured as log 1/C where C is the molar concentration of drug producing a standard response.

Selection of Dataset and Design of Training and Test Series

The selection of dataset for a CoMFA analysis is to be carried out carefully to obtain a robust 3D QSAR model. The selection should be such that the compounds or ligands in the dataset should be as much varied as possible implying that various kinds of substituents on the ligands should be incorporated. The dataset should be divided into two sets, the training set and the test set. The training set spans a parameter space in which all data points are more or less equally distributed. A test set is not too far from training set in terms of both chemical nature and biological activity.

Generation of Three Dimensional Structures of the Ligands

To start a CoMFA analysis the starting structure has to be generated and optimized. The different methods are X ray crystallography or molecular modelling. In X ray crystallography the appropriate receptor structure, if available in the Protein Databank (www. rcsb.org) can be downloaded,the ligand extracted from the downloaded receptor and is taken as the starting structure from which all the other ligands are generated. In cases when the receptor structure is not known, for example the GPCR receptors, the ligands are drawn from scratch with the help of molecular modelling techniques which have been discussed in detail in the next chapter. Each structure has to be energy minimized, in other words to be optimized so as to get the most stable structure. The various methods for optimization of structure are molecular mechanics methods, semi empirical and *ab-initio* methods. A discussion of all these methods has been covered in the next chapter.

Conformational Analysis of each Molecule

Conformational analysis of each molecule in the training set is to be carried out and the conformer with the least energy is to be considered for further steps in the CoMFA analysis. The conformational analysis can be carried out with the help of various methods like systematic search method, molecular dynamics method, the MC (Monte Carlo) method, and the distance geometry approach. However, the preferred conformation of an isolated molecule may not always correspond to the bioactive conformation.

What is the bioactive conformation? The bioactive conformation of a molecule is the conformation in which it is bound to the target receptor. The bioactive conformation can be obtained by X ray crystallography or by NMR spectroscopy, if the receptor structure is known. However, if the receptor structure is not known we have to revert back to the systematic search, distance geometry method or the molecular fitting technique. Various software such as DISCO, CATALYST, APEX –3D can be used to find bioactive conformations of the molecules in the selected data set.

Alignment

Alignment or superimposition is one of the most crucial steps in CoMFA. The whole dataset can be aligned at a time known as the "Database Alignment method" or the ligand can be aligned by matching the atoms better known as the atom fit technique. Other methods of alignment include field fit technique which uses the technique of aligning the fields or psuedofields. While aligning the molecules of the selected dataset it is to be remembered that results of CoMFA analyses depend on the alignment of the molecules

Force Fields

A force field is an empirical fit to the potential energy surface. A force field uses a combination of bond distances, bond angles, torsion angles and interatomic distances to describe both bonds as well as van der waals and electrostatic interactions between them. The force field parameters are obtained from an empirical data of a small set of molecules. Before understanding the force fields let us understand what major forces are involved in the interactions of the ligand with the receptor. Steric and electrostatic interactions of the ligand with the receptor are considered for a CoMFA analyses. Electrostatic fields use the Coulomb potential whereas steric fields use Lennard-Jones 6-12 Potential. Additional fields are Hydrogen bonding fields (GRID) and Hydrophobic Fields (HINT) which are integrated as additional modules in SYBYL.

Grid Box

Once the molecules have been drawn, energy minimized and aligned, a grid is built around the molecules (Fig. 18.7, Colour Plate 1). The grid behaves as a pseudo receptor. The intersections of the grid are called grid points. The grid point defines the position of the molecule with respect to space. By default the size of grid spacing is 2 Å and that of grid box is 3-4 Å. A probe atom such as water or methyl group is added at one of the grid points. The interaction energies, i.e. the steric and electrostatic interactions are calculated between the probe atom and the molecules for all the lattice points.

The steric and electrostatic interaction energies of all the molecules can be calculated and are obtained as CoMFA values for each molecule.

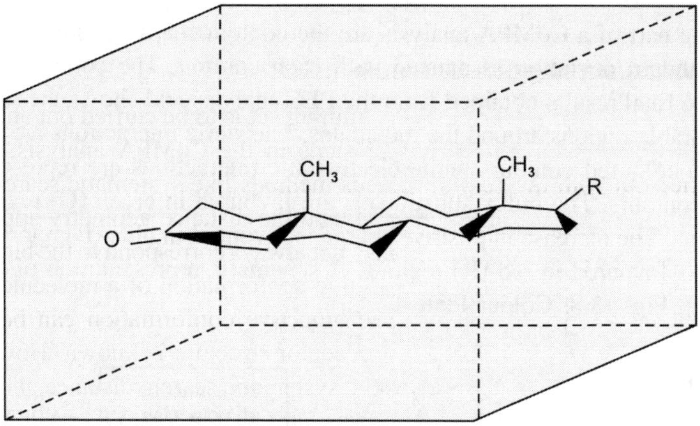

Fig. 18.7 Grid box with aligned ligands inside

Partial Least Squares Analysis (PLS)

After the generation of the CoMFA values of all the molecules a statistical analysis is to be carried out. However, multiple linear regression analysis cannot be applied as it cannot deal with a large number of descriptors being used to explain the biological activity of a small number of compounds.

PLS can be applied to hundreds or thousands of variables involving only small number of biological data and can be used with variables which exhibit a high degree of collinearity among them. It is an iterative procedure and uses a method known as "**Leave One Out**" method which finds out the model which can best correlate the biological property with the different variables.

In the Leave One Out method when the software strives to derive a relationship between the interaction energies of the molecules in the dataset with the biological activity, one of the molecules is left out every time and the formula derived is tested against the left out molecule to predict its biological activity. Next time, the same molecule is included in the calculations and a different molecule is left out and the same procedure is repeated to predict the biological activity of that left out molecule. This procedure is repeated again and again until all the molecules have been left out once. This is known as cross validation.

The results are obtained in the form of the following parameters, namely the Cross-validated Correlation Coefficient (r^2_{cv}) (leave-one-out, leave-group-out), Standard Error of Prediction (SDEP), Conventional (Non Cross-Validated) Correlation Coefficient (r^2), Standard Error of Estimate (SEE) and Predictive Correlation Coefficient of the (r^2_{pred}) based on molecules of test set, defined as,

$$r^2_{\text{pred}} = (\text{SD-PRESS})/\text{SD} \qquad \text{... (Eq. 17)}$$

where SD is the sum of the squared deviations between the biological activities of the test set and mean activities of the training set molecules and PRESS is the sum of squared deviation between predicted and actual activity values for every molecule in test set. To further test the robustness of the model developed, a bootstrapping analysis is also carried out. Bootstrapping involves the generation of many new data sets from original data set and is obtained by randomly choosing samples from the original data set. The result of the bootstrapping analysis is represented as r^2_{bs}.

Contour Maps

The most interesting part of a CoMFA analysis are the contour maps generated as a scalar product of coefficients and standard deviation associated with each column. The contour maps are a graphical representation of the final results obtained from the PLS analysis and shows the steric and electrostatic favorable or unfavorable regions around the molecules. The steric interactions are represented by green (G) and yellow (Y) coloured contours while electrostatic interactions are represented by red (R) and blue (B) coloured contours. The bulky substituents are favoured in green (G) regions and disfavoured in yellow (Y) regions. The increase in positive charge is favoured in blue (B) regions while the increase in negative charge is favoured in red (R) regions. A schematic representation of the steps involved in CoMFA is shown in Fig. 18.8, Colour Plate 1

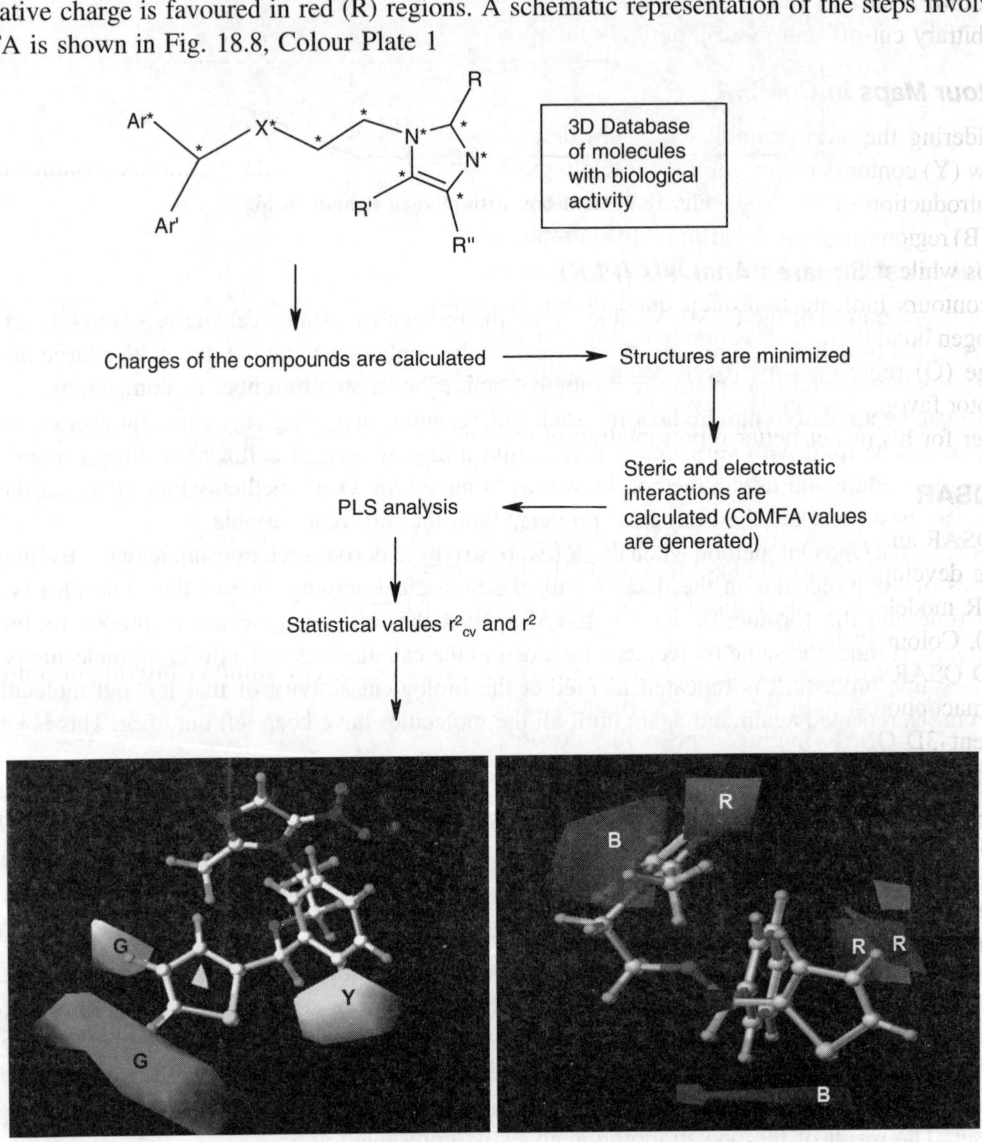

Fig. 18.8 Schematic representation of CoMFA steps

CoMSIA (Comparative Molecular Similarity Indices Analysis)

The CoMSIA method was introduced by Klebe and this method differs by the way the molecular fields are calculated and by including additional molecular fields, such as lipophilic and hydrogen bond potential. CoMSIA introduces the Gaussian function for the distance dependence between the molecular atoms and the probe atom in order to avoid some of the inherent deficiencies arising from the Lennard-Jones and Coulomb potential functional forms. In CoMSIA, five different similarity fields viz., steric, electrostatic, hydrophobic, hydrogen bond donor and hydrogen bond acceptor fields are calculated. These fields are selected to cover the major contributions to ligand binding. It has several advantages over CoMFA such as greater robustness regarding both region shift and small shift within the alignments, no arbitrary cut-off and more intuitively interpretable contour maps.

Contour Maps in CoMSIA

Considering the steric contours of CoMSIA, green (G) contours indicate favourable regions while yellow (Y) contours indicate unfavourable regions for bulkier substituents. In the electrostatic contours, the introduction of electronegative substituents in red (R) regions may increase the affinity while in blue (B) regions decrease the affinity. In hydrophobic contours, the yellow (Y) regions favour hydrophobic groups while white (W) regions favour hydrophilic groups. In the hydrogen bond donor contours cyan (C) contours indicate hydrogen bond donor favourable regions while purple (P) contours indicate hydrogen bond donor unfavourable regions for substituents. In case of hydrogen bond acceptor contours orange (O) represents hydrogen acceptor disfavored region and magenta (M) represents hydrogen acceptor favored region. However, the contour colours can be customized according to the needs of the worker for his or her better representation of the favored or disfavored regions.

4D-QSAR

4D-QSAR analysis incorporates the conformational, alignment, and pharmacophore degrees of freedom in the development of 3D-QSAR models. It is used to create and screen against 3D-pharmacophore QSAR models and can be used in receptor independent or receptor-dependent modes (Figs 18.9 and 18.10, Colour Plate 2).

3D-QSAR methods lets us understand the mechanisms of activity while identifying ligand-receptor pharmacophores and also act as virtual screens to process libraries of real or virtual compounds. Current 3D-QSAR methods, however, do not include multiple conformations or alignments and pharmacophores of the ligands of the data sets in the construction of the QSAR model. 4D-QSAR strives to remove these shortcomings by considering the multiple conformations or alignments and pharmacophores of the ligands in the selected dataset. In explicit 4D-QSAR approaches, the ligands of both training and test set are provided as an ensemble of conformations, orientations, and protonation states. The most likely bioactive representation is then genetically evolved from this reservoir using a Boltzmann-weighted selection criterion.

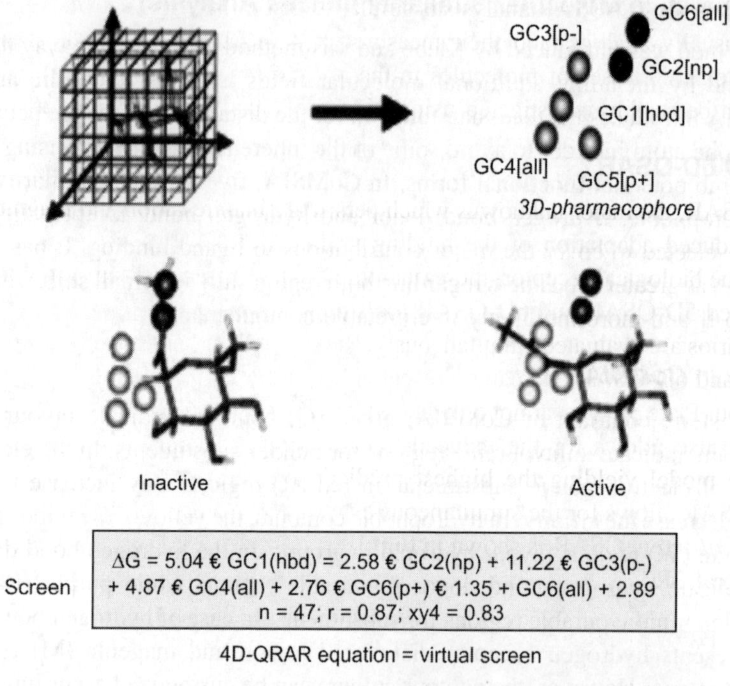

Fig. 18.9 4D QSAR process
(*Source:* www.seascapelearning.com)

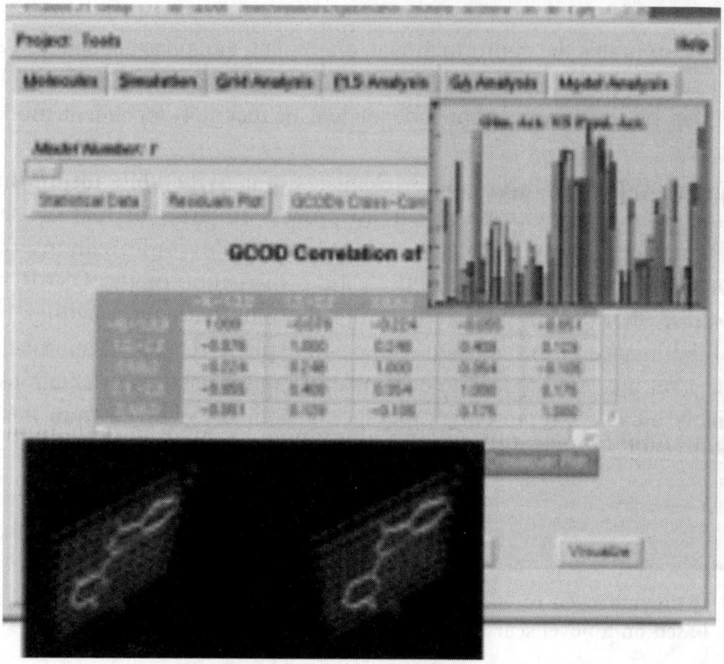

Fig. 18.10 4D-QSAR interface
(*Source:* www.seascapelearning.com)

The required data for 4D-QSAR analysis is similar to that of 3D-QSAR which includes a training set of compounds, usually analogs, and their measured biological activities in a common screen/assay. Both rigid and flexible classes of molecules in the normal range of size and structural complexity of current drugs can be readily investigated using 4D-QSAR analysis.

5D-QSAR AND 6D-QSAR

Even with 4D-QSAR, the major unknowns which persist are manifestation and magnitude of the induced fit, the ligand-induced adaptation of the binding site to the topology of the small molecule. In the absence of the true biological receptor, these quantities cannot unambiguously be determined. The most recently developed 5D-QSAR and 6D-QSAR tools offer a possible solution to the problem as several induced-fit scenarios are evaluated simultaneously. Raptor and Quasar are software programmes dealing with 5D-QSAR and 6D-QSAR and can represent an ensemble of up to six different induced-fit models (Fig. 18.11, Colour Plate 3). Quasar not only allows for the simultaneous evaluation of different induced-fit scenarios but also allows for the induced-fit crossover and linear combination of the individual hypotheses. The model yielding the highest predictive surrogates is selected during the simulated evolution. 6D-QSAR allows for the simultaneous evaluation of different solvation models. A schematic representation of different QSAR is shown in Fig. 18.12. For further reading the readers can consult the websites of Biograf 3R.

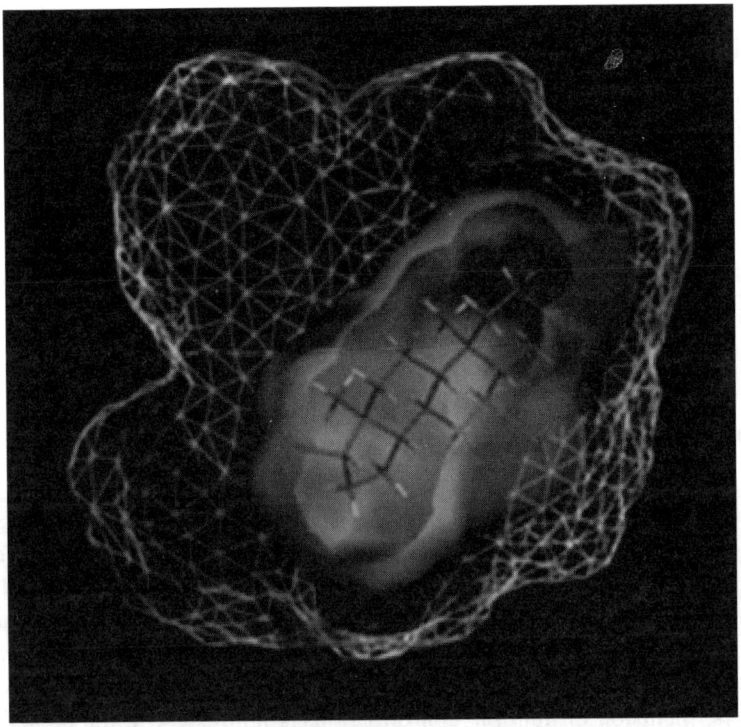

Fig. 18.11 A model of the androgen receptor produced using Raptor, a 5D-QSAR tool. Raptor is a receptor-modeling technology based on a novel scoring function. (*Source:* Biographics Laboratory 3R)

Colour Plate 4

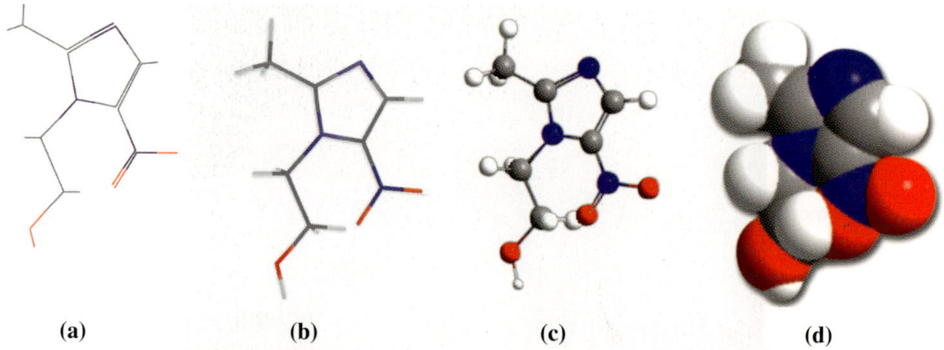

Fig. 19.6 The structure of metronidazole in different modes (a) Lines (b) Sticks (c) Ball and Stick (d) Space filling (CPK model). Image generated by Chem3D Ultra of ChemOffice 10

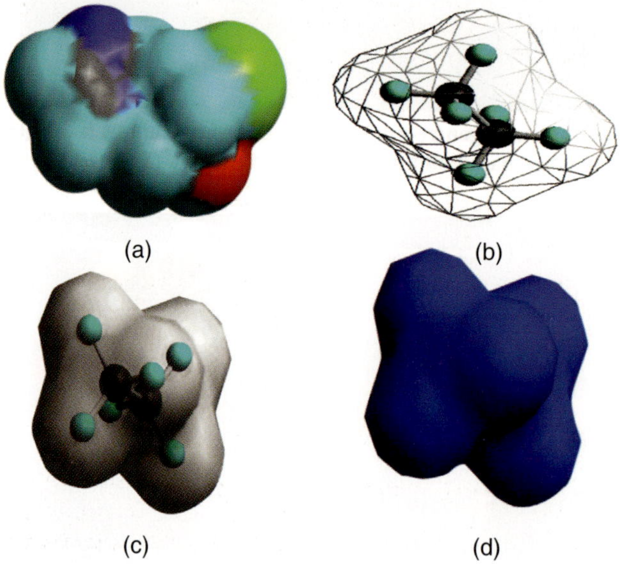

Fig. 19.7 Various surfaces (a) Solvent accessible surface of ethane (b) Wire mesh Connolly surface of ethane (c) Translucent Connolly surface of ethane (d) Solid Connolly surface of ethane. Image generated by ChemOffice 10

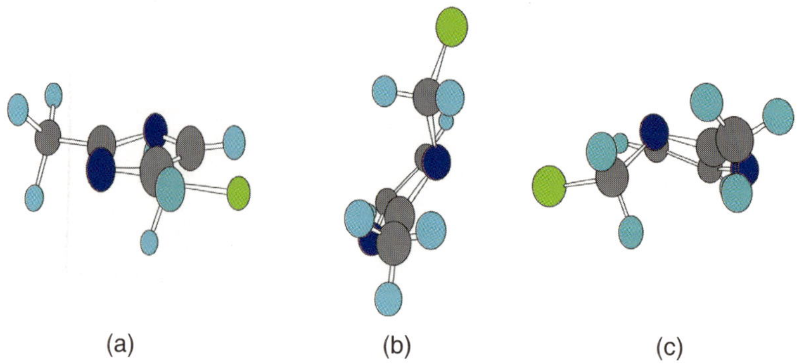

Fig. 19.8 Rotation of a molecule in three planes (a) Rotation in X axis (b) Rotation in Z axis (c) Rotation in Y axis. Image generated by ChemOffice 10

Colour Plate 5

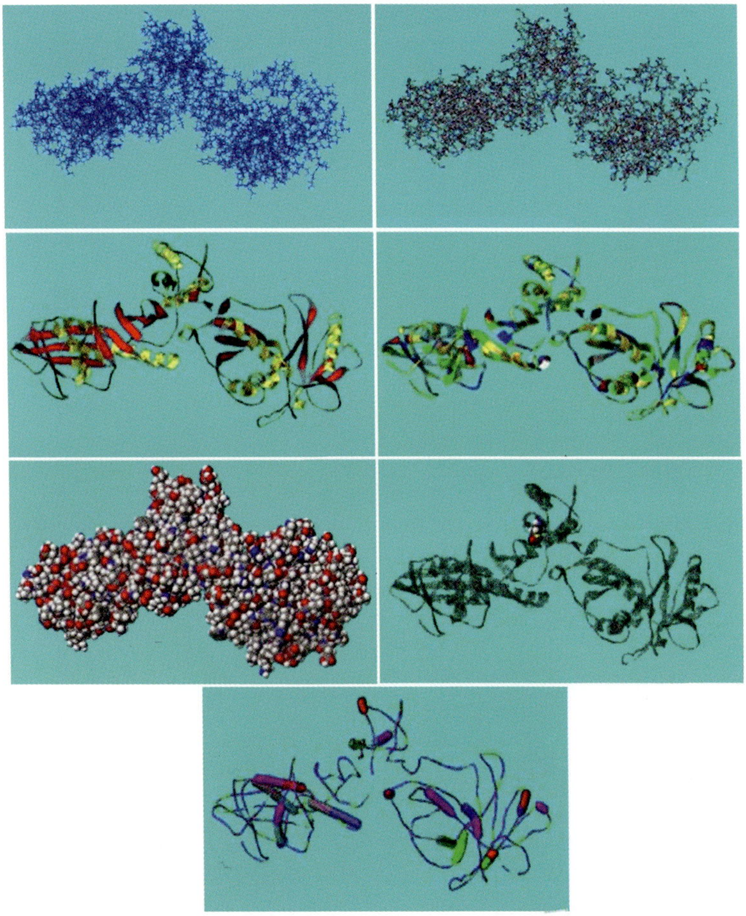

Fig. 19.9 Crystal structure of Reverse Transcriptase (PDB code 1RT2) ; Clockwise, from top left: lines, stick, flat ribbon of secondary structure, solid ribbon colored by Karpus and Schulz flexibility, CPK/ space filling, Threaded pod, Threaded spools of Chou-Fasman Alpha helix. Image generated by Scigress Explorer Ultra 7.0

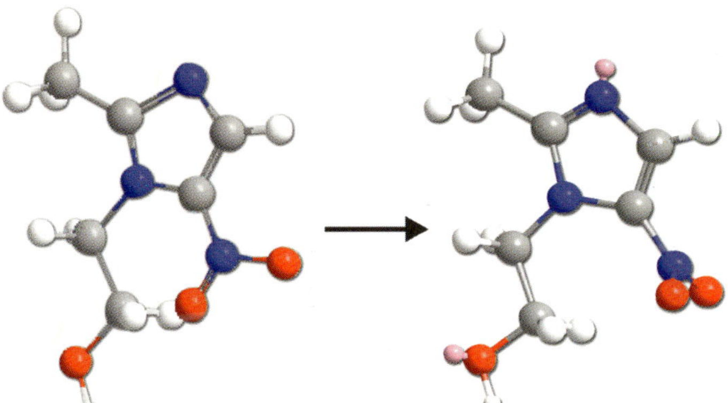

(a) (b)

Fig. 19.10 The process of energy minimization a) Molecule before minimization b) Molecule after minimization. Image generated by Chem 3D Ultra of ChemOffice 10

Colour Plate 6

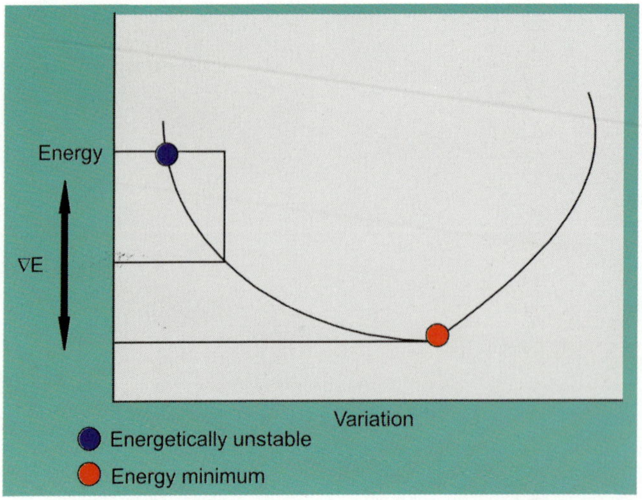

Fig. 19.11 **Energy minimization** (Reproduced from Introduction to Medicinal Chemistry, by J.L. Patrick, page 323)

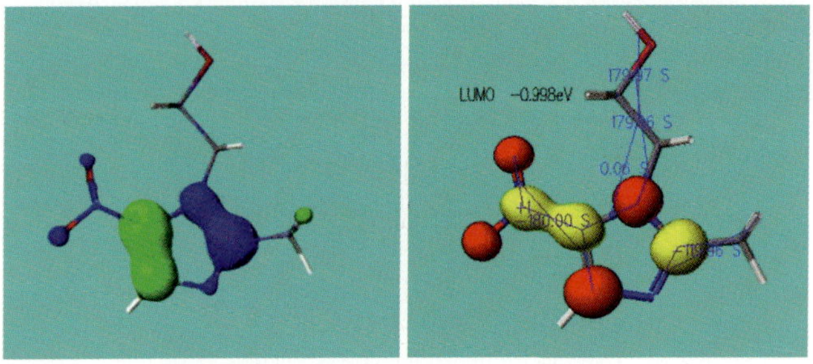

(a) (b)

Fig. 19.13 **(a) HOMO orbitals of metronidazole and calculated energy (b) LUMO orbitals of metronidazole and calculated energy. Image generated by Scigress Explorer Ultra 7.0**

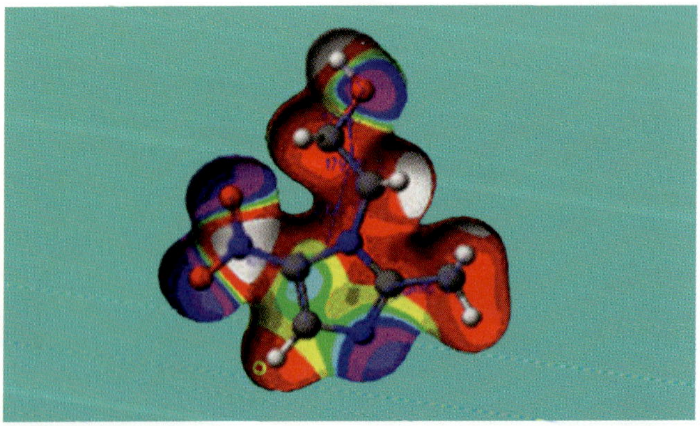

Fig. 19.14 **Electron density surface for metronidazole colored to show the electrostatic potential which indicates charge distribution of metronidazole. Red and white colored areas indicate positive electrostatic potential whereas green, blue, purple and cyan colored areas indicate negative electrostatic potential. Image generated by Scigress Explorer Ultra 7.0**

Fig. 19.15 Electrophilic susceptibility for metronidazole superimposed on the molecule of metronidazole. Image generated by Scigress Explorer Ultra 7.0

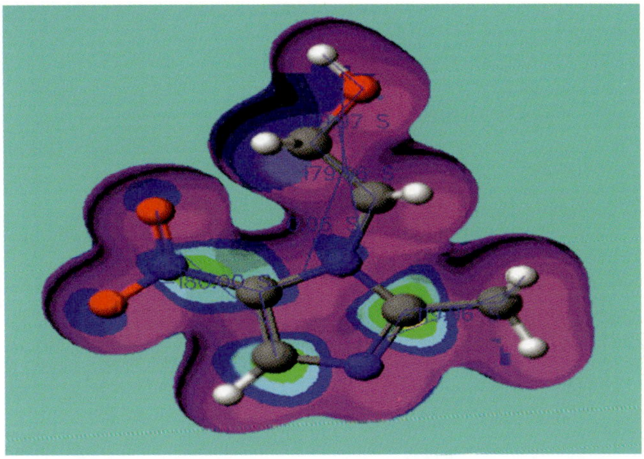

Fig. 19.16 Nucleophilic susceptibility for metronidazole superimposed on the molecule of metronidazole. Image generated by Scigress Explorer Ultra 7.0

Fig. 19.17 Partial charges calculated for metronidazole. Positively charged atoms are colored by red and negatively charged atoms are colored by yellow. Image generated by Scigress Explorer Ultra 7.0

Colour Plate 8

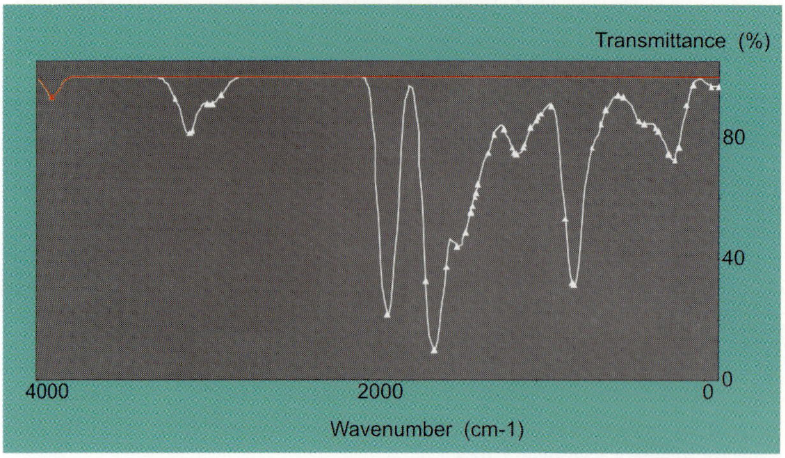

Fig. 19.18 IR spectral transition for metronidazole. Image generated by Scigress Explorer Ultra 7.0

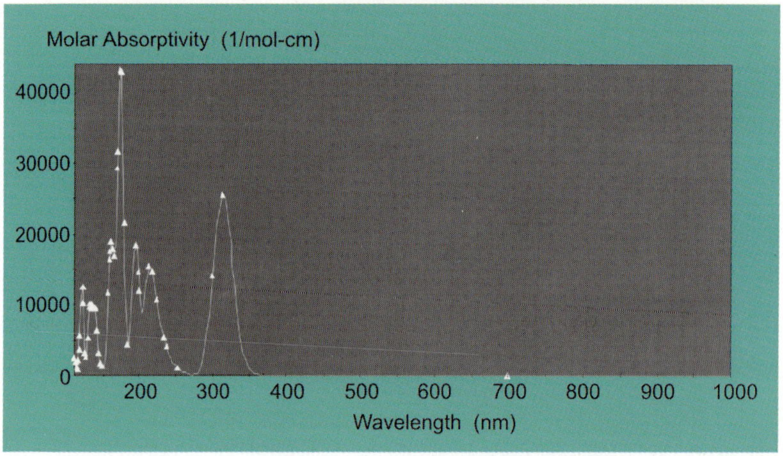

Fig. 19.19 UV visible spectral transition for metronidazole. Image generated by Scigress Explorer Ultra 7.0

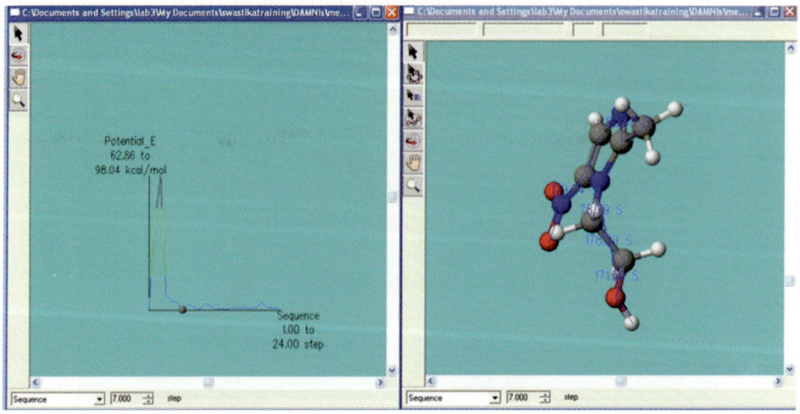

Fig. 19.20a Conformational search of metronidazole. Left window shows the potential energy map and right window shows the least energy conformer

Colour Plate 9

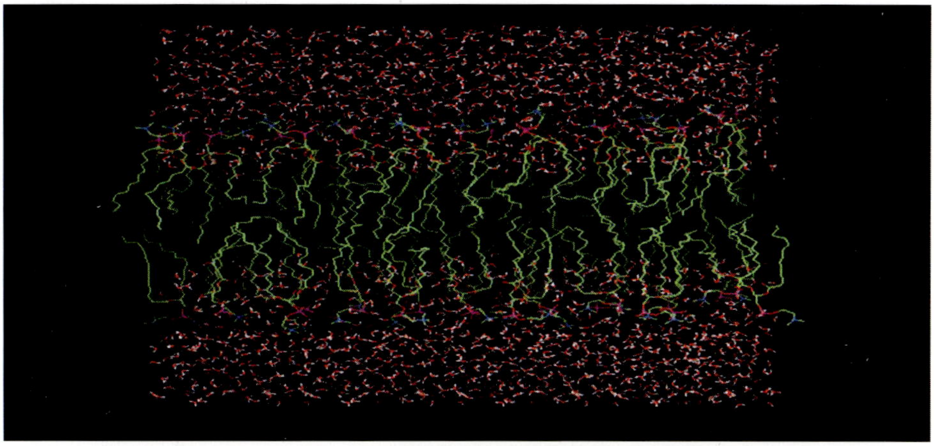

Fig. 19.22 Snapshot from molecular dynamics simulation of a solvated lipid bilayer (http://www.booksites.net/leach1/molecular lipids.gif.last visited on 18/04/2011)

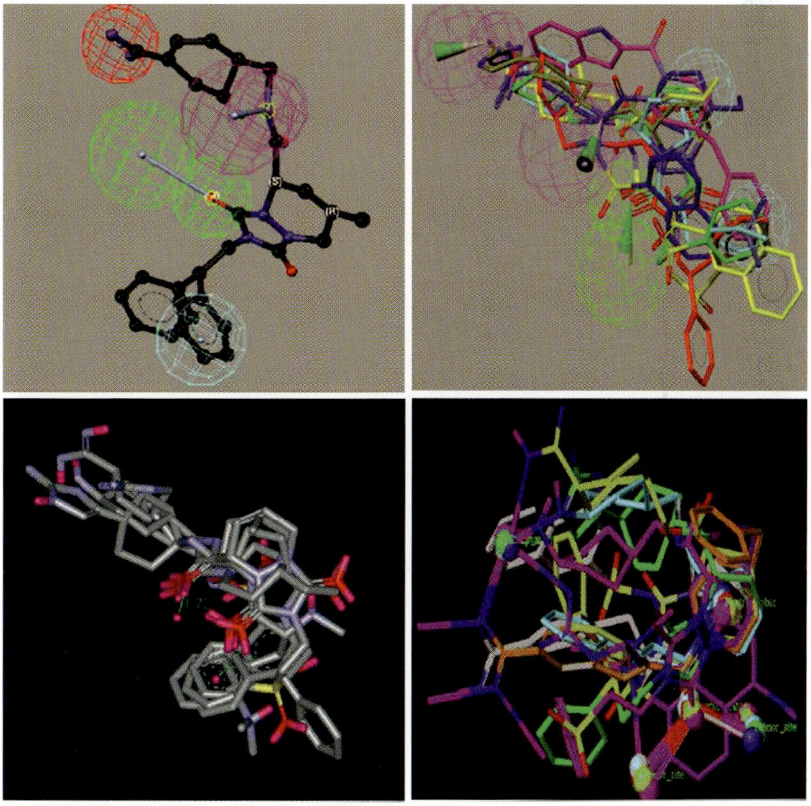

Fig. 19.23 The best hypotheses for thrombin: the manually generated pharmacophore that represents the target pharmacophore (top left); the best hypothesis generated for Catalyst (top right); GASP (bottom left); and DISCO (bottom right). (*Source:* Journal of Computer-Aided Molecular Design, **16**: 653–681, 2002)

Colour Plate 10

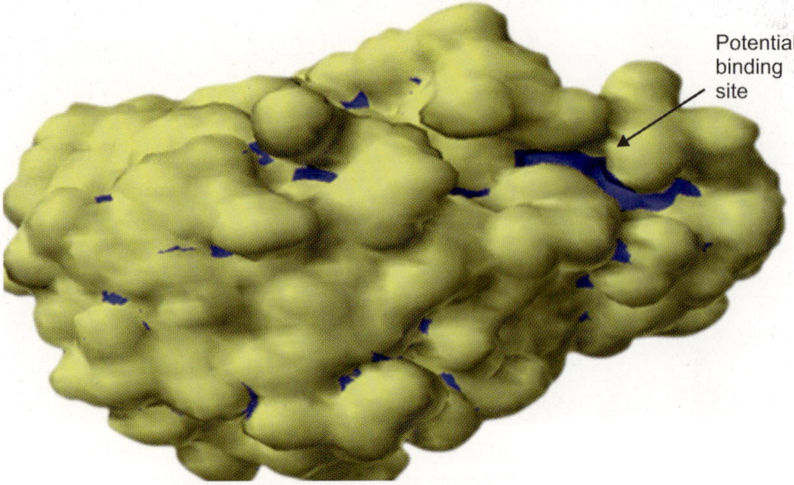

Fig. 19.25 **Active site in a receptor. Image generated by Scigress Explorer Ultra 7.0**

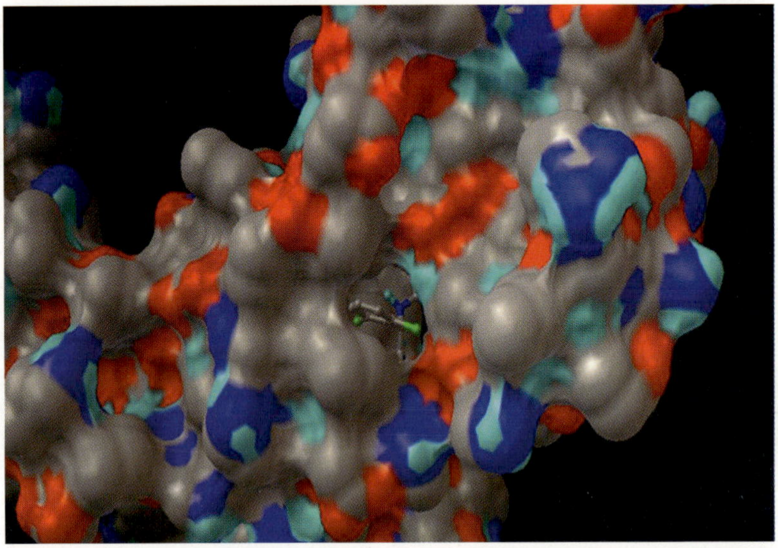

Fig. 19.26 **Snapshot of loviride docked into the non nucleoside inhibitory binding pocket of Reverse transcriptase enzyme of Human Immunodeficiency virus. The active site is represented by molecular surface mode whereas loviride is in ball and stick mode. Image generated by Autodock 4.0**

Colour Plate 11

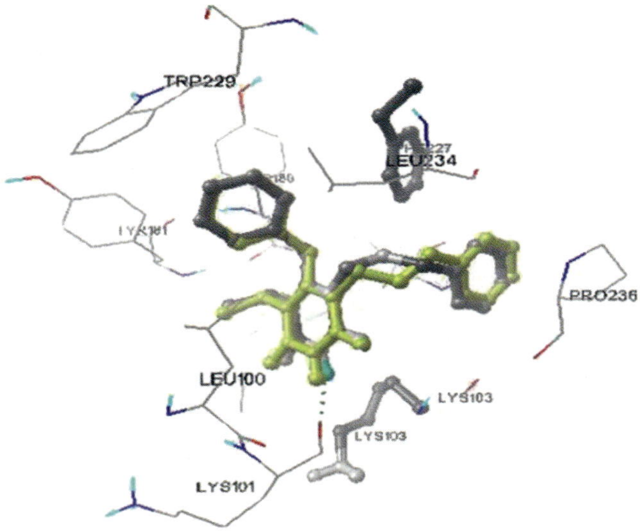

Fig. 19.27 Validation of docking protocol of TNK 651 into the active site pocket of Non nucleoside Inhibitory binding pocket of Reverse Transcriptase by Autodock 4.0. Docked conformer coloured by atom type, co-crystallised ligand coloured yellow, active site amino acid residues represented by sticks. [RMSD 0.46 Å (100 runs)]

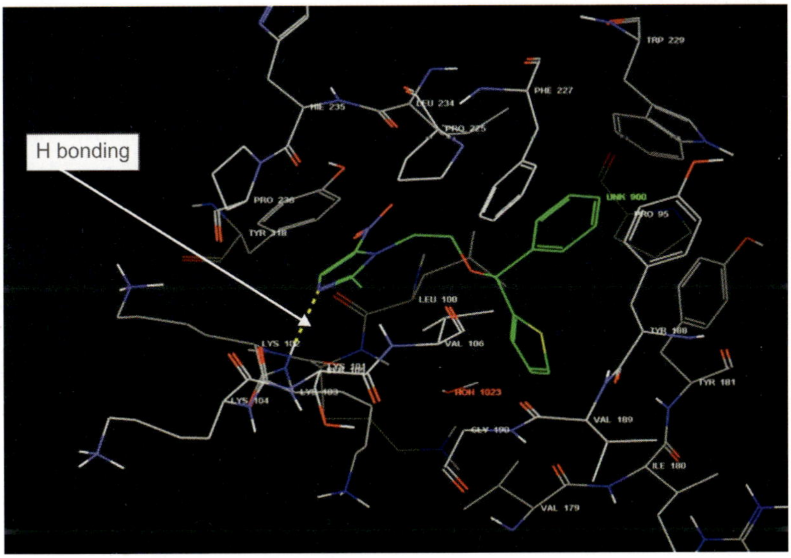

Fig. 19.28 Docked conformer of molecule in the active site pocket of non nucleoside Inhibitory binding pocket of Reverse Transcriptase. The ligand is shown in green while the active site amino acid residues are represented in sticks. Image generated by Glide

Colour Plate 12

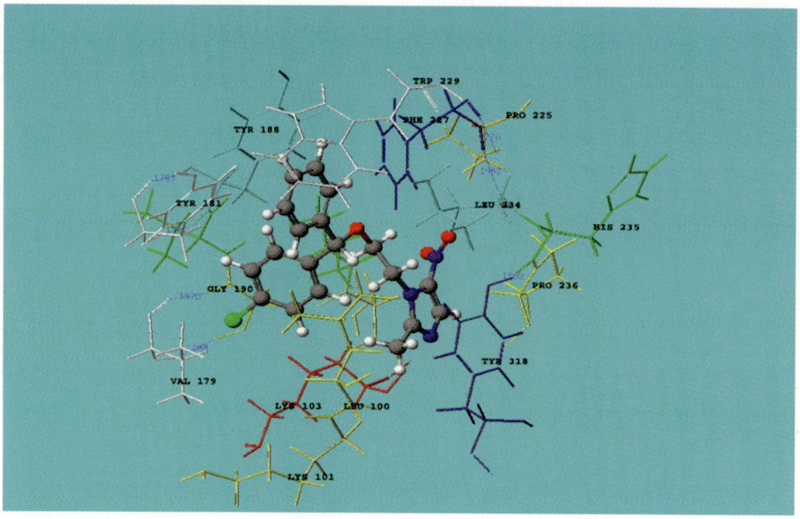

Fig. 19.29 **Docked molecule in the active site pocket of Reverse Transcriptase. Active site amino acid residues are represented as sticks colored according to labeled residue type (Sequence protocol-Karplus and Schultz Flexibility). The ligand is colored with the atoms as carbon: grey, hydrogen: white, nitrogen: blue, and oxygen: red (ball and stick model). Image generated by Scigress Explorer Ultra 7.0**

figures into the computer will not produce "**drug candidates**" neither will it provide an explanation of the mechanism of the action of the drug to its full intent. The medicinal chemist along with the computational chemist,the molecular biologist and other team workers with their experience, will still have to improve QSAR models, make a correct interpretation of results, propose hypotheses and prove the hypotheses with correct experimentation and validation of results.

FURTHER READING

1. C. Hansch and A. Leeo, "Exploring QSAR," American Chemical Society, Washington D.C., 1995.
2. H. Kubini, G. Folkers, and Y.C. Martin, (Eds.), "3D QSAR in Drug Design," Kluwer, Dordecht, 1998.
3. R.B. Silverman, "The Organic Chemistry of Drug Design and Drug Action," 2nd ed., Elsevier India Pvt. Ltd., 2004, p. 66.
4. C.D. Selassie in "Burger's Medicinal Chemistry and Drug Discovery," Vol. 1, D.J. Abraham, Ed., John Wiley & Sons, N.Y., 2003, p. 1.

19

Molecular Modelling

Swastika Ganguly*

Molecular modelling comprises of two words " Molecular" and "Modelling". "Molecular" implies that molecules are involved, whereas "modelling" can be defined as very simply as a process of representing molecular structures numerically and mimicking their behavior, thus helping in calculations and predictions of the behavior of the molecules in various systems using equations of quantum and classical physics. It is also described by different terms such as Computer Aided Drug Design (CADD), Computer Assisted Molecular Design (CAMD), Molecular Simulation and so on.

Fig. 19.1 Plastic models used in the past
(*Source:* http://www/kubmyl.de/last visited on 08/02/2010)

* Associate Professor, Department of Pharm. Sciences, Birla Institute of Technology, P.O. Mesra 835215, Ranchi (India).

In the not so distant past modeling was accomplished by plastic models (Fig. 19.1, Colour Plate 3). The first molecular 'models' were those which had been devised by Dreiding or Corey, Pauling and Koltun (CPK models). These models strove to represent the three dimensional structure of the molecules and were of good use as teaching aids and in understanding the behavior of molecules in research. However, all physical models suffered from limitations like tedious and time consuming construction with appropriate scale, difficulty in manipulating molecules, large occupancy of storage space and problems in transport from one location to another, thus making them unpopular with researchers.

With the advent of computers, molecular modelling has become a much easier process and spectacular advances have been made in the field of rational drug design.

Molecular modelling has opened up various ways of discovering new molecules with potential biological activities and its role in the rational drug design cannot be ignored. Today's molecular modelling covers various aspects like quantum chemical equations, three dimensional visualization and simulations of small molecules and macromolecules in virtual systems, conformational analyses, database search, computer software and hardware, computational methods to calculate properties of molecules, detailed information about the ligand receptor interactions and binding mode analyses of the active ligands to the receptor structure, receptor mapping, homology modelling of hitherto unknown targets, superimposition, ADME (absorption, distribution, metabolism and excretion) modelling, structure property relationships, etc. Molecular modelling considers the three dimensional structures of the molecules and it is hoped that this discipline can contribute significantly to the discovery of "intelligent" molecules in the field of pharmaceutical research.

Molecular modelling is defined as a range of computerized methods based on theoretical chemistry principles and experimental data that can be used either to analyze molecules and molecular systems or to predict molecular and biological properties. It is a virtual tool for understanding the function of a biological system and also for the prediction of specific activities of potential drug candidates.

Since long time, medicinal chemists have faced a number of challenges. Mankind has been combating deadly diseases like AIDS (Acquired Immunodeficiency syndrome), cancers of ovary and prostrate, MDR (Multiple drug resistant) and XDR (Extreme drug resistant) tuberculosis, Hepatitis B and C to name a few of them. Till date very few drugs are there in the market to combat these diseases and in most cases, aggressive therapy like radiation and surgery is required to help the patient survive. However, mortality rate is increasing day by day and there is a dearth of inexpensive and effective drugs in the market. As such, there is a burning need for investigation of the underlying causes of these diseascs and discovery of newer therapeutic molecules with maximum therapeutic activity and minimum side effects. The traditional methods of drug discovery have been expensive, tedious and time taking. Most of the time medicinal chemists have relied on their intuition and experience and resorted to trial and error methods in the synthesis of a large number of compounds finally embarking over one lead molecule after years and years of intensive research.

Molecular modelling looks at the biological processes at the molecular level while trying to understand the root causes of a disease. Here, the molecules are modeled based on the structure of the target, i.e. a receptor or an enzyme. This technique has, to some extent, narrowed down the search for potential molecules, decreased the unnecessary waste of chemicals and the irrational use of animals, saved precious time required in synthesis and evaluation of newer analogs and have given a considerable speed to drug discovery and development in the 21st century.

The first generation of rational drug design comprised of 1DQSAR (1 dimensional Qunatitative Structure Activity relationships) and 2D QSAR (2 dimensional Qunatitative Structure Activity relationships). However, these methods had their own limitations in that they were restricted only to the two dimensional approach and were restricted in their use when it came to providing information about the interactions of the ligand with the receptor. The limitations in these approaches and the use of computers in medicinal chemistry led to increasing interest in the field of molecular modelling since 1980s. Thus, this approach was known as the second generation of rational drug design, which could lead to a better representation of the ligands and the receptors in three dimension and biological activities could be better perceived.

Molecular modelling can be classified into two parts, direct drug design and indirect drug design (Fig. 19.2). Direct drug design is based on the fact that the three dimensional structure of the receptor is known. Indirect drug design is used when the receptor structure is not known and molecules are designed based on the comparative analyses of the structures of the active and inactive ligands and interpreting these by analyzing their interactions with a hypothetical receptor site.

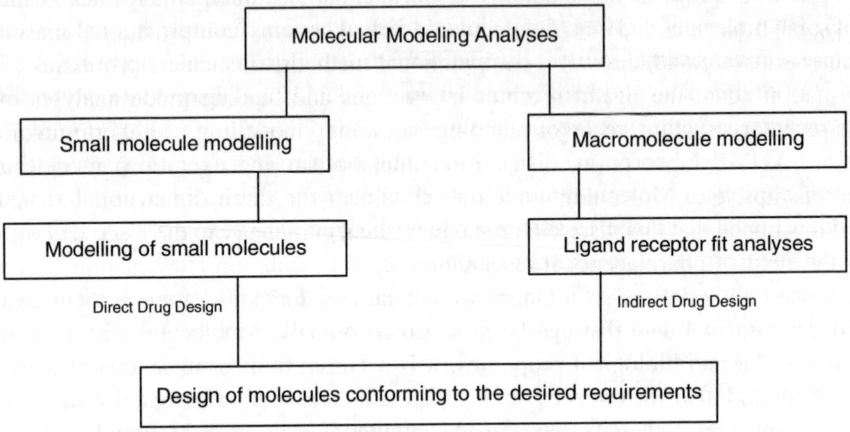

Fig. 19.2 Conceptual frame used in molecular modeling

(Reproduced from N. Claude Cohen, ed., Guidebook on Molecular Modelling in Drug Design, Academic Press Inc., p. 5.)

SOFTWARE FOR MOLECULAR MODELLING

Many companies have developed and marketed commercial software for molecular modeling. Every molecular modelling software should have minimum five basic modules as shown in Fig. 19.3.

Molecular modeling was once left to the expertise of computer scientists, but over the recent years, modeling tools have become well designed, user friendly and integrated for R & D efforts of pharmaceutical companies. Molecular modeling is strongly linked with the internet in various web based client server systems.

Drawing Chemical Structures

Drawing chemical structures had been a tedious job in the past. Today drawing structures has become relatively easy with the help of software available for this purpose. Most of the software programmes have the option of "cleaning the molecule" which implies that the molecule is checked for correct valency, correct hybridization, correct ring structure in case of ring compounds and the correct geometry of the molecule (Fig. 19.4).

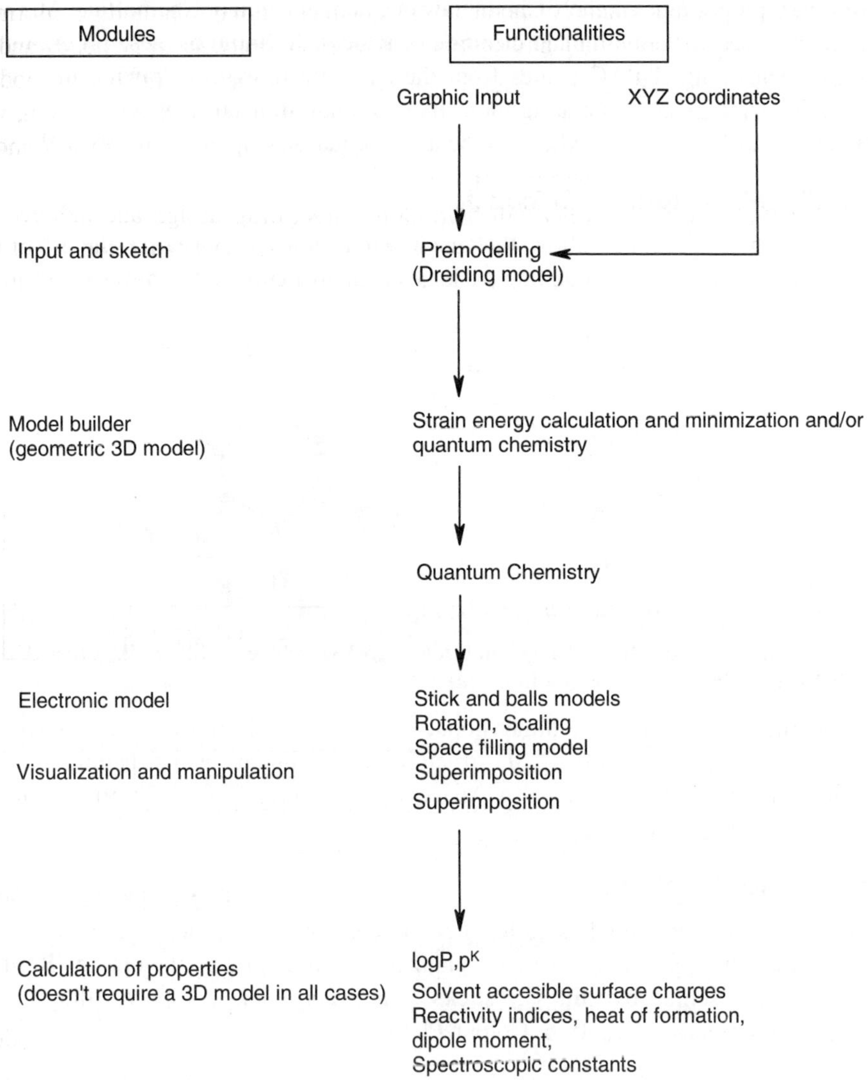

Fig. 19.3 Basic modules of a molecular modeling system

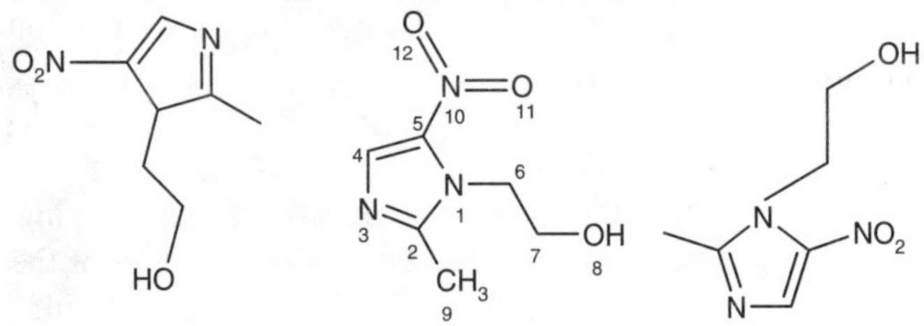

(a) (b) (c)

Fig. 19.4 (a) Structure of metronidazole generated by Chemoffice 10.0 (b) Structure of metronidazole generated by ACD Chemsketch (c) Structure of metronidazole generated by ISIS draw

Various software programmes namely ChemDraw or Chem 3D ultra of Chemoffice, ACD Chemsketch, ISIS Draw, etc. are used for drawing and cleaning of structures. Some of these programmes also have the provision of generating IUPAC names from the structure drawn or drawing the structure of the molecule from the name given, generating molecular formula, molecular weight, theoretical elemental analyses, ^{1}H NMR and ^{13}C NMR predictions, heat of formation, dipole moments and log P.

Conversion of 2D-Structure to 3D-Model

Molecular modelling programmes allow the medicinal chemist to visualize the structures in three dimensions. Almost all molecular modelling packages available contain the provision of visualizing 3D

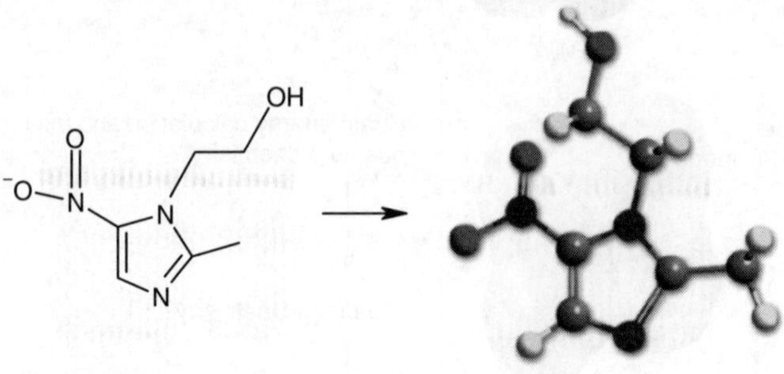

Fig. 19.5 Conversion of 2D-structure of metronidazole to 3D-structure in Chem 3D Ultra (Carbon in grey; Oxygen in red; Nitrogen in blue; Hydrogen in green)

structures of the molecules. The three dimensional structures can be drawn from scratch, i.e. drawing each bond and every atom to construct a 3D structure or two dimensional structures can be converted to three dimensional structures automatically. An example of conversion of 2D structure to 3D structure is illustrated in Fig. 19.5, Colour Plate 3.

Visualization of 3D-Structures

The beauty of molecular modelling lies in the three dimensional visualization of the molecules. In most of the molecular modelling programmes this visualization is provided by the option "**Rendering**". The molecules can be represented by "lines", "sticks", "ball and sticks", "space filling" (CPK)," solid spheres" or "dotted surfaces" (Fig. 19.6, Colour Plate 4).

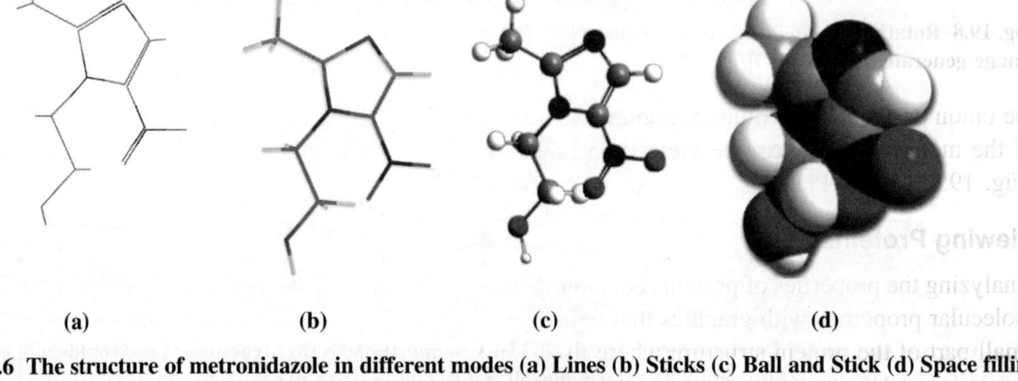

(a) (b) (c) (d)

Fig. 19.6 The structure of metronidazole in different modes (a) Lines (b) Sticks (c) Ball and Stick (d) Space filling (CPK model). Image generated by Chem3D Ultra of ChemOffice 10

The solvent accessible surface as well as the various Connolly surfaces (solid, translucent, wire mesh) (Fig. 19.7, Colour Plate 4) can also be visualized and these can be used for various modelling operations, like union, intersection or subtraction, helping in the easy determination of parameters like

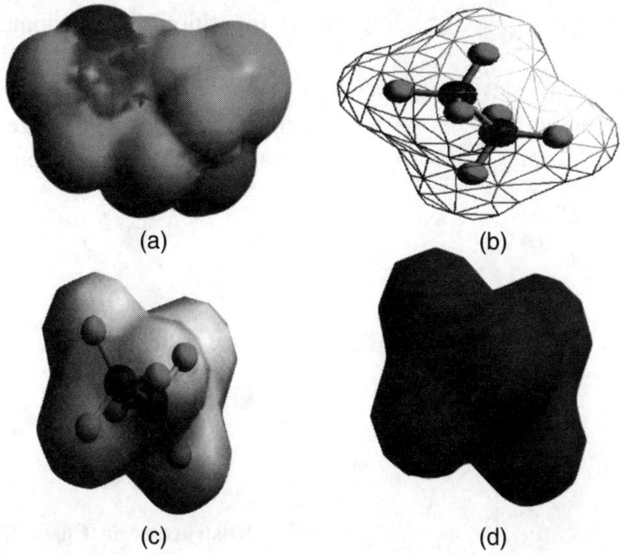

Fig. 19.7 Various surfaces (a) Solvent accessible surface of ethane (b) Wire mesh Connolly surface of ethane (c) Translucent Connolly surface of ethane (d) Solid Connolly surface of ethane. Image generated by ChemOffice 10

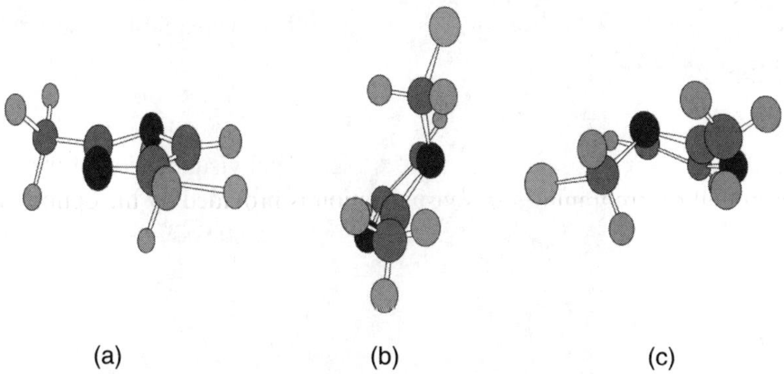

Fig. 19.8 Rotation of a molecule in three planes (a) Rotation in X axis (b) Rotation in Z axis (c) Rotation in Y axis. Image generated by ChemOffice 10

the union or difference volumes among a series of molecules. For better understanding of the structure of the molecules, they can be viewed and rotated in different planes, viz., X axis, Y axis and Z axis (Fig. 19.8, Colour Plate 4).

Viewing Proteins

Analyzing the properties of proteins containing thousands of atoms is best accomplished by representing molecular properties with graphics that reduce complexity. Drug design focuses only on that relatively small part of the protein structure where the ligand binds, therefore it is important for the modelers to

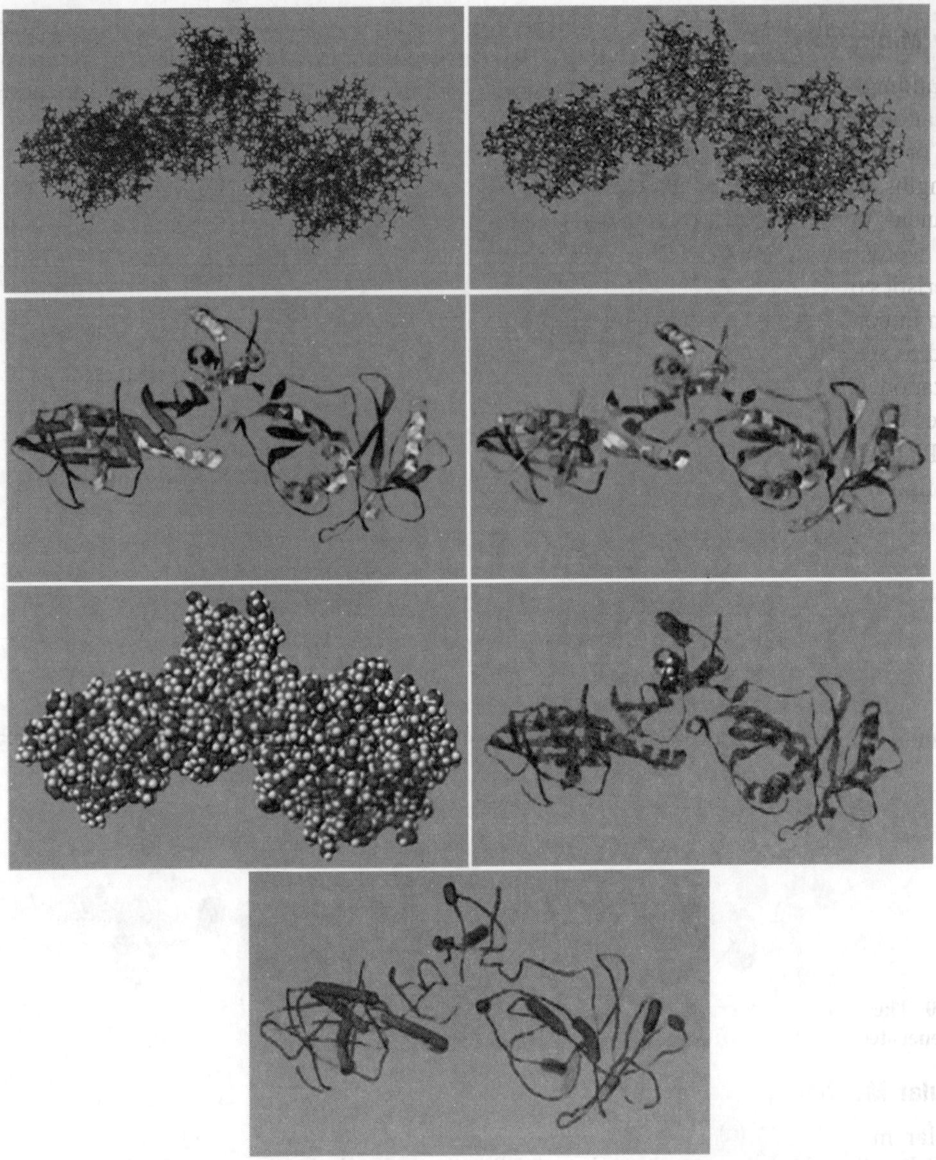

Fig. 19.9 Crystal structure of Reverse Transcriptase (PDB code 1RT2) ; Clockwise, from top left: lines, stick, flat ribbon of secondary structure, solid ribbon colored by Karpus and Schulz flexibility, CPK/space filling, Threaded pod, Threaded spools of Chou-Fasman Alpha helix. Image generated by Scigress Explorer Ultra 7.0

easily visualize and identify only the active binding sites and their ligands, to visualize and manipulate groups of atoms in the protein (Fig. 19.9, Colour Plate 5), display important hydrogen bond interactions of the receptor with the ligands, manipulate the sequences of proteins for modelling of unknown proteins, color the protein by different properties, e.g., hydrophobicity and hydrophilicity, label atoms that have bad steric interactions amongst themselves and extract important information from sequence alignments.

Energy Minimization

After building the 3D structure of the molecule, the first step to be carried out is called energy minimization. Most molecular modelling programmes contain the option in the form of "**Minimize energy**" or "**Optimize the molecule**". While building the molecule the process may result in unfavourable bond lengths, bond angles, torsion angles, etc. The energy minimization process strives to correct these discrepancies of the molecule and obtains an optimum structure which is most stable with least energy. In other words the optimum structure of a molecule is that which displays the correct properties and characteristics of a molecule. The process involves the calculation of the energy of the starting molecule, variation in bond lengths, bond angles, torsion angles, and generation of a new structure, which is then analyzed to see whether the new structure is energetically more stable or not. The process of energy minimization will further continue if it is found that the structure still remains unstable and will terminate only after the most stable structure with the least energy (energy minimum) is obtained (Fig. 19.10, Colour Plate 5). Both classical molecular mechanics and semi-empirical quantum mechanics can be used to find minimum energy conformations of the molecule.

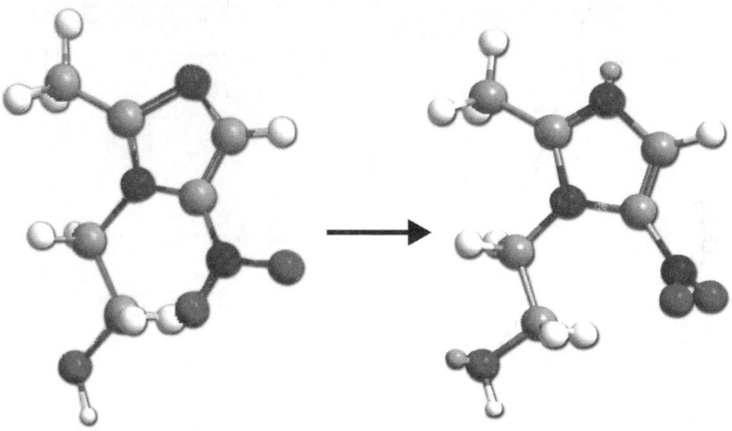

(a) (b)

Fig. 19.10 The process of energy minimization a) Molecule before minimization b) Molecule after minimization. Image generated by Chem 3D Ultra of ChemOffice 10

Molecular Mechanics Methods

Molecular mechanics methods, also known as classical mechanical methods, do not take into consideration the electronic motions and calculate the energy of a system by considering only the nuclear positions of the molecule. A molecule is treated as series of spheres (atoms) connected by springs (bonds). The different interactions and energies resulting from bond stretching, angle bending, torsional energies and non bonded interactions are known as force fields (Figs 19.11 and 19.12, Colour Plate 6). These force fields are such that they can reproduce the structural characteristics of the molecule as well as predict other properties of the molecule. However, the force fields are empirical and there is no correct form of force field.

The equations which are derived from the molecular mechanics methods are used to compare the geometry of the given molecule to the classical mechanical ideal value. Differences from the ideal value are summed up to a relative energy quantity known as potential energy. The molecule is then optimized by moving and adjusting its atoms to lower the sum of the differences in energy, thus lowering the potential energy until energy changes become minimum.

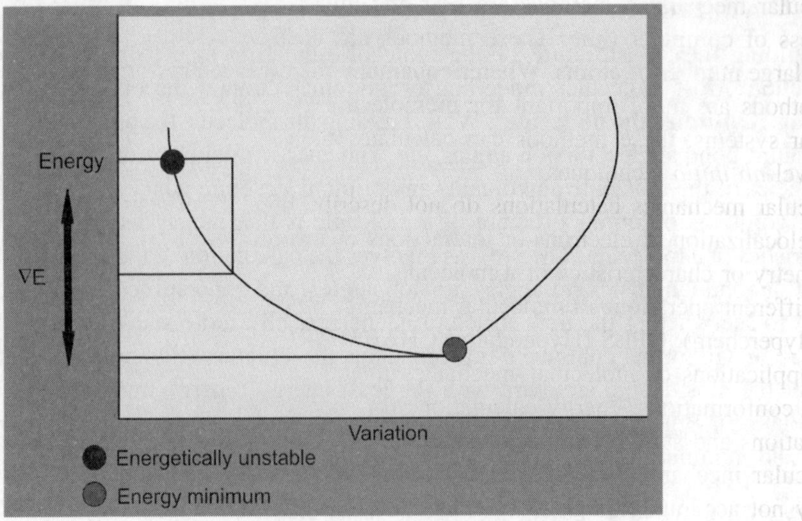

Fig. 19.11 Energy minimization (reproduced from Introduction to Medicinal Chemistry, by J.L. Patrick, page 323)

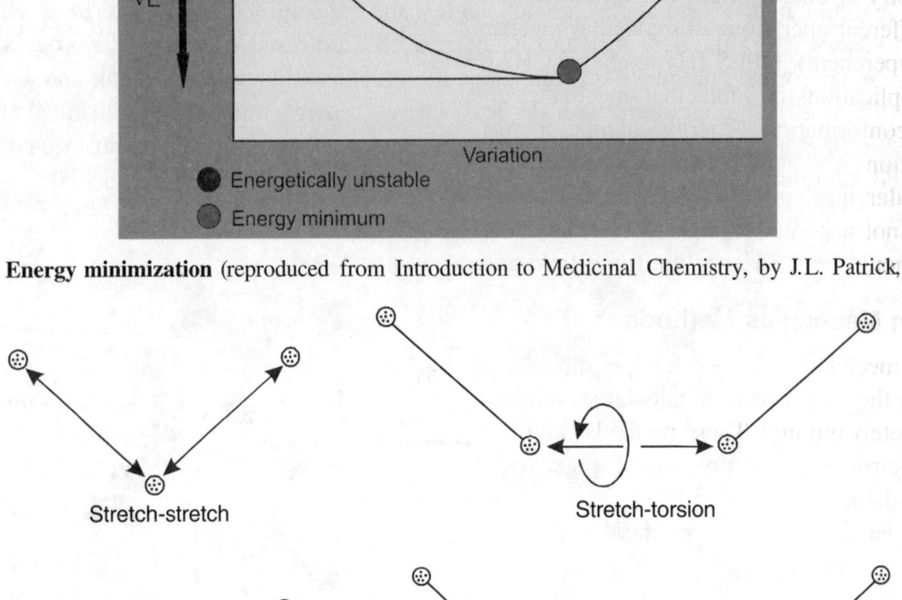

Fig. 19.12 Schematic representation of four key contributions to molecular mechanics force field: bond stretching, angle bending, torsional energies and non-bonded interactions

(*Source:* http://chem.wayne edu%7Ehbs/Chm6440/chem6440basis.ppt.last visited on 18/04/2011.)

Molecular mechanical methods are however, much faster than quantum mechanical calculations, taking less of computer time. These methods are used to calculate the energy of a system which contains large number of atoms. Whereas quantum chemical methods can be used for small molecules, these methods are more important for biomolecules. Moroever, for specific and well-parameterized molecular systems, these methods can calculate values that are nearer to experimental values than lower level *ab initio* techniques.

Molecular mechanics calculations do not describe bond formation, bond breaking, or systems in which delocalization of electrons or interactions of molecular orbitals play a decisive role in defining the geometry or characteristics of a molecule.

The different operations in molecular mechanics methods are MM2, MM3, AMBER (Hyperchem), BIO+ (Hyperchem), OPLS (Hyperchem) CHARMM, COSMIC, SYBYL, MMFF, DREIDING etc.

The applications of molecular mechanics methods lies in minimization of energy, generation of different conformations, energy calculations for specific conformations, identification of most stable conformations and study of molecular motion.

Molecular mechanics works well for ordinary organic compounds. However these methods are generally not accurate enough to calculate reaction energies. If it is at all practicable, an electronic method should be used after the force field geometry optimization.

Quantum Mechanics Methods

Quantum mechanics uses the laws of quantum physics to calculate the properties of the molecule and represents the electrons in a calculation unlike the molecular mechanics methods where the electrons are completely ignored. These methods can be used to obtain the properties of the molecule that depend on the electronic distribution and also specifically to study chemical reactions in which the bonds are broken and formed.

Molecular properties can be derived from the Schrodinger equation (Eq. 1),

$$H\Psi = E\Psi \qquad \text{... (Eq. 1)}$$

where, E = energy of the system relative to one in which all atomic particles are separated to infinite distances

Ψ = wave function which defines the Cartesian and spin coordinates of the atomic particles

H = Hamiltonian operator which includes terms for both potential and kinetic energy.

However, as this equation can be solved for very small molecules a number of approximations have to be made for calculations of polyatomic systems. The first approximation lies in assuming that the nuclei are motionless and electrons move around the fixed nuclei (the Born Oppenheimer approximation). The second approximation allows the wave function Ψ to be represented as the product of one-electron (or spin) orbitals. Basis functions are the functions that are used to describe these orbitals and are referred to as the Linear Combination of Atomic Orbitals (LCAO) theory. After derivation of the orbitals the orbital coefficients defining the energy of the system are calculated by means of Hartree-Fock theory.

Ab Initio Methods

Ab initio means "from first principles". These methods are repetitive processes based on SCF (self consistent field) methods in which an initial guess for the value of the coefficients is progressively refined until it provides consistent values. The more the orbitals used for the calculation, the more accurate the results are but the calculations are slower.

These methods are most useful for cases where there is no experimental data to work upon, but the main disadvantage of this method is that more computer power is needed. Ab initio method is much more rigorous, and are useful for systems containing less number of atoms (tens of atoms). In general, *ab initio* methods are able to reproduce laboratory measurements for properties such as the heat of formation, ionization potential, UV/Visible spectra and molecular geometry.

Semi Empirical Methods

These methods use approaches similar to *ab initio* methods and some experimental data also. Semi empirical methods use the types of wave functions which include the Slater type orbitals (STO) and Gaussian type orbitals (GTO). Semi empirical methods treat the linear combination of orbitals by repetitive computational processes, which establish a self-consistent field (SCF) and minimize the energy of the system. The earlier methods were not reliable for calculating geometry, neither gave reliable energies but were useful for calculating shapes of molecular orbitals and charges. Various improved methods such as CNDO (Complete Neglect of Differential Overlap), INDO (Intermediate Neglect of Differential Overlap), MNDO (Modified Neglect of Differential Overlap), MNDO-3, AM1, PM3 are used. For ordinary molecules AM1 or PM3 are probably the best to try. Semi empirical methods are most useful for better geometry optimization than force fields, geometries for molecules including atoms, which are not parameterized in a force field, qualitative prediction of IR frequencies, and total electron density surface for graphical display. They are not really good enough for reaction energies and equilibrium constants.

While semi empirical methods require less computer resources than *ab initio* methods, they still require more computer time than molecular mechanics methods. In general, calculations are routinely performed on compounds which contain up to 100 atoms. Semi empirical methods are also cheaper than *ab initio* electronic structure methods, but not as accurate. Along with this, the main disadvantage of the method is that its application is restricted to systems for which appropriate parameters have been developed.

Molecular Properties

Once the molecular structure is built and energy minimized, various properties of the molecule can be calculated. Steric energies, heat of formation, dipole moment, electron density, electrostatic potential, partial charges, log P, HOMO and LUMO energies can be calculated for further molecular modelling

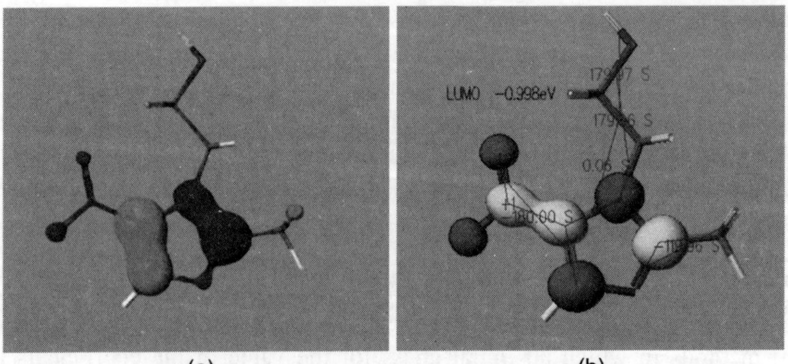

(a) (b)

Fig. 19.13 (a) HOMO orbitals of metronidazole and calculated energy (b) LUMO orbitals of metronidazole and calculated energy. Image generated by Scigress Explorer Ultra 7.0

(Figs 19.13 to 19.17, Colour Plates 6 and 7). IR and UV visible spectra can also be visualized using some molecular modeling programmes (Figs 19.18 and 19.19, Colour Plate 8).

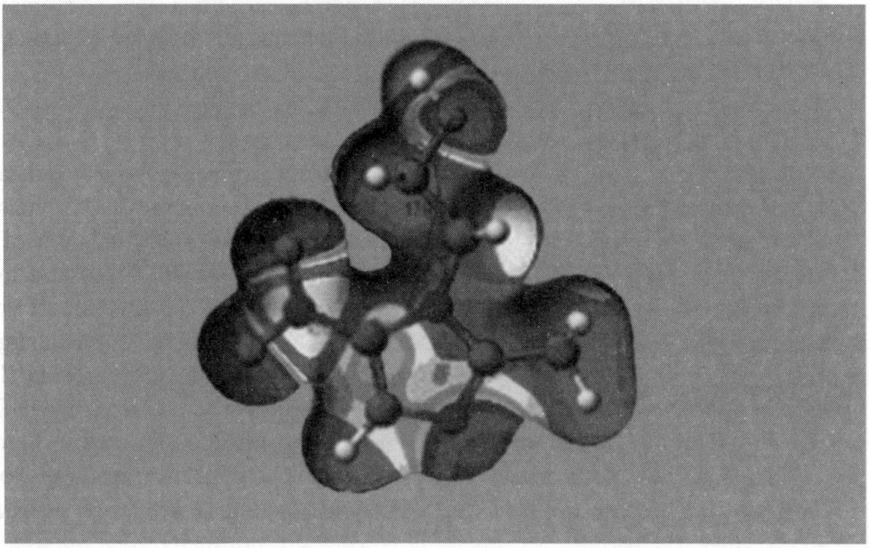

Fig. 19.14 Electron density surface for metronidazole colored to show the electrostatic potential which indicates charge distribution of metronidazole. Red and white colored areas indicate positive electrostatic potential whereas green, blue, purple and cyan colored areas indicate negative electrostatic potential. Image generated by Scigress Explorer Ultra 7.0

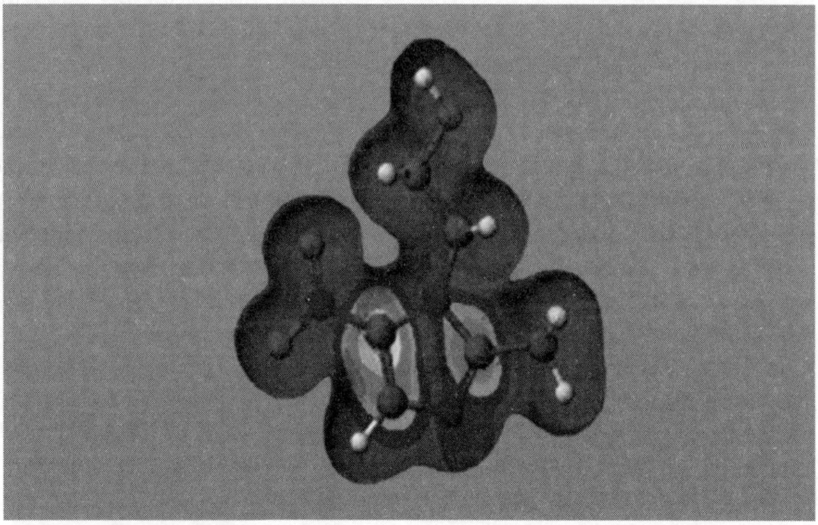

Fig. 19.15 Electrophillic susceptibility for metronidazole superimposed on the molecule of metronidazole. Image generated by Scigress Explorer Ultra 7.0

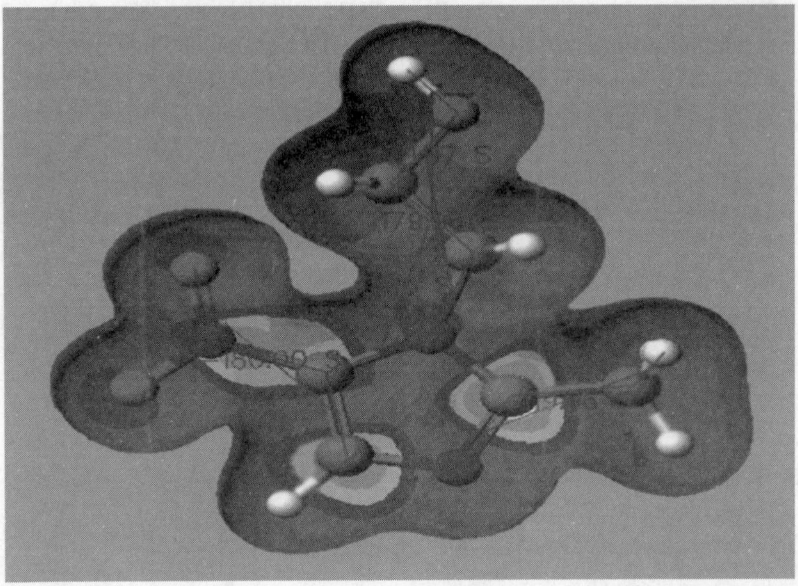

Fig. 19.16 Nucleophillic susceptibility for metronidazole superimposed on the molecule of metronidazole. Image generated by Scigress Explorer Ultra 7.0

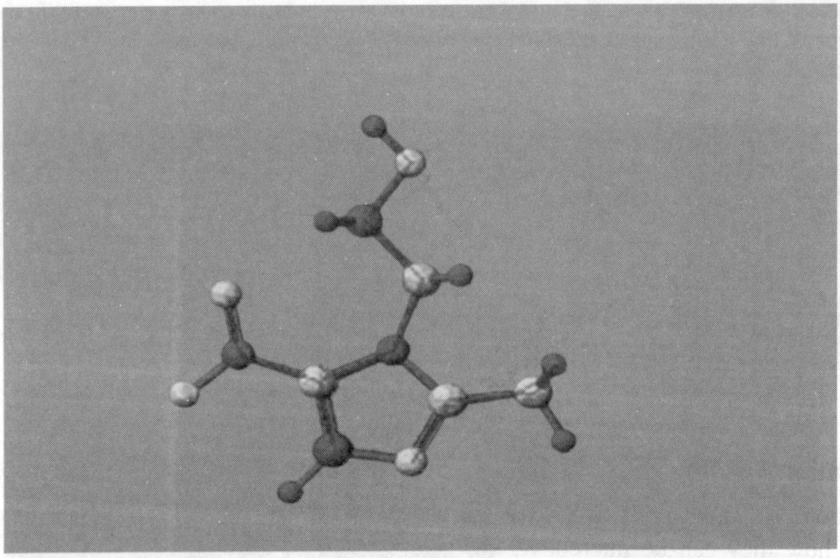

Fig. 19.17 Partial charges calculated for metronidazole. Positively charged atoms are colored by red and negatively charged atoms are colored by yellow. Image generated by Scigress Explorer Ultra 7.0

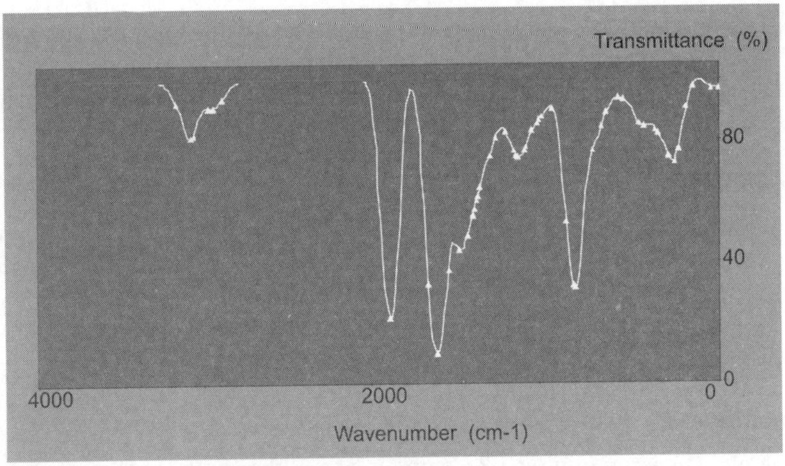

Fig. 19.18 IR spectral transition for metronidazole. Image generated by Scigress Explorer Ultra 7.0

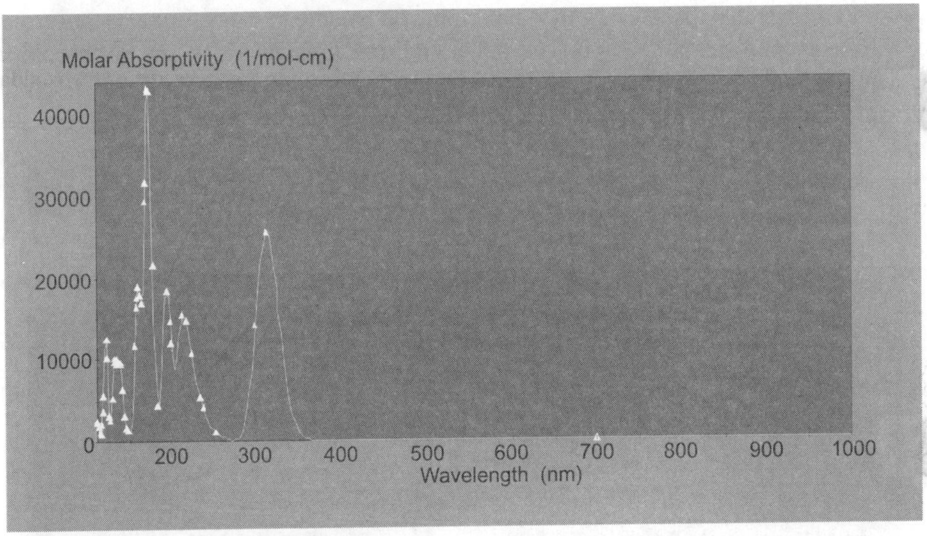

Fig. 19.19 UV visible spectral transition for metronidazole. Image generated by Scigress Explorer Ultra 7.0

Conformational Analysis

Conformation of a molecule is defined as the way in which the atoms of the molecule are arranged in space and how they can be interconverted by rotation about the single bonds. The properties of a molecule depend on the conformation it can adopt. Conformational analysis is the study of the conformers of a molecule and the way they influence the behavior of a molecule. A principal component of the conformational analysis is conformational search, a search which can identify the preferred conformers, that is, the conformers which determine the actual behaviour of the molecule. A conformational search is extremely important as the conformations generated are typically used as starting points for biomolecular docking, pharmacophore modeling, 3D database searching, 3D-QSAR, and other molecular modeling techniques.

Currently various methods of conformational search for small molecules are systematic search, random search, distance geometry methods and molecular dynamics methods.

Before we embark on learning about different methods of conformational search we should know what the local energy minimum is and what the global energy minimum is.

Local Energy Minima

When energy minimization is carried out of a molecule, the least energy structure is obtained which is considered to be the most stable one. This is however, not the least energy structure. Energy minimization stops as soon as it finds the first and foremost stable conformer. It is like dropping water from a particular point on the hill and the first place where the water accumulates downhill is considered to be the lowest point of the hill.

Global Energy Minima

What is, then, the global energy minimum? Continuing from the above, to measure the lowest point of a hill we need to drop water from each and every point on the hill, and then measure all the distances where the water accumulates downhill for each and every particular point of the hill. The lowest point will be the one where the distance is the maximum.To obtain the most stable conformation of a molecule, different conformations should be generated and their energies are to be compared. The conformer with the least energy is the one with the global energy minimum (Fig. 19.20, Colour Plate 8).

The global minimum is thus, the most interesting, and often a representative of an equilibrium conformer found at room temperature. However, the best conformation depends on our lookout and our needs. Conformational analysis may ignore many other variables like the effect of solvent and the quality of the energy reported at the given theory level.

(a)

Fig. 19.20a Conformational search of metronidazole. Left window shows the potential energy map and right window shows the least energy conformer

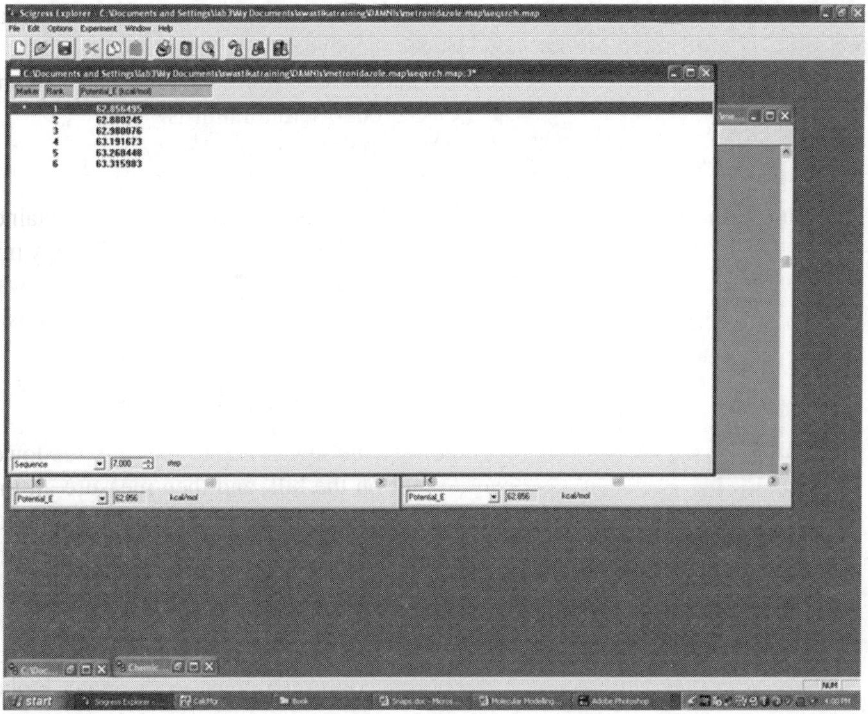

(b)

Fig. 19.20b The conformational analysis window shows that the least energy conformer is obtained at an energy value of 62.856

Systematic Search

In traditional systematic search, as the words imply, in the starting geometry of the molecule, the atoms are represented as rigid spheres and the bonds are represented by lines connecting the atoms. The torsional angles are varied at regular increments. Conformations are generated by rotating the bonds by the fixed increment. At each conformation, each and every atom pair are analysed to determine the steric interactions between them and the steric energies generated as a result of the interactions. The total number of conformers calculated by a systematic search is based on $(360/A)^T$, where A is the torsional angle increment, T is the rotatable number of bonds.

These conformations are tabulated in order of their stability. High energy (sterically unfavored) conformers are rejected. Unlike molecular dynamics and distance geometry methods where conformers can be allowed over a broad range, the systematic search method is based on the all or none concept, i.e. the conformers are either allowed or not allowed. The most stable conformers are selected, energy minimized and their structures are compared.

Random Search Methods

Whereas systematic search methods explore the energy surface of the molecule in a predictable fashion, random search is the opposite of systematic search. The steps are represented in the flow chart in Fig. 19.21. The user provides a certain conformation, which is the starting conformation. A random change is made in this conformation and a new structure is generated, which is energy minimized. If this structure has not been generated before, it is stored and iteration is started on the next conformer, this procedure goes on until there are no new structures generated.

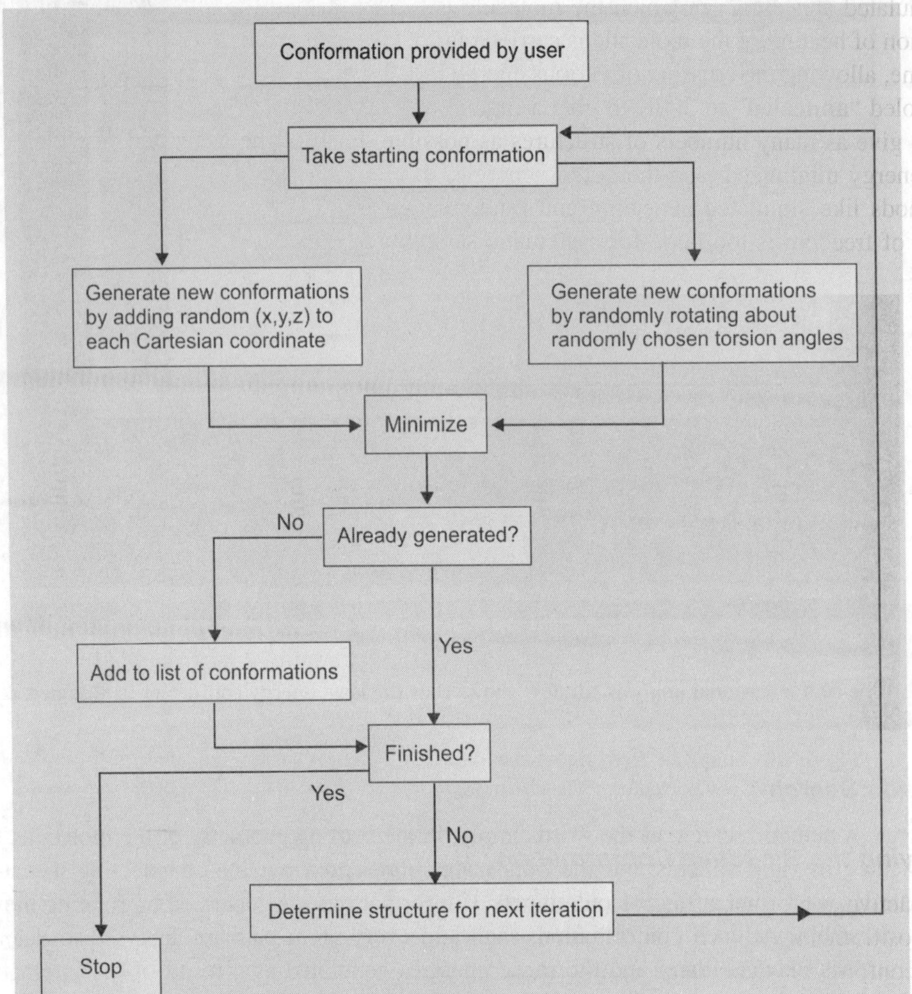

Fig. 19.21 Flow chart steps followed by a random conformational search

(Reproduced from Molecular Modelling, Principles and Applications by Andrens R. Leach, Addison Wesley Longman Limited, England, 1996, p. 423)

Distance Geometry Methods

In distance geometry methods, a matrix of upper and lower interatomic distance bounds is calculated. This matrix contains the maximum and minimum values permitted to each interatomic distance in the molecule. Values are randomly assigned to each interatomic distance between its upper and lower bounds. The distance matrix is then converted into a trial set of Cartesian coordinates and the fourth step is the refinement of the trial set of coordinates. The distance geometry methods do not guarantee generation of all possible conformers and are not practical for large structures.

Distance geometry along with MM methods gives superior results to MM methods alone.

Molecular Dynamics Methods

In molecular dynamics methods a number of conformers can be generated by using a method named as "Simulated annealing" in which the molecule is heated virtually to a temperature of 800-1000K.A simulation of heating of the molecule is carried out by the programme, and the energy barriers, are thus overcome, allowing the crossing of various energy saddle points. After a certain time, the molecules are then cooled "**annealed**" to 300K to give a final structure. The process can be repeated as many times so as to give as many numbers of structures as possible. Each of the generated structures can then be taken, energy minimized, and their steric energies are measured (Fig. 19.22, Colour Plate 9).

Methods like simulated annealing and random search should be considered when the number of degrees of freedom is too large for systematic sampling.

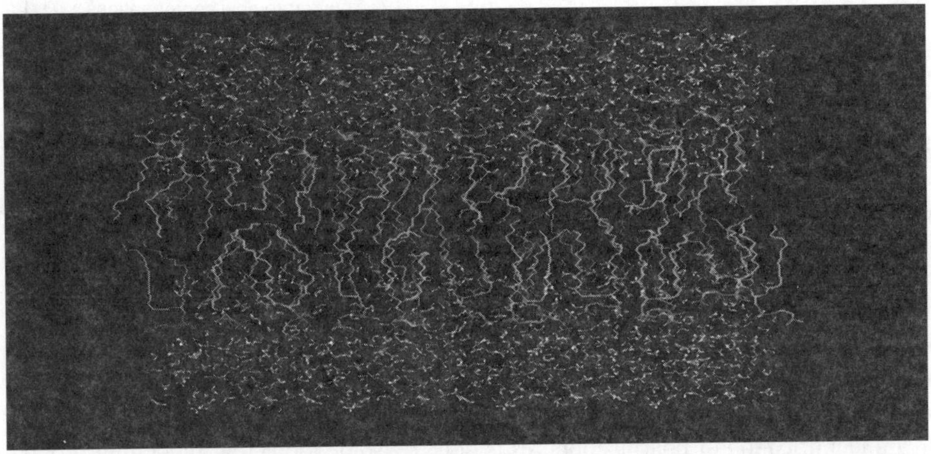

Fig. 19.22 Snapshot from molecular dynamics simulation of a solvated lipid bilayer (http://www.booksites.net/leach1/molecular lipids.gif.last visited on 18/04/2011)

Identifying the Bioactive Conformation

The bioactive conformer of a molecule is the conformation in which it binds to the receptor, i.e., the actual position in which the molecule binds to the receptor. Though, we may tend to think that the least energy conformer is the bioactive conformer, it is just possible that the bioactive conformer may not be the least energy conformer. There are different methods of identification of bioactive conformation like X-ray crystallography (known method for determining the exact three-dimensional shapes of macromolecules), NMR spectroscopy, active analog approach and ensemble distance geometry approach.

Pharmacophore Identification

A pharmacophore is defined as the essential arrangement of functional groups necessary to produce a biological response. The traditional approach of identifying pharmacophores is through structure activity relationship studies. A set of biologically active molecules producing a certain activity by the same mechanism are thought to have the same pharmacophoric features. Pharmacophores may be topologic or topographic. Topologic are based on connectivity indices and topographic are based on 3D or geometric patterns.

Pharmacophore generation programs are particularly used when a series of active compounds is known but the three-dimensional structure of the receptor site is unknown.

The identification of pharmacophoric groups involve steps like selection of a set of active analogs, division of the structure into different classes of pharmacophoric groups, analysis of the maximum number of common pharmacophoric groups in all the selected active analogs, ascertaining the geometric feasibility in aligning the equivalent pharmacophoric groups in different analogs and finally testing the pharmacophore hypothesis.

Different methods of identifying a pharmacophore like X-ray crystallography, structure alignment, and automatic identification by various software programmes exist.

In X-ray crystallography, the crystal structure of a target protein can be downloaded from the Protein Data Bank (www.rcsb.org) and the protein ligand complex can be studied to identify the binding interactions of the ligand with the active site in the receptor. The distances between the binding groups of the ligand and the complimentary groups of the receptor are measured to see whether they are within the bonding distances. Once the groups responsible for binding are identified, their positions can be mapped to find the pharmacophore.

Structural alignment methods are based on conformational search of the active molecules, obtaining the preferred conformer and defining the common groups which have some property in common. The molecules are aligned and superimposed at specific points in a particular way. The common points are then joined, the distances between them are calculated by a least squares calculation and the pharmacophore is derived. At the least, the pharmacophore needs three points of connection represented by a triangle, though a pharmacophore may have more number of common points. Several different superpositioning procedures such as manual or automatic fitting by rigid body rotation or flexible fitting procedures where both r.m.s. (root mean square) deviation between the fitted atom pairs and the conformational energies are minimized (FITIT method).

Automatic identification of pharmacophores is done by some molecular modelling programmes like DISCO, CATALYST, HIPHOP and GASP, etc. (Fig. 19.23, Colour Plate 9.) The programmes can identify the important binding centres in a particular molecule for example, H bond donors, H bond acceptors, aromatic rings, acidic groups, basic groups, positively charged centres and hydrophobic centres involving hydrocarbon skeletons of three or more carbon atoms. The main differences between the programs lie in the algorithms used for the superimposition of the dataset and in the way in which conformational flexibility is handled.

Pharmacophore models are very useful for medicinal chemists during novel lead identification as well as lead optimization. The pharmacophore geometry can be extremely important and can serve as a reference point for searching compounds with the same geometry in the available chemical library or a chemical database. If one is interested in synthesizing a few compounds with similar pharmacophoric geometry, the linking bonds to the pharmacophores may be used to search for scaffolds. A pharmacophore hypothesis can also be useful to generate a library of compounds with some small variations in the geometry. The library becomes useful for the search of finding an improved compound. Several programs described in the literature like NEW LEAD, SPROUT and HOOK can carry out this procedure to a certain extent. In 3D QSAR techniques, superimposition or alignment is an important step (as discussed in the previous chapter). A pharmacophore model can well serve as the basis for such a alignment. In approaches like CoMFA, where there is no definite algorithm for alignment of the dataset, the pharmacophore modelling can be a good initiator. The limitations of pharmacophore modelling is the existence of multiple binding modes of the ligands to the receptors, restrictions in variation from the pharmacophore geometry in design of newer compounds and constraining of the conformations.

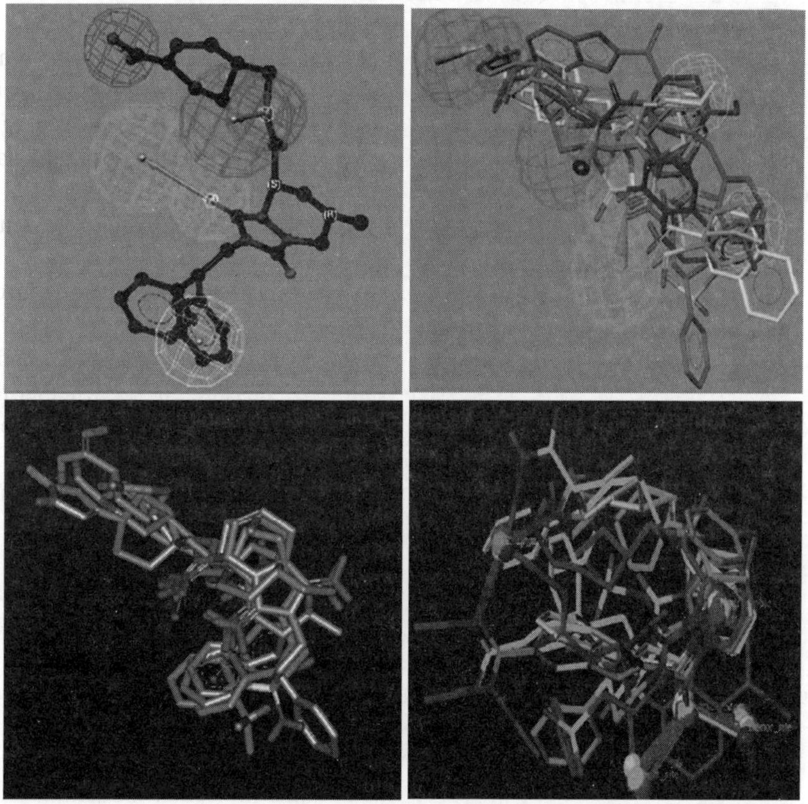

Fig. 19.23 The best hypotheses for thrombin: the manually generated pharmacophore that represents the target pharmacophore (top left); the best hypothesis generated for Catalyst (top right); GASP (bottom left); and DISCO (bottom right). (*Source:* Journal of Computer-Aided Molecular Design, **16**: 653–681, 2002)

Docking

In the last few years various methods of calculating receptor ligand interactions have been developed and applied. The decision tree in Fig. 19.24 gives an idea about the choice of appropriate methods for protein ligand docking.

Docking is a method which gives an idea about how the ligand is going to bind to the active site of the receptors and also about the extent to which conformational changes can be brought in the receptor structure when the ligand binds to it and hence the response elicited by the drug can be measured.

Active site is the site where a ligand binds to the receptor to produce a particular response (Fig. 19.25, Colour Plate 10).

Docking comprises of two distinct tasks. The first task is the prediction of favourable binding geometries for a small molecule in the binding site of a target protein and the estimation of the binding free energy of the complex so formed. The latter task, which is usually referred to as scoring, is one of the major challenges in the development of docking programs.

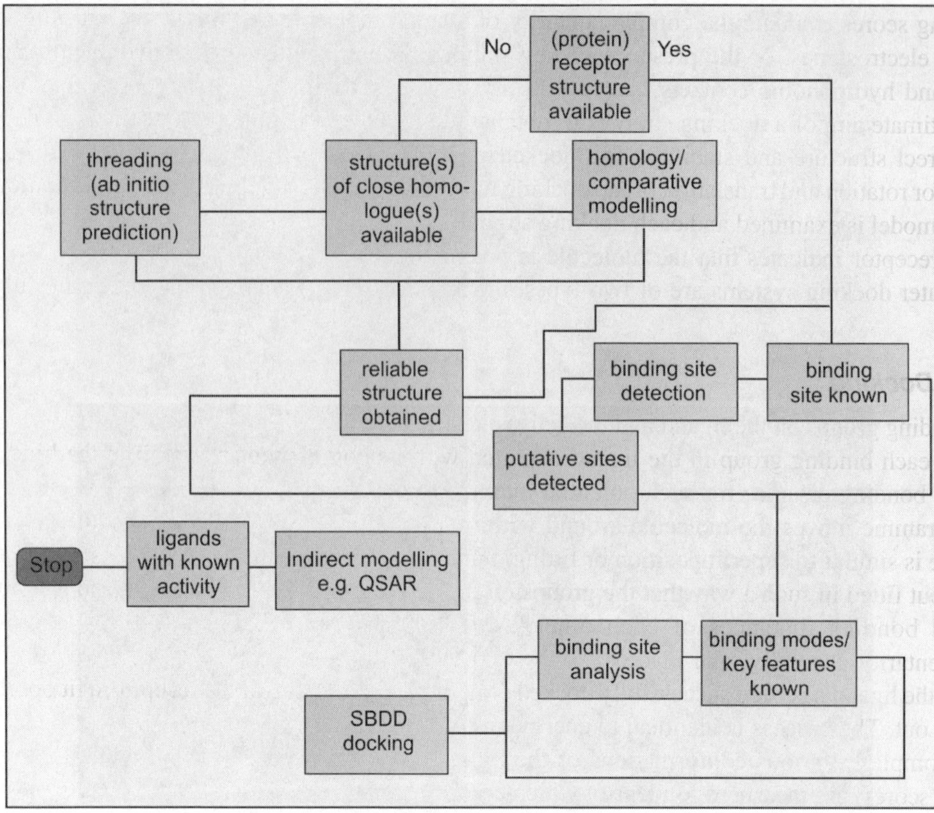

Fig. 19.24 Decision tree for choosing appropriate methods for protein ligand docking
(*Source:* Biochemical Society Transactions (2003) Volume 31, part 5)

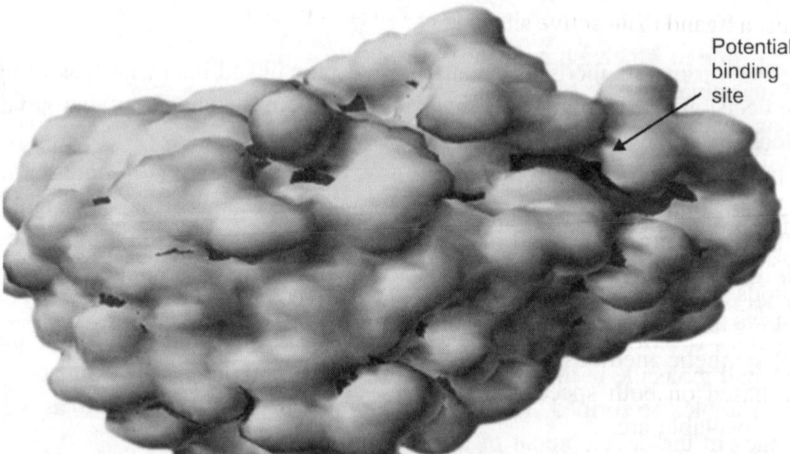

Fig. 19.25 Active site in a receptor. Image generated by Scigress Explorer Ultra 7.0

Docking scores evaluate the complementarity of a small molecule and the target structure in terms of shape, electrostatics, or the presence of key stabilizing interactions such as hydrogen bonds, salt-bridges, and hydrophobic contacts.

The ultimate aim of a docking study is to obtain the global energy minimum docking model as well as its correct structure and stability. The docked model should be searched by taking all degrees of freedom for rotation and translation of the docking mode of the ligand along with the ligand conformation and each model is examined and each docking structure is evaluated. Good complementarity of a ligand with the receptor indicates that the molecule is potentially a good binder.

Computer docking systems are of two types, the manual (direct) type and the automatic (unbiased) type.

Manual Docking

When binding groups on the ligand and the active site are known, they can be defined by the programme such that each binding group in the ligand is paired with its complimentary group in the binding site. The ideal bonding distance for each potential interaction is defined and the docking procedure started. The programme moves the molecule around within the binding site trying to obtain the best fit. The procedure is similar to superimposition or fitting, the difference being the paired groups are not directly aligned, but fitted in such a way that the groups on the active site and those on the ligand are within the preferred bonding distances of each other. At such positions hydrogen bonding and/or steric complimentarity generally take place.

When the ligand has been successfully docked or fit to the binding site of the receptor, a fit optimization is carried out. The process is identical to energy minimization, but this is carried out on a ligand- target protein complex. Various conformations of the ligand can be docked in similarly and the interaction energies (scores) are measured to identify which conformation is the best fit. In manual docking, a rigid fit is obtained as both ligand and protein remain in a particular conformation.

Automatic Docking

Automatic docking is an unbiased type of docking in which a user does not specify the active site, neither has to direct a ligand to an active site, and can place a ligand randomly. The system automatically finds an optimal position in which a ligand and a macromolecule bind. Autodock is a programme which is an example of an unbiased type of docking.

Depending upon the extent to which it takes account of molecular flexibility, a docking algorithm can be categorized into one of four classes: ligand and protein rigid, flexible ligand and rigid protein, rigid ligand and flexible protein, and both ligand and protein flexible. The simplest of these four cases i.e. both ligand and protein rigid was studied earlier, but current research has provided several ways of removing this restriction.

Docking methods are generally docking algorithms to assess and rationalize the protein ligand interactions. Docking has been a very useful tool in virtual screening of libraries of compounds obtained by combinatorial synthetic methods. The potential for a docking algorithm to be used as a virtual screening tool is based on both speed and accuracy. Based on the search algorithms, the principal methods currently available are:

- Molecular dynamics,
- Monte Carlo methods,
- Genetic algorithms,
- Fragment-based methods,

Fig. 19.26 Snapshot of loviride docked into the non nucleoside inhibitory binding pocket of Reverse transcriptase enzyme of Human Immunodeficiency virus. The active site is represented by molecular surface mode whereas loviride is in ball and stick mode. Image generated by Autodock 4.0.

- Point complementarity methods,
- Distance geometry methods,
- Tabu searches and
- Systematic searches.

Molecular dynamics (MD) methods: Molecular dynamic (MD) method involves the calculation of solutions to Newton's equations of motions. Using standard MD methods like AMBER and CHARMM to find the global energy minimum of a docked complex is difficult since traveling the rugged hyper surface of a biological system can be problematic. The problem is solved using standard optimization algorithms including direct searches which are, impractical for large molecules, suitable only for crude optimization of small molecules far away from the minimum, gradient methods recommended for initial optimization, steepest descent method, conjugate-gradient methods, Newton-Raphson method and least squares method. Mangoni *et al* have docked flexible ligands to flexible receptors in solution using MD simulations. Many times a combination of methods as mentioned above can be used, for example a combination of a gradient method for initial optimization and a conjugate-gradient method when nearing the minimum.

Monte Carlo methods: Monte Carlo (MC) technique was used to perform the first computer simulation of a molecular system. MC methods are among the most established and widely used stochastic optimization techniques. In molecular docking, the expression Monte Carlo usually means importance sampling or Metropolis method. In this method, random moves are generated to the system. The move may be accepted or rejected based on a Boltzmann probability. Molecular Modeling programs using MC methods are AutoDock, ProDock, ICM, MCDOCK, DockVision, QXP and Affinity.

Genetic algorithms: A genetic algorithm may be defined as the evolution of a population of possible solutions via genetic operators (mutation, crossovers and migrations) to a final population, leading to optimization of a predefined fitness function. Degrees of freedom are encoded into binary strings. A random initial population of solutions created, to which are applied genetic operators to create a newer population. The new populations are scored and ranked and these are then scored and ranked accordingly and their probability to go to the next iteration depends upon the score. Programs like GOLD, DIVALI, and DARWIN use genetic algorithms.

Fragment based methods: In this method the ligand is divided into separate portions or fragments, docking the fragments, which is then followed by the linking of fragments. However, the importance of the functional groups has to be analyzed and careful choice of the fragments is important. The base fragment should predominantly interact with the receptor. Previously, the fragments were selected manually but things have been automated now. The programs using this method are FlexX, DOCK, LUDI, ADAM, SLIDE and SPETICOPE.

Point complementarity methods: These methods evaluate the shape and/or chemical complementarity between the protein and the ligand. The ligand is rotated and translated to obtain maximum number of matches between ligand and protein surfaces, subtracting the number of volume overlaps.

Sometimes a 3D grid is used, which is placed over the protein and over the ligand. Each grid point is then labeled either in open space or inside the ligand or protein. A correlation function is then created which is optimized using rigid body translation and rotation. A high correlation score denotes good surface complementarity between the molecules. Because many of the methods were originally created for protein-protein docking, the rigid body assumption is usually made. This is a limitation in ligand-protein docking. FTDOCK, SANDOCK,LIGIN are programmes which use this method.

Distance Geometry methods: In distance geometry methods the distances are assembled and three-dimensional structures consistent with them to be calculated. However, it is not possible to arbitrarily assign values to the inter-atomic distances in a molecule and always obtain a low-energy conformation. The inter-atomic distances may be closely interrelated and many combinations of distances can be geometrically impossible. Conformational space is thus sampled fast although this method does not result in good results. DockIt is a program which uses the distance geometry method.

Tabu searches: An initial random ligand conformation is generated which is the **current solution** and then scored. New states are randomly generated from an initial state. These states or solutions are then scored and ranked in ascending order. The highest ranking solution is the new **current solution**, *i.e.,* one with the lowest energy. A new random population is then generated from this new **current solution**, and the same process is repeated for a certain number of iterations defined by the user. A "tabu" list is used which ensures the diversity of the **current solution**. This list stores the information of the last 25 **current solutions**. A new solution is rejected if it reminds a previous solution too much. A move is considered '*tabu*' if it is within an RMSD of 0.75 Å of any of the solutions stored within the tabu list. This tabu list is updated on a first in first-out basis. A program called PRO_LEADS uses the Tabu search.

Systematic searches: These methods systematically search all possible conformations. All molecules are usually assumed to be rigid and interaction energy is evaluated from a force field model.

Some restrictions can be used to reduce the dimensionality of the problem. EUDOC is a program which uses this method.

Steps to be followed in a Docking Procedure

Protein preparation: The components required for a docking procedure include, the three dimensional structure of a target protein with or without a ligand, few molecules of interest or a database of existing or virtual molecules and a computational program which shall achieve the desired docking poses and scores. The three dimensional structure of a protein is downloaded from the Protein Data Bank (www.rcsb.org). The Protein Data Bank (PDB) maintained by the Research Collaboratory for Structural Bioinformatics (RCSB) contains various x-ray crystal structures for proteins and other biomolecules. Once the protein is downloaded it is to be corrected for missing residues, missing atoms, alternate locations, added water molecules and incorrect bonding types and charges are to be balanced. This is known as the "cleaning" of the protein. Once the protein has been cleaned, it is then further refined by molecular mechanics calculations, to be finally prepared for use in docking purposes.

Ligand preparation: Some programmes like Autodock require the ligand to be prepared in a particular format, even after energy minimization and conformational analysis, for correct visualization of the hydrogen bonds and other interactions. The ligands can be prepared in online PRODRG server (http://davapc1.bioch.dundee.ac.uk/cgi-bin/prodrg/prodrg.cgi) and then used for docking analyses.

Validation of the docking protocol: Every docking program or method is to be validated everytime a docking procedure is to be carried out. Validation requires that the cocrystallized ligand should be extracted from the protein, corrected and redocked to the same protein (Fig. 19.27, Colour Plate 11). The redocked conformer is then compared with the original one by superimposition or by visualization as well as the RMSD (root mean square deviation) is calculated which provides the deviation between the redocked conformer and the original cocrystallized ligand with the protein. Generally RMSD may be acceptable if it is upto 3Å, but it is always better if the RMSD is less than 1Å.

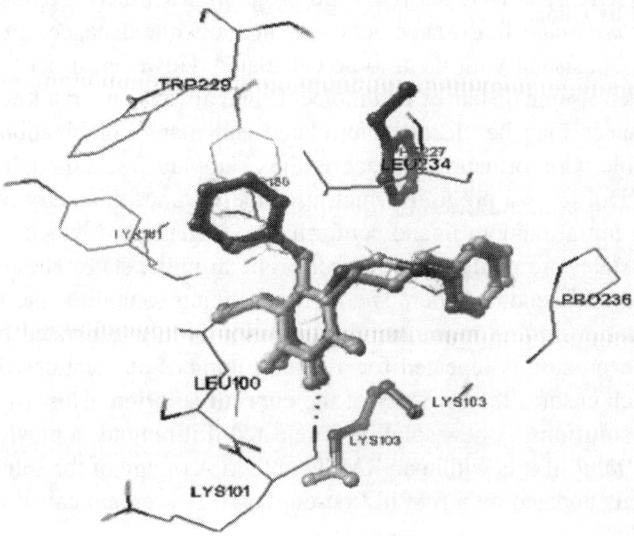

Fig. 19.27 Validation of docking protocol of TNK 651 into the active site pocket of Non nucleoside Inhibitory binding pocket of Reverse Transcriptase by Autodock 4.0. Docked conformer coloured by atom type, co-crystallised ligand coloured yellow, active site amino acid residues represented by sticks. [RMSD 0.46 Å (100 runs)]

Docking Analyses and Scoring

Docking is carried out by searching for the correct binding mode of a molecule with a number of trial and keeping the energetically favorable poses (Figs 19.28 and 19.29, Colour Plates 11 and 12). After a certain number of trials have been carried out and/or a sufficient number of poses have been found for a molecule, the search stops.

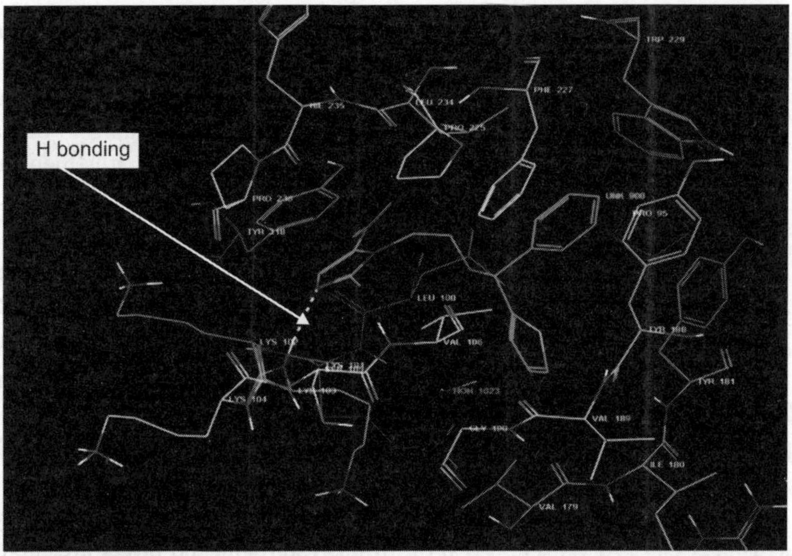

Fig. 19.28 Docked conformer of molecule in the active site pocket of non nucleoside Inhibitory binding pocket of Reverse Transcriptase. The ligand is shown in green while the active site amino acid residues are represented in sticks. Image generated by Glide.

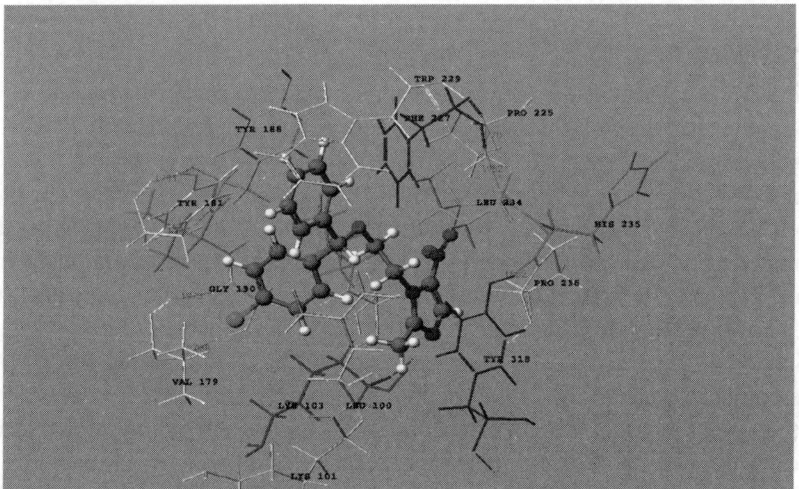

Fig. 19.29 Docked molecule in the active site pocket of Reverse Transcriptase. Active site amino acid residues are represented as sticks colored according to labeled residue type (Sequence protocol-Karplus and Schultz Flexibility). The ligand is colored with the atoms as carbon: grey, hydrogen: white, nitrogen: blue, and oxygen: red (ball and stick model). Image generated by Scigress Explorer Ultra 7.0.

The decision to keep a trial pose is based on the computed ligand–receptor interaction energy (score) of that pose. The programs then calculate the dock score (a score based on a simple energy function such as a force field with an electrostatic term and repulsive and attractive van der Waals terms), which identifies and ranks many different poses of a molecule during the search in a reasonable time, which can then be analyzed rapidly during the docking process, while a more sophisticated function calculates the final 'affinity score' for that molecule.

Affinity scoring functions are then applied to the energetically most favorable pose or *n* energetically most favorable poses found for each molecule, and comparison of the affinity scores for different molecules gives their relative rank-ordering. For a given molecule the best pose according to the affinity score is among the *n* saved poses identified with the dock score. According to the affinity scores, the docked poses having the best scores are then analyzed by visualization to see how the groups are oriented to the active site residues of the protein of the groups and the kind of interactions which are taking place between the ligand and the receptor. These poses as well as the scores are compared with that of the redocked original cocrystallized ligand to understand the binding mode of the virtual molecules and also to exploit this information for further design of more potent compounds.

Receptor Mapping

Many a times the receptor structure is not known, in these cases model receptors and binding sites are constructed to aid in drug design processes. The most prominent examples where receptors are still not known are the G-protein coupled receptors, which play an important role in many physiological and pathophysiological processes. At present, 50% of all recently launched drugs are targeted against G-protein coupled receptors. One of the techniques is the active analog approach. In this technique, bioactive conformations are derived for both active and inactive analogs. The volumes of each set are superimposed. The active analog volume is subtracted from combined inactive volume. The remaining volume is the receptor map where the active analogs fit.

Homology Modelling

A model protein can be constructed if the primary amino acid sequence of a protein is known and the X-ray crystallographic structure of an analogous protein is already determined. This technique is also known as Homology modelling. This technique relies on the observation that in nature the structural conformation of a protein is more highly conserved than its amino acid sequence and that any small or medium changes in sequence will typically result in only small changes in the 3D structure .The process of homology modeling consists of four steps – fold assignment, sequence alignment, model building and model refinement (Fig. 19.30). The fold assignment process identifies template structures which are proteins of known 3D structure that are related to the target sequence. Next, a sequence database of proteins with known structures (e.g. the PDB-sequence database) is searched with the target sequence using sequence similarity search algorithms or threading techniques. Once a defined correlation has been observed between the target protein and a protein of known three dimensional structure, the two protein sequences are superimposed or aligned to identify the optimum correlation between the residues in the template and target sequences. The next stage is the model-building phase. A model of the target protein is then constructed from the substitution of amino acids in the 3D structure of the template protein and the insertion and/or deletion of amino acids according to the sequence alignment. Alternatively, a loop may be generated to connect two known regions. Once the backbone of the target protein has been constructed, side chains may be added in energetically favourable conformations. After this, the constructed model is checked with regard to conformational aspects and is corrected or energy minimized using force-field approaches.

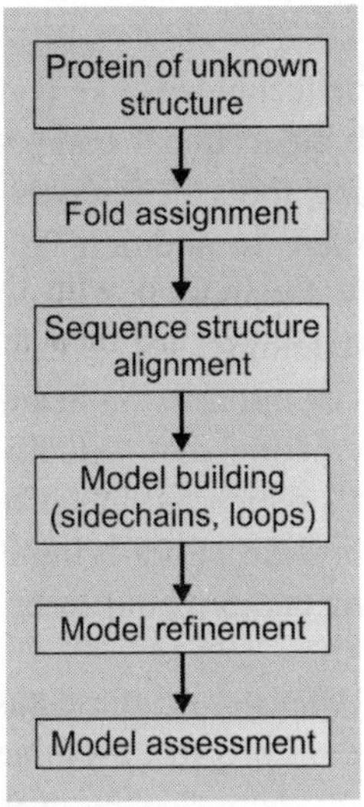

Fig. 19.30 The steps involved in the prediction of protein structure by homology modeling
(*Source:* DDT Vol. 9, No. 15 August 2004, p. 660)

This constructed model is then checked for its validity .If the model indicates that certain amino acid residues are important for activity, some of these may be mutated and the effect on the binding of the model receptor to the ligand may be analyzed to see if there is any change.

Homology modelling has a number of applications at various stages of drug design and discovery process. This kind of technique has stupendously helped to identify or to optimize compounds that have subsequently progressed to clinical trials or to the drug market. Homology models have had considerable impact on target identification and/or validation, lead identification and lead optimization.

Modelling a Binding Site

At times a model binding site can be designed, for this a range of structurally diverse molecules of interest with a range of activities are chosen. A conformational analysis is carried out and the active conformations should be identified as far as possible. A 3D pharmacophore may be obtained and the molecules should be superimposed with each other such that their pharmacophores match. Each molecule is then placed in a potential energy grid and different probes are placed at each grid point in turn to measure interaction energies between the molecule and the probe atom. Different kinds of probes are used for measuring different kinds of interactions. An aromatic CH probe could be used to measure hydrophobic interactions whereas an aliphatic OH probe could be used to measure polar interactions. Interactions may then be displayed as isoenergy contours similar to contours generated by CoMFA and CoMSIA. Fields for all molecules in the study can then be compared to identify fields common to all the molecules. Once the fields are identified, suitable amino acids can be positioned to allow the required interaction. Once a binding site is built with help of suitable analysis of hydrogen bonding interactions, ionic and hydrophobic binding interactions along with structure activity relationships, known molecules can be docked to the model binding site, the complex minimized, and binding energies calculated. These can then be compared with experimental values to examine the validity of the model binding site. If results are close to the experimental values, the model can be used for design and synthesis of novel molecules.

CONCLUSIONS

Today, molecular modelling with synthetic techniques like combinatorial processes and high throughput screening influence the efforts of all pharmaceutical companies. As the computational technologies advance, the role of molecular modelling tools in improving the efficiency of the drug discovery process will become increasingly important. In addition, as the amount of structural information on potential therapeutic targets dramatically expands, it will act as a driver in the development of the various techniques of computational modelling. There will be increased use of automation, faster algorithms will be developed, and improved information management techniques will be used to handle the sheer volume of target-related information that will need to be processed. However, it should always be remembered that these are tools which aid in the drug design and development process and one should not believe a model just for the sake of believing it. A model is useful if the guidance given by it in carrying out the required experiments turns out to be correct, with possibly a few explainable deviations.

Statistically, if the model does not predict the results which are obtained experimentally it is not a useful model and it should be discarded.

FURTHER READING

1. A.R. Leach, "Molecular Modelling," 1st ed., Longman China Ltd., Harlow, England, 1996.
2. P.M. Dean, "Molecular Similarity in Drug Design," 1st ed., Blackie Academic & Professional, Glasgow, 1995.
3. N.C. Cohen, "Guidebook in Molecular Modelling in Drug Design," 1st ed., Academic Press Ltd., London, 1995.
4. N.C. Cohen, J.M. Blaney, C. Humblet, P. Gund, and D.C. Barry, *J. Med. Chem.*, **33**, 883 (1990).
5. P. Gund, D.C. Barry, J.M. Blaney and N.C. Cohen, *J. Med. Chem.*, **31**, 2230 (1988).

Index

Reader's Notes

Reader's Notes

Reader's Notes

Reader's Notes

Reader's Notes